RELUCTANT COSMOPOLITANS

THE LITTMAN LIBRARY OF
JEWISH CIVILIZATION

MANAGING EDITOR
Connie Webber

Dedicated to the memory of
LOUIS THOMAS SIDNEY LITTMAN
who founded the Littman Library
for the love of God
and in memory of his father
JOSEPH AARON LITTMAN
יהא זכרם ברוך

'*Get wisdom, get understanding:*
Forsake her not and she shall preserve thee'
PROV. 4: 5

The Littman Library of Jewish Civilization is a registered UK charity
Registered charity no. 1000784

RELUCTANT COSMOPOLITANS

◆

The Portuguese Jews of Seventeenth-Century Amsterdam

◆

DANIEL M. SWETSCHINSKI

London · Portland, Oregon

The Littman Library of Jewish Civilization

2000

The Littman Library of Jewish Civilization
74 Addison Road
London W14 8DJ, UK

———

Published in the United States and Canada by
The Littman Library of Jewish Civilization
c/o ISBS, 5804 N.E. Hassalo Street
Portland, Oregon 97213–3644

A catalogue record for this book is available from the British Library

Library of Congress Cataloging-in-Publication Data
Swetschinski, Daniel, 1944–
Reluctant cosmopolitans : the Portuguese Jews of seventeenth-century Amsterdam /
Daniel M. Swetschinski.
p.   cm.—(The Littman library of Jewish civilization)
Includes bibliographical references and index.
1. Sephardim—Netherlands—Amsterdam—History—17th century.
2. Jews—Netherlands—Amsterdam—History—17th century.
3. Judaism—Netherlands—Amsterdam—History—17th century. 4. Amsterdam
(Netherlands)—Ethnic relations. I. Title. II. Littman library of Jewish civilization
(Series)

DS135.N5 A684 2000   949.2'352—dc21   99-088379
ISBN 1–874774–46–3

Publishing co-ordinator: Janet Moth
Production: John Saunders
Design: Pete Russell, Faringdon, Oxon.
Copy-editing: Gillian Bromley
Proof-reading: George Tulloch
Indexes: Daniel Swetschinski
Typeset by Footnote Graphics, Warminster, Wilts.
Printed in Great Britain on acid-free paper by
Biddles Ltd., Guildford & King's Lynn

for
Galia, Sasha, and Lucien

———

The thought of our past years in me doth breed
Perpetual benediction: not indeed
For that which is most worthy to be blest;
Delight and liberty, the simple creed
Of Childhood, whether busy or at rest,
With new-fledged hope still fluttering in his breast:—
        Not for these I raise
        The song of thanks and praise;
      But for those obstinate questionings
      Of sense and outward things,
      Fallings from us, vanishings;
      Blank misgivings of a Creature
Moving about in worlds not realised,
High instincts before which our mortal Nature
Did tremble like a guilty Thing surprised:
        But for those first affections,
        Those shadowy recollections,
      Which, be they what they may,
Are yet the fountain-light of all our day,
Are yet a master-light of all our seeing . . .

WILLIAM WORDSWORTH
'Ode: Intimations of Immortality'

Acknowledgements

There is no question that I have often cherished the solitude of doing research. It is equally true that I would have found it too much of a good thing, if it were not for the friends I made along the way. I do not know exactly why this should be so, but I remember my travels with fondness in no small measure because of the professional archivists I met along the way. Few went as far as Dr J. van Roey at the municipal archives in Antwerp, who personally greeted every researcher in the reading room at the beginning of his and our working day. Almost daily and over a very long period, Dr Simon Hart and Dr Wil Pieterse, directors of the Amsterdam municipal archives, gave unstintingly of their time, advice, and personal research notes. In Amsterdam, too, Dr Bas Dudok van Heel guided me over all the un-anticipated obstacles a novice researcher inevitably runs into. In Madrid, at the Archivo Histórico Nacional, Dr Pilar Leon Tello aided me in overcoming my initial bafflement at the foreign ways of that great institution. In Lisbon, I waited many hours one afternoon alone in a silent and barren room for Professor Virgínia Rau, because her maid did not know how to communicate with me nor I with her. When I finally met the historian, she made me feel at home so readily that I will always associate the impersonal concept of a 'community of scholars' with her reception of this totally unknown foreign graduate student. At the archives of the Torre do Tombo I had the good fortune of meeting Dr David Grant Smith, then a fellow graduate student, who gave generously of his knowledge and research data on Luso-Brazilian trade.

Only after emerging from the dungeons of archival research did I learn that I was not alone in pursuing an understanding of Amsterdam's Portuguese Jews. If I ever found the discovery annoying and a little threatening, I have long since learned to suppress any memories of my flawed reaction, not least because of the wonderfully personal friendships I have formed with my principal rivals. Professors Yosef Kaplan and Jonathan Israel may never know how much they have taught me about the subject of our shared devotion—not only through their publications, but perhaps even more through casual conversations over tea or beer, in a taxi between Tel Aviv and Jerusalem, on a stroll through the palace at Versailles. If I could have chosen the friends with whom I was going to share what has become a rather large part of my life, I could not have picked any better comrades.

At the very beginning of my journey I received a most encouraging send-off from my revered teachers. Professors Alexander Altmann, Nahum Glatzer, Ben Halpern, and Yosef Yerushalmi treated me with respect long before I was deserving of it. The strength and vitality of their personal commitments to Jewish scholarship have been—and will for ever remain—an inexhaustible source of inspiration. Their encouragement, faith, and affection gave my research the momentum without which it would never have got off the ground. And at the very end of this voyage I have found the warm welcome of the staff at the Littman Library of Jewish Civilization. Connie Webber, Janet Moth, and Gillian Bromley have given me all the consideration I could have wished for and prodded me gently when-ever I hesitated. I only hope that it is not true that you can only be lucky once.

DANIEL M. SWETSCHINSKI

Contents

A Note on Orthography, Transliteration, and Special Usages

In the seventeenth century spelling was generally not yet standardized: not in Portuguese, nor in Spanish, nor in Dutch. It is not a matter that goes to the heart of the century, but does form a sufficiently lively part of it that I thought it worthwhile to retain some sense of it in this description of the doings of the Portuguese Jews of seventeenth-century Amsterdam. Initially I thought to retain as much as possible the spelling used by the individuals themselves. Within the same family, for instance, the surname was often spelled differently by father and son or husband and wife. But too many confusions resulted. Joseph Athyas spelled his surname Athyas when signing a letter or a deed, but used the spelling Athias on the title pages of the books he published. I was therefore led to standardize surnames within the same family, but leave a modicum of variation in the spelling of forenames. Thus you may find side by side one family Pereyra and another Pereira; one individual Moseh, another Mosse, or Moise, for example.

Another peculiarity led me to use an ampersand (&) in order to indicate the names of business firms—in imitation of such modern usages as 'So-and-so & Co.' There have been, in the historiography of Dutch Jewry, a few scholars who have been misled by firm names to believe that the individuals named were actually present in the city whenever such names were used, making the mistake of taking any mention of such a firm to refer to the persons in the firm's title. To take the example of André de Azevedo & João de Pas: a bank account in the name of André de Azevedo & João de Pas says little about their whereabouts. Whether André or João or a third person was ever present in person at the location of the bank cannot be determined from the mention of the firm's name alone. In using the ampersand it will be clear that I refer to a non-human entity and any such confusion will be avoided.

Portuguese Jews used a small number of Hebrew terms regularly and transliterated them almost always in our roman script, according to rules that made sense from their perspective as primarily Portuguese-speaking individuals. Romance languages, for instance, rarely pronounce the 'h', which is therefore dropped where we might expect it, as in Bet aHaim (cemetery); where we do encounter an 'h' it usually corresponds to the Hebrew *het* or *khaf*, as in *haham* (rabbi). They pronounced a thicker 's' than we do, which makes them transliterate the Hebrew *shin* as well as the *tsade* with an 's'. In the following pages these spellings have been retained as much as possible. They give the English narrative a measure of local colour, and constitute, as it were, a kind of shortlist of those religious and communal concepts whose Jewishness Portuguese Jews particularly emphasized, for one reason or another. Many of these terms continued to be used and spelled in the traditional way even when most Portuguese Jews no longer spoke Portuguese. They are also terms that the various communities of the Portuguese Jewish diaspora tended to spell in a similar fashion, for they all spoke the same Portuguese mother tongue.

To transliterate such terms in accordance with the rules for the transliteration of Hebrew employed elsewhere in this book would have created the impression that

Portuguese Jewish culture was more Hebraic than it really was. It would have robbed us of this revealing nuance of authenticity. Portuguese Jewish transliterations of key Hebrew terms have therefore been retained in this book:

beraha for *berakhah*—'minor' excommunication;
Bet aHaim for beit haḥayim—'House of Life' or cemetery;
bodeca for *bedikah*—inspection;
escava for *hashkavah*—requiem;
haham for *ḥakham*—the Portuguese Jewish title for a rabbi;
hekhal for *heikhal*—synagogue ark for the Torah scrolls;
herem for *ḥerem*—excommunication;
jesiba for *yeshivah*—academy;
Mahamad for Ma'amad—governing board;
misva (pl. *misvot*) for *mitsvah* (pl. *mitsvot*)—commandment;
nedava for *nedavah*—donation;
sedaca for *tsedakah*—charity and, more generally, the community's charity chest;
sehita for *sheḥitah*—ritual slaughter;
teva for *tevah*—raised platform in the synagogue;
yahid for *yaḥid*—member of the congregation.

A final point, with regard to the way this book refers to the Portuguese Jews themselves. Some works on the Portuguese Jews of the seventeenth century refer to them as 'Sephardim'. I have some reservations about this usage and have not adopted it in the pages to follow. Amsterdam's Portuguese Jews never referred to themselves as 'Sephardim'. Although I am not always in principle wedded to authenticity as an end in itself, this is my main reason. The use of 'Sephardi' gives in my opinion a truly different and false flavour. It over-emphasizes the Sephardi–Ashkenazi dichotomy and obscures the essential rootedness of our seventeenth-century Jews in the Iberian peninsula. But I have another, more idiosyncratic, motive. The use of the designation 'Sephardi' in relation to the Portuguese Jews of northern Europe acquired especially negative connotations for me as a result of its over-eager application by Hermann Kellenbenz in his *Sephardim an der unteren Elbe*. Unfortunately, this otherwise excellent study of the Portuguese Jews of Hamburg had originally been sponsored by the Reichsinstitut für Geschichte des neuen Deutschlands, that is, as a Nazi-supported project entitled 'Das Hamburger Finanzjudentum und seine Kreise'.[1] Kellenbenz did his initial research during the war years, amid the deportations of western European Jewry. After the Second World War he attempted, as it were, to remove the moral stench of his earlier antisemitic associations by employing the ultra-Jewish designation 'Sephardi'. For me, this has given the term, whenever used inappropriately in relation to the Portuguese and Spanish Jews of northern Europe, an uncomfortably double and disingenuous connotation that in no way fits the image I have of Amsterdam's Portuguese Jews. 'Portuguese Jewish' is no doubt more cumbersome than 'Sephardi'; but it has the distinct advantage of being correct, in the dual meaning of that word.

'Sephardi' is here used only to refer to the Jews of medieval Spain and Portugal and their immediate descendants among the exiles who fled the Iberian peninsula in the years of the expulsions from Spain (1492) and Portugal (1497).

[1] Heiber, *Walter Frank*, 456–7, 1189.

List of Tables

List of Abbreviations

AGR	Archives Générales du Royaume, Brussels
AHN	Archivo Histórico Nacional, Madrid
AJHQ	*American Jewish Historical Quarterly*
AM	*anno mundi*
ANTT	Arquivo Nacional de Torre do Tombo, Lisbon
Bibl. Nat. Paris	Bibliothèque Nationale, Paris
BMGJWN	*Bijdragen en Mededeelingen van het Genootschap voor Joodsche Wetenschap in Nederland*
BN Madrid	Biblioteca Nacional, Madrid
BRAH	*Boletín de la Real Academia de Historia*
GAA	Gemeentelijke Archiefdienst, Amsterdam
DTB	Doop-, Trouw-, en Begrafenisboeken
NA	Notariële Archieven
ORA	Oud Rechterlijke Archieven
PA	Particuliere Archieven
PIG	Portugees-Israëlitische Gemeente
HUCA	*Hebrew Union College Annual*
JQR	*Jewish Quarterly Review*
JSS	*Jewish Social Studies*
NRPJA	'Amsterdam Notarial Deeds Pertaining to the Portuguese Jews', ed. Pieterse and Koen
PAAJR	*Proceedings of the American Academy for Jewish Research*
PAJHS	*Proceedings of the American Jewish Historical Society*
REJ	*Revue des Études Juives*
RHR	*Revue de l'Histoire des Religions*
SR	*Studia Rosenthaliana*
TJHSE	*Transactions of the Jewish Historical Society of England*
VA	*De Vrijdagavond*

INTRODUCTION

THE DUTCH JERUSALEM
The Distortions of History

One would expect people to remember the past and to imagine the future. In fact, when discoursing or writing about history, they imagine it in terms of their own experience, and when trying to gauge the future they cite supposed analogies from the past: till, by a double process of repetition, they imagine the past and remember the future.

SIR LEWIS NAMIER

O^N Shabat Nahamu of 5435 (2 August 1675), the senior *haham* of the Kahal Kados de Talmud Tora, the Portuguese Jewish religious community of Amsterdam, delivered the first sermon in the recently completed Esnoga.[1] In his appropriately baroque Portuguese discourse Ishac Aboab da Fonseca compared the newly erected structure to the two Temples of ancient Israel and expressed the hope that 'this celebrated house, though [only] a small Temple . . . be rendered great by the greatness of God' ('esta famoza caza ainda que piqueño Templo . . . que a sua grandeza a fassa grande'),[2] echoing the opinion of his Portuguese Jewish contemporaries who regarded their community as striving for and approaching, if only in miniature, the ancient glory of Jerusalem. A little more than a hundred years later Dutch *maskilim* (that is, Jews espousing the philosophy of the Enlightenment) gave a wholly new twist to the Amsterdam–Jerusalem analogy. Upon receiving the coveted equality of rights in 1795, these enlightened Jews sang:

> Triumph! O Rights of Man.
> Now you obtained, Brothers, your wish
> After so many vicissitudes!
> Freedom speaks! Tyranny trembles!
> Yes, woe to him, who strives against her!
> Now Brotherhood, and Reason, rejoice!

---

[1] *Haham*, 'wise/sage one', is the Portuguese Jewish designation for rabbi. For this, and a number of other terms commonly used in seventeenth-century documents of the Portuguese Jewish community, I have retained the original spellings rather than applying standard principles of transliteration from Hebrew. For a full list of terms and an explanation of the system of transliteration followed elsewhere in this book, see pp. xi–xii.

[2] Ishac Aboab da Fonseca's sermon is included in *Sermões*, 1–14; abbr. Dutch trans. by J. H. Hillesum in *Nieuw Israelietisch Weekblad*, 61 (31 July 1925). The quotation may be found in *Sermões*, 7.

Thus she addresses you, hear her voice!
Amsterdam! she [is] Jerusalem!
The Messiah! this Constitution!
The Temple! Virtue and Honour!
The Truth! the Sacred Law!
Repentance for sin! Absolution![3]

A new Jerusalem of freedom, brotherhood, and reason replaced the ancient
Jerusalem of the Temples of Solomon, Ezra, and Herod. And the new Jerusalem
was here and now, neither in miniature nor in expectation, in Amsterdam. Another
century later, after the exaltation of the emancipation had worn off, Amsterdam
came to be known deceptively simply as 'Mokum' (the Dutch spelling of the
Ashkenazi pronunciation of the Hebrew *makom*, 'place'), an appellation which
affectionately expressed the place Amsterdam occupied in the hearts of the then
mostly Ashkenazi Jews.

   The image of Amsterdam as the 'Dutch Jerusalem' has persisted in modern
Jewish historiography, at least from Heinrich Graetz to Salo W. Baron—and not
merely as a rhetorical flourish.[4] The modern usage, of course, makes no reference
either to divine providence or to rational self-confidence; rather, it seeks to convey
two quintessential elements of Jewish history that appear uniquely combined in
the history of Amsterdam's Jews. 'Dutch' refers to the special toleration extended
by Amsterdam's burghers to their Jewish fellow residents; an exemplary toleration
by any seventeenth-century, and many modern, standards. 'Jerusalem' recalls the
dynamic commitment to Judaism exhibited by Amsterdam's Portuguese Jews; a
faithfulness bred and nurtured in the shadow of the extreme intolerance of Iberian
inquisitions. In modern Jewish historiography, the phrase 'Dutch Jerusalem' symbolizes Jewish steadfastness in the face of persecution and Jewish dynamism in the
fertile environment of a liberal bourgeois society.

   On the threshold of the modern era Amsterdam's Portuguese Jews appeared to
demonstrate all the positive features of the changes associated with modernity and,
as yet, very few of the drawbacks. As early as the days of Moses Mendelssohn and
Naphtali Hirsch Wessely in the late eighteenth century, Amsterdam's Portuguese
Jews were lauded as the first modern Jewish community within which secular life
and Judaism managed to co-exist relatively peacefully and successfully.[5] However,

   [3] Gans, *Memorboek*, 281.
   [4] Graetz, *Geschichte der Juden*, vol. x, ch. 1, 'Das holländische Jerusalem'; Baron, *Social and
Religious History*, vol. xv, ch. 63, 'Dutch Jerusalem'.
   [5] On Mendelssohn's introduction to Menasseh ben Israel's *Vindiciae Judaeorum*, see Altmann,
Moses Mendelssohn, 463–74; on Wessely's appreciation of Amsterdam's Portuguese Jewry in his *Divre
shalom ve'emet*, see Melkman, *David Franco Mendes*, 9–16. Ironically, Richard Popkin, otherwise no
mean critic of the Enlightenment, arrives at a similar assessment: 'The quest within [the Amsterdam
Sephardic community] represented on a minor scale the vital concern of the whole Western World
from then until now: the crucial attempt to find a *modus vivendi* between, on the one hand, modern
interests and scientific understanding, and, on the other, the desire for a life rooted in and growing
from traditional religion': 'Historical Significance', 27.

conceiving of Amsterdam as 'the first modern Jewish community' introduced a whole set of largely extraneous issues into the discussion of its history. Specifically, much of the discourse around the Jewish encounter with modernity—an encounter for which central European Jewish history has long served as the paradigm—was imported into Dutch Jewish historiography. In particular, the economic history of the Portuguese Jews and the examination of the excommunications of Uriel da Costa and Spinoza, discussed in Chapter 5 below, drew much unwarranted attention on account of the 'lessons' that might be drawn from them. The broad scope of economic activities undertaken by these Jews highlighted the positive contribution they made—and would always make, when given the opportunity—to the evolution of one of the most advanced national and international economies, 'in contrast to their money-lending ancestors'. At a minimum, it seemed, here was a group of Jews for whose economic activities no one needed to apologize. The da Costa and Spinoza affairs served as reminders, for liberal Jews, of the non-orthodox creative potential within Judaism and perhaps of its universalist aspirations; and, for more traditional Jews, of the pitfalls either of rabbinic fanaticism or of heterodox flights of the imagination. In short, until very recently, much of Dutch Jewish history depicted the 'Dutch Jerusalem' as viewed from Berlin or from New York, by former Berliners.

Even when placed more squarely within its own context, the history of Amsterdam's Portuguese Jews is beset by its own peculiar problems. The very dramatic story of the Marrano past hangs as a dark cloud over the quite remarkable success of the Amsterdam settlement. The contrast between the two actually leads almost inevitably to a reliance upon that past as a convenient explanation for any and all aberrations, real or imagined. While there can be no question of ignoring the real terror experienced in the face of inquisitorial persecution, it is quite something else to infuse these experiences with all the doom and gloom of our contemporary obsession with trauma. A final 'distortion', if so common a human failing can be called that, comes with an inclination to look for external factors first and to resort to an investigation of internal ones only when the first cannot plausibly be identified. The most common 'external factor' widely cited as having greatly affected the history of Amsterdam's Portuguese Jews is the inherently unstable position of the Jews in society. As we will see, the leaders of the community had no difficulty in expressing their concern that this or other aspects of the Jews' situation or behaviour might have deleterious consequences for Jewish–Christian relations and might undermine the much appreciated toleration; but they actually expressed such fears on only a very few, clearly justified occasions. Only someone quite unfamiliar with the sources could maintain that 'political instability' played a major role in guiding the actions of Amsterdam's Portuguese Jews; and indeed, my own clear and unambiguous preference is for an exploration of internal dynamics before seeking explanations elsewhere.

The recent emphasis upon archival research has made it difficult to sustain extravagant claims for the significance of extraneous notions imported from other eras or areas of Jewish history. The publication of the earliest notarial records, beginning with those for 1595, as well as the ready availability of notarial and other Amsterdam records and the post-war deposition of the archives of the Portuguese Jewish community at the City Archives, allow everyone today an immediate acquaintance with the realities of seventeenth-century Portuguese Jewish history. Compared with the false certainties of previous generations, the conditions of contemporary Jewish historiography may seem chaotic—especially, perhaps, with regard to the early modern period. This study seeks, in the first instance, to add a more authentic vision of the Portuguese Jews of Amsterdam to the panorama of early modern Jewish history and hopes, secondarily, to suggest new ways of linking the medieval and modern periods in Jewish history.

What follows is the story of several thousand refugees from the Spanish and Portuguese inquisitions who settled in Amsterdam in the course of the seventeenth century. They were the descendants of Spanish and Portuguese Jews most of whom were forcibly baptized in the century between 1391 and 1497. It was to interrogate these converts, suspected of being insincere Christians, that the Spanish Inquisition was established in 1480 and the Portuguese Inquisition in 1536. From the early 1590s increasing numbers of Portuguese and Spanish New Christians—as the converts (conversos) were then officially designated—began settling in northern Europe, and particularly in Amsterdam and Hamburg. The Dutch and German ports offered not only basic economic opportunities but also a degree of freedom of religion absent in the Iberian peninsula.

Fairly soon after the initial settlement in the 1590s, the Portuguese New Christians who had come to Amsterdam began manifesting themselves as Jews. True to the principle of freedom of conscience—formulated as part of the Union of Utrecht (1579), the founding document of the Republic of the United Provinces—the Amsterdam authorities put no real obstacles in the way of the return to Judaism of the erstwhile New Christians. By the 1610s, the Amsterdam Jews had established three distinct Jewish congregations. But almost as soon as these *kehilot* were founded, the elders began discussing plans to bring them together, and from 1639 the unified Amsterdam Portuguese Jewish community was known as the Kahal Kados de Talmud Tora. In 1675, as already noted, this congregation moved into the famous and magnificent Esnoga; as the same year also roughly marks the point at which the immigration of New Christians began to taper off, it may be taken to represent the attainment of communal maturity, in both numerical and religious terms.

Economically speaking, Amsterdam's Portuguese Jews did very well for themselves—and for the city. From fairly humble and uninspiring beginnings as merchants trading primarily between their former homeland and their new place of residence, frequently in the service of Iberian principals, some of the most successful emerged as important merchant bankers whose activities reached into the inner workings of national and international politics. Not only were they very successful as merchants, they also managed to explore other entrepreneurial avenues in industry, army purveying, and brokerage. They survived the wars between the Republic and, at various times, Spain, Portugal, France, and England and emerged as economically worthy and politically loyal 'citizens' of the United Provinces, that is, burghers of several cities in Holland: Amsterdam, The Hague, and Rotterdam.[6]

In their cultural as well as their religious life, of course, these immigrants remained a group apart. They wanted it that way; and the people among whom they lived did not seem to be bothered by their self-sufficiency. Neither group viewed it as an implicit rejection of their own values or exerted even subtle pressure for some form of assimilation. Under these conditions, cultural creativity flourished. Amsterdam's Portuguese Jews were the first Jews to create a significant body of religious and secular literature. Joseph Penso de la Vega's quirky introduction to the mysterious world of stock trading is still, and justly, admired as a work of quintessentially seventeenth-century genius. The poetry and plays of Daniel Levi de Barrios have not fared so well with the passage of time, yet they too deserve respect. The voluminous output of Menasseh ben Israel forms, as it were, a religious corrective to our preoccupation with these secular creations; and while his works may fall short of the highest creative achievements in religious thought of the contemporary Ashkenazi world, they have their own idiosyncratic merits and charms. And, possibly after some initial hesitation, we must also reckon as an expression of Portuguese Jewish creativity the trail-blazing philosophical reflections of Baruh de Spinoza.

These few examples suffice to illustrate the point that the Portuguese Jews of seventeenth-century Amsterdam reached unparalleled heights both economically and culturally; that though relatively few in number, they made their indelible mark; and that there remains as ever the mystery of accounting for their success, for their worldliness and their parochialism, for their integration and their separation.

With the exception of Chapter 1, the focus in the following pages is on the Portuguese Jews themselves, their religious community and other informal groupings. Economic and religious studies of the community abound; now it is the social dimension of their history which deserves our attention. From the earliest days of the three separate congregations the community was plagued by disputes, provoked in part, perhaps, by ideological differences, but mostly by personality or kin conflicts. Even within the unified Kahal Kados de Talmud Tora, individual members continued to quarrel with the leadership of the community: sometimes

---

[6] The word 'citizen' is an anachronism. At that time the most any Dutch person could be, if he or she chose to file the application and pay the fee, was a burgher of her or his place of residence.

over taxes, at other times over political matters, and on a few occasions over profoundly religious issues. In this respect, with the exception of the religious altercations, the Amsterdam community was not very different from most other Jewish communities of the time. The extraordinary nature of the religious tensions may never cease to attract scholarly and lay curiosity; yet, when all is said and done, it is the generally smooth re-integration of the New Christians into a traditional Jewish community more than the quarrelsomeness of a few individuals that deserves our attention.

To subsume, in some sense, both the quarrel with and the acceptance of the Jewish tradition in a single evocative term, it has become fashionable of late to refer to the Portuguese Jews of this period as 'New Jews'. This label has the advantage of distinguishing them from other contemporary Jews and of simultaneously referring to that which makes for the distinction—their past as New Christians and their recent conversion to Judaism. The phrase 'from New Christians to New Jews' definitely has a satisfying ring to it; however, when it is also used to give new life to Gebhardt's old definition of the split consciousness, its usage becomes reminiscent of distortions of a similar kind to those that plagued the old history. One recent devotee of the term speaks of Uriel da Costa's case

as a manifestation (albeit extreme) of a specific internal schism inherent in the Marrano experience per se. Wherever he turns, the Marrano is an outsider and someone 'new' (he is a New Christian or a New Jew). He does not belong to any cultural context simply or naturally, and feels both inside and outside of any one of them. If he seems to have solved his problem and found an identity for himself (through assimilation into Christian society or by returning to the Jewish fold), this identity does not adhere to him simply or directly, for he must constantly struggle to engender and preserve it, overcoming the internal contradictions it entails. Hence he is doomed to a life of mental ferment and upheaval, to manifestations of doubt, and to rupture with himself, his past, and his future.[7]

Through these eloquent and stirring lines echo once again the problems of an alien dynamic—that of a certain kind of modern man. The evident rush to abstraction, before any of the evidence has been examined or on the basis of just one single case, reflects contemporary ideological realities and styles of scholarly and political argumentation far better than it reflects the situation of Amsterdam's so-called 'New Jews'. But the term is also used more judiciously to describe two possible interrelated characteristics: 'that institutional Judaism was something entirely new to them', and 'that the Jewish life they created for themselves possessed new characteristics which one might consider harbingers of modern European Judaism'.[8] It hints at the paradox of 'converts' to Judaism embodying some of the quintessential features of modern Jewish existence. To put it another way, Amsterdam's Portuguese Jews were modern Jews without ever having been medieval Jews. If this proves to be true, it calls into question the terms of the debate within which Jewish modernity is seen as saddled with a host of problems deriving

[7] Yovel, *Spinoza and Other Heretics*, i. 49.   [8] Kaplan, in Blom *et al.* (eds.), *Geschiedenis*, 129.

from the delayed, conditional, and gradual emancipation of the Jews at the end of the eighteenth century and the beginning of the nineteenth.

To redress a tendency to study Amsterdam's Portuguese Jewish community through its 'pathological' cases, the following communal portrait focuses on the obvious rather than on the exceptional. At the outset it avoids terms like 'New Jews'. Rather than emphasizing the abnormal or even the unusual, it seeks the norm. It sets out to unearth the underlying premises on which the toleration exercised by the city's magistrates and population were based; it attempts to identify the major trends and dimensions of the *converso* immigration; it looks for patterns within the disparate array of economic activities; it examines the appeal of Judaism and the congregation, notwithstanding initial obstacles, occasional flirtations with outside influences, and the allure of competing loyalties; it sketches a cultural profile of men and women who, by and large, were quite comfortable living with an allegedly split mind. Above all, it seeks the centre from which it may be possible to grasp the interrelationship of all the constituent parts, both the functioning and the malfunctioning elements.

ONE

'THE TRUE BOOK OF EXPERIENCE'

Amsterdam's Toleration of the Jews

The city of Amsterdam reaps the fruit of this freedom [of conscience] in its own great prosperity and in the admiration of all other people. For in this most flourishing state and most splendid city, men of every nation and religion live together in the greatest harmony, and ask no questions before trusting their goods to a fellow-citizen, save whether he be rich or poor, and whether he generally acts honestly, or the reverse. His religion and sect is considered of no importance: for it has no effect before the judges in gaining or losing a cause, and there is no sect so despised that its followers, provided that they harm no one, pay every man his due, and live uprightly, are deprived of the protection of the magisterial authority.

BENTO ALIAS BARUH DE SPINOZA

To this very day both Jewish and non-Jewish Amsterdammers colloquially refer to their city as 'Mokum'—'the place'. Nothing expresses so simply and eloquently the very special place of Amsterdam in Jewish history. This reputation derives, in large measure, from the city's centuries-long toleration of Jews and the flourishing of Jewish life that this attitude made possible.

Toleration is as old as Jewish diasporic history itself. Not, admittedly, toleration as we have come to know and value it where it has existed in the last two centuries: prior to the modern era no toleration, anywhere, was ever absolute. Unlike the modern concept of toleration, in which religious liberty is based on acknowledgement of the individual's natural or inalienable rights, pre-modern toleration was more nearly synonymous with permission, granted by an authority. Whether the case involved Jews or, in Europe, fellow Christians, the authority more or less seriously disapproved of the tolerated belief or practice, but had, for reasons of its own, decided not to press its case and apply the full weight of its coercive power against the dissenting group.[1]

Needless to say, there was a great deal of variety in the reasons inspiring dominant groups to extend toleration to dissenting minorities. Sometimes toleration was based on tradition, as, for instance, when the Christian Roman emperors inherited the doctrine of Judaism as *religio licita* from their pagan

---

[1] Jordan, *Development of Religious Toleration*, i. 15–19; Lecler, *Toleration*, vol. i, p. x.

predecessors.[2] At other times, a policy of toleration was dictated by reason—whether the reason of theology, as in Augustine's doctrine of the Jews as witnesses to the truth of Christianity, or the more mundane reason of economic welfare, as in the medieval charters inviting Jews to settle in certain towns.[3] It is in these terms—of tradition, and of theological or economic reason—that the history of premodern Jewry toleration is generally couched.[4]

In the case of Amsterdam and Holland, the common argument runs something like this: as Amsterdam had never harboured Jews prior to the 1590s and Jews had only been short-term and occasional residents of the medieval county of Holland, there existed no local tradition either for or against the toleration of Jews;[5] so, when it became apparent that Jews wished to settle in Amsterdam and other cities in Holland, the authorities must have had either intellectual or economic reasons for allowing them to do so. As Protestants, the Dutch authorities may have disapproved of Judaism and Jews less strongly than Catholic authorities, and may therefore have been less passionate and more rational in their deliberations. The precise nature of the intellectual or economic rationale behind Holland's toleration of Jews remains a matter of dispute. Some stress the influence of the allegedly tolerant tradition of Erasmian humanism. Others point to certain chiliastic expectations based, in part, on the ultimate conversion of the Jews—a conversion thought to be more readily achievable in an atmosphere of genuine Christian (i.e. Protestant) charity than in that of Catholic idolatry, exploitation, and greed. Yet others highlight the significance of religious freedom as a general political principle in Dutch history ever since it had become a central issue in the early stages of the Revolt of the Netherlands (1568–c.1620). Most emphasize the economic argument that toleration was not only good but even necessary to guarantee the economic prosperity of a small province like Holland.

Whatever variant of the argument is adduced, its proponents for the most part fail to consider the practical application of Jewry toleration in seventeenth-century Amsterdam—that is to say, the actual legislation put in place and operated. The fairly elaborate, wholly speculative, and never implemented Jewry law proposal of the famous jurist Hugo de Groot (Grotius) further skewed attention away from contemporary practice. Unfortunately, but not uncharacteristically, the burgomasters and city councillors who actually determined Amsterdam's policy had

[2] Juster, *Juifs dans l'empire romain*, i. 243–51, 409–12.

[3] Blumenkranz, 'Augustin et les juifs'; Kisch, *Jews in Medieval Germany*, 135–9. For the later example of Venice, see Ravid, *Economics and Toleration*.

[4] As it has become customary to distinguish between Jewish law, i.e. law by Jews for internal governance, and Jewry law, i.e. law of others governing Jews, it may be useful to distinguish Jewish toleration, i.e. by Jews of others, from Jewry toleration, i.e. by others of Jews. For discussions of Jewry toleration along lines different from those guiding the following discussion, see J. Katz, *Exclusiveness and Tolerance*, 156–96; Baron, 'Medieval Heritage and Modern Realities'; Ettinger, 'Beginnings of the Change'.

[5] For a summary of Jewish settlements in the Netherlands during the Middle Ages, see Speet, 'De middeleeuwen', in Blom *et al.* (eds.), *Geschiedenis*, 19–49.

very little to say on the subject. Nevertheless, from their thoughts on other subjects and from those of others more representative than Hugo de Groot, in conjunction with an examination of the evidence of what actually went on, we may yet infer the precise nature and scope of their toleration.

THE LAW IN PRACTICE

In 1579 the seven rebel provinces of the Northern Netherlands assembled in Utrecht to draft the so-called 'Union of Utrecht' which was to give their rebellion against Spain greater cohesion and force. Article XIII of that agreement is often presented as a general declaration of freedom of conscience. In fact the article primarily concerns the mutual toleration of Protestants and Catholics in the five provinces other than Holland and Zeeland. The latter were given the right 'to conduct themselves as they liked', which in effect meant to outlaw the public practice of Catholicism. Freedom of conscience makes its appearance almost as an aside: 'on condition that each one in particular will remain free in his choice of religion without fear of investigation'. This proviso was intended to preclude the promulgation of heresy laws or the establishment of an inquisition, hated instruments by which the duke of Alba had tried to quell the rebellion, only to stir up ever more discord. In the minds of many, however, freedom of conscience, perhaps more than any other issue, had emerged as the great goal of the rebellion.[6] Clearly no thought of Jews, however remote, entered the consideration of the signatories to the Union of Utrecht. On the other hand, freedom of conscience became such a powerful slogan and the prospect of interminable religious squabbles so unappealing that many a magistrate in Holland must have grown wary of scrutinizing the religious convictions of his city's or town's residents any more closely than was necessary to maintain peace and order. In so far as Article XIII of the Union of Utrecht had any bearing on subsequent toleration of Jews, therefore, it did so indirectly in tending to inhibit action on the part of the authorities on any subject relating to religion.

The city of Amsterdam had joined the rebels rather late, in 1578, and the immigration of Portuguese merchants began not long thereafter, in the early 1590s.[7] On 31 March 1597 Manuel Rodrigues became the first Portuguese *poorter* (burgher) of Amsterdam. About the same time the Jewish background of the Portuguese immigrants became apparent. In 1598 Hugo de Groot wrote that 'the refugees from Portugal, a part of the Jews who have remained in that country, have preferred the great city of Amsterdam over others, some for fear of an inquisition into their ancestral religion and others in expectation of greater gain'.[8] In a

---

[6] Motley, *Rise of the Dutch Republic*, iv. 159–65; Geyl, *Revolt of the Netherlands*, 169–78; Lecler, *Toleration*, i. 220–1.

[7] Brugmans, *Geschiedenis van Amsterdam*, ii. 113–27; Koen, 'Earliest Sources'.

[8] Quoted in Seeligmann, 'Marranen-probleem', 106.

resolution adopted on 4 September 1598 the burgomasters of Amsterdam implicitly recognized the special character of Portuguese immigrants. 'Trusting that
[the Portuguese merchants] are Christians and will live an honest life as good
burghers', they allowed them to purchase burgher rights, 'on the condition that
before making the oath they be warned that in this city no other religion can nor
may be practised than that practised publicly in the churches'.[9] The first part of
the resolution regarding the presumed Christianity of the Portuguese merchants is
rather vague, probably intentionally so. For the time being, as long as the incomers
lived 'an honest life', the burgomasters appear to have been willing to accept at face
value the Christian façade that Portuguese New Christians presented wherever
they settled. It is doubtful, moreover, whether the Amsterdam burgomasters
either had or were interested in gaining any substantial understanding of the
ancestral ties binding some, perhaps many, New Christians to Judaism. In the
second part of the resolution the burgomasters merely reiterated the principle of
freedom of conscience. The resolution distinguishes between public and private
worship, restricting the freedom of the former, but allowing a large measure of
freedom in the latter. Freedom of conscience, as defined by Article XIII of the
Union of Utrecht—namely, as the absence of persecution—required no greater
degree of explicitness on the part of Amsterdam's burgomasters than this resolution exhibited, and the subject was never taken up again. Freedom of worship,
however, remained another matter, for Jews and for others.

   Freedom of worship was never formally granted to the Jews of Amsterdam. The
city's magistrature dealt with the issue of Jewish worship—whose emergence is
discussed in Chapter 4—as it came up and in so far as it presented problems. As
early as 1603 Amsterdam's officials learned (by accident, while questioning Philips
Joosten, alias Moses Uri Halevi, on an accusation of theft and being a fence or
pawnbroker) that he practised Judaism in private.[10] No action was taken. In 1606
and 1608 Amsterdam's burgomasters denied a request by the Portuguese nation
to be allowed to buy land for burial grounds in the vicinity of the city.[11] The
Portuguese nation continued to use its existing burial grounds in Groet near
Alkmaar. As the reasons for the refusal are not stated, they may have rested on
other grounds than the denial of the right of public worship to Judaism.

   While other cities in Holland—Alkmaar in 1604, Haarlem in 1605, and
Rotterdam in 1610[12]—had already favourably, if conditionally (pending the settlement of larger numbers of Jews), settled the issue of Jewish worship, Amsterdam
did not deal with the Portuguese as Jews until the 1610s, and then only after the
Portuguese themselves had emerged publicly as Jews. The initial response was
negative. In 1612 members of the Portuguese nation hired the carpenter Hans

   [9] Bontemantel, *Regeeringe van Amsterdam*, vol. i, p. cxxxii.
   [10] Zwarts, 'Eerste rabbijnen', 172–9, (documents) 251–4.
   [11] Ibid. 195, 203–4, (documents) 256–8.
   [12] Ibid. 186–96, 204–9; de Groot, *Remonstrantie*, ed. Meijer, 37–46.

Gerritsz. to build a large house, apparently to be used as a synagogue.[13] (Gerritsz. was explicitly instructed not to work on the building between sunset on Friday and Sunday night.) When the project was brought to the attention of the City Council by the elders of the Reformed Church, the councillors decided, on 8 May 1612, 'that no one of that [Portuguese] nation may live in that building and that no gatherings may be convened there nor any ceremonies of their religion practised, under penalty of demolition, to the ground, of that house or building and the prohibition to practise their religion in any other places within this city and its jurisdiction'. Notwithstanding this injunction, the building was finished and used as a synagogue. It was, however, no longer owned by the Portuguese nation but rather by Nicolaes van Campen, himself a member of the City Council. The transfer of ownership may have enabled the Portuguese Jews to claim that they were still practising their Judaism in private; or it may at least have made it very difficult for the elders of the Church to persist in their protest. More importantly, the council resolution of 1612, in its very threat to prohibit the practice of Judaism altogether, fully and explicitly endorsed the interpretation of freedom of conscience first hinted at in the magistrature's earlier resolution of 1598. Surprisingly, in view of the formalistic interpretation of 'freedom of conscience' implied in these two resolutions, no other official statement, formal or informal, ever granted or denied the Portuguese, German, or Polish Jews the right to practise Judaism publicly.

Given the *de jure* recognition of the Jews' right to practise their religion in private, the council did not carry out its threat of 1612, privacy of worship being assured either by the transfer of ownership or by the absence of any further public complaint from the Reformed Church. In any event, as the building came to be used as a synagogue, the Portuguese nation gained *de facto* recognition of their right to practise Judaism publicly; and once *de facto* recognition had been granted, the right of public worship no longer needed to be translated into law. Such seems to have been the characteristic procedure of Amsterdam's authorities; a procedure which, when properly understood, at no stage involved a principled reluctance to grant the Jews full right to public worship.

In 1614 the magistrates tacitly acknowledged public worship by Jews. In that year the leaders of the Portuguese nation purchased land for burial grounds in Ouderkerk aan de Amstel, some five miles from Amsterdam.[14] A petition by the villagers of Ouderkerk to prohibit the Jews from burying their dead there was ignored by the magistrate of Amsterdam. Another tacit acknowledgement occurred in 1618–19. A conflict had arisen in one of the two then existing Portuguese Jewish communities, resulting in the creation of a third community.[15] When the two factions could not arrive at a mutually satisfactory division of their

---

[13] Zwarts, 'Eerste rabbijnen', 209–16, (documents) 260–4; Koen, 'Waar en voor wie' and 'Nicolaes van Campen als huiseigenaar'.

[14] Pieterse, *Livro de Bet Haim*, pp. xii–xiv.   [15] D'Ancona, 'Komst der Marranen', 228–39.

former common property, they appealed to the city authorities to settle their dispute. On 6 August 1619, the three arbiters appointed by the magistrature arranged an agreement that both parties accepted. Other recognitions of Jewish worship followed. On 25 March 1659 the justices of the city granted a Portuguese Jewish request to excuse them from appearing in court on Saturdays.[16] Cases involving Jews were to be postponed until the following Tuesday. The States of Holland were occasionally asked on behalf of either the Portuguese Jewish community as a whole or one of its charitable organizations to rule on issues involving exemption from certain taxes. For instance, in 1691, the *parnasim* (synagogue leaders) of the Portuguese Jews of Amsterdam requested the States that they be exempted, like other religious congregations, from the impost on the 8,000 tons of peat which they annually distributed among their poor. In 1693 the request was granted.[17]

Such were the only legal enactments pertaining to the public practice of Judaism or regarding the Jewish community as a religious association. Other laws, by-laws, and legal decisions affected the Jews as individuals, in their capacity as dissenters, as people with differing customs, or as non-natives. In other words, the vast majority of 'Jewry laws' concerned the Jews not as a distinct category, but in so far as various other more general definitions applied to them.

Regarding the Jews as dissenters, Amsterdam's burgomasters passed a general regulation in 1616 that remained on the books until the emancipation of Dutch Jewry in 1795. According to this sweeping resolution, the closest Amsterdam ever came to formulating a 'Jewry statute', the Jews were warned (1) 'not to speak or write (and to make sure that is not spoken or written) anything that may, in any way, tend to the disdain of our Christian religion'; (2) 'not to attempt to seduce any Christian person from our Christian religion nor to circumcise one'; and (3) 'not to have any carnal conversation, whether in or out of wedlock, with Christian women or maidens, not even when such are of ill repute'.[18] These particular restrictions, first introduced in the days of the Christian Roman Empire, had formed part and parcel of traditional Jewry law.[19] Similar restrictions were contemplated or enacted in other parts of the United Provinces around this time with regard to

[16] Noordkerk, *Handvesten*, ii. 472–3.

[17] *Gedrukte resolutiën der Staten van Holland en West-Friesland*, 25 Aug. 1691, 8 Apr. 1693.

[18] Noordkerk, *Handvesten*, ii. 472.

[19] The prohibition on converting Christians to Judaism dates from Constantine the Great. Sexual relations between Christians and Jewish women were first prohibited at the Council of Elvira (about 300). During the Middle Ages the prohibition was enlarged to include any and all sexual relations between Jews and Christians. In the days of the Christian Roman emperors specific forms of blasphemy by Jews were prohibited. For instance, Jews were not to disturb the Christian sacraments nor were they to mock the Cross during Purim. From the days of the Visigothic kings of Spain onwards, however, Jews were forbidden to criticize Christian doctrine in general. See Juster, *Juifs dans l'empire romain*, i. 259–63; S. Katz, *Jews in the Visigothic and Frankish Kingdoms*, 89; Parkes, *Conflict of the Church and the Synagogue*, 174; Kisch, *Jews in Medieval Germany*, 197–200, 205–7.

Christian dissenting minorities.[20] Their introduction into Amsterdam at this juncture, in a form altogether milder than in previous centuries, does not seem to have been prompted by any awareness of their history in Christian tradition but rather by specific contemporary incidents. On numerous occasions prior to 1616 the Council of the Reformed Church had complained about the Jews as blasphemers and had brought to the attention of the burgomasters cases of certain Christian individuals who had converted to Judaism and/or were having sexual relations with Jews.[21] The similarities between the Amsterdam provisions and their medieval precursors must not be seen as embodying a conscious imitation, but merely reflect the dominant position, politically and socially, of a particular brand of Christianity, and the normal desire to protect that position. Only the third stipulation interfered in the social life of the Jews, and this was the sole social barrier ever erected between the Christian and Jewish populations of the city.

According to the preamble to the 1616 law, sexual relations between Jewish males and Christian females were the immediate reason for its introduction. Indeed, such relations with Christian women, of good and ill repute alike, are reported very frequently throughout the seventeenth century. We learn of such intimate contact only when something went wrong—for example, when the woman became pregnant and sued her former lover or employer for childbirth expenses or child support, or when the man and woman were caught in the act by the bailiff's men.[22] Pregnancy seems to have resulted frequently in the case of sexual relations between a Portuguese Jew and his or the family's Christian maid. The inopportune arrival of the police was a frequent occurrence in Amsterdam's many brothels. Such raids were not carried out specifically with the aim of trapping Portuguese Jews, but any apprehended were fined. In view of the frequency of such illicit 'carnal conversation', the action of Amsterdam's city fathers in promulgating the law of 1616 is notable for its restraint. Almost everywhere else in Europe Jews were prohibited from employing Christian servants;[23] not surpris-

[20] Brandt, *History of the Reformation*, ii. 10–14, tells of remonstrances by the ministers of the South and North Holland synods presented to the States of Holland and West Friesland. In the remonstrances, the ministers address questions of censorship, marriage to unbaptized persons, and adultery in a context having nothing to do with Jews.

[21] Zwarts, 'Eerste rabbijnen', 217–20, (documents) 258, 265.

[22] The following are a few notarial deeds referring to illegitimate children fathered by Portuguese Jews with Christian women: GAA, NA 645, pp. 1113–15 (11 Nov. 1620; S. Cornelisz.); 941, fos. 497–9 (23 Dec. 1631; D. Bredan); 1556 A, p. 35 (5 Feb. 1643; J. V. Oli); 2269, fo. 514 (31 July 1654; A. Lock); 2231, p. 817 (21 Nov. 1669; A. Lock); 4078 (18 Apr. 1674; D. v. d. Groe); 4077 (6 Dec. 1673; D. v. d. Groe); 4253 A, p. 349 (21 Apr. 1707; D. v. d. Groe). The confession books of the Amsterdam court are replete with references to Portuguese Jewish visitors of the city's brothels: GAA, ORA 307, fo. 183ᵛ; 308, fo. 234; 309, fos. 120, 214; 310, fo. 276; 311, fos. 264ᵛ, 274; 314, fos. 55ᵛ, 67ᵛ; 316, fos. 101ᵛ, 187, 187ᵛ, 188; 317, fo. 127; 318, fos. 37, 96, 254ᵛ; 319, fo. 60; 320, fos. 121ᵛ, 124, 126ᵛ; 322, fos. 124, 138ᵛ, 153ᵛ, 156, 212ᵛ; 323, fo. 11ᵛ; 328, fo. 183; 331, fo. 43; 335, fos. 14, 128ᵛ; 336, fo. 93ᵛ; 337, fo. 255ᵛ; 338, fo. 88ᵛ; 339, fos. 73ᵛ, 74ᵛ; 341, fo. 191, 191ᵛ; 342, fo. 2ᵛ; 346, fo. 175; 347, fos. 63ᵛ, 242ᵛ, 256.

[23] Kisch, *Jews in Medieval Germany*, 300–1, 336, 350; Dubnov, *History of the Jews in Russia and Poland*, i. 49, 82, 87, 160; Vogelstein, *Rome*, 160–1, 165, 268.

ingly, therefore, the Christian maids in the service of Portuguese Jewish families in Amsterdam continually elicit remarks from foreign visitors, most notably from German travellers.[24]

As mentioned above, Amsterdam had no tradition of Jewish residence whatsoever. The New Christian colony of Antwerp, whose settlement dated from the time when the Northern and Southern Netherlands were still united and shared the same overlord, was the closest precedent at hand.[25] However, the differences between the New Christian colony of Antwerp and the Jewish community of Amsterdam precluded any simple transposition of legal provisions from the former to the latter. Not only had the Portuguese lived in Antwerp as Christians and now lived in Amsterdam as Jews, but also in Antwerp they had been organized as a factory with the backing of the king of Portugal, whereas Amsterdam did not recognize the factory institution for any of its foreign mercantile colonies, nor did the émigrés any longer enjoy royal protection. Perhaps the most salient example of Amsterdam's legal inexperience *vis-à-vis* the Jews is the obscurity surrounding the degree of autonomy exercised by the Jewish community. Autonomy had been— and still was in eastern Europe—the mainstay of the medieval Jewish community.[26] Provisions regarding its nature and extent were never absent from medieval Jewry charters. It is, therefore, all the more surprising that the Amsterdam officials ignored the issue almost completely. On a few occasions when the authorities were asked or forced to intervene in the internal affairs of the Jewish community, Amsterdam's justices had to face some of the issues traditionally associated with the autonomy of the Jewish community, in particular concerning the use of the *herem* (ban) by the *parnasim* in order to force compliance with the community's rules and regulations. In 1670 a dispute between the *parnasim* and the heirs of Jacob Delmonte (alias Jacob del Sotto) resulted in the excommunication of the heirs, who then organized their own, private prayer meetings and purchased their own cemetery.[27] The *parnasim* applied to the Court of Amsterdam to confirm their regulations prohibiting the formation of any synagogue or *minyan* (prayer meeting of at least ten adult males) outside the existing community. The court granted the request without stating why, but stipulated that it exempted the heirs of Jacob Delmonte, if they desired to meet separately.

A little over a decade later a much less serious dispute produced more reflection by higher authorities. A dispute between Jacob Pereyra and his sons concerning the inheritance of his wife and their mother seems to have prompted the sons to steal their mother's *ketubah* (marriage contract)—for what purpose is not entirely

[24] 'Es wuert disen Juden zugelassen, Christen maegt zu ihren diensten zu halten, welches ich an keinen orth noch gefunden noch gehoert habe': Heeres, 'Jörg Franz Müller's reisindrukken', 195.

[25] Prins, *Vestiging der Marranen*; Goris, *Étude sus les colonies marchandes méridionales*; Pohl, *Portugiesen in Antwerpen*.

[26] Baron, *Jewish Community*, i. 208–82.

[27] Noordkerk, *Handvesten*, ii. 473–4. The dispute between the *parnasim* and the heirs of Jacob Delmonte is discussed in Chapter 5 below.

clear.[28] Jacob Pereyra asked the *parnasim* to threaten the thieves (he did not identify them as his sons) with excommunication. Pereyra's sons objected to the procedure and appealed to the Court of Amsterdam. The court endorsed their protest
on 27 January 1683, but on 14 May its decision was overturned by the burgomasters at the request of the *parnasim*. Pereyra's sons then appealed to the Court of
Holland, and just prior to that court's decision the deputies of Amsterdam (representatives of the burgomasters and city council at the States of Holland,
the provincial assembly) brought the dispute to the attention of the States (on
26 January 1686), arguing the case of the *parnasim*, and requested the States to
prevent the court from interfering in the internal affairs of the Portuguese Jewish
community. In the course of this minor but heated dispute the Amsterdam authorities revealed their conception not only of the extent to which excommunication
may be used as a punitive measure but also, albeit less clearly, of where the boundaries lay of what they considered 'internal' to the community and therefore subject
to its autonomous action.

In overturning the Amsterdam court's judgment the burgomasters argued that
it had, unfortunately, been interpreted as intended to interfere 'in the free management of synagogal affairs' (the Dutch text has *Kerkelijke zaaken*, 'church affairs')
and 'to reduce the authority and free disposition of those to whom these are
entrusted in accordance with the rules and regulations adopted by the Spanish and
Portuguese Jewish Nation'. The burgomasters wished to declare 'that all such
freedoms, rights, and prerogatives as have been enjoyed up to now, and especially
those concerning the administration of the synagogue and what relates to it, remain
with the members of that Nation, and especially with the *parnasim* appointed to
manage its synagogal affairs'. These extracts reveal the difficulties Amsterdam's
burgomasters experienced in formulating a general approach to the issue in question. The word 'especially' introduces the substantive point they wished to make.

In their statement before the States of Holland, the Amsterdam deputies were a
little more specific. With regard to the 'freedoms, rights, and prerogatives', they
say—in one characteristic seventeenth-century sentence—that

those of the Jewish Nation have been tolerated for a number of years, also with regard to
their liturgy and synagogal affairs, including those solemnities and ceremonies which, in
accordance with the Mosaic laws and otherwise from of old, they still observe daily, among
which the exercise of synagogal discipline has always been one of the most important, such
as, also, the exercise of the ban or excommunication which has been as effective (in the
experience of the burgomasters) as the strictest political laws in maintaining quiet and unity
and curtailing disturbances among the said Nation.

The disturbance feared most was the community's inability to enforce payment of
its taxes, which, in turn, could result in the community's poor becoming a burden

---

[28] Noordkerk, *Handvesten*, ii. 474; *Gedrukte resolutiën der Staten van Holland en West-Friesland*,
26 Jan. 1686.

to the city at large.[29] The Pereyra dispute, Amsterdam's deputies argued, was not a matter of ordinary ('political') justice, but was in essence a synagogal, domestic affair. It was not right—it was even harmful—to grant to the courts final disposition of disciplinary measures essential to preserving synagogal discipline.

Clearly the authorities did not express an opinion regarding the general right of the *parnasim* to adjudge or adjudicate a dispute such as that between Pereyra and his sons. The conflict had not yet taken a course which raised this question. The *parnasim* had exerted their disciplinary authority to resolve a domestic squabble and to prevent it from becoming a public issue. They had not adjudicated a crime, but had merely tried to clear the air of the suspicion that a crime, namely the theft of the *ketubah* by Pereyra's sons, might be involved. Amsterdam's officials addressed themselves explicitly to that preliminary, disciplinary intervention only. The 'autonomy' of the Jewish community discussed in the burgomasters' statements on the Pereyra dispute was not a judicial autonomy. On the contrary, everything in the texts quoted points to the absence of any judicial autonomy within the Jewish community. Had judicial autonomy been the accepted norm, the Pereyra dispute could not have given rise to the discussion that it evoked among the various Dutch authorities.

In their submission to the States of Holland, the Amsterdam deputies defined the Jewish community narrowly as a voluntary religious association governed by Mosaic laws and ancient customs. The use of excommunication in order to discipline the members of the association was regarded as one such ancient custom, one by which members of the association had to abide *ipso facto*, because of their voluntary membership and the voluntary delegation of authority to the *parnasim*. The crux of the problem lies in the conception of discipline: for the Amsterdam authorities understood synagogal discipline to cover not merely behaviour connected with the 'religious' nature of the association (as we would understand the term 'religious' today) but also other social behaviour that was not fully 'political', that is, regulated by the municipal or provincial authorities. Social behaviour such as the domestic squabbles between the Pereyras fell outside the scope of Dutch political authority, at least as long as the charge of theft was not formalized. Such behaviour lay within the scope of communal responsibility because of the voluntary agreement, sanctioned by religious custom, of the members of the Jewish nation. The ban, elsewhere a powerful instrument of Jewish autonomy invested with political authority, was in Amsterdam a disciplinary measure, hallowed by religious custom, encompassing certain forms of social behaviour not immediately within the purview of Dutch political authority. Conscious of the fact that over-zealous use of the weapon of excommunication might result in problems that would ultimately affect the city authorities, on 14 May 1683 the burgomasters

---

[29] Noordkerk, *Handvesten*, ii. 474: '. . . diminution in the respect for synagogal discipline such that it would no longer have the proper effect regarding the support of the poor and other necessary matters'.

counselled the *parnasim* 'to take special care not to disturb the quiet and unity among the [Portuguese] Nation by capriciously exercising the synagogal ban beyond customary moderation and by being more rigorous than is necessary and proper'.

Another traditional domain of Jewish autonomy subjected to official scrutiny concerned the legalization of marital bonds. Two separate issues arose in this regard: the imposition of obligatory civil marriage upon the Jews, and the differences in the degrees of consanguinity between marriage partners allowed by Jewish law as opposed to Dutch law. A political ordinance of 1 April 1580 laid down the marriage laws of Holland and West Frisia in conformity with the new ideas of the Reformation.[30] According to Reformed theory, marriage was no longer a sacrament; it was therefore removed from the domain of grace to that of 'natural life' and, concomitantly, from the jurisdiction of the Church to that of the state. Henceforth, all marriages contracted in Holland had to be legalized before the secular, that is to say the city, authorities. An exception was made with regard to marriages between men and women of the Reformed Church, who were allowed to choose between secular and religious legalization; and, since even civil marriages were followed by religious ceremonies, the great majority of Reformed marriages were legalized in church rather than at the city hall. Thus the curious situation emerged in which the dominant religious group followed the exception rather than the rule, having inherited, as a result of legal inertia, the privilege of ecclesiastical marriage from previous Catholic practice.[31] In other words, the obligatory civil marriages required of the Jews did not constitute an arbitrary deviation from established legal practice motivated by any particular, negative concern. On the other hand, making the legality of Jewish marriages conditional upon their confirmation by the civil authorities did signify some encroachment, however unintentional, upon the traditional autonomy of the Jewish community.

Two official warnings were necessary to remind Amsterdam's Jews of the implications of the political ordinance of 1580. In 1622 the Portuguese Jews were told that their marriages had to be registered and confirmed at the city hall in order to become legal.[32] Even those men and women already married in Amsterdam before the rabbis had to have their marriages legalized retroactively. The exhortation was repeated in 1656 when, during an inheritance dispute, one of the parties claimed that the daughter of a marriage that had not been duly registered was illegitimate.[33] Unfamiliarity with the novel practice of civil marriage—stemming more likely from the exclusive experience with Catholic practice in Spain and Portugal rather than from a wish to assert traditional Jewish autonomy—necessitated these two courteous reminders from the city authorities, who merely reiterated legal norms adopted before the settlement of the Portuguese Jews in Amsterdam.

[30] Van Apeldoorn, *Geschiedenis van het Nederlandsche huwelijksrecht*, 70.
[31] Ibid. 84–9.   [32] Noordkerk, *Handvesten*, ii. 470–1.
[33] *Gedrukte resolutiën der Staten van Holland en West-Friesland*, 30 Sept. 1656; Noordkerk, *Handvesten*, ii. 471–2.

With regard to the issue of consanguinity, for over a century neither the Amsterdam justices nor the Portuguese Jews realized that the political ordinance of 1580 contained other, even more restrictive, clauses than that requiring civil legalization of marriage. Eventually it was discovered that the ordinance explicitly prohibited marriages of various degrees of consanguinity allowed by Jewish law. In particular, it forbade marriages between uncles and nieces, frequent occurrences among Portuguese Jews.[34] It is not clear who or what brought the discrepancy to the attention of the authorities, but in 1712 the States of Holland assembled testimony in order to resolve this issue once and for all.[35] The Portuguese Jews argued that such marriages, allowed according to Leviticus 18 and 20, were permitted everywhere that Jews lived, specifically in France and even in Rome. Individual Portuguese Jews intimated that, were the States to rule unfavourably on their request to grant the Jews exemption from these provisions of the political ordinance, they might have to move elsewhere. The States also heard the advice of jurists and professors of theology of the University of Leiden, but the content of their replies is not reported. On 14 May 1712 the States of Holland decided that the Jews did have to observe, in all strictness, the clauses of the political ordinance of 1580 and ruled against the legality of uncle–niece marriages, excepting those already contracted. Neither the States of Holland nor the city authorities of Amsterdam considered marriage an internal communal affair; and, once marriage was removed from the domain of Jewish ecclesiastical jurisdiction, Dutch matrimonial law governed the Jews indiscriminately as individual members of the polity.

Two other significant aspects of traditional Jewish autonomy—residential rights and censorship—were never openly discussed in Amsterdam. Permission to reside in Amsterdam ultimately rested with the city authorities. As far as I know, no Jew, other than one convicted of a crime, was ever denied the right to live and work in Amsterdam. Nor did the Jewish communal authorities there ever adopt any rule or regulation resembling the medieval institution of the *ḥerem hayishuv*, the restriction (literally, ban) on settlement.[36] If anything, the Jewish authorities' attempts to lure indigent immigrants into re-emigration by offering to pay their travel expenses (a topic discussed more fully in Chapter 4) seems to indicate their lack of authority simply to withhold residential rights from undesired immigrants.[37]

Censorship is a somewhat more complex area. Never did the Amsterdam authorities formally grant the Jewish communal leaders the right to censor the publications of their congregants. Yet the *parnasim*, aided by the rabbis, did on a

---

[34] Van Apeldoorn, *Geschiedenis van het Nederlandsche huwelijksrecht*, 160–1.

[35] *Gedrukte resolutiën der Staten van Holland en West-Friesland*, 27 Nov. 1710, 19 Feb., 7 May, 14 May 1712; van Apeldoorn, *Geschiedenis van het Nederlandsche huwelijksrecht*, 73; van Apeldoorn's note in de Groot, *Inleidinge tot de Hollandsche rechts-geleerdheid*, ii. 5–6. In 1622, 1656, and 1712, the authorities declared all marriages previously contracted in contravention of the political ordinance legal. The States agreed to this dispensation in order to avoid inheritance disputes.

[36] Baron, *Jewish Community*, ii. 5–11; Rabinowitz, *Herem hayyishub*.

[37] D'Ancona, 'Komst der Marranen', 245–6; Baron, *Jewish Community*, i. 363–4, ii. 332–3, iii. 212–13.

great number of occasions exercise their statutory right (according to haskamah 37) to censorship.[38] Unfortunately, the community leaders' arrogated right to censorship was never tested. No Portuguese Jew censored by the Mahamad (the board of six *parnasim* and a treasurer or *gabai*) ever appealed against its decision to the secular authorities. Writers who wished to avoid censorship could do so by publishing abroad, especially in Antwerp. Publications of strictly Jewish interest would inevitably be subject to censorship within the intended audience, even if the author obtained permission to distribute the work from outside the community; authors of such work therefore had no reason to resort to the secular courts. Publications of more general interest were generally geared towards a Spanish-reading audience, and their publication in Antwerp was no handicap; on the contrary, if effectively divested of Jewish associations, it might even have helped their distribution, especially in the Iberian peninsula. These authors too, then, could expect no immediate benefit from court procedures in Amsterdam. Because the *parnasim*'s right to censorship was never formally disputed, it is impossible to say whether censorship constituted a weapon of communal autonomy sanctioned by government approval or whether it remained uncontested because of voluntary submission prompted by common sense.

In sum, the autonomy of the Jewish community was limited to internal administrative and some disciplinary matters. Its scope was defined by communal concerns such as synagogue worship, education, charity, and, possibly, censorship. In all other, individual, respects Amsterdam's Jews were expected to abide—and did generally abide—by the laws of Holland and Amsterdam.

In contrast, the laws of Amsterdam did not always apply equally to the Jews. Amsterdam's Jews were always permitted to become *poorters* (burghers).[39] But the acquisition of burgher rights did not follow the same rules for Jews as for others, nor did possession of these rights entitle Jews to the same privileges as Christian *poorters*. Unlike the Christian *poorters*, Jewish *poorters* could not transmit their *poorterschap* (burghership) to their children, nor could a Jew become a *poorter* by marrying the daughter of a *poorter*.[40] More serious was the exclusion of Jewish *poorters* from the right to engage in *poortersneringen* (literally, livelihoods of a *poorter*) since this right was the single most important reason for wanting to become a *poorter*.[41] Although they were never very clearly defined, in practice *poortersneringen* came to include all trades and crafts organized in guilds.[42]

---

[38] GAA, PIG 19, p. 110. The censorship exercised by the *parnasim* is discussed in Chapter 5 below.

[39] Excepting the resolution of 1598, the Amsterdam magistrature never passed a law preventing Jews from purchasing the *poortersrecht* (burgher rights). The 1598 resolution was passed prior to the city authorities' acknowledgement of the Jews' presence in the city and therefore has no bearing on the subsequent period. Bloom's statement on this issue (*Economic Activities*, 22) has absolutely no basis in fact: 'In certain exceptional cases important merchants were granted the privilege of buying "poorters-recht" (right of citizenship).'   [40] Reijnders, *Van 'Joodsche natiën'*, 24.

[41] Noordkerk, *Handvesten*, i. 138. The resolution is dated 29 Mar. 1632.

[42] Van Dillen, *Bronnen*, i. 796.

Occupational restrictions upon Jews are a common, albeit not universal, feature of pre-modern history.[43] Exclusion from guilds in particular limited Jewish economic activities in a great many cities and towns. Amsterdam's enforcement of similar limitations undoubtedly represents the closest single correspondence between its otherwise liberal legislation and traditional discriminatory practices. On the other hand, the similarity must not be allowed to obscure the specifically local conditions out of which this occupational discrimination in Amsterdam emerged.

Throughout the seventeenth century, Amsterdam's rulers protected the interests of the guilds.[44] Themselves mainly engaged in commerce, the burgomasters and City Council members hoped thereby to prevent the guilds from spreading their political and economic sphere of influence while at the same time co-opting guild members into accepting political and economic policies tailored primarily to the interests of the mercantile community. In guild-related matters the city fathers tended to adopt a somewhat conservative stance, agreeing to those guild demands that did not immediately encroach upon their own commercial domain.

This give and take between the burgomasters and City Council on the one hand and the guilds on the other affected the Jews in various ways. The particular by-law excluding Jewish *poorters* from *poortersneringen* was passed in 1632 in the wake of protests by the Christian retailers' guild in 1629 and 1631 that Jews were setting up tobacco shops.[45] At that point retailing seems to have been the only trade in which Jewish immigrants wished to engage. In 1668, however, under more substantial Jewish pressure, the 1632 by-law was modified to allow Jews to open tobacco retail stores.[46] In 1655, notwithstanding Christian claims that sugar refining was included among the prohibited *poortersneringen* of 1632, Abraham Pereyra, one of the city's most prominent Portuguese Jewish merchants, received permission, for himself and for other Jews, to establish a refinery.[47] To the best of my knowledge, guild exclusiveness was not tested by Jews in other trades or crafts. The brokers', physicians', surgeons', apothecaries', and bookdealers' guilds never excluded Jews,[48] who were particularly numerous in these professions, regardless of the exclusiveness of other guilds. They were admitted because in these occupations Jewish guild members did not compete with their Christian counterparts— or did so to only a small degree. The clientele of Jewish physicians, surgeons, pharmacists, and bookdealers was almost exclusively Jewish, and that of the Jewish brokers was restricted by law to Jews. Finally, with regard to most new industries that appeared on the Amsterdam scene in the course of the seventeenth century the

---

[43]   In the absence of a general and satisfactory economic history of the Jews, a rapid overview may be gained from Baron, Kahan, *et al.*, *Economic History*, 57–9, 61–9, 72–3.

[44]   Van Ravesteyn, *Onderzoekingen*, 163; Brugmans, *Opkomst en bloei*, 142; Barbour, *Capitalism in Amsterdam*, 71.

[45]   Van Dillen, *Bronnen*, ii. 690–1.   [46]   Bloom, *Economic Activities*, 31.

[47]   Noordkerk, *Handvesten*, i. 138; Bontemantel, *Regeeringe van Amsterdam*, ii. 498; Reesse, *Suikerhandel*, 127.

[48]   Bloom, *Economic Activities*, 23, 55; van Eeghen, *Inventarissen*, 23, 30, 83.

city government successfully resisted guild formation. Consequently, the sugar refining (as seen by the 1655 decision), tobacco manufacturing, and diamond industries were never closed to Jews. And not insignificantly, for reasons solely related to the particular concentrations of Portuguese Jewish commerce and having nothing whatsoever to do with guild exclusivism, these were the industries that attracted the largest amounts of Jewish financial and labour investment. Guild restrictions hardly ever affected the most important spheres of the economic life of Amsterdam's Jews. Where they did, the restrictions were lifted or modified.[49] The attitude of the guilds was formed more by fear of competition than by Church-inspired anti-Jewish sentiments, and their generally discriminatory stance affected non-native Christians as well as Jews, though admittedly less radically.[50]

Jewish merchants were not affected by the 1632 exclusion from *poortersneringen*, for Amsterdam residents did not need to buy burgher rights in order to engage in commerce. When, during the 1650s, the Spanish authorities began to question the provenance of goods imported into Spain from the Dutch Republic, Portuguese Jewish merchants of Amsterdam did acquire burgher rights, solely in order to safeguard the legality of their commerce.[51] Hence the city's decision in 1654 to grant Jews only minor burgher rights—in other words, all that was needed in the circumstances; for the major burgher rights included no additional commercial privileges.[52]

Only in one minor respect were Amsterdam's Portuguese Jewish merchants discriminated against. In 1620 the Court of Amsterdam decreed that all insurance policies contracted by merchants of the 'Portuguese and Jewish Nation' had to be registered.[53] For other merchants registration was optional. The law, which remained in effect for a brief period only, undoubtedly owed its existence to the peculiar nature of the trade of the Portuguese Jews. This trade was concentrated almost exclusively on Spain and Portugal and was therefore particularly susceptible to enemy interception. As so many cargoes were owned jointly by Portuguese and Dutch—whether Jewish or not—merchants or were registered under one name to enable their cargo to leave the port of origin and under another to enable it to enter the destination port, it became difficult to sort out what might and what might not be considered a 'good or lawful prize'. Neither the Dutch admiralty nor the merchants relished the protracted court battles that ensued when a Dutch navy ship captured a Portuguese ship. The law singled out Portuguese Jews for special treatment not because their commercial practices were considered inherently suspect, but because their commercial associations were generally different from

---

[49] Seeligmann comes to a similar conclusion on the basis of events in Haarlem: 'the Amsterdam Jews, had they wished to, would have been able, in many respects, to break through [the exclusivist wall of] guild ordinances': 'De gilden en de Joden', 137.

[50] Van Dillen, *Van rijkdom en regenten*, 291–3.

[51] Swetschinski, 'Spanish Consul', 158–65; GAA, DTB 685, p. 260 (2 Mar. 1663), DTB 682, p. 122 (26 Mar. 1654).

[52] Bloom, *Economic Activities*, 23 n. 106.   [53] Van Dillen, 'Vreemdelingen', 15.

those of Holland's Christian merchants. The law, of course, in no way interfered with the legitimate commerce of Amsterdam's Portuguese Jews.

The guilds were not the only segment of Amsterdam society favouring restrictive measures against the Jews. The most vociferous expressions of anti-Jewish sentiment came from the ministers and aldermen of the Reformed Church.[54] However, with the exception of the 'Jewry statute' of 1616, discussed above, their complaints went largely unheeded. The unresponsiveness of Holland's political establishment to ecclesiastical pressures illuminates a most important aspect of the quality of seventeenth-century Dutch tolerance.

Although the Reformed Church had been declared the official state church in 1580, Holland's political leaders took great pains to keep it out of the political arena. Apart from the Synod of Dort (1618), national synods were prohibited, and provincial synods and local councils were not permitted to discuss political issues. Moreover, a considerable social gap separated the political leaders from the religious establishment: the City Council drew its members largely from the mercantile community, while both the lay and the ecclesiastical leaders of the Reformed Church were for the most part rooted in the artisan class.[55] While the City Council made concessions to guild interests, it consistently refused to do so vis-à-vis the claims of the Church—again excepting the 1616 statute.

Rarely do Church council minutes go into detail about the specific anti-Jewish measures advocated. In a singularly hostile tone, they frequently refer to the insolence of the Jews, their blasphemy and licentiousness. But this strong language yielded no legal fruits. The Church-inspired warnings of the 1616 statute did not result from verbal agitation but were based on specific proven allegations. Nor was the Church successful in its attempts to prevent public Jewish worship. Although it probably proposed that Christian maids be prohibited from working or living in Jewish households, lacking support from the city authorities the Church council could only instruct its members to visit these maids, warn them against the danger to their souls, and exhort them to go and live with Christian families.[56] Conversion of Jews to Christianity, elsewhere often an activity actively sponsored by the state, was permitted only to adults. Minors who wished to convert to Christianity against the will of their Jewish parents were not allowed to do so, much to the dismay of the Reformed ministers.[57] Attempts in the 1670s by various synods to obtain governmental sanction for their conversionist programmes, however mild in comparison with the compulsory sermons imposed elsewhere, were never successful.[58]

[54] Zwarts, 'Eerste rabbijnen', 221–6; van Eeghen, 'Gereformeerde kerkeraad'; and Swetschinski, 'Tussen middeleeuwen en Gouden Eeuw', in Blom et al. (eds.), Geschiedenis, 82–4.

[55] Romein and Romein, Lage Landen, ii. 128–9; Boxer, Dutch Seaborne Empire, 126–7.

[56] Van Eeghen, 'Gereformeerde kerkeraad', 171.   [57] Ibid. 172–3.

[58] Koenen, Geschiedenis der Joden, 258–67; sources published in Knuttel, Acta der particuliere synoden, i (1621–33), 49, 75–6, 103–4, 137–8; ii (1634–45), 269, 323, 336, 367, 415, 417; iii (1646–56), 103, 166, 339; iv (1657–72), 571; v (1673–86), 161, 208–11, 254–5, 277, 293, 327, 334–5, 365, 369, 406, 408, 443, 445, 490–1, 532, 572; vi (1687–1700), 22, 56, 93, 134, 169, 221, 265, 307, 344, 393, 431, 484, 531, 585.

Excepting the 1616 statute, the synods and Church council had little more to report than is found in the minutes of the Synod of Hoorn (1641): 'The Church of Amsterdam has not been able to obtain, from the magistrature, satisfaction of the issues raised.'[59] In the eyes of Holland's political leaders the Jews were no concern of the Reformed Church. Only in a few rare cases where Christians had demonstrably been wronged by Jewish actions, such as the conversion of Christians to Judaism and the impregnation of Christian women by Jewish men, did the authorities yield to ecclesiastical pressures.

Church-inspired law was not the only legislation conspicuous by its absence. A host of medieval laws whose effects proved so very discriminatory and debilitating in many other countries never found their way on to Holland's statute book. Consciously and explicitly, the States of Holland deviated from medieval practice only in prohibiting in 1619 the imposition of a 'distinguishing sign' on the Jews.[60] But such staples of traditional Jewry law as the prohibition on owning real estate, the imposition of special taxes, inequality before the law (whether as plaintiff, defendant, or witness), residential and numerical restrictions, building limitations on synagogues, and the prohibition on hiring Christian domestic or other labour were never adopted in Holland and seem never even to have crossed the minds of its political guardians.

This, then, was the practical application of Jewry toleration in seventeenth-century Amsterdam. The unquestionably favourable mixture of explicit restrictions and implicit freedoms clearly did not follow any plan or order. Neither religious nor secular traditions, nor any allegedly paradigmatic Christian preconception of Jewish infamy, inspired whatever censures or restrictions on Jewry did find their way into the law books of Amsterdam.[61] After the public worship of Judaism had become a fact, legislation impinged on Jewish beliefs and practices only in the interrelated areas of autonomy and marriage law. In both instances the Jews and their association were treated no differently from any other religious congregation in Holland. Most of the restrictive legislation resulted from pressure coming from outside the ruling oligarchy, when the burgomasters succumbed to clerical and guild pressures for reasons of political expediency or necessity, from

---

[59] Van Eeghen, 'Gereformeerde kerkeraad', 174.

[60] *Gedrukte resolutiën der Staten van Holland en West-Friesland*, 13 Dec. 1619.

[61] Cf. Bloom's statement: 'Even in Calvinist Amsterdam relics of the old church law were enforced. The civil government would have accorded more liberties to the Jews, had it not been that the Calvinists and Arminians still felt the Jews to be the "enemies of Christ", in spite of the broadening influence of the Renaissance and the rebellion from Spain and Rome': *Economic Activities*, 24. Many years later Baron, Bloom's teacher, came to a far more judicious conclusion: 'No longer were they considered primarily as a corporate body within other corporate bodies, each endowed with a special system of rights and duties. They were now admitted to that growingly uniform society as individuals basically equal to other citizens': *Social and Religious History*, xv. 72. Although essentially correct, Baron's judgement is as intuitive as that of Bloom and erroneously, I believe, based on his interpretation of de Groot's Jewry statute. Bloom's remark must be regarded as another example of his general 'medievalist' orientation.

fear of popular challenges to their authority and pre-eminence. More importantly, the resulting legal restrictions proved decidedly mild, milder certainly than hoped and pressed for by the clergy and the guilds. In responding to quite substantial clerical demands, the burgomasters accepted only those which conformed to their own sense of propriety, outlawing, for example, not the hiring of Christian domestics, but only 'carnal conversation'. In enforcing restrictions on guild membership, the burgomasters' decision affected only a very small number of Jews. Whenever and wherever Jewish claims to specific occupational freedoms gained substance, guild restrictions were lifted. At no time did the burgomasters allow popular prejudices to snowball a minor conflict or complaint into an ever-expanding accumulation of repressive legislation.

On only one occasion, it seems, was Jewry legislation inspired neither by a general legal principle nor by external pressure: in the 1632 law preventing Jews from transmitting their *poorterschap* from parents to children and from acquiring it through marriage with the daughter of a *poorter*. In effect, this stipulation rendered the Jews permanent first-generation immigrants, inasmuch as it prevented them from ever becoming second-generation *poorters*; and as first-generation immigrants the Jews were excluded from official posts in the political, legal, and military administration, that is to say, the power base and aristocratic preserve of the ruling oligarchy. Political authority in seventeenth-century Holland was a precarious affair. It had been divorced only recently, and as yet imperfectly, from religious authority. The full political and intellectual implications of this change were only beginning to be felt and digested at the time of the 1632 law. Hugo de Groot's major and influential theoretical statement *De imperio summarum potestatum circa sacra* (*Of the Authority of the Highest Powers about Sacred Things or the Right of the State in the Church*, as the English translation of 1651 was entitled) was not published until 1647, posthumously. Under the prevailing circumstances Amsterdam's burgomasters could not conceive—nor should we expect them to have been able to conceive—of giving political influence and power to so different a religious and cultural group as the Portuguese Jews. What may surprise us is that they limited their discrimination against Amsterdam Jewry to this sensitive area of political authority, intending thereby more to defend their own aristocratic monopoly of power than to segregate the Jews from the rest of the population.

TRADITIONS OF TOLERATION

Early modern Jewry toleration followed a course both related to, and yet separate from, that of toleration in general. In so far as Jews were tolerated they were at best classed with such peripheral Christian dissenters as Anabaptists, Socinians, and the like, minorities of which the theoreticians disapproved sufficiently to make their toleration an issue distinct from toleration as a general principle. Theoretically, on the level of disapproval, substantial and essential differences to the disadvantage of minorities continued to prevail in the distinction between major denominations and minor sects. In practice, on the level of authority, it often proved far easier to tolerate a minor sect than a rival denomination. As Johan Uytenbogaert, a leader of the Remonstrants, remarked in 1604: 'You [Hollanders] are a strange kind of people; you bear harder upon those that differ but little from you, than upon those who differ much.'[62]

Obviously there are other factors to be taken into account; religious disapproval may have been mitigated by other forms of approval, and the laws may reflect much more than a sense of security *vis-à-vis* a relatively small minority. Between individual religious concerns and reasons of state lies the vast and compelling arena of social and economic interaction where other forms of approval and a sense of security may have been established. Unfortunately for us, the burgomasters were not much given to talking or writing about their religious, ethical, or political principles. They were doers, primarily active participants in the daily humdrum life of the city's economy and society. Indeed, it is in their doings, rather than in the musings of economically inactive contemporaries, that the key to their toleration of Jewry lies. As noted above, the reflections of Hugo de Groot can be shown to have been out of step, in significant ways, with the realities of Jewry law in seventeenth-century Amsterdam.

Two philosophies of toleration prevailed in late sixteenth- and early seventeenth-century Holland: the one, 'irenic', going back to Desiderius Erasmus; the other, 'politique', inspired by Sebastian Castellio and Michel de L'Hospital. Both influenced, in varying ways, the progress of Jewry toleration.

Erasmus (1469–1536) advocated tolerance in order to avoid discord and war. 'Peace and unanimity are the *summa* of our religion', he wrote in 1523. Peace meant the suspension of the prosecution of heretics, and unanimity entailed the reduction of the canon of principles, the so-called fundamentals of Christianity, by which people were judged heretics. The *animus* (hence 'unanimity'), the rational soul, lay at the root of Erasmus' toleration; it was the *animus* that distinguished means from ends and fundamentals from 'indifferent things'. Reason and toleration were the means to peace and religious harmony. The many religious colloquies, primarily of the sixteenth century, represent the irenicists' hopeful, but largely futile, attempts at religious conciliation. Religious differences cut deeper than Erasmus' rational soul, and no amount of reason sufficed to heal the political, social, and psychological wounds of the wars of religion. As far as the Jews were concerned, Erasmus' scheme of toleration proved doubly exclusive. For Jews, Erasmus implied, lacked reason, and religious harmony was defined in purely Christian terms. Erasmus' toleration is 'a Christian virtue, which leaves Judaism as "the most pernicious plague and the bitterest enemy of the doctrine of Christ" no room in a Christian society'.[63]

---

[62] Brandt, *History of the Reformation*, ii. 30.

[63] On Erasmus and toleration, see Ferguson, 'Attitude of Erasmus'; Lecler, *Toleration*, i. 114–33; Kamen, *Rise of Toleration*, 22–8. On Erasmus and the Jews, see Kisch, *Erasmus' Stellung*; Oberman, *Wurzeln*, esp. 48–51 (quotation on p. 51).

If later Erasmians were none the less to exert a more or less positive influence on Jewry toleration in Amsterdam, it was because the Erasmian definition of toleration came to be modified on both exclusivist counts. Even in Erasmus' own day, humanists with a more than superficial knowledge of and interest in Judaism and its philosophical and mystical literature—men such as Johann Reuchlin (1455–1522), Philipp Melanchthon (1497–1560), and Andreas Osiander (1498–1552)—were equipped and ready to refute Erasmus' assertion of the Jews' irrationality and their implacable hatred of Christianity. Rightly or wrongly, they perceived in Jews a potential for conversion—that is, future conciliation—which their exclusion from Christian society would render impossible of achievement.[64] In the generations after Erasmus, the men of the so-called Third Reformation themselves suffered persecution and exile and came to regard that condition as proof of the strength and value of their religious conviction. The traditional interpretation of the dispersion of the Jews as a sign of divine punishment gave way to notions of a potential, as yet 'hidden community of fate [*Schicksalsgemeinschaft*] between Jews and Christians', especially the Reformed.[65] Finally, radical, spiritualistic humanists such as Sebastian Franck (1499–1542) and Guillaume Postel (*c*.1510–81) had begun to extend the Erasmian search for fundamentals beyond reason and beyond the limits of Christianity to include Judaism, Islam, and even paganism. But their quest for religious universalism focused primarily on the individual and proved difficult to reconcile with the social focus of the Erasmian tradition.[66] When it did make its appearance in Holland, it did so in conjunction with Castellio's views on toleration as personal freedom of conscience.

We must begin our account of the Erasmian tradition's part in the story of Amsterdam's Jewry toleration with François du Jon, better known as Franciscus Junius (1545–1602), a French Calvinist who spent the last ten years of his life in Holland. Born in Bourges, Junius was educated at Geneva (1562–5) and sent to Antwerp as minister of the small Walloon community in 1565. Because of his outspoken opposition to attempts at establishing an inquisition in Flanders and his disapproval of the iconoclastic riots, Junius was forced to flee in 1566; he settled in Germany, where he served first as a minister and later as a professor. At Heidelberg he collaborated with Emmanuel Tremellius, a convert from Judaism, on a new Latin translation of the Hebrew Bible (published in Frankfurt, 1575–9). In 1592, while passing through Holland, he accepted the offer of a professorship in theology at the University of Leiden and remained there until his death. Apart from his Bible translation, which went through twenty editions in almost as many years, Junius is best known for his *Eirenikon sive de pace ecclesiae catholicae inter Christianos* (Leiden, 1593; translated into French, in the same year, as *Le Paisible*

[64] Baron, *Social and Religious History*, xiii. 159–296; id., 'Medieval Heritage and Modern Realities'; Stern-Taeubler, 'Vorstellung vom Juden'; Kisch, *Zasius und Reuchlin*; Oberman, *Wurzeln*, esp. 30–47.
[65] Oberman, *Wurzeln*, 189.   [66] Lecler, *Toleration*, i. 166–76; ii. 32–9.

Chrestien; and into Dutch, in 1612, as *Den vreedsamen Christen*). Though containing no new ideas, the *Eirenikon* was widely read and appreciated for its advocacy of peace and unity and its truly Christian—as opposed to political or indifferent—treatment of religious issues.[67]

The *Eirenikon* does not directly deal with toleration of Jews. Nevertheless, in a few passing asides, one begins to recognize in Junius a distinct change in attitude from his great forebear Erasmus. In a revealing passage quoted by Gerard Brandt, the seventeenth-century Remonstrant historian of the Reformation in the Northern Netherlands, we read:

What advantage then hath the Jew? [Rom. 3: 1] . . . Much every way: chiefly because, that unto them were committed the Oracles of God. For from hence we are clearly instructed, that they to whom the Oracles of God are committed (though they be mostly Unbelievers) do yet retain that privilege or advantage, not for their own sakes, but thro' that wonderful faithfulness of God, which their unbelief cannot render null or of no effect, whilst he vouchsafes to wait for them with long suffering. This external form is imprest by God, when he commits to us his Holy Word; and they who retain that Word must be esteemed so long as they do retain it, to retain the principle of that form which God has imprest: just as one does not scruple to receive an old worn piece of Money, as long as there remains any face or figure upon it.—And it cannot be otherwise, but that those who retain the Holy Scripture will at the same time admit, at least in part, the contents of it.[68]

Not only does Junius, the Calvinist and humanist with a knowledge of Hebrew, differ from Erasmus in his more positive evaluation of the Old Testament; he also draws traditional conclusions from the historical and divine interrelation between the Old and New Testaments for the present and future of the Jews. In the present, the Jews 'must be esteemed'—and tolerated, we learn from another fragment—for having received and retained part of the word of God. So far, however great the difference between Jews and Christians—Jews approaching 'nearest to an entire alienation from and desertion of God'—it is still one only of degree and not of essence.[69] And therefore Junius, the friend of Tremellius (an Italian Jew who converted first to Catholicism and then to Protestantism), trusts—'knows'—the Jews to be susceptible to future amplifications of the divine word and eventual conversion to Christianity.

Consistently, but more negatively, Junius reiterated his opinion in response to a question directly concerning the Jews:

That they ought to be tolerated among Christians; First, Because they are poor ignorant creatures, and that no man living ought to be extirpated from the earth on account of Religion, since Faith is the gift of God, and since all men are by nature our brethren. Secondly, that although the Body of the Jews is in general rejected by God, yet it is not to be inferred from thence, that the particular Members of that Body are not to be tolerated among Christians; for the Church must be gathered out of both. Consequently they are to

---

[67] Haag and Haag, *La France protestante*, iv. 381–91; Cuno, *Franciscus Junius der Aeltere*; Lecler, *Toleration*, ii. 269–71.   [68] Brandt, *History of the Reformation*, ii. 22–3.   [69] Ibid. 23.

be tolerated, not only on the account of Nature, but of Grace. From their unfruitful works we ought indeed to abstain. There is much said about their Synagogues, but there is nothing to be found in them that so greatly wounds the reputation of Religion.[70]

We do not know the context of this question and answer. By definition, the question implied a difference between Christians and Jews and thus almost dictated the negative point of departure assumed by Junius. On the other hand, the references to faith as the gift of God and the future conversion of the Jews tally with the passage from the *Eirenikon* cited above. Otherwise, the most striking and thoroughly characteristic feature of Junius' statement is his consideration of only the humanitarian and religious—that is, the non-political—dimensions of the problem. 'All men are by nature our brethren' expresses a lofty sentiment but cuts very little political ice. Similarly, judging the synagogue in terms of the reputation of religion, however favourably, ignores the socio-political context of religious conflict. The same references and features recur, with varying emphases, in Junius' heirs in the Erasmian tradition.

Among the prominent Erasmians of seventeenth-century Holland were Gerard Joannes Vossius and his sons, Caspar Barlaeus, Hugo de Groot, and such notable Remonstrants or Arminians as Simon Episcopius, Philip van Limborch, and Jean Le Clerc.[71] For Vossius, Barlaeus, and de Groot the connection with Junius was personal as well as intellectual; others embraced him indirectly through his works or reputation. All were personally acquainted with individual Jews. This is not the place to analyse in detail their multifarious relations with Jews or their subtly different attitudes towards Judaism. What we need to do here is merely to identify certain of the main and recurring features of the Erasmian 'school' of Jewry toleration before we turn to examining Hugo de Groot's famous proposal for a Jewry law.

None of the seventeenth-century Erasmians ever questioned Jewry toleration as practised in Amsterdam. The Jews' right to reside and worship in the city was taken for granted. Yet, if none was explicitly negative, not all were equally positive. The gamut of their evaluations ranged from cautious acknowledgement to a wholehearted embrace. The youthful van Limborch warned against 'this carnal and worldly nation mindful of nothing but the domination over all peoples'.[72] Barlaeus welcomed the Jews with his 'let us live God as friends, and may learning everywhere receive the recognition it deserves'.[73]

---

[70] Ibid. 20 (in English); Koenen, *Geschiedenis der Joden in Nederland*, 137–8 (in Dutch).

[71] Lindeboom, 'Erasmus' Bedeutung'; Mansfield, *Phoenix of his Age*, 115–51.

[72] Polak, 'De betekenis der Joden voor de wijsbegeerte', in Brugmans and Frank (eds.), *Geschiedenis*, 682 n. 1.

[73] A famous poem mistakenly attributed to Barlaeus was almost certainly written by the artist Romeyn de Hooghe, many of whose etchings illustrating various aspects of Portuguese Jewish life have come down to us. The poem is worth citing: 'The tyranny of the inquisitors rages against all of you, o Juda, and by extortion and by fire and by the sword, and is not satisfied that you hide yourselves. Neither on the Seine nor on the Tagus do you find security. But the city on the Amstel is more

Most of the Erasmians maintained more or less intimate relations with individual Jews. Although several of these associations grew into genuine friendships, they initially and primarily served the humanist thirst for intellectual exchange. Vossius and Barlaeus recognized in Menasseh ben Israel a gold mine of Jewish erudition.[74] Van Limborch found in Don Baltasar Orobio de Castro an eager and intelligent conversationalist with whom he indulged his passion for serious discussion of religious matters.[75] These exchanges were more than professional; they were sincerely and mutually respectful of the interlocutor and his tradition. Vossius and most explicitly Barlaeus exhibited real warmth and friendship in their relations with Menasseh ben Israel. Every such relation, however, remained one between individuals and entailed neither a forgetting of the religious difference nor an extension of sympathy beyond the individual at hand.

Finally, each and every one of the Erasmians favoured and expected the ultimate conversion of the Jews. Van Limborch sought most actively to contribute to this goal. In 1687 he published his private dialogue with Don Baltasar against the latter's wishes and with *ex post facto*, unilateral emendations to strengthen his alleged refutation of the Jew's arguments. Even though the *De veritate religionis christianae amica collatio cum erudito Judaeo* strikes modern readers as the first truly respectful and balanced disputation between a Christian and a Jew, its publication was unquestionably intended to serve the cause of Christianity against Judaism.[76] Dionysius Vossius, the son of Gerard Joannes, the student (in Hebrew and rabbinic literature) of Menasseh ben Israel and the translator into Latin of the latter's Spanish works, planned to write an *Adversus Judaeos*, 'to refute the Jews and thereby convert them'. Gerard Joannes Vossius himself counselled his Polish student, Christophorus Słupecki, to immerse himself in rabbinic literature, as a Christian duty, with an eye to the conversion of the Jews. In another, friendly, note, Gerard Joannes Vossius refers to Menasseh as 'a learned and pious man: if only he were a Christian'.[77]

Only Barlaeus, unquestionably the most liberal of the humanists discussed here,

---

prudent: it recognizes and shelters your temples within its walls. And hearing the psalms intoned, the spouse of Zion exclaimed: indeed, here are the people and the city of God. Preserve yourself well and long, sacred temple, you who elsewhere are detested by the monarchs. May distant generations still admire your gables.' Blok attributes the poem to Barlaeus, following in the footsteps of the Dutch editor of Basnage's *Histoire des Juifs*; see 'Quelques humanistes', 22, 31–2. Meijer shows conclusively that the poem must have been written by de Hooghe on the occasion of the 1675 opening of the Esnoga; see his 'Barlaeus overgewaardeerd'.

[74] Blok, 'Quelques humanistes'; id., 'Caspar Barlaeus en de Joden'; Rademaker, *Life and Work of Vossius*, 264–6.

[75] Kaplan, *From Christianity to Judaism*, 270–85; Barnouw, *Philippus van Limborch*; Schoeps, 'Isaak Orobio de Castros Religionsdisput'.

[76] Van Limborch's emendations and intentions are referred to in his letters to John Locke; see Locke, *Correspondence*, esp. nos. 958, 959, 963, 964. The *De veritate* appeared in Latin (Gouda, 1687) and in Dutch (Amsterdam, 1723). Voltaire judged the disputation 'respectful': Polak, in Brugmans and Frank (eds.), *Geschiedenis*, 683 n. 2.   [77] Rademaker, *Life and Work of Vossius*, 264–5.

appears to have been content to leave things as they were: 'Even though our opinions differ, let us live God as friends, | and may learning everywhere receive the recognition it deserves. | This is the *summa* of my faith; be convinced of it, Menasseh. | Thus I will be a [spiritual] son of Christ and you one of Abraham [*Sic ego Christiades, sic eris Abramides*].' Barlaeus' epigram must not be understood as an expression of the kind of sceptical relativism later to develop into deism. When called upon to explain and defend his statement, Barlaeus carefully distinguished *pietas universalis et legalis*—founded on natural knowledge of God and shared by all moral beings of whatever religion—from *pietas Christianorum quae ex fide est*—stemming from the belief in Jesus Christ and based on supernatural, revealed knowledge. Barlaeus' toleration, in scope the widest formulated by any seventeenth-century Dutch Erasmian, is based on unanimity of morality through natural knowledge of God, a reduction of the fundamentals of religion *per se* rather than just those of Christianity. Barlaeus embraced the Jew Menasseh ben Israel because he showed himself endowed with natural reason and because the harmony of civil society depended more on morality than on dogmatic unity.[78]

Though reiterating several of the themes encountered in Erasmian circles, contemporary Calvinists show us a distinctly different variety of seventeenth-century toleration of Jewry. Calvinists, too, accepted the Jews' right to reside in Holland and, likewise, subscribed to the expectation of their ultimate conversion. In almost all other respects Erasmians and Calvinists were miles apart.

Either because of theocratic predilections or from socio-economic distrust bred by envy, Calvinists particularly sought to restrict the public worship of Judaism, by limiting the number of synagogues or by confining Jewish worship to a reading of the Torah (Pentateuch) and the Prophets, or even to prohibit it altogether. As early as 1608 Abraham de Coster published his *Historie der Joden* to forewarn his fellow Christians, in the most unambiguous terminology, about '[the Jews'] absurd and foolish ceremonies and their horrendous blasphemies against Christ and his Gospel as well as their curses against Christians and Christian authorities'.[79] Whereas de Coster recommended only a restriction of Jewish immigration, Gisbertus Voetius, professor of theology at the Illustre School in Utrecht, favoured the closure of all synagogues, censorship of Jewish books, the dispersion of Jewish residents through the city to avoid conglomerations that might threaten the established order, and a halt to any and all future immigration of Jews.[80]

It is obvious that the limitations urged by Calvinist preachers and theologians reflect their strong disapproval of Judaism and Jews. Calvinists referred to Judaism at best as foolish and silly; more commonly, they labelled it scandalous and blasphemous, and the Jews deceitful. Nicolaus Vedelius, Voetius' counterpart at

---

[78] Blok, 'Caspar Barlaeus en de Joden'. Barlaeus' poem appeared among the laudatory poems in Menasseh ben Israel's *De creatione problemata xxx* (Amsterdam, 1635).

[79] Jaspers, 'Schets van Abraham Costerus' leven'. The passage cited may be found in the introduction of de Coster's *Historie*.   [80] Van den Berg, *Joden en christenen*, 22–3.

the Illustre School in Deventer, gives us a full view of Calvinist disapproval in his attack on the above-cited poem by Barlaeus on behalf of Menasseh ben Israel. A Jew, according to Vedelius, cannot be pious, for Judaism is synonymous with impiety. A Jew cannot be good, for without faith in Christ there are no good works. Whatever honesty Jews do exhibit is nothing but an external appearance. Without Christ's revelation there is no knowledge of God. The God of the synagogue, therefore, is another, fictitious, God, an idol. Modern Jews are no longer included in God's covenant, for they have been rejected. Positive remarks such as those voiced by Barlaeus cannot but encourage Menasseh ben Israel in his unbelief. Thus Vedelius distanced not only Christianity from Judaism but also the contemporary Christian from the contemporary Jew.[81] Not surprisingly, then, personal relations between Calvinists and Jews, of the sort so characteristic between Erasmians and Jews, were few and far between. Even the study of Jewish sources, encouraged for reasons of apologetics and mission, was lamented when the time spent by Jean de Labadie on the study and teaching of Hebrew and rabbinic literature threatened to exceed the proprieties of apologetics.[82]

In other Calvinist circles, especially during the latter half of the century, the desired and expected conversion of the Jews often assumed apocalyptic proportions. To cite only two among several examples, Johannes Coccejus (1603–69), professor of theology at the University of Leiden, believed that the imminent mass conversion of the Jews would bring special blessings to the Church. The Jews would be elected to combat Satan's kingdom and, as Christians, return to the Holy Land. Pierre Jurieu (1639–1713) went further and saw in the conversion of Paul an 'exemplar' of that of the entire Jewish people. As Paul became the most zealous of Christians, so the Jews will too; as Paul became an apostle to the heathens, so will the Jews. All this was to occur in the days of the Fifth Monarchy. In the end, the Jewish people were to be elevated above all peoples and rule through their prophets and apostles.[83] The pitch of these expectations is so high, almost menacing, that we must wonder whether they promised any truly positive improvement beyond the strong disapproval of less apocalyptic Calvinists.

Thus we encounter two quite different traditions of Jewry toleration in seventeenth-century Holland. The Erasmian tradition expressed no apparent socio-economic concerns, nor did it voice opposition to public Jewish worship. Of Judaism as a religion it disapproved to some degree, but more for spiritual than for dogmatic reasons. Erasmians welcomed personal relations with Jews and remained generally optimistic about the chances of conversion through rational persuasion. The Calvinists clamoured for major social and religious restrictions and harboured a strong, dogmatic, almost physical dislike for Judaism and the Jews. They showed no interest in social or intellectual conversation with Jews, and, in so far as the issue

[81] Blok, 'Caspar Barlaeus en de Joden', 85–92.
[82] Bovenkerk, 'Nederlandsche schrijvers', 732–5; van den Berg, *Joden en christenen*, 40–1.
[83] Van den Berg, *Joden en christenen*, 25–35; Eng. trans. in id., 'Eschatological Expectations'.

concerned them at all, viewed conversion of the Jews as an end to be achieved either by act of God or by missionary zeal and militancy.

During a brief period of time, from the publication by Uytenbogaert and fellow Arminians of the 'Remonstrance' in 1610 until the execution of Johan van Oldenbarnevelt, Grand Pensionary of Holland, and the life imprisonment of Hugo de Groot, Pensionary of Rotterdam, in 1619, Holland was in the throes of a major political and religious conflict pitting Calvinists against Remonstrants. Part of this basically factional strife revolved around the issues of the proper relation of state and Church and the degree of toleration to be extended to religious dissenters, that is, the Arminians. The residence of Jews in Amsterdam and their public worship became a point of contention as the city's toleration of Judaism contrasted so sharply with its intolerance towards the Remonstrants. To make matters worse, in 1614 the authorities of Hoorn discovered three Mennonites who had converted to Judaism, and similar incidents were reported from Amsterdam. As a consequence of these events, in 1615 the States of Holland 'directed and commissioned the Pensionaries of Amsterdam [Adriaen Pauw] and Rotterdam [Hugo de Groot] to design . . . a set of regulations with which the Jews (residing in these lands) will have to comply for the prevention of all scandals, offences and sanctions'.[84]

De Groot's proposal, *Remonstrantie nopende de ordre dye in de landen van Hollandt ende Westvrieslandt dyent gestelt op de Joden* ('Remonstrance concerning the regulations to be imposed upon the Jews in Holland and West Frisia', written sometime between 1615 and 1619), the only one of the two proposals extant, embodies a curious blend of positive and negative attitudes towards Jews.[85] Because of Hugo de Groot's stature as one of the great luminaries of seventeenth-century Holland, there has been a great deal of second-guessing as to whether the negative or the positive represents the writer's own position. More often than not the negative views reflected in the *Remonstrantie* are seen as concessions by de Groot to the opinions of contemporary Calvinists; concessions he was inspired or forced to make because of the contentious times. On this interpretation, a positive Hugo de Groot could then be added to the all too slender list of illustrious men who tolerated the Jews on ethical rather than self-interested grounds, the harbingers of the emancipation.[86]

Certainly, there can be no doubt that Hugo de Groot was an Erasmian; arguably the greatest Erasmian of his generation. As a student he had boarded with Franciscus Junius, and during his exile in Paris he maintained an extensive correspondence with the major humanists in Holland and some indirect contacts with Menasseh ben Israel. Many testimonies to his appreciation of Erasmus could be cited. It will suffice here to quote a letter to Uytenbogaert, written in 1631 during a brief return from

[84] Geyl, *Netherlands*, i. 41–63, 70–83; de Groot, *Remonstrantie*, ed. Meijer, 47–51.

[85] De Groot, *Remonstrantie*, ed. Meijer; Meijer, 'Hugo Grotius' "Remonstrantie"'; van Eysinga, 'De Groots Jodenreglement'.

[86] Kuhn, 'Hugo Grotius and the Emancipation'; Baron, *Social and Religious History*, xv. 25–33; Oberman, *Wurzeln*, 189, 194–5 n. 9.

exile: 'My first visit to Rotterdam was to show my affection for the memory of Erasmus. I went to see the statue of the man who had so well shown us the way to a measured reformation, never binding himself on disputable questions to one side or the other. We Hollanders cannot thank this man enough, and I hold myself fortunate that I can from afar understand his virtue.'[87] Many of his arguments in the *Remonstrantie*, positive and negative alike, clearly reflect de Groot's Erasmian approach to the problem. What remains may be explained in terms of personal idiosyncrasy, caution resulting from a lack of familiarity with the practice of Jewry toleration, or possibly concessions to placate Calvinist clerical and popular opinion.

Hugo de Groot's *Remonstrantie* falls into three parts. The first discusses at length and in detail whether the Jews ought to be tolerated at all; the second addresses itself briefly to the issue of Jewish worship; and the third suggests forty-nine specific laws by which their presence might be regulated. The writer opens his discussion with the thoroughly Erasmian statement that unity of religion is one of the greatest strengths of a state, for diversity breeds doubt and sterile inquisitiveness. At the end of the first part he counters this statement of the ideal by saying that diversity is already a fact in Holland and that the dangers associated with diversity are the less, the more different the divergent religion is from the main faith. This is the sum of de Groot's consideration of the socio-political dimensions of the issue. Otherwise, with the exception of one humanitarian appeal to the natural brotherhood of man echoing that of Junius, the *Remonstrantie* is devoted to reviewing at length the ethical and religious dimensions of Jewry toleration. De Groot first enumerates a great deal of evidence, from antiquity and the Middle Ages, showing the Jews' 'general, irreconcilable hatred toward Christians'. He then softens his indictment and suggests that not all of this evidence can be verified, that Christians are themselves partly to blame, and that Christian authorities used the Jews for their own greedy purposes and caused much of the mutual antagonism. On the positive side of the religious argument de Groot lists a number of 'excellent reasons which, perhaps, ought to outweigh those preceding':

The major reason is this: that, although the Jews as a whole seem to have been rejected by God to this very day on account of their unbelief, some individuals nonetheless convert to the true faith daily, as the prophets of old predicted that the remnant be saved. Moreover, the Apostle Paul explicitly says that one can ultimately expect a general conversion of the Jewish people, for which purpose also God seems to preserve the Jewish nation miraculously, on its own and separated from all other people, in order to show in due time the certainty of His promises. All Christians must do their best for this individual and general conversion which cannot happen if one cuts the Jews off from intercourse with Christians. For how will they believe without hearing and hear without preaching?

Moreover, de Groot continues, this conversion is most likely to occur among Christians who, like the Jews, reject idolatry—in other words, the Reformed.

---

[87] Mansfield, *Phoenix of his Age*, 137–44 (quotation on p. 143); Lindeboom, 'Erasmus' Bedeutung', 11–12.

Furthermore, Jews differ from other unbelievers in that they are the descendants of Abraham, Isaac, and Jacob, the ancestors of Christ himself. Unlike the pagans the Jews worship the true God; unlike the Muslims they honour the true prophets. The Jews share a great deal of what the Christians believe. It is also God's apparent will that the Jews remain. So they may as well stay here as anywhere else. Finally, the Christians may profit from the presence of the Jews, who can help improve their knowledge of the Hebrew language; also, observing the Jews' unbelief, Christians will be induced to thank God even more for the grace He has shown them. Thus de Groot weighs up the religious side of the question. On the whole, the argument for Jewry toleration is characteristically Erasmian, and fairly close to that of Junius, in the scant consideration it gives to socio-political issues and in the emphasis it places on the religious links as well as difference between Jews and Christians and on the ultimate conversion of the Jews.

In the second, shorter part of the *Remonstrantie* de Groot argues in favour of allowing the Jews to practise their religion. (From the practical legal proposals we learn that he had only private worship in mind.) Unlike Catholicism, whose practice de Groot, it seems, thought justifiably denied, Judaism is not idolatrous and does not recognize a supreme, terrestrial authority inimical to the Republic. More importantly, if Jews were denied the practice of their religion, they would either have to accept Christianity or be left without any form of divine worship. The first is inadmissible: religion may not be forced and God deems hypocrisy a greater sin than ignorance. The second would open the door to atheism, which is worse than Judaism. Divine worship is necessary to maintain God-fearing piety. Finally, history shows that Jewish worship has traditionally been allowed. In these arguments de Groot echoes the sentiments of the Arminians, who as a religious minority sought the same freedom of worship and who, like Barlaeus, recognized in Judaism at least some form of piety. Also characteristic is de Groot's restricted use of the slogan 'religion may not be forced' in the context of worship only, rather than as a general principle of toleration.

Nowhere in the *Remonstrantie* does de Groot argue for toleration as an end in itself, as some of his more radical contemporaries did. He is conservative in his definition of the issue in terms of morality and religion. His argument is with tradition and with his book-lore, not with the reality of seventeenth-century Holland. Thus he misunderstands and distorts as mere greed the socio-economic underpinnings of contemporary toleration. As Johan Huizinga noted, citing Fruin: '"He was not alive to his time." His vision was directed towards an ideal that was the mirror of an imaginary past. The obsession with antiquity obstructs his view. The flaw in his great mind is its one-sidedness. He personifies only one half of our Golden Age. What to us appears its most lively part he lacks . . . He lacks a firm grip on reality and the radiant warmth of sentiment.'[88]

---

[88] Huizinga, 'Hugo de Groot', 399.

The same emphases and distortions characterize the forty-nine regulations and their explications contained in the final section of the *Remonstrantie*. The explications consist largely of references to the Roman law codices so admired by de Groot and so inappropriate in the contemporary context and practice. The regulations themselves in part confirm the existing content of Amsterdam's statute book, and for the rest spell out de Groot's strictures upon Judaism and his hopes for the Jews, and—unrealistically—grant economic freedoms beyond what was attainable within the limits of Amsterdam's political realities. De Groot shared the Calvinist attitude reflected in Amsterdam's Jewry statute of 1616 and probably knew of its existence. He prohibited the blaspheming against Christianity (sections 14–16), the conversion of Christians to Judaism (sections 25, 28, and 33), and the marriage or cohabitation of a Jew and a Christian (sections 27–8 and 38). On the basis of Justinian's Novella 146, he counts the Talmud among the Jewish books containing blasphemous material that would thus have to be prohibited.[89] In this instance, where there was no need for him to make concessions to Calvinist opponents, he showed himself as reactionary as the theology professor Voetius. At other points, too, de Groot's religious sensibilities resemble those of Calvinist preachers more than those of the burgomasters. Thus he preferred to restrict Jewish worship to duly registered private houses (sections 8 and 10) and to limit the number of congregants at any one time and place to 100 (section 9). He would have required of Jews a declaration of faith against which no Jew was allowed to teach (sections 2 and 13).[90] He shared the Calvinist clergy's strictures upon Christians working in Jewish households (section 29) and upon Christians attending Jewish religious services (section 12). He included no fewer than four statutes detailing the legal status of future Jewish converts to Christianity (sections 34–7), another unnecessary excursion revealing a personal predilection. And the full force of his traditional and negative attitude towards Judaism stands revealed in the regulation providing for conversionist sermons (section 21):

The ministers of the Christian religion will be allowed to enter the assembly of the Jews, with the knowledge of the Magistrate and after the worship of the Jews, to instruct and admonish them in the Christian religion, while the Jews are obliged to listen and remain present; under a penalty of 100 gulden for every person who leaves. [explanation:] This is being practised in Rome, to wit: the Jews are forced to listen to Christian sermons. This is not unreasonable since their law does not prohibit them from listening to a person of another religion, especially if the authorities order so. And, truly, this is the only means to make these poor people understand their error, provided that one uses for this purpose learned and wise people well versed in the Hebrew language. Let us do to the Jews as God did to us in letting the Heathens find Him without them looking for Him and in making Himself known to them without them asking for Him. The weakness of the Jews is accom-

---

[89] Juster, *Juifs dans l'empire romain*, i. 369–77; Parkes, *Conflict*, 392–3.
[90] The required declaration coincides with the articles of faith enumerated by Joseph Albo: see *Sefer ha'ikarim*, i. 120–3 (Bk. I, ch. 13).

modated in that they are not, in principle, forced to come to our churches, but they will be admonished in their own houses.

De Groot has much less to say about the practical, non-religious side of Jewish residence. Like other Erasmians, he had no interest in economic affairs and therefore flatly granted in a much-celebrated statute that 'the Jews will live freely in the cities of their residence and gain a living by whatever trade, craft, or industry they please' (section 6)—a magnanimity inspired by economic ignorance rather than a modern spirit of toleration. The *Remonstrantie* requires registration of all past and future immigrants (section 1), for 'registration is very useful to keep an eye on people of another religion', and registration of all births and deaths (section 44).

In sections 4 and 5 de Groot lays down a general principle of Jewish residence that stands in stark contradiction to actual practice:

Section 4. That all Jews will have to take up residence within closed cities;

Section 5. That each city in Holland and West Frisia will not be allowed to have more than 200 families, excepting Amsterdam which, because of its size, may have 300 families. When this number is exceeded, either by births or by new arrivals, these will have to depart for other cities.

[The explanation adds:] This serves to compel the Jews better to obedience and to prevent any conspiracy as might be entered into in solitary places or, also, in cities where they would become too strong.

This regulation is not only more restrictive than any ever entertained in Holland, but completely reverses the procedure adopted in Haarlem, Rotterdam, and (implicitly) Amsterdam. For, in contrast to de Groot's ceiling on the number of Jews allowed to reside in each city, these cities stipulated conditions for a bottom figure of Jewish residents below which Judaism could not be practised publicly. In 1605 Haarlem stipulated 'at least fifty excellent families', while a Rotterdam proposal of 1610 reduced the minimum requirement to thirty families.[91] Amsterdam allowed the worship of Judaism in a public synagogue, in the 1610s, as soon as the number of Jews reached a fairly sizeable figure—somewhere between fifty and a hundred families, according to modern estimates. At first sight the contrast appears to involve two separate issues: number of residents and public worship. But both, as we will see, revolve around the issue of trust: not more or less trust, but different kinds of trust.

The customary explanation for the minimum numerical requirement laid down by Haarlem and Rotterdam views the use of a synagogue and the free exercise of Judaism as bait held out to entice wealthy Jewish families to settle there.[92] De Groot may have had this line of reasoning in mind when he wrote: 'They [the Jews] have been pampered by the towns with promises of great liberties and privileges, as each having in mind its private gain and economy, and little the honour of God and

---

[91] De Groot, *Remonstrantie*, ed. Meijer, 38–46.
[92] e.g. Zwarts, 'Eerste rabbijnen', 193.

the common weal.'[93] Amsterdam, of course, did not need to lure immigrants—it was attractive enough in itself—and never made such conditions. But the main difference between the approaches of de Groot and of the cities does not lie in their divergent assessments of economic factors: for the same minimum residence requirement may be found, about the same time, elsewhere and in a context having nothing to do with Jews.

The famous Article XIII of the Union of Utrecht (23 January 1579) which established freedom of conscience throughout the seven United Provinces refers in its consideration of the matter of public worship to a previous attempt at settling the religious conflict: the so-called *Religionsvrede* (religious peace). The *Religionsvrede*, in turn, represents an attempt to break the deadlock occasioned by the Pacification of Ghent (8 November 1576), which promised the Protestants a certain measure of freedom in Holland and Zeeland and a suspension of anti-heresy legislation elsewhere. Ensuing disturbances having proved the Pacification insufficient to stem the tide of religious conflict, on 10 July 1578 the prince of Orange presented to the States General his *Religionsvrede*, which proposed to resolve the issue in a highly original fashion.[94] The prince's proposal opened with a general proclamation of freedom of conscience, that is, private worship, and then turned to public worship:

Section 3 . . . The Roman Catholic Religion will again be allowed, both in the cities of Holland and Zeeland as in other cities and places where it has been abandoned, to be practised peacefully and freely by those who desire to do so, without any disturbance or hindrance, *provided that they are not fewer in number than one hundred households in each large city or town* and have been domiciled there for at least one year . . .

Section 4. Similarly will the Reformed Religion be allowed to be practised publicly etc. (*ut supra*).[95]

The principles of the *Religionsvrede* proved unworkable, but what concerns us here is its statement of a principle of toleration obviously unrelated to economic considerations of any kind.

On a general level the thinking of the *Religionsvrede* parallels that of the French Politiques of the same decade. Originally a somewhat crude plea for the suspension of religious intolerance for reasons of state, the programme of the Politiques was sharpened and sophisticated to the point where it became a fully fledged theory of

[93] De Groot's remark has a striking parallel in the following observation made by the Spaniard Don Juan in the early days of the Rebellion: 'The Prince of Orange has always insisted on impressing on the people that freedom of conscience is essential to commercial prosperity, and as these people are vitally interested in this aspect, they usually side with the party that protects their interests, without giving a thought to God or Your Majesty': Lecler, *Toleration*, ii. 208.

[94] For the history and text of the *Religionsvrede*, see Motley, *Rise of the Dutch Republic*, iii. 290–3; iv. 108–9; Geyl, *Revolt of the Netherlands*, 149–63; Lecler, *Toleration*, ii. 203–19; Elkan, 'Über die Entstehung'; Gachard, *Bibliothèque nationale*, i. 190–7; Hubert, *De Charles-Quint*, 165–78; van Meteren, *Historie van de oorlogen*, iii. 162–77; Brandt, *History of the Reformation*, i. 340–2.

[95] Translated from van Meteren, *Historie van de oorlogen*, iii. 167; emphasis added.

toleration. At the root of the *politique* theory of toleration lay the distinction between civil and religious or dogmatic toleration.[96] Irenicists, that is, advocates of religious toleration, advocated the acceptance of a minimum of doctrinal unity, of a few fundamentals of (Christian) faith, as a means of ironing out the rivalries between the churches. The Politiques favoured treating the religious issue with 'benign neglect', accepting the status quo of two religions in one state, and concentrating attention on fostering peaceful civil interaction (as opposed to war) between members of different churches. They created the idea of civil toleration: the delimitation of a sphere of public life in which religious opinions are not of primary concern. The particulars of this ideology were worked out in a wide variety of ways, depending on the social and political situation of the moment. Considering the realities of the Netherlands, the prince of Orange reasoned somewhat along the lines of Jean Bodin's *La République* (1576) that 'the more a man's will is forced, the more it will rebel', and that powerful minorities are less dangerous if tolerated publicly than if condemned to practise in secret.[97] The prince apparently felt that the presence of a small religious minority did not warrant irritating the sensitivities of the majority. Once a minority reached a more significant number, the dangers it might represent to the state if forced to remain underground (or indoors) outweighed the annoyances its presence might create in the eyes of the majority. The dividing-line of 100 households is, of course, arbitrary, but the real significance of this approach lies in its recognition of reality. Reality, not dreams, determined the thinking of these Dutch Politiques, and to that extent their pragmatic approach represented a significant advance over the ideological clarity of the Middle Ages.

De Groot, it seems, did not sufficiently appreciate the idea of civil toleration. His failure to recognize the implications of the minimum residence requirement clauses (with which he was no doubt familiar) nullifies the significance of his appeal to other familiar *politique* arguments, such as the faint allusion to a natural community. No doubt, in the context of the juridico-political history of the Jews, de Groot's basic acceptance of the Jews as 'citizens' represents a noteworthy step towards Jewish emancipation.[98] When considered in the light of contemporary actions and views, however, the conservative de Groot appears awkwardly out of step. His religious sentiments and prejudices, as well as an unrealistic view of social and political issues, set him apart from his less learned contemporaries.

The resurfacing of the *politique* approach in the explicit and implicit conditions of Jewry toleration in Haarlem, Rotterdam, and Amsterdam contains a faint yet unmistakable indication that the burgomasters were not 'baiting' the Jews for reasons of economic advantage but were actually weighing the social pros and cons of Jewish settlement. The allegedly close interrelation between toleration of the Jews and calculations of economic profits—the favourite alternative to a humanist explanation of Jewry toleration—needs to be re-examined. As moderate

---

[96] Lecler, *Toleration*, ii. 40–156; Kamen, *Rise of Toleration*, 131–45.
[97] Lecler, *Toleration*, ii. 108–9.   [98] Baron, *Social and Religious History*, xv. 29.

Politiques, the burgomasters may actually have subscribed to a theory of toleration different from those of either the Calvinist clergy or the Erasmians and Remonstrants.

Dirck Volckertsz. Coornhert's name does not figure in the history of Jewry toleration in seventeenth-century Holland. Yet more than any of his contemporaries, Coornhert represents Dutch toleration at its finest and its most modern.[99] As secretary of the burgomasters of Haarlem and of the States of Holland (at the recommendation of William of Orange), Dirck Volckertsz. Coornhert (1522–90), a nominal Catholic throughout his life, was well established in political life. As translator of some of the works of Sebastian Castellio into Dutch, he represents the less conservative and more positive trend in early modern toleration. Unlike Erasmus, Castellio advocated an almost universal toleration limited only to believers in God.[100] (Coornhert, it seems, was willing to tolerate even atheists.) What made Castellio and Coornhert more liberal than Erasmus, however, was not primarily their extension of the limits of toleration but their emphasis on the individual conscience rather than on religious unity. Given the inability of humanity to arrive at universally accepted religious truths, Erasmus was inclined to counsel submission to 'the way of authority' for the greater *summa* of peace and unanimity. For Castellio and Coornhert, the individual is the ultimate judge of what to believe true and false. In their eyes, hypocrisy is the greatest sin against God. They rejected the concept of heresy as a social and political crime. They valued peace as highly as did Erasmus but, having lived through religious war, were not as sanguine about achieving it, unless the search for unanimity gave way to an acceptance of variety. Not surprisingly, Coornhert proved particularly susceptible to the teachings of Sebastian Franck, whose emphasis on the spiritual unity of the various religious traditions rendered arguments over religious differences less urgent. Ultimately Coornhert's advocacy of toleration, with certain *politique* emendations, did more to further the solution of the social and political problems raised by the religious wars than the Erasmian quest for conciliation.

In his *Synod on Freedom of Conscience* (1582) Coornhert presents a major statement of his position on toleration. Amid an imaginary multitude of anonymous and historical participants, Coornhert himself appears in the person of Gamaliel, the Pharisaic member of the Sanhedrin who spoke in defence of the early Christians: 'Keep clear of these men, I tell you; leave them alone. For if this idea of theirs or its execution is of human origin, it will collapse; but if it is from God, you will never be able to put them down and you risk finding yourselves at war with God' (Acts 5: 38–9). In other words, the fundamental problem resides in (clerical and lay) men's inability to determine whether a religious conviction is 'of human origin' or 'from God'. In nineteen sessions devoted to as many separate issues

---

[99] Bonger, *Motivering van de godsdienstvrijheid*; Lecler and Valkhoff (eds.), *A l'aurore des libertés modernes*; Lecler, *Toleration*, ii. 271–86

[100] Bainton *et al.*, *Castellioniana*; Buisson, *Sébastien Castellion*; Lecler, *Toleration*, i. 336–60.

Coornhert establishes that every church, even the true one, can err; that only Scripture does not err, but no one church has yet found the key to its truths; that in recognizing the possibility of one's own error any church must, in accordance with the Golden Rule, acknowledge another's 'right' to err; that no earthly authority is capable of judging either persons or doctrines. Coornhert counsels against any restriction of public worship or censorship of printing, lest the secret dissemination of error escape refutation and secret sects be inspired to mutiny, treason, or other disturbances. For in the end, so the optimistic Coornhert believed, freedom of conscience and expression will lead to the triumph of the truth.

Written shortly after the *Religionsvrede* of 1578 and the Union of Utrecht in the following year, Coornhert's *Synod* may be regarded as a major plea for the policy of toleration embodied in those treaties, an optimal state of toleration to which the prince of Orange and the political leadership of the Republic aspired. Notwithstanding his radicalism, Coornhert was more representative of the thinking that prevailed in those circles than was Hugo de Groot. Coornhert attempted to lift the discussion of toleration from the traditional framework of authority and disapproval, in removing religious matters from the authority of the state and reserving disapproval for social and political 'vices'. He arrived at his novel conclusions in a particularly noteworthy manner.

Toleration being a new idea in the sixteenth century, its theorists were forced to bolster their rational arguments with other, preferably traditional, reasons. Reason alone was not yet sufficient; nor, in theory, was the urgency of terminating the religious wars. In this regard Erasmians had a great advantage over Castellians, for the reasons they advanced strayed less from the tradition of a unified Christendom. When all is said and done, Coornhert's rational arguments did no more than destroy the rational or traditional arguments of his opponents, and only experience could prove the necessity and viability of his alternative: the negative experience of religious war and the positive experience of his personal tolerance based on the Golden Rule and an optimistic evaluation of his fellow citizens' motivation for seeking religious diversity.

There are also things one can know indubitably, by the proper use of reason or by experience. By the proper use of reason he knows evidently that the space must be greater than the body which occupies it, that the whole is greater than the part . . . But by experience he knows what is good or bad, for the health of the soul as well as for that of the body. For example, everyone may know that his stomach is empty, when he is very hungry; that he is ill, when his body suffers. Similarly anyone who is attentive may be sure when his conscience is ill at ease, that he is without God or impious, as he lacks the nourishment of souls, namely the Word of God.[101]

History, as the record of human experience, has for Coornhert a value comparable to that of Scripture and is, therefore, designated 'the true book of experience' or

---

[101] Lecler and Valkhoff (eds.), *A l'aurore des libertés modernes*, 157.

'genuine mirrors of experience'.[102] If and in so far as Coornhert's approach represents an important strand in the thinking of the political leadership of Holland's cities and towns, it lies in viewing political authority untraditionally as not merely inferior or superior to, but truly autonomous of religious authority and in relying on experience rather than reason to determine 'what is good or bad', to measure levels of disapproval.

Cornelis Pietersz. Hooft (1547–1626), twelve-times burgomaster of Amsterdam (1588–1610), has left us a substantial collection of his thoughts and opinions.[103] Several of his extant writings deal with toleration, of which Hooft was one of the staunchest supporters within the city's magistrature. On the occasion of the excommunication of one Goosen Vogelsang for 'divers Heresies and gross Errors' in 1597, Hooft submitted a memorial to the Vroedschap (city council) in which he makes the following observation:

We should have thought our selves very happy formerly, if we could have brought our affairs to the condition they are now in; the design of our taking up Arms extending it self no further than to the shaking off force and tyranny, but not the lording it over the consciences of others; as seeking (if I may use the words of a great Historian [Livy]) *a shelter for liberty, but not an unbounded power of invading others.* Neither had we ever been able, nor even Prince William himself, of glorious memory, to have set foot again in this country, from whence we were driven, had not the inhabitants, and among them, a great many *Romanists*, who abhorred the cruelty of the Spaniards, opened the Gates to us themselves, in a firm persuasion, that every man's conscience would be free: for which reason I cannot yet be convinced that we ought to do violence to the conscience of any man, but adhere to my opinion, that every one should be left to his liberty as far as may consist with the preservation of that liberty which, through the favour of God, we have obtained for our selves.[104]

Although he never quotes Coornhert, Hooft placed a commensurate emphasis upon experience as the source of his tolerance. Like Coornhert, he believed, quoting a burgomaster predecessor, that 'No Princes, nor Magistrates, had any authority over the consciences of their subjects in matters of religion.'[105] Echoing an anonymous defence of the *Religionsvrede*, Hooft argued that the excommunicated Vogelsang yet remained a member of civil society from whom the city had nothing to fear, 'he being a stranger and without support'.[106] It was not religion but common political opposition to Spain that created unity within the body politic of Holland, and Hooft therefore condoned the contemporary discrimination against Catholics on political rather than religious grounds.

The similarities and differences between Coornhert and Hooft are illuminating. Rationally, both accepted the respective autonomy of the political and religious

---

[102] Bonger, *Motivering van de godsdienstvrijheid*, 95–106.

[103] Van Gelder, *Levensbeschouwing*; Lecler, *Toleration*, ii. 292–7; Brandt, *History of the Reformation*, i. 461–74.

[104] Brandt, *History of the Reformation*, i. 463. The original Dutch text may be found in Hooft, *Memoriën*, ii. 38.   [105] Brandt, *History of the Reformation*, i. 472.   [106] Ibid. 469.

spheres. Experientially, on the other hand, they had less in common. The lack of common experiences must indeed be regarded as a major and—at this early stage in the development of toleration—unavoidable weakness in the crystallization of a coherent *politique* theory of toleration. Coornhert sought religious truth, Hooft political independence; the first found the seed of unity and peace in an optimism that the truth would triumph, the latter in a shared determination never again to suffer foreign domination; the first disapproved of hypocrisy and indifference, the latter of treason and political meddling. In other words, in their search for a common non-religious bond of social and political unity, non-Erasmians and non-theocratically-inclined Calvinists were guided by their personal store of experiences and disapproved accordingly of whatever contradicted their per-ception, based on those experiences, of the basic ingredients of unity.

A few disparate phrases uttered during the early years of Portuguese settlement reveal another dimension of approval/disapproval. In the 1598 resolution remind-ing the Portuguese immigrants that only the Reformed religion could be publicly practised in the city, the Amsterdam burgomasters expressed their expectation that the immigrants 'are Christians and will live an honest life as good burghers'. Likewise, the Haarlem charter of 1605, which explicitly recognized the Judaism of the petitioners, refers to the future settlers as 'people with honour and of good conduct and [honest] dealings' ('Luyden met eere ende van goeden handel and wandel').[107] These deceptively platitudinous phrases hint at honesty, honour, and proper conduct as the prerequisites for approval, overriding whatever immeasur-able disapproval Judaism may have engendered. And when, in another seemingly innocuous aside, the Haarlem charter speaks of 'people of esteem and of property', we are led to wonder whether the references do not hint at some implied relation between honesty and property.

Much is made in the literature of the interrelation between the quest for eco-nomic prosperity and religious tolerance. The argument that commercial pros-perity requires a fairly large measure of religious liberty has a long history. It was a particular favourite with advocates of toleration in the Netherlands, whether Catholic or Protestant, whether in the south or in the north.[108] It tended to stand alone, however, proffered with some *gêne* as tainted with morally questionable self-interest. Hugo de Groot chid the Holland towns for having 'pampered' the Jews 'with promises of great liberties and privileges, each having in mind its private gain and economy and little the honour of God and the common weal'.[109] But contemporary opponents of the argument and modern historians alike have failed to grasp the presuppositions of social and political unity according to which these advocates operated. The fact that the premisses were not yet fully articulated during the early seventeenth century does not mean that they were not already

---

[107] De Groot, *Remonstrantie*, ed. Meijer, 40.
[108] Lecler, *Toleration*, ii. 498; Hassinger, 'Wirtschaftliche Motive'.
[109] De Groot, *Remonstrantie*, ed. Meijer, 107.

operative. They had, after all, first to be experienced before they could emerge to the level of consciousness. Indeed, the fact that these presuppositions do eventually surface only confirms that they had already been in effect.

The economic argument for religious toleration came into its own in political theories of the second half of the seventeenth century following the introduction of the ideas of Thomas Hobbes (1588–1679), who had made self-interest the pivot of his political philosophy. In Holland, the brothers de la Court and Spinoza were most responsible for disseminating, applying, and modifying Hobbesian ideas. Taken as a whole, their works represent the most explicit and passionate defence of freedom and toleration ever published in seventeenth-century Holland. Pieter de la Court praises Machiavelli, Descartes, and Hobbes because they took man as he was and not as old-fashioned professors chose to see him.[110] In other words, he commended their reliance upon experience.

Pieter de la Court (1618–85), a Leiden cloth manufacturer and partisan of Johan de Witt's 'Freedom' party, propounded his ideas most notably in his *Interest van Holland* (1662; English translation: *The True Interest and Political Maxims of the Republic of Holland*, attributed to John de Witt).[111] By nature, he declared, men are driven primarily by self-interest, and his central purpose in this work is to demonstrate that the self-interest of the republican state best coincides with the self-interests of its subjects. A harmonious chain of interests binds rulers and ruled. Prosperity and populousness are important conditions for the maintenance of this harmony and unity; and one of the best means to procure prosperity and immigration is toleration, along with occupational freedom, the removal of monopoly companies and guilds, and the abolition of taxation for 'fishers, manufacturers, merchants and owners of freight-ships'.

Chapter 14 of part one of the *Interest van Holland* is entitled: 'That freedom or toleration in, and about the service or worship of God, is a powerful means to preserve many inhabitants in Holland, and allure foreigners to dwell amongst us.' Here, de la Court regards the churches and their ministers as one more interest group within the totality of the state; a group, moreover, whose interest might easily run counter to that of the state. Civil and ecclesiastical authority are clearly distinguished, in both ends and means:

the coercive power is given only to the civil magistrate; all the power and right which the ecclesiasticks have, if they have any, must be derived from them . . . Indeed the essential and only difference between the civil and ecclesiastical power is this, that the civil doth not teach and advise as the other doth, but commands and compels the inhabitants to perform or omit such outward actions, or to suffer some certain punishment for their disobedience . . . Whereas on the other side, the duty of Christian teachers is to instruct and advise men to all

---

[110] Kossmann, *Politieke theorie*, 30–58.

[111] On Pieter de la Court, see van Tijn, 'Pieter de la Court'. The following translations are quoted from the 1746 London edition of *The True Interest*, because this is the version most readily available in reprint (New York, 1972).

Christian virtues . . . Which virtues consisting only in the inward thoughts of our minds cannot be put into us by any outward violence or compulsion.[112]

Enforcement of a single divine worship would breed atheism, and the public use of force would undermine the faith of the faithful. On the other hand, de la Court sees very little reason to assume that religious dissenters would be particularly drawn to sedition:

the honest dissenting inhabitants, who fare well in this country, or possess any considerable estates, ought not to be presumed to fall into such seditious thoughts, so destructive to themselves and the country, so long as they are not imbittered by persecution; but on the contrary will be obliged by such liberty, easy and moderate government, to shew their gratitude to so good a magistracy.[113]

If anything, the presence of such groups must be seen as an asset to the political stability of the Republic.

There will be found naturally among the inhabitants diversities in religion, nations, tongues and occupations: so that there would be no occasions ministred to the few aristocratical rulers who govern our republick and cities, of dividing the people by artificial, and often impious designs, in order to govern them: for by these natural divisions, and the diversity of the peoples occupations, they may as peaceably and safely govern them, as in the open country; for in the great cities of Holland, and other cities filled with foreign inhabitants, as Amsterdam, Leiden, Haarlem, etc. there have been nothing near so many seditions against the rulers, as in other countries, and much less and worse peopled cities, unless when they have been stirred up to mutiny or sedition by a sovereign head.[114]

Finally, Pieter de la Court sums up his ideas and sentiments in these designedly poetic and impassioned lines:

There is an absolute necessity that the commonalty be left in as great a natural liberty for seeking the welfare of their souls and bodies, and for the improvement of their estates, as possible. For as the inhabitants of the most plentiful country upon earth, by want only of that natural liberty, and finding themselves every way encumber'd and perplexed, do really inhabit a bridewel or house of correction, fit for none but miserable condemned slaves, and consequently a hell upon earth. Whereas a power of using their natural rights and properties for their own safety, provided it tends not to the destruction of the society, will be to the commonalty, tho' in a barren and indigent country, an earthly paradise: for the liberty of a man's own mind, especially about matters wherein all his welfare consists, is to such a one as acceptable as an empire or kingdom.[115]

A more concise formulation of the centrality of civil toleration in the thinking of many a Dutch patrician can hardly be imagined.

De la Court's argument may seem rather confused. The *Interest van Holland* is a political pamphlet. Above all it seeks to hammer home the dangers to the United Provinces of monarchy, specifically of an idea of monarchy with which large segments of the Republic's population flirted at that time. Because de la Court argues

---

[112] Ibid. 51.   [113] Ibid. 320–1.   [114] Ibid. 329.   [115] Ibid. 416–17.

for one political system over another, he emphasizes the influence of the political upon the social and obfuscates the complexities of cause and effect. None the less, he does give a description (and not a prescription) of the coincidence of the true interest of Holland's republican leaders with that of the 'fishers, manufacturers, merchants and owners of freight ships' and, in doing so, reveals a sense of certain social and political interrelationships that might plausibly be imputed to other members of his patrician class.

Economic prosperity and religious freedom, on the one hand, and social diversity and political unity, on the other, are so multifariously intertwined as to constitute an acutely sensed, if not logically coherent, integral whole. The missing links in de la Court's argument between prosperity and freedom, between diversity and unity, are never explicated. But the fact that he implies a link only adds value to his perception. Freedom and prosperity may be connected, and give rise to civil toleration, provided the apparent diversity of socio-economic self-interests coincides with the real unity of economo-political interdependence. Otherwise, only an apparent—that is, a coerced—unity such as that which must be feared from the restoration of the monarchy will be able to control the very real diversity that has evolved from the natural and historical conditions of Holland. In the truly prosperous and free republic of the future, self-interest will somehow and naturally produce interdependence—as it has, by implication, in that of the past and the present. On several occasions de la Court attributes special significance to 'faring well', 'possessing any considerable estates', and 'the improvement of their estates' as motivating men to shy away from sedition. The self-interest of property ownership induces a realization of interdependence and of the value of unity. Economic pursuits, but especially the pursuit of property, inspire ratiocination and predictability in serving self-interest, seeking integration into unity rather than diffusion into chaos.

In his unfinished *Tractatus politicus*, Spinoza addresses the same problem in more abstract terms.[116] Spinoza, too, held that self-preservation was conducive to rationality. In the treatise's discussions of monarchy and aristocracy (of the discussion of democracy only a fragment remains) Spinoza then takes great pains to ensure the interdependence of rulers and ruled by insisting on royal councillors or patricians remaining dependent upon commerce.[117] Thus the self-interest of the rulers will be wedded to that of the ruled, and a common centripetal interest 'in promoting peace and concord'—the *summa* of Spinoza's political organization—will bind and sustain the polity. In sum, both de la Court and Spinoza interrelate economic prosperity and religious freedom via the coincidence of a diversity of self-interests and a unity of interdependence; a coincidence engendered by the 'natural' rationality of economic, and especially commercial, pursuits.

Neither Coornhert nor Hooft nor de la Court nor even Spinoza had anything

---

[116] Wernham, intr. to Spinoza, *Political Works*.   [117] Ibid. 341–3, 385–7.

specific to say on the subject of Jewry toleration. Each in his own way was concerned to find a non-religious basis upon which to restructure political society after the demise of religion as the great unifier. From Erasmus' 'peace and unanimity' to Spinoza's 'peace and concord' we witness not only the emancipation of political from religious concerns, but also the discovery of the 'concordant' search for prosperity rather than the 'unanimous' quest for salvation as the 'natural' nexus of the body politic. Coornhert and Hooft were still restricted by the religious parameters of the socio-political debate inherited from the past and too narrowly preoccupied with safeguarding the gains of the rebellion against Spain. Yet both already pointed to social and political 'vices and crimes' as the basis for disapproval of fellow residents. After several decades of peace and the consolidation of the Republic's independence, unity ceased to be a need and emerged as a given. A new generation of political theorists was then able to venture a more dispassionate explanation of how the bewildering array of social differences and economic interests had produced the relative political stability and social tranquillity of seventeenth-century Holland. They discovered what political practitioners had 'trusted', from experience, to be the case all along: that the pursuit of self-interest generally renders a resident an honest member of society. There were undoubtedly different levels of this 'trust'; and the trust was the more secure, the more that self-interest coincided with the self-interest of the ruling class and the more obviously that self-interest was visible in the accumulation of 'considerable estates'. Trust and distrust replaced approval and disapproval in the judgement of fellow residents. The real significance of the *politique* theory of civil toleration lies not only in its redefinition of authority, but more importantly in its novel articulation of approval or disapproval in terms of trust. And, however little the Politiques had to contribute to the discussion of Jewry toleration, their general approach to problems of toleration makes better sense of the evolution of the liberal Jewry legislation of Amsterdam's magistrature than the alternately traditional and modern approach of Hugo de Groot.

A DISTINCTIVE LIBERALISM

Amsterdam's toleration of Jewry was not just liberal in the relatively small number of restrictions it imposed upon Jewish settlement in the city: it was truly liberal in spirit, and as such represents an intermediary and distinctly variant and original stage between the toleration-with-disapproval of the past and the emancipation-with-equality of the future. Its liberalism stands revealed in the nearly consistent separation of Church and state, in the latitude allowed to the immigrants in their economic activities, and, above all, in the pervasively empirical attitude of the legislators.

   In concrete terms, the choice between a political or a religious definition of the Jews and their community arose in connection with the issues of excommunication, marriage, and *poorterschap*. The burgomasters never excluded Jews from the *poorterschap* and recognized their basic political rights as residents of the city. In insisting that Jewish marriages be legalized at the city hall, the burgomasters applied a new standard according to which marriage was primarily a political rather than a sacramental contract. And in disallowing marriages involving degrees of consanguinity permitted only by Jewish law, the magistrates in Amsterdam— and elsewhere in Holland—followed the same political principle that applied to Christians. The Amsterdam authorities did accept the Jewish community's right to excommunication, a right considered by some to represent a curtailment of the political rights of the individual; but—and in this respect the burgomasters acted as Collegialists—they viewed a religious community as a voluntary association whose members freely committed themselves to abide by its rules and regulations.[118] Excommunication was one such legitimate rule, instituted to secure discipline and compliance with communal statutes. On no occasion did excommunication entail a concomitant loss of political status. The case of Spinoza demonstrates that it was possible to live in seventeenth-century Holland without any formal affiliation to a religious community.[119] And finally, the Amsterdam authorities, adhering to the separation of Church and state, never lent any support to the conversionist plans entertained by the clergy. In all these instances the burgomasters and the Vroedschap clearly distinguished between the political burgher and the religious Jew, as they then defined the distinction between religion and politics. According to the laws of Amsterdam, the Jewish resident was a burgher by nature and a Jew by will.

In economic matters, Amsterdam's liberalism may be recognized, characteristically, in the burgomasters' silence rather than in their declared decisions. At no time did the authorities ever interpose an obstacle in the way of the economic development and expansion of the Portuguese Jews; nor did they ever interfere in any way with the Jews' right to acquire property. Jewish settlement in Dutch Brazil, the Caribbean islands and Surinam, and Nieuw Amsterdam met with the full approval of the Amsterdam authorities, on a few occasions over the objections of an illiberal local official such as Peter Stuyvesant. Industrial initiatives undertaken by Jews in Amsterdam itself likewise found favour with the burgomasters. No laws prohibiting or restricting Jewish ownership of real estate, no enactments tapping Jewish wealth through special taxation, no procedural rules creating inequality in a court of law were ever introduced. Only on the lower rungs of the economic ladder did Jews run into difficulties, and then often only temporarily. *Poortersneringen* from which Jews were excluded would have meant an economic and social step backwards. That exclusion, however, as noted above, served more to protect the guilds than to curtail Jewish economic activity.

[118] On Territorialism and Collegialism, see Altmann, 'Moses Mendelssohn on Excommunication'; on the Collegialism of burgomaster Hooft, see van Gelder, *Levensbeschouwing*, 70–3.

[119] This fact leads Baer to label Spinoza the first modern Jew: *Galut*, 105.

The empiricism of Amsterdam's city fathers may well be the feature most indicative of their liberalism. We encounter this trait negatively in the lack of any plan or order in the Jewry legislation actually passed. But we also find it more positively in the 1616 statute's yielding to clerical pressure only in so far as an actual rather than an imaginary impropriety was involved; in the decision to legalize retroactively marriages not recorded at the city hall; and in the temporary requirement to register insurance policies. The most salient indication of the authorities' empirical level-headedness must surely be recognized in what Hugo de Groot lamented as 'an error of judgement [*een saecke van quade insichte*], [namely] that the Jews have already come to this country in large numbers without public resolution or prior decree'.[120] For the very ambiguity which attended the earliest settlement of Portuguese immigrants, and the fact that it was eventually resolved in favour of the Jews, bespeaks a reluctance to act out of preconception and a courage to face reality as it comes. The initial hesitation was no 'error of judgement' but a suspension of judgement. The Amsterdam authorities operated within a framework of trust rather than of disapproval; and trust, unlike disapproval, is by definition open to empirical validation. The immigrants' 'honest life as good burghers' proved, in the end, a more basic and more important condition than their alleged Christianity. By the 1610s, when the public practice of Judaism came to be condoned, the burgomasters had seen sufficient first-hand evidence of honesty and trustworthiness in the commercial dealings of the Portuguese settlers to render the question of religion moot and of consequence only in so far as it affected the realities of power in political life; that is, in so far as it posed empirical problems.

Toleration caused political problems on two fronts. In the colonies, where Calvinists were often in prominent positions of power, local *predikanten* (ministers) and, sometimes, governors quite vocally questioned the toleration of the directors of the great trading companies.[121] In a famous letter, dated 22 September 1654, Governor Peter Stuyvesant of the New Netherlands refers to the Jews as 'that deceitful race [*dat bedriegelijck geslachte*]—such hateful enemies and blasphemers of the name of Christ' (deceitful because of 'their customary usury and deceitful trading with the Christians') and calls for them 'not to be allowed further to infect and trouble this new colony'.[122] Similar remarks and requests were voiced in Brazil and even on Curaçao, and echo the sentiments of Calvinist ministers in Holland itself.[123] The standard reply of the directors of the West India Company and the burgomasters of Amsterdam was to point out the contribution to the prosperity of the city or the colony made by or expected from the Jews. It was an argument that did not so much reflect their personal thinking as bridge the gap between

---

[120] De Groot, *Remonstrantie*, ed. Meijer, 107.   [121] Boxer, *Dutch Seaborne Empire*, 148–72.

[122] Oppenheim, 'Early History of the Jews in New York', 4–5.

[123] Van Dillen, 'Economische positie', 605; Emmanuel, *History of the Jews of the Netherlands Antilles*, 84–7; Teensma, 'Resentment in Recife'.

the prejudices of the Calvinists and the empirical understanding of the merchant class. For the Calvinists as artisans generally distrusted commerce and denounced it as deceitful across the board. The directors or burgomasters could therefore not 'disprove' Calvinist prejudices on empirical grounds. Wittingly or unwittingly, they were forced to appeal to the one goal both sides had in common: prosperity. Always appearing in such contexts of justification, the utilitarian argument tells us more about the dialogue between the classes involved than about the sentiments of Holland's merchant class.

In the colonies a verbal retort sufficed, for there were no other, more specific, conflicts between Calvinists and Jews; both groups shared in the common colonizing enterprise. In Amsterdam itself, however, Calvinist opposition to the Jews assumed more concrete forms, and the magistrates were forced to deal with this opposition as such conflicts constituted a potential threat to their own position in power. The Amsterdam magistrature was an oligarchy whose authority, because of religious and social changes, could no longer be justified in traditional, semireligious terms. For the time being its authority rested on the voluntary consent of the population and on the empirical fact that it created peace and concord and prosperity. At the same time the recent separation of Church and state and the increasing divergence of mercantile and artisan interests produced both the potential for challenges to that authority and the environment in which such challenges could be mounted. This somewhat precarious balance forced the magistrature to make a number of substantial compromises, involving departures from their liberal creed. Prominent among these were the recognition of Calvinism as the religion of the state and acceptance of the continued existence of the guilds, neither of which subsequently came under attack until in the eighteenth century freedom became linked with equality. The surrender of the Amsterdam magistrature to ecclesiastical and guild pressures for discriminatory legislation against the Jews represents less a survival of traditional prejudices than a balancing of contemporary realities rendered necessary by the very nature of oligarchical power in the days of incipient liberalism.

Similarly, the refusal of the authorities to allow Jews to become second-generation *poorters* and the concomitant exclusion of Jews from official posts safeguarded the tenuous base of their own authority. Popular opposition to Catholics and Remonstrants had occasioned severe restrictions upon their religious assemblies as the Calvinist oligarchy feared its authority being tarnished by association.[124] Both groups already belonged to the ruling classes and therefore could not be excluded from political power by any other means. Equally disliked by the Calvinist populace, Jews were both dissenters *and* foreigners, and thus doubly ineligible for insider status. This combination of disqualifications suggested another solution. For as long as Jews were forced to stay foreigners, they remained excluded from political power. This arrangement had advantages beyond the immediate political

---

[124] Brugmans, *Geschiedenis van Amsterdam*, ii. 130–8, 227–47; iii. 39–48, 140–6.

necessity. Not only did it allow the Amsterdam magistrature to tolerate the Jews who, in Uytenbogaert's words, 'differ much', where it acted more harshly against dissenters 'that differ but little', it left the other rights of the Jews as burghers unaffected. Even the very liberal Pieter de la Court, who argued for a nearly total toleration of all dissenters and for complete freedom of occupation, finds some 'empirical' justification in excluding dissenters 'from all government, magistracies, offices and benefices',

which is in some measure tolerable for the secluded inhabitants, and agrees very well with the maxims of polity, in regard it is well known *by experience* in all countries to be necessary, as tending to the common peace, that one religion should prevail and be supported above all others, and accordingly is by all means authorised, favoured, and protected by the state, yet not so, but that the exercise of other religions at the same time be in some measure publickly tolerated, at least not persecuted.[125] [emphasis added]

And, paraphrasing Machiavelli, a very level-headed Spinoza, perhaps echoing his own experiences, explicates the other side of the coin, the foreigners' acceptance of their exclusion: 'The new-comers [*peregrini*], for their part, make no objection to this; since it is not to be rulers, but to further their own private interests, that they join the settlement, and they are quite content as long as they are given freedom to conduct their own business in security.'[126]

Lest I be accused of having painted too positive a picture of Amsterdam's toleration of Jewry, let me conclude by pointing out that this brand of liberal toleration was not an isolated phenomenon. However apparent the impact of local events and developments on the history of Jewry toleration in Holland, we must not lose sight of the fact that the Amsterdam example is not unique. It can be shown that the histories of the New Christian and Jewish communities of Bordeaux, London, and the European settlements in the western hemisphere exhibit some of the same peculiarities encountered in Amsterdam.[127] The same *laissez-faire*, haphazard treatment of problems of Jewish immigration, a comparable reluctance rigorously to define the juridico-political status of Jewish residents, and a similar unwillingness to cater to prejudice, as well as a number of particular regulations (such as the narrower than traditional definition of Jewish autonomy) seem to have prevailed throughout western Europe. The prevalence of these features in widely scattered and historically distinguishable places suggests the common and independent emergence of liberalism as the basis of similar manifestations of toleration of Jewry. In so far as concrete differences show up, they resulted demonstrably from variations in the position of the 'liberals' in the societies in question—that is, from

[125] De la Court, *True Interest* (London, 1746), 52.

[126] Spinoza, *Political Works*, 379.

[127] On Bordeaux, see Blumenkranz (ed.), *Histoire des Juifs en France*, 22–33; Malino, *Sephardic Jews*, 1–26. On London, see Wolf, 'Status of the Jews'; Roth, 'Resettlement'; Samuel, 'First Fifty Years'; Henriques, *Jews and the English Law*; Endelman, *Jews of Georgian England*, 13–49. On New York, see Marcus, *Colonial American Jew*, i. 397–411.

empirical conditions, not from ideological principles. This liberal, western European toleration stands in stark contrast to the brand of toleration of Jewry, inspired by purely utilitarian, narrowly defined motives, that prevailed in contemporary Italy and Germany.[128] Though allegedly subscribing to the same economic rationale credited for Holland's and England's toleration, Italian and German toleration is characterized by ghettoizing, severely restricting legislation addressing a legally limited number of Jews of whom the tolerators expected specific economic contributions and who were truly considered aliens and only on that account allowed a large measure of autonomy.

As an explanation of these substantive differences between western European and southern and central European Jewry toleration, secularization may seem to describe a great deal, but explains little and then only negatively. Variations in the rates of secularization account, negatively, for the greater or lesser persistence of traditional prejudice, in so far as secularization contributed to removing matters relating to Jews from a purely religious framework; and, of course, secularization created the ideological space for the emergence of principles other than religious ones. The contrast in the kinds of toleration accorded to Jewry owes its starkness not to negative variations in secularization, but to positive principles employed in viewing society and the polity from another than a religious perspective. The evolution of liberalism and the related rise of capitalism furnished western European Jewry toleration with its distinctive features. Pivotal among these were a new idea of authority, reverberating in definitions of the Jew as burgher and of the Jewish community as a voluntary association, and the new market model of society evidenced in the basic trust and the wide range of economic opportunities accorded the Jews.[129]

As a dynamic openness to experience replaced the static circularity of preconception, toleration of Jewry passed into a new phase. The intermediacy of this phase and its lack of ideological clarity have all too often led to its being ignored in the history of the transition from medieval toleration-with-disapproval to modern emancipation-with-equality. The retrieval of an intermediate stage which we may characterize as toleration-with-trust-and-inequality calls into question the very framework of that historiography. It is no longer sufficient to describe the toleration and emancipation of Jews in terms of tradition and reason, however dynamically one recounts their admixture. Nor will the problem be wholly solved by paying due tribute to experience in the history of positive relations between Jews and non-Jews—the kind of tribute it customarily receives only in accounts of anti-Jewish

---

[128] On Germany, see Stern, *Court Jew*; Priebatsch, 'Judenpolitik'; Mahler, *Modern Jewry*, 129–35, 140–6. On Italy, see Pullan, *Rich and Poor*, pt. 3; Ravid, *Economics and Toleration*; Roth, *History of the Jews of Italy*, 329–53.

[129] On the idea of authority, see Krieger, 'Authority' and 'Idea of Authority in the West'. On the market model, see Macpherson, *Political Theory of Possessive Individualism*; various essays in Schochet (ed.), *Life, Liberty, and Property*; and Appleby, *Economic Thought and Ideology*.

violence. The three dimensions of history—tradition, reason, and experience—ought to be taken for granted as modes of description, not as history itself. The proper history of toleration and emancipation must focus on the three-dimensional interplay of authority and power, on the one hand, and the moral and/or 'natural' circumscriptions of the body politic, on the other.

TWO

REFUGE AND OPPORTUNITY
The Geography of a Jewish Migration

Te Deum laudamos Sancto, Sancto, Sancto,
Adonai, Sabaoth, Omnipotent.
Let my soul chant forthright
The heavenly and never-ending hymn of praise:
    For without delay and terror,
Shipwreck, storm or other misfortune,
My eyes now gaze on Amsterdam before me,
And I am free of the Pit and of so many enemies.
    A worthy and divine analogy,
My spirit recognizes the evidence
That he who puts his faith in you finds you:
    In your infinite and holy Providence
Protection sought is found,
If sought with just and proper reverence.

DAVID JESURUN, the 'Child Poet'

THE overwhelming majority of the immigrant settlers of seventeenth-century Amsterdam's Portuguese Jewish community were born in Portugal, Spain, the Spanish Netherlands, or France. Most, if not all, of the immigrants from Spain, Antwerp, and France were themselves the sons and daughters or grandchildren of Portuguese parents and grandparents. On the one hand, then, almost all Portuguese Jewish settlers in Amsterdam were Portuguese natives, at varying removes. On the other hand, not all Portuguese expatriates, nor even all New Christian émigrés, settled in Amsterdam or even in a Jewish community. Some remained in Christian countries where Judaism was proscribed; others settled in other Jewish communities; and still others stayed in Amsterdam for only a short time, before settling in Jewish or Christian communities elsewhere. Before, during, and after the establishment of the Portuguese Jewish community in Amsterdam, there existed a larger Portuguese New Christian and Jewish diaspora spreading across geographical and religious boundaries in ever-changing configurations.

THE GENESIS OF A DIASPORA

The origins of this Portuguese diaspora go back to events in Spain in 1492. In that year the remaining Jews of Spain who had hitherto contrived to evade or resist the

forces, pressures, or temptations of a century of conversions were expelled from
the lands of the Catholic monarchs Isabel of Castile and Ferdinand of Aragon.
An uncertain percentage converted at the last moment in order to gain permission
to remain in Spain. A great many, probably the majority, decided to leave and
sought refuge in North Africa, in Italy, in Ottoman Greece and Turkey, and,
especially, in Portugal. Thus came into being the first Iberian Jewish or Sephardi
diaspora.[1]

Unfortunately, we cannot retrieve the factors that made any given group of Jews
decide in favour of one territory over another. Nevertheless, several characteristics
of this first migration stand out and identify it, not unexpectedly, as a dispersion of
displaced persons. Nobody who follows the paths of the exiles can avoid being
struck by the aimlessness of much of the wandering that preceded settlement in
any of the communities of the emerging diaspora. Some exiles never found rest
abroad and, perforce, drifted back to Spain where a new law permitted duly
converted exiles to resettle. A somewhat pathetic, yet salient example of aimless
wandering highlighting the hardship and confusion of unplanned emigration may
be found in the story of Luys de la Ysla of Illescas, a town halfway between Toledo
and Madrid.[2] At the time of the expulsion Luys was about 8 years old. We do not
know whether he left with his parents or an acquaintance, or alone. After a short
stay in Algiers, Luys made his way to Venice, where he spent three and a half years.
Around 1496, perhaps despairing of ever being able to improve on his hand-to-
mouth existence, perhaps reduced to utter helplessness by the loss of parents or
friends, he decided to return to Spain, converted to Christianity in Genoa prior to
embarkation, and resettled in his native district of Toledo. After a few menial jobs
as a servant, he eventually acquired some skill in silk spinning and, as a spinner,
wandered from job to job throughout southern and central Spain. In the plague
year of 1506 he again decided to leave Spain, boarded a ship at Cartagena, and
sailed for Italy. Unfortunately, Italian silk manufacturing procedures turned out to
be different from the ones Luys had learned in Spain, and he was forced to become
a servant once more, this time to two Portuguese merchants, whom he later discovered to be Jews—or so he testified. In the service of these merchants he came to
Salonika, where he ran into several acquaintances from his post-expulsion days in
Valencia. These, in turn, helped him find another job in service with a Turkish
merchant travelling to Adrianople. After that journey he wandered around for
a time in the area of Constantinople until another merchant took him on for a
journey to Alexandria. Throughout this period, from his arrival in Italy until
reaching Alexandria, Luys had feigned—or so he testified—being a Jew, because
it was only among Jews that he stood any chance of finding employment. In
Alexandria, however, he found a community of Spanish Christian merchants
at the Alhóndigo de Catalanes (the grain market and hostel of the Catalans).

---

[1] Useful and detailed summaries may be found in Baron, *Social and Religious History*, x. 167–219;
xiii. 64–158.   [2] Fita, 'Judío errante'.

Henceforth he refused to associate with Jews, who must have disappointed Luys's expectations of economic security. Two Spanish ladies became fond of him and took him into their service, but Luys lost his sight—a misfortune Alexandrian Jews attributed to his betrayal of Judaism. Blind and now 30 years of age, Luys returned to Spain, where he was imprisoned by the Toledo Inquisition and subjected to questioning on the legitimacy of the absolutions he claimed to have received for his Judaizing in Italy, Greece, and Turkey. And before the inquisitors he told this woeful tale of his wanderings. Whether they were moved or not, we do not know.

One may be tempted to dismiss the example of Luys de la Ysla as atypical in that Luys had neither skill nor family. But in his case it was not so much the wandering itself as Luys's failure to settle down that was attributable to these personal factors. Some wandering was inevitable, and structurally rather than personally determined. Even so prominent a Spanish Jewish grandee as Isaac Abrabanel, otherwise the only kind of exile to leave behind traces of his biography, spent many years moving from Naples to Corfu to Monopoli before settling down in 1503 in Venice, where he died in 1508.[3] The wanderings of Luys de la Ysla and Isaac Abrabanel alike, and of many other Spanish Jewish exiles besides, betray more aimlessness than pattern, their direction determined more by accident than design. Where a plan or pattern does emerge, it follows the dispersion of already established Jewish communities within the Mediterranean world.

It may appear natural that those Jews who were expelled as Jews should choose to settle in already established Jewish communities. This tendency also suggests that as exiles the Spanish Jews had had neither time nor opportunity, nor, perhaps, desire or inclination, to fashion the pattern of their dispersion to their own political, economic, or cultural advantage. The exigencies of a sudden, unanticipated, and unwanted exile reduced their options to what was most readily available.

The 1492 dispersion gave rise to an unevenly distributed diaspora whose various segments pursued separate paths and disintegrated into more or less independent sub-diasporas loosely related to one another. Generally speaking, the larger the number of exiles in a particular segment and the more different culturally the host Jewish community, the more recognizably Spanish that segment of the diaspora remained. In Constantinople, Adrianople, and Salonika, the exiles established their own Spanish Jewish congregations.[4] In Italy, most exiles joined the existing Levantine communities until such time, around the middle of the sixteenth century, as a new wave of Iberian Jewish émigrés settled in Italy. In North Africa, too, the exiles merged with the host communities. In those regions closest to the Iberian peninsula the immigrants predominated at first; elsewhere

---

[3] Netanyahu, *Don Isaac Abravanel*, chs. 3–4.

[4] Emmanuel, *Histoire des Israélites de Salonique*, esp. i. 64–5, 144–51; Galante, *Histoire des Juifs d'Istanbul*, ii. 170–224; Todorov, *Balkan City*, 57–8, 68; Heyd, 'Jewish Communities of Istanbul'.

the refugees assimilated into the existing communities.[5] In Portugal, to which the majority of Spain's expelled Jews fled, the exiles outnumbered the local Jewish communities and merged into one proportionally very large Portuguese Jewish community, many families of which retained for generations the memory of their Spanish descent.[6]

According to some estimates as many as 80 per cent of the Spanish Jewish exiles, or some 85,000–115,000 individuals, preferred the neighbouring Iberian monarchy over a more radical and inevitably harsher exile elsewhere.[7] Portugal was more than simply the most convenient resettlement option, and it was certainly not only—nor even principally—the impecunious who settled there. Portugal provided a chance of escaping the alarming uncertainties of total uprootedness. It offered opportunities of continuity: the retention of traditional economic and cultural ways and the avoidance of the social disintegration that threatened the more far-flung exiles. But Portugal also harboured political dangers. Although in the past the Portuguese king may have appeared a more consistently clement lord than his Castilian counterpart, the close ties between the two monarchies did not bode well for the future. Even the expulsion decree of the Catholic kings had been an about-face after a decade in which they had consistently defended Jewish rights.[8] If the migration of Spanish Jewish exiles to Portugal reflects their determination to continue living as Jews, it also reveals a commitment to Iberia as their economic, social, and cultural homeland.

The history of Spanish Jewish settlement in Portugal after the expulsion has yet to be written. If the figures of contemporary Spanish chroniclers are to be trusted, most of the exiles entered Portugal in the northern and central regions of the country. Many established themselves initially in the towns relatively close to the Spanish frontier and continued trading across the border into Spain or along the routes connecting the Portuguese ports with the Spanish hinterland. Throughout the sixteenth and seventeenth centuries there are records of substantial New Christian communities in Beira and Trás-os-Montes, some of which survived even into the twentieth century.[9] At the time of the expulsion, other exiles undoubtedly made their way to the larger coastal centres of Lisbon and Oporto, but large-scale New Christian settlement in these ports probably came later in the sixteenth century. Meanwhile, in 1497, the Portuguese king forcibly converted all

[5] Hirschberg, *History of the Jews in North Africa* (Heb.), i. 285–329; Abbou, *Musulmans andalous*, 350–88; Chouraqui, *Histoire des Juifs en Afrique du Nord*, 127–9. Chouraqui lists as cities where the Iberian immigrants determined local culture Meknès, Debdou, Fès, Tangier, Tetuan, Salé, Arzilla, Larache, Rabat, and Safi.

[6] Ferro Tavares, *Judeus em Portugal no século XV*, 43–105. Throughout Alves, *Judeus no distrito de Bragança*, one comes across the designation 'originario[/a] de Castela' after the names of many who appeared in *autos-da-fé* until at least the beginning of the eighteenth century.

[7] The estimates cited here derive from the contemporary chroniclers Andrés Bernaldez (93,000) and Alonso de Santa Cruz (113,000).

[8] Suárez Fernández, *Judíos españoles*, 252–71; id., *Documentos*, 9–64.

[9] Paulo, *Criptojudeus*; Novinsky and Paulo, 'Last Marranos', and the older literature cited there.

of Portugal's Jews, the natives as well as the immigrants. He thereby satisfied both the Spanish demand that he rid his kingdom of the Jews and the Portuguese need to draw the Jewish population into the country's grand schemes of colonial expansion. At the same time, in order to avoid a mass exodus of recent converts, Manoel I promised to refrain from enquiring into the religious beliefs of the now 'New' Christians for a period eventually to last until 1536.[10]

The conversion of the Jews provoked two responses. Many, committed to remaining Jews or distrusting royal promises, fled the country and joined the Jewish communities of the previously established Sephardi diaspora. In an attempt to arrest this flight, the Portuguese Crown closed the borders and ports to New Christian emigration from 1499 until 1507; but the attempt proved ineffectual, for in the face of popular outbreaks of anti-*converso* violence such as the Lisbon riots of 1506 those who wished to flee sought every opportunity and exploited every stratagem to do so.[11] On the other hand, the majority of the Portuguese New Christians accommodated themselves to the new situation as best they could. Some consolidated their economic position in their original places of settlement; others—many were not yet rooted economically—eagerly pursued the new opportunities created by Portugal's colonial explorations. The latter gravitated from the interior of the country towards the bustling markets of the coastal plain and beyond towards the African and Asian settlements of the Portuguese empire. Samuel Usque, an eyewitness to these developments in New Christian history, observed that 'the New Christians had become immersed in power and its deceits. They had nearly forgotten their ancient faith, and lost the fear of that Fountain whence our life flows because of the vast riches and the status and rank they were acquiring in the kingdom.'[12] Because of the difficulties in distinguishing New from Old Christians during this era, we cannot be specific about the inroads made by New Christians into colonial commerce and settlement. One thing is quite clear, however: the integration of the New Christians into Portugal's national and colonial economies occasioned a new pattern of emigration. Following and accompanying the first wave of emigration to Jewish communities was a second emigration characterized by planned, voluntary settlement in places offering distinct economic advantages. Until well into the eighteenth century the two strands of emigration continued to run side by side.

During the first quarter of the sixteenth century the pursuit of economic opportunities prompted Portuguese New Christians to settle in Antwerp, then the most important market in northern Europe, where Iberian merchants exchanged colonial wares for European foodstuffs and manufactures.[13] During the second quarter of the century, exploiting links with the Iberian diaspora of the eastern Mediterranean, New Christian merchants began to seek opportune havens of

---

[10] Lucio d'Azevedo, *Historia dos Cristãos Novos portugueses*, 17–40.
[11] Ibid. 58–62; Yerushalmi, *Lisbon Massacre*.
[12] Usque, *Consolation*, 206.   [13] Goris, *Étude sur les colonies marchandes*, 37–55.

settlement in Italy, notably in Ancona, Ferrara, and, though less systematically, Venice.[14] In 1532, alarmed by the exodus of New Christians and their establishment of contacts with and flight to the Ottoman empire, the Portuguese king again—and until 1538—prohibited emigration.[15] At about the same time he began to lobby in Rome for the establishment of a Portuguese Inquisition, an institution which, when inaugurated in 1536, put new pressure upon Portuguese New Christians to seek refuge from religious persecution.[16] Thus the diaspora of commercial entrepreneurs became intertwined with that of refugees from the Portuguese Inquisition.

The flight from inquisitorial persecution differed in significant ways from the earlier exodus in the wake of conversion and popular violence. Whereas the latter disasters befell all New Christians of the country or of a given place indiscriminately, inquisitorial persecution was directed specifically at particular families— in many cases, families conspicuous by virtue of wealth, profession, or status, all features likely to represent ties of varying degree to Portugal. On the other hand, the Inquisition presented a constant and somewhat distant danger, as opposed to the sudden and immediate dangers of physical violence. Its approach could to some degree be anticipated, and a response planned. Indiscriminate violence is more likely to engender a flight towards safety than is a wish to escape the reach of a specific enemy; and inquisitorial persecution could be evaded, for example by withdrawal to territories not under the jurisdiction of the Inquisition or under less rigorous surveillance. Allowing for some measure of anticipation and deliberation, flight from inquisitorial persecution was much less chaotic than the earlier exodus. Flight from violence had been a personal choice, by people for whom that choice was made less difficult by their freedom from social or economic ties to the country; but the inquisitors' selected victims were usually families who valued their connections with other Portuguese families and with the Portuguese economy. The former were accordingly able to uproot themselves more readily; the latter tried to keep in touch as much as possible, socially and economically, with their homeland.

As escape from the Inquisition became a more pressing concern than a return to Judaism, and as the new exiles sought to maintain their connections to Portugal, religious refugees naturally settled in those areas which already had or were likely to offer relations with the home country, which meant first and foremost those communities established by the second, commercial diaspora—especially given that refugees from the Inquisition already had established commercial relations with these communities. Thus there emerged a truly interlocking diaspora, a veritable network held together by common ties to Portugal and peopled by merchants who settled abroad for one of two basic reasons: 'some for fear of an

---

[14] Milano, *Storia degli Ebrei in Italia*, 267–85; Roth, *History of the Jews of Italy*, 177–93.

[15] Lucio d'Azevedo, *Historia dos Cristãos Novos portugueses*, 76, 86.

[16] Ibid. 73–111; Herculano, *History of the Origin and Establishment*.

inquisition into their ancestral religion and others in expectation of greater gain',
as Hugo de Groot phrased it in 1598.[17] Indeed, it becomes well-nigh impossible,
except in rare cases, to determine whether a given individual's emigration was
prompted by inquisitorial persecution or inspired by prospects of commercial
gain.

In the decades following the establishment of the Portuguese Inquisition, New
Christians flocked to the Portuguese colonies in Africa, Asia, and America.
Apparently their number was substantial enough to warrant the establishment of
an Inquisition at Goa in 1560.[18] It remains a curious fact, however—and one unex-
plained to this day—that the Portuguese refrained from establishing permanent
inquisitorial branch offices in those colonies where New Christians appear to have
been most numerous: Madeira and Brazil. Possibly the New Christians' pioneer-
ing contributions there dictated a more tolerant policy than was required in Asia,
where the New Christians served more as brokers and interlopers. In Europe,
meanwhile, Antwerp and the Italian communities continued to attract Portuguese
immigrants until, around the middle of the century, Emperor Charles V's suspicions of New Christian collaboration with the Ottoman enemy, arising from the
apparent links between the Portuguese of Antwerp and Italy and the Iberian
diaspora in the Turkish empire, suddenly gave rise to a backlash. Temporarily the
communities of Antwerp, Venice, and Ancona suffered setbacks in the form of
expulsion and/or imprisonment.[19] At the same time, however, the French king,
Henry II, decided to issue *lettres patentes* to Portuguese merchants wishing to settle
in the south-west of France—a move in which it is possible to discern the beginnings of a more positive evaluation of the economic contributions to be anticipated
from Portuguese immigrants and their dispersed, international connections.[20]
Whatever its motivation, the large-scale emigration of Portuguese New Christians
during the third quarter of the sixteenth century provided the expatriates and
refugees with a rudimentary network more or less safely beyond the reach of the
Inquisition yet sufficiently interconnected with Portugal itself to permit the maintenance and exploitation of those economic opportunities they had come to value
during the first half of the century.

The union of Spain and Portugal in 1580 significantly altered the extent and
directions of Portuguese New Christian emigration. It opened up new territories
to Portuguese immigration, within Spain and its colonies, at a time when the ever-
intensifying persecutions of the Portuguese Inquisition were giving more and
more New Christians cause to emigrate. At first it was primarily the sheer attrac-
tiveness of Spain and its colonies that lured a fairly substantial influx of Portuguese
New Christians. Seville–Cádiz and Madrid, especially, offered promising commercial and financial opportunities. Other New Christians settled in Málaga,

[17] Cited in Seeligmann, 'Marranen-probleem', 106.   [18] Baião, *Inquisição de Goa*, i. 17–51.
[19] Goris, *Étude sur les colonies marchandes*, 560–71, 574–6; Pullan, *Jews of Europe*, 172–82; Milano,
Storia degli Ebrei in Italia, 250–3.   [20] Blumenkranz (ed.), *Histoire des Juifs en France*, 224–5.

Valencia, and the Spanish interior. Once in Spain, Portuguese New Christians also became interested in Spanish American settlement, contriving to evade a fairly restrictive immigration policy by entering Spanish America either illegally or through the back doors of Buenos Aires and Cuba. By the turn of the century substantial numbers of Portuguese merchants had infiltrated the commercial centres of Peru and Mexico.[21]

This influx of Portuguese New Christians did not go unnoticed. At first the Spanish government reacted positively. It allowed the New Christians to buy pardons for inquisitorial offences (in 1601, 1627, and 1630) and freedoms of movement (in 1601 and 1630). It also, increasingly, drew Portuguese financiers into state contracts as it phased out the Crown's dependence on Genovese bankers. In a *consulta* dated 17 August 1626, the Council of Finance recommended accepting the offer made by a number of Portuguese merchant bankers of a loan in exchange for certain privileges, 'since once these men have been introduced to the contracting of *asientos* with His Majesty and have opened commercial establishments in the court [i.e. Madrid] they will be very useful because of the competition in which they will be able to engage the Genovese and the benefits one will be able to draw therefrom'. Between the state bankruptcy of 1627 and the dismissal of the Conde-Duque de Olivares in 1643, the Portuguese became such important bankers and tax farmers as to create a second New Christian diaspora centred in Spain and branching out to the colonies of the Portuguese diaspora in Spanish America, Antwerp, France, and Italy.[22]

In the meantime the suspicions against the Portuguese New Christians that were eventually to engulf the entire Iberian world began to mount, producing a very serious anti-*converso* backlash. It began in Portugal as early as the *cortes* of Tomar (1581), when Portuguese officials voiced their fear that the new Spanish authorities might not be as strict in their discrimination against the New Christians as the Portuguese had grown accustomed to deem necessary. In the ensuing years, as the Spanish Crown appeared to be favouring the New Christians while it allowed the Portuguese economy to deteriorate, the Portuguese Inquisition stepped up its persecution. Between 1584 and 1640—not counting the years from 1606 to 1616, when inquisitorial zeal was curtailed in the wake of a general pardon granted by Pope Clement VIII and King Philip II in 1604—the Portuguese inquisitors sentenced an average of 224 victims annually; in the two decades from 1620 to 1640, the period of the most intensive persecution, a total of 5,676 individuals were sentenced. In Brazil, too, the Portuguese inquisitors pursued their campaign against the *conversos*, making two impromptu visitations in 1591 and 1618. The 1618 visitation coincided with a major persecution in Oporto that

[21] Swetschinski, 'Conflict and Opportunity', 218–22.
[22] Lea, *History of the Inquisition of Spain*, iii. 268–74; Lucio d'Azevedo, *Historia dos Cristãos Novos portugueses*, 158, 162–4, 185–92; Domínguez Ortiz, *Política y hacienda*, 128–30; Boyajian, *Portuguese Bankers, passim*.

seriously weakened one of the economic pillars of the Portuguese diaspora. In 1626 the Portuguese Inquisition even sent a *visitador* (inspector) to Angola, but the results of his investigations are unknown.[23]

In Spain, too, popular opposition to the Portuguese immigrants was quick to emerge. In 1605 Spanish officials of the province of Guipúzcoa complained that

since these people have entered this region, they have usurped the business and the profits of its natives, in the shipments made to Seville and to the Indies as well as in the commerce and exploitation of Terra Nova and that of the foundries and harvests of the country, buying everything cheaply in anticipation of the price [rise], and moreover, as wealthy people, they consume and buy the merchandise coming from abroad and sell it at great profits, forcing the natives to live by the labour of their hands.

Murcia de Llana, a contemporary Spanish economist, voiced a similar complaint: 'None of them cultivates the land, nor is a farmer, nor breeds animals of any kind, nor exercises a mechanical profession [i.e. is an artisan or craftsman], but they manage money, causing a shortage of every kind of merchandise.' The Spanish Inquisition soon joined the chorus, showing a renewed interest in 'Judaizers', a preoccupation that had all but disappeared more than a generation earlier. The upswing in Spanish inquisitorial persecution—directed almost exclusively against Portuguese New Christian immigrants—commenced in the 1630s with the revelations in the case known as *El Cristo de la Paciencia* (1630) and the arrest of the *asentista* Juan Nuñez Saravia (1631). It gained momentum after 1640 when the successful rebellion of Portugal placed the Portuguese in Spain in an awkward position and motivated a previously sympathetic government to have second thoughts about the loyalty of the Portuguese merchant bankers. Echoing the sentiments current in government circles, Pellicer observed in 1640:

It was thought that the evils brought about by the Genovese financiers could be cured by resorting to the Portuguese, for since they were at the time subjects of the Crown to make use of them would also benefit the Crown. But this was only to go from bad to worse. For since most of the Portuguese merchants were Jews, fear of the Inquisition made them establish their main trading houses in Flanders and cities of the north, keeping only a few connections in Spain. The result was that far from Spain benefiting, most of the profits went to the Dutch and other heretics.

Finally, the Spanish American authorities too began to take serious action against the Portuguese New Christian 'interlopers' of Peru and Mexico. The Dutch conquest of a part of Brazil in 1630 set in motion a frenzy of anti-Portuguese inquisitorial persecution. Spanish American authorities imagined and then 'discovered' a *complicidad grande* (great conspiracy) between the Portuguese of Latin America and those of Holland which they claimed had inspired and rendered successful the Dutch victory in Brazil. Between 1635 and 1650 more than 250

[23] Lucio d'Azevedo, *Historia dos Cristãos Novos portugueses*, 149, 225; Veiga Torres, 'Longa guerra social', 63–4; Siqueira, *Inquisição Portuguesa*, 183–93; Vasco Rodrigues, 'Judeus portuenses', 26.

Portuguese merchants were sentenced and robbed of their wealth by the Lima and Mexico City inquisitions.[24]

At the end of the sixteenth century, at the time of Portuguese settlement in Amsterdam, the Portuguese diaspora constituted a truly international network, solidly ensconced in two centres in Portugal and Spain, with branches in the Portuguese and Spanish colonies, links to the two major European entrepôts of Venice and Antwerp, and an as yet minor outlet in south-western France. Interlocking economic strategies gave the network its cohesion; religious (and political) persecution contributed to its diffusion. Neither economic nor religious nor political realities alone can account for the delicate balance between these opposing forces that rendered the network so peculiarly dynamic, creative yet conservative. Only the fact that the economic adventurers and the religious refugees hailed from the same or related families can explain the Portuguese diaspora's success in retaining so much of its cohesiveness over several generations, notwithstanding pressures that would ordinarily have led to its fragmentation.

How large were the sixteenth-century settlements? Their number in Portugal and the Portuguese colonies cannot be estimated. The New Christian mercantile community of Lisbon, to take just one example, was continuously replenished by new arrivals from the interior as it sent others to the overseas settlements of the diaspora. Of 140 New Christian merchants of the seventeenth century about whom we have information, 76 (54.3 per cent) were born outside Lisbon; 81 fathers (73.6 per cent) of the 110 fathers whose origins are known came from the provinces; 62 (90 per cent) of 69 grandfathers were not natives of the capital.[25] Throughout most of the period under consideration there existed a large and mobile New Christian population ready, for one reason or another, to delve locally into international commerce or to venture abroad. As to the Portuguese New Christian immigration into Spain, we are not much better informed. The Spanish economist Murcia de Llana, mentioned above, obviously exaggerated when he reported an immigration of some 70,000 Portuguese, 40,000 of whom supposedly went to live in Madrid alone.[26] Though somewhat closer to the mark, an estimate of 2,000 Portuguese families in Seville prior to 1640 would still seem too high.[27] Sporadic and incomplete figures abstracted from inquisitorial documents, however, clearly reveal the total immigration to have been in the thousands, perhaps as high as 10,000. The Toledo tribunal sentenced 802 Judaizers between 1631 and 1695; that of Galicia 454 in 1560–1700; that of Llerena 647 in 1562–1679; that of

[24] Domínguez Ortiz, *Política y hacienda*, 128; Lucio d'Azevedo, *Historia dos Cristãos Novos portugueses*, 463; Yerushalmi, *From Spanish Court*, 105–22; Domínguez Ortiz, 'Proceso inquisitorial'; Pellicer, *Avisos*, cited in Kamen, *Inquisition and Society*, 224; Liebman, 'Great Conspiracy in Peru'; id., 'Great Conspiracy in New Spain'; Cross, 'Commerce and Orthodoxy'; Hordes, 'Inquisition as Economic and Political Agent'.   [25] Smith, 'Mercantile Class', 34–42.

[26] Lucio d'Azevedo, *Historia dos Cristãos Novos portugueses*, 463.

[27] Domínguez Ortiz, *Judeoconversos*, 69.

Granada 538 in 1560–1695; and that of Córdoba 378 in 1574–1666.[28] Though these periods cover several generations, most of the Judaizers thus documented were Portuguese New Christian immigrants of the period of union and their descendants. The Portuguese New Christian migration to the Spanish American colonies again appears to have been quite substantial. The Lima tribunal convicted 221 Judaizers between 1571 and 1696; that of Mexico City 158 in 1574–1696 and that of Cartagena 70 in 1614–90.[29] Though almost certainly a minority among an estimated total of 10,000–12,000 Portuguese Old and New Christians in all of Mexico, the number of New Christians here must again have run into the thousands. Were we to estimate the Portuguese New Christian population of Mexico roughly and conservatively at 2,000 and use the inquisitorial figures to indicate the relative size of the various New Christian communities, we would arrive at a gross figure of some 6,000 Portuguese New Christians for all of Spanish America.[30] In comparison to these figures, those for the European settlements of Portuguese New Christians are tiny indeed. Antwerp, the largest and oldest expatriate community, counted 94 members of the Portuguese *feitoria* (factory) in 1572, or at most some 500 individuals.[31] Around 1610, according to the denunciations of Hector Mendes Bravo, Venice harboured six single and ten married Portuguese New Christians, or at most 100 individuals, if we add some Mendes Bravo failed to name.[32] Figures for other Italian communities are not available. Nor do we know much about the dispersed small communities along the eastern Adriatic and in the Balkan interior. Around the 1630s, the south-western region of France may have been home to as many as 1,500 Portuguese New Christians.[33] The vast majority of these, however, were very recent immigrants and were part of the same mass exodus of the first half of the seventeenth century that also furnished Amsterdam with most of its Portuguese immigrants.

However tentative or downright speculative the figures cited above, it is clear that there existed, around the end of the sixteenth century, a wide numerical gap between the intra-Iberian (including colonies) and the European migrations of the Portuguese New Christians. Migrations to Spain and the Portuguese and Spanish colonies are measured in the thousands, those to Atlantic and Mediterranean communities in the hundreds.

GEOGRAPHICAL AND HISTORICAL ORIGINS

The settlement of Portuguese New Christians in Amsterdam in the 1590s coincided with similar experiments elsewhere. Middelburg, Cologne, Hamburg,

---

[28] Dedieu, 'Causes de foi', 171; Contreras, *Santo Oficio*, 466; Henningsen, '"Banco de datos"', 564.   [29] Henningsen, '"Banco de datos"', 564.

[30] Israel, 'Portuguese in Seventeenth-century Mexico', 17–20.

[31] Révah, 'Pour l'histoire des Marranes à Anvers', 135–8.

[32] Roth, 'Strange Case', 232–3; Pullan, *Jews of Europe*, 195.

[33] Blumenkranz (ed.), *Histoire des Juifs en France*, 230.

London, and Rouen all received small numbers of Portuguese immigrants between 1585 and 1610. These attempts at settlement inaugurated a new chapter in the history of the Portuguese diaspora. As they occurred within a relatively short radius of the northernmost Portuguese colony of Antwerp, it seems safe to assume—and has always been assumed—that they were occasioned by the closure of the port of Antwerp in 1585 by a rebel naval blockade. Yet it is equally clear that the Antwerp Portuguese community suffered only a temporary setback at the time. In 1598 Antwerp still harboured ninety-three Portuguese commercial firms, as many as there had been in 1572.[34] Thereafter their number does indeed slowly decline, but apparently as a result more of attrition than of emigration. By and large, therefore, the Portuguese settlement attempts at the turn of the century were not direct offshoots of the Antwerp community, but were related to events in that northern port more indirectly.

Several of the settlements were only of short duration or took a while to get off the ground. Middelburg, strategically situated on the maritime route into Antwerp, had harboured a few Portuguese merchants throughout the latter part of the sixteenth century. This obscure settlement briefly grew in size and significance in the wake of Antwerp's closure, but shortly afterwards suffered irreparably from the prohibition on trade with the enemy (including the Spanish Netherlands) promulgated by the Republic in 1599.[35] Cologne temporarily offered a safe haven for Portuguese fleeing the dangers of war in Antwerp. Most returned once the expectation of an imminent attack proved to have been unwarranted; only a very few moved on to Hamburg.[36] The Portuguese settlement in London in the days of Elizabeth I and James I never succeeded in gaining a sure foothold. Aside from cloth—which could also be had elsewhere—and fish, the London market offered as yet little opportunity for a substantial exchange to take root. Moreover, from the very first attempts at settlement here, the Portuguese merchants found themselves the target of serious political suspicions of court intrigue and spying for Spain.[37] Rouen witnessed an abortive attempt at settlement by Portuguese merchants between 1603 and 1607. Little is known about its failure. A more enduring settlement was initiated in 1609 and persisted at least into the 1650s, notwithstanding an unpleasant episode in 1633 which is discussed below.[38] In the long run, only the settlements in Hamburg and Amsterdam proved successful, and these grew into fairly substantial communities.

Northern Europe, however, was not the only theatre of substantial Portuguese New Christian settlement in the early seventeenth century. During the same period, communities of varying size emerged in south-western France: at Bordeaux, Bayonne, Labastide-Clairence, Saint-Jean-de-Luz, Peyrehorade,

---

[34] Pohl, *Portugiesen in Antwerpen*, 67.
[35] Prins, *Vestiging der Marranen*, 141, 155–6, 170.
[36] Kellenbenz, *Sephardim*, 42, 106, 117.
[37] E. Samuel, 'Jews in Jacobean London'; Wolf, 'Jews in Elizabethan England'.
[38] Révah, 'Premier établissement'.

Bidache, Biarritz, and a few smaller towns and villages.[39] In Italy, Ferdinand de' Medici, grand duke of Tuscany, invited Portuguese New Christians to settle and live as Jews in Pisa-Livorno, and in the ensuing years the Portuguese Jewish settlement of Livorno blossomed into a thriving community.[40] After 1589 Venice, too, became more receptive to Portuguese New Christian or Jewish immigration. Throughout most of the seventeenth century the Ponentine Jews of Venice constituted the weightiest segment of the city's Jewish population, though it was never quite as substantial, numerically or commercially, as other Portuguese communities of the diaspora.[41] And, of course, there was the contemporary and large-scale migration of Portuguese to Spain and the Spanish colonies, discussed above. In sum, in the northern European context, the rise of the Jewish communities in Amsterdam and Hamburg may be linked to events surrounding Antwerp; in the larger international context, it ties in with what was happening in Portugal.

Among all the Portuguese settlements of the seventeenth century Amsterdam has a special place not only because it grew into the most important community but also because it allows us to study its immigration and growth in unusual detail. For, as noted in Chapter 1, Amsterdam law required all non-Calvinists to register their intention to marry at the city hall. At the time of registration the 'commissioners of marital affairs' recorded not only the names of the bride and groom but also their place of origin, profession, age, and address, as well as the names and relationships of witnesses. The bride and groom then appended their signatures to the registration. The plethora of information contained in the *puyboecken* (registration ledgers)—the most extensive we possess for any Portuguese colony in the world— provides us with a solid basis for a thorough demographic analysis.[42] The data allow us to identify the channels of migration, the relative strengths of migratory movements, their vicissitudes over time, their sexual as well as, to some degree, social compositions, and the general size and rate of growth of the community.

Between 1598 and 1699, 1,354 Portuguese marriages were registered, involving 2,579 men and women.[43] Using the information they supplied at the time of regis-

---

[39] Blumenkranz (ed.), *Histoire des Juifs en France*, 225–9.

[40] Milano, *Storia degli Ebrei in Italia*, 322–8.

[41] Pullan, *Jews of Europe*, 187–92; Ravid, 'First Charter of the Jewish Merchants'; Roth, *Venice*, 66–70.

[42] See above, p. 18. 'Puy' refers to the steps of the city hall from which announcements were read; in this case, the banns read thrice to afford third parties an opportunity to lodge complaints against the intended marriage.

[43] The information was culled from thirty-seven *puyboecken* (GAA, DTB 665–701, DTB 1008, pp. 95–102) of some 250–500 pages each, containing three registrations per page. The extraction of Portuguese Jewish marriages is facilitated by the obvious dissimilarity between Portuguese and Dutch surnames as well as by the conspicuous difference in the handwriting of the signatures appended to the registration. In all but a very few cases the certainty that the marriage in question is really between Jews is virtually absolute. Some doubts exist with regard to Portuguese Jewish men marrying Dutch women. But their registration at the Puy (city hall) rather than at the church indicates that the man had not (yet) converted to Calvinism, although there is no certainty that he was still a member of the

tration for purposes of studying immigration patterns will of necessity involve certain arithmetical manipulations. The actual immigration of each of these individuals into Amsterdam may have taken place at any time within the twenty to twenty-five years which on the average separated the date of marriage from the date of birth. First, therefore, we must assume the distribution to have been statistically symmetrical and place the date of immigration ten to twelve years before the date of marriage. Second, this rule of thumb clearly has more validity in cases involving the immigration of entire families. Where individual immigrants predominate, the curve will, of course, peak closer to the date of marriage. I do not know of any simple arithmetical formula that will allow for an entirely accurate translation of marital data into immigration curves. In the ensuing discussion, therefore, I have assumed the marriage figures to reflect immigration trends with a ten-year lag for areas furthest removed from Amsterdam and a five-year lag for cities as close as Antwerp, Hamburg, and London.[44]

Table 2.1 highlights the geographical variety in the paths traversed by the Portuguese New Christians who came to form the Portuguese Jewish community of seventeenth-century Amsterdam. The variety reflects the distribution of the Portuguese diaspora of the late sixteenth and early seventeenth centuries, and indeed confirms the existence of that dispersion as an interrelated unit. Certain

Portuguese Jewish community. These Portuguese men have been included in the tally. With regard to Jews from Italy with Italian rather than Portuguese surnames, one cannot always be certain that they were members of the Portuguese Jewish community. If the partner of an Italian man or woman was Portuguese, however, his or her name was included in the survey. Otherwise, for the vast majority both names are clearly recognizable as those of members of the Portuguese Jewish community. If only one partner was recognizably Portuguese or Spanish, the less familiar name was included also. Finally, widows and widowers whose first marriage could be traced back to Amsterdam—not always an easy task in view of the name changes—were not counted a second time.

The data for the first two decades of the seventeenth century are deficient. Owing to unfamiliarity with Dutch law, reluctance to make their marriages public, or conviction that the Jewish marriage contract was legally sufficient, the earliest immigrants were negligent in registering at the city hall. In 1622 the authorities became aware of these omissions and demanded that these Portuguese Jews register retroactively. Unfortunately, these *post factum* registrations omitted the customary data. For a few individuals I was able to find some relevant information which was included in the survey. Otherwise, most of these are listed under 'unspecified, unidentifiable'. In general, subsequent generations appear to have complied with the law more conscientiously, if never without some omissions. See also Koen, 'Earliest Sources', 31–3.

Since I first did this research, the Dutch Jewish marriage records have been published in part in Verdooner and Snel (eds.), *Trouwen in Mokum*, which lists the names of the bride and groom, the respective years of birth, places of origin, and witnesses. It omits the information on signatures used later in this chapter and reads certain names slightly differently from my reading. I have throughout relied upon my own original research.

[44] Throughout this chapter the tables adhere to the periodization according to date of registration. The explanatory text, however, will interpret the tables in accordance with the factors outlined in this paragraph, so that the table will indicate increases in immigration from Spain after 1640 and the text will interpret these as having occurred after 1630.

Table 2.1. Places of origin of Portuguese Jews married in Amsterdam, 1598–1699

	1598–1609	1610–19	1620–9	1630–9	1640–9	1650–9	1660–9	1670–9	1680–9	1690–9	Total	% of foreign-born[a]
HOLLAND	—	—	8	24	63	100	162	191	351	297	1,196	
FOREIGN-BORN[b]	37	104	119	98	153	197	162	166	176	171	1,383	
(the Portuguese New Christian/Jewish heartlands)												
France	—	1	3	15	33	39	26	22	45	43	227	18.0
Italy	—	—	2	1	9	7	15	17	27	45	123	9.7
Portugal	32	17	67	59	66	66	33	30	14	11	395	31.3
Spain	1	1	1	10	21	37	39	41	33	25	209	16.5
(the Portuguese Jewish diaspora of northern Europe)												
Antwerp	—	4	5	4	13	14	12	5	16	2	75	5.9
Hamburg	—	—	—	2	5	20	15	21	25	19	107	
London	—	—	—	—	1	—	2	1	3	6	13	
(the Portuguese Jewish diaspora at large)												
Morocco/ Africa	—	—	—	—	1	—	2	2	3	2	10	
Ottoman empire	—	1	1	—	—	1	—	2	—	2	7	
Transatlantic colonies	—	—	—	2	2	6	11	18	9	10	58	
Unknown[c]	4	80	40	5	2	7	7	7	1	6	159	
TOTAL	37	104	127	122	216	297	324	357	527	468	2,579	

Note: 'Places of origin' refers to the cities named in response to the clerk's question where the individual originated from. In many cases the question was understood to refer to one's place of birth; in some cases to the place where one grew up.

[a] For the purpose of these percentages, Hamburg and London have not been included among the foreign-born. Portuguese Jews from these two cities essentially belonged to the same northern European diaspora community.

[b] All of the unknown have been included in the foreign-born totals.

[c] This category includes individuals who failed to mention a place of origin as well as some whose place of origin could not be identified. The large numbers of the 1610s and 1620s reflect people who had failed to register their marriage at the time of its occurrence and did so summarily and retroactively, without the customary specifications.

areas, of course, are more strongly represented than others, but the proportions rarely correspond to the relative strength of that part of the diaspora. For example, the Portuguese New Christian communities of Spain and Spanish America—and Brazil, as we shall see—though much larger settlements than those of France or Antwerp, contributed smaller numbers to the emerging colony of Amsterdam. On the other hand, unlike Portuguese New Christians elsewhere, Antwerp New Christians gravitated so strongly towards Amsterdam as to bring about the virtual demise of the Antwerp community at the end of the seventeenth century. The very large Sephardi communities of the eastern Mediterranean and, to some extent, even the smaller ones of Italy are decidedly under-represented. Their relative insignificance helps to define the Portuguese New Christian and Jewish diaspora of which Amsterdam was a member as a distinctly western European phenomenon with rather weak links via Italy to the eastern Mediterranean. Finally, it would appear that the migratory link between Portugal and Amsterdam ran more or less naturally through France. For many, settlement in France probably represented only an intermediate goal, either satisfying the pressing desire to flee from Portugal or necessitated by the lack of sufficient resources to reach a more distant location, becoming an ultimate destination whenever opportunities in France warranted permanent settlement. Alongside the major, direct, and seemingly resolute Portugal–Holland migration, therefore, ran a parallel and more hesitant Portugal–France–Holland migration. This dual migratory stream received separate influxes from Spain, Italy, and Antwerp. The Portuguese Jews from Hamburg and London do not truly denote distinct immigrations. To all intents and purposes—socially and economically as well as culturally—Amsterdam–Hamburg–London must be considered one single community.

Chronologically, too, the immigration statistics show significant fluctuations and conspicuous differences from area to area. The 1620s witnessed a slight but noticeable decrease in immigrants in general; otherwise immigration continued to climb until about 1650, after which it dropped back to a more or less constant influx at the relatively high level of about 1640. These broad trends cannot be attributed to any one or two conditions, but rather conceal a multitude of individual tendencies and fluctuations that somehow combined to create a relatively even flow of immigration. No common factor appears to exist that can explain the confluence of individual fluctuations. Not even the ups and downs of inquisitorial persecution in Portugal (see Table 2.2) correlate well with the ebbs and flows of immigration to Amsterdam, even if we allow for indirect routes taken by refugees from the inquisitors via Spain or France. Clearly, events in Spain and France intervened in the flow of refugees to Amsterdam differently at different times during the century. It is also possible that inquisitorial repression in Portugal affected different classes of New Christians at different times. In short, the various migrations may indeed have had a common source; but once removed from that source, each became subject to its own internal and external dynamics. Each geographical source of immigrants merits separate consideration here.

Table 2.2. Number of persons sentenced by the Inquisition of Portugal, 1584–1699

Tribunal	1584–9	1590–9	1600–9	1610–19	1620–9	1630–9	1640–9	1650–9	1660–9	1670–9	1680–9	1690–9	Total
Coimbra	255	801	350	295	1,359	697	164	274	1,128	622	289	325	6,559
Évora	397	961	425	199	912	1,210	814	524	1,390	579	312	74	7,797
Lisbon	177	297	500	371	562	836	448	329	489	178	308	131	4,626
TOTAL	829	2,059	1,275	865	2,833	2,743	1,426	1,127	3,007	1,379	909	530	18,982

Portugal

For the first half of the seventeenth century, the number of immigrants from Portugal does, to some degree, correspond with the figures of inquisitorial victims: immigration was higher during periods in which those victims were more numerous. The peak periods of inquisitorial ferocity in 1584–1605 and 1620–40, and the respite of 1606–19, coincide with the increased level of arrivals in Amsterdam of the decades 1600–20 and 1630–50 and with the decline in numbers arriving during the 1620s.[45] Proportionally, however, the two sets of figures diverge, with the lower figures for inquisitorial sentences in 1584–1605 corresponding to a higher number of immigrants than the massive totals for 1620–40. Two unrelated phenomena may explain the divergence. The earliest immigration may have drawn on, or even been inspired by, a substantial number of commercially adventurous immigrants as the port of Antwerp was ever more tightly closed. Next, the relative decline of the 1630s and 1640s may have been brought about by the simultaneous expansion of other Portuguese New Christian centres in Spain and France. In other words, the immigration of the earlier period consisted of both refugees and adventurous merchants, while the later wave of migrants had more places of destination to choose from. The increased numbers of immigrants from Spain and France during the 1640s may reflect the intensification of inquisitorial activity from 1620 to 1640, though it is worth noting that the resurgence of inquisitorial repression between 1660 and 1674 found no immediate reflection at all in Amsterdam. Again, the increased immigration from France in the 1670s and 1680s is probably attributable to the same twin causes as that of the previous period. On the whole, Portuguese New Christians migrated to Amsterdam, over the course of the seventeenth century, not only in declining numbers but also increasingly less directly.

Broken down into regions, cities, towns, and villages, the small figures become less indicative, to the point of losing almost all significance, in determining general trends.[46] Additional difficulties stem from the alleged tendency of some registrants to name as their place of origin a large city such as Lisbon or Oporto, if some time of their lives had been spent there—if only to accommodate the Dutch clerk, who apparently had a great deal of difficulty in deciphering, by ear, the names of unfamiliar Portuguese places.[47] Nevertheless, the figures given in Table 2.3 do have useful information to impart.

[45] The figures are derived from Veiga Torres, 'Longa guerra social', 63–6.

[46] As mentioned above, most of the 120 'unspecifieds' of 1610–30 should probably be included as originating from Portugal. 'Unidentifiable' in this table includes the simple designation 'from Portugal'. I have chosen to place 'Linhares' in Beira as the Linhares in Trás-os-Montes was a tiny hamlet.

[47] To mention but a few examples: Trancoso is spelled as Villa de Tarrancosa, Tranquoso, Tranko; Guimarães as Guimerijns, Gimarijns, Guymerens, Guymereys; Caminha as Caminige; Vila Real as Vileraer; São João da Pesqueira as Sint Jan de Paskera, St de Pasquere; and Setúbal as St Vy.

Table 2.3. Portuguese Jewish immigration from Portugal to Amsterdam, by place of origin, 1598–1699

	1598–1609	1610–19	1620–9	1630–9	1640–9	1650–9	1660–9	1670–9	1680–9	1690–9	Total	%ᵃ
Alentejo	1	1	3	4	8	12	4	3	—	1	37	10.2
Abrantes	—	—	—	1	—	1	—	—	—	—	2	
Alvito	—	—	2	—	—	—	—	—	—	—	2	
Elvas	—	—	—	—	—	2	—	1	—	—	3	
Estremoz	—	—	—	—	1	6	1	1	—	1	10	
Évora	—	—	—	—	—	1	—	—	—	—	1	
Fronteira	1	—	—	—	2	—	3	1	—	—	7	
Moura	—	1	1	—	1	—	—	—	—	—	3	
Portalegre	—	—	—	1	3	2	—	—	—	—	6	
Salvaterra	—	—	—	1	—	—	—	—	—	—	1	
Setúbal	—	—	—	1	—	—	—	—	—	—	1	
Vidigueira	—	—	—	—	1	—	—	—	—	—	1	
Algarve	—	—	—	—	4	—	—	—	—	—	4	1.1
Faro	—	—	—	—	4	—	—	—	—	—	4	
Beira	3	2	11	17	9	8	5	4	2	1	62	17.1
Castelo Mendo	—	—	2	2	1	—	—	—	—	—	5	
Castelo Rodrigo	—	—	2	—	—	—	—	—	—	—	2	
Celorico	—	—	—	—	—	—	1	1	—	—	2	
Covilha	—	—	—	—	—	1	—	—	—	—	1	
Fundão	—	—	—	2	2	1	—	—	—	—	5	
Gouveia	—	—	—	3	—	—	—	—	—	—	3	
Guarda	—	1	2	—	—	2	3	—	2	—	10	
Lamego	1	—	—	—	2	—	—	—	—	—	3	
Linhares	—	—	—	—	—	—	1	—	—	—	1	
Melo	—	—	1	—	—	1	—	—	—	—	2	
Pinhel	—	—	2	—	—	—	—	—	—	—	2	
São João da Pesqueira	—	—	—	2	1	1	—	1	—	—	5	
Trancoso	2	1	2	3	2	—	—	2	—	1	13	
Viseu	—	—	—	5	1	2	—	—	—	—	8	
Douro-e-Minho	19	3	17	14	8	4	—	3	1	2	71	19.6
Amarante	1	—	—	—	—	—	—	—	—	—	1	
Caminha	—	—	1	—	—	—	—	—	—	—	1	
Guimarães	—	—	3	1	—	—	—	—	—	—	4	
Oporto	13	3	12	11	7	4	—	3	1	2	56	
Ponte-de-Lima	5	—	—	—	—	—	—	—	—	—	5	
Viana	—	—	1	2	1	—	—	—	—	—	4	
Estremadura	6	8	16	20	29ᵇ	26	23	12	8	4	152	42.0
Aveiro	2	—	—	—	1	—	—	—	—	—	3	
Coimbra	—	—	—	—	—	—	1	—	—	—	1	
Lisbon	3	7	13	15	27	26	21	12	8	4	136	
Pinheiro	—	—	—	—	—	1	—	—	—	—	1	
Santarém	1	—	—	4	—	—	—	—	—	—	5	
Tomar	—	1	2	—	—	—	—	—	—	—	3	
Vila Franca	—	—	1	1	—	—	—	—	—	—	2	
Madeira	3	1	2	—	—	—	—	—	—	—	6	1.7
Trás-os-Montes	—	1	1	4	8	12	1	1	1	1	30	8.3
Bragança	—	1	—	1	—	2	1	—	—	—	5	
Miranda	—	—	1	—	—	—	—	—	—	—	1	
Mogadouro	—	—	—	—	1	—	—	—	1	1	3	
Torre de Moncorvo	—	—	—	—	2	1	—	—	—	—	3	
Vila Flor	—	—	—	1	—	3	—	—	—	—	4	
Vila Real	—	—	—	2	5	6	—	—	—	—	13	
Vinhais	—	—	—	—	—	—	1	—	—	—	1	
Unknown	—	1	17	—	—	4	—	7	2	2	33	
TOTAL	32	17	67	59	66	66	33	30	14	11	395	

ᵃ Percentage of total less 'Unknown'.

ᵇ Includes one individual who named only this region.

The place-names of origin for the immigrants from Portugal are for the most part known from other sources as having been centres of New Christian settlement: some by virtue of their inclusion on special tax lists or other such records, some by virtue of the unwelcome distinction of having had most of their New Christian population successfully prosecuted by the Inquisition. In 1652 Luys de Melo asserted that the activity of the Inquisition had virtually depopulated the cities of Coimbra, Oporto, Braga, Lamego, Bragança, Évora, Beja, and part of Lisbon, as well as the towns of Santarém, Tomar, Trancoso, Aveiro, Guimarães, Vinhais, Vila Flor, Montemór o Velho and o Novo, and many others not named.[48] All of those, except for the cities of Beja and Braga and the two towns of Montemór, are to be found in Table 2.3. Braga may not have been a large *converso* centre to begin with, but Beja and Montemór o Novo are located in the region of Alentejo, which was densely populated with *conversos* at the time of Luys de Melo's writing. According to an incomplete *finta feita no ano de 1631*, a list of contributors to the pardon of 1630, which regrettably includes little from Beira and nothing from Trás-os-Montes, the *comarcas* (administrative districts) of Beja, Elvas, and Portalegre in Alentejo counted no fewer than ten towns with more than twenty-five contributors—Elvas (179), Estremoz (136), Portalegre (100), Olivença (94), Moura (50), Vila Viçosa (38), Évora (35), Crato (31), Beja (29), and Serpa (26)—more than in any other part of Portugal.[49] Nor do the discrepancies between the Beira and Alentejo figures appear to be accidental. In Madrid, too, where the Toledo tribunal had gathered information on Portuguese New Christians who had appeared as defence witnesses in the trials of other Portuguese defendants, we encounter a similar preponderance of Beira and Trás-os-Montes places of origin such as Lamego, Trancoso, Guarda, Viseu, and Moncorvo (in Beira), and Vila Flor, Bragança, Mogadouro, and Vila Real (in Trás-os-Montes).[50] In fact, none of the thirty-four Madrid *conversos* hailed from Alentejo. But Alentejo New Christians constituted the highest proportion (some 42 per cent) of the non-natives among the New Christian merchants of Lisbon.[51] In so far as Alentejo *conversos*

---

[48] Lea, *History of the Inquisition of Spain*, iii. 274.

[49] Mendes dos Remedios, *Judeus em Portugal*, ii. 144–8; Caro Baroja, *Judíos en la España moderna*, iii. 322–4. It may be of interest to list the places that occur in both the 1631 *finta* and the Amsterdam registries as well as those that are mentioned only in the 1631 *finta*. Listed in the *finta* and the *puyboecken*: in Alentejo, Moura (50), Alvito (17), Vidigueira (2), Evora (35), Estremoz (136), Elvas (179), Portalegre (100); in Algarve, Faro (80); in Estremadura, Coimbra (1), Aveiro (5); in Douro-e-Minho, Oporto (19), Guimarães (6), Viana (11). Listed in the *finta* only: in Alentejo, Beja (29), Serpa (26), Vila Viçosa (38), Olivença (94); in Algarve, Tavira (99), Lagos (42), Portimão (27); in Estremadura, Alcobaça (20); in southern Beira, Castelo Branco (34), Penamacor (29), Idanha-a-Nova (40); in Douro-e-Minho, Chaves (42).

[50] Caro Baroja, *Judíos en la España moderna*, iii. 326–9. Forty-three of the fifty-seven individuals listed are mentioned with places of origin. Thirty-four originated from Portugal: Lisbon (7), Lamego (6), Trancoso (4), Guarda (4), Vila Flor (2), Oporto (2), Bragança (1), Viseu (1), Moncorvo (1), Mogadeiro (1), Vila Real (1), others (4). Nine originated from elsewhere: Ciudad Rodrigo (5), Talavera (2), Toledo (1), and Rouen (1).   [51] Smith, 'Mercantile Class', 34–6.

emigrated, therefore, they appear to have done so either in two stages—first to Lisbon and then abroad—or, perhaps, to Andalusia rather than to Madrid.[52] It is also possible that Alentejo New Christians were simply less intimately involved in commerce and had fewer contacts with the outside world. Finally, in view of the fairly sizeable *converso* centres of Tavira, Faro, Lagos, and Portimão, the nearly complete absence of Algarve émigrés in Amsterdam comes as somewhat of a surprise. The Algarve was certainly not lacking in commercial relations with Holland. If the emigration trends of the general population of Portugal are any indication, we must perhaps assume that Algarve émigrés gravitated primarily to Madeira and Andalusia.[53]

While there may appear overall to be a certain correlation between the figures of inquisitorial activity and the waves of New Christian emigration, it becomes difficult to correlate various regional waves of migration with local variations in the intensity of inquisitorial persecution. Portuguese immigrants from towns known to have suffered from especially intense inquisitorial attention cannot readily be classed as refugees in contradistinction to others from more stable New Christian centres who might be thought to have left under less immediate pressure. It would seem that there can be no doubt about a correlation between the intensity of inquisitorial activity and the size of New Christian emigration; however, at present we cannot go much beyond this general statement. The regional variations are interesting to note, but provide as yet few clues about the motivations of the emigrants.

The first wave of Portuguese New Christian immigration, up to about 1620, appears to have come from Douro-e-Minho. During the same period also occurred the only immigration from Madeira. Then, simultaneously with increases in the number of Lisbon immigrants, follows the immigration from Beira, especially from 1610 to 1630. Between 1630 and 1650, we encounter *conversos* from Trás-os-Montes and Alentejo. At present it is not possible to determine whether these regional shifts reflect changing economic conditions, varying levels of overpopulation, differences in occupational structure of the respective New Christian communities—those of Beira, for instance, may very well have been more commercially active than those of other interior regions—or variations in Jewish loyalties and concomitant fluctuations in inquisitorial persecution.

With regard to the immigration from Douro-e-Minho—a region with an economic basis for ties with Amsterdam—we can be fairly certain that its decline corresponds to the depletion of its New Christian communities as a result of

---

[52] The suggestion that Alentejo New Christians may have emigrated to Andalusia derives from the fact that, of the ten Portuguese who obtained a licence to trade with the Indies and whose origins are listed, five came from Castelo Branco and one from Estremoz. The figures are, of course, very small, but Castelo Branco, though in southern Beira, is not only very close to Alentejo but also absent from the Amsterdam registries. Domínguez Ortiz, 'Extranjeros en la vida española', 397–413.

[53] Magalhaes-Godinho, 'Émigration portugaise', 259–60.

excessive inquisitorial vigilance.[54] The *finta* of 1631, mentioned above, lists only a few small centres: Oporto (19 contributors), Soalhães (2), Guimarães (6), Braga (5), and Viana (11). Only Chaves (42) in the far and isolated east of the region escaped mass persecution. By 1631 most *conversos* of Douro-e-Minho were either in the dungeons of the Inquisition or had fled to Galicia in Spain, whence some of them had reached France.[55] Inquisitorial vigilance in Douro-e-Minho appears to be linked to that region's prominence in trade with the recently and rapidly developing colony of Brazil. The Douro-e-Minho émigrés who settled in Amsterdam rather than in Galicia may have done so to enable them to maintain their interest in the Brazil trade while at the same time eluding the Inquisition. Similarly, the later, but eventually larger, immigration from Lisbon may combine elements of escape from the reach of the inquisitors and of economic interest. The economic interests of the Lisbon émigrés, however, may have been different in so far as they were inspired by the general commercial crisis in Portugal during the mid-century and less by a specific desire to continue exploitation of a threatened trade route.[56]

One final and general observation needs to be made. Leaving aside the large ports of Lisbon and Oporto, the largest numbers of immigrants hailed from the *comarcas* of Guarda, Portalegre, Viseu, Bragança, Vila Real, and Évora—market towns in rural areas relatively close to the Spanish border. It is somewhat surprising, especially in view of the major (in geographical terms) migration being studied here, to find large concentrations of New Christians still so near their land of origin more than a century after the expulsion from Spain. The question arises: was emigration to Amsterdam favoured by New Christians with Jewish loyalties, or was it a general New Christian phenomenon? The answer depends to some degree on how one views the retention of Jewish loyalties, that is, as a voluntary predilection or as a coerced stigma. It is at least clear that the exiles themselves, as well as the Portuguese Inquisition and, probably, the Portuguese population, retained well into the eighteenth century an awareness of their Spanish and thus Jewish descent.[57] This mostly ethnic awareness was stimulated by the condition of exile and, as such, was shared by almost all Portuguese New Christians, but perhaps

[54] As mentioned above, there existed a special and intimate link between Douro-e-Minho and the burgeoning mercantile community of Brazil. The Brazil 'visitations' of 1591 and 1615 coincided with an intensification of inquisitorial activity in Douro-e-Minho. The precise interrelations between the two sets of events have yet to be examined. In the interim, see the sources listed in n. 23 above; and Smith, 'Mercantile Class', 273–96. As Smith admits (p. 281), many of those known in Bahia as Old Christians were possibly of New Christian descent. I am inclined to think that many more of the Douro-e-Minho emigrants to Brazil were in fact New Christians than Smith seems to believe. Indeed, much of Smith's thesis is to argue for substantial Old Christian participation in Portuguese and Brazilian trade.

[55] Contreras, *El Santo Oficio*, 591–5.   [56] Mauro, *Portugal et l'Atlantique*, 487–90.

[57] See n. 6 above. Moreover, many of the genealogies retained by Portuguese Jews traced the family back to the forced conversions of 1496–7. See e.g. Révah, 'Pour l'histoire des "Nouveaux Chrétiens" portugais', 290–2; Salomon, ed. and intr., 'The "De Pinto" Manuscript', 10.

more consciously by those who remained where they had first settled after the expulsion, in the regions closest to the Spanish border. At the same time, it seems entirely plausible to assume that the vast majority of exiles settled close to the Spanish border, moving only gradually towards the Atlantic coast and then primarily to the larger ports. In sum, the regional distribution of the émigrés to Amsterdam does not in itself necessarily reflect a bias in favour of *conversos* with Jewish loyalties. In so far as specific Jewish loyalties are to be suspected as a motive behind the decision to move to Amsterdam, they must be looked for in individual, not in regional differences.

Spain

The list of origins of Portuguese New Christian immigrants from Spain (Table 2.4) harbours few surprises. By and large, their distribution corresponds to the cursory observations of contemporaries. About two-thirds of all Spanish-born immigrants came from Madrid and Seville–Cádiz. Another sizeable contingent was born in Málaga. The prominence of these cities reflects the primarily mercantile character of the Portuguese migration to Spain. Whether or not the migration of Portuguese to the universities of Alcalá de Henares, Valladolid, and especially Salamanca—in part from fear of or repulsion at the strongly anti-*converso* sentiments pervading the university and student body at Coimbra[58]—is reflected in the few who listed these cities in Amsterdam is not certain. Other Spanish (admittedly, none too rigorous) sources indicate substantial Portuguese New Christian settlement in places other than the capital, the ports, and the university towns.[59] The geographical distribution of these interior settlements—including the lack of Portuguese New Christian penetration in Aragon and Catalonia—is mirrored in the variety of the remaining towns listed. Those in Old Castile, Extremadura, and Andalusia conform to expectations and hints of settlement in Spanish regions not too distant from the Portuguese border. Numerically the immigrants from the Spanish interior seem to be markedly under-represented. It is possible that Spanish inquisitorial persecution at first hit primarily the large and relatively conspicuous Portuguese New Christian communities of the administrative and commercial centres. But emigration from the provincial towns does not really increase after the initial persecution of Madrid and Seville New Christians. A more plausible explanation for the small numbers of provincial émigrés is the fact that these Portuguese New Christians were primarily local merchants, skilled craftsmen, and physicians or barber-surgeons. They lacked the kind of international connections that enabled the Madrid, Seville–Cádiz, and Málaga Portuguese to emigrate with some measure of confidence and security. They may

---

[58] Yerushalmi, *From Spanish Court*, 66–7. On Coimbra, see de Oliveira, 'Motim dos estudantes'.

[59] Bennassar (ed.), *Inquisition espagnole*, 162, 164; Caro Baroja, *Judíos en la España moderna*, in recounting innumerable trials of the mid-seventeenth and early eighteenth centuries, gives the distinct impression of widespread Portuguese New Christian settlement.

Table 2.4. Spanish and Portuguese Jewish immigration from Spain to Amsterdam, 1598–1699

	1598–1609	1610–19	1620–9	1630–9	1640–9	1650–9	1660–9	1670–9	1680–9	1690–9	Total	%[a]
Andalusia	—	1	—	2	4[b]	14	13[b]	13	11	9	67	32.5
Andújar	—	—	—	—	—	—	1	—	—	—	1	
Cádiz	—	—	—	1	—	3	2	3	3	3	15	
Córdoba	—	—	—	—	—	—	—	—	—	1	1	
Huelva	—	—	—	—	—	1	—	—	—	—	1	
Jaén	—	—	—	—	—	—	—	—	1	—	1	
Osuna	—	—	—	—	—	—	—	—	—	1	1	
Pto de Sta Maria	—	—	—	—	1	—	—	—	1	—	2	
Seville	—	1	—	1	2	10	9	10	6	4	43	
Basque provinces	—	—	—	1	—	—	—	—	—	—	1	0.5
Vitoria	—	—	—	1	—	—	—	—	—	—	1	
Castile (New)	—	—	1	—	11	16	19	13	13	7[b]	80	38.8
Madrid	—	—	1	—	11	15	19	13	13	6	78	
Toledo	—	—	—	—	—	1	—	—	—	—	1	
Castile (Old)-León	1	—	—	2	2	2	5	2	2	3	19	9.2
Arévalo	—	—	—	—	—	—	—	—	—	1	1	
Burgos	—	—	—	—	—	—	—	—	—	1	1	
Ciudad Rodrigo	—	—	—	1	—	—	—	—	—	—	1	
Medina del Campo	1	—	—	—	—	1	2	—	—	—	4	
Salamanca	—	—	—	—	—	—	1	1	—	—	2	
Segovia	—	—	—	—	1	1	1	—	—	—	3	
Soria	—	—	—	—	1	—	—	1	—	—	2	
Valladolid	—	—	—	1	—	—	—	—	2	1	4	
Zamora	—	—	—	—	—	—	1	—	—	—	1	
Extremadura	—	—	—	—	—	1	—	3	1	—	5	2.4
Badajoz	—	—	—	—	—	1	—	—	—	—	1	
Cáceres	—	—	—	—	—	—	—	—	1	—	1	
Don Benito	—	—	—	—	—	—	—	2	—	—	2	
Trujillo	—	—	—	—	—	—	—	1	—	—	1	
Galicia	—	—	—	—	—	1	—	—	1[b]	—	2	1.0
Pontevedra	—	—	—	—	—	1	—	—	—	—	1	
Granada	—	—	—	5	3	2	2	6	3	4	25	12.1
Antequera	—	—	—	3	1	—	—	1	1	1	7	
Granada	—	—	—	—	—	—	—	—	—	1	1	
Málaga	—	—	—	2	2	2	2	5	2	2	17	
Murcia	—	—	—	—	—	—	—	—	2	1	3	1.5
Lorca	—	—	—	—	—	—	—	—	1	—	1	
Murcia	—	—	—	—	—	—	—	—	1	1	2	
Navarra	—	—	—	—	—	—	—	1[b]	—	—	1	0.5
Valencia	—	—	—	—	1	—	—	1	—	1	3	1.5
Valencia	—	—	—	—	1	—	—	1	—	1	3	
Unknown	—	—	—	—	—	1	—	2	—	—	3	
TOTAL	1	1	1	10	21	37	39	41	33	25	209	

[a] Percentage of total less 'Unknown'.
[b] Includes one individual who specified only region of origin.

also not have felt the need. Referring to the Portuguese in Extremadura and Old Castile, Murcia de Llana observed negatively but, in stressing the basically regional framework, probably correctly: 'What shall I say of the Portuguese who live in Extremadura, which forms the boundary with Portugal, in such towns as Trujillo, Cáceres, Llerena, Badajoz, Soria, Zamora, and Ciudad Rodrigo? They buy the meat and other animals at cheap prices and, bringing it to Portugal, resell it to Castile at excessive prices.'[60] The geographical distribution of immigrants from Spain reveals a decided slant in favour of those Portuguese New Christians with international commercial or financial contacts. The other Portuguese were trapped between their regional roots and the vigilance of the inquisitors.

In general, the chronology of emigration from Spain corresponds closely with the increasing activity of the Spanish Inquisition. Not until the 1630s, and especially after 1640, is the impact of Spanish-born immigrants noticed in Amsterdam. Given that the first serious threats of an impending anti-*converso* campaign by the Spanish Inquisition were felt in Madrid with the arrest of the *asentista* Juan Nuñez Saravia (1631), the slightly earlier emigration from the capital, as compared with that from Seville–Cádiz, comes as no surprise. After 1640, a number of circumstances combined to spell disaster for the Portuguese New Christians in Spain: the successful rebellion of Portugal and the contemporaneous but ultimately failed revolt of the Catalans; growing discontent with the Conde-Duque de Olivares, who had been most instrumental in attracting the Portuguese to Madrid as a replacement for the Genovese; and Portuguese losses to the Dutch in Brazil, rumoured to have been the doing of treacherous New Christians.[61] Slowly, surely, and unjustly—as a result of growing paranoia—the features of financial deceitfulness and political treason attached themselves to the already not very positive image of the Portuguese New Christians in Spain.[62] Inspired by this popular and governmental paranoia rather than by any evidence of imminent and dangerous eruptions of Judaizing, the Spanish Inquisition launched its second major anti-*converso* campaign—the first having occurred shortly before and for some time after the 1492 expulsion—between 1640 and about 1665. As with the emigration from Portugal in the late seventeenth century, substantial numbers of refugees from Spain probably fled to France and either settled there or moved to Amsterdam later. Some, such as the famous Cardoso brothers, emigrated to Italy.[63] We have no figures or any other data to enable us to compare—either in motivation or in numbers—the Holland-bound with the Italy-bound emigration.

[60] Lucio d'Azevedo, *Historia dos Cristãos Novos portugueses*, 463.

[61] In addition to the articles on the *complicidad grande* listed in n. 24 above, see Cyrus Adler, 'Contemporary Memorial', and Lope de Vega's *comedia El Brasil restituido*.

[62] Herrero Garcia, *Ideas de los españoles*, 134–78; see also the virulently anti-*converso* sentiments expressed in *La Isla de los Monopantes* (1639), attributed to Quevedo, and considered by one historian a precursor of *The Protocols of the Elders of Zion*: van Praag, 'Protocolos de los sabios de Sion'.

[63] Yerushalmi, *From Spanish Court*, 192–4.

According to the *bachiller* (university graduate) Nájera, himself a Judaizing but not commercially active New Christian, the ideal of the typical Portuguese *converso* had been to amass a fortune of 8,000–10,000 *ducados* and then to 'retire' to lands where freedom of conscience existed and live a life of Jewish orthodoxy.[64] The near-perfect coincidence of emigration and inquisitorial persecution belies this allegedly calculating strategy. It seems more likely that the heads of firms who were near 'retirement' age found it easier than younger members of the family to give up the lure of further profits. The persistence with which so many *conversos* stayed in Spain is further reason to doubt this motivation. It is very clear that, however substantial in number and wealth they may have been, only a relatively small minority of the Portuguese New Christians living in Spain chose to emigrate, and then only at a fairly slow, hesitant rate. Spain, it would seem, had never been meant as a temporary refuge. If the 1492 migration of Spanish exiles to Portugal reveals a strong attachment to the Iberian peninsula on the part of the Jews of Spain, the late sixteenth- and early seventeenth-century migration of Portuguese commercial and financial adventurers and inquisitorial refugees to Spain similarly bespeaks the strengths and depths of the *conversos*' roots in Iberian society and culture.

France

In the course of the sixteenth century, a variety of interests had given rise to the establishment of several Portuguese colonies in France. Iberian merchants had been motivated by the potential of trade between the peninsula and France, including smuggling across the Pyrenees; New Christian refugees had sought to escape the pressures of the Spanish and Portuguese inquisitions; and individual professors and students had been lured by France's humanistic revival. These groups founded notable Iberian centres in France, especially in the south-west (Saint-Jean-de-Luz, Peyrehorade, Biarritz, Bayonne, and Bordeaux), around the University of Toulouse, and in the Atlantic ports of La Rochelle, Nantes, and Rouen.[65] In 1550 Henry II had officially recognized their presence and issued *lettres patentes* for their protection: 'Since it pleases us to accord them letters of naturalization and the right to enjoy the privileges which other strangers enjoyed and are enjoying in Our Said Kingdom, We, liberally inclined to listen to the supplication and request of the said Portuguese, as persons whose good zeal and affection we recognize, make known that they shall live under Our Sovereignty like Our other subjects.'[66] These *lettres patentes* were reconfirmed in 1575, 1656, 1723, and 1776, and remained the legal basis of New Christian, and later Jewish, settlement in France right up to the French Revolution.

---

[64] Beinart, '*Converso* Community', 475–6; Caro Baroja, *Judíos en la España moderna*, i. 480.

[65] Francisque-Michel, *Portugais en France*, 38 ff., 187–8; Lapeyre, *Famille de marchands*, 46–57; Léon, *Histoire des Juifs de Bayonne*, 16–19; Malvezin, *Histoire des Juifs à Bordeaux*, 88–123; Serrão, *Portugais à l'Université de Toulouse*; Mathorez, 'Notes sur les Espagnols en France'.

[66] Nahon, '*Nations' juives portugaises*, 21–6.

This is not to suggest that these immigrants lived happily ever after. The increased immigration of Portuguese after 1580, as well as the mounting political tensions between the Spanish and French monarchies, caused sporadic eruptions of anti-Portuguese, anti-New Christian sentiments. In 1602 Henry IV ordered the expulsion of the Portuguese from Bayonne and generally their removal from the area closest to the Spanish border. But the Bordeaux *parlement* failed to register the decree and no action was taken.[67] In 1615 Louis XIII ordered a general expulsion of disguised Jews from France.[68] Although this decree remained a dead letter, largely because of the ambiguity of the term 'disguised Jews', it does seem to have occasioned the 'voluntary' emigration of a few individual New Christian families. Lopo da Fonseca and his family, for instance, who as refugees from the Portuguese Inquisition had settled in Saint-Jean-de-Luz, joined the son of his brother-in-law, Jeronimo Henriques, in Amsterdam, allegedly as a result of the 1615 decree.[69]

The distribution of the Portuguese immigrants in France is reflected in the estimates of Juan Bautista de Villadiego, a Spanish priest and secretary of the Inquisition of Llerena, who reported the following numbers of Judaizing *converso* families in several towns in 1633: Paris—10 to 12; Rouen—22 or 23; Bordeaux—about 40; Bayonne—more than 60; Dax—10 to 12; Biarritz—a few families; Peyrehorade—more than 40; La Bastide—more than 80; Nantes—6 or 7.[70] In relative terms, these figures are fairly similar to the Amsterdam statistics (Table 2.5), which merely accentuate the importance Bordeaux was to gain subsequently at the expense of Peyrehorade and La Bastide. Yet the Amsterdam figures cannot simply be explained in terms of a general attraction, that is, in terms affecting all Portuguese New Christians in France equally. For we know of several local incidents that precipitated emigration in specific cases, at least in those of Saint-Jean-de-Luz and Rouen, and at the very end of the century.

The town of Saint-Jean-de-Luz is conspicuous by its absence from the 1633 report of Juan Bautista de Villadiego. At the very beginning of the seventeenth century, Saint-Jean-de-Luz had been the 'pivot' of the New Christian emigration northward.[71] But in 1619, one Catarina Fernandes of Trancoso was alleged to have desecrated the host and was burned by an angry mob, led by sailors of fishing ships from Newfoundland, on the day before the court was to pronounce its sentence. Juan Bautista de Villadiego, who had been sent to spy on Spanish and Portuguese expatriates in France in the wake of the trial of Juan Nuñez Saravia and others, visited Saint-Jean-de-Luz in December 1632, and recounts in his report the horrid details of the 1619 incident as he had personally heard them from the mouth of the guardian of the Franciscan monastery. The guardian had also given him an

---

[67] Léon, *Histoire des Juifs de Bayonne*, 19–20.
[68] Malvezin, *Histoire des Juifs à Bordeaux*, 121–2.
[69] GAA, NA 396, fos. 361–2 (5 Apr. 1628; N. and J. Jacobs).
[70] Révah, 'Marranes', 66.　　　　　　　　　　　[71] Révah, 'Premier règlement', 664.

Table 2.5. Portuguese Jewish immigration from France to Amsterdam, 1598–1699

	1598–1609	1610–19	1620–9	1630–9	1640–9	1650–9	1660–9	1670–9	1680–9	1690–9	Total
Bayonne	—	—	1	2	2	5	5	8	9	19	51
Bordeaux	—	1	—	2	13	14	13	6	13	6	68
Carpentras	—	—	—	—	—	—	1	—	1	1	3
La Bastide	—	—	—	—	—	2	—	—	1	—	3
La Rochelle	—	—	1	1	—	—	—	1	—	—	3
Lille	—	—	—	—	—	—	—	—	1	—	1
Marseille	—	—	—	—	—	2	—	—	—	—	2
Nantes	—	—	—	3	—	3	1	—	—	—	7
Nice	—	—	—	—	—	—	—	—	1	1	2
Paris	—	—	—	—	3	2	1	4	4	1	15
Peyrehorade	—	—	—	—	1	1	1	3	7	12	25
Rouen	—	—	—	3	10	7	4	—	8	2	34
Saint-Jean-de-Luz	—	—	1	3	4	3	—	—	—	—	11
Toulouse	—	—	—	1	—	—	—	—	—	1	2
TOTAL	—	1	3	15	33	39	26	22	45	43	227

account of the upshot of the episode: 'The next day all the people assembled and went to the said church and they sent to speak to the judges, governor, and councillors and by public decree they decided that not a single Portuguese remain in this town and so it was executed, for they proclaimed that no one could rent them a house or house them in his, on pain of burning them in it, and thus within three days all left . . . and they did not return.'[72]

All but three of the eleven persons recorded in Table 2.5 as having originated in Saint-Jean-de-Luz were born before 1619. It is not certain whether they moved directly from that town to Amsterdam, but in view of the earlier, intimate connections between the two places it seems quite plausible that they did. The other three individuals were born in the 1620s, contradicting the assurance Villadiego received that the town had been free of Portuguese since 1619.

Before leaving Spain, Villadiego had been instructed to pay particular attention to the Portuguese New Christians of Rouen, with whom those of Madrid were alleged to maintain suspicious relations. The drama in Rouen unleashed by his visit constitutes a complicated story—superbly unravelled by I. S. Révah—replete with religious, commercial, and political overtones.[73]

Rouen had received a more or less permanent and commercially relatively important influx of Iberian immigrants after 1609. For various reasons that are

[72] Domínguez Ortiz, 'Proceso inquisitorial', 568–71. The majority of refugees from Saint-Jean-de-Luz appear to have settled in Biarritz; see Loeb, 'Notes', 107–11.

[73] Révah, 'Autobiographie d'un Marrane', 58–85. Révah's account concentrates on religious tensions primarily and economic rivalries secondarily. I would like to suggest that the contemporary political conflict between France and Spain may have added to the tense situation within the Rouen New Christian community, if only in so far as it assured the highest French governmental attention.

difficult to trace, the Rouen settlement was divided into two factions along religious lines, though probably also reflecting commercial rivalries: one Catholic, the other Judaizing. Until 1633 the factions had lived peaceably side by side, but with the arrival of Villadiego the Catholics began to denounce the others as Judaizers. The Judaizers countered by denouncing the Catholics as spies of the Spanish Inquisition, which intended, in Spain, to confiscate the property belonging to the Judaizers—a move which would be detrimental to the interests of the king of France. Some of the Judaizers were imprisoned and their goods sequestered, but they were eventually released after the offer of 'the sum of 250,000 *livres* to be employed towards the foundation of a seminary for poor children and other works of charity . . . as further proof of their piety, zeal, and perseverance in the Catholic religion'.

Unlike the Saint-Jean-de-Luz affair, the Rouen episode unsettled the New Christian community only temporarily. The threats, of course, were of a different nature, and so were the options. The incident highlights two noteworthy factors. On the one hand, it demonstrates the continued precariousness of the New Christian colonies on Catholic soil; on the other hand, the assertiveness exhibited by the Judaizing New Christians, before and during the trial, underscores the depth of their roots in this favourable economic environment, as demonstrated by their choice to 'purchase' the opportunity to remain in the city. Strategically lodged between the busy trade routes of the Atlantic and the luxury and political and intellectual excitement of Paris and its court, Rouen appealed to a particular type of New Christian immigrant attracted by a lifestyle of affluence and splendour. If some none the less moved to Amsterdam in response to the 1633 harassments, they did so haltingly, keeping in touch with Rouen as much as possible.

Finally, there were marked increases in immigrants from France from 1630 to 1650 and again during the last quarter of the century. These increases unquestionably resulted in large part from the earlier Portuguese and Spanish emigrations referred to above. As for the immigration of the 1680s and after, we have specific evidence that 93 Portuguese families were expelled by royal *arrêt* from Bordeaux (20), Bayonne (19), Bidache (15), Dax (3), and Peyrehorade (36) in 1684.[74] This expulsion affected only the poor who had recently arrived and who were of no use to the commercial development of the port (*d'aucune utilité au commerce*). All in all, we can recognize in the immigration from France a second wave of Portuguese and Spanish émigrés of lesser means and an occasional influx occasioned by the as yet somewhat tenuous status of even the more substantial *nouveaux chrétiens*.

Antwerp

The proximity of Antwerp to Amsterdam and the cultural ties between the two cities have predisposed some historians to attribute an inordinate significance to

---

[74] Nahon, *'Nations' juives portugaises*, 3–7.

Antwerp's role in populating the Portuguese Jewish community of Amsterdam.[75] The statistics (see Table 2.1 above) do not support this claim. It is true that Spanish repression following the Dutch rebellion sent streams of émigrés from Antwerp to the Northern Netherlands;[76] but it is equally clear that Spanish and Portuguese New Christians were conspicuous by their absence from this initial mass migration. The period of relatively extensive New Christian movement falls somewhere between 1630 and 1660 and seems to have been occasioned by the resumption of hostilities between the Republic and Spain after the Twelve Years Truce (1609–21) and by changes in the world economy owing to the inroads made by the Dutch into the Portuguese colonial empire, especially in Brazil, and the decline of the Brazil sugar trade as a result of Caribbean competition.

The Brazil trade was one important branch of commerce in which Antwerp had been able to retain much of its former pre-eminence and was the major commercial preoccupation of the city's New Christian merchants.[77] But the Dutch capture of Brazil's sugar and wood trade, followed by Portugal's achievement of independence from Spain in 1640, destroyed the economic base of these Portuguese merchants on Spanish territory. At the same time the rekindled Dutch–Spanish war, fought largely on Flanders territory, quelled any expectation of an imminent recovery. To cite the most illustrious example—and one for which we have first-hand information—the famous de Pinto and Teixeira families began winding up their affairs in Flanders in 1643 and emigrated from Antwerp in 1646, the Pintos to Amsterdam by way of Rotterdam and the Teixeiras to Hamburg.[78] For a short while following the Peace of Westphalia (1648), and notwithstanding the conference's ratification of the closure of the Schelde, emigration to Amsterdam tapered off, but it was resumed a decade or so later, ostensibly because Antwerp's decline by then had become a *fait accompli*. The delay before the Portuguese New Christians of Antwerp took this final, geographically short step reveals again their attachment to the familiar past and their reluctance to embark on a new future, whether for the sake of adventure or salvation.

Italy

More than 75 per cent of all the immigrants from Italy came from Venice and Pisa–Livorno–Florence, a predominance that becomes particularly marked towards the very end of the seventeenth century (Table 2.6). The increase does not, as in the case of France, signal a second wave of Portuguese and Spanish refugees; it was more directly related to the general decline of these once notable communities as a result of the protracted commercial crisis of the later part of the century and, more particularly, in the wake of the Venetian–Turkish war over Crete (1645–69), which disrupted commercial activity in the eastern Mediterranean.

[75] For the first critical refutation of this view, see Vaz Dias, 'Stichters van Beth Jaacob'.
[76] Van Dillen, *Van rijkdom en regenten*, 12; Hart, 'Historisch-demografische notities', 68.
[77] Pohl, 'Zuckereinfuhr', 348–73.   [78] Salomon, ' "De Pinto" Manuscript'.

Table 2.6. Portuguese Jewish immigration from Italy to Amsterdam, 1598–1699

	1598–1609	1610–19	1620–9	1630–9	1640–9	1650–9	1660–9	1670–9	1680–9	1690–9	Total
Ancona	—	—	—	—	—	—	—	—	—	1	1
Ferrara	—	—	—	—	—	1	—	—	2	1	4
Florence	—	—	—	—	1	1	2	1	—	1	6
Genoa	—	—	—	—	—	—	—	—	1	2	3
Livorno	—	—	—	—ʹ	3	3	2	4	10	16	38
Mantua	—	—	—	—	—	—	—	—	—	1	1
Naples	—	—	—	—	—	1	—	—	—	—	1
Padua	—	—	—	—	—	—	2	—	—	4	6
'Piedmont'	—	—	—	—	—	—	—	—	1	—	1
Pisa	—	—	—	—	3	—	1	1	—	—	5
Reggio	—	—	—	—	—	—	—	—	—	1	1
Rome	—	—	—	—	—	1	—	—	2	—	3
'Sicily'	—	—	—	—	1	—	—	—	—	—	1
Venice	—	—	2	1	1	—	8	9	9	15	45
Verona	—	—	—	—	—	—	—	1	1	3	5
TOTAL	—	—	2	1	9	7	15	17[a]	27[a]	45	123

[a] Includes one individual who specified only country of origin.

Otherwise small numbers of Italian immigrants hailed from a variety of communities. By and large, their immigration occurred after 1650 and cannot be attributed to a single apparent factor. The establishment of ghettos in most Italian towns and cities in the course of the first half of the seventeenth century, the plague that struck northern Italy in 1629–31, and the increasing number of economic restrictions and mob attacks upon the peninsula's Jews must have had a devastating effect on recent Spanish and Portuguese immigrants.[79] Dwindling opportunities in Italy contrasted sharply with rumours of the booming community in Holland.

Brazil

Forty-two of the immigrants from the Americas were born in Brazil. The remaining sixteen comprised four from New Spain or Mexico, two from Guyana, and ten from the Caribbean islands of Curaçao, Barbados, Martinique, and Jamaica. The Caribbean immigrants were themselves the descendants of northern European Portuguese Jews and need not detain us. The astonishingly low number of immigrants from Spanish America reveals how utterly cut off from the rest of the Portuguese diaspora the Portuguese *conversos* of Mexico and Peru had become.

Brazil's stormy political history in the first half of the seventeenth century makes it difficult to determine whether particular immigrants originated from Portuguese or from Dutch Brazil. The immigration as a whole post-dates the Dutch loss of its Brazilian foothold in 1654. Thirty-three of the Brazilian

[79] Roth, *History of the Jews of Italy*, 329–94; Milano, *Storia degli Ebrei in Italia*, 286–322.

immigrants gave their place of birth simply as Brazil; the nine others listed Pernambuco, Recife, Paraíba, and Bahia. Only four immigrants can definitely be identified as of Portuguese Brazilian origin: two men and one women born before the Dutch occupied Brazil and one woman born in Bahia, a town the Dutch never captured. The other thirty-eight were born during the period when the Dutch were established in Brazil (1630–54). The lack of more individuals of identifiable Portuguese Brazilian origin, the occurrence of most births during the period of Dutch occupation, and the nearly complete absence of Christian first names (otherwise quite common) must incline us to believe that the majority of the Brazilian immigrants were the descendants of Dutch Jewish colonizers, that is, Portuguese Jews from Amsterdam who had settled in Dutch Brazil. If large-scale conversions of New Christians back to Judaism took place in Brazil, their echo in these Amsterdam statistics is undetectable.[80] For we have no reason to assume that most Brazilian immigrants intentionally hid their Portuguese origin, as Portuguese and Spanish immigrants apparently never felt a need to do so.

Hamburg

In view of Hamburg's proximity to Amsterdam, migration may be too big a word for what must often have been little more than a temporary displacement, for the duration of the betrothal and the wedding only. Moreover, during certain periods of the first half of the seventeenth century, Hamburg and Amsterdam exchanged small numbers of their respective Portuguese Jewish populations depending on the fortunes of the Republic's war with Spain. Immigration from Hamburg, though, clearly gained some momentum after 1640, perhaps especially after the Peace of Westphalia in 1648. Although the Hamburg Portuguese Jewish community continued to grow until the mid-1660s, this merely indicates that its rate of immigration continued to exceed its rate of emigration.[81] The same migratory wave that flooded the Amsterdam community after 1640 undoubtedly had its impact in Hamburg. From the late 1640s onwards, however, the security of Hamburg's Portuguese Jewish community began to be eroded by the increasing hostility of the local authorities, clergy, and populace.[82] The failure to procure permission for the building of a public synagogue symbolizes the difficulties placed in their way. This change in Hamburg's hitherto tolerant attitude appears to have occurred in the wake of the large-scale immigration of Ashkenazi refugees, uprooted by the havoc of the Thirty Years War and by the murder and plunder of Polish Jews by Chmielnicki's Cossack hordes and the Swedish and Muscovite armies, and is definitely related to post-1660 emigration.

---

[80] Wiznitzer, *Jews in Colonial Brazil*, 60–1, speaks of such conversions. More recent studies, however, reveal the basic loyalty of the Brazilian New Christians to Portugal: d'Oliveira França, 'Um problema'.

[81] Kellenbenz, *Sephardim*, 40–1.   [82] Ibid. 45–54.

Other Origins

The remaining foreign-born brides and grooms fall into two groups. First there are the London-born, whose relation to Amsterdam was very similar to that of the Hamburg Portuguese Jews. Relations among these three communities were so intimate as to render movement of individuals from one to another normal rather than exceptional. Second, there are the immigrants from the distant communities of the Ottoman empire and North Africa—and two stray individuals from the furthest reaches of the Portuguese empire, one from Angola, another from East India.

The small number of immigrants from the Ottoman empire highlights the 'otherness' of the first Sephardi diaspora of the Mediterranean as distinct from the second New Christian diaspora of the Atlantic. Clearly, Amsterdam was beyond the horizon of the Sephardim of Greece, Turkey, and Palestine. Of the six immigrants from the eastern Mediterranean, David Pardo of Salonika was the son of a rabbi who had been 'imported' specifically because the Atlantic diaspora lacked Jewish scholars;[83] another immigrant from Jerusalem married a Dutch woman;[84] and the remaining four listed simply Turkey (two), Smyrna (one), and Constantinople (one).

All but three of the nine immigrants from North Africa were born in Salé. David Palache from Fez was the son of the Moroccan envoy to the Republic.[85] Two others came from Ceuta and Masa. Salé, a pirate republic along the Barbary Coast heavily populated by Moriscos who had been expelled from Spain after 1609, maintained important commercial relations with Amsterdam in the seventeenth century, especially through the Portuguese Jews. As a distinctly Iberian enclave it may have drawn the attention also of Portuguese New Christians, who saw in the port's pirate activities an opportunity to tap the American wealth of Spain either through direct piracy or through the commercial distribution of pirate booty. The six immigrants from Salé are but a faint echo of the vigorous trading that linked the Portuguese Jews of Salé with those of Amsterdam.[86]

GENDER AND PROSPERITY

By and large, the Portuguese immigrants did not arrive singly but in families. In theory, therefore, the number of males was about equal to that of females. In practice, of course, imbalances occurred as they do in any sizeable migration. Until very recently men were infinitely more mobile than women, and any migration, whatever its motive or goal, inevitably produced communities in which men

[83] D'Ancona, 'Komst der Marranen', 211–12.

[84] GAA, DTB 669, p. 101 (27 June 1622); registration by Jacob Callas (of Jerusalem, 27 years old, living in Nieuwe Hoogstraat) and Annetien Bastaer (25 years old, accompanied by Beertien Thijsen her mother, living for the last twelve years in Gasthuismeulensteeg).

[85] Gans, 'Don Samuel Palache'; Hirschberg, *History of the Jews in North Africa* (Heb.), ii. 228–43.

[86] Terrasse, *Histoire du Maroc*, 220–1; Lapeyre, *Géographie*, 206–8; Penella, 'Transfert des Moriscos'.

outnumbered women. The Portuguese Jewish settlement in Amsterdam was no exception.

Although not without pitfalls, the Amsterdam marriage statistics offer possible ways of approaching the question of male–female imbalances with some precision. The first caveat to enter is that we lack any data on the numbers of unmarried men and women. These numbers need not have been the same proportionally for each geographical group nor for every social class. Second, the numbers in several cases are fairly small and may exaggerate a minor discrepancy. Nevertheless, bearing these points in mind, we may make potentially important observations on the basis of these figures.

The male majorities among the immigrants from Italy (69.1 per cent of the total), Portugal (57.2 per cent), and Spain (57.9 per cent) come as no surprise. Given the great distance between these lands and Amsterdam, the more or less substantial imbalance in favour of men simply reflects their greater mobility and, if anything, seems somewhat less marked than might have been expected. More importantly, only among the Italian immigrants was the imbalance a fixed and characteristic feature, highlighting the basically opportunistic impulse behind this migration; in the other groups it was not a constant phenomenon, but appears more pronounced at some times than at others.

Table 2.7. Portuguese Jewish immigration to Amsterdam, by place of origin and gender, 1598–1699

	1598–1609	1610–19	1620–9	1630–9	1640–9	1650–9	1660–9	1670–9	1680–9	1690–9	Total	(% women)
Antwerp												
Men	—	3	1	3	4	4	7	2	9	1	34	
Women	—	1	4	1	9	10	5	3	7	1	41	54.7%
France												
Men	—	1	2	5	15	23	15	8	22	23	114	
Women	—	—	1	10	18	16	11	14	23	20	113	49.8%
Hamburg												
Men	—	—	—	1	5	8	8	10	12	8	52	
Women	—	—	—	1	—	12	7	11	13	11	55	51.4%
Italy												
Men	—	—	1	—	5	4	9	11	21	34	85	
Women	—	—	1	1	4	3	6	6	6	11	38	30.9%
Portugal												
Men	17	8	38	33	38	42	19	18	7	6	226	
Women	15	9	29	26	28	24	14	12	7	5	169	42.8%
Spain												
Men	1	—	1	7	14	20	21	23	16	18	121	
Women	—	1	—	3	7	17	18	18	17	7	88	42.1%

As far as the Portuguese and Spanish immigrations are concerned, significant imbalances occurred between 1630 and 1650, for Portugal, and before 1640, for Spain. On the whole, of course, the figures underscore the basic male–female balance in these migrations, presumably reflecting their essentially familial nature. The individual male immigrants from Portugal and Spain are harder to characterize than those from Italy. Significantly, this particular Iberian migration occurred at a time (1620–40) when the Portuguese Inquisition markedly increased its persecution of New Christians. For this relatively brief period, the explosion and virulence of Portuguese inquisitorial activity gave rise to a truly panic-stricken emigration. At the same time, the Amsterdam settlement had become established, had been recognized by the political authorities, and had gained a reputation as a safe and prospering refuge. Both these facts, relating respectively to Portugal and Amsterdam, combined to steer at least some of the 'panicking' refugees in the same direction as the rather more deliberate, if only slightly less anxious, refugees of the earlier and later seventeenth century. The majority of contemporary Portuguese refugees probably settled in Spain and south-western France. The reason for the imbalance in the Spanish immigration during the first half of the seventeenth century—numerically small to begin with—remains uncertain.

The immigration from France stands out in that relatively large proportions of these arrivals were individual men and women. This highlights an important difference between the migrations from the Iberian peninsula and those from other western European communities. While some of the immigrants from France were undoubtedly Portuguese and Spanish refugees who for one reason or another had made or had been forced to make a temporary stopover in south-western France, others of them had moved for more particular reasons. Certain men were attracted by the economic opportunities provided by reciprocal trade relations between south-western France (and its Spanish hinterland) and Holland, or simply by the more expansive economy of Amsterdam as compared with that of Bordeaux or Bayonne. Individual women were often 'imported' specifically for the purpose of alleviating the Amsterdam community's shortage of females. This 'importation' of women occurred through informal channels, with more or less distant relatives in south-western France being encouraged to send their daughters to the northern metropolis for marriage, and more formally, with the establishment in 1615 by the Amsterdam community, in conjunction especially with the Portuguese of Hamburg, of the so-called Santa Companhia de Dotar Orfans e Donzelas Pobres (Holy Society for the Dowering of Orphans and Poor Maidens), commonly known as Dotar.[87] According to the statutes of Dotar, the society invited applications from any women 'of the Portuguese and Castilian nation' from 'between Saint-Jean-de-Luz and Danzig, from France as well as from Flanders, England, and Germany'. In practice, the majority of non-native women so dowered came from

[87] Révah, 'Premier règlement'; Pieterse, *350 jaar Dotar*.

south-western France, whose New Christian communities formed, so it appears, from an Amsterdam perspective, a kind of halfway house between the Iberian peninsula and more far-flung settlements to the north and east. They still retained direct and uninterrupted connections with Spain and Portugal while simultaneously being drawn into the emerging Portuguese diaspora, socially and economically. For much of the seventeenth century these French communities existed in a state of flux, susceptible to local accommodations as well as to the lures of distant horizons.

The proximity of Antwerp to Amsterdam made it a natural community from which to draw prospective brides during the 1630s and 1640s, when the Amsterdam community suffered its most acute shortage of women. The brides born in Antwerp, whose Portuguese had never really been a refugee community, appear to have been of a distinctly higher social class than those 'imported' from France. Eventually this initial migration of primarily single women may even have facilitated the subsequent transfer of almost the entire Antwerp Portuguese community to Amsterdam during the second half of the century.

It has already been emphasized that the Hamburg community must not be regarded as too separate from the one in Amsterdam. Only with the Hamburg Portuguese, and later with those of London, did the Amsterdam Portuguese maintain truly reciprocal relations. Probably as many Amsterdam brides and grooms married in Hamburg as vice versa. The figures are an almost perfect reflection of this reciprocity.

In addition to geographical origin and male/female ratios, the statistics allow us to chart to some degree, albeit by indirect means, the influx of poorer than usual immigrants.

The general level of literacy among the Portuguese immigrants was very high, very much higher than that of the population of Amsterdam as a whole. Male illiteracy was only 1 per cent as compared with 43 per cent, 36 per cent, and 30 per cent for the male population of Amsterdam as measured during the single years 1630, 1660, and 1680.[88] Although substantially higher at about 30 per cent, female illiteracy, too, compares favourably with the Amsterdam rates of 68 per cent, 63 per cent, and 56 per cent. Although illiteracy may not be hard and fast evidence of poverty, and the social status of the bride may not always have been a reflection of that of her husband, in our case female illiteracy (see Table 2.8) must suffice as an indicator of the relatively low social status of a particular group of immigrants.[89]

The arrivals from Italy, among whom the poor were a more or less constant

[88] Hart, 'Enige statistische gegevens', 4. The statistics for Amsterdam's Portuguese Jews are based on a slightly different criterion from that applied to the general population of the city. In computing the Amsterdam figures, Hart counted every semblance of a signature, including illegible scribbles and initials, among the literate. As I am more concerned with literacy as a relative indicator of wealth than with literacy per se, I have considered illiterate any person unable to sign a full name. Thus first-name-only signatures were included among the literate, initials were not.

[89] Cf. the interesting discussion in Rodriguez and Bennassar, 'Signatures et niveau culturel'.

Table 2.8. Illiteracy among Portuguese Jewish women in Amsterdam, in relation to place of origin, 1598–1699

	1598–1609	1610–19	1620–9	1630–9	1640–9	1650–9	1660–9	1670–9	1680–9	1690–9	Total	(% illiterate)
Amsterdam												
Total	—	—	6	15	41	63	94	107	202	185	713	
Illiterate	—	—	1	4	11	17	26	40	81	47	227	31.8%
Antwerp												
Total	—	1	4	1	9	10	5	3	7	1	41	
Illiterate	—	—	—	—	—	2	—	—	1	—	3	7.3%
France												
Total	—	—	1	10	18	16	11	14	23	20	113	
Illiterate	—	—	—	4	3	3	2	7	8	7	34	30.1%
Hamburg												
Total	—	—	—	1	—	12	7	11	13	11	55	
Illiterate	—	—	—	—	—	5	2	2	1	—	10	18.2%
Italy												
Total	—	—	1	1	4	3	6	6	6	11	38	
Illiterate	—	—	—	—	2	2	1	3	4	7	19	50.0%
Portugal												
Total	15	9	29	26	28	24	14	12	7	5	169	
Illiterate	1	4	10	14	7	2	1	5	7	1	52	30.7%
Spain												
Total	—	1	—	3	7	17	18	18	17	7	88	
Illiterate	—	—	—	2	1	4	8	—	4	3	22	25.0%

presence, and from Antwerp, among whom the poor were almost entirely absent, form the two extremes on this spectrum. These data have already enabled us to characterize the Italian immigrants as basically motivated by the search for economic opportunity, and the Antwerp brides—indeed, the Antwerp community as a whole—as basically prosperous.

The Hamburg brides, too, were generally prosperous. The Hamburg Portuguese community probably never experienced as relatively large an influx of poor immigrants as Amsterdam did.[90] The overall prosperity of the German branch of the northern European diaspora was therefore probably higher to begin with than that of the Holland Portuguese. Second, marriages among families of the sister communities of Amsterdam, Hamburg, and London were presumably more common among the well-to-do than among the poor, who lacked connections outside their place of settlement.

The illiteracy rates of Portuguese, Spanish, and French immigrants hover around the average for the total Portuguese Jewish population, at a level which,

[90] Kellenbenz, *Sephardim*, 36–7. Fifty-two poor in Hamburg in 1652 constituted about 10 per cent of the Portuguese Jewish population.

compared with the Amsterdam rates, confirms the general prosperity of the immigrant settlers. Nevertheless, it must come as some surprise that fully one-quarter to one-third of the immigrants managed to make the long and often hazardous migration on relatively meagre means. Some, no doubt, came as servants of the wealthy families. Others must have travelled the long distance in stages: from the Iberian peninsula to the south-west of France, thence to Flanders, and thence to Amsterdam. And some at least arrived directly, by means which will probably always remain hidden, as the poor are so much less likely to leave traces in our historical records than the well-to-do. Our general lack of knowledge regarding the poor immigrants is all the more regrettable as their presence—in fairly large numbers—in seventeenth-century Amsterdam is one of the features that distinguish that settlement from others in northern Europe.

Only with regard to the immigration from Portugal are we in any position to specify the chronology of the poorer arrivals. Poor immigrants were particularly numerous (that is, constituting more than one-third of the total number of immigrants from Portugal) between about 1610 and 1635, and again after 1660. These periods coincide roughly with the decades during which the Portuguese Inquisition intensified its prosecution of New Christians and presumably acted less discriminately in its choice of victims. Whether or not other, particularly economic, factors also played a role is difficult to say. Among the Spanish and French immigrants the poor were more evenly distributed. No specific factors other than the steady trek away from Portugal would seem to have been at play here.

SIZES OF COMMUNITY

It remains in this chapter only to establish the overall population development of the Amsterdam community and place it in the context of the Portuguese diaspora as a whole.

Previous research attempting to chart the overall population growth of the Amsterdam Portuguese Jewish community relied on the estimates of visitors such as Will Brereton or of the Amsterdam rabbi Menasseh ben Israel, or on the numbers of members of the synagogue or of Portuguese account-holders at the Bank of Exchange.[91] Surprisingly, the figures thus arrived at are fairly close to the mark; but they are sporadic and provide only the most general view of the evolution. One estimated the size of the population at four accidentally more or less equidistant dates (1609, 1630, 1655, 1674) and gained from the respective figures (number of individuals: 200, 1,000, 1,800, 2,500) the impression of a deceptively steady growth rate in absolute figures of some 800 persons per two decades, until the community stabilized at about 3,000 during the last quarter of the century. The only nuance added to this picture consisted in the observation that during the 1620s and 1630s there had actually been a decline in the number of

---

[91] Bloom, *Economic Activities*, 5, 11, 203–5.

Table 2.9. Portuguese Jewish account-holders at the Amsterdam Bank of Exchange, 1609–1674

	1609	1611	1612	1615	1620	1625	1627	1631	1641	1646	1651	1661	1674
Account-holders	24	28	43	57	106	76	92	89	89	126	197	243	265

Table 2.10. Portuguese Jewish marriages and estimated population, 1610–1699

	1610s	1620s	1630s	1640s	1650s	1660s	1670s	1680s	1690s
Number of marriages	52	66	62	110	155	169	187	278	255
Estimated population	600–50	775–825	725–75	1,300–75	1,825–1,925	2,000–2,100	2,200–2,325	3,275–3,475	3,000–3,175

Portuguese account-holders at the Amsterdam Bank of Exchange (Table 2.9)—and presumably a concomitant decline in population—due to emigration, particularly to Hamburg.[92]

We lack data on birth or death rates and must again fall back on our marriage statistics to arrive at more satisfactory estimations of the overall size of the population. Demographers have examined the relation between population and annual number of marriages. As in any demographic rates, they have found a great deal of variation, from a low of five marriages per year per 1,000 persons to a high of eleven or even fourteen.[93] On the basis of known rates among culturally similar people during the early modern era, I have chosen to assume the rate among the Amsterdam Portuguese to have been between 8 and 8.5 per cent.[94]

The growth of the Amsterdam community (Table 2.10) occurred in spurts. Following the initial settlement of some 200 Portuguese, the community grew appreciably during the 1610s to about 800 individuals and then remained more or less stable throughout the 1620s and most of the 1630s. The next significant growth occurred during the 1640s and 1650s and raised the size of the community

[92] Van Dillen, 'Vreemdelingen', 14, 16–17.

[93] Henry, *Techniques d'analyse*, 152. Schraa, 'Onderzoekingen', 26–7, arrives at a marriage rate of 14 per cent.

[94] Henry, *Techniques d'analyse*, 152, cites a rate of 8.5 per cent for France, 1740–89. Hollingsworth, *Historical Demography*, 190, gives 7 per cent as the normal rate. Bennassar, *Valladolid*, 197, cites 8 per cent as the rate 'en période normale' (1570–89). Finally, Herrero Martínez de Azcoitia, 'Población palentina', gives the following figures: 8.53 per cent between 1585 and 1590; 10 per cent between 1626 and 1650; 9.14 per cent between 1651 and 1675. I have chosen the rate of 8–8.5 per cent because it seemed the one prevalent in France and Spain. I have chosen a figure at the lower end of the scale in consideration of the fact that a certain number of marriages escaped registration.

to about 2,000 individuals. Then the 1660s and 1670s witnessed a tapering off of growth to about 2,200 individuals. Finally, during the 1680s the community reached its peak at about 3,350 and settled down during the 1690s at slightly over 3,000. This stop–go development of the community can be explained only partially in terms of immigration. Emigration from Amsterdam must be considered to complete the picture.

Immigration from southern Europe—from the Iberian peninsula and south-western France combined—was highest during the 1610s and the period from about 1630 to 1655. For the rest of the century, with the exception of a temporary and minor decline in the 1620s and a more permanent fall towards the end of the century, this immigration remained fairly stable. Inquisitorial persecutions in Portugal and Spain have already been mentioned to explain the particular surges in immigration. Moreover, the Twelve Years Truce (1609–21) between Spain and the Republic and the temporary relaxation of anti-*converso* collaboration between state and Church in Portugal in the wake of the 1609 pardon added extra momentum during the 1610s.

Notwithstanding a continued immigration between 1620 and 1640, the emigration of Portuguese to Hamburg and, after 1630, to Brazil helped stabilize the population during that period.[95] The interplay of immigration and emigration during the 1620s and 1630s, however, gave rise to a community in which poor immigrants began to constitute an ever larger proportion. Hence the discrepancy between the decline in the number of Portuguese account-holders (Table 2.9) and the basic numerical stability of the community (Table 2.10) during the same period. The upsurge of immigration from southern Europe between 1630 and 1655 made its dramatic impact in conjunction with the immigration of Antwerp Portuguese and the return of many of the Brazilian émigrés. During the same period some emigrants continued to settle in Hamburg and even founded small communities in the nearby towns of Glückstadt, Altona, and Emden. The stability of the 1660s and 1670s again owed much to the emigration of Portuguese Jews to London and the Dutch and English islands of the Caribbean.[96] At about the same time, however, increasing numbers of Portuguese Jews from Hamburg and its environs made Amsterdam their final place of settlement in northern Europe. The last spurt in population growth during the fourth quarter of the seventeenth century owed a little to the immigration of a substantial number of Italian Jews, but much more to the coming of age of the descendants of the large immigration of the middle of the century. The Amsterdam community, as it were, had settled down to its own rhythms of natural growth and a balanced, undramatic ratio of immigration and emigration.

Placing Amsterdam in the context of the entire Portuguese diaspora in Europe during the seventeenth century presents a great many problems. No community

---

[95] On emigration to Hamburg, see van Dillen, 'Vreemdelingen', 16–17.
[96] See nn. 109–10 below.

other than Amsterdam allows us to be very specific about the evolution of the population over the century. Such population estimates as do exist—whether hard or soft—are based on wildly diverse criteria.[97] An inconsistent application of relatively arbitrary multipliers further adds to the confusion.[98]

Four broad but fairly distinct regions must be considered: Italy, south-western France, northern Europe, and the transatlantic colonies. In Italy, two major centres of Iberian expatriates had emerged during the second half of the sixteenth century and flourished during the seventeenth: Venice and Livorno. For Venice, more or less reliable figures estimate the total number of Jews at 1,700 in the 1580s, 2,650 in the 1640s, and 4,000 in the 1660s.[99] The city's Jewish community consisted of three separate congregations of Levantine, Iberian, and Ashkenazi Jews, and no method of computation has yet established the proportion of each. The Spanish and Portuguese Jews certainly did not constitute a majority. It may be safe to say, none the less, that the Iberian Jewish community of Venice harboured one of the largest populations—possibly alongside Antwerp—within the emerging Portuguese diaspora at the very beginning of the seventeenth century, as befitted the last link with the earlier Sephardi diaspora. It would appear definitely to have been surpassed by Amsterdam in the 1640s when that city's Iberian Jewish population passed the 1,000 mark. Livorno, too, probably eclipsed Venice about the same time. Much less reliable figures estimate the Jewish (Ashkenazi, Levantine, and Iberian) population of Livorno at 100 around the beginning of the century and that of nearby Pisa at 500 in 1617.[100] By the end of the century the Jewish community of Pisa had been absorbed by that of Livorno, and the prosperous harbour counted some 3,500 Jews among its inhabitants. In Livorno, the Spanish and Portuguese Jews did form a majority, though in what proportion is not known. In general, therefore, the rise of the Livornese community of Iberian Jews paralleled that of Amsterdam. Livorno, however, was somewhat more isolated as an Iberian Jewish community than was Amsterdam and never played the same kind of dynamic role in the global scheme of Iberian migration. Although the two cities were of approximately comparable size, far more Iberians passed through the gates of Amsterdam to settle there or in one of its satellites than ever settled in Livorno.

Throughout most of the seventeenth century the Iberian New Christian and Jewish population of south-western France consisted of an ever-changing mosaic of smaller communities. Not only did many New Christian expatriates, as noted above, settle in south-western France only temporarily while in transit to some

[97] Such as the number of families, or of households, or of taxpayers, or of bank-account-holders, or of *yehidim* (paying members of the synagogue), or mortality rates.

[98] Estimates about the average size of a Portuguese Jewish family range from 3.5 to 6.4 persons. The confusion is compounded by the frequent lack of clarity as to whether the reference is to family in the narrow sense or to household. Households may have included, on average, 1.5 persons each more than families. In subsequent calculations I have consistently applied a rate of 5 persons per family.

[99] Ravid, *Economics and Toleration*, 75–6; Pullan, *Jews of Europe*, 156–7.

[100] Milano, *Storia degli Ebrei in Italia*, 324.

final and more promising destination, separate communities also experienced different treatment at various times, with an expulsion from one place balanced by a more tolerant reception somewhere else. During the first half of the century the most important communities of Bayonne, Labastide-Clairence, Peyrehorade, Bidache, and Bordeaux each harboured Iberian populations of about 200–400 individuals. All the communities combined totalled at most 1,500 people. Around the middle of the century several communities witnessed a sizeable influx of new immigrants, with Bayonne and Peyrehorade alone apparently increasing their combined populations to about 1,500 people. Other communities experienced a less dramatic growth. Bordeaux, for instance, only doubled its population to about 400–500 Portuguese and Spanish expatriates by the end of the century. Obviously, substantial numbers of the mid-century immigrants had moved on to the east or north and beyond. On the whole, the Bordeaux rate may have been typical of the region, and the large-scale immigration of the middle and later seventeenth century generally doubled the Iberian population to approximately 3,000 individuals at most.[101] In other words, at this period the entire south-western region of France harboured about the same number of Portuguese and Spanish immigrants as Amsterdam. Chronologically, during the earlier two-thirds of the century, the figures dovetail with those for Amsterdam: that is, a rise in population in south-western France preceded a similar rise in Amsterdam. During this part of the century the communities of south-western France played the same dynamic role vis-à-vis the rest of the Iberian diaspora that Amsterdam was to play later vis-à-vis the English and Caribbean diaspora, without the economic dimensions of the latter relationship.

In northern Europe at the end of the sixteenth century the established Iberian community of Antwerp totalled about 500 individuals.[102] No substantial numbers of new immigrants subsequently settled there, and the once famous community slowly died out, as a result first of attrition and then of emigration.

Around the beginning of the seventeenth century more or less equal numbers of recent émigrés from Portugal established small and tentative communities of about 100 in Rouen, Amsterdam, and Hamburg. Still smaller settlement attempts were made in Middelburg, Rotterdam, Haarlem, and London. Rouen witnessed a setback at first, and the later, more successful community of the 1630s never numbered more than 200 individuals.[103] Only Amsterdam and Hamburg proved truly viable, but until at least 1640 neither emerged as decisively more promising than the other. During this early period both communities—Hamburg in conjunction with neighbouring settlements—grew to some 700–800 individuals each.[104]

[101] Blumenkranz (ed.), *Histoire des Juifs en France*, 230–3; Révah, 'Marranes', 66; and the interesting calculations in Nahon, 'Inscriptions funéraires', 127: 228–9, 355; 128: 354–6, based on mortality rates.

[102] Pohl, *Portugiesen*, 66–71.

[103] Révah, 'Premier établissement'; Brugmans and Frank (eds.), *Geschiedenis der Joden in Nederland*, 383–95; E. Samuel, 'Portuguese Jews in Jacobean London'; Révah, 'Autobiographie d'un Marrane', 72–3.   [104] Kellenbenz, *Sephardim*, 41, 65.

Although Hamburg continued to grow thereafter until the 1660s, Amsterdam suddenly grew much faster. By 1660, Hamburg and its environs harboured about 900 Iberians, while Amsterdam had expanded to accommodate double that figure.[105] The favourable position of Holland *vis-à-vis* Portugal (after the 1640 rebellion) and Spain (after the 1648 Peace of Westphalia) and the western colonies, that is, in respect of Atlantic trade in general, gave Amsterdam once and for all the competitive edge over Hamburg. Slowly, the Hamburg community of Portuguese and Spanish Jews declined to the level of some 300 members,[106] while Amsterdam became the largest community of expatriate Iberians of the seventeenth-century, predominantly Atlantic, diaspora. With the decline of Hamburg in northern Europe came the rise of London, more favourably situated in relation to Portugal and the transatlantic colonies. From a meagre beginning of some 120 individuals in 1660, the Iberian community of London expanded quite rapidly to 414 in 1684 and about 550 in 1695.[107]

Finally, the second half of the seventeenth century also witnessed the emergence of sizeable Jewish communities in the Caribbean and of as yet tentative ones in North America. At the end of the century, Curaçao harboured some 625 Jews, Jamaica 400, and Barbados 300.[108] Nieuw Amsterdam (and later New York) counted at most seventy-five Jews during the same period.[109] Over-population problems in the seemingly ever-expanding community of Amsterdam are often cited as the inspiration behind the settlements in London and the Caribbean.[110] Certainly, the 2,000 or so individuals who settled in these colonies might have stretched the resources of the Amsterdam community beyond a tolerable level; but this is not the same as saying that over-population or problems associated with it consciously motivated these further migrations abroad. In the first place, most of the London and many of the Caribbean settlers emigrated for specific purposes of expanding trade. This expansion was not a vaguely anticipated consequence of emigration inspired by over-population. London and Caribbean merchants did not flee the overly congested and fiercely competitive market of Amsterdam to try their luck elsewhere. Mostly, they migrated in deliberate consultation with Amsterdam and other Portuguese merchants seeking to maximize their advantages or to maintain their positions in international trade.[111] Nor will simple over-population do as an explanation of the emigration of poorer settlers. As early as the 1620s, when the Amsterdam community was only a third or a quarter the size it was to attain after 1660, the leaders of the community had made attempts to 'bribe' poor immigrants to migrate abroad, primarily to Italy in those early

---

[105] Ibid.   [106] Ibid. 52, 68.

[107] E. Samuel, 'First Fifty Years', 28; Cohen, 'Jewish Demography', 13–34.

[108] Emmanuel, *History of the Jews of the Netherlands Antilles*, 93; W. Samuel, 'Review of the Jewish Colonists', 8, 13; Rosenbloom, 'Notes on the Jews' Tribute', 247; Cohen, 'Jewish Demography', 35–62.

[109] Hershkowitz, 'Some Aspects of the New York Jewish Merchant', 10; Cohen, 'Jewish Demography', 66.

[110] Israel, 'Spain and the Dutch Sephardim', 35; Fuks-Mansfeld, 'Bevolkingsproblematiek'.

[111] Swetschinski, 'Conflict and Opportunity', 230–2.

days.[112] Size as such, therefore, was not the determining factor. Far more important were the employment opportunities in Amsterdam and the ability and willingness of the wealthy members of the community to support, through charity or otherwise, their destitute fellow exiles. The first factor was tied in with the economic development of Amsterdam as a whole and the role of the Portuguese in particular; the second depended on a wide variety of social and cultural factors. Neither was directly or inevitably linked to over-population. In later chapters we will have occasion to return to these questions of employment and charity.

We may now distinguish three relatively distinct types of community. The first, of approximately a hundred individuals, remained tentative. It could not subsist on its own; it either grew or disappeared. It survived as a tentative community—as for instance in Middelburg and Nieuw Amsterdam—only in so far as it was intimately and subserviently linked to a much larger community. The second type, with a population of several hundreds, was more independent and able to sustain itself longer. Though still dependent on links to other centres, communities of this type established roots and thereby gained a measure of stability that allowed them to adjust to changes in the international configuration of links. The third and truly sizeable type of community, harbouring more than 2,000 people, may be called dynamic. Not only did it possess the qualities of rootedness, stability, and flexibility, it was positively able to create its own new links. Its measure of control over its own destiny—barring extraordinary events such as war or a sudden and radical reversal of tolerant attitudes—was exponentially greater than that of the middle-sized community. Such, at least, appear to have been the realities of Portuguese New Christian and Jewish history.

COMPLEXITIES OF FLIGHT AND ATTRACTION

Migration is a complex phenomenon. Notwithstanding its ubiquity in Jewish history, Jewish historians have given relatively little attention to its distinctive features. In so far as they have worked with a model, it has been the simple push–pull model: either the Jews were more or less explicitly forced to migrate or they took to the roads, seas, or skies from a desire to reach some 'promised' land. As far as the Portuguese Jews of Amsterdam are concerned, little attention was focused on the 'push'. No more or less explicit order of expulsion was issued after those of 1492 and 1497, and only sporadic, localized mob violence appeared to have threatened the Iberian New Christians. It remained, therefore, to identify the 'pull'. Was it the promise of economic betterment or that of religious liberty? An interminable debate ensued.[113] It may not be possible to settle the issue here once

---

[112] GAA, PIG 13, pp. 7–9: *imposta* regulations chs. 22–9, dated 4 February 1622.

[113] To cite but two examples, Seeligmann, 'Marranen-probleem', and da Silva Rosa, 'Van Marranen tot Portugeesche Joden'. In some form or other, often implicitly rather than explicitly, almost every study of the Portuguese Jews of Amsterdam assumes either one or the other of these two positions.

and for all; indeed, it may very well lie in the nature of the phenomenon that the question cannot easily be resolved.

We must recognize that the Portuguese New Christians as a group were fairly mobile to begin with and continued to remain so throughout the seventeenth century. There is, of course, no question here of arguing for some kind of racial propensity towards nomadism.[114] But it cannot be denied that for these New Christians, having been uprooted by the expulsion from Spain and thus compelled to seek new avenues of economic and social improvement, migration became a widely experienced, a group rather than an individual reality. As a mobile group, the Portuguese New Christians at once received more information about opportunities elsewhere and were readier than other groups of Portuguese to take these opportunities. Among the most mobile of the Portuguese New Christians were the merchants who ventured into international waters. The Portuguese merchants who settled in the Portuguese colonies of Asia and America and then in the Spanish colonies of America and in Spain itself—not to speak of those who peopled the islands of Madeira, the Azores, and the Canaries—testify to the great mobility of this segment of the New Christian population.[115]

Then we must not underestimate the constant and present danger presented by the Portuguese and Spanish inquisitions to the New Christians both as individuals and as a group. While inquisitorial prosecution may not have amounted to an explicit order of expulsion, for many its consequences, such as confiscation of property and social stigmatization, not to mention imprisonment and the threat of the death penalty, rendered continued life in its shadow intolerable; as intolerable as famine, for instance. But inquisitorial prosecution also had an uncertainty, an element of mere potentiality, indeed a kind of unreality about it: for no particular individual or family could ever be absolutely certain where he, she, or they stood in the eyes and minds of the inquisitors until the very moment of arrest. Between complete ignorance of a potential arrest and the certainty of its imminence lay a wide spectrum of partial (un)certainties, of vast ambiguity. Undoubtedly, New Christians coped with this ambiguity in a wide variety of individual ways. One event, however, stands out as having often (perhaps always) tipped the scales of ambiguity towards heightened expectation of imminent victimization: the arrest of a relative or friend. For inquisitorial procedure (written and unwritten) was such that unless he or she denounced others, the accused was unlikely to be treated with any but the harshest consideration.[116] Yet even so, the present danger of inquisitorial prosecution threatened primarily the more or less immediate family and

---

[114] As argued, for example, by Sombart, *Juden und das Wirtschaftsleben*, esp. 403–26. Unaware of its antisemitic connotations, the term was unfortunately misapplied by García Cárcel, *Herejía y sociedad*, 220: 'Estos judaizantes portugueses se caracterizaban . . . por su afición al nomadismo'.

[115] The importance of this kind of mobility as a precondition of migration is recognized by Taylor, 'Migration and Motivation', 110–11.

[116] Révah, 'Marranes', 41–5. On the fear of denunciation, see also Ribeiro Sanches, *Christãos Novos*, 7–9. Ribeiro Sanches, himself a New Christian, wrote down his observation in 1735.

circle of friends, relatively small groups. This situation changed during periods of mass prosecution such as Portugal witnessed between 1620 and 1640 and in the 1660s, and Oporto in 1618. In these times, the expansion of the number of small groups under imminent suspicion created ever-increasing, interlocking chains of anxiety. This in turn gave rise to a diffuse group panic gripping large segments of the New Christian population in a given locality or region, or even the whole land. In sum, when considering the impact of inquisitorial prosecution, we must carefully distinguish the levels of unease it instilled, the kinds of people it affected, and the degree of manoeuvrability it left the person, family, or group under real or imagined suspicion. The people affected determined the selection of potential émigrés, their room for manoeuvre the options available.

Two groups stand out among the immigrants of Amsterdam: the merchants and the poor. And the question arises whether the selection of these particular groups derived from the situation in Portugal, was somehow determined by the nature of Amsterdam, or resulted from events in any of the places of settlement in between. Merchants were to be found throughout the Iberian diaspora, but poor immigrants appear to have been common only in some places. We know almost nothing of the social composition of the Iberian communities in Italy. Elsewhere, poor immigrants constituted a small minority in Antwerp, Hamburg, and London, but formed sizeable minorities in south-western France and Amsterdam. Of these two the south-west of France was, in several important respects, distinctly more heterogeneous than Amsterdam. For unlike any other part of the Iberian diaspora, south-western France harboured small but relatively self-sufficient rural communities of 200–400 Iberians in Labastide-Clairence, Bidache, and Peyrehorade. Moreover, the religious commitments of these as well as the port communities of Bayonne and Bordeaux remained in a certain state of flux, oscillating between a lukewarm Christianity and an unfamiliar Judaism, until the final third of the century, when many declared themselves Jews more openly. The example of the religious hybrid family of Lopes–Mendes Sotto may serve as a case in point. Two sons became merchants, settled in Amsterdam and London, and returned to Judaism. A third son became a clergyman in Bordeaux, and the fourth a (Christian) physician and professor at the Medical College of Bordeaux. The four daughters all married merchants, settled in northern Europe, and joined Jewish communities.[117] These facts suggest the interaction of several processes of selection resulting in communities of varying degrees of social and religious uniformity.

The heterogeneity of the south-western French communities highlights a flight from Portugal by a broad range of people, while the relative homogeneity of the northern European communities implies some measure of attraction exercised by these ports.[118] The two processes, of course, are not mutually exclusive and may

---

[117] The data derive from 'Genealogia do velho M. Lopes' extant in manuscript, c/o Ms J. C. E. Belinfante, Amsterdam.
[118] On selectivity in migration, see Jansen, 'Some Sociological Aspects', 64.

frequently have operated simultaneously. There are some indications that flight or attraction were not always equally important motives at all times and for all groups of people. For instance, we have every reason to assume that the kind of commercial calculations which had induced Portuguese merchants to settle in Antwerp in the sixteenth century continued to motivate some to emigrate to northern Europe in the seventeenth. Especially during the early settlement period, before the realities of international trade had changed as radically as they were to do later, Amsterdam and Hamburg must have attracted the same kind of commercial agents as had previously represented Lisbon and Oporto merchants in Antwerp. After the 1630s, however, political and commercial matters become exceedingly confused. The expansion of Amsterdam as an international entrepôt held greater promise than ever before, but less and less so from the particular point of view of Portugal–Holland trade. Merchants who emigrated during the middle of the seventeenth century did so because the economic decline of Portugal provoked an adventurous response or, more frequently, because the imminence of inquisitorial prosecution made them seek safety abroad. Emanoel Gomes Pessoa, a fairly substantial merchant of Lisbon, stealthily fled the city in fear of arrest, heading first for Rouen and ultimately for Amsterdam, and was forced in the process to try his hand at a variety of economic endeavours only loosely connected with his previous commercial activities in Portugal.[119] Often prompted into departure by the same set of circumstances, the immigrant merchants from Spain must have found Amsterdam particularly attractive as it promised them a certain measure of continuity in the exploration of trade with Spain, the Spanish Netherlands, and the Spanish colonies in America.[120] Whereas most Portuguese and Spanish merchants fled the peninsula for fear of inquisitorial prosecution, they were generally able to consider their options carefully and choose the one most attractive from an economic point of view.

The matter was not so easy and clear for New Christians not engaged in commerce, unaccustomed to a certain degree of mobility, and therefore having less information and fewer options. Such New Christians may not have been singled out for inquisitorial prosecution quite so frequently as the more prosperous, or may have felt themselves somewhat less conspicuous, and were therefore generally less fearful. They also lacked the means to act upon anything but the strongest fears. In their case, the harsh realities of economic life and the uncertain perceptions of inquisitorial dangers combined to retard rather than accelerate the search for refuge or economic opportunity abroad. Not surprisingly, vast numbers of poorer New Christians fled Portugal only at times of mass prosecutions (1620–40, the 1660s) and then primarily to the nearest places of refuge: to Spain and to south-

---

[119] ANTT, Inq. de Lisboa, Proc. 10794 (Processo de Francisco Gomes Henriques) (I owe this reference to Dr David Grant Smith); Roth, 'Marranes à Rouen', 134, on the Pessoas' temporary stay in Rouen. On the bankruptcy of Jeronimo's son, Isaac Pessoa, see Ch. 3 below.

[120] Swetschinski, 'Conflict and Opportunity', 229–38.

western France. Spain was the nearest and the most familiar, and sometimes—perhaps often—allowed the migrants to continue engaging in local or retail trade and specialized crafts, and had as yet not made the less affluent Portuguese a prime target of inquisitorial vigilance. South-western France must have attracted the hardier ones capable of a long journey on foot, the more adventuresome, those who had the least to lose, those without family, the more fearful, and those with a religious desire to return to Judaism. But the south-west of France could not possibly provide employment for so many non-commercially active immigrants, and local authorities sporadically proved hostile to any but the merchants among the *nouveaux chrétiens*. These refugees' options were limited; no particular economic interest guided their choice. They stayed as long as they could or moved on to Italy and Amsterdam. What inspired them to migrate to Italy is uncertain. As far as Amsterdam is concerned, initial connections with the refugees in south-western France were established through Dotar for the specific purpose of furthering the through-migration of poor girls and orphans to northern Europe. Having formed this migratory link, Amsterdam acquired an aura of accessibility and promise in the minds of the refugees, and more and more 'uninvited', poor Portuguese New Christians travelled to the north, finding the atmosphere in Amsterdam far more hospitable than it was in the other major northern European settlement of Hamburg. Amsterdam Jewry enjoyed greater security and less (if any) scrutiny from the authorities than did its counterpart community in Hamburg, where toleration depended more narrowly on specific commercial profits expected from the Portuguese New Christian settlement.

In the end, migration to Amsterdam was neither entirely a voluntary nor wholly an involuntary act. The decision to flee the Inquisition had always, in large measure, remained a voluntary one. This act of volition, even if initially nothing but an escape from the most agonizing ambiguity, had produced a most distinct and peaceful clarity; it generally paid off. Something of this sentiment may be recognized in David Jesurun's hymn of praise, reproduced at the opening of this chapter. 'Free of the Pit', having escaped the Inquisition, he has found 'protection', security, in God's 'infinite and holy Providence', in Judaism. Many, perhaps even most, other Portuguese Jews retold their flight from Portugal as a heroic quest for religious freedom.

In certain ways, the legends purporting to tell the story of this undaunted pursuit of the singular objective of returning to Judaism—the details of which will be discussed in a later chapter—express some of the uniqueness of the Portuguese Jewish experience in Amsterdam. For no other community in the Iberian diaspora seems to have felt a need for similar legendary flourishes. If Amsterdam's Portuguese Jews did so, it may have been to resolve the tension between the individual's recognition of a voluntary act and the group's awareness of an involuntary decision. The first prevailed unquestioned in the homogeneous communities; the second inevitably arose and produced dissonance in a more heterogeneous

community like Amsterdam. Moreover, at least two of the three legends acknowledge the tolerance of Amsterdam's authorities—one even specifically in contrast
to the intolerance of the Lutherans in northern Germany. They highlight the very
security which had made Amsterdam attractive and receptive to immigrants of
lesser means and fewer international connections. These immigrants may have felt
more gratitude and greater loyalty to their city of refuge than those primarily in
search of opportunity.

THREE

COMMERCE, NETWORKS, AND OTHER RELATIONS

The Inner Workings of Portuguese Jewish Entrepreneurship

The Hanover merchant Meyer Michael-David once told David Prager of Amsterdam that the difference between London and Amsterdam, on the one hand, and the German states, on the other, was comparable to that between Heaven and Hell.

YOGEV, *Diamonds and Coral*

THE single most salient feature of the economic history of Amsterdam's Portuguese Jews during the seventeenth century is the relatively narrow range of activities explored by these immigrants. Even during the second half of the century, the settlement's most flourishing period, some 80 per cent of the Portuguese Jews were more or less directly engaged in commerce (see Table 3.1). Many of the non-commercial activities encountered will be shown to have been recent accretions from around the middle of the century. During the first half of the century, therefore, commerce unquestionably figured even more prominently as the core form of Portuguese Jewish economic activity.

This very high degree of specialization has been explained in a variety of terms. Some analyses, focusing on the later seventeenth and eighteenth centuries, saw the then prevailing concentration on the trade in precious stones, jewels, and bills of exchange simply as the continuation of a Jewish economic tradition reaching back to the Middle Ages. Others emphasized the second-class political status even the Portuguese Jews suffered and their concomitant exclusion from the 'native' economy and particularly from industry. Thus many Jews—the Portuguese Jews of Amsterdam included—concentrated their efforts in commerce *faute de mieux*. Finally, it is suggested that the very diffuse nature of Jewish settlement across Europe and around the Mediterranean harboured such distinct commercial advantages as to have almost naturally 'sucked' Jews into its exploration. And, of course, there are many who resort to various combinations of these explanations. The concentration on commerce of Amsterdam's Portuguese Jews was definitely

Table 3.1. Occupations of Portuguese Jewish males, 1655–1699

Occupation	No.	%	Occupation	No.	%
Commerce			*Labour*		
Book-keeper	2		Coral polisher	3	
Broker	31		Diamond cutter/polisher	20	
Cashier	8		Gilder	1	
Factor	9		Hatmaker	1	
Jeweller	6		Musician	2	
Merchant	498	71.9	Packer	1	
Money changer	1		Painter	1	
Sugar refiner	2		Silk carder	2	
Tobacco wholesaler	4		Silk sashmaker	1	
	561	81.0	Sugar refinery worker	1	
Retail			Tobacco worker	13	
Butcher	2		'Worker'	1	
Confectioner	3			47	6.8
Distiller	1				
Grocer	3		*Other*		
Pharmacist	4		Ḥazan	1	
Tobacconist	13		Letter carrier	1	
Undertaker	1		Officer	1	
	27	3.9	Slaughterer	1	
Professions			Student	7	
Barber	2			11	1.6
Physician	10		Profession listed	693	100
Professor	1		No profession listed	193	
Solicitor	2		TOTAL	886	
Surgeon	10				
Teacher	22				
	47	6.8			

not a matter of Jewish traditions. Nor did it result primarily from political marginality and powerlessness. And the diaspora will at times prove to have been a product of commercial enterprise, at others an invitation to new pursuits.

In approaching the economic history of Amsterdam's Portuguese Jews, we must guard against laying too great an emphasis upon the merchants' Jewishness. In this case, Jewishness obscures the fact that, as *conversos*, the Portuguese had already been members of European society and stood outside the main traditions of Jewish history. It also insinuates *a priori* a degree of solidarity with other communities of the diaspora rather than questioning the precise nature of inter-communal relations. In the end, the economic history of Amsterdam's Portuguese Jews will tell us more about Jewish history than vice versa.

In large measure, as we saw in the previous chapter, the concentration of Portuguese merchants in Amsterdam was the result of pre-selection. The example of the Lopes-Mendes Sotto family, cited in Chapter 2, illustrates how only those members of a family already inclined towards commerce chose to settle in Amsterdam. To a great extent, the same holds true for the larger group of Portuguese and

Spanish New Christians. Sometimes migration occurred for reasons of commerce; at other times it did not seriously interrupt, and often merely redirected, what had already been a commercial career. Only rarely, and then primarily among second-generation immigrants, does settlement in Amsterdam as such inspire commercial aspirations—even more rarely, successful ones—in individuals with no prior experience.

'Commerce' is a deceptively simple designation for a broad spectrum of activities. The Portuguese Jews themselves applied the term *mercador* or *koopman* (merchant) with a singular lack of discrimination. A few claimed to be merchants for want of a more specific occupation. The 'merchant' Rephael Montesinos of Venice, for instance, was employed as a labourer in the sugar refinery of Abraham Pereyra. Unlicensed brokers like Juda Obediente, Ishac Brandon, Joseph de Leão, and Isaac Cohen de Lara naturally registered as merchants. But even with regard to those who legitimately called themselves merchants, the category was so broad as to include the multifarious international activities of a Jeronimo Nunes da Costa and the diamond 'peddling' of a Semuel Rosa. Introducing subtler distinctions would hardly be helpful, for seventeenth-century merchants rarely stuck to one type of activity or role. In this respect, the sweeping connotations of the term 'merchant' are an apt reflection of contemporary realities.

At the most basic level, commerce involves the exchange, by merchants and their factors and brokers, of goods between two or more markets at some distance from one another. In the seventeenth century the nature of the goods was perhaps the least significant variable in the equation. Distances and people determined the contours of commerce. Because of advances in communication, transportation, insurance, law enforcement, and international payment mechanisms, a merchant was now able to move goods over smaller or greater distances without having to accompany the wares himself or (in exceptional cases) herself. To trade effectively one needed collaboration between two or more individuals more or less permanently stationed in the markets between which exchanges took place. Notwithstanding the advances mentioned above, distances remained enough of a barrier to make collaboration feasible only between such individuals as could for one reason or another truly trust one another. Legal guarantees were rarely if ever sufficient, in the long run, to establish the kind of trust and collaboration without which international commerce could not function. Primarily, such trust was based upon kin ties or upon mutual interdependence. In short, the commercial enterprises of the Portuguese Jews of seventeenth-century Amsterdam must first and foremost be circumscribed in terms of their routes—the distances between Amsterdam and other markets—and their networks of associates. Neither one nor the other exclusively can make sense of the countless number of transactions recorded.

TRADE CIRCUITS AND KIN NETWORKS

In the seventeenth century commerce was reckoned in circuits. Merchants concentrated, by and large, on whatever goods were exchanged within a given circuit.
The primary circuit, by a very very wide margin, in which the Portuguese Jewish
merchants were engaged comprised Portugal and its dependencies in the south,
and the larger northern European market encompassing Rouen, London,
Antwerp, Amsterdam, and Hamburg. In principle any exchange or combination of
exchanges between one of the northern ports and one in the south might be
involved. Thus goods might leave Hamburg to be delivered in Lisbon, and a
return cargo be picked up in Madeira to be returned to Amsterdam. In practice
political obstacles as well as seasons determined more precisely the preponderance
of any given route at any particular time. No individual merchant or commercial
firm, moreover, ever truly covered the entire circuit. But as a group, as a small
mercantile colony whose members interconnected with one another and with the
neighbouring settlements—in ways yet to be determined—the Amsterdam
Portuguese Jewish merchants became a major component of an increasingly
important and complex commercial circuit.

The viability of the Portugal–Holland circuit was first explored by Christian
merchants from the Dutch Republic in the last quarter of the sixteenth century.
These Dutch merchants established a minor presence in various Portuguese ports,
much as the Portuguese New Christians were to do on a larger scale in the north.[1]
The circuit's economic viability was founded on Portugal's increasing needs to
export its colonial wares and to import wheat during ever more frequent times of
harvest failure. Especially during the 1590s Portugal and the Azores—whence the
mainland imported wheat whenever its own production fell short—suffered a
series of bad harvests (as did other parts of the Mediterranean) which made the
country semi-permanently dependent on imported cereals.[2] Northern Europe,
meanwhile, was rapidly developing a sweet tooth and utilized various raw
materials from Brazil, the Azores, and East India for dyestuffs. Amsterdam as
an entrepôt was always looking for new export opportunities, and the industrial
producers of other northern European towns found eager buyers for their output
in southern Europe and the transatlantic colonies. The ingredients of this circuit
are somewhat different from those that had formed the basis of a Portugal–
Antwerp circuit during the sixteenth century. The latter had been governed to a
very large degree by Portugal's needs to distribute the rich cargoes of Asian spices
(especially pepper), traffic which was at that time largely monopolized by the
Portuguese king. Then, too, harvest failures were not yet a semi-permanent
feature. Sugar was on its way to becoming a very important Portuguese commodity

---

[1] IJzerman (ed.), *Journael*, p. xxiv; Nanninga Uitterdijk, *Een kamper handelshuis*.
[2] Mauro, *Le Portugal et l'Atlantique*, 294–306, and tables, pp. 308–17, illustrating the rise in wheat
prices during the 1590s.

on the Antwerp market, but this was primarily 'old' sugar from the traditional cultivation areas of the Canary Islands, São Tomé, Madeira, the Azores, and North Africa. The real boost in Brazilian sugar production made itself felt in the 1580s, at about the same time that the Dutch rebels began increasing their pressure on Antwerp.[3] As most goods were now to be transported over land, the Dutch blockade of Antwerp in 1585 and subsequent measures to impede its commerce were more successful against high-bulk items like sugar than against smaller ones such as pepper or precious stones. The Dutch measures were at first not sufficiently threatening to induce Antwerp Portuguese merchants to close down their offices in that city. The viability of a Portugal–Amsterdam circuit emerged not as an alternative to Antwerp but as an addition. It was to take another fifty years for Amsterdam and especially London to oust Antwerp from this circuit completely and permanently.

The first Portuguese merchants to settle in Amsterdam were not immigrants from Antwerp nor even primarily representatives of the major Antwerp Portuguese firms. They were merchants, especially from northern Portugal, who had been most actively engaged in the Brazil trade. Indeed, a surprisingly large number had personally lived in Brazil shortly before settling in Holland. There was in Portugal itself a real rivalry between the port of Oporto and that of Lisbon. Oporto had been particularly instrumental in the exploitation of Brazil, 'the accidental colony', originally used as little more than a way station along the *carreira da India*. Most of the major merchant bankers who were involved in Crown contracts resided in Lisbon and had considered Brazil at first too small to bother with. Thus it fell, to a significant degree, to the Oporto community by default. In 1622 Portuguese merchants in Amsterdam confirmed, in a so-called *deductie* (memorandum) to the admiralty, the supremacy of Oporto and Viana in the Brazil trade as follows: 'This agreement [by which the States General allowed them to trade with Portugal and Brazil] inspired a great many burghers and inhabitants of this land to conduct a large trade with Brazil, with their ships and manufactures, most made in this country, in conjunction with the Portuguese via the kingdom of Portugal; principally via the cities of Viana and Oporto, more so than via Lisbon, as the King of Spain imposed a higher levy on the sugar there than in the said cities of Oporto and Viana.'[4] The relative prominence during the earliest period of Portuguese Jewish trade of Viana, Oporto, and Aveiro (see Appendix, Table A.1) corresponds directly to the immigration of merchants from the northern province of Douro-e-Minho.

Trade between Holland and Portugal was not without its hazards. Portugal,

---

[3] The first sugar mill in Brazil started operations in 1542. By 1585 Pernambuco had sixty sugar plantations in operation. See Lockhart and Schwartz, *Early Latin America*, 189.

[4] IJzerman (ed.), *Journael*, 99. The letter from which this passage is taken forms part of the same debate about the status of the Portuguese merchants as hostilities resumed as reflected in the requirement of 1621, quoted above, that Portuguese Jewish merchants register their insurance policies. See pp. 22–3 above.

which had been annexed by Philip II of Spain in 1580, was forced to implement the same measures—various prohibitions on trade with the enemy—that the Spaniards had imposed against the Dutch rebels. But these restrictions, as prohibitions inevitably do, also created opportunities for enterprising individuals who found ways of circumventing the embargoes. The means were fairly easy to come by. A ship travelling under other than a Dutch passport was able to sail safely past Spanish and Portuguese officials—officials who, moreover, were quite susceptible to bribes and who, especially in Portugal, were often not quite as committed politically as a modern reader might deem proper. A foreign passport might be obtained by chartering a German, English, Scottish, or French ship and having the voyage actually commence abroad or merely having it seem in the papers as if it had. The 1622 *deductie* adds the following vivid details:

In order to facilitate this trade [between the Republic and Brazil] many good and trustworthy Portuguese, mostly from Viana and Oporto, offered the merchants of this country a helping hand and conducted this trade conjointly and in their name. Their loyalty to this country was indeed so great that, during the war, when all our ships and goods were in their name and under their control, they could have—had they so desired—kept them for themselves and we were in no position to claim them back . . . They made such a good record, proof, and account of the freight our ships had earned as well as of the profits of our manufactures, as if they had been our fathers and had lived amidst us. The magistrature of Viana itself shut one eye and secretly warned our associates and factors to guard them from damage by the Spaniards. Just now, three days before the end of the Truce, they decreed publicly in our favour that every Portuguese who owed us anything was to pay us promptly . . . Thus many Netherlanders were paid their debts; which in many years of litigation they would have been unable to collect.[5]

In so far as there were hazards, then, they came more from the measure of uncertainty engendered by the politically inspired legislation than any serious impediment to traffic. Uncertainty, however, must not be underestimated as a feature that might discourage trade. Only such merchants as were very securely connected with partners at the other end of the trade route were likely to be able to surmount and even profit by these circumstances. Thus it may have been that the Portuguese Jewish merchants who did venture in this area gained a decided advantage over their Dutch counterparts.

Prior to the Twelve Years Truce, only one other circuit drew Portuguese Jewish involvement and that was the grain trade with Italy in 1606–8 (see Appendix, Table A.1). Earlier in the 1590s, when Florence had been in dire need of grain imports, the duke had turned to the Antwerp Portuguese firm of Ximenez. Rumour had it that the Ximenez had raked in profits of 300 per cent in the emergency operations to relieve Florence.[6] In 1606–8 all shipments (by a Portuguese Jewish merchant) of grain and beans from Amsterdam to Livorno (primarily) and Venice were ordered by one man, Manoel Carvalho, who, as far as can be

---

[5] IJzerman (ed.), *Journael*, 99–100.   [6] Pohl, *Portugiesen in Antwerpen*, 151.

established, had no relations of any sort with the Antwerp Portuguese. Carvalho (born c.1565) had spent part of his earlier years in Brazil and had settled in Amsterdam in 1604. He was a bachelor and had a child by a Dutch servant. Most of his trade concerned the importation of Brazilian sugar via Oporto, where he had a relative, Paulo Mendes Carvalho. The names of his associates in Italy are not mentioned, and the precise origins of this expansion beyond the Portugal–Holland circuit remain obscure. It was undoubtedly a spin-off from the Portugal–Italy circuit, recently established and firmly managed by New Christians in Portugal and expatriate Portuguese Jewish brethren in Livorno and Venice. Although these and many other Dutch shipments signalled a new phase in the expansion of Dutch trade throughout the Mediterranean, the Portuguese Jewish merchants of Amsterdam at first played only a peripheral role, contrary to the opinion of an eighteenth-century observer who wrote: 'It was only in 1612, in imitation of certain Jews who had taken refuge among them, and who had it was said set up counting houses everywhere, that the Dutch began to set up their own and to send their ships all over the Mediterranean.'[7]

As mentioned above, the Amsterdam settlement coincided with others in Rouen, Middelburg, London, and Hamburg. In some instances the alternative settlement attempts were made by the same families, in others they concerned different but similar individuals. By and large, these various colonies, including that of Antwerp, collaborated rather than competed with one another. All shared the need to surmount the handicaps of the various trade embargoes that had been issued. Networks of relations—many personal, others commercial—were formed, and their necessity, stability, and success are what made the Portuguese Jewish/New Christian diaspora of northern Europe a diaspora. The operations of Duarte Fernandes, born in Oporto in 1541, will serve as an example. Fernandes settled in Amsterdam in 1598 with four of his sons. Another son, Antonio Fernandes Homem, remained in Portugal, in Lisbon, until 1604, when he joined his father. Two others, Manuel Lopes and Simão Henriques, settled in Florence or Livorno. Simão subsequently settled in Madrid. Of the four sons who came with Duarte Fernandes to Amsterdam, Bento Rodrigues stayed with his father as his assistant. Miguel Lopes Fernandes and Francisco Fernandes Homem travelled back and forth between Antwerp, Amsterdam, and Hamburg as business required. Gaspar Lopes Henriques returned to Lisbon. Thus this small family was able to build a miniature network covering the major bases of the northern Europe–Portugal circuit as well as the Portugal–Italy circuit. Few families, of course, counted as many as seven sons. More often than not miniature networks of this sort consisted of two or three families, intermarried and interchanging stations within the circuit as the situation warranted. If not actually created by kin relations, the burgeoning diaspora comprising Hamburg, Amsterdam, Antwerp, and Rouen (and, later, London) soon came to be reinforced and maintained by intermarriage. It became,

---

[7] Quoted in Braudel, *Mediterranean*, i. 641.

indeed, one fairly large supranational town of some considerable magnitude. The communities of Hamburg and Amsterdam in particular formed an axis against which the Spanish and Portuguese trade embargoes proved singularly ineffectual. One supplied the goods, the other the transportation and the legal papers; other combinations were applied as needed. The technique, certainly, was not new. Its application throughout much of the seventeenth century on a larger than individual or temporary scale is one of the major distinguishing features of the new Portuguese Jewish diaspora.

If it grossly distorts reality to view Portuguese Jewish history too narrowly from one city's perspective only, it would likewise be a grave mistake to chart the subsequent evolution of Portuguese Jewish trade in northern Europe in isolation from developments in Portugal and Spain. In fact, during most of the first half of the seventeenth century, the northern European Portuguese merchants were the lesser partners of the Iberian merchants who controlled most of the circuit. It was not political developments so much as what happened to these Iberian merchants that determined the direction the trade of Amsterdam's Portuguese merchants would take.

The Twelve Years Truce of 1609–21, during which all previous trade restrictions in Spain and Portugal were lifted, set in motion the full blossoming of Portuguese Jewish trade. The period coincided with an increased immigration from Portugal and the simultaneous migration of many Portuguese New Christians to Spain and the Spanish colonies in America. These movements of so many people could not fail to produce an intensification and broadening of trade. Many merchants, in fact, were so encouraged by the new security that attended their trade that they purchased ships or shares in ships to sail between Brazil, Portugal, and the north. Portugal itself was solidly covered from the northern ports of Viana and Oporto to the southern harbours of Lagos, Portimão, Albufeira, Faro, and Tavira (see Appendix, Table A.1). Especially significant was the inclusion of Setúbal and its salt exports in the circuit. This came about as the result of an increased interest in Amsterdam on the part of the Lisbon–Antwerp merchant bankers, who controlled many of the Crown contracts. Several important firms decided to dispatch a factor to Amsterdam to explore the new opportunities. Miguel de Pas represented the Antwerp firm of André de Azevedo & João de Pas. Bento Osorio, who very rapidly grew to be the wealthiest member of the Portuguese Jewish community in Amsterdam, was the factor of the famous de Pinto firm. He settled in Amsterdam in 1610. As the factor of André Lopes Pinto, *contratador* of the supplies for Tangier and Ceuta, two Portuguese garrison towns in North Africa, and of the new salt and brazilwood contracts, Bento Osorio soon presided over trade activities surpassing those of any of his fellow Portuguese Jews. In the three years 1616–18, he freighted some 200 ships, hauling salt from Setúbal (some also from Aveiro and Castro Marim) to Flanders, Holland, and the Baltic ports of Riga, Königsberg, and Danzig; shipping in return rye, wheat, wood, and ammunition either directly from the Baltic region (grain) or Norway (wood), or from Amsterdam to Tangier and Ceuta. These were exceptional shipments characteristic of the large merchant bankers who controlled the Portugal–northern Europe circuit. In addition, Bento Osorio was active in the more common sugar trades between Portugal and Holland, in the north, and Italy, in the Mediterranean. Bento Osorio's settlement in Amsterdam signals that port's promotion into the circuit of the major Portuguese merchant bankers.

It was during the Twelve Years Truce that Amsterdam's Portuguese Jewish trade with Brazil gained its greatest boost and catapulted the community to a new level of commercial significance in the city. Once more the 1622 *deductie* provides us with a close-up view:

During these twelve years [of the Truce] this shipping and trade increased so strongly that annually more than ten, twelve, and fifteen ships were built and rigged out, here in this country, to carry here from Brazil annually thousands of crates of sugar, not to mention the brazilwood, ginger, cotton, pelts, and other goods—mostly via Viana and Oporto, as much as three-quarters by estimation, and about one-quarter via Lisbon; during the Truce in our ships, now partly in ours, under French, English, and Eastern names. This effort has been so successful that in the course of these twelve years the Portuguese caravels have been bested by the competency of our ships and we were able to claim half, even two-thirds, of this trade, thanks to the management of our factors in Portugal, under Portuguese names, who shared part and parcel with us in this trade. Although the King of Spain put several obstacles in our way—prohibited the French, English, and Easterners from bringing the sugar from their lands here, even made them post bail—he was always deluded, as our gifts corrupted his officials; particularly in towns where the magistrature was not well disposed towards the Spaniards such as Viana and Oporto . . . We will demonstrate how different all other commerce of the Spaniards with the West Indies and that of the Portuguese with the Cape Verde Islands, Saõ Tomé, Elmina (Guinea), Angola, Congo, East India and elsewhere was. All these routes are travelled by their own ships. Your subjects have not the least part in it. This shipping and trade takes place for their account only, such that when ships and cargoes are captured, brought to this country, and declared 'a fair prize', the inhabitants of this country, suffer no damage or harm. Things are very different with regard to the ships and goods travelling to Brazil, in which we are mutually and inseparably attached, commingled, and intertwined with the Portuguese and they with us.[8]

The 1622 *deductie* was not meant to give a history of this trade, but to argue the case against the Dutch navy declaring ships captured on the Brazil–Portugal–Holland route 'a good, lawful prize'. Certain facts are, perhaps, overstated in favour of showing the cargoes as preponderantly belonging to merchants residing in the Republic. None the less the overall theme of the highly intimate collaboration between Portuguese and Dutch merchants that helped them secure a dominant position in the Brazil trade cannot be contested. The document honestly shows how this particular form of partnership made it relatively easy to circumvent unfavourable legislation and how unique it was in the scheme of international commerce.

<hr />

[8] IJzerman (ed.), *Journael*, 100–1.

During the Twelve Years Truce the first manifestations of commercial relations with Spain itself made their appearance (see Appendix, Table A.1). They are not particularly dramatic and serve as a reminder that it takes more than the removal of trade restrictions to generate a viable trading circuit. The two areas in Spain with which the Amsterdam Portuguese traded were in themselves relatively peripheral: Galicia in north-western Spain and Málaga on the south-east coast. Galicia was basically an extension of trade with northern Portugal. The Portuguese Jewish merchants supplied primarily wheat, rye, and barley as well as shipbuilding materials to that region. The return cargoes were invariably loaded in Viana or Oporto. Málaga at the beginning of the seventeenth century was the major target of a fairly large number of Portuguese New Christian émigrés. Why it was so has yet to be investigated. Perhaps it offered better commercial prospects, from a Portuguese mercantile and Spanish newcomer perspective: it may not have had the entrenched mercantile establishment that controlled the southern ports of San Lúcar, Cádiz, and Seville; it did not specialize in such a highly desirable and heavily controlled traffic as the wool exports that dominated the northern ports of San Sebastian, Bilbao, and Santander; it was, moreover, the centre from which the Spanish towns of North Africa were supplied and maintained important contacts with Italy. Málaga matched the commercial profile of many of Portugal's merchants and did not too strenuously resist new immigrants with international connections. From Málaga a handful of Amsterdam's Portuguese Jewish merchants imported primarily wine, raisins, and wool. Exports to Málaga were insignificant. The Málaga return voyages complemented voyages to Portugal and Italy in a manner similar to the relation of the Galicia voyages to Viana and Oporto. Essentially, this Spanish trade broadened the southern component of the basic Portugal–northern Europe circuit.

This period of expansion in the south promised more significant changes for the future. For it was during this first quarter of the seventeenth century that the New Christian merchant bankers of Portugal managed to establish themselves on the Iberian peninsula and in the American colonies as a formidable economic force. The first major direction in which Portuguese merchants expanded was southwards into Africa. Commercial relations between Portugal and north-western Africa date back to the fifteenth century. But as North and West Africa underwent changes, so did their relations with Portugal. There was first the increased demand for slaves, generated especially in Portuguese Brazil by the labour-intensive sugar plantations. These demands sent Portuguese explorers down the western coast to Guinea and Angola. Some Amsterdam Portuguese ventured along and sent representatives (so-called supercargoes) to Guinea to sell and buy for the Dutch or the Italian markets.

Further north, the Lisbon merchants established very important contacts with the corsairs of the Barbary Coast and North Africa (see Appendix, Table A.1). The recent expulsion of the Moriscos (forcibly converted Spanish Muslims) in the years after 1609 appears to have laid the foundation for a Portuguese–Morisco collaborative effort (alliance is too strong a word) aimed at preying on the Spanish fleets returning from Spanish America. The subject deserves some day to be examined in depth. The Portuguese merchants who settled in Andalusia found it difficult to gain access to the extremely lucrative but well-protected America trade. In Spanish America itself, however, they were succeeding in becoming major interlopers, that is, merchants who through other than legal, Sevillan channels imported and exported to and from Europe. Some contraband channels ran from Peru through the Argentinian interior to Buenos Aires and Brazil; others utilized the opportunities for trans-shipment offered by the Azores and the Canary Islands; and still others landed European vessels on the Caribbean islands (especially Cuba) whence the goods were transported to Mexico, Cartagena, or Peru. Some manifestation of these connections does surface in Amsterdam in the form of insurance policies and abandonments concerning voyages between Italy and Tunis, Algiers, or Salé. During the first quarter of the seventeenth century these African and American ventures were new ones for the Portuguese New Christians themselves and do not, therefore, as yet reverberate loudly in the still somewhat peripheral Portuguese mercantile communities of northern Europe. But they were establishing certain patterns of trade that, although hard to detect by virtue of their questionable legality, were to become prominent in the future of the Amsterdam Portuguese as well.

For the present, the termination of the Twelve Years Truce signalled a return to the more troublesome years of the early settlement, and many merchants chose to move their headquarters to Hamburg. Duarte Fernandes, for instance, moved to Hamburg, as did, judging by the steep decline in Portuguese Jewish accounts at the Amsterdam Bank of Exchange (Table 2.9 above), approximately 25 per cent of his fellow Portuguese merchants. Indeed, the 1620s witnessed a marked upsurge of German shipping to Portugal. There is also some evidence of financial difficulties suffered by some Amsterdam merchants, possibly as a consequence of the reopening of hostilities. Manoel Carvalho, whose commercial activities were perhaps a little more far-flung than those of most contemporary Portuguese in Amsterdam, was forced to sign over to his debtors contracts that had not yet been completed.[9] The Amsterdam Portuguese, meanwhile, continued to avail themselves of the same old tricks and sail their goods on foreign ships, under false flags, or with falsified passports. Witness the frequent occurrence of phrases like: 'If the bills of lading, freight-contracts, certificates of registry or other documents mention a different country of departure than the Netherlands or a different place of destination than Amsterdam, this will merely be done pro forma because of the war between Spain and the Netherlands.'[10] In any case, the resumption of war proved to be only a temporary disruption. In 1630 Portugal decided that the prohibition against Dutch shipping hurt the Portuguese more than the Dutch and agreed to

[9] NRPJA 2572.   [10] NRPJA 2652.

issue special licences to permit a certain number of Dutch ships to dock at Portuguese harbours;[11] licences which in turn offered a new opportunity for contraband. It does appear that during this period especially, between the end of the Twelve Years Truce (1621) and Portuguese independence (1640), the Amsterdam Portuguese succeeded in gaining on the Dutch merchants. Their personal connections allowed them to circumvent annoying restrictions more easily than the Dutch were able to do; and no doubt the same relatives also had a better grasp of the demands of the Portuguese market and were in a better position to regulate the circuit.

Apart from the tax records of the Portuguese Jewish community, we possess very few truly hard economic data. In 1622 the three Portuguese Jewish congregations then in existence agreed to set up an umbrella organization to take care of the new, poor immigrants flocking to the city and other matters affecting the *nação* as a whole.[12] This organization collected an *imposta* (tax) on imports and exports as well as on a number of other commercial transactions. Recently published figures show that the total volume of Portuguese Jewish trade increased more than four-fold from the 1620s to the 1650s.[13] The most rapid growth occurred between 1637 and 1651, the years of the largest influx of immigrants, in particular because of large numbers of new settlers from Spain and France. Towards the end of the 1650s the total volume of commerce begins to decline steadily until by the early 1670s the level regains that of the early 1640s. The quarter-century from 1640 to 1665 emerges as the heyday of Portuguese Jewish commercial success. These are the years immediately following Portuguese independence in 1640; they coincide, in part, with the West India Company's successes in Brazil; and they gave rise to the most aggressive exploitation of trade opportunities in Spain.

None of that success to come was predictable in the 1620s. What little information we do have for the relatively calm 1620s and 1630s makes it clear that the corsairs of North Africa and the Barbary Coast were rapidly becoming major clients of the Amsterdam Portuguese. A link had first been established by Portuguese New Christians who drew on their northern European factors to supply goods and transportation that were not to be had in Portugal. Through this channel the Moroccan and Algerian privateers bought foodstuffs, textiles, and, especially,

[11] Rau, *Exploração e o comércio do sal*, 165–76.

[12] See below, pp. 182–7.

[13] Vlessing, 'Portuguese-Jewish Merchant Community', 228. On the basis of these very valuable figures, Vlessing tries to estimate the total value of Portuguese Jewish trade and compare it with other data pertaining to the Dutch East India Company and the city at large. For 1634 she arrives at the following conclusion: 'The Portuguese controlled about 4–8% of the total trade in that year and about 10–20% of the Amsterdam trade, excluding the East and West India Companies, and 3–6% of the total trade and 8–16% of the Amsterdam trade including those companies.' The percentages seem high to me, which is, of course, exactly her point. There are, to my taste and at first glance, too many uncertainties about matters of significant detail to allow one to make the assertions she makes with comfortable confidence. I have, however, not yet had an opportunity to check the details of her calculations and must therefore withhold final judgement.

ammunition and shipbuilding materials. They paid for these imports with the booty acquired in raids on transatlantic and Mediterranean shipping, especially in minted and unminted gold and silver. Most of this bullion, at that time, was then transported in the same Dutch or other ships to Italy, where it yielded, during the first half of the seventeenth century, a higher price than in Amsterdam. Much of this traffic, of course, was conducted primarily on the account of major Lisbon merchant bankers, the same ones who after 1627 became the financiers of the Spanish Crown.

In the late 1610s the Amsterdam Portuguese increased their participation in the trade between Brazil and Portugal as well as, in some cases, directly between Brazil and Holland. Brazil had always loomed very large in the background of the Portugal–Holland circuit, had indeed made it viable to begin with. This latest, more active participation may have come about as the result of the Portuguese Inquisition's crackdown on much of the Oporto mercantile community in 1618. Many of the Amsterdam Portuguese were the immediate relatives and partners of these Oporto merchants and had few options but to try to maintain their position in the Brazil trade through direct involvement. Whether or not the Amsterdam Portuguese were able to extend these activities beyond the end of the Truce is not certain.

In any case, in 1630 the Dutch West India Company succeeded in conquering an important section of north-eastern Brazil, the region where many of the lucrative sugar plantations were located. The plantations were at first destroyed but managed to restore operations relatively quickly. At that time many in Portugal and Spain were convinced that the Portuguese Jews of Amsterdam had played a major role in the Dutch conquest of Brazil. In 1633, in a denunciation before the inquisitors of Toledo, one Estevan de Ares de Fonseca, a relative of Lopo Ramirez for whom he had spent several years working in Amsterdam, told fantastic tales of a Portuguese Jewish company of soldiers that he said had been part of the Dutch invading force. The evidence to date does not bear him or his Spanish contemporaries out. It is quite possible that the company obtained some intelligence reports from Portuguese Jews who had been in Brazil. But the company had been trying for several years to establish a foothold on the Brazilian coast and was probably as well informed about its properties as any Portuguese Jewish merchant. That a few individual Portuguese Jews sailed with the company's invaders as interpreters seems plausible. But neither a few bits of intelligence nor sundry feats of interpretation made a major contribution to the company's success. Nor should we necessarily expect the Amsterdam Portuguese to have been very enthusiastic supporters of the company's scheme.[14] To most merchants on the Portugal–northern Europe circuit the Dutch conquest of a major portion of Brazil could only herald their displacement from prominence in the sugar trade. The Dutch route

---

[14] Kellenbenz, *Participação da Companhia de Judeus*, gives more credence to the denunciation of Estevan de Ares de Fonseca.

would inevitably be cheaper than the roundabout voyages via Portugal, and the competition would be much more formidable.

As we saw, the 1620s and 1630s had seen a fairly constant influx of new immigrants from Portugal, many of whom were refugees from the Portuguese Inquisition. Among these were an increasing number of poor immigrants, and, as we shall see, the communal leaders began, as early as 1622, to discuss measures to cope with the increasing burden of poor relief. Other than the poor in need of communal aid, there were no doubt many who were more or less self-sufficient but, while lacking the commercial connections that the first generation of merchants and factors possessed, were eager to explore the economic possibilities offered in the new context of Holland and its colonies. Many of these impecunious craftsmen and retail tradesmen were the Portuguese Jews of Amsterdam who, later in the 1630s, especially after John Maurice of Orange became governor of Dutch Brazil in 1637, moved to settle in Brazil. They continued, as it were, a Portuguese tradition but on Dutch soil. Menasseh ben Israel, the well-known *haham*, was such a Portuguese Jew who was forced 'by stress of circumstances' to consider this not always attractive option 'for he is far from affluent'.[15] In the end, Menasseh ben Israel did not go, but Manoel Mendes de Castro (in 1638) and Haham Ishac Aboab da Fonseca and Rubi Moseh Rephael de Aguilar (in 1642) led substantial parties of Portuguese Jewish émigrés prompted by similar exigencies.[16] A small number of Brazilian New Christians continued to live on their plantations in Dutch Brazil. Of these, some seem to have converted to Judaism while others remained Catholics. Finally, the Dutch colony in Brazil also attracted some merchants who saw it as a propitious station from which to engage in contraband trade with Spanish America. Duarte Saraiva, a major tax farmer in Dutch Brazil and no mean merchant, maintained relations with known Portuguese interlopers in the Rio de la Plata region such as the Lisbon merchant Jorge Lopes Correa. From Buenos Aires there was a lively, largely illegal exchange with Peru.[17] All in all, the Jewish community of Dutch Brazil, numbering some 850–1,000 in the mid-1640s, may have come to total as much as half the white civilian population of Recife. At the time the Amsterdam community probably had somewhat over 1,300 members. If we assume that about two-thirds of the Brazilian Jewish community had originally migrated from Amsterdam, we see that fully one-third of the Amsterdam community had been drawn to Brazil, a clear measure of the extreme importance of Brazil in the evolution of the mother community.

Some Portuguese Jews who settled in Brazil bought deserted sugar plantations auctioned by the West India Company; others engaged in trade, for themselves or for Amsterdam Portuguese principals, shipping sugar, tobacco, and brazilwood; a few, such as Duarte Saraiva, became tax farmers; and some took the opportunity

---

[15] Quoted in Roth, *Life of Menasseh ben Israel*, 59.
[16] Wiznitzer, *Jews in Colonial Brazil*, 81, 86, 129. Two hundred emigrants are said to have accompanied Manoel Mendes de Castro.   [17] Swetschinski, 'Conflict and Opportunity', 238.

of relative freedom in Brazil to establish retail stores. Thus most Brazilian Jews pursued traditional endeavours, already familiar to them from their Dutch or Portuguese past. While the retail trade may generally have been closed to the Portuguese Jews in Holland, many New Christians had been successful retailers in Portugal before fleeing to Holland. In the end, the Brazilian settlement proved insufficiently attractive to the West India Company, which shifted its interests to the Caribbean and especially Curaçao and the very much more lucrative trade in slaves. It therefore put up very little of a fight to defend the territory when it was reclaimed by the Portuguese in 1654. Dutch Brazil might otherwise have spawned one of the truly great Jewish communities of pre-modern times.

Of course, the Brazilian interlude was significant to the Amsterdam Portuguese as well, some of whom owned sugar mills in Brazil. Domingos da Costa Brandão and his wife, Maria Henriques Brandoa, authorized Joseph de Abraham Lumbroso to travel to Brazil and manage their mill; David do Vale inherited a mill from his brother, Felipe Dias do Vale. The ownership of both these mills seems to pre-date the Dutch occupation. Many more Amsterdam Portuguese availed them-selves of the 'free-trading' opportunities afforded by the West India Company. Almost from the inception of the Dutch occupation of Brazil the company's monopoly had come under heavy fire from so-called 'free-traders' and Brazilian plantation owners who strongly favoured the opening of trade between the Republic and Brazil to free competition.[18] (Trade between Dutch Brazil and other parts—such as the French and English islands in the Caribbean and the Spanish territories in the Gulf or in the Rio de la Plata region—was entirely free.) Excepting provisions (from 1634 to 1638), war supplies and dyewood (from 1634), and slaves (from 1637), Amsterdam interests secured a wide measure of free trade. In exchange for this accommodation, free-traders were to use only company ships to carry their cargoes to and from Brazil (until 1648) and had to pay freight, convoy tax, and other dues to the company. Shareholders of the West India Company received certain minor advantages, so that free-trading encouraged investment in company shares.

As most of the West India Company records were destroyed at the time of its reorganization in 1674, it is impossible to gauge the share of Amsterdam and Brazilian Jews in these free-trading operations. It was no doubt substantial and continued beyond 1648, when the company lifted all restrictions as it had lost interest in the colony. In 1648–52 Amsterdam Portuguese were still privately chartering ships to export (curiously, the contracts do not speak of a return voyage) supplies to Brazil. With regard to shareholding we are only slightly better informed. Few bought shares in the earliest days of the company. Of the 7,108,106 gulden original capital of the West India Company (subscribed between 1623 and 1626), the Amsterdam chapter received subscriptions totalling 2,846,582 gulden, to which eighteen Portuguese Jews contributed a total of 36,100 gulden (1.27 per

---

[18] Van Dillen, 'Vreemdelingen te Amsterdam', 21, 32; Boxer, *Dutch in Brazil*, 75–82.

cent);[19] a cautious but prudent investment in view of the profits reaped by the older East India Company. In the 1630s and 1640s Portuguese Jewish investment in the West India Company undoubtedly increased, if only because it yielded certain small advantages. Truly substantial investments did not come until later, with the arrival in Amsterdam of some major Portuguese Jewish merchant bankers—mostly after the loss of Dutch Brazil. Some measure of the increase may be gained from the published lists of *hoofdparticipanten* (main participants), that is, shareholders owning more than 6,000 gulden in shares: in 1656, of 167 *hoofdparticipanten* seven were Jews (4.9 per cent); in 1658, of 169 listed eleven were (6.5 per cent); and in 1671, of 192 ten were (5.2 per cent).[20] In 1674 the Portuguese Jews constituted approximately 1.5 per cent of the population of Amsterdam and 13 per cent of the account-holders at the Bank of Exchange, so their share of about 5 per cent in the West India Company does not constitute a disproportionate investment. Whether Jewish *hoofdparticipanten* owned larger blocks of shares than their Dutch contemporaries remains doubtful; but it is certain that some Portuguese Jews had invested large sums. Witness the amounts mentioned in the 1674 list: Antonio Lopes Suasso 107,667 gulden; Jeronimo Nunes da Costa 46,200; Jacob de Pinto 42,000; Simão & Luis Rodrigues de Sousa 30,000; and Jacob Delmonte 30,000. The status of *hoofdparticipant* carried sufficient weight for the West India Company to reprimand Peter Stuyvesant, the governor of New Netherlands, for his anti-Jewish measures, at the request of its Portuguese Jewish *hoofdparticipanten*.[21] The directors of the West India Company no doubt knew exactly how much the Portuguese Jews had invested in the company. If they reacted favourably to the request, it was not so much because of the size of that investment as because major participation as such conferred a certain status, putting the petitioners in the same class, so to speak, as the directors.

During the same period, between the Twelve Years Truce and the Peace of Westphalia, an important Spain–Holland circuit came into being. As mentioned above, many Portuguese New Christian immigrants had risen to positions of considerable prominence in Spain. From 1627 until 1647, Portuguese merchant bankers in Madrid were the main financiers of the Spanish government.[22] They were in an excellent position to organize various clandestine ways of trading with their more or less distant relatives—or, more commonly, the more or less close relatives of their family and business associates in Lisbon—in Amsterdam. The Portuguese Jews of Amsterdam were eager to trade with Spain as the embargoes

---

[19] Wätjen, *Judentum und die Anfänge der modernen Kolonisation*, 32–3.

[20] Ibid. 33. Bloom, *Economic Activities*, 126, finds eleven Jewish names on a 1674 list of 111 *hoofdparticipanten*, i.e. *c.*10 per cent. But Abraham Alewijn, Jeronimias Noiret, and Isaac Jan Nijs are most definitely not Jews. Moreover, Simon & Luis Rodrigues de Sousa and Jacob & Moseh Nunes Rodrigues are names of firms and must not be counted as separate individuals. Thus there are at most six Jewish firms (5.4 per cent) on this incomplete list—the same percentage as calculated for the other lists.   [21] Oppenheim, 'Early History', 4–37.

[22] Boyajian, *Portuguese Bankers at the Court of Spain*.

had made such exchanges all the more profitable. They also recognized in the roundabout connections they had with the Madrid merchants a means of gaining an advantage over Dutch competitors who would have a harder time distributing their illegal exports in Spain. Some made use of the subterfuges familiar from the Portugal trade; Manoel Lopes Pereira reported to his superiors in Madrid other tricks employed by Portuguese Jewish and Dutch merchants.[23] Wherever possible, Dutch goods were mixed in with goods from elsewhere to hide their Dutch origins. For instance, Dutch and Flemish goods were hard to distinguish; so Dutch goods were shipped to Calais, whence they were traded to Spain as Flemish goods. The ruse worked because the harbours of Dunkirk and Ostend, from where Flemish goods were normally exported to Spain, were under a Dutch blockade, and Flemish goods had therefore also to be shipped from the French and neutral harbour of Calais. Similarly, Dutch and north German linens and woollens were very much alike, and Dutch cloth was thus billed as German and easily passed Spanish inspection. Many of the major articles traded between Holland and Spain could be readily disguised without too many additional costs. As early as 1621 reports circulated about an extensive contraband network connecting Amsterdam to Madrid via Bayonne and Saint-Jean-de-Luz in south-western France.[24] In May and September 1621 a Spanish customs official warned the Madrid Council of War that Dutch cloth was being unloaded at Bayonne for transportation to Castile via Pamplona and the *puertos secos* (custom stations in the Castilian interior). 'Portuguese merchants in Holland and at Bayonne' were behind the scheme, acting in consort with the *arrendadores* (tax farmers) of the *puertos secos* who were 'of the same nation'. What was true of imports applied also to exports. Notwithstanding the efforts of Spanish administrators to close the loophole, it continued to flourish and became the major channel through which Portuguese merchants in Spain smuggled silver and wool to their factors in northern Europe. The Spanish wool trade in particular became a major element of the Portuguese Jewish Spain–Holland circuit and eventually gained a status equal to that held by sugar in the pre-1630 days.

The Portuguese rebellion of 1640 served to infuse the Portugal–Holland circuit with new energy (see Appendix, Table A.2). The Dutch conquest of north-eastern Brazil had done much to throw the circuit off balance. The independent Portugal of 1640, however, was in dire need of war materials, and few suppliers were willing to advance moneys under the prevailing insecure conditions. Here the Portuguese Jews of northern Europe stepped in and seized the opportunity not only of making a profit but also of improving their status, politically and economically, within the new Portugal by putting the new regime in their debt. In 1649 (after the rebellion of Portuguese plantation owners in Dutch Brazil that inaugurated the demise of the rival colony) Portuguese New Christian merchants were able to pressure the government into accepting the foundation of a monopolistic Companhia Geral do

---

[23] Israel, 'Manuel López Pereira', 118–19.   [24] Israel, 'Spain and the Dutch Sephardim', 20–1.

Comércio do Brasil.[25] This company was to have exclusive rights over the importation of wine, olive oil, flour, and salted fish to Brazil and over the collection and
exportation of brazilwood. The merchants were also able to extract a temporary
suspension of the Inquisition's confiscatory powers. The organization of the
Companhia is reminiscent of the Dutch trading companies' monopolies and
undoubtedly owed much to the conversations Frey António Vieira had in
Amsterdam with several important Portuguese Jews and the correspondence
between Amsterdam and Lisbon merchants. Portuguese Jews of Amsterdam and
Hamburg may actually have raised considerable funds to help establish the
Companhia, but factual evidence to that effect has so far not been found.[26] Father
and son, Duarte and Jeronimo Nunes da Costa, became representatives of the
Companhia in Hamburg and Amsterdam respectively and derived huge personal
benefits from their efforts on its behalf. In later years, Jeronimo Nunes da Costa
was the major importer of brazilwood in Holland.

The Portuguese Jews of Amsterdam, Hamburg, and Rouen—and especially the
Nunes da Costa family under the inspiration of the brothers Lopo Ramirez of
Amsterdam and Duarte Nunes da Costa of Hamburg—made themselves indispensable to the new Portuguese king and his government. The efforts exerted by Duarte
Nunes da Costa and his brother to obtain the release of the king's brother, Dom
Duarte, who was held hostage by the Spaniards in Milan, symbolize that family's
dedication to the Portuguese cause as well as the trust reposed by the highest govern-
ment circles in this family of renegade expatriates. The 1640s otherwise witnessed
the resumption of a more or less normal exchange within the Portugal–Holland
circuit and, simultaneously, the emergence of increased competition from England.
Much Portuguese Jewish trade with Portugal, moreover, concentrated on the
Azores rather than the mainland. In the preceding decades the Azores had become a
major centre on various contraband routes connecting northern Europe to Spanish
America, Brazil, and Portuguese East India. Amsterdam's Portuguese Jews, it would
seem, were fairly active players in this lucrative game of international contraband.

The Peace of Westphalia may also serve as a convenient turning-point in the
history of the economic activities of Amsterdam's Portuguese Jews. The peace
itself promised obvious advantages in the removal of all obstacles to trade between
Spain and Holland, and explicitly permitted, at the insistence of the States
General, the Portuguese Jews of Amsterdam to participate in this trade (albeit
through non-Jewish intermediaries) without having to fear confiscation of their
cargoes. (The States General's advocacy of the Jewish cause in this instance highlights the prominence the Portuguese Jews had gained in the Spain–Holland
circuit.) Far more momentous, however, were changes in the position of the

---

[25] On the foundation of the Portuguese Brazil Company, see Boxer, 'Padre António Vieira and the
Institution of the Brazil Company'; de Freitas, *Companhia Geral*; Révah, 'Jésuites portugais'; Smith,
'Old Christian Merchants'. On Vieira's visits to Amsterdam, mentioned below, see Lucio d'Azevedo,
História de António Vieira, i. 102–6, 129–52.   [26] Kellenbenz, *Sephardim*, 157–8.

Portuguese New Christian merchant bankers of Madrid (and, to a lesser degree, of Seville). The events have been recounted many times. The Portuguese rebellion of 1640 had made the status of the Portuguese living in Spain precarious. From that date the Spanish population, then the Church, and finally the Inquisition grew ever more suspicious of these Portuguese interlopers; a paranoia no doubt aggravated by the contemporaneous rebellion of the Catalans and the instability engendered by the two rebellions occurring simultaneously. The Conde-Duque de Olivares—the Spanish prime minister and, in the absence of any strong royal authority, the effective ruler of Spain—had been the mentor of the Madrid Portuguese; his control of the Spanish government had helped ward off a major backlash. But in 1643 the Conde-Duque fell from grace, and the Portuguese New Christians throughout Spain found themselves without a protector. To make matters worse, taking advantage of the political weakness of these merchant bankers, the Spanish government declared a state bankruptcy in 1647 and thereby abruptly ended the era of the Portuguese financiers. The Spanish Inquisition, meanwhile, began to act on its suspicions with ever greater vehemence and instigated ever more trials, often on the flimsiest evidence, against some of the most prominent of these financiers. These various pressures eventually set in motion a massive exodus of Portuguese New Christians from Spain. In their wake came the migration of Portuguese New Christians from Antwerp, not so much because they were directly exposed to similar negative reactions as because the collapse of the Madrid centre removed their reason for remaining in Antwerp. At about the same time large numbers of Brazilian Jews were returning to Amsterdam. These three substantial migrations shifted the centre of gravity of the Portuguese New Christian/Jewish diaspora irrevocably from the Madrid–Lisbon axis to the triangle of Amsterdam, Hamburg, and (shortly) London.

During the turbulent years of the 1640s and 1650s when these changes were taking place, Portuguese Jewish commerce with Spain reached an all-time high (see Appendix, Table A.2). Portuguese New Christian merchant bankers in Madrid poured large sums of money—formerly reserved for *asientos* (state loan contracts)—into European trade, either in anticipation of their imminent emigration or as a more or less sensible alternative business venture. The Amsterdam Portuguese faithfully acted as their factors until such time as the Madrid New Christians themselves settled in Amsterdam. The high stakes of this commerce drew considerable attention not only from the New Christian and Jewish merchants but also from Spanish government officials, who feared as they had done in the 1620s that behind the link between the Portuguese of Madrid (and Seville) and those of Amsterdam lay sinister schemes to defraud the Spanish treasury.

On his own initiative and by his own means, the Spanish consul in Amsterdam, Jacques Richard, an ambitious and commercially not very knowledgeable native of Franche-Comté, began to investigate the relations between Amsterdam's Portuguese Jews and their Portuguese New Christian correspondents in Spain.

Obtaining most of his information from an Amsterdam notary clerk, Emmanuel de Lavello, who later himself became a notary, he wrote extremely negative reports about what he learned to the Spanish ambassador in The Hague, Don Estevan de Gamarra y Contreras, who in turn reported whatever he thought noteworthy to his superiors in Madrid. Much of this correspondence is still extant.[27] Stripped of their hostile tone and misunderstandings, Richard's reports are a very valuable source.

The Spanish government was particularly keen on preventing goods of 'enemy' origin from entering the country. Portuguese, French, and English merchandise were all at various times declared contraband. At the same time, the peace treaty of Münster (1648) had stipulated that the Spanish customs officials would forgo their inspection of imports if the goods were accompanied by a certificate of origin. Thus were created both the desire and the opportunity for illicit trade. The Amsterdam Portuguese had already been involved, before 1648, in extensive contraband transactions with their Portuguese New Christian correspondents in Spain. The same network could easily be put to use in the new ventures. Most of Richard's self-interested complaints concerned the issuance of false certificates of origin. (Richard exposed the frauds in the hope of being entrusted by the Spanish authorities with the sole right of issuing such certificates; for a small fee, obviously.) 'The more oaths and witnesses, the more falsehood' is how he summed up what in his mind was a sordid affair. The Amsterdam admiralty, lacking competence in Spanish, had entrusted the issuance of certificates to Amsterdam notaries, who, in cahoots with Portuguese Jewish and, no doubt, Dutch merchants, disguised both the Portuguese origins of the Jewish merchants and the enemy origins of the merchandise. In one example cited and witnessed by Richard, a Portuguese Jewish merchant wanted a certificate for Brazilian tobacco being exported to Spain. He was told by the notary that tobacco, as a Portuguese product, was contraband and that it was therefore necessary to claim in the certificate that the tobacco came from the booty of Zeeland privateers who had captured several Portuguese vessels.[28] On another occasion a merchant decided to claim that the tobacco in question had been brought to Amsterdam by Dutch Brazilians at the time of the expulsion of the Dutch from Brazil in 1654.[29] According to Richard's report there lived in Amsterdam a professional falsifier named Juda Machabeu who was able to forge any Spanish or other official document that might be required.[30] Richard also kept a careful record of the Dutch aliases used by the

---

[27] Brants ('Une page de sémitisme'), the first to study some of these documents which were then stored at the Archives du Royaume de Belgique in Brussels, uses the information to questionable, almost antisemitic, purposes.   [28] Brants, 'Une page de sémitisme', 583.

[29] GAA, NA 1552, p. 23 (31 Mar. 1655; J. V. Oli) and many of the certificates drafted in the office of B. Baddel; GAA, NA 977B and C.

[30] The family name Machabeu does occur in Amsterdam. The only Juda Machabeu I have come across was born in 1663 and married Rachel Machorro, of Salé, in 1689: DTB 696, p. 257 (18 Feb. 1689). His father, Moseh Machabeu, was born in Amsterdam in 1640: DTB 684, p. 26 (29 Mar. 1658). Richard may possibly have been referring to Juda junior's grandfather of the same name.

Portuguese Jewish merchants in their mostly illegal trade with Spain to avoid alerting the Spanish authorities to the Portuguese connections of which they were so suspicious. Sometimes a merchant employed two different aliases simultaneously in the same certificate: one as the sender and one as the witness. To cite a few examples of particularly active merchants on the Holland–Spain circuit: Joseph de los Rios called himself Michel van der Rivieren (actually a Dutch translation of de los Rios); Abraham Pereyra, Gerardo Carlos van Naerden; Jacob Delmonte, Jacob Vandenberg (also a Dutch translation); Andres Christoval Nunes, Henrique & Roberto Moyenberg; Manuel de Toralto, Albert Dirksen den Ouden. The use of aliases seems to have been restricted to the Spain circuit. Witness the explicit proviso: 'David Henriques Faro alias and in his Spanish trade employing the name of Reyer Barentsz. Lely.'[31] It is possible by means of these Dutch aliases to measure the share of Amsterdam's Portuguese Jews in trade on the Holland–Spain circuit. Thus it emerges that as much as 20 per cent of this very considerable volume of trade was in Portuguese Jewish hands.

The major Spanish export article traded by Amsterdam's Portuguese remained wool. Most of this wool was exported via the northern harbours of Santander (the primary outlet), Bilbao, and San Sebastian. The Portuguese Jewish merchants proportionally traded more frequently with those ports than did their Dutch competitors (see Appendix, Table A.2): about 50 per cent of Dutch Christian trade with Spain concerned the northern coast, against 70 per cent of Portuguese Jewish trade. About one-quarter of the wool exports handled by Dutch merchants, then, passed through Portuguese Jewish hands. If, as has been claimed, two-thirds of all wool was exported through Dutch channels, the Portuguese Jews controlled close to one-fifth of the country's total wool exports. In addition, Amsterdam's Portuguese imported substantial amounts of silver, cochineal, and indigo, products of Spanish America. Some of these American goods were also obtained more directly either from Central America itself or from trans-shipments in the Canary Islands.

The major Dutch export to Spain in the late 1640s and early 1650s was Brazilian tobacco, none apparently deriving from Dutch Brazil. Because Brazilian tobacco was considered contraband, it was particularly highly prized in Spain. Portuguese New Christian tobacconists in Madrid were major buyers of this product and during the second half of the 1650s were one of the major targets of the Spanish Inquisition. 'There is not a single seller of tobacco in Madrid whom the Inquisition has not arrested. The other day they took away two entire families, both parents and children', noted a Madrid diarist on 23 October 1655.[32] Much of the illegal tobacco trade no doubt collapsed in the wake of these arrests. For most of the second half of the seventeenth century more common goods such as spices and other commodities bought from the Dutch East India Company, wood, cordage

---

[31] GAA, NA 1552, p. 182 (13 June 1673; J. V. Oli).
[32] Quoted in Kamen, *Spanish Inquisition*, 221.

and other naval stores, army supplies, various kinds of linen and woollen cloth, dairy products, and artefacts formed the bulk of Portuguese Jewish exports to Spain.

If the figures in Table A.2 of the Appendix are to be trusted—and I think they are, by and large—the Portugal trade remained the mainstay of the commercial activities of Amsterdam's Portuguese Jews until at least the 1660s. (If it did decline in the course of the second half of the seventeenth century, other trades, with the exception of that with the Caribbean which is discussed below, declined along with it. For, beginning in the 1660s, commerce as such appears slowly but surely to have lost much of its appeal for the Amsterdam Portuguese.) The Portugal trade concentrated in the main on the Lisbon–Setúbal connection and, with surprising regularity, on the smaller harbours of the Algarve (see Appendix, Table A.2). Contacts with the Azores and Oporto were much less significant, and trade with Madeira became an intermittent affair, while Aveiro (except for several salt voyages in the early 1650s) disappears entirely from the commercial horizon. Grain continued to be the major export commodity. During the years in which the Azores had good harvests, Amsterdam's Portuguese even chartered ships to transport its surpluses to the mainland. Increasingly, too, some of the major Portuguese Jewish merchants such as André d'Azevedo & João de Pas, Juan Nunes Henriques, Antonio Lopes Gomes, and Jeronimo Nunes da Costa chartered so-called *deurgaende* (through) voyages between the Baltic and southern Europe, exchanging directly Baltic wheat, barley, or rye against Setúbal salt. Other voyages of this type concerned wood from Norway or Sweden and iron from Sweden. These *deurgaende* voyages are an indication of the degree to which the northern European Portuguese remained vital to the Portuguese economy, yet also signal some measure of decline in the importance of Amsterdam or Hamburg as such, reduced as they were to supplying merely transportation rather than the actual goods exchanged. Increasingly, that kind of intermediation between the Baltic and Portugal was to be undertaken by the Portuguese Jews of London, who were in a better position to handle this trade. Otherwise, the Amsterdam Portuguese contracted to have dried fish shipped to Portugal, either directly from Newfoundland or from England. Not mentioned in the freight contracts—because not bulk items—but undoubtedly important were various kinds of cloth and sundry artefacts. In return, the Portuguese Jews imported figs, almonds, fruit, wine, and olive oil (from the Algarve), salt (mostly from Setúbal, but also from Aveiro), linseed (from Aveiro), sumac (from Oporto), and the traditional colonial products such as sugar, tobacco, and dry ginger (from Brazil), woad (from the Azores), and ivory (from Africa), which were loaded in any major Portuguese port.

A variety of factors conspired to bring about the inevitable decline of the Holland–Portugal circuit. Temporarily, during the 1650s and 1660s, until the final peace settlement in 1669, the salt trade suffered from a certain instability (resulting from short supplies, high prices, and wars) and thus weakened the circuit as a

Table 3.2. Salt prices at the Amsterdam
Exchange, 1650–1669

Year	Salt price (gulden)[a]	No. of Dutch ships[b]	No. of *moios*[c]
1650	352.20		
1651	432		
1652	474		
1653	698		
1654	831		
1655			
1656			
1657	309		
1658			
1659		69	33,640
1660		68	27,953
1661	426	98	60,079
1662	362.70	145	85,876
1663	345	135	76,669
1664	357.30	114	62,323
1665	666.60	12	7,168
1666	978.75	42	22,433
1667	987.38	42	22,738
1668	1,080	108	60,852
1669	377		

[a] The salt prices are per hundredweight of 404
measures. The figures are derived from Posthumus,
Nederlandsche prijsgeschiedenis, i. 92–3.

[b] Figures in Rau, *Exploração e o comércio do sal*.

[c] One *moio* equals 828 litres.

whole. The figures in Table 3.2 make the point clearly. After the 1669 settlement, in which Portugal committed itself to making reparations in the form of salt and salt dues, normal traffic resumed. Between 1680 and 1690, of some 1,500 ships that loaded salt at Setúbal, 1,069 were Dutch.[33] In the 1670s and 1680s only the largest of the former Portugal merchants were still in business, and most of the salt trade in those years was controlled by Jeronimo Nunes da Costa, the political and commercial agent of the Portuguese Crown in the Republic. The problems in the trade of the other major export article, sugar, were more serious. The Portugal sugar trade had been in jeopardy ever since the Dutch conquered the north-eastern section of Brazil. After the Dutch lost Brazil, from about the mid-1660s, imports of Caribbean sugar became a formidable competitor and eventually edged most Brazilian sugar out of the Amsterdam market. As the sugar trade had once been the very heart of the Portugal–Holland circuit, its decline created a serious imbalance and caused the stagnation which would have doomed the circuit even if other factors had not contributed as well.

[33] The other ships included 169 English, 70 German, 60 Norwegian and Danish, 38 Swedish, 10 Spanish, and 6 French.

Around the middle of the seventeenth century the balance of Portugal's north–south trade had begun to shift to England.[34] By means of two favourable treaties concluded in 1642 and 1654—such as the Dutch were only able to conclude in 1661—England had consolidated its position as Portugal's major client for agricultural and colonial products, filling the vacuum created on account of the Dutch conquest of Brazil. England had earlier figured as Portugal's major supplier of dried fish, a much appreciated source of protein in Portugal and the colonies, and even in the first half of the century England had had a slight edge over the Dutch in trading with the Algarve, an advantage which became steadily more pronounced from the 1640s onwards.[35] By the 1680s English ships outnumbered Dutch ones even in the port of Lisbon.[36] The emergence of England as Portugal's major trading partner was no doubt one of the major changes in the international commercial configuration of Amsterdam's Portuguese Jewish merchants that inspired some to establish a settlement in London.

Finally, and this was a factor affecting the Spain trade as well, the declining numbers of new immigrants from the Iberian peninsula meant a weakening of those personal ties so vital to seventeenth-century trade circuits. The nature of the religious climate of Portugal and Spain prevented any large-scale movement of New Christian or Jewish merchants back and forth between the mother country and the expatriate colonies. The movement of people was one-directional, away from the Iberian peninsula. This emigration, moreover, tended to include fewer and fewer substantial merchants as the century wore on. Thus the various circuits operating between Holland and the Iberian peninsula suffered on three counts: first because émigrés were not truly able, through personal contacts or an effective marital strategy, to establish new contacts; second because Portugal and Spain were, as a result of the intensified persecutions of the inquisitions, losing much of their commercial class and reducing the potential pool of new contacts; third because the latest immigrants were not of the kind to bring with them connections upon which others in the community might have been able to draw.[37] It is telling that only a merchant like Jeronimo Nunes da Costa was able to maintain and even expand his Portugal trade. In his case, his official function as an agent of the Portuguese Crown and a representative of the Companhia Geral do Comércio do

---

[34] Shillington and Chapman, *Commercial Relations*, 205–26.

[35] Rau, 'Subsidios para o estudo do movimento dos portos de Faro e Lisboa', 236–7.

[36] Ibid. 241, 253.

[37] The general deterioration of the Dutch–Portuguese trade balance is unmistakably reflected in the decline of the exchange rate of the cruzado: from 103 groats (40 groats = 1 gulden) in 1642, to 81 groats in 1645, to 66 groats in 1668, to 59 groats in 1677, to 50 groats in 1692; it remained slightly below 50 groats throughout most of the eighteenth century. Posthumus, *Nederlandsche prijsgeschiedenis*, i. 590–5. The figures for the 1660s (not in Posthumus) may be found in Bibl. Nat. Paris, MSS Portugais 25, p. 483: 'Copea do parecer e exemplos mercantis que dej [Jeronimo Nunes da Costa] em Flamengo ao Pensionario sobre a duvida dos Cruzados.' Jeronimo Nunes da Costa had made this presentation to John de Witt at the time of the negotiations concerning the 1669 treaty in which the aforementioned reparations in the form of salt were determined.

Brasil make up for what he had lost in personal contacts. Most of his commercial relations were with merchant bankers with whom he had had to deal in one of his official capacities. After his death in 1697 no Portuguese Jewish merchant in Amsterdam was ever to come anywhere close to the scope of his commercial dealings with Portugal.

The second half of the seventeenth century witnessed two Portuguese Jewish trade initiatives that made up somewhat for the losses in Portugal and Spain: settlement and trade in London and in the Caribbean. Both occurred in the course of the 1650s and are to some degree interrelated. In those years the Amsterdam community had gained by immigration the important addition of very wealthy refugees and émigrés from Spain and Antwerp. Several had been involved in various aspects of the America trade before their migration and were thus familiar with its potential as well as with its ways and, especially, its byways. In the early 1650s many Portuguese Jews returned from Brazil with substantial gains they had made there. Several had been engaged, while in Brazil, in the trade with Spanish America. At the same time, because of Spain's war with Portugal and its government's refusal to do any more business with Portuguese merchants, the Dutch West India Company was drawn, by Italian merchant bankers who had bought the slave *asiento*, into the supply of slaves to Spain's American colonies. The company turned the neglected and barren island of Curaçao into a major slave entrepôt and sent ships from there to the harbours of Central and South America. This official slave trade provided, at times, a perfect cover for contraband trade of the sort for which the Portuguese New Christians had been known before. In Europe, meanwhile, the impending trade conflict between England and the Republic did not bode well for the future of the main trading activities of Amsterdam's Portuguese in southern Europe. Settlement in England was an absolute necessity for those Portuguese Jewish merchants who sought to weather this storm. As they had previously managed to circumvent trade restrictions by simultaneous settlement in Hamburg and Amsterdam, so the English Navigation Act of 1651 could similarly be subverted through the collaboration of London- and Amsterdam-based merchants working in consort. The Portuguese Jewish settlement in London enabled them both to continue the traditional Iberian trades, as England was rapidly becoming Portugal's major trading partner, and to expand their Caribbean operations beyond the Dutch islands and gain entrance to Jamaica and Barbados where the English were busily expanding sugar and (to a lesser degree) tobacco production and from which some contraband operations might also be mounted.

As is well known, settlement neither in London nor in the Caribbean, not even on the Dutch island of Curaçao, proceeded without protests from competing commercial interests. By the 1650s, apparently, the fame of Amsterdam's Portuguese as international merchants had grown so significantly—no doubt somewhat beyond proportion—that rival merchants, not without a heavy dose of religious hypocrisy, sought to block their initiatives in England and the Caribbean. If the

Amsterdam Portuguese none the less succeeded, it was because, for the officials of the English government and the Dutch West India Company making the ultimate decision, the stimulation of commerce and all that that entailed in the international political arena was far more important than which particular individuals were going to benefit from it.

The Caribbean and London settlements came to play different roles in the continuing evolution of Amsterdam Jewish enterprise. Whereas formerly Iberian and Latin American ventures were often linked, after 1648 this proved to be less and less the case. Maintaining whatever was left of the Portugal and/or Spain–northern Europe circuit became a joint Amsterdam–London effort. Holland continued to import Spanish wool and some of the Portuguese export goods needed for local consumption, while England eventually became the main distribution centre of most other goods from the Iberian peninsula. The Spanish New Christian merchant Felipe de Moscoso of Alicante, for instance, was already trading more extensively with London than with Amsterdam during the 1660s and 1670s.[38] As far as goods exported to the Iberian peninsula were concerned, the balance of Dutch and English cloth and other manufactures was probably fairly even. Trade between London and Amsterdam was a by-product and restricted almost exclusively to jewels and precious stones. Especially after the ascension to the English throne of William III of Orange in 1688–9, this commercial collaboration in the jewellery trade between Amsterdam and London grew into one of the major endeavours of the Portuguese Jewish diaspora of northern Europe. Originally little more than a branch of the Amsterdam-centred diaspora, the London Portuguese Jewish community became a fully fledged partner only in the eighteenth century.

The Caribbean islands of Curaçao, Jamaica, and Barbados harboured an estimated total of several hundred Portuguese Jewish families in the 1680s—their sum is unlikely ever to have exceeded 1,000 individuals. This veritable mini-diaspora played a disproportionately large role in the commercial evolution of the Dutch and English Caribbean.[39] Curaçao in particular, always better stocked with European goods than the English islands and the slave entrepôt of the Spanish colonies throughout the remainder of the seventeenth century, proved extremely useful. The contraband opportunities afforded by Curaçao's and Jamaica's propitious locations, geographically, commercially, and politically, were so substantial as to attract the major Portuguese Jewish merchants of Amsterdam and, to a lesser degree, of London, and especially some who had been involved in the Latin American trade prior to settlement in northern Europe. Much of the intelligence reporting of the Spanish consul Jacques Richard concerned these contraband activities in the Caribbean, which afforded a most welcome outlet for much of the

[38] Kamen, *Spain in the Later Seventeenth Century*, 140–4.
[39] See esp. Fortune, *Merchants and Jews*, esp. 99–150; Loker, 'Jewish Presence, Enterprise and Migration Trends in the Caribbean'; Swetschinski, 'Conflict and Opportunity'.

capital the most recent immigrants from Spain, Antwerp, and Brazil had brought with them to Amsterdam. Some of the goods smuggled in volume by the Caribbean Portuguese were cacao and tobacco from Caracas and cochineal, indigo, and various dyewoods from Central America. The Caribbean and European Portuguese Jews even came close to monopolizing much of the cacao trade, and the fame of the Portuguese Jewish *chocolatiers* of Amsterdam was widespread in seventeenth-century northern Europe. The Spanish ambassador in The Hague considered it a singular honour to receive a gift of Pacheco chocolates. However difficult it may be to obtain any reliable figures on the contraband trade, the returns on these investments must have been among the highest available.

Within the Caribbean, and especially on the English islands, the contraband activities of these Portuguese Jews met with a great deal of resentment, not from the authorities but from mercantile competitors. More often than not the smuggling took place with the connivance of, if not in active collaboration with, the Dutch West India Company and the English South Sea Company. The competitive edge of the Portuguese Jewish merchants over the local English merchants, even in other areas of trade, as a more or less direct result of their prominence in the contraband trade, gave rise to bitterness. The major share of the sugar trade was mostly in the hands of London merchant bankers and local planters, but large shares of other trades fell into Portuguese Jewish hands by virtue of their connections with the Spanish colonies and the level of organization that connection entailed: the organization of major supply routes between the Caribbean and the European metropolis, of a warehousing system, and of intra-Caribbean exchanges. Locally, in intra-Caribbean trade, the Portuguese Jewish merchants succeeded in becoming the main wholesalers and retailers of European dry goods. During the following century or so, these Caribbean endeavours came to occupy first place among the commercial pursuits of the Portuguese Jewish diaspora of northern Europe.

The success of the various commercial activities also lent support to the lasting establishment of a largely agricultural Portuguese Jewish colony in Surinam which might otherwise have languished in the distance of the Surinam interior. Surinam sugar plantations had first been modestly settled by Portuguese Jewish refugees from Dutch Brazil in the 1650s and 1660s, while the territory was under English rule. Neighbouring Dutch-governed territories had also attracted small numbers of Portuguese Jewish planters. When Surinam changed hands in 1675 and came under the control of the Dutch West India Company, the two powers competed to lure these planters either to move to English Jamaica or to remain in Dutch Surinam. Most congregated in Surinam's 'Jooden Savanne', as the settlement came to be known, and many others were subsequently drawn to this unusual settlement up the Surinam river in the bush of Dutch Guyana, some three hours' rowing from the town of Paramaribo. In 1694 the Jooden Savanne counted ninety-two Portuguese Jewish and ten German Jewish families as well as some fifty single individuals; they owned forty sugar plantations and about 9,000 slaves. The Surinam plantations offered the Amsterdam Portuguese some further investment opportunities, but otherwise remained an unusual and peripheral phenomenon of little far-reaching consequence other than as a historical curiosity. The price of Surinam sugar, quoted on the Amsterdam exchange from 1683, was lower than that of other imports and the sugar profits almost certainly paled in comparison with those of the contraband trade of the islands.

Very clearly, Portuguese Jewish commerce towards the end of the seventeenth century had come a long way from the almost exclusive involvement in the Portugal–Holland circuit with which it had started. As Brazil had ceased to be an important supplier of sugar, the bottom had dropped out of the circuit. Trade with the Algarve and the island of Madeira, always an important element of the circuit, continued (see Appendix, Table A.2); but only a major merchant like Jeronimo Nunes da Costa maintained extensive commercial relations with the mother country. His imports of salt and brazilwood were as substantial as they had been in the past and remained so until the very eve of his death in 1697. However, as we have seen, Nunes da Costa's official responsibilities placed him in a uniquely favourable position to pursue this trading activity.

The Spanish circuit that had become so vital in the years following the Peace of Westphalia had also lost a great deal of its erstwhile substance as a result of the migration of some of the major Portuguese New Christian merchant bankers from Madrid and Seville to Amsterdam and London (see Appendix, Table A.2). Some of the major wool importers no doubt persisted in their highly profitable endeavours and, in conjunction with their London relatives, managed for some time to maintain a more or less favourable balance of trade with Spain. But their number began to dwindle as more and more of the wealthiest Portuguese Jews—in other words, the very same individuals who had been so active in the wool trade—chose to withdraw from commerce and live off their investments, enjoying a more aristocratic lifestyle. Some minor connections certainly continued to be explored. Felipe de Moscoso of Alicante, for instance, developed a lucrative trade in soap in association with the Amsterdam Portuguese Rephael de Arredondo. Similar commercial relations were doubtless maintained with the other, less important, provincial centres in which the remaining Portuguese New Christians had sought refuge after the inquisitorial onslaught of the mid-century.

Trade with Morocco and Italy was affected only slightly by the decline of the Portugal and Spain circuits (see Appendix, Table A.2). Although the Moroccan connection may have been initiated by New Christians in Portugal earlier, in the 1620s, the Amsterdam–Salé (and also, later, Santa Cruz) exchanges had rapidly become independent and continued to remain viable as long as the Moroccan privateers continued to prey on Spanish and Portuguese shipping. The corsairs of the Barbary Coast still needed war and food supplies as well as a market for their booty. The Amsterdam–Italy connection had also started as a spin-off from the main Holland–Portugal circuit. Though it never acquired the size of the Moroccan trade, with the growth of the Portuguese Jewish settlement in Livorno and its connections with the eastern Mediterranean it settled down to a fairly steady rhythm (see Appendix, Table A.2). Jacob de Pinto and other equally substantial Amsterdam merchants were the most active pursuers of trade with Italy. Towards the end of the century the Morocco trade seems still to have attracted some individual initiative on the part of enterprising young merchants whose other opportunities, particularly in Portugal and Spain, had become increasingly limited.

The latter part of the seventeenth century also saw the emergence of some measure of trade between the various branches of the Portuguese Jewish diaspora. The jewel trade in particular, originally again a spin-off of the Portugal circuit, became a major independent field of endeavour in which Rouen, Antwerp, Amsterdam, Hamburg, and London merchants (some of whom were Ashkenazi Jews) co-operated on a fairly large scale. The raw materials for this trade (especially diamonds and pearls) were purchased directly from India via London or from the Dutch or English East India Companies, or imported from the Caribbean. Another new branch of commerce that was to gain somewhat in significance during the eighteenth century concerned the Portuguese Jewish settlements of south-western France (see Appendix, Table A.2). At the beginning of the eighteenth century Abraham Lopes Colaso and his relatives established trade connections between Bayonne and Amsterdam; the Amsterdam Portuguese sent to France especially tobacco and cacao and oriental goods purchased from the East India Company, receiving in return small quantities of wine.[40] This French trade, however, never attained much more than tertiary status at best.

The Caribbean trade, as already noted, became the main arena of Portuguese Jewish commercial enterprise during the last quarter of the seventeenth century. In so far as the practice of hands-on commerce had a future among the Amsterdam Portuguese, it was primarily exercised in the Caribbean. Most of the money employed in the Caribbean trade belonged to the wealthiest Amsterdam merchants of yesteryear, while the individuals involved consisted for the most part of the younger cousins and other more distant relatives of that elite which had by and large retired from commerce and devoted itself to the management of its investments and the pleasures of a life of leisure.

INTERNATIONAL ALTERNATIVES TO COMMERCE

After 1648, the second major and arguably more significant turning-point in the economic history of Amsterdam's Portuguese Jews came in 1672. If 1648 brought peace between the Republic and Spain, 1672 forged a true alliance between the

---

[40] Pieterse, 'Abraham Lopes Colaso'.

former enemies—an alliance which radically altered, in unforeseen ways, the options open to the Portuguese Jewish entrepreneurs.

In 1668, in response to the threats and actions of the king of France against the Spanish Netherlands, the States General and England—Sweden's participation was merely symbolic—had entered into a defensive alliance (the so-called Triple Alliance) to thwart French pretensions. In the previous year, Louis XIV had informed the Spanish that he planned to claim—and had indeed moved to claim— his wife's rightful share in the Southern Netherlands, especially her alleged right (according to the law of devolution) to the provinces of Hainault and Brabant. In a secret clause whose contents were soon leaked to the French, the Triple Alliance committed itself to defend the Southern Netherlands in the event of French advances going beyond an acceptable line, namely to include the province of Brabant and certain coastal regions. In 1671 the French, offended by the audacity of the Republic's rulers, entered into a collaboration with the English, who relished the opportunity to deal the Republic's dominance in international trade a decisive blow, and declared war on the States General, attacking first at sea, in vain, and then, in 1672, on land with such success that the Hollanders were forced to flood large areas of low-lying terrain at short distances from Amsterdam in order to halt the advances of the French troops. The French invasion caused a minor revolution in the Republic, leading to the elevation of Prince William III of Orange to the stadholdership of Holland and Zeeland and the captaincy-general of the United Provinces, and the murder of the Grand Pensionary and his brother, John and Cornelis de Witt. A second attempt by the English and French navies to attack Holland from the sea was decisively repelled by the Dutch fleet under the command of its two most famous admirals, Michiel de Ruyter and Cornelis Tromp. In November 1673 the States General, the German emperor, and the Spanish governor of the Southern Netherlands, the Conde de Monterey, formally signed an anti-French alliance—the Hague Alliance—in which Spain committed itself to assisting the States General in liberating the Republic from French occupation and the States committed themselves to defending Spanish lands in the Southern Netherlands. Early in 1674 the French occupation of the Northern Netherlands came to an end and a separate peace was concluded with England. But from 1674 until the Peace of Nijmegen in 1678 Dutch, Spanish, and German troops continued to fight the French in the Southern Netherlands where Louis XIV was unwilling to surrender his claims. The Peace of Nijmegen might have resolved the various outstanding issues between France and the Spanish Netherlands, had it not been for Louis XIV's excessively personal and idiosyncratic interpretation of the peace agreement. Louis's obduracy led to new skirmishes almost as soon as the agreement had been signed, and throughout the early 1680s the Spanish governor continued, under the Hague Alliance, to call on the assistance of the States General and the stadholder, William III. In 1688–9, as a result of unrelated developments, William III ascended the throne of England and eventually, as

stadholder-king, became 'the soul of European resistance against Louis XIV'.[41]
The Nine Years War, from 1688 to 1697, pitted a France insistent upon its
claims in the Spanish Netherlands against all the major powers of Europe: William
III of the Republic and England, the German emperor, Spain and the governor
of the Southern Netherlands, the electors of Bavaria and Brandenburg, the duke
of Brunswick, the landgrave of Hesse, and a number of other German princes.
The protracted, monotonous campaigns of that war, driven by William III
much against the desires and interests of war-weary and tax-worn cities like
Amsterdam, yielded few dramatic results and did little to advance either cause.
The Peace of Rijswijk (1697), therefore, was little more than a concession to
fatigue and boredom and again failed to resolve the underlying issue of French
claims to certain Spanish territories. Eventually, the ever more complex bundle
of claims and counter-claims by an increasing number of participants was
settled, after the War of the Spanish Succession, at the Peace of Utrecht (1713)
between France and England, and that of Rastadt (1714) between the emperor and
France.

These major international conflicts might seem to be far removed from the lives
of the small settlement of Portuguese Jews in Amsterdam. But nothing could be
further from the truth. The tensions and wars created by the French–Spanish
conflict and the Republic's interventions drew several wealthy Amsterdam
Portuguese into the maelstrom of world politics, international finance, and the
high-stakes enterprise of army purveying.

At least two Amsterdam Portuguese had, in one form or another, been involved
in diplomatic affairs prior to the 1672 invasion. Jeronimo Nunes da Costa (alias
Moseh Curiel) had been an official agent—in modern terms, a *chargé d'affaires*—of
the Portuguese Crown since 1645.[42] Moving from Hamburg, he had settled in
Amsterdam at the suggestion of his father, Duarte Nunes da Costa, who represented the Portuguese Crown there and whose brother in Amsterdam, Lopo
Ramirez, had been showing signs of leaning towards Spain. The Nunes da Costas
were a large and substantial mercantile family, particularly active on the Portugal–
northern Europe circuit and its colonial branches in Asia, Africa, and South
America. Almost immediately after the Portuguese rebellion of 1640 the father had
been drawn into helping the Portuguese purchase various war materials and naval
equipment and into negotiations for the release of the Portuguese king's brother,
Dom Duarte, who was held hostage by the Spaniards in Milan. Jeronimo's role in
Amsterdam at first was to assist his father in supplying the Portuguese army and
navy. But Jeronimo was in many respects a very loyal Portuguese subject: 'I will
always show myself a good Portuguese and faithful servant of His Majesty' ('bom

---

[41] Geyl, *The Netherlands in the Seventeenth Century*, ii. 255.
[42] Detailed investigations of Jeronimo Nunes da Costa's diplomatic activities may be found in
Swetschinski, 'An Amsterdam Jewish Merchant-Diplomat', and Israel, 'The Diplomatic Career of
Jeronimo Nunes da Costa'.

portuguez e fiel servidor de Sua Magestade').[43] Beyond his services in purchasing the requested materials he proved himself an invaluable source of information, particularly regarding events in Spain; information he garnered, no doubt, from fellow Portuguese Jews with high-level contacts in Madrid. Information was arguably an even more valuable commodity in the seventeenth century than it is today;[44] for at that time reliable data were hard to come by, with nations increasingly encountering one another on far-flung, even transatlantic, commercial and military battlefields. Advance notice of army and navy movements to these distant outposts, as well as first-hand reports of trading operations, were essential to the maintenance of empires spread across the known world. Amsterdam's Portuguese Jews, as substantial members of the city's transatlantic trading community, were in a position to help and, in so far as the provision of such information did not run counter to their own interests, apparently quite willing to do so.

The Portuguese ambassador in The Hague, Francisco de Sousa Coutinho, recognized Jeronimo's potential and cultivated his collaboration, drawing him into the service of the Portuguese diplomatic corps in north-western Europe. Following the Portuguese reconquest of Brazil, Jeronimo began to play an increasingly important role in the negotiations that were then set in motion between Portugal and the United Provinces, and during much of the 1650s was Portugal's sole representative in Holland. In 1660–1, as an assistant to the new Portuguese ambassador, the Conde de Miranda, Jeronimo played a crucial role in bringing the peace negotiations to a successful conclusion. Somehow, he (rather than his ambassador superior, it appears) was able to move a Portuguese government split between a pro-English faction opposed to a peace with the Republic and a pro-Republic faction towards accepting an agreement that settled more than half a century of conflict. The 1661 peace agreement therefore earned Jeronimo the gratitude of both the Portuguese king, in the form of an annual pension of 700 *cruzados*, and the Grand Pensionary of the Republic, in the form of a chain worth 800 gulden. Between 1661 and his death in 1697 Jeronimo continued to fulfil the normal duties of *chargé d'affaires*, again often as the only Portuguese representative in the United Provinces.

The career of the other Portuguese Jew who had become active in international political affairs before 1672, Manuel de Belmonte, truly took off as a direct consequence of the Spanish–Dutch alliance of 1673. Manuel and his brother Andres, who had settled in Amsterdam around 1650, were not particularly wealthy; they had no direct involvement in commerce and seem to have lost some funds in the course of their migration from Spain to Holland. Little else is known of their background. Andres de Belmonte was the first to make contact with the Spanish ambassador in The Hague, Don Estevan de Gamarra y Contreras. As early as 1660 he

[43] Biblioteca da Ajuda, Lisbon, MS 49-X-24, fo. 339ᵛ (20 Oct. 1645), quoted more fully in Swetschinski, 'An Amsterdam Jewish Merchant-Diplomat', 15.
[44] Roosen, *The Age of Louis XIV*; Mattingly, *Renaissance Diplomacy*, 181–256.

corresponded with the ambassador, in particular on the subject of Jeronimo Nunes da Costa and his and other Portuguese Jews' activities in behalf of Portugal and 'el Tirano', as Spanish officials were wont to refer to King João. Andres's informants in those early days were the same shady characters who had helped the Spanish consul Jacques Richard: a petty villain and ex-convict nicknamed 'the devil of Vloyenburgh', the former messenger boy of Jeronimo Nunes da Costa who had been fired for swindling, and a notary's clerk who was an alcoholic. When Andres died suddenly in early 1666, his duties were assumed by his brother Manuel. Official letters of nomination came only later. In 1671 the Conde de Monterey, governor-general of the Spanish Netherlands, nominated Manuel de Belmonte *agente* of the Spanish embassy in The Hague; in 1676, the same nomination was confirmed by King Carlos II; and in 1679 Manuel de Belmonte was elevated to the rank of *residente* of the Spanish Netherlands. In the same year the emperor and the Hanseatic resident at the court in Madrid raised objections against the Spanish king's employment of Jewish agents in various European cities. The complaints were primarily directed against the Spanish agent in Hamburg, Antonio Enriquez. On 23 December 1679 the Council of State resolved to fire all Jewish consuls, agents, and residents, but deferred, for the time being, its decision on Manuel de Belmonte. 'For the time being' eventually lasted until Manuel's death in 1705.

Even more than Jeronimo Nunes da Costa, Manuel de Belmonte functioned primarily as an informant. He maintained a fairly extensive correspondence—much of which is still extant—with Don Juan of Austria and his secretary, Don Mateo Patiño, with the respective governors-general of the Spanish Netherlands, with the Spanish ambassador in The Hague, and with other Spanish ambassadors such as Pedro Ronquillo in London and Baltasar de Fuenmayor in Copenhagen, reporting on anything of political or military significance that he had learned, whether at first hand or from acquaintances such as the Amsterdam burgomasters Gillis Valckenier and Andries de Graeff, both fairly strong supporters of the coterie favouring the Republic's support of the Spanish Netherlands against the French. Manuel also gave extensive information on the numerous 'illegalities' he discovered in the trade with the Spanish Indies, an area in which he made himself such an expert as later to be able to join in that trade himself. Occasionally he ventured a more personal piece of advice: in 1666 he lobbied for the establishment of a Spanish Crown monopoly on the sale of Campeche wood; in the same year, he argued in favour of a revaluation of the Spanish silver denomination the *patacon*; and in 1667 he argued at length for a massive trade embargo against France. Most of these proposals were clearly self-serving: he saw himself as the agent of the Campeche wood monopoly in northern Europe and as the 'inspector' of the anti-French embargo.

To demonstrate how valuable Manuel de Belmonte's information was to the Spanish officials, we may refer to a minor incident that occurred in 1668. Following the successful negotiation of the Triple Alliance, including its secret stipulations mentioned above, the English envoy, Sir William Temple, returned to his post in Brussels only to learn

that a Jew of Amsterdam had sent him [the governor-general, the Marques de Castel Rodrigo] a copy of them [the secret articles], by which he [Castel Rodrigo] must needs be well informed of our [English and Dutch] mutual obligations, as well as of our intentions, not only to assist Spain, in case of a refusal from France, but to engage ourselves in the quarrel, by an open war with all our forces against the Crown.[45]

And in the years immediately following the French invasion of the southern Netherlands in 1667 Manuel de Belmonte became a very vociferous advocate of a Dutch–Spanish anti-French alliance. It is clear from his correspondence that he spoke at length and with great persistence and vigour with the magistrates of Amsterdam on the importance, for Amsterdam, of such a coalition. When the Hague Alliance eventually became a reality, Manuel de Belmonte's status—as well as that of a small number of other influential Portuguese Jews—took a marked turn for the better.

The small coterie of Portuguese Jewish diplomats, financiers, and entrepreneurs who rose to prominence in the wake of the Hague Alliance does not appear to have had any family or other intimate ties prior to this period. They shared a Spanish rather than a Portuguese background, a fact which in their predominantly—and, until recently, proudly—Portuguese community may have been enough to forge a bond. They had either been born in Spain or had had in their youths direct, personal contact with that country. For instance, Antonio Lopes Suasso, the most prominent of the group, was born and raised in and near Bordeaux, a second-generation émigré from Portugal, but had as a young man been directly engaged in smuggling primarily wool between Spain and France and beyond. Often working in close consort with one another, this coterie became a crucial link in relations between the administrations of the Northern and Southern Netherlands and the Spanish government in Madrid.[46]

It is difficult to be precise about where and with whom the involvement of the Amsterdam Portuguese in these official communications began. Clearly Manuel de Belmonte was the first to have had formal contact with the governments involved. But Manuel was not a particularly wealthy person. It is probable that Manuel's acquaintance with Antonio Lopes Suasso pre-dated 1672 and that Lopes Suasso had been the financier behind Manuel's bid for the agency of the Campeche wood monopoly in 1666. Antonio Lopes Suasso had settled in Amsterdam in 1653 at the time of his marriage to Rachel de Pinto, daughter of Gil Lopes Pinto alias Abraham de Pinto, widow of Ishac Pereyra, son of the famous merchant banker

[45] Sir William Temple, *Works*, i. 367–8.
[46] The coterie eventually and informally attempted to give itself semi-institutional status in the organization of the literary academies, under the auspices of Manuel de Belmonte, the Academia de los Sitibundos (founded in 1676) and the Academia de los Floridos (founded in 1685). See below, pp. 299–302.

and moralist Abraham Pereyra alias Tomé Rodrigues Pereyra (of Madrid).[47] By this marriage Antonio received the handsome dowry of 130,000 gulden. As mentioned above, Antonio had previously been active in the wool trade and continued that pursuit after his settlement in Holland, often in partnership with his cousin Jacob Delmonte. He also imported bullion and Campeche wood from southern Spain and was involved in the contraband trade centred in the Azores. Locally, and often in partnership with his de Pinto in-laws in Amsterdam or his brother Francisco de Liz and cousin Manuel Dormido in London, he was a major dealer in diamonds, precious stones, and jewellery. Together these activities, otherwise not at all different from many another Portuguese Jewish merchant's, made Antonio an extremely wealthy man. Even in 1655 his account at the Amsterdam Bank of Exchange had been larger than that of any other Portuguese Jew. In 1674 an extraordinary levy (of 0.5 per cent of each individual's property) occasioned by the war against France lists Antonio as the wealthiest member of his community, with an estimated—that is to say, a grossly under-estimated—value of 231,000 gulden.

After 1672 Antonio Lopes Suasso became one of the major financial backers of the Spanish government in northern Europe. (He actually began, in the 1670s, to refer to himself as a *marchand-banquier*.) He was, at first, primarily the commissioner of major Madrid bankers, forwarding large sums of money to pay for the mercenary troops supplied by various German rulers and 'subsidies' (i.e. bribes) for the neutrality of others.[48] Thus he was nominated 'Factor of His [Spanish] Majesty in Amsterdam' by the Conde de Monterey on 13 February 1674. In 1675 both Antonio Lopes Suasso and Manuel de Belmonte actively lobbied for, on behalf of the Spanish government, and eventually secured the services of a Dutch fleet under the great admiral Michiel de Ruyter. The Dutch fleet sailed to Sicily (then part of the Spanish kingdom) and chased away the French fleet that had captured the port of Messina. (Michiel de Ruyter was mortally wounded during this campaign, in 1676, and died shortly thereafter.) Manuel de Belmonte had negotiated the basic agreement with the admiralty of Amsterdam, but it was Antonio Lopes Suasso's financial guarantees that persuaded the admiralty to accept the agreement in the face of serious misgivings about Spain's ability to pay for the hire of the fleet. A few years later, while negotiating the Peace of Nijmegen (1678), a rift occurred within the Dutch delegation as a result of Spain's failure to honour its financial commitments to the admiralty. One faction favoured a separate peace agreement between the Republic and France, while the other, led by the prince of Orange, advocated holding out until France and Spain had come

---

[47] For an extensive biography of Antonio Lopes Suasso and his son Francisco, see Swetschinski, 'Worthy Merchants, Keen Bankers, Loyal Courtiers'.

[48] Antonio Lopes Suasso does not seem to have had any major dealings with any of these bankers prior to the 1670s. It is possible that he was drawn into these financial transactions by his in-laws the de Pintos, who had had a great deal of experience in Spanish finance during their Antwerp days, before 1646.

to an agreement. The latter prevailed only because the Spanish ambassador, Don Emanuel de Lira, was able to reassure the admiralty that his government would fulfil its obligations. Without these payments—which, so far as contemporary documents show, were handled by Antonio Lopes Suasso—'the Prince', according to Sir William Temple, 'would have found difficulties to carry on the war without endangering a mutiny at Amsterdam'. The de Ruyter episode shows Amsterdam Portuguese Jewry at its most prominent. In gratitude for their services, the Spanish government elevated Antonio Lopes Suasso to the rank of baron (d'Avernas-le-Gras, a barony in the Southern Netherlands), Manuel de Belmonte to the rank of *residente* (in 1679), and Michiel de Ruyter posthumously to the rank of duke, an honour his family declined.[49]

In the years following the Peace of Nijmegen, Manuel de Belmonte and Antonio Lopes Suasso continued to labour on behalf of the joined cause of Spain and the Republic: that is, the cause of the Republic as it was viewed by the prince of Orange. Undoubtedly the various negotiations of the late 1670s had occasioned several more or less formal encounters between these Portuguese Jews and the prince. Socially, too, they moved in the same aristocratic circles in Antwerp and The Hague. In the 1680s the relationship between William III and Antonio Lopes Suasso and his son, Francisco Lopes Suasso, became a particularly close one. First, on 15 February 1682, Baron Suasso lent Prince William the sum of 200,000 gulden at 4 per cent. He made this loan on orders from the Marques de Castelmoncayo, ambassador extraordinary of Spain, who was seeking to encourage the prince's continued support for the Spanish cause. On 7 March the prince made a passionate speech before the States of Holland, endorsing the Spanish request for support under the Hague Alliance. On 20 March the French backed down, thus rendering the issue moot. And on 15 April the Marques de Castelmoncayo repaid Antonio Lopes Suasso the 200,000 gulden loan (plus 1,333 gulden interest for two months). It is unlikely that the Spanish moneys had radically influenced the prince's opinion, but the incident did forge some more intimate connection between the prince and the Portuguese Jewish *marchand-banquier*.

Antonio Lopes Suasso died on 9 February 1685 and was succeeded, as a merchant banker and as a baron, by his only son, Francisco Lopes Suasso. By and large, Francisco followed in the footsteps of his father. He had married, in 1682, Jeudit Teixeira of Hamburg, daughter of the wealthy merchant banker Manuel Teixeira. In addition to the services he rendered the Spanish government, Francisco Lopes Suasso increasingly aided the prince of Orange, whenever— which was quite often—he found himself in financial difficulty. Thus in 1689–90, shortly after William III had ascended the throne of England, Francisco lent the king at least 1.5 million gulden, possibly to cover debts resulting from his recent

---

[49] De Ruyter's son, however, accepted the title of baron. The family also received a *merced* (benefice) of 6,000 ducados: AHN, Estado, leg. 1702[1] (document dated 9 June 1676); and Balbian Verster, 'Waar was het hof?', 180–1.

campaign, possibly to finance the war in Ireland. This exceedingly large sum is the source of the famous story according to which Don Francisco had given William III 2 million gulden before he sailed for England without asking for as much as a receipt: 'If you succeed,' Francisco is reported to have said, 'I know you'll repay me; if you do not, I'll agree to lose the money.' Wealthy as the Baron Suasso undoubtedly was, there is no evidence that he could gamble 2 million gulden. The story underscores the very special relationship that existed between the king-stadholder and the baron-banker. Henceforth, until William's death in 1702, Don Francisco remained a welcome and appreciated courtier in London and in The Hague.

Perhaps even more significant than the meteoric rise of the Suasso father and son—which after all remained a singular phenomenon—was the emergence of army purveying as a novel Portuguese Jewish enterprise and the exponential expansion of the jewellery trade of northern Europe's Portuguese Jews. The joint war effort in the Southern Netherlands and the provisioning and foraging of large numbers of Dutch, German, and Spanish troops, on an unprecedented scale, called into being a new class of entrepreneurs. Portuguese Jews were not the only merchants to venture into this business, but they do seem to have been among the most competitive and were quite successful. That they prospered in this enterprise was due, no doubt, to their extensive network of commercial and financial relations, not merely between the Northern and the Southern Netherlands—relations they shared with many a Dutch merchant—but also with Spain, which under the prevailing circumstances gave them a competitive edge. With regard to the jewellery trade, the entrance of a substantial number of Portuguese Jews into the court circles of Holland, England, and the Spanish Netherlands gave them ready access to the main clientele for diamonds, precious stones, and jewellery for several decades at the end of the seventeenth century and the beginning of the eighteenth.

Portuguese Jewish army purveying is first and foremost associated with the partnership of Antonio Alvares Machado and Jacob Pereyra. Nothing is known about the antecedents of Machado. Jacob Pereyra, the son of Abraham Pereyra, was born in Madrid in 1629. Jacob's brother, Ishac Pereyra, had been married to Rachel de Pinto, who after Ishac's death had married Antonio Lopes Suasso. Rachel's daughter from her first marriage, Sara Pereyra de Pinto, in turn married Jacob's other brother, Moise Pereyra.[50] The army purveying of Machado & Pereyra required large investments in personnel, money, and time, often requiring the purveyors to be personally present on the scene. As such it runs somewhat counter to the trend away from commerce and towards retirement and the rentier's life. On 23 May 1692, for instance, William III personally informed Jacob Pereyra (in French) that 'as it could easily happen at present that the purveyor Machado will not be able to be in the vicinity of this army [near Brussels], it will be necessary that you come here quickly in order to receive, from time to time, orders which I

[50] GAA, DTB 685, p. 260 (2 Mar. 1663); DTB 682, p. 122 (26 Mar. 1654).

will have to give'.[51] The note seems to imply that it was more customarily Machado who worked in the field, while Pereyra took care of financial and other matters in Amsterdam or The Hague. Whatever their precise arrangement, Machado & Pereyra employed a number of lieutenants who managed day-to-day logistics in the field. Many, if not all, were Portuguese Jews, such as Jacob Pereira da Silva, Francisco de Cordova, Antonio de Caceres, Manuel Mercado Salasar, and Jacob Teixeira.[52] Sometimes the actual purveying of bread to the troops and fodder to the horses involved a fairly elaborate network of mobile 'ovens, wagons, and storehouses'; at other times Machado & Pereyra subcontracted the work to local bakers and merchants. The army purveying activities of Machado & Pereyra extended beyond the Southern Netherlands into Northern Ireland, where in 1689–90 William III fought and defeated James, the Catholic pretender to the English throne. These English and Irish operations were handled by Abraham and Ishac Pereyra and, later, Solomon de Medina.[53] The provisioning of this Irish campaign, according to one source, required at least twenty-eight bakers, 700–800 horses, and some 300–400 wagons.[54]

Aside from these unusual operational dimensions, army purveying entailed a high-stakes financial game as well. Over the years the contracts made—in Brussels, The Hague, or London—ran into the millions of gulden.[55] Much of the time Machado & Pereyra advanced the moneys themselves or with the help of Portuguese Jewish investors. One notarial deed of 1698 refers to a 40,000 gulden investment by Jacob de Mercado, Michiel Senior, and Juda Senior Henriques.[56] There were no doubt hundreds of other such contracts. Government payments were notoriously slow, which caused Machado & Pereyra endless financial problems. On some special occasions they insisted on payment in advance;[57] by and large, however, it was their very willingness to juggle their own and their investors' financial resources to meet governmental arrears that won them the special gratitude of William III. And it was the king-stadholder personally who often insisted contracts be awarded to Machado & Pereyra even though other purveyors had submitted lower bids.[58] Only once, so far as I know, did the financial negotiations between the partners and the English government cause more than ordinary friction. In 1690, on the occasion of a contract for the supply of William's troops in Ireland, Machado & Pereyra asked for payment in advance. The request did not go

[51] The letter may be found among certain uncatalogued letters in the Ets Haim-Montezinos library of the Portuguese Jewish community of Amsterdam. It was published in Meijer, 'Provéditeur Pereira', 151.

[52] Meijer, *Zij lieten hun sporen achter*, 83; Hyamson, *Sephardim of England*, 68; GAA, NA 4081 (3 Dec. 1675; Dirck van der Groe).   [53] Hyamson, *Sephardim of England*, 68.

[54] *Calendar of State Papers, 13 February 1689–April 1690*, 514, 556; *May 1690–October 1691*, 234.

[55] Ten Raa and de Bas, *Staatsche Leger*, vi. 28, 42, 51, 54, 62, 66; vii. 11, 22, 39, 51, 64, 82–3, 108, 123. A fairly complete record of the contracts and payments made by the English government with Machado & Pereyra may be found in the British *Calendar of Treasury Books*, vols. ix–xxiv.

[56] Vaz Dias, 'Approviandeeren', 413–14.

[57] Ten Raa and de Bas, *Staatsche Leger*, vii. 11.   [58] Ibid. 108, 123.

down well with the English officials, who privately aired some ominous complaints of the sort never heard in the United Provinces. On 10 February 1690 the earl of Shrewsbury wrote to the lord mayor of London:

Taking into consideration that the Jews residing in London carry on, under favour of the Government, so advantageous a trade, it was thought that they ought to be called upon to shew their readiness to support that Government by advancing such sums of money under the late Acts of Parliament as they are agreeable to lend. They have been asked what they are willing to furnish towards supplying one of their brethren, Mons. Pereyra, in part of the contract made with him for providing bread for the army and have made an offer only of £12,000 which is below what his Majesty expected from them, and he directs you to send for their elders and principal merchants to let them understand the obligation they are under to his Majesty for the liberty and privileges they enjoy, and how much it is to their advantage to make suitable returns of affection and gratitude for the kindness they have received and may expect. And since the money demanded carries with it more than the ordinary interest allowed, it was supposed they would, without difficulty, raise among them £30,000, or if not that amount, that they could not propose less than £20,000; and his Majesty believes that, upon second thoughts, aided by such representations as your Lordship may make to them, they will come to new resolutions and such as may be accepted by his Majesty.[59]

This forceful expedient seems to have worked, for an entry in the Treasury Book on 11 April 1690 refers to £36,000 to be issued to Mr Pereyra 'out of such loans as shall be made into the Exchequer in the name of Monsieur Pereira'.[60]

Whatever the financial hazards, army purveying was unquestionably a very lucrative enterprise. Investors usually gained a slightly higher rate of interest than was available elsewhere. Antonio Alvares Machado himself fared well indeed. A provisional distribution of his estate shows him to have amassed a fortune of at least 367,656 gulden; and the distribution covered, to all appearances, only a portion of the total estate.[61] Jacob Pereyra, we know, lived a very luxurious life in The Hague, in a house which later was to become the residence of the queen mother. However, while Machado & Pereyra were not the only Portuguese Jews actively engaged in army purveying—in 1675 Ishac Pessoa contracted to supply horses and, in 1676, Jacob Coutinho fodder[62]—none of these other efforts seems to have paid off: indeed, Ishac Pessoa went bankrupt in 1679. To round off this section on the phenomenal successes of a small number of Portuguese Jewish merchant bankers and the subject of Portuguese Jewish commerce in general, the account of Pessoa's bankruptcy affords us a valuable glimpse at the hazards and failures of Portuguese Jewish enterprise during the third quarter of the seventeenth century. Much of history tends to record only the successes, if only because

---

[59] *Calendar of State Papers, Domestic Series, William and Mary, 13 February 1689–April 1690*, 453.
[60] *Calendar of Treasury Books*, vol. ix/2: 576.
[61] GAA, NA 4254B, pp. 1805–16 (3 Nov. 1710; D. van der Groe).
[62] Ten Raa and de Bas, *Staatsche Leger*, vi. 58; GAA, NA 2251, p. 94 (18 Jan. 1677; A. Lock).

failures leave fewer traces. Yet the story of Ishac Pessoa is fairly typical of the average Portuguese Jewish merchant of the second half of the seventeenth century.

Ishac Pessoa, as he was most commonly known in Amsterdam (his Portuguese name was Emanoel Gomes Pessoa), had settled in Amsterdam in the mid-1650s. His father, Jeronimo Gomes Pessoa alias Abraham Israel Pessoa, had been one of Lisbon's more prominent merchants, a member of the small circle who had financed the foundation of the Portuguese Brazil Company.[63] Notwithstanding the freedom from confiscation of property by the Inquisition that the Lisbon New Christian merchants had been able to negotiate in exchange for their participation in the Brazil Company, Jeronimo seems to have feared inquisitorial prosecution and stealthily fled the country.[64] His wife and children followed him in 1651, accompanied by two male servants and two black maids, and the family came to Le Havre in France.[65] The Pessoas probably lived in Rouen for several years before permanently settling in Holland.[66] In Amsterdam, Rifica Pessoa (b. 1641, Lisbon) married Ishac Cohen Caminha alias Simão Correa (b. 1633, Pernambuco) in 1659; Emanoel Gomes alias Ishac Israel Pessoa (b. 1638, Lisbon) married Sara de Pas alias Sara Salom (b. 1636, Amsterdam) in the same year; David Pessoa (b. 1642, Lisbon) married Raquel Cardosa (b. 1642, Lisbon) in 1660; and Moseh Pessoa (b. 1644, Lisbon) married Sara Pensa (b. 1650, Lisbon) in 1664.[67] These marital arrangements do not indicate any prior connection between the Pessoas and other Portuguese Jews of Amsterdam, nor do they reveal an acceptance of the family into the upper echelons of Portuguese Jewish society.

We do not know Jeronimo's financial status at the time of his settlement in Holland, so it is impossible to determine whether or not he lost a great deal in his sudden flight. Unfortunately, he died very shortly after his arrival on 16 August 1661, leaving Ishac Pessoa, aged 23, to establish himself commercially. His activities are best recounted in his own words as he explained his situation to the administrators of the Chamber of Desolate Estates.

As a young man he [Ishac Pessoa] traded, in partnership, for the account of his father and, after the latter's death, for the account of the estate. In 1659, in the month of June, he married Sara Salom, daughter of Michiel de Pas and Rachel Salom, and received a dowry of 30,000 gulden. His father had added to that another 25,000 gulden. With these means he

---

[63] Smith, 'Old Christian Merchants', 239–40. Jeronimo Gomes Pessoa had also been among the financiers of the expedition of Salvador de Sa: ANTT, Inq. de Lisboa, Processo 8132 (Processo de Duarte da Silva). I owe this information to Dr David Grant Smith.

[64] According to testimony before the Lisbon tribunal, in 1651, Jeronimo Gomes Pessoa left Portugal because he had heard that he was about to be arrested. The witness mistakenly thought that Pessoa had fled to Italy: ANTT, Inq. de Lisboa, Processo 10794 (Processo de Francisco Gomes Henriques). On 28 November 1650 Jeronimo was still in Lisbon, for on that day he appeared before the Inquisition as a defence witness in favour of Luis Lopes Franco: ANTT, Inq. de Lisboa, Processo 8187 (Processo de Luis Lopes Franco). I owe both references to Dr David Grant Smith.

[65] Vaz Dias, 'Blik in de Marranen-historie', *VA* 9: 121–2.   [66] Roth, 'Marranes à Rouen', 134.

[67] GAA, DTB 684, p. 144 (28 Jan. 1659); p. 208 (25 July 1659); p. 268 (13 Feb. 1660); DTB 686, p. 101 (20 June 1664).

traded, between here [Amsterdam] and other places, both in merchandise and in bills of exchange, as well as in East India shares, both fixed and option ones. In the course of these commercial activities he suffered many damages and losses.

Thus, in the month of March 1662, he drew up his balance sheet and discovered no longer to own, of his own as well as his wife's means, more than 39,517 gulden in all; over and above his household effects, silverware, and jewels which are also registered in his books and of which he subsequently sold one part and pawned another. The balance sheet of his father's estate having also been drawn up in 1662, that estate was found to total, in good as well as in bad debts, the sum of 107,900 gulden.

Having continued in the afore-mentioned trades he suffered again many damages and losses which were quite substantial in view of [the size of] his capital. In the course of the same trades in shares and other articles, however, he also made a profit in the sum of 45,355 gulden and 9 shillings. At the same time, he has also always needed, in order to effect the afore-mentioned trades, to receive moneys on deposit on East India shares, bills of exchange as well as otherwise, which has caused him excessive damages in conjunction with commissions and broker's fees. Moreover, he has lived here in this city, for the period of nineteen years, which has also set him back noticeably.

Not having been able to collect outstanding debts, he has been forced to withdraw and surrender his books to the Chamber of Desolate Estates.[68]

The attached meticulous list of debtors, creditors, losses, and bankruptcies reveals the full extent of Ishac Pessoa's commercial activities. The single largest debtor—owing 47,355 gulden for bills of exchange and merchandise—was Fernando Rodrigues Penso of Lisbon, probably a relative.[69] Other debtors, outside Amsterdam, resided in Rouen, Hamburg, Frankfurt, Copenhagen, and Barbados. Ishac Pessoa suffered losses on account of bankruptcies of persons in Paris, London, Rouen, and Antwerp. He had shipped cargoes to Oporto, Viana, Lisbon, Archangel, Barbados, and Goa. As far as merchandise was concerned, diamonds, pearls, and jewels are mentioned most frequently; but the list also speaks of Indian cotton, wool, sugar, musk, cloves, and hats. Ishac Pessoa underwrote insurance and owned an eleven-twentieths share in a house in Hamburg and a one-sixth share in a sugar refinery in Rouen. As the above deposition makes clear, his traffic in bills of exchange and East India Company shares was extremely extensive.

Under the heading of losses the document lists no less than 18,243 gulden in interest paid over the years. His parents' household had cost him 46,314 gulden, his own about 34,000 gulden. Among his creditors was his maid, Catharina Jansen, whom he owed five years' salary at 60 gulden per annum. Ishac Pessoa had also ventured into army purveying. According to the bankruptcy papers, his four-fifths share in a contract to supply horses had cost him a loss of 30,271 gulden. The docu-

[68] GAA, NA 4089, pp. 30–47 (4 Jan. 1679; D. van der Groe).

[69] During the trial of Francisco Gomes Henriques a witness declared that he had learned that Fernão Roiz Penso had planned to flee with Jeronimo Gomes Pessoa, but had waited in order to collect money owed him by the Conde de Villa Franca. (I owe this information to Dr David Grant Smith.) Moreover, Jeronimo's son Moseh married a Sara Pensa of Lisbon.

ment does not state who had owned the other one-fifth share, but the papers do mention some of Ishac Pessoa's other partners. Thus, a third of almost all his debts and a third of almost all his assets belonged to David Pessoa, 'presently residing in London', 'with whom he had formed a partnership'. Another brother, Moseh Pessoa, who had died in 1676 'without leaving behind anything in the world', had entered into occasional associations with Ishac Pessoa. In the jewel trade Ishac collaborated intensively with Aron and David Senior of Hamburg, who seem to have been responsible for his Copenhagen connections.

It is difficult to pinpoint exactly where Ishac Pessoa made his biggest mistakes or where things turned sour on him. No doubt his failure was due in part to bad luck, in part to bad judgement. It would appear that the general decline of the Portugal–Holland circuit upon which so much of Pessoa's commercial activity had depended was one important factor. Unlike the other new immigrants from Spain who were drawn to the Caribbean, Pessoa's Portuguese background proved more of a hindrance than an asset in the second half of the seventeenth century. Another major factor was an over-extension on Pessoa's part in areas of volatile speculation. His losses in the army purveying contract and, especially, in his trade in bills of exchange—a trade he may again have taken up in an over-estimation of the value of his Portugal connections—account for the contribution of bad judgement or inexperience.

BROKERS AND INTERLOPERS AT THE LOCAL EXCHANGE

The thirty-one brokers recorded in Table 3.1 at the beginning of this chapter and the countless unrecorded 'interlopers', that is, unlicensed brokers, attest to the attraction exercised by this line of activity on Amsterdam's Portuguese Jews. Although Jews were admitted to the brokers' guild from the days of its foundation, their number was restricted by law; hence the large number of interlopers. Jews, moreover, did not enjoy the full benefits of guild membership if they fell ill. At the very beginning of the seventeenth century two Jews were admitted among a total of 250 brokers. When, in 1612, the total number of brokers was raised to 300, the Jewish quota was fixed at ten. In 1643 there were thirty Jews among 430 brokers; in 1657, fifty Jews among 500 brokers. In other words, the percentage of Jewish brokers rose from an insignificant 0.8 per cent to a respectable 10 per cent in half a century, reflecting quite faithfully the relative significance—in numbers and in trade volume—of the Portuguese Jewish mercantile community in the city and the virtual absence of anti-Jewish discrimination.[70]

[70] The percentage of Portuguese Jewish merchants among the merchants of Amsterdam may be calculated from the number of account-holders at the Bank of Exchange as provided in van Dillen, 'Vreemdelingen', 14. Thus we arrive at the following percentages of Portuguese Jewish account-holders: 1609—3.3 per cent; 1611—4.0 per cent; 1612—5.7 per cent; 1615—6.7 per cent; 1620—8.8 per cent; 1625—5.9 per cent; 1627—7.9 per cent; 1631—6.6 per cent; 1641—5.9 per cent; 1646—8.0 per cent; 1651—10.5 per cent; 1661—11.6 per cent; 1674—13.1 per cent.

To judge from the Kahal's financial records, brokers constituted the lower middle to middle class of the community's social pyramid. The *finta* (communal tax) list shows the payments made by Jacob Rodrigues Nunes, a licensed broker from 1674 to 1704, rising from 6 gulden in 1677 to 10 gulden in 1691.[71] Jacob Senior Henriques (b. 1631, Amsterdam), a broker from 1676 to 1699, remained at a *finta* of 8 gulden;[72] Ishac Treviño (b. 1642, Portugal), a broker from 1679 to 1719, at 14 gulden;[73] and Semuel Pereira (b. Madrid), a broker from 1665 to 1685, at 20 gulden.[74] Abraham da Fonseca (b. 1638, Hamburg), a son of a *haham*, constitutes the exception that proves the rule.[75] He was a broker from 1670 until 1693.[76] During these years his *finta* assessments rose from 24 gulden in 1677 to 50 gulden in 1691. Upon his 'retirement' from brokerage, da Fonseca became one of Amsterdam's most prominent Portuguese Jewish jewellers.[77] It is more than probable that he had begun his jewellery trading while still a broker, even though guild regulations forbade members from engaging in commerce. Abraham da Fonseca's membership of the brokers' guild was inherited by his son, Ishac da Fonseca, upon the recommendation of all of Amsterdam's burgomasters.[78]

Little has been recorded about the day-to-day activities of these brokers, but there is no reason to assume that they acted very differently from their unlicensed colleagues. As the interlopers' meddling in brokerage was illegal, it was subject to denunciation and exposure—and registration: the brokers' guild tried interlopers before its own judges and duly registered the charges, including the articles the interloper had been caught selling. These data (Table 3.3 lists all articles mentioned more than once) demonstrate clearly that Amsterdam's Portuguese Jewish brokers, licensed as well as unlicensed, specialized in articles traded on the Portugal–Holland circuit and its branches. Sugar, tobacco, olive oil, raisins, syrup, diamonds, plums, and silver coins were directly imported from Portugal or Spain. Rice, pepper, cloves, silk, and cassia fistula represent related branch activities, imported from Italy or bought at East India Company auctions. The greatest volume of business during this roughly third quarter of the century was transacted in bills of exchange (by an overwhelming margin), West and East India Company

[71] GAA, PA 366, no. 1190, p. 86; PA 366, no. 1115 (admitted: 21 Dec. 1674; died: 4 Oct. 1704). The *finta* lists used for this and the following remarks are those of 5438 (1677/8), 5441 (1680/1), 5448 (1687/8), 5452 (1691/2), 5455 (1694/5), 5458 (1697/8), and 5463 (1702/3); GAA, PIG 19, pp. 779–83; PIG 20, pp. 13–17, 121–4, 153–5, 185–7, 237–41, 345–50, respectively.

[72] GAA, DTB 684, p. 21 (28 Feb. 1658), where he registered as a merchant; GAA, PA 366, no. 1190, p. 112; GAA, PA 366, no. 1115 (admitted 25 Sept. 1676; quit 29 Jan. 1699).

[73] GAA, DTB 690, p. 64 (10 May 1675), where he registered as a broker, although he became a broker only in 1679; GAA, PA 366, no. 1115 (admitted 10 Nov. 1679; died 24 Oct. 1719).

[74] GAA, DTB 687, p. 171 (9 Mar. 1668), where he registered as a broker; GAA, PA 366, no. 1115 (admitted 29 Apr. 1665; quit 16 Oct. 1685).

[75] GAA, DTB 688, p. 11 (6 Sept. 1669), where he registered as a merchant.

[76] GAA, PA 366, no. 1190, p. 39; PA 366, no. 1115 (admitted 5 Feb. 1670; quit 26 Nov. 1693).

[77] Vaz Dias, 'Joden in den Amsterdamschen diamanthandel', 281–3; Bloom, *Economic Activities*, 42–3; GAA, NA 4256 (24 Jan. 1712; D. v. d. Groe).   [78] GAA, PA 366, no. 1190, p. 207.

Table 3.3. Commodities and financial
instruments traded by Portuguese Jewish
interlopers, 1641–1682

Commodity	Occurrence
Bills of exchange	57
Cassia fistula	2
Cloves	3
Debentures	2
Diamonds	3
Oil (prob. olive)	4
Pepper	3
Plums	2
Raisins	4
Rice	3
Silk	2
Silver coins	2
Sugar	15
Tobacco	7
VOC shares	2
WIC shares	3

From GAA, PA 366, nos. 1288–90.

shares, and debentures. The activities of the licensed and unlicensed brokers are a faithful reflection of those of the merchants of the community, and these figures from the second half of the century clearly reveal the decline of the Portugal–Holland circuit and the concomitant shift of mercantile activity towards speculation and the intra-diasporic trade in bills of exchange.

During the first half of the seventeenth century, Amsterdam's Portuguese Jews had not been particularly active in stockbroking and the trade in bills of exchange. The increasing concentration on these endeavours was no doubt inspired by the influx of wealthy immigrants around the mid-century and the shrinking of commercial opportunities, especially for those Portuguese Jews born in Amsterdam. In 1641, stocks and bonds were added to the list of trading articles subject to a community *imposta*, and by 1662 stock dealing had become such a common profession that the Mahamad was obliged to halve its tax on stockbrokerage fees, 'because this trade in stocks has become much more common and frequent' ('por quanto este neg⁰ de acções se a feitto mucho mais commun e frequente').[79] According to most accounts, the Portuguese Jewish stockbrokers were particularly instrumental in the promotion of the speculation in so-called *ducaton* shares, costing one-tenth the value of a full share. Joseph Penso de la Vega refers in his *Confusion de confusiones* to this speculation as having become more widespread, especially among the members of 'a certain nation which is as boisterous as it is quick-witted'. The introduction of trading in *ducaton* shares in turn brought a great many smaller

[79] GAA, PIG 19, p. 507 (22 Elul 5422/6 Sept. 1662).

investors into the market, accounting for some of the volatility for which the Portuguese Jews were to be blamed. Portuguese Jewish brokers and interlopers may indeed have become the main stockbrokers at the exchange in the course of the 1670s and 1680s. In any event, they rose to sufficient prominence to attract the blame for the second great drop of the century in stock prices in 1688—here and there even provoking a degree of rancour that smacked of antisemitism.[80] Penso de la Vega's colourful and expert description of this trade and the people involved in it affords us a characterization of a certain element within the Portuguese Jewish community whose nuances tend otherwise to get lost amid the formal dullness of notarial and other official documents.

Some younger members [of the profession] discovered that the speculation in ordinary shares . . . was too hazardous for their slight resources. They began, therefore, a less daring game in which they dealt in small shares. For while with whole shares one could win or lose 30 guilders of bank money for every point that the price rose or fell, with the small shares one risked only a ducaton [3 guilders] for each point. The new speculation, called trading in *ducaton shares*, began in 1683 . . . Payment is made in cash, and is more punctual than with the large shares, so that many of the most upstanding [burghers] [*los mas eregidos*] take part in this trade in small shares, for, tempted by the punctuality, they overlook its dubious nature [*indecencia*] and become entranced . . .

Therefore, the means devised to reduce hazards has in fact made the dangers more widespread. The speculation has been so extended that one deals in whole regiments of [*ducaton*] shares, as if they were matchsticks. And I fear one day they may well become matchsticks and kindle a fire in which the participants of these machinations will be consumed . . .

The two main motivations for the introduction of this kind of speculation was the greed of the brokers and the need of those who invented the gambit. And so as to engrave this axiom the better in your memory, know that there are three forms of greed among the brokers, and that on their count many have already been ruined. First, they want to earn the brokerage fees; secondly, they wish to make quick gains [on their own dealings] out of the price fluctuations; and thirdly, they wish to amass fortunes.

(1) If they try to achieve all these ends, they will easily meet with failure, for, when seeking to secure a large brokerage income, they have to offer or to take large batches of stock [on their own account] and thus they may easily be caught [holding the bag] and become dependent on news and rumors and thus exposed to ruin.

(2) The brokers who intend to seek quick gains through price changes, i.e., by getting large orders from their customers and speculating extensively [on their own account] in executing these orders, experience the same fate. For, although it is not their intention to keep the shares [brought for their clients] for any length of time at their own risk, they cannot foresee incidents that may occur suddenly during this time.

(3) They who devote themselves voluntarily to this business, because they have sufficient capital and intelligence to withstand its blows gracefully and to rebuff its snubs constantly, will experience their triumph more gloriously the more formidable an attack they must devise, but in the end they [too] will have to confess that this business is such that they are always in the dark, that it is always risky, and that it is always frightening . . .

---

[80] Israel, 'The Amsterdam Stock Exchange', esp. 416–20, 428–39.

Although brokers were the original inventors of this gambit, people who needed it [as a source of income] came [a close] second. For although the greater part of the profits from this gambling are spent on cards, dice, wine, gifts, excursions, women, calèches, elegant clothing, and other extravagances, there are also numerous people in this business simply for the reason of supporting their enterprises, their status, and their families . . .

Some gamble for the fun of it, some for vanity, many are spendthrifts, many find satisfaction in their occupation, and quite a few make a living here. If they are hit by bad luck and are unable to prevent their own downfall, they at least try to save their honour. They ask premiums, refund the invested money, pay the differences, the furore subsides, their troubles ease, the confusion is overcome, and the attack defeated.

This is the reason why so many jump into this whirlpool. And it is easier to count those who do not deal with ducaton shares than those who do.[81]

This portrait of the gambling, pleasure-seeking, luxury-loving Portuguese Jews alongside the responsible family men provides a more authentic complementary view of the community than is likely to be obtained elsewhere.

Increasingly, during the second half of the seventeenth century, Amsterdam's Portuguese Jews moved away from commerce itself towards increasing engagement—directly or indirectly—in the financial aspects of commerce. Directly, Amsterdam investors bankrolled the large contraband trade of their brethren in the Caribbean and jewellery ventures in northern Europe. Less directly, Portuguese Jewish 'merchants' (for want of a better term) began dealing in bills of exchange, issuing insurance policies of various sorts, and changing foreign moneys. The trade in bills of exchange confined itself, as we have seen, to such bills as were drawn on other cities within the northern European diaspora (see Table 3.4). Surprisingly, notwithstanding this vigorous trade, it was rare that any Portuguese Jew rose to the rank of banker. Their bill-trading operations, it would seem, remained relatively small-scale. Their connections across the diaspora gave them a narrow advantage that enabled them to establish themselves on this low level with a relative ease not available to fellow Dutchmen. The only Portuguese Jew whom one might wish to label a banker would be Don Francisco Lopes Suasso—whose father Antonio had still proudly called himself a *marchand-banquier*. The son had no commercial interests whatsoever and, by virtue of an advantageous marriage to the daughter of the Hamburg Portuguese Jewish banker Manuel Teixeira, and with the occasional help of de Pinto and del Sotto relatives, established himself as a private banker to Dutch and foreign members of the nobility (including, as we saw, William III himself) as well as a commissioner of the financial affairs of the Spanish Crown.

With regard to Portuguese Jewish involvement in insurance and money-changing transactions we are rather poorly informed. Portuguese Jews certainly underwrote insurance policies, frequently—as was the custom—in consort with

---

[81] De la Vega, *Confusion de Confusiones*, ed. Smith, trans. Geers, 115–16, 123–6 (Spanish part); 202–4, 212–16 (Dutch part); a slightly different English translation, from which I borrowed the 'summary' of the last two paragraphs, is *Confusion de Confusiones*, ed. and trans. Kellenbenz, 26–9.

Table 3.4. Places mentioned in bills of
exchange traded by Portuguese Jewish
interlopers, 1641–1682

City	Occurrence
Antwerp	15
Bayonne	2
Bordeaux	2
Frankfort	1
Hamburg	6
La Rochelle	1
Lille	5
London	7
Madrid	1
Paris	4
Rouen	2
'Spain'	1
Venice	2
'Zeeland'	2
No city mentioned	6

From GAA, PA 36, nos. 1288–90.

many other merchants, Dutch as well as Jewish. Quite frequently, too, Portuguese
Jewish merchants issued 'bottomry bonds', a common form of maritime insurance
then in vogue in the Netherlands.[82] Bottomry bonds were loans to skippers or
ship-owners on the security of the vessel and its cargo at relatively high rates of
interest, but at the risk that, if the ship was lost, the bond-holder lost all his money.
Of the money-changers we know only the names; their transactions have otherwise
left no traces. The firms of Moseh & David Jeuda Leon and of David & Jonatan
Levi are recorded in this context.

Brokerage, the trade in bills of exchange, and the insurance operations reflect
the response of Amsterdam's Portuguese Jews to the decline of commerce after the
middle of the century. As brokers, the Portuguese Jews removed themselves from
the centre to the periphery of trade. In focusing on bills of exchange, they moved
from the substance to the instruments of trade. And their transactions tended to
confine themselves ever more narrowly to the geographical area of the northern
European Portuguese Jewish diaspora and its Caribbean daughter communities.

INDUSTRIES OF MASS CONSUMPTION AND LUXURIES

In pre-modern European history Jewish engagement in industrial activities,
whether as employers or as employees, is relatively rare. Guild exclusivism virtu-

---

[82] See e.g. GAA, NA 1551, 17 (26 June 1652; J. V. Oli); NA 2214B, 868 (24 Apr. 1663; A. Lock);
NA 2271, 874ᵛ (7 Dec. 1656; A. Lock); NA 4093 (3 Jan. 1680; D. v. d. Groe); NA 6000, no. 47 (9 May
1697; P. Schabaelje).

ally everywhere in northern and central Europe kept the door shut on any Jewish industrial initiative. The industrial endeavours of Amsterdam's Portuguese Jews have therefore received a certain measure of undue attention, in particular for the purpose of demonstrating that under the proper tolerant conditions Jews were capable of, even attracted to, the so-called 'useful' professions. This argument, left over from the earlier days of the emancipation debates, has little to do with our subject here.

A certain degree of guild exclusivism existed also in Amsterdam; but traditional guild regulations were tolerated and safeguarded by Amsterdam's city fathers only to prevent them from becoming too large an impediment to new industrial initiatives. Theoretically speaking, Jewish ambitions in industrial areas not yet—and thus never—governed by guild laws were in no way curtailed or thwarted. In practice, those areas of industrial initiative to which the Portuguese Jews were most attracted were relatively new fields not restricted by existing guild regulations, and these entrepreneurs pursued particular industrial initiatives not because these happened to be free of guild exclusivism but because their commercial concentration on the importation of colonial products suggested specific industries which by their very nature were of relatively recent vintage and, therefore, free of guild traditions.

Before the middle of the seventeenth century, industrial initiatives had been rather limited. There had been an attempt very early in the century to transplant a silk industry from the Iberian peninsula to Holland. Manuel Rodrigues and the partners Estevão Cardoso & Diogo da Vilar obtained official permission to set up silk mills after demonstrating their expertise in this field. In 1604 three Portuguese merchants from Oporto declared 'that they remember how their [da Vilar's and Cardoso's] grandparents brought, from their native Córdova and Granada, the silk mills on which they made all kinds of silk . . . and that they had heard their ancestors say that the grandparents of the petitioners had been the first to bring the silk mills to Oporto in Portugal'.[83] This impressive tradition notwithstanding, we hear little or nothing of the silk industry in subsequent years.[84] The Dutch East India Company's regular supply of silks from the Far East probably formed too formidable a competition.

Aside from this premature foray into the textile industry, printing was chronologically the first more or less successful industrial enterprise on the part of the Portuguese Jews. Its significance lay largely in highlighting the general level of literacy and the seriousness of the religious preoccupations of the community; its economic value was far smaller. In the lists of the Jewish community's *finta* payers, printers rank near the bottom of the scale, below the brokers and slightly above the 'barber-surgeons'. Only Joseph Athias, whose *finta* was assessed at 40 gulden at

[83] NRPJA 165.

[84] Bloom, *Economic Activities*, 33–5. Bloom and others have made far too much of the importance of the Jews in the silk industry; see van Dillen, 'Economische positie', 571.

one point in his career, rose to the rank of a more or less successful merchant.[85] Printing establishments emerged first in immediate response to a local need and very soon thereafter expanded beyond the boundaries of the northern European Portuguese diaspora to include much of central and eastern European Jewry. This was in many respects a truly Jewish industry, by Jewish entrepreneurs for Jewish consumption; hence its prominence in Jewish historiography. Amsterdam's Jewish printing industry deservedly stands out for its financial involvement of many Christian financiers and for the successes Joseph Athias scored in 'mass marketing'.[86]

In the course of the seventeenth century, Holland became 'probably the greatest centre of book production in the whole of Europe'.[87] Amsterdam especially harboured an unprecedented abundance of printing materials and expertise. The supply opportunities were plentiful and the demand growing. First and foremost, as concerns Portuguese Jews, there was a need for the most basic religious texts. Some prayer-books were available from Italy, but the quantities must have been small and the supplies unable to keep pace with the growth of the northern European diaspora; and why resort to such circuitous routes when the same materials might readily and more cheaply be made available at home? In its earliest days, printing did not generally involve publishing as we understand it. An investor or author or author's benefactor would commission a printer to deliver a certain number of books at a certain price per job. Often the paper was supplied by the contractor; and often the paper merchant was himself a partner in the project. Not infrequently proofreaders, too, were furnished by the contractor or the author. The printer was paid for his services as printed reams came off the press. Only texts for which the demand was more constant and predictable might be printed at the printer's expense and risk, without financial backing.

The earliest prayer-books and a reprint of the famous Spanish translation of the Bible, the so-called Ferrara Bible, were printed by non-Jewish printers. The first Jewish printer in Amsterdam was the Haham Menasseh ben Israel, and his first 'publication' (1626–7) a miniature prayer-book in duodecimo format, the pocket-book size of the seventeenth century.[88] Menasseh ben Israel had ventured into printing to supplement the inadequate rabbinical salary he received from his community. The venture entailed only a relatively small investment in fonts and

---

[85] Between 5435 (1674/5) and 5455 (1694/5), the *fintas* paid by David de Castro Tartas and Uri Phoebus Halevi ranged between 3 and 9 gulden, and between 2 and 4 gulden, respectively. That of Joseph Athias, on the other hand, started at 30 gulden and rose to 40 gulden in his heyday (5448–55/1687/8–1694/5).

[86] For authoritative histories and bibliographies, see Fuks and Fuks-Mansfeld, *Hebrew Typography*, i. 99–135 (Menasseh ben Israel), 135–40 (Daniel de Fonseca), 146–84 (Imanuel Benveniste); ii. 233–86 (Uri Phoebus ben Aaron Witmund Halevi), 286–339 (Joseph Athias and his son Imanuel), 339–82 (David de Castro Tartas).   [87] Price, *Culture and Society*, 171.

[88] On Menasseh ben Israel the printer, see Roth, *Life of Menasseh ben Israel*, 73–83 and esp. Fuks and Fuks-Mansfeld, *Hebrew Typography*, i. 99–135.

printing presses, while his clientele was expanding and his monopoly assured, at least for the foreseeable future. At first Menasseh ben Israel limited himself to producing primarily bibles, prayer-books, and his own writings for local consumption—that is, within the northern diaspora. Whether through the contacts with his German Jewish compositors or after running into the censorious restrictions of his own Mahamad in the course of printing Yosef Delmedigo's writings, Menasseh was motivated to expand his activities and attended the Frankfurt book-dealers' fair in 1634,[89] whether to seek a Jewish or a Christian market we do not know. He found a Jewish market, began printing Ashkenazi prayer-books, and later, in 1651, wrote his own *Nishmat ḥayim* in Hebrew and dedicated it to the German Emperor Leopold, for a German Jewish audience. Menasseh's son and partner in his printing endeavours died in Lublin in 1650, on a business trip. For reasons that are not quite clear, Menasseh never became a truly successful printer. Notwithstanding a fairly substantial, if intermittent, output of possibly forty-four Hebrew and twenty-six vernacular titles between 1627 and 1655, he continued to complain, all through the 1640s, of financial worries and the lack of opportunities in Amsterdam.

The 1640s brought an expansion of printing not only beyond the boundaries of Holland, but also as a result of the immigration of the Venetian Jew Imanoel Benveniste.[90] Benveniste's arrival coincided with substantial increases in immigration from the Iberian peninsula and especially, after 1648, from Poland. The new arrivals created a greater demand for Hebrew texts, brought with them new and more direct contacts with eastern European centres, and last but not least provided Amsterdam's Hebrew printers with a number of first-class Hebrew compositors, men who moreover knew many of the religious texts by heart. German and Polish as well as Portuguese Jewish printers availed themselves of the services of these experts, who moved from one atelier to another as work became available. Like many craftsmen, some worked in father–son pairs. Their names are—or where they are not, should be—almost as familiar as those of the printers themselves: Judah Leib ben Gimpel Mordecai of Posen and his son, Gimpel Mordecai ben Judah Leib of Amsterdam; Joseph ben Alexander of Witzenhausen and his son, Simon ben Joseph; Reuben bar Eljakim of Mainz, Moses ben Aaron of Worms, Uri Phoebus ben Abraham Bermans, and Issachar Ber ben Eliezer of Minden, to name but the most frequently mentioned. David de Castro Tartas and Jacob de Cordova are among a very small number of Portuguese Jews who actually learned the craft of setting type. Both eventually opened their own print shops. Otherwise, the printing ateliers relied upon a staff of mostly Christian workmen to man the actual presses; the foremen were either Ashkenazi or Portuguese Jewish or Christian.

Imanoel Benveniste was active as a printer from 1640 until 1664. He brought to

---

[89] Bloom, *Economic Activities*, 46 n. 60. The censorship of Yosef Delmedigo is discussed in Ch. 6 below.

[90] Bloom, *Economic Activities*, 48. On Venice as a printing centre, see the article 'Printing, Hebrew', in *Encyclopedia Judaica*, xiii. 1102–3.

his efforts greater skill—probably acquired in Venice—and a more single-minded dedication than Menasseh ben Israel had been able to exert. But even he was unable to make printing a wholly successful enterprise, and he ended his days a small-time farmer, outside of Amsterdam. Uri Phoebus Halevi—from 1673 a member of the Portuguese Jewish community, on the merits of his grandfather's catalytic role in the earliest days of the settlement—moved more comfortably in both Ashkenazi and Portuguese circles, and ran a moderately successful atelier, printing mostly Hebrew books, from 1658 until his emigration in 1689 to Zolkiew in Poland, where he founded an apparently more successful printers' dynasty. David de Castro Tartas printed both Hebrew and Spanish or Portuguese publications and for much of the period 1662–98 worked in the shadow of both Joseph Athias, who had branched out to the non-Jewish world, and Uri Phoebus Halevi, who had better access to the German and Polish Jewish markets. De Castro Tartas was, perhaps, more typically the printer of his own community, supplying the limited demand for Portuguese Jewish ritual texts and printing the vernacular literature of Daniel Levi de Barrios and Joseph Penso de la Vega, which was primarily of local interest. In 1693, after the emigration of Uri Phoebus Halevi and the bankruptcy of Joseph Athias, de Castro Tartas, seeking to become Uri Phoebus' successor in the export markets, obtained a fifteen-year States of Holland privilege for the printing of Hebrew prayer-books. But when his rights were successfully contested by two other printers—one Jewish, the other not—de Castro Tartas seems to have rather quickly lost his appetite for the business, and in 1698 left the city for an unknown destination.

Joseph Athias was unquestionably—and despite his ultimate bankruptcy—the most successful of Amsterdam's Jewish printers. His production included Jewish religious books in Hebrew and the vernacular, untold thousands of bibles (including, no doubt, the text of the New Testament) in English, and even liturgical literature for the Church in Portugal. In part he operated in much the same way as the other Jewish printers in town. In 1697, for instance, Wolf Samuel, Isaack Meyer, Salomon Jonasz., and Hirts Abrahamsz., 'rabbis of the German Jewish Nation', contracted with Moyses Josephs that the latter would have Athias print Isaiah Hurwitz's *Shenei luḥot haberit*.[91] The rabbis would supply 1,000 gulden for the edition, to be covered later by the proceeds from the sales. They also accepted responsibility for the proofreading. Moyses Josephs would sell the copies and cover his expenses from the profits. He would also receive a commission of 100 copies. According to the contract drawn up between Moyses Josephs and Joseph Athias, the latter would print six reams a week at thirteen and a half gulden per ream, to be paid upon completion of every six reams. Upon finishing the edition, Athias was to receive six complete copies, and at the end of the contract he bound himself, under penalty of 5,000 gulden, never to print any more copies for himself.

[91] Kleerekoper and van Stockum, *Boekhandel te Amsterdam*, i. 12–13; da Silva Rosa, 'Joseph Athias', 109.

Athias concluded similar contracts with David Nunes Torres for the printing of Joseph Caro's *Shulḥan arukh*; with the Christian merchant Lazarus Schiller for the printing of Maimonides' *Mishneh torah* (500 copies at 26 gulden per copy); and with Johan Coenraed Reus and Hartog Abraham Veronike for the printing of a 3,000-copy edition of *Yalkut re'uveni*.[92]

To begin with, Athias' contribution to the published book lay primarily in its quality, and for this he drew heavily upon the expertise provided by Dutch type-founders, compositors, and printers. For instance, he was able to purchase the entire Elsevier font collection, among which the fonts of Christoffel Van Dijck were particularly highly regarded. Under the direction of the Portuguese Jewish shop-owner and his (mostly) Portuguese Jewish assistant the print shop was supervised by, in the case of Athias, such Dutch workers as Jan Bruyningh, Jan Bus, and Herman Mandesloo.[93] The actual printers were either Dutchmen or Ashkenazi Jews, occasionally a Portuguese Jew.[94] Athias' print shop must have been among the more cosmopolitan establishments in seventeenth-century Amsterdam. But his success went far beyond running a better atelier, producing a higher-quality product. Joseph Athias was perhaps the first printer to introduce the practice of stereotyping. In order to meet the massive demand for English bibles he had bought, at considerable capital expense, large quantities of type, so that he could store entire pages of text in their frames and even an entire bible ready to be printed at very short notice. He boasted, without exaggeration, that he could produce a complete bible in a matter of a few hours. That his achievement was due to the efficiency of the process and the quality of the product is beyond dispute, though how he obtained such prominence in the printing of bibles in English is not clear. Athias' introduction of stereotyping was only the best-known aspect of his entrepreneurship. He also experimented—ultimately without success, but more than a century before its general introduction—with printing textiles using copper plates; and he was the first Jewish printer to advertise in a Dutch paper. When he was unable to assert his monopoly in the export of English bibles, he entered into a fruitful partnership with his Dutch rival, Widow Schippers. Joseph Athias was the only Jewish printer to exhibit in his printing ventures the same kind of entrepreneurial ambition and inventiveness that certain merchants and particularly the army purveyors demonstrated in their affairs. Both socially and temperamentally

---

[92] Kleerekoper and van Stockum, *Boekhandel te Amsterdam*, i. 13–17; da Silva Rosa, 'Joseph Athias', 109–10.

[93] GAA, NA 2206, p. 991 (27 June 1659; A. Lock); Kleerekoper and van Stockum, *Boekhandel te Amsterdam*, i. 17–18.

[94] Da Silva Rosa, 'Joseph Athias', provides the following names: Gimpel Mordechai ben Juda, Jacob de Cordova, Jacob ben Mordechai Gimpel, Jacob ben Alexander Witzenhausen, and his son, Simon. My records, moreover, supply in addition: Govert Spaeck, Pieter Harmensz., Jacob Marchena, Jacob da Costa, Tymen Hendricksz., Hendrick van der Sael, and Marcus Levy: GAA, NA 2206, p. 194 (3 Feb. 1659; A. Lock); NA 206, p. 991 (27 June 1659; A. Lock); NA 2225, p. 1315 (15 Dec. 1667; A. Lock). Jacob Guadaloupe, whom J. S. da Silva Rosa lists as a printer, was Joseph Athias' servant/messenger boy.

he belonged to the same class, even if in the end, in 1695, bankruptcy plunged him into disgrace. After the ensuing settlement in 1696, he spent the few remaining years of his life, until 1700, helping his son Immanuel Athias establish himself in the printing business.

The sugar refineries, tobacco workshops, and diamond-processing ateliers established by Portuguese Jews were a direct offshoot of Portuguese Jewish commercial activities. With regard to all three of these industries, the raw materials came from the lands of the Portuguese empire—sugar and tobacco from Brazil, and diamonds from the Portuguese colonies in the east—and their importation to Holland was to a significant degree controlled by Portuguese Jewish merchants. These facts, of course, created particularly favourable conditions for Portuguese Jewish entrepreneurship. Some merchants themselves became involved in industry and had an obvious advantage over competitors who bought their materials wholesale. Other Portuguese Jews had the potential advantage of being able to purchase these materials on credit. This appears to have played an important role, most notably in the diamond industry.

Of the three industrial initiatives, sugar refining had the briefest life. It appeared on the Portuguese Jewish scene rather suddenly in the mid-1650s, many years after sugar refineries had become quite commonplace in Amsterdam, where the first sugar refinery had been founded in 1597 by refugees from the southern Netherlands. In 1605 the city counted three refineries, in 1650 forty, in 1661 sixty, and at the end of the century about twenty.[95] The first Portuguese Jewish refinery was established in 1655 by Abraham & Ishac Pereyra.[96] In that year the city authorities overruled the protests of Dutch sugar refiners and declared sugar refining not to be covered by *poortersneringen* and thus open to Jewish initiative. Pereyra was, however, allowed only to wholesale the production of his refinery, for retailing remained restricted. Shortly after Pereyra's overture, other Portuguese Jews followed: Martin Rodrigues alias Joseph de los Rios; Selomoh, Moseh & Isaac de Pina; Ishac Mocatta; Abraham da Vega and David de Aguilar.[97] Most of these refineries remained in Portuguese Jewish hands for only relatively short periods of time. The Pereyra firm sold its refinery in 1664; the de Pinas theirs in 1669. The Mocatta family, on the other hand, still possessed its refinery in 1710.[98]

During the first half of the century, sugar had rapidly become a mass-consumed article. However, sugar refining was, and is, a capital-intensive industry, and thus appeared relatively late among the activities of Amsterdam's Portuguese Jews, with the mid-century immigration of wealthy settlers from Spain and Portugal.

[95] Reesse, *Suikerhandel*, 105, 107.

[96] Noordkerk, *Handvesten*, i. 138; Bontemantel, *Regeeringe*, ii. 498; Reesse, *Suikerhandel*, 127.

[97] Bloom, *Economic Activities*, 39; GAA, NA 2280, p. 673 (5 May 1660; A. Lock); NA 2226, p. 452 (23 Feb. 1668; A. Lock); NA 2234, p. 811 (3 Dec. 1670; A. Lock); NA 2271, fo. 40ᵛ (24 Jan. 1656; A. Lock); NA 4254B, p. 1263 (28 May 1710; D. v. d. Groe).

[98] Reesse, *Suikerhandel*, nos. cxlvi, cxlviii, cxlix; GAA, NA 4254B, p. 1263 (28 May 1710; D. v. d. Groe).

During the 1650s the sugar trade and refining absorbed larger capital investments than any other industry in the city. Owing to the Dutch occupation of Brazil, Amsterdam had emerged as the major sugar market of Europe; and those of Amsterdam's Portuguese Jews who had become engaged in Dutch commerce were particularly active in Brazil and, later, in the West Indies, at the very source of Holland's sugar supply. In Surinam, many Portuguese Jews became personally involved in the cultivation of sugar.[99]

The real value of the sugar-refining initiatives, however, appears to have been limited to the Portuguese Jewish capitalists involved. In comparison to the total output of all of Amsterdam's sugar refineries, that of the Portuguese Jewish ones was negligible. Sugar refining was not a particularly labour-intensive industry and so did not create many jobs for the ever-increasing number of Jewish poor. Table 3.1 above shows only one Portuguese Jew who described himself as a 'sugar refinery worker'. Clerical posts apart, most jobs in the refineries were held by Dutch workers, who, after all, had far greater experience in this field.[100]

The tobacco trade and associated industry produced a longer-lasting and further-reaching impact. At the beginning of the seventeenth century tobacco originated from both Portuguese and Spanish lands. It was in Portugal and Spain, too, that tobacco had first become a luxury article of consumption. It became an article of mass consumption more slowly than sugar; indeed, for that reason, entire tobacco growing areas—in Brazil and on Cuba—were converted into sugar plantations to cash in on the much larger profits deriving from sugar cultivation, trade, and refining. Compared to sugar, tobacco had always been traded in much smaller quantities. The tobacco trade lent itself to exploitation by the less wealthy merchants, while tobacco processing required neither expensive facilities nor advanced technology, but relied heavily on manual labour which, for most of the century, was abundant and cheap. Thus tobacco trade and tobacco processing were often combined in the same mercantile hands.

Portuguese Jewish merchants had traded in tobacco from the very beginning of the seventeenth century and, although the evidence is slim, they do seem to have been engaged in processing as well even in those early days: as noted earlier, in 1629 and 1631 Christian retailers complained that Jews were selling tobacco products retail. This complaint had resulted in the formal exclusion of Jews from *poortersneringen* in 1632—an exclusion which did not include the processing and wholesaling of tobacco, nor did it stop the street-peddling of cigars.[101] The

---

[99] Van Dillen, 'Economische positie', 602–13.

[100] Izaque Baruh listed his profession as *suikerbakkersknecht*: GAA, DTB 686, p. 364 (16 July 1666). Among the workers in the Pereyra refinery, we encounter one Rafael Montesinos. The others were all Dutchmen: Jan Hartman, Hans Eggersz., Hendrick Anckerman, Dirck Penne: GAA, NA 2272, fo. 46 (23 Jan. 1657; A. Lock); NA 2890A, p. 351 (22 Sept. 1661; P. Padthuysen). Isaac Coronel kept the books at the de los Rios refinery and Claes Lodewijcx served as its foreman: GAA, NA 2271, fo. 40ᵛ (24 Jan. 1656; A. Lock); NA 2208, p. 673 (5 May 1660; A. Lock).

[101] Van Dillen, 'Economische positie', 572–3.

restriction on tobacco retailing was lifted in 1668, in perhaps the clearest indication that the tobacco trade, in all its inter-related aspects, had become a very important occupation among the Jews. As early as 1620 the brokers' guild had licensed two Jewish tobacco brokers,[102] and Table 3.1 lists four tobacco wholesalers (*tabaks-kopers*), thirteen tobacconists (*tabaksverkopers*), of whom one specialized in snuff, and thirteen tobacco workers. In the 1650s Portuguese Jewish merchants became heavily involved in the smuggling of Brazilian tobacco into Spain, and Portuguese New Christian retailers were the most prominent tobacconists in Madrid. Locally, in Holland, Portuguese Jews did much to further the expansion of tobacco growing in the region of Amersfoort and Nijkerk. Not only were they major buyers of local tobacco, they also invested in the conversion of farm land to tobacco cultivation.[103] In 1694 the board of elders of the community—the Mahamad of the Kahal Kados de Talmud Tora—explicitly allowed tobacco workers the practice, prevailing in tobacco workshops (*ofisinas de tabaco*), of praying the afternoon and evening prayers at their place of work; otherwise the Mahamad very strictly forbade any and all prayer meetings outside the Esnoga, except in cases of weddings or of mourning.[104] This regulation, too, may serve to highlight the significance the tobacco industry had acquired in Portuguese Jewish life.

Tobacco stemmed from the same geographical area as sugar, namely Brazil and the Caribbean, two areas in which Portuguese Jewish merchants were deeply involved at various times throughout the entire seventeenth century. There was therefore a more or less accidental continuity in the tobacco supply over a time when relations between Holland and Brazil and the Caribbean went through drastic changes; a continuity which must account for the longevity of Portuguese Jewish—and later also Ashkenazi—engagement in this industry. As already noted, it took relatively little capital to set up a tobacco shop; but, as the case of Joseph Fernandes Reynoso demonstrates, it was not necessarily that easy to turn a profit. Joseph Fernandes Reynoso alias Luis Fernandes Nunes had started to deal in tobacco in 1659, 'in spinning, pressing, as otherwise', with a capital of slightly over 8,000 gulden; 4,873 gulden he had brought with him from Seville in 1658 and another 3,260 gulden he had received as a dowry with the daughter of Dr Reynoso. By 1662 he was bankrupt, because of a drop in tobacco retail prices.[105] Only some of the labourers who worked in tobacco workshops—that of Widow Sara Dias da Fonseca employed no fewer than fourteen workers—were Portuguese Jews, many of whom occupied supervisory jobs. Rafael da Silva and Semuel Rosa are mentioned as foremen. Many German and Polish Jews were employed in these shops as well and eventually, in the eighteenth century, these groups came to dominate the industry. There is no mention of non-Jewish employees. Whereas sugar refining was primarily a capital venture, tobacco processing was a *métier*, largely a family

[102] Bloom, *Economic Activities*, 61.
[104] GAA, PIG 20, p. 147.
[103] Israel, 'Economic Contribution', 519–20.
[105] GAA, NA 2261B, p. 935 (Mar. 1662; A. Lock).

enterprise; the sons of tobacco dealers were often apprenticed in their fathers' shops. All in all, and despite its lack of brilliance in an age of transatlantic commerce, large-scale smuggling, army purveying, and international finance, the tobacco industry formed a key link in the total configuration of Portuguese Jewish and Ashkenazi life. Its opportunities were open to the less affluent among the community; it offered employment to the poor; and it established contacts, on a fairly large scale and with relative frequency, between Portuguese and German and Polish Jews.

Like the sugar and tobacco industries, the diamond industry owed its rise to Portuguese Jewish trade with Portugal. Until the discovery of diamonds in Brazil in 1725, all diamonds came from India, where the Portuguese colony of Goa—and, later, the English settlement at Surat—served as a major channel of supply for the European markets. In the course of the seventeenth century the Dutch East India Company imported increasing numbers of diamonds. In the diamond trade, therefore, there existed the same fortuitous possibilities of continuity as in the tobacco trade. The diamond and jewel trade, moreover, was particularly attractive to Portuguese Jewish merchants because of the international nature of its market and the opportunities for smuggling. The diamond industry was both capital- and labour-intensive. It also required a great deal of skilled labour—indeed, the process of working the stones was so skilled that it developed into several sub-specializations. The combination of capital and skill accorded the diamond industry its unique place in the history of Amsterdam's Portuguese Jews.

At the end of the sixteenth century and the beginning of the seventeenth, the diamond industry in Amsterdam was practised primarily by refugees from Antwerp.[106] As Portuguese Jews controlled a great deal of Amsterdam's diamond trade, they soon began to think of introducing their sons to the art of diamond polishing and cutting. Thus, typically, a Portuguese Jewish merchant supplied the raw material and the necessary equipment, hired an Antwerp master diamond cutter/polisher, and apprenticed his son with the Antwerp master.[107] This appears, by and large, to have been the manner in which Amsterdam's Portuguese Jews gained supremacy in the diamond business; and they remained a significant force in this industry longer than in any other. Until well into the eighteenth century, various specializations within the diamond industry remained the occupations of choice for Portuguese Jewish orphans sponsored by the charitable foundation Aby Jetomim.[108] The six jewellers and twenty diamond workers (listed in Table 3.1) together made up the largest specialized occupational group within the Portuguese Jewish community during the second half of the seventeenth century. To this tally we must, of course, add all the unrecorded middlemen, such as brokers and 'pedlars'—whom the diamond trade, with its erratic profitability, attracted in substantial numbers—as well as, at the top, the great financiers and other investors.

---

[106] Van Dillen, 'Economische positie', 574.
[107] NRPJA 460, 544; GAA, NA 2212A, p. 615 (28 Mar. 1662; A. Lock).
[108] GAA PIG 1211, *passim*.

Although Portuguese Jews controlled most of the international trade and throughout most of the seventeenth century filled the majority of positions, high and low, in the industry, Ashkenazi Jews played an important intermediary role in exporting the finished product to central and eastern Europe.[109] Some of these middlemen rose to prominence—as, for example, the Gumpers family did—and eventually introduced Ashkenazi workers to the skills of the diamond industry. But this slow replacement of Portuguese Jewish with Ashkenazi jewellers and workers did not assume truly significant proportions until the eighteenth century. During much of the seventeenth century, the Hamburg–Amsterdam–Antwerp–Rouen–London interconnections of the Portuguese Jews and, increasingly, the entry of many of the wealthiest of them into court circles enabled them to keep in very close touch with the major aristocratic markets of northern Europe; and the relatively high level of education even among the less affluent Portuguese provided a readily available skilled labour force. Together, these factors merged to create a virtual domination of this important industry by Portuguese Jews.

SOME FORMS OF JEWISH SOLIDARITY

Much of the success of Jewish enterprise was—and in some quarters still is—commonly attributed to the close relations between members of a despised minority, the kind of closeness forged by persecution and common cultural traits, that allowed Jewish communities to link up and interlock over great distances. Commenting specifically on the Jewish prominence in stock trading, an anonymous Frenchman—a 'neerlandophobe', in the words of the 1698 report's editor, L. Vignols—observed:

This Judaic sect, these Jews, are numerous and substantial in Amsterdam and maintain a very intimate relationship with [members of] the government. Because they are as concerned with news as with commerce, they are so far superior in both that, on big occasions, they succeed in making their suppositions prevail over the truth. In both—news and commerce—they maintain relations with their [sister] congregations, as they call them; the one of Venice—though less wealthy and less populous—is nonetheless reckoned the first among the major congregations because it links the West to the East and the South via the congregation of Salonika which governs their nation in these two other parts of the world; correspondingly the Venice congregation, with the Amsterdam one, governs all communities of the North (amongst which they count the [Jews] tolerated in London and the secret [Jews] in France). In these two regards—in commerce and news—one might say that they are the first and best informed about all that 'moves' in the world. With that [information] they construct their scheme, every week, in their meetings which they hold very appropriately the day after Saturday, their Sabbath, and consequently the day before Monday, i.e.,

---

[109] Bloom, *Economic Activities*, 40–4; GAA, PIG 679: 'Letters received by Athias & Levy', pp. 156–248. Athias & Levy was, perhaps, the greatest of the Amsterdam jewellers' firms. It corresponded in Germany with Elias Gumpers, Reuben Elias Gumpers, Cosmanus Elias Gumpers, and Maria Benedict, widow Gumpers.

Sunday, when the Christians of all the sects devote themselves to their religious exercises. These schemes, which consist of the 'subtlest' news they have received that week refined by their rabbis and congregational leaders, [these schemes] are, on Sunday afternoon, issued to their Jewish brokers and agents—the most adroit men in the world in this field—who, having made another agreement amongst themselves, go separately, from that day [Sunday], and spread the news fitted to their aims (which they start pursuing the next day, Monday morning, according to the dispositions of the various detailed aspects: purchase, sale, change, and stocks, in all which genres, having always amongst them substantial amounts, at hand or readily available, they are instructed to make a move actively, passively, or both ways at the same time).

Surely these are the sentiments of a foreigner. Amsterdam merchants would never have expressed themselves in this way. If we strip the observations of their biases against Jews and against commerce, there remains an apposite assertion regarding the solidarity of the Jews and the fact that it was this solidarity, transcending regional boundaries, that made the Jews such successful businessmen. The Frenchman was uncomfortable with that solidarity, but otherwise he was not expressing anything very different from what is frequently implied in commentaries on Jewish economic activities. All too often the solidarity of the Jews remains unexamined, either for fear of feeding an antisemitic stereotype or because it appears too self-evident. As it constitutes so significant an aspect of their economic successfulness, it deserves to be discussed dispassionately.

During the seventeenth century, the Portuguese Jews of Amsterdam manifested several varieties of solidarity. In some respects these variations continued to exist side by side over time, in others they clearly succeeded one another chronologically. Once more, albeit by chance, the major turning-point came roughly at mid-century.

During the first half of the century, Portuguese Jewish enterprise was confined—with the significant exception of the Dutch Brazilian interlude—to an exploration of the commercial Holland–Portugal circuit. Commercial overtures in Spain and Morocco and collaborations with other northern European communities were directly related to that central trade route. And the Holland–Portugal circuit was explored, primarily, by a number of mutually independent, relatively small family firms. On innumerable occasions the Amsterdam merchants naturally shared with one another the costs of transportation, the risks of insurance, and information on ways of circumventing whatever obstacles came their way; and did so, most likely, more often with fellow Portuguese merchants than with Dutch ones. The basic unit remained the primary network of relatives; some were closer than others, but the closeness of the relationship was less important than the fact of kinship. A small number of related nuclear families settled as much of the circuit as was feasible, and the more extensively they did so the more successful they were as commercial firms. Sometimes the network was the result of an explicit settlement strategy; at others it came about by happenstance, as the result of an unexpected threat of inquisitorial prosecution or of a fortuitous foray into unknown harbours. Whatever the circumstances, the family network remained, throughout the first half of the seventeenth century, the dominant mode of solidarity at the base of Portuguese Jewish enterprise. This is not to deny the importance of other merchants appearing on the scene, for example the agents and commissioners representing some of the major merchant-banking houses of Lisbon or Antwerp; their relation to their firms was frequently not one of kinship. But their number was at first small compared to that of the family firms.

The second major characteristic of the earlier period is the parallels that existed among those individual merchants, which gave rise to frequent collaboration between Portuguese merchants. Given the economic realities of that time there were only a limited number of feasible strategies open to the Portuguese Jews. Settlement in Stockholm or Riga, for instance, made no sense, whereas London remained a temptation, whatever the difficulties and setbacks. The existence of parallel networks, then, engendered a second and more ambiguous level of solidarity. On the one hand, it augured the inescapable prospect of ceaseless competition; on the other, it promised, in days of a favourable market, opportunities of joint exploration beyond the financial or organizational abilities of a single firm. The first was not to be avoided, while the second harboured substantial promises. There is nothing particularly mysterious and certainly nothing especially sinister or ominous in the fact that the Portuguese merchants sought to bolster this solidarity by establishing various religious congregations and found in religious rituals the means of resolving the ambiguities of their mercantile careers. This is not to argue that the religious commitments of the Portuguese were nothing but an outgrowth of the problems they faced as merchants. For, as we have seen already and will see again, Portuguese Jewish existence was beset by at least one other major over-arching problem—the problem of exile: what had occasioned it in the past, and what it entailed for the future.

During the second half of the century, there occurred a transformation of these basic solidarities through contraction and solidification. The immigration of the wealthy merchant bankers, from the late 1640s onwards, shifted the centre of gravity and with it the determinants of the solidarity that had prevailed hitherto. The decline of the Portugal–Holland circuit and the emergence of the Caribbean connections occasioned further changes. Gradually, Amsterdam metamorphosed from a branch of an Iberocentric network into the centre of the northern European diaspora communities and their far-flung transatlantic offshoots. Under these new conditions, Amsterdam increasingly ceased to regard itself as 'diasporic'; it was now the centre of its own network and thus forged its social groupings along new lines. The change is marked by the gradual intermarriage of the wealthiest families of the northern diaspora. Whereas earlier families intermarried on the basis of kin ties that went back to the Iberian past, the de Pintos, Pereyras, Suassos, Teixeiras, and others established marital connections on the basis of the new realities encountered in their new 'homelands'. Within a relatively short period, these families constituted themselves into a local elite whose composition remained remarkably fixed and unchanged throughout much of the eighteenth century. The settlement of family branches throughout the northern communities of Amsterdam, Hamburg, and London had nothing in common with the old networks of the first half of the century. The very proximity of these communities allowed for almost constant interchange and made possible marital strategies that had been impractical under the previous conditions of a more widespread and thinner dispersion of family members. During this period the elite became virtually a closed circle of a limited number of families so extensively intermarried that within a few generations almost everyone became a cousin of everyone else.

This cousinhood constituted a novel type of solidarity and as such engendered new economic initiatives. For as commercial opportunities dwindled and families sought to maintain their wealth and status, they were drawn to investments in stocks and bonds, in industry, and, for the more adventuresome, in Caribbean smuggling operations. They also committed themselves to ever further intermarriage to prevent the inevitable dispersal of the family fortune. Instead of the parallel networks of the previous generations we now find concentric circles of increasingly less exclusive and poorer clusters of intermarrying families. During this time, the Portuguese Jewish diaspora of northern Europe became a small world unto itself. This new configuration lent itself, as external opportunities disappeared, to an increasing exploitation of the new forms of internal interdependence. Thus the second half of the seventeenth century is characterized by an exploration of all the opportunities within the Portuguese Jewish settlement itself, by efforts to squeeze all potential advantages out of the diaspora communities' very close and increasingly closer inter-relationships as well as the mutual dependencies within each community.

None of the economic activities of Amsterdam's Portuguese Jews can truly be classified as at or near the forefront of emergent capitalism. Their commercial operations in the Portugal and Spain circuits represented nothing out of the ordinary. In terms of Jewish history the scale of their contributions in these fields was, no doubt, unprecedented. And even locally the substantial share of the Portuguese merchants in these vital areas proved a boon to the continued prosperity of the city. In particular, the salt (from Portugal) and wool (from Spain) imports were crucial to the viability of some of the most important local industries. Aside from commerce, the Portuguese Jews specialized primarily in smuggling in the Caribbean, in stock trading, and in the diamond industry. In the diamond industry, as we have noted, the Portuguese merchants had been relative latecomers, while smuggling, of course, was as old as commerce itself, and in the particular case under consideration was considered illegal only on the Spanish side; that is to say, as far as the Dutch authorities and fellow Dutch merchants were concerned, it was an entirely honourable occupation. In all likelihood, Amsterdam's Portuguese Jews showed greater staying power than other merchants in this branch of commerce. As in the days following the end of the Twelve Years Truce, when Portuguese merchants had emerged better equipped to deal with the adversities of the war situation, so now in the Caribbean the mutual reinforcement of the parallel networks of Portuguese smugglers gave them a resilience in these troubled waters that proved hard to beat.

Only with regard to the trade in stocks and other financial instruments, perhaps, can we speak of an original Portuguese Jewish contribution. The attraction stock trading exercised for Portuguese Jews during the last quarter of the seventeenth century, as documented in Joseph de la Vega's *Confusion de confusiones*, is not easily explained. Leaving aside the stock exchange, the Portuguese Jews had always been inveterate gamblers, far more than their Dutch contemporaries. It was, perhaps, not quite a national trait; but it was certainly more than a temporary or individual idiosyncrasy. Maybe it was a quality that had been acquired in Portugal in the anarchic, fortune-hunting days of the sixteenth-century expansions. But perhaps more salient than the gambling itself was the intensity with which Portuguese Jews threw themselves into speculation. Much of the sophistication and abstraction for which the Amsterdam exchange became famous derived from this intensity. As de la Vega's *Confusion de confusiones* had been written, quite publicly and without subterfuge, to initiate his English brethren into the secrets of stock trading, there clearly existed within the Portuguese Jewish community itself a 'code'—more than just a jargon—of thinking and acting with regard to stocks and bonds and bills of exchange that owed much of its innovative sophistication and abstraction to the very limited circle and cultural homogeneity of the major practitioners. Similar 'codes' are a fairly common phenomenon among specialized traders who are also ethnically similar—flea-market merchants or the textile wholesalers with whom I grew up, to cite just two contemporary examples. Portuguese Jewish brokers had first become involved as the representatives of major investors who were turning away from commerce and seeking the life of the rentier. The trade in *ducaton* shares—with the exponential growth in sophistication and abstractions that that entailed, if only because of the latitude this trade afforded and the element of gambling it increasingly acquired—was originally inspired by the thought of having smaller investors within the Portuguese Jewish community ride piggy-back, as it were, on the investments of the major financiers. (For, as Iberians, Amsterdam's Portuguese Jews had hankered after the life of leisure from the day they had become engaged in commerce.) The new solidarity of a Portuguese Jewish diaspora in northern Europe turned in on itself created, it seems to me, the impetus behind the novelties in the stock-trading field and generated much of the intensity with which Portuguese Jews threw themselves into the stock exchange, providing the framework for the rapid codification of increasingly more complex procedures.

It must be clear that most of the theories hitherto employed to explain the peculiar role played by Jews in general, and by Amsterdam's Portuguese Jews in particular, do not fit the descriptions and discussions set out in this chapter. The extravagant claims made by Werner Sombart have long been laid to rest. The emergence of Dutch capitalism clearly owes almost nothing to the Jewish immigrants, and one would be hard put to recognize in the Portuguese refugees any peculiarly Jewish type of rationality whose origin lies in the biblical days of wandering through the desert ('ein ganz besonders geartetes Volk—ein Wüstenvolk und ein Wandervolk, ein heißes Volk—unter wesensverschiedene Völker—naßkalte, schwerblütige, bodenständige Völker—verschlagen', as Sombart describes the Jews in his introduction to *Die Juden und das Wirtschaftsleben*).[110] Max Weber's critique of Sombart does not get us much further. In a famous passage, Weber declares the Jews to have been speculative pariah-capitalists, as opposed to the Puritans who were bourgeois organizers of labour.[111] One will find in Amsterdam precious little evidence that whatever remained of the 'pariah' status of the Jews—their alleged social segregation from the rest of the bourgeoisie—contributed in any form or fashion to their penchant for speculative capitalism.[112] Nor have I found any trace of the so-called 'double ethics' according to which Jewish businessmen supposedly acted differently *vis-à-vis* fellow Jews and towards Christian merchants. The particular economic endeavours in which Amsterdam's Portuguese Jews specialized and, to some degree, excelled had little to do with the nature of their relations as a minority with the majority and nothing to do with their descent from the wandering tribes of ancient Israel. There is, perhaps, more value in Abram Leon's concept of the 'people-class': 'Above all the Jews constitute historically a social group with a specific economic function. They are a class, or more precisely, a people-class.' I do not think, as Leon does, that the Jews were always and everywhere a 'people-class'; their economic function was not group-specific at all times, certainly not in the vast majority of Portuguese Jewish activities in Amsterdam. But when a particular economic function—for one reason or another, not necessarily a negative one—became co-terminous with the Jewish community, we do encounter, perhaps, a specifically Jewish contribution to the evolution of capitalism.[113]

On the whole, Amsterdam's Portuguese Jews derived their main impetus from the internal evolution of the community and its response to the evolution of basic commercial realities. To return to the Frenchman's observations quoted at the beginning of this section, there was indeed a special kind of solidarity—to a suspicious outsider, solidarity and conspiracy can look very much alike—behind

---

[110] Sombart, *Die Juden*, p. vii.

[111] Weber, *Gesammelte Aufsätze zur Religions-Soziologie*, ii. 39.

[112] My fear is that in the theories regarding the rise of capitalism 'speculative capitalism' continues to be invested with negative connotations and its evolution consequently attributed to social outsiders.

[113] See in this connection also the argument presented by Bovenkerk in favour of a *sui generis* treatment of the peculiar contribution made by trading minorities in modern capitalistic societies: 'Shylock of Horatio Alger'.

the success of Portuguese Jewish enterprise. Ironically, this solidarity owed its innovative force to a conservative instinct to stay with the fundamentals of the Portugal–Holland circuit—namely, the personal relations more than the goods—and its multifarious ramifications for as long as the changing times allowed. In the end, only the personal relations of fellow exiles remained, giving rise to the special solidarity, from within, not from without, that sparked the peculiar frontier activities in smuggling and in stock trading for which the community should be duly famous.

FOUR

NAÇÃO AND KAHAL
A Religious Community in the Making

Let the truth never part from your mouth, for God loves the truth and those who speak it and abhors mendacious lips. Thus, He is called, by one of His attributes, God of Truth. Do not say out of mockery anything other than what you know and hold in your heart, for you will acquire a bad name and reputation and, when you do speak the truth, you will not be believed and you will be held in low esteem. So always deal very truthfully so that they will similarly deal with you. Thus you will acquire a good reputation and name which is worth more than riches, as Solomon says (Prov. 22: 1).

Do not scorn the advice of old and wise men. Because of their large experience with the things of this life, it is sounder than that of young men. Listen to them attentively. If they give you advice about your business, accept their counsel; if the matter does not concern you, always try to remember what they said so that you can take advantage of it on another occasion. Do not trust your own opinion for you can easily deceive yourself...

My son, always keep in mind where you come from and who you are, so that you will never grow arrogant, as God abhors arrogance. Be humble toward everyone, which is a very pleasing virtue to Him. Never boast about yourself, for praise from one's own mouth is despicable.

DR PEDRO GOMES DE SOSSA

THROUGHOUT the sixteenth and seventeenth centuries, the Antwerp colony of Portuguese merchants was designated a *natie* (nation). In fact, in Antwerp all colonies of foreign merchants—those of Spain, of Lombardy, of Genoa, and of Lucca—were known as 'nations'; and so was the nation of stevedores. In Antwerp, it seems, the term 'nation' denoted a group on the margin of society proper, structurally less integrated than the guilds but more fully recognized than incidental associations.[1] In Portugal during the same period New Christians were frequently referred to as *homens da nação* (men of the nation). There, it seems, the term 'nation' had an even less well defined meaning. The phrase *homens da nação* may simply have been analogous to *homens de negocio* (men of trade), another frequently used name for New Christians; alternatively, it may have implied a *nação hebrayca* or *judayca* (Hebrew or Jewish nation), with connotations of ethnicity. Almost certainly it owed something to the historical coincidence of these associations. In Portugal, then, the term *nação* referred to a more or less coherent group on the

---

[1] Goris, *Étude sur les colonies marchandes*, 32–3.

periphery (or, at least, not in the centre) of society, coherent by virtue of ethnic affiliation and occupational specialization. *Nação*, therefore, suggests both a distinctiveness from society at large and an identity of interest and purpose within the group.[2]

In Amsterdam and Holland the authorities, as well as the city's Portuguese Jews, also employed the designation *natie* or *nação*. The usage of the term in Holland had none of the ambiguity it possessed in Portugal nor any of the legal connotations it carried in Antwerp. 'Nation' simply denoted a distinct group without a specific legal status as such. It was always accompanied by an adjective highlighting the particular distinctiveness deemed appropriate in the context. Thus in city and state documents, the *natie* with which we are concerned here is called Portuguese or Jewish or Portuguese Jewish. The adjectives are applied with surprising and telling consistency: 'Portuguese' only rarely and at the very beginning of the seventeenth century; 'Jewish' frequently and most commonly until the 1670s; and 'Portuguese Jewish' always and exclusively thereafter, as a result of the emergence of a second, German Jewish *natie*. The standard practice of the eighteenth century speaks of the Portuguese Jewish *natie*, of the German Jewish *natie*, and occasionally of the Jewish *natiën*.[3] In other words, as far as the Dutch authorities were concerned, the distinctiveness of this group lay principally in its Jewishness, in its adherence to a religion other than Christianity.

The Portuguese Jews themselves applied slightly different adjectives to the term *nação*. They spoke either of a *nação portuguesa*, sometimes *e espanhola* (or *castelhano*), or of a *nação ebrea*. The two designations are not co-terminous, nor are they used with more or less equal frequency. *A nação portuguesa* is unquestionably and by far the more favoured and the more all-embracing expression. It included occasionally, but significantly, Portuguese or Spaniards not yet or only loosely affiliated with a Jewish community. *A nação ebrea*, on the other hand, occurs in certain specific contexts only to denote and stress the religious aspect of the group.[4] Both expressions were commonly used long before the arrival of the German Jews. In the self-perception of the Portuguese Jews, it was principally their 'Portugueseness' (or 'Spanishness') which distinguished them from society at large, and not just from the German Jews as in the view of Holland's non-Jewish authorities.

Characteristically, 'Portugueseness' is not readily definable. Its associations, of

---

[2] See also the interesting evolution sketched in Zernatto, 'Nation'.

[3] Noordkerk, *Handvesten*, ii. 470–95; *Gedrukte resolutiën . . . Holland*, ('Hebrew Nation') 12 Dec. 1619, 13 Dec. 1619; ('Jewish Nation') 27 July 1649, 23 Mar. 1651, 26 Mar. 1652, 30 Sept. 1656, 12 July 1657, 8 July 1677, 24 July 1677, 26 Jan. 1686, 28 Sept. 1691, 23 May 1703; ('Portuguese Jewish Nation') 10 Dec. 1676, 17 Dec. 1676, 31 July 1680, 21 Sept. 1680, 25 Aug. 1691, 8 Apr. 1693, 27 Nov. 1710, 24 Nov. 1719, 8 Feb. 1720, 29 Feb. 1720; ('German Jewish Nation') 17 Feb. 1748, 17 Mar. 1769; ('Jewish Nations') 19 Feb. 1712, 7 May 1712, 14 May 1712.

[4] GAA, PIG 13, pp. 14 (3 Sivan 5382/12 May 1622), 78 (5 Iyar 5392/26 Apr. 1632), 114 (25 Elul 5394/18 Sept. 1634).

course, are not political but almost wholly cultural. They include such general elements as a common language and literature and the *Weltanschauung* associated with them as well as the distinct historical experiences of the *gente da nação*: experiences of social discrimination, inquisitorial persecution, and common ancestry. *A nação portuguesa* is an appropriately fluid concept with fuzzy boundaries, including at once Portuguese not yet Jewish, wholly Jewish Portuguese, and renegade Portuguese Jews. If 'Portugueseness' is closely associated with religion, the term *nação ebrea* likewise has distinct ethnic overtones; for in the choice of the adjective *ebrea* we must surely recognize an analogy with the linguistic and historical associations implied in the adjective *portuguesa*. Even in their Jewishness, it seems, the emphasis was placed, consciously or not, on the language and biblical, historical origins of the religion rather than on its contemporary doctrinal and practical contents. Thus, whether joined by *portuguesa* or by *ebrea*, whether with reference to society at large or to the group itself, the term *nação* implies a strong awareness of ethnic distinctiveness.

The term *a nação ebrea* occurred especially during the early part of the seventeenth century, at a time when the *nação* was split into three separate congregations. It was used as an overarching concept comprising three *kehilot kedoshot*.[5] Eventually, with the unification of the three congregations into one, *nação ebrea* was replaced by Kahal Kados. *Nação* and *kahal* are not wholly synonymous terms. The first stresses affiliation, the second institutionalization. In other words, the modes of institutionalization of the Portuguese Jewish community must be seen within the larger context of the *nação ebrea*, which in turn represents a condensation of the even broader and fuzzier *nação portuguesa*. As such, institutionalization and all it meant for Amsterdam's Portuguese Jews was a process subject to both the internal dynamics of the *nação* and the exigencies of Holland's political and religious structure.

THE GENESIS OF A KAHAL KADOS

That the Portuguese expatriates who settled in Amsterdam established a Jewish community cannot be denied, and indeed has never been disputed. Whether they came to Amsterdam with the intention of doing so is another question. Some have argued that the establishment of a Jewish community or communities was by no means a premeditated objective and occurred only gradually as a result of a variety of largely unanticipated and unrelated events.[6] Others find it impossible to ascribe such a momentous change as the conversion to the generally despised religion of Judaism and the establishment of a peripheral, minority community to anything but the most deep-seated desires.[7]

---

[5] e.g. ibid. 78 (5 Iyar 5392/26 Apr. 1632). *Keilot kedosot* was the most common spelling used. Portuguese Jews had difficulty pronouncing the 'h' and pronounced the 's' almost like 'sh'.

[6] Seeligmann, 'Marranen-probleem'.   [7] Da Silva Rosa, 'Van Marranen tot Portugeesche Joden'.

For obvious reasons, answers to this question were most assiduously sought in the actions of the first generation of immigrants. It was these people, after all, who had made the momentous decision to create the Jewish community out of nothing. Their decision and creation, in many respects, pre-determined the choice of subsequent immigrants. Scrutiny of the motivations of the earliest settlers goes back to the seventeenth century. Within the Portuguese Jewish community itself a number of accounts circulated about those very early days. They are the only contemporary documents explicitly discussing the issue at hand and, as we shall see shortly, without exception stress the steadfast commitment of the earliest settlers to establish a Jewish community. Traditionally, researchers have been content to check these seventeenth-century traditions against other established facts in an effort to determine whether they were largely factual or fictitious. They generally sought too hard for solutions, failing to recognize that the traditions themselves may be part of the story.

The accounts are three and have come down to us in late seventeenth-century versions two or three generations removed from the events they recount. It is worth devoting a few paragraphs here to retelling these stories in some detail.

The first narrative extols the initiative of Moses Uri Halevi.[8] According to this most detailed account, ten Spanish merchants and four boys landed at Emden in East Frisia in 5364 (1603/4). Accidentally learning of the presence of one Jewish family, that of Moses Uri Halevi and his son Aron, in the otherwise Lutheran town of Emden, they revealed to him their desire to be circumcised and practise Judaism. But, since Emden did not permit such practices, Halevi instructed them to settle in Amsterdam and promised to join them in due course. And so the Spaniards moved to Amsterdam. Upon Moses and Aron Uri Halevi's arrival there, the ten men and four boys were circumcised, and the group rented a room for daily prayer meetings. Christian neighbours denounced these assemblies, and Moses and Aron were arrested. Brought before the burgomasters, they spoke as follows:

It is true that we did what you said we did [circumcise people and practise Judaism], but it was done for the profit and benefit of this city of Amsterdam so as to let it share in a large trade; we could very well have gone to another city, which wanted to give us complete freedom, but we did it here so that it might share in large maritime trade activities, for these Spaniards carried large sums of money and riches with them; if the burgomasters see fit to grant these Spaniards the freedom to live here, we assure them that within one year there will be more than fifty families of this Spanish and Portuguese nation with large capital resources, who would make Amsterdam the leading commercial city of Europe.

The burgomasters verified Halevi's story by questioning the Spaniards and decided 'to give [them] all the freedom in the world to live here, to observe [their] Law and religion freely and to maintain a house for [their] prayers'. The story ends:

8   Uri ben Aron Halevi, *Narração*.

After this many families came from Spain and Portugal to live here in this city. My grand-father [the author is a son of Aron Uri Halevi] was their *haham* and my father their *ḥazan*; they circumcised them and were the creators of this K[ahal] K[ados]. They arranged their prayers and *haskamot* on how to govern themselves in observance of the precepts of God. May He increase them forever. AMEN.

Finally, two appended affidavits—one by David de Ishac Cohen de Lara, dated the thirty-second day of the Omer 5433 (3 May 1673), and the other by Ishac Aboab, dated the twentieth day of the Omer 5434 (11 May 1674)—attest to the virtue of Moses and Aron Uri Halevi. The account was first published in 1711.

A second account praises the constancy and determination of one Maria Nunes.[9] It begins with the flight of Miguel Lopes and his nephew and niece, Manoel Lopes Pereira and Maria Nunes, from the Iberian peninsula in 1590 or 1593. Their Spanish ship was captured by the English, and the travellers were brought ashore in England. There an English duke fell in love with Maria Nunes and proposed to marry her. Having learned of Maria's exceptional beauty, the queen released the prisoners and 'took Maria Nunes in her carriage to show the citizens of London this prodigy of beauty who, refusing offers of love and material reward, preferred the Jewish faith she practised in Amsterdam to all the pomp of the English court'. Shortly afterwards Maria Nunes was joined in Amsterdam by the rest of her family. In 1598 she married her cousin Manoel Lopes Homem. The story appeared, in the 1670s, in Daniel Levi de Barrios' *Triumpho del govierno popular*.

The third account celebrates the attachment to Judaism of a secret *minyan* (prayer meeting) led by Jacob Tirado.[10] In 1595 a group of Amsterdam Jews met in secret to celebrate Yom Kippur. The city police, mistaking the meeting for an underground Catholic church, burst in on the penitents and found not idolatrous images but only Hebrew books. Realizing their blunder, 'The Schout, or Praetor, . . . asks them to pray to the God of Israel for the government of Amsterdam'. And at the end the story announces the foundation of the first Jewish congregation in Amsterdam:

The Israelites, with prudent rejoicing, promise through their spokesman Yahacob Tirado to do so; and the Praetor with his much feared henchmen goes to inform the magistrates who, by allowing the Jews to practise their religion openly, inspired the said Yahacob Tirado to found Bet Yahacob, which translated is the House of Yahacob, with the sons of Yahacob, who gave due thanks to the Divine Mercy who delivered them from human justice and assured the continuance of their faith amidst the indescribable horrors they suffered when they were surprised by those righteous ministers.

In another version the raid of the Tirado story is merged with that already mentioned in the account given by Moses Uri Halevi's grandson.[11] Both versions were published, in the 1670s, in Daniel Levi de Barrios' *Triumpho del govierno popular*.

[9] De Barrios, *Triumpho del govierno popular*, 455–6.
[10] Ibid. 460–5.   [11] Ibid. 286–91.

It would lead us too far from our purpose to examine these accounts in minute detail. Their various degrees of veracity have been discussed by others. Thus, it can be established:

1. that all the personalities mentioned lived in Amsterdam at one time or another and that most of them were members of the Jewish community after it was founded at some unknown date;

2. that Moses Uri Halevi—who calls himself a rabbi from Emden and who is called a *haham*, but only after 1617, in some documents of the Jewish community—settled in Amsterdam in 1602, where he worked as a slaughterer and lived as a Jew; that he was, indeed, arrested, and declared before the court in 1603 that he had never circumcised anyone, nor ever taken anything in pawn or sold stolen goods;[12]

3. that four Portuguese merchants and a (noble) daughter in men's clothing were captured by English ships and brought to London in 1597; that they were on their way to Amsterdam, where the girl was to be married; that her parents had been imprisoned by the Inquisition, 'the Holy House as they call it'; that Maria Nunes and Manoel Lopes Homem did, indeed, register their intention to marry in Amsterdam, on 28 November 1598;[13]

4. that the eve of Yom Kippur fell on a Sunday evening—the most likely time for it to have been confused with a Catholic mass—in 1597 (21 September) and 1603 (14 September).[14]

However, before we jump to the conclusion that these sparse facts are sufficient to verify these accounts, we must enter a number of equally significant caveats. On the one hand, Daniel Levi (alias Miguel) de Barrios, who may or may not have been the 'embellisher' of two of the legends, wrote primarily to the greater glory of God, the synagogue, and individual families and persons. His entire *Triumpho del govierno popular* is a panegyric on his community and its members, from whom he derived most, if not all, of his livelihood.[15] Drama, courage, steadfastness, and praise of God occur again and again and form the main background against which de Barrios sang his poems. The account of Moses Uri Halevi's grandson owes its existence to a different set of circumstances. During the latter part of the seventeenth century relations between Amsterdam's Portuguese and German Jews worsened considerably, and the descendants of Moses and Aron Uri Halevi became embroiled in a controversy concerning their rights of membership in the Kahal Kados de Talmud Tora.[16] Quite likely, the account's claim that Moses and

[12] Zwarts, 'Eerste rabbijnen', 166–86; Pieterse, *Daniel Levi de Barrios*, 44.
[13] Prins, *Vestiging der Marranen*, 174–5; Pieterse, *Daniel Levi de Barrios*, 45.
[14] Zwarts, 'Eerste rabbijnen', 171; Seeligmann, *Bibliographie en historie*, 14–20.
[15] Pieterse, *Daniel Levi de Barrios, passim*; Scholberg, *Poesia religiosa*, 58–80.
[16] GAA, PIG 20, p. 293 (14 Elul 5460/26 Aug. 1700).

Aron Uri Halevi had actually been 'the creators of this K. K.' (substantiated, in part, by two affidavits) originated with this latter-day dispute.

Unfortunately, an attempt to balance these contrary indications does not yield an easy compromise, for the elements are too disparate. It will be more fruitful to step back from the all-too-eager search for origins and view the accounts as reflections of how Portuguese Jews of seventeenth-century Amsterdam saw themselves or wished to see themselves. Thus the heroic deeds of Maria Nunes and Jacob Tirado may be seen as part of a collective memory, an ideal history which, if it was not actually true, 'ought', so to speak, to have been true. The archetypal history of Portuguese Jewish settlement in Amsterdam included the perils and vagaries of the voyage (the privateers encountered by Nunes and her party; the ship blown off course to Emden), the lures of wealth and aristocratic life (the offer of marriage to Nunes by an English duke), the determination to pursue as planned one's desire to return to the ancestral faith (Nunes's pre-arranged marriage; the Spaniards' second-lap migration from Emden to Amsterdam), the misunderstandings between the Dutch authorities and the Portuguese immigrants (the denunciation of Halevi's prayer meetings; the *schout*'s raid on Tirado's *minyan*), and finally the establishment of mutual trust (Halevi's speech to the burgomasters; Tirado's receiving permission to establish the first public synagogue).

Restated in this fashion, the collective memory of Amsterdam's Portuguese Jews appears to have mixed elements of pre-migration Portuguese experience with others from the period after settlement in Amsterdam. 'Portuguese' echoes may be recognized in 'the lures of wealth and aristocratic life', staple sins of which the Portuguese New Christians often accused themselves, and in 'the misunderstanding of their domestic gatherings and celebrations', of which they undoubtedly accused the Inquisition.[17] 'Dutch' elements surface most clearly in the appreciation of the burgomasters for the newcomers' economic contribution and their toleration of public Jewish worship. The perilous voyage and the unswerving determination dramatically represent the tensions between the discomforts of a Portuguese past and the rewards of a Dutch present. In short, the multifarious ambiguities stemming from the experience of migration and expatriation, the dissonance produced by an irrevocable and often involuntary decision, were boiled down to a most elementary, clear-cut dichotomy, sufficiently 'realistic' in its echoes of past and present to be acceptable to a wide variety of individuals. This dichotomous, black-and-white formulation, in turn, logically implied the kind of determination attributed to the first immigrants.

I am inclined to suspend any investigation of the emergence of Jewish communal life on the basis of these particular accounts—especially as we have at our

---

[17] Regarding 'the lures of wealth', see Usque, *Consolation*, 206; Révah, 'Autobiographie', 109; Méchoulan, 'Abraham Pereyra, juge des marranes'; Teensma, 'Fragmenten uit het Amsterdamse convoluut'.

disposal other, 'unfiltered', facts. Shorn of drama and hindsight, these actually give us more freedom of interpretation and allow us to view the establishment of a Jewish community or communities as a social rather than a personal event.

The simple facts are as follows. A Jewish congregation and, later, congregations were founded in Amsterdam during the first two decades of the seventeenth century. The exact founding year of the first congregation, called Bet Jacob, is unknown, but it must have occurred during the very first decade of the century.[18] A Brussels document of 1610 mentions that 'Jacob Thirado alias Guimes Lopes' (da Costa) had put his house in Amsterdam at the disposal of Portuguese Jews to meet for prayers.[19] Bet Jacob almost certainly owed its name to this Jacob Tirado. The second congregation, Neve Salom, seems to have been founded in or just before 1612. In that year there appeared a prayer-book carrying the vignette of Neve Salom and printed at the expense of Ishac Franco, a known member of that congregation.[20] During the same year three known members of Neve Salom commissioned the building of the synagogue referred to in Chapter 1, whose construction was temporarily stopped on orders of the city authorities.[21] Neve Salom counted among its founders some of the same men who had earlier, in 1605, petitioned the Haarlem magistrature for permission to practise Judaism publicly in that city. There may very well have existed a disagreement among those of the Portuguese nation about whether to accept the restrictions on public worship or to push for greater acceptance. In that case Bet Jacob represented the Portuguese who were content for the time being to accept that the practice of Judaism should be a legally sanctioned but private matter. This might explain why no more explicit data confirming the existence of Bet Jacob exist for the earliest period. The third congregation, Bet Israel, was definitely founded in 1618. Thus, within a period of roughly fifteen years, three Jewish congregations arose in Amsterdam.

The circumstances that gave rise to the foundation of the first two congregations are unknown. The foundation of Neve Salom is sometimes attributed to shortage of space within the synagogue of Bet Jacob. We are ostensibly better informed on the conflict within Bet Jacob that occasioned the foundation of Bet Israel. The conflict seems to have originated in a jurisdictional dispute between a *parnas* of Bet Jacob and the two rabbis of Bet Jacob and Neve Salom.[22] To quote a summary of a responsum of R. Joel Sirkes of Brest:

a physician who was at the same time *parnas* of one of the communities [Bet Jacob is meant] had given someone permission to act as *shohet* [ritual slaughterer]. The leaders of the two

[18] There is some discussion as to whether Bet Jacob was really the first congregation. Some indications favour the primacy of Neve Salom. Daniel Levi de Barrios, in his *Triumpho del govierno popular*, purports to repeat local traditions and names Bet Jacob the first congregation. Vlessing, 'New Light on the Earliest History', shows that the sources do not straightforwardly support de Barrios' contention. There is, however, nothing in the sources she mentions that squarely contradicts it either.

[19] Vaz Dias, 'Verzoek', 187.

[20] Seeligmann, *Bibliographie en historie*, 41–4.   [21] See above, p. 12.

[22] Vaz Dias, 'De scheiding'; d'Ancona, 'Komst der Marranen', 228–39.

communities had entrusted the two rabbis with the task of investigating the aforesaid slaughterer. When it appeared that the man was entirely ignorant of the regulations, it was proclaimed in the two synagogues that the meat slaughtered by this man was unfit for consumption. On hearing this the physician had mounted the *teva* [raised part of the synagogue intended for the reader] and called out in a loud voice that the proclamation had no value and that the people could continue to eat the meat. Furthermore, this physician had mocked the aggadic sayings of the Jewish sages, was opposed to the Kabbalah [Jewish mysticism], and interested only in philosophy. He reportedly also converted others to his point of view. The question was whether the rabbis had the right to place the *parnas*-physician under a ban.[23]

We do not know whether or not the physician in question, Dr David Farrar, was ever excommunicated, but in July 1618 two factions—one led by Baruh (alias Bento) Osorio supporting the rabbi of Bet Jacob, Haham Joseph Pardo, and the other led by David Curiel (alias Lopo Ramirez) seconding Dr David Farrar—began arguing about possession of the synagogue and its inventory. Emotions ran so high that the Farrar–Curiel faction, locked out of the synagogue, appealed to the Amsterdam authorities. A complicated legal battle ensued. In August 1619 the Amsterdam justices reached a compromise decision recognizing the Farrar–Curiel faction as representing Bet Jacob. The property of Bet Jacob was divided to the general advantage of its legal heirs, and the Osorio–Pardo faction founded the new congregation of Bet Israel.

It has been customary to view most conflicts within Amsterdam's Portuguese Jewish community almost exclusively in intellectual terms.[24] Thus the split within Bet Jacob was allegedly occasioned by irreconcilable differences between the rationalist faction of Dr Farrar and Haham Saul Levi Morteira and the mystically inclined followers of Haham Isaac Uziel. Following the lead of Carl Gebhardt, the overall contentiousness of the Portuguese Jews was attributed to the peculiarities of their Marrano past, for in the context of Jewish history this argumentativeness appeared perhaps somewhat excessive. (In another context, of course, strife of this sort might easily have been considered less noteworthy.) According to Gebhardt, in an introduction to his edition of the writings of Uriel da Costa, 'the Marrano problem is a unique religious–psychological problem'. In a pithy formula he summarized the split personality (*Spaltung des Bewußtseins*) of the Marrano: 'The Marrano is a Catholic without faith and a Jew without knowledge, but a Jew by will.'[25] The lack of a Jewish education and a certain distrust of religious authority bred divergent, idiosyncratic approaches to religion in general and Judaism in particular: hence a conflict such as that within Bet Jacob as well as the critiques of Judaism and religion by Uriel da Costa and Spinoza. Today we are no longer so sanguine as our predecessors about the prospects of solving religious–psycho-

[23] D'Ancona, 'Komst der Marranen', 229.
[24] Vaz Dias, it must be admitted, did not. He saw the conflict as a power struggle within the Mahamad.
[25] Gebhardt, *Schriften des Uriel da Costa*, p. xix; pp. xxiii–xxv deal with the Bet Jacob conflict.

logical problems in terms of faith and knowledge, even leaving aside the ambiguities and complexities we have come to associate with the human will. Especially in their application to the Marranos the terms, awkwardly, have more negative than positive value. As merchants, for instance, their faith may not have been too profound or very sophisticated to begin with; as sixteenth-century Iberians, their knowledge of matters religious was probably perfunctory across the board; and as persecuted individuals, they willed perhaps most to be left alone.[26] Even if there was some intellectual divergence of opinion, we do better to consider first whether other, more elementary, tensions were at play.

The multiplicity of congregations within a single Sephardi or Portuguese Jewish colony is quite a common phenomenon. If we compare the various settlements for overall size, number of congregations, and date of foundation, we clearly discern a pattern. The earlier and larger communities of Salonika and Constantinople harboured many separate congregations and continued to be so divided throughout the sixteenth and seventeenth centuries.[27] Hamburg and Amsterdam, both established at the end of the sixteenth century and of decidedly smaller size, each had three congregations at first which united at a later date—in Amsterdam in 1639, in Hamburg in 1652—at a time when the community was still increasing in size.[28] Finally, the Jewish communities of London, the Caribbean, and North America, founded after the mid-seventeenth century and the unifications of the Amsterdam and Hamburg communities, never had more than one single congregation.[29] Obviously the divisions and fusions of communities were not a simple correlate of the size of the settlement.

In the communities founded during the period immediately following the expulsion from Spain (1492) and the mass conversions in Portugal (1496–7), that is, those in Salonika and Constantinople, the most conspicuous feature of the different congregations is their members' common region or place of origin rather than any intellectual compatibility. It was not loyalty to their former locality so much as kinship ties between people from the same area that occasioned these expatriates to assemble in separate synagogues. The size of the settlement as a whole and of the congregations individually enabled this internal division to persist. Numerical strength and kin loyalties enabled and encouraged each congregation to finance such communal responsibilities as the rabbi, education, and poor relief.

---

[26] On faith, see Pullan, ' "Ship with Two Rudders" '; id., *Jews of Europe*, 206–28. On knowledge, see Dedieu, ' "Christianisation" en Nouvelle Castille', who shows the deplorable state of knowledge of even the most basic elements of Christian doctrine among large sections of the population. On will, we need only refer to the numerous attempts to curb the power of the Inquisition and the pardons purchased at great expense.

[27] Emmanuel, *Histoire des Israélites de Salonique*, i. 64–5, 144–51; Galante, *Histoire des Juifs d'Istanbul*, ii. 170–224; Heyd, 'Jewish Communities of Istanbul'.

[28] D'Ancona, 'Komst der Marranen'; Kellenbenz, *Sephardim*, 25–57.

[29] Emmanuel, *History of the Jews of the Netherlands Antilles*, 51–61; Hyamson, *Sephardim of England*, 24–35; Oppenheim, 'Early History of the Jews in New York'.

The proliferation of congregations in the relatively small colonies of Hamburg and Amsterdam must likewise be ascribed to social rather than intellectual factors. Otherwise we must assume that somehow similar intellectual disputes plagued both communities and mysteriously never contaminated those of London and Curaçao. The fact of the ultimate unifications of the Hamburg and Amsterdam communities points to somewhat different social factors from those operating in the eastern Mediterranean.

As we saw earlier, kinship played a major role among the Portuguese Jews of northern Europe. As a result of several generations of New Christian mobility, their kinship was less geographically based than that of the descendants of the traditional communities of Spain and Portugal. Among the sixteenth- and seventeenth-century expatriates these ties had been forged as elements in an economic and ethno-religious strategy of survival and improvement. Their kin relations were at once narrower and more rational than the regional, primordial ties of the Salonika and Constantinople Sephardim. At the same time, there existed among the Portuguese Jews of northern Europe a diffuse sense of belonging to the *nação portuguesa e espanhola*, that peculiar Portuguese New Christian and Jewish collectivity whose boundaries were then—and are now—so hard to draw. And much of the communal history of the Portuguese Jews of the Atlantic diaspora must be seen in the light of the dynamics of kin clusters or clans and the *nação*.

For many years after the settlement of the first Portuguese in Amsterdam, a great many of them remained unaffiliated with any of the congregations that emerged. For example, one of the most substantial merchants of the early period, Manoel Carvalho, stated in 1643 that he had settled in Amsterdam in 1603 or thereabout and had not become a practising Jew until 1616, when apparently he joined Bet Jacob.[30] A similar wavering in religious no man's land also characterized many Portuguese expatriates in the Venice area.[31] The formation of the earliest congregations, therefore, by no means involved the entire *nação* then living in Amsterdam. Those who assembled in the congregations Bet Jacob and Neve Salom were a self-selected group, a small number of families among whom, for one reason or other, Jewish loyalties were particularly strong. As a matter of course, consciousness of Jewish descent may have been particularly strong among New Christian families that had been endogamous prior to settlement abroad. During these early days, moreover, the emphasis of Amsterdam's toleration on private worship fostered the emergence of small, domestic nuclei. Only after the building of the synagogue of Neve Salom in 1612 and the purchase of a Jewish cemetery at Ouderkerk in 1614—that is, when Jewish worship became public

---

[30] Pieterse, *Daniel Levi de Barrios*, 57. Carvalho's name first occurs in notarial deeds in 1604. In 1618 Carvalho was among the members of Bet Jacob leasing the building 'Antwerpen', where the congregation assembled for services; NRPJA 126, 1460–3.

[31] Pullan's ' "Ship with Two Rudders" '; id., *Jews of Europe*; id., 'Inquisition and the Jews of Venice'.

and recognized as such by the authorities—did other Portuguese join the two congregations.

As larger numbers joined the two congregations, a more or less clear distinction between Bet Jacob and Neve Salom became apparent. Neve Salom emerged as the more narrowly kin-based, and the majority of late joiners and newcomers appear to have linked up with Bet Jacob.[32] The latter congregation may have been more loosely based—on friendship, or regional ties, or common economic interest—from the start. The conflict which erupted in Bet Jacob in 1618 therefore comes as no great surprise. We will probably never know the precise nature of its underlying causes. It may have been set off by two family clusters or circles of friends or associates vying for supremacy in the community. More likely, it was sparked by the kind of economic tension discussed above. The Twelve Years Truce had drawn a greater variety of merchants to Amsterdam. With them and their often conflicting interests—especially now that the truce was drawing to a close—came an increase in volatility over and above the already substantial level of competitiveness and friction normal to mercantile communities.[33]

In the end, the division of the colony into three separate congregations established sufficient tranquillity for common concerns of the *nação* to emerge. As the Amsterdam authorities had explicitly declined any responsibility for indigent Iberian immigrants, poor relief became the major common preoccupation transcending congregational differences. To a large degree, the survival of the community depended on its ability to solve this problem within, of course, the bounds of its charitable impulses and resources. Hence the pious refrain, in the documents, of *tranquilidade* (tranquillity) and *conservação* (preservation) as the supreme objectives of the community's leadership. These were not hollow, platitudinous words. More often than not, they addressed themselves positively to the value of the *nação* rather than negatively to the fear of a governmental backlash. Ultimately, this co-operation on behalf of the *nação* laid the foundation for the unification of 1639; and significantly, the main unifying impulse came from Bet Jacob, not because of its rationalistic outlook, as has been suggested, but because it was the congregation with the broadest social base.

The division of the community into three congregations concerned worship primarily and education and charity secondarily. Each congregation had its own synagogue and its own rabbi, or *haham*, as the Portuguese Jews were wont to call him.[34] These rabbis occasionally also delivered sermons in congregations other

[32] D'Ancona, 'Komst der Marranen', 211.

[33] The sources necessary to unravel the background to the conflict are available. The major difficulty remains how to 'translate' the Jewish names of the congregational records into the Christian ones used in commercial and other transactions.

[34] The names and dates of the first *hahamim*, commonly the source of extensive and tiresome debate, are of little importance here. Zwarts, 'Eerste rabbijnen', d'Ancona, 'Komst der Marranen', and Seeligmann, *Bibliographie en historie*, discuss the relevant data.

than their own. We know from the voluntary contributions they made on such occasions that individual members often attended services at another synagogue, probably to participate in festivities of a private character.[35]

The first common concern to which the *parnasim* or elders addressed themselves seems to have been the provision of ritually slaughtered meat. As early as 1603, Philips Joosten (better known as Moses Uri Halevi) declared before the justices of Amsterdam that he slaughtered animals at the house of the butcher Marten Pietersz. and his brothers.[36] On 17 November 1610 various members of the Portuguese nation entered into a formal agreement with the Dutch butchers Hans Pietersz. and Jan Hermansz. according to which Uri Halevi or his son would slaughter and bone meat, paid for by the Portuguese, at the premises of these butchers. The Portuguese committed themselves not to buy meat from any other butcher.[37] As Jews were excluded from the butchers' guild, the only means by which they could obtain kosher meat was to have a *shohet* or ritual slaughterer working under Christian auspices. After 1622, with the foundation of the *imposta* board, communal supervision became more direct and stricter.

The next documented incidence of co-operation between Bet Jacob and Neve Salom occurred in 1614. On two occasions prior to that year the Portuguese had been refused permission to purchase land for a cemetery in or near the city.[38] The Portuguese dead were at that time buried in Groet, a village in the vicinity of Alkmaar, some twenty-five miles north of Amsterdam. Early in 1614 the *parnasim* of Bet Jacob and Neve Salom purchased (without prior permission, it seems) a plot of land at Ouderkerk, only about three miles from the city, to be used as a cemetery.[39] Some protest from the local population ensued, but the provincial authorities, *ex post facto*, granted the Portuguese Jews officially the right to bury their dead at Ouderkerk. Bet Israel later joined Bet Jacob and Neve Salom in the use of the Ouderkerk cemetery, which has remained the burial ground of the Portuguese Jewish community of Amsterdam to this day. After 1622 the administration of the communal cemetery was placed in the hands of the *imposta* board.

As regards charity and education, the early period is clouded in obscurity. Prior to 1615–16 Bet Jacob and Neve Salom seem to have organized rudimentary charitable and educational activities separately. According to Daniel Levi de Barrios, Bet Jacob members had instituted a sodality, Bikur Holim (dedicated 'to visit the sick, both rich and poor, to provide the things necessary to alleviate their difficulties of support and medicines, to watch over the dying, to wash and embalm the dead, and to accompany the mourners'), as early as 1609.[40] From the complaints of the Church Council we learn that there existed a Jewish school (we are not told whose) in 1614.[41] More definite information has been preserved regarding

[35] GAA, PIG 8 (Bet Jacob) contains a list of the members of the other congregations who pledged money to Bet Jacob.

[36] Zwarts, 'Eerste rabbijnen', 252.

[37] NRPJA 436.   [38] See above, p. 12.   [39] See above, p. 11.

[40] De Barrios, *Triumpho del govierno popular*, 479–86.   [41] Zwarts, 'Eerste rabbijnen', 265.

the period after 1615–16, for in those years the two congregations decided on a significant reorganization of their charitable and educational activities.

The first impetus came from the foundation of Dotar, initiated at the suggestion of Jacob Coronel of Hamburg after the example of the Hebra Kedossa de cazar orfans, founded in Venice in 1613.[42] The Santa Companhia de Dotar Orfans e Donzelas Pobres, commonly referred to as Dotar, was founded by twenty Portuguese Jews, sixteen of whom were residents of Amsterdam, two of Pernambuco, one of Hamburg, and one of Florence. According to the provisional regulations drawn up and approved on 12 February 1615, the society was to dedicate itself to marry orphans and poor maidens of the Portuguese and Castilian nation residing between Saint-Jean-de-Luz and Danzig, whether in France or in Flanders (i.e. the Low Countries), England or Germany. All those 'wishing to support such a pious work who are of our Hebrew nation, whether Portuguese or Castilian, or their descendants in masculine or feminine line, residing anywhere in the world', could become members of the society, if they contributed at least 20 Flemish pounds in Amsterdam money.

The ultimate regulations, running to twenty-seven chapters and covering all the details of the organization, were published on 12 March 1615.[43] Dotar was to be and to remain a free association, 'neither subject nor obligated to any of the *kehilot* of this city, neither the two which presently exist nor those which may come into being in the future'. Having no punitive power whatsoever, Dotar placed itself under the protection of the *parnasim*, who, if necessary, would censure recalcitrant members. Obviously the concerns which had inspired the foundation of Dotar transcended the boundaries of the two congregations and of any congregations, for they included the entire expatriate Iberian community of western Europe.

The focus of Dotar's concern was not without significant limitations. Eligibility for the annual drawings (by lot) of the society was regulated with meticulous detail and was restricted to

orphans and maidens . . . who are poor and need support for their marriage; [who are] of the Portuguese or Spanish nation; Hebrews who confess the unity of the Lord of the World and the truth of His Most Sacred Law; [who are] of good conduct and manners, honest and honourable, without any taint of vileness; who live and dwell, during the year in which they are admitted, in the area designated in the preamble to these *haskamot*.

Most significant here are the limitations to girls and women who had emigrated from the Iberian peninsula and had settled in France, the Southern Netherlands, the Republic, England, or Germany, and to those who had rejected Catholicism and inclined towards Judaism. Conscious of the existence of the Hebra Kedossa of Venice, Amsterdam's Dotar did not need to spread its activities also over Italy and the Levant. Moreover, as the immigration statistics have shown, Italy and the Levant did not really constitute a significant social reality from the perspective of

[42] Révah, 'Premier règlement'; Pieterse, *350 jaar Dotar*; d'Ancona, 'Komst der Marranen', 221–3.
[43] Révah, 'Premier règlement', 668–91.

Amsterdam's Portuguese Jews. France seems to have received most of Dotar's attention. Among the correspondents abroad enlisted by the society's administrators so as to inform its leaders in Amsterdam of worthy candidates, the French outnumbered all the others. In October 1615 correspondents were designated for Saint-Jean-de-Luz, Bordeaux, Paris, Nantes, Rouen, Antwerp, and Hamburg. Saint-Jean-de-Luz especially figured most prominently in supplying candidates for the Amsterdam drawings (thirteen in 1616, thirty-five in 1617). The reasons for the prominence of France in general and Saint-Jean-de-Luz in particular are not hard to find. France, after all, bordered Spain and was therefore the most likely place of refuge for those émigrés unable to afford costlier voyages; Saint-Jean-de-Luz, being the first major French town across the Spanish border, could even be reached on foot. The percentage of poor Iberian émigrés was probably nowhere as high as in France. Otherwise, the most significant limitation concerned the exclusion of Spain and Portugal as areas of recruitment. The reason for this can only be guessed at. The Amsterdam administrators may have wished for greater certainty as to the religious inclinations of the prospective candidates than could be provided under the clandestine and volatile conditions that prevailed in Spain or Portugal. Or they may have viewed their relations with the expatriate community of Iberian New Christians as qualitatively different from those with the New Christians of Portugal and Spain. The latter were still primarily private. The various New Christian settlements of western Europe—all abstracted in a similar vein from the Iberian context—could be viewed as separate communal entities sharing many problems with the community of Amsterdam.

This is not to say that religion played no role at all in the thinking of Dotar's founders. The limitation restricting eligibility to those girls and women 'who confess the unity of the Lord of the World and the truth of His Most Sacred Law' clearly indicates that it did. The phrase circumscribes the Marranos' minimal Judaism perfectly. Another clause of the regulations which must be seen in conjunction with this restriction went one step further. According to chapter 15, a woman whose lot had been drawn would be paid her dowry 'as soon as the administrators and treasurer had received reliable information that she had married a circumcised Jew with *beraha* [the customary Jewish ceremony], in conformity with our Sacred Law' and within a certain amount of time. In other words, Dotar allotted dowries only to those women willing to make a more definite commitment to Judaism than was possible in those countries where Judaism could not be practised. This, as well as the explicit inclusion of the contingency that the woman might choose to get married in Venice or the Levant, seems to indicate that Dotar's primary concern was to draw people to Judaism in general. But we may be making too much of a minor contingency if we leave our conclusion in that abstract form. In reality, the eligibility restriction to women residing near or along the Atlantic coast weighed the chance of a future Jewish marriage heavily towards Amsterdam and Hamburg.

Another set of explicit regulations tipped the scale even more decidedly in Amsterdam's favour. Chapters 11–14 of the regulations treat, at great length and with revealing meticulousness, of the various categories of candidates, the respective degrees of preference they would enjoy, and the differential payments to be reserved for each category. Alongside the classification into orphans (by which is meant fatherless girls) and maidens, Dotar also distinguished between *parentas* and *particulares*. *Parentas* were such girls and women who were related, in any of three degrees, to a *companheiro* of Dotar, that is, a member who had contributed at least 20 Flemish pounds. First-degree *parentas* included daughters and sisters of *companheiros*; second-degree, granddaughters and nieces; and third-degree, first and second cousins. *Particulares* were the girls and women not related, in any of these degrees, to a *companheiro*. These two classifications—into orphans and maidens, and into *parentas* and *particulares*—were superimposed upon each other to create an unmistakable system of preferential treatment, both in terms of selection among the final candidates and in terms of the amount of dowry to be allotted.

A sole recipient for each dowry was drawn from among six candidates, four orphans and two maidens. A drawing among the *particulares* determined which were to be included among the finalists. *Parentas*, orphans as well as maidens, were admitted to the finalists without prior drawing. The amounts of money for each category's dowry reveal a similar scale of preference (see Table 4.1). On the whole, therefore, the geographical as well as the eligibility restrictions, coupled with the preferential treatment of *parentas*, reveal a calculated Amsterdam-centred bias. The main concern of Dotar may thus be summarized as the Amsterdam-bound migration of unmarried New Christian women ready to adopt Judaism.

The source of this concern is not far to seek. As pointed out in Chapter 2, single male immigration from Portugal seems to have commenced in the 1610s and remained a fairly constant feature of that particular immigration until about 1650. Single female immigration becomes noticeable from about 1620 onwards, and is most pronounced from France and Antwerp. Dotar's primary function was to redress the gender imbalance that naturally emerged among the immigrant community in Amsterdam. Similar associations were a common feature of Portugal's colonial empire. During the sixteenth century, for instance, the Portuguese Crown instituted the system of 'orphans of the king', that is, 'orphans of marriageable age sent from Lisbon to India to be married', with the blessings of a royal dowry.[44] On a private level, too, brotherhoods such as the Misericórdias, the largest charitable organization of the Portuguese empire, administered dowries in a fashion closely paralleling, in execution and in function, the activities of Amsterdam's Dotar.[45] The provision of dowries as a concomitant of migration resembles these Portuguese examples more closely than contemporary Jewish sodalities, whose provision of dowries was an element in their general aid to the needy.[46]

[44] Russell-Wood, *Fidalgos and Philanthropists*, 32.   [45] Ibid. 173–200.
[46] Baron, *Jewish Community*, i. 363–4; ii. 332–3; iii. 212–13.

Table 4.1. Dowries set by the
statutes of Dotar, 1615

Category	Range (gulden)
Parentas	
Orphans	
1st degree	600
2nd degree	360–500
3rd degree	350–450
Maidens	
1st degree	400–500
2nd degree	360–450
3rd degree	300–360
Particulares	
Orphans	300
Maidens	240

In the statutes of Dotar we recognize the first more or less explicit circumscription of the *nação* from the point of view of the northern European Portuguese. This *nação* consisted of two clearly distinguished and unequal elements: kin-related, but geographically separated, individuals; and the general poor of the communities of the Atlantic diaspora. The first were by far the more prominent centre of attention; the second inhabited a grey area at the boundaries. The latter's inclusion in the *nação* may be seen as a consequence of their participation in the same historical and geographical movement, or of pressures by non-Jewish authorities in whose undiscriminating minds these poor were obviously part of the *nação*. Generally, poor relief within the Amsterdam Portuguese Jewish community has been interpreted as a necessary, almost forced response to external pressures, as inspired by the fear that the poor might tarnish the image of the wealthier and more 'advantageous' merchants in the eyes of the local authorities. The inclusion, however self-serving, of some of these poor within the parameters of Dotar suggests, I believe, that the Portuguese themselves already possessed a sense of common bonds created by having shared in the same fate. On one, most important, level the *nação* was a community of blood ties; on another, a community of fate. It was a network of cousinhoods created—as a network—by fate.

In terms of the history of Amsterdam's Portuguese Jewish congregations, the foundation of Dotar had other reverberations as well. It seems that the Bikur Holim society of Bet Jacob protested against the creation of the new sodality, probably fearing encroachment upon its monopoly in the field of charity. Subsequently, as a result of the foundation of Dotar and the protest by Bikur Holim, the two congregations then existing entered into negotiations regarding possible co-operation in the fields of charity and education.[47] The agreement they reached,

[47] D'Ancona, 'Komst der Marranen', 211, 222, 239–43; Pieterse, *Daniel Levi de Barrios*, 95–8.

in 1616, separated the formerly united charitable and educational activities and established one single society, called Talmud Tora, in which the two congregations together co-operated to provide religious instruction for the poor. The more affluent Portuguese Jews seem to have relied on private instructors. For that reason Bet Jacob, most likely the congregation with the greater number of poor, dominated the administration of the Talmud Tora society. With regard to Bikur Holim, the two congregations agreed to retain their independence.

The conflict within Bet Jacob that resulted in the foundation of Bet Israel interrupted the process of ever-increasing co-operation. In the long run, the fragmentation that attended the existence of three separate congregations ultimately drove home to the various *parnasim* the necessity of sharing responsibilities. Changes in the pattern of immigration certainly contributed to this realization. During the Twelve Years Truce (1609–21) the Portuguese Jewish community of Amsterdam witnessed a sudden increase of both wealthier and less affluent immigrants; and, as the Bank of Exchange figures indicate, the end of the truce was accompanied by an exodus of commercially important Portuguese Jews from Amsterdam, making the growing problems of poor relief all the more salient for the reduced population of better-off merchants. It is in this light that we must view the next co-operative phase, initiated by the formation of the *imposta* board.[48]

On 4 February 1622 the *parnasim* of the three congregations of Amsterdam met 'to discuss matters general and necessary to the nation and its preservation'.[49] They resolved to institute an *imposta* (impost), the revenue from which was to help 'the common weal and general benefit of the nation and to enable us better to preserve ourselves'. The *imposta* was levied, in various percentages, on the import and export of merchandise, silver and gold (minted and unminted), diamonds, pearls, amber, and jewels; on money transactions, insurance policies, and brokerage fees. It was administered by a board of six members, consisting of two former *parnasim* from each of the three congregations. Articles 19–29 of the statutes, which ran to thirty-two paragraphs in all, specify the purposes for which the *imposta* revenue was to be used. Aside from all other self-imposed obligations, 30 gulden a month was contributed to the almoners of the city of Amsterdam for their poor (Article 21). In general, the funds were to be used exclusively for 'general cases of the nation' ('os casos gerais da nação') and 'particular cases having occurred on account of deficiencies of the nation' ('hos casos particulares subcedidos por defeitos da nação') (Article 19). Articles 22 and 23 explain the 'general cases' and suggest the solution envisaged:

Article 22. And since the main object and reason of this *imposta* is to alleviate the excessive financial burden placed on us by the poor of our Portuguese and Spanish nation, as they completely lack relief or livelihood, [the founders of the *imposta* board] resolve to attempt to

[48] D'Ancona, 'Komst der Marranen', 243–54.
[49] GAA, PIG 13: 'Libro dos termos da ymposta da naçao principiado em 24 de Sebat 5382 [4 Feb. 1622]'.

get them to re-emigrate [*se procure encuminhalos*] to countries of Judaism where they can live more easily [*para terras de Judezmo aonde mais commodamente possão pasar a vida*], as follows: the poor who will, in the future, arrive directly [i.e. only by way of sea] from Portugal and Castile will be considered as general poor, even though they join one of the three *kehilot*. For these [general poor] the *imposta* board [*diputados*] will provide some aid in conformity with what is presently being given from the *sedaca* to similar families, while trying to get them to re-emigrate within the shortest time possible. These [future poor] are to be preferred over those already in the country . . .

Article 23. The poor presently residing in this country, belonging to our Portuguese and Spanish nation, who are not registered on the *sedaca* rolls which each *kahal* is to submit (even though they will be so in the future with any of the *kehilot*) are also considered as general [cases]. Of these the board will send away [*yrão despachando*] those who themselves understand its necessity and agree to be the first to re-emigrate.

Each person over 13 years of age would receive 60 gulden, children 30 gulden, and babies 20 gulden, with the proviso that a single household, however large, would never receive more than 400 gulden. The minimum possible amount was to be disbursed upon departure from Amsterdam, the rest to be paid along the way, 'it being well understood that no person will be sent away to a country of Judaism closer than Italy or Poland' ('bem entendido que nenhua pesoa sera encaminhada para mais proxima terra de Judezmo que Ytalia ou Polonia') (Article 25). Recipients of *imposta* aid were given six months within which to emigrate (Article 26).[50] Finally, Article 29 defined those poor who would not be eligible for *imposta* assistance:

The board will immediately write to France and to other regions they see fit, warning them that no poor person coming from there will receive aid or be helped to settle elsewhere, for there [in France] he is much closer to the route to Italy and Turkey [*como nenhu pobre que delas venha sera provido nem encaminhado por quanto ali esta mais perto do caminho direito de Ytalia e Turquia*], and [the board will explicitly] state that no poor person coming from those regions or any other where Judaism is practised, whoever he may be, can be assisted or helped to settle elsewhere, not only as far as the *imposta* is concerned, but he will also not be admitted to the *sedaca* of any of the *kehilot*. Thus, they might save themselves the trouble of coming to such an expensive and inconvenient country as this is, to live or undertake a voyage [*para que assi escusem de se vir meter em terra tam cara e yncomoda como esta o he para viverem ou fazer caminho*]. For [the *sedaca* and the *imposta*] are only for those who are already here and for those who will directly come from Spain, persecuted by [inquisitorial] proceedings, looking for a refuge to observe the Law of God [*perseguidos de tarbalhos a buscar a observancia da Ley del Dio*].

Unrelated to these measures of poor relief, the *imposta* board was also to be the official spokesman of the nation (Article 30). In the ensuing years, the board also assumed control over the slaughtering and selling of ritual meat and the administra-

---

[50] The fate of some of the families who emigrated under this programme may be studied in Cohen, 'Passage to a New World', and Bartal and Kaplan, 'Emigration of Indigent Jews'.

tion of the cemetery.[51] It expanded its relief efforts to include the ransoming of Jews and Iberian exiles captured in the Mediterranean and the provision of assistance to Jewish communities such as those of Jerusalem and Mantua which had fallen on hard times; and locally it helped Ashkenazi refugees (Tudescos) and Portuguese Jewish poor who had fallen sick, and gave special assistance such as the hiring of a wet-nurse for an orphaned baby.[52] It also maintained a rudimentary pawn shop (*emprestimo*) to aid the slightly less or only temporarily destitute.[53] Once in place as a central committee of the three congregations, the *imposta* board took upon itself other matters concerning the *nação* as a whole. Thus it issued warnings against conflicts between licensed and unlicensed brokers as well as against the buying and selling of illegal coinage.[54] It delegated to itself the right of censorship over religious disputes with non-Jews and the printing of Hebrew and vernacular books.[55] It imposed restrictions on gambling, on festivities—whether private or within the synagogue—and on the carrying of arms within or in the neighbourhood of the synagogues.[56] It ruled against the issuance of divorce certificates without the permission of the board.[57] Finally, it upheld the traditional Jewish communal safeguard of *jus hazaka*, the protection of Jewish tenants.[58]

There is nothing unique in the *imposta* board's intermingling of religious and socio-economic concerns *per se*. After all, the Portuguese Jewish community of Amsterdam was at once an association of religious exiles and a colony of foreign merchants. But what model did the *imposta* board follow in its deliberations regarding the organization of the community? As religious exiles Amsterdam's Portuguese Jews might have organized their community upon the model of a traditional, more or less autonomous Jewish community. As foreign merchants they might have wished to establish themselves as a privileged 'nation' or 'factory' in accordance with the practice of other foreign merchants elsewhere. Early modern Europe was replete with foreign mercantile communities that maintained separate religious establishments. Even where there existed no religious difference between the foreign merchants and the host country, the former tended to congregate in their own houses of worship. Either model, the Jewish community or the factory, would account for the far-reaching religious and socio-economic concerns expressed by the *imposta* board. We may, however, consider certain factors that possibly rendered the *imposta* board an institution *sui generis*, neither fully reflecting the model of traditional Jewish communities nor faithfully mirroring the contemporary factory.

---

[51] On ritual meat, GAA, PIG 13, pp. 16, 19–24, 29, 32, 52, 58, 72, 120; on the cemetery, ibid. 16, 29, 34, 42, 63, 67, 80–1, 108.

[52] On ransoms, ibid. 31, 99, 100, 121; on aid to foreign Jewish communities, ibid. 40, 56, 59, 116, 136; on Tudescos, ibid. 44, 78, 102; on the Portuguese Jewish sick, ibid. 130, 131; on the wet-nurse, ibid. 92.   [53] Little is known about the *emprestimo*. Mention of it occurs ibid. 109.

[54] On brokers, ibid. 18, 71; on illegal currencies, ibid. 109, 112, 114, 141.

[55] On religious disputes, ibid. 61; on printing, ibid. 50, 53, 78.

[56] On gambling, ibid. 25, 62, 87, 131; on festivities, ibid. 48, 62, 86; on arms, ibid. 82–3, 112, 123–7.

[57] Ibid. 133.   [58] Ibid. 36, 139; and Baron, *Jewish Community*, ii. 291–301.

The Amsterdam authorities viewed the Portuguese Jewish community primarily as a religious association. Unlike other cities, in Holland and in other parts of Europe, Amsterdam never granted factory status to any colony of foreign merchants. As far as the Amsterdam government was concerned the religious character of the Portuguese Jews determined their communal organization. The Amsterdam authorities had also left the communal status of the Portuguese Jews sufficiently ill defined to allow them to define themselves as more than a mere voluntary religious association. The Portuguese Jews were undoubtedly familiar with the factory status of their fellow Portuguese in Antwerp and that of foreigners in Portugal and Spain. If anything, personal experience must have made the factory model more familiar than that of the Jewish community. At the same time, significant political and religious realities militated against the adoption of the factory model. First, of course, Amsterdam realities ruled out the establishment of a factory. More importantly, in terms of self-definition, Amsterdam's Portuguese Jews had no formal political ties to either Portugal or Spain. Other foreign merchant colonies remained subject to their national sovereigns. Because of their conversion to Judaism and settlement in enemy territory, Amsterdam's Portuguese Jews had lost their status as subjects of the Iberian kings. Therefore, even if the Amsterdam government had been accustomed to grant factory status to foreign merchants, the Portuguese Jews would have been in no position to accept such a grant. Yet the political realities of their own expatriate situation forced Amsterdam's Portuguese Jews to introduce into their religious communal structure elements commonly associated with foreign merchant colonies.

Thus, lacking the right to restrict immigration into Amsterdam, the *imposta* board resorted to encouraging the re-emigration of undesired immigrants. Neither in Amsterdam nor in Portugal or Spain could the *imposta* board hope or wish to find assistance in its endeavour to curb immigration. Never did the *imposta* board invoke the traditional, halakhically sanctioned principle of *herem hayishuv*, the threat of excommunication against any person who had not acquired, from the Jewish community, the legal right to reside in that community. True, the *herem hayishuv* had never been adopted in medieval Spain; but its widespread application in early modern Europe makes Amsterdam's silence on this score at least unexpected.[59] The non-implementation of *herem hayishuv* is less surprising if we assume the *imposta* board to have thought along the lines of a factory. The taxation of imported and exported goods reflects common practice in many factories of foreign merchants, while Jewish communities more regularly taxed property or income, or relied on consumer taxes.[60] Finally, the *imposta* board's role as representative of the entire nation before the Dutch authorities resembles the factory's

[59] Rabinowitz, *Herem Hayyishub*, 78–9.
[60] For a general survey of taxation, see Baron, *Jewish Community*, ii. 246–65. The factory type of taxation may conveniently be studied in Goris, *Étude sur les colonies marchandes*, 51–2; Pohl, *Portugiesen in Antwerpen*, 54–6.

election of consuls who acted on its behalf before the authorities. The *imposta* board's representatives were not *shtadlanim*, 'temporary or permanent envoys in charge of external political relations' employed by traditional Jewish communities;[61] they were 'consuls', duly elected representatives who shared in the entire administration of the community. The particular forms in which the *imposta* board mixed religious and commercial concerns expose the hybrid character of a religious association imbued not primarily with traditional, Jewish communal practices but with a residue of commercial customs as practised by foreign merchants throughout Europe.

The problems of poor relief that had led to the establishment of the *imposta* board did not disappear. The re-emigration policy adopted by the board seems to have been effective only for a short period of time. Emigrants sent to Italy were unable to find employment there and often returned to Amsterdam. In 1628, therefore, the board decided to send emigrants at least as far as North Africa or the Ottoman empire.[62] To ensure compliance, emigrants received only one-quarter of their assistance in Holland, another quarter in Italy, and the remainder at their destination. In 1629 the board decided to help immigrants from France to re-emigrate, but in 1631 this assistance had to be withdrawn for lack of funds.[63]

In 1633 the congregation Neve Salom requested—and was granted—a reduction of its contribution to the *imposta*,[64] and the following year the representatives of the three congregations agreed, in principle, to work towards the unification of the community.[65] During the next five years the Mahamadot of Bet Jacob, Neve Salom, and Bet Israel discussed the terms of unification. On 28 Elul 5398 (7 September 1638) they reached an agreement; on 29 Heshvan 5399 (6 November 1638) they completed the draft of that agreement, whose forty-two articles were read in the respective synagogues on 6 Kislev 5399 (13 November 1638). On 28 Veadar 5399 (3 April 1639) the articles of the unification agreement were approved by all the married members of the three congregations.[66]

There can be little doubt that it was the burdens of poor relief that prompted the communal leaders of Amsterdam's Portuguese Jews to relinquish the socially preferred division of the community in favour of an economically more equitable and administratively more manageable unity. The social composition of the immigrations of the 1620s and 1630s blurred the clan-like divisions of the early community. At first the Amsterdam congregations sought to resolve this problem by advocating and supporting the re-emigration of these immigrants; when that proved ineffectual, unification emerged as the only solution that was both socially feasible

---

[61] On the *shtadlan*, see Baron, *Jewish Community*, ii. 115–16. On the consuls, see Goris, *Étude sur les colonies marchandes*, 39–44, and Pohl, *Portugiesen in Antwerpen*, 44–52.

[62] GAA, PIG 13, p. 45.

[63] Ibid. 50–1.   [64] Ibid. 93.   [65] Ibid. 111.

[66] D'Ancona, 'Komst der Marranen', 261, 262, 266–7, 268–9; Wiznitzer, 'Merger Agreement', 109–11.

and economically justified. The motives behind the unification are clearly stated in a 1670 decision of the Amsterdam burgomasters:

Many years ago there being among them divisions of churches, it was discovered that many and sundry inconveniences resulted therefrom, both in terms of disagreements and disturbances which arose among each other (which also created some unrest within the city) and with regard to the poor, who presented a greater burden to one [congregation] than to the other and who, therefore, did not receive the proper relief on account of the impecuniosity and frequent lack of means of that congregation which was bearing the heaviest burden, so that many had to take recourse to and importune the public *comptoiren* of the poor.

In order to safeguard [against this happening again], they concluded already in 1638 a certain agreement according to which all [members] of the Jewish, Portuguese and Spanish *natie* bound themselves to have and attend one church or synagogue and to support communally the poor of the nation without anyone being allowed to pray with ten men outside the church and to establish separate congregations again.[67]

MEMBERSHIP AND ADMINISTRATION

The forty-two *capitolos* of the merger agreement and the fifty-six *haskamot* (agreements) of the Kahal Kados de Talmud Tora lay down in detail the manner in which the community was henceforth to conduct itself, in both religious and other matters.[68] These paragraphs, selected and amended from the statutes and regulations of the former congregations and of the *imposta* board, perpetuated the hybrid structure of communal governance discussed above, namely that of a voluntary religious association governed, in part, as a mercantile colony.

Talmud Tora was formed for 'the Jews of the Portuguese and Spanish nation who presently live in this city and will come here in the future' ('os judeos da nação portugeza e espanhola que ao prez^te estão nesta cidade e de novo vierão a ella') (cap. 3). The male members of this group were generally referred to as the *yehidim* (literally, the singular ones; the worshippers). In 1639 the definition required no specification. Not much later, the influx of a wide variety of Jews from Italy, North Africa, Germany, and Poland prompted the *parnasim* to introduce a number of telling distinctions. All Jewish males, of course, were permitted to pray in the synagogue; Jewish women, as we shall see, possessed this right to a more limited degree. The level of participation in special rites, however, differed from group to group.

---

[67] Noordkerk, *Handvesten*, ii. 473.

[68] Merger agreement: GAA, PIG 19, pp. 1–7; *haskamot*, ibid. 21–6. There exist two paginations of GAA, PIG 19: one modern, in pencil, ending on p. 289, and the original, in ink, which sometimes numbers folios and then pages. As the modern one is incomplete I have throughout used the original pagination. Furthermore, throughout this chapter and the next, paragraphs of the merger agreement will be identified as 'cap.' and those of the *haskamot* as 'hask.' The merger agreement has been published in Pieterse, *Daniel Levi de Barrios*, 155–67. Abbreviated versions of both the merger agreement and the *haskamot* may be found in de Castro, *Synagoge*, pp. xxi–xliii, and Mendes dos Remedios, *Judeus portugueses*, 189–97. A topical summary in English exists in Wiznitzer, 'Merger Agreement'.

Firstly, black and mulatto Jews—probably circumcised former slaves—were assigned an inferior status. They were buried in a separate section of the cemetery and could not be called to the reading of the Sefer Torah or participate in the lottery of other *misvot*.[69] The sources say nothing of the celebrations of circumcisions or weddings. Italian and North African 'Berberisco' Jews eventually came to be considered a group apart. In 1697, in the wake of a fairly large-scale Italian immigration, the *parnasim* observed that too many immigrants came to Amsterdam for the sole purpose of seeking aid from the Portuguese Jewish community. They resolved that members of other nations could no longer be admitted to Talmud Tora, not even those who married a Portuguese man or woman.[70] This resolution was difficult to enforce, as documents proving membership of one or another nation were difficult to come by or verify. In the end, certain Italian Jews were admitted as *congregantes* and others, of better social standing and with more positive documentation, as *yehidim*.[71] *Congregantes* possessed, as it were, a limited membership. They were taxed, but could not claim an assigned seat in the synagogue or participate in the lottery of *misvot*. They could, however, be called to read from the Torah on the occasion of circumcisions and weddings, and were buried at the Bet aHaim 'na carreira ordinaria' (in the common row). A special prayer (*rogativa*) could be said at the time of their death, but no *escava* (*hashkavah*; requiem) in the synagogue after the burial. (An exception was made for Italian *hahamim*.) *Congregantes* lost their limited membership if they married anyone not of the Portuguese and Spanish nation.

Ashkenazi Jews—Tudescos and Polacos, of German and Polish origin—were totally and unquestioningly excluded from any form of membership of Talmud Tora. So were Ashkenazim 'intermarried' with Portuguese Jewish women or men, and their descendants. Originally, it appears, such intermarriage occurred primarily between Ashkenazi men and Portuguese women. Exclusion of such Ashkenazim provoked no protests.[72] When, towards the end of the eighteenth century, Portuguese men began to marry Ashkenazi women, these sometimes prominent Portuguese accepted their exclusion less quietly. Thus in 1798 Moseh Curiel sought, in vain, to force the *haham* of Talmud Tora to consecrate his marriage to Rebeca Abraham Polak, 'mulher da nação tudesca'.[73] Finally, in 1805, it was decided that an 'intermarried' *yahid* lost his membership, but that his sons

---

[69] GAA, PIG 19, pp. 173 (20 Sivan 5404/24 June 1644), 224 (24 Nisan 5407/29 Apr. 1647).
[70] GAA, PIG 20, p. 230 (1 Elul 5457/18 Aug. 1697).
[71] Ibid., p. 243 (6 Adar 5458/17 Feb. 1698): Abraham, Ishac, Jacob, and Moseh Bassan admitted as *congregantes*; ibid., p. 305 (10 Adar Sheni 5461/20 Mar. 1701): Daniel Fresco, Moseh Sarfatin di Girona, and Aron de Manuel Marsella admitted as *congregantes*; GAA, PIG 21, p. 387 (Tishri 5487/1726): Selomoh de Mosseh Franco admitted as *yahid*.
[72] GAA, PIG 19, p. 643 (24 Kislev 5432/26 Nov. 1671).
[73] GAA, PIG 22, p. 317 (5558/1797/8). Since 1791, Portuguese Jewish fathers married to Ashkenazi women had been allowed to bury their children at the Ouderkerk Bet aHaim; ibid., p. 308 (28 Tevet 5551/4 Jan. 1791).

could reclaim membership if they married a woman 'de nossa nação de pae e mae', Portuguese paternally and maternally.[74] The only Ashkenazim ever formally accepted as *yehidim* were Moses Uri Halevi, his son Aron, and their descendants, including the printer Uri Phoebus Halevi, until their right of membership (*hazaka*) came to an abrupt end in 1700. In that year, around the same time that restrictions began to be placed on the membership of Italian Jews, the *parnasim* checked the records and found no document promising the descendants of Uri Halevi membership in perpetuity. Henceforth, no new descendants were to be admitted.[75]

The *parnasim* also considered the rights of Portuguese and Spanish New Christian refugees who had died on their way to joining Talmud Tora in Amsterdam. New Christians who died at sea without having set foot in any other country where they might have returned to Judaism were—in all matters pertaining to burial, mourning, and other mortuary rites—to be treated as Jews, even though uncircumcised, 'if it could be established by trustworthy witnesses that said persons had known *el Dio benditto*, had served Him in so far as was possible in said lands, and had undertaken this journey solely for the purpose of placing themselves under the wings of *el Dio benditto* and His service' ('constando por testemunhas fidedignas q dittas peças conheçião al dio bendito e o servião no que era posible fazerse en dittas terras e que aquelle viage não era com otro fin que porse debaxo das azas del dio bendito e seu serviço').[76] But when certain *yehidim* extended the letter of this resolution to recite *escava* for other New Christians who had died 'outside of Judaism' ('fora do Judesmo'), that is, not en route to Holland, the *parnasim* put an immediate stop to the practice. They feared that treating all New Christians potentially as Jews in this respect would undermine the significance of circumcision.[77]

The various modifications of the criteria for membership of the Kahal Kados de Talmud Tora highlight the two dimensions of ethnic particularism in Portuguese Jewish consciousness. It made them acutely aware of their difference, not only— and not even primarily—from Dutch Christians, but also, and just as strongly, from Jews of other parts of Europe; and it never allowed them to forget that the *nação* was larger than the Kahal. In their inclusion of 'almost' Portuguese Jews as well as 'renegade' Portuguese Jews, the *parnasim* applied the same criteria used earlier in the century by the founders of Dotar and the *imposta* board. It would be a mistake to view Portuguese Jewish exclusivism simply as a haughty and negative reaction to threats posed by Ashkenazi immigration. Prior to the rejection of German, Polish, and Italian Jews there had been and always remained an affirmation of something peculiarly and positively Portuguese. The sadness lies not so

---

[74] Ibid., p. 326 (21 Shevat 5565/21 Jan. 1805).

[75] GAA, PIG 20, p. 293 (14 Elul 5460/29 Aug. 1700). Isaac Leendert van Leewaerden, a descendant of Uri Halevi, however, was allowed to bury his child at the Bet aHaim; ibid., p. 328 (13 Iyar 5462/11 May 1702). [76] GAA, PIG 19, p. 191 (4 Sivan 5405/29 May 1645).

[77] Ibid., p. 195 (21 Av 5405/10 Aug. 1645).

much in their stubborn exclusivism—which harmed no one—as in their retention of this affirmation for its own sake.

Having succeeded in unifying the community in order to gain better control over the problems of poor relief, the *parnasim* were adamant in safeguarding this unity in the face of mounting financial pressures within the Kahal proper as well as within the Jewish community at large. Capitolo 2 of the agreement forbade the formation of any other congregation in the future. Any *minyan*, or embryonic association, outside the synagogue was regarded with suspicion and allowed only under the strictest of conditions. Prayer meetings outside the synagogue were allowed only at the homes of bridegrooms and mourners, in the Medras (the religious schools), and in tobacco workshops, and then only for those who worked there.[78] In Chapter 5 we will have occasion to examine the circumstances and consequences of the formation of a private *minyan* by the del Sotto family in 1670. In response to the disruptions generated by this incident the burgomasters saw fit to confirm capitolo 2 of the merger agreement, as follows:

I. That no one of the Portuguese or Spanish Jewish *natie* who until now has observed their religion in their Church or Synagogue as well as those who in the future will arrive from abroad and join them may separate himself from that Church or Synagogue and community in order to pray or congregate with ten or more persons.

II. Much less that any one of them may form or keep another Church without approval and explicit consent of the Gentlemen Burgomasters, after consultation with the Parnasim or Elders of that time.

III. That no one of those who break with the aforesaid Church may go and pray outside their community in one of the other Jewish Churches, whether German or Polish.[79]

This became the only statute of the Kahal formally ratified in municipal law. It proved sufficient to prevent any further schisms within the Portuguese Jewish community, but less effective, as we shall see, in stopping individuals from occasionally and temporarily joining the German Jewish community in prayer.

The Kahal Kados de Talmud Tora was to be governed, directed, and administered by a board of 'seven worthy, devoted, and God-fearing persons', six *parnasim* and one *gabai* (treasurer), known collectively as the Mahamad (cap. 4). Each new Mahamad was elected by the previous one, changing half of its members every half year (cap. 6). In order to be eligible to serve on the Mahamad, a prospective *parnas* or *gabai* had to have lived as a Jew for at least three consecutive years and could not be re-elected to another term until three years after his previous one (cap. 10). A person elected to serve on the Mahamad could not refuse to do so, nor could he quit after having accepted his nomination, without penalty (hask. 3). Finally, certain degrees of consanguinity among members of the same Mahamad were explicitly forbidden (hask. 2): 'In one Mahamad will not be elected a father

---

[78] GAA, PIG 20, p. 147 (27 Sivan 5451/24 June 1691; and 5454/1693/4).
[79] Noordkerk, *Handvesten*, ii. 473–4; GAA, PIG 19, p. 628 (5431/1670/1).

together with his son, a brother with a brother, a grandfather with a grandson, an uncle with a nephew, a father-in-law with a son-in-law, cousins in the first degree, a brother-in-law with a brother-in-law. Neither can a relative in these degrees cast a ballot in favour of such a relative nor judge an issue which concerns him.' In ensuing years several changes in the severities of penalties and in certain rules of consanguinity elaborated what may have seemed a simple enough matter on paper, but proved a sensitive issue in reality. A 1727 *reformação* (amendment) pertaining to the election of the Mahamad and certain honorary offices consisted of thirty-two paragraphs.[80]

'Worthy, devoted, and God-fearing persons'—'Pesoas benemeritas, zelozas e tementes del Dio': this abstract and pious formula does not come close to revealing the values and prejudices that went into selecting candidates for the Mahamad.

Two groups were definitely excluded—and so 'naturally' that their exclusion required no special mention: women and unmarried men. Ishac Nunes Belmonte, better known as Don Manuel de Belmonte, a nobleman and the king of Spain's resident, was the only bachelor for whom an exception was made.[81] Age, too, came to be a significant factor: a preference came to be expressed for prospective *parnasim* to be over 40 years of age and the *gabai* between 28 and 38.[82] *Parnasim*-elect over the age of 70 were the only ones who could legitimately refuse to serve.[83]

But sex, marital status, and age were only the most obvious restrictions. Far more important and less immediately apparent were the requirements of wealth and status. Table 4.2 clearly shows the preponderance of the wealthiest 5 per cent of the community among the *parnasim*.[84] Not only did the wealthiest proportionately furnish the largest number of *parnasim*, but these wealthy men also served more frequently. In fact—and this may be the most telling statistic of all—none of the wealthiest members of the community was ever passed over for selection on to the Mahamad, unless by his own choice.

Indeed, contrary to the noble-sounding words of capitolo 4 of the agreement, service on the Mahamad was less a privilege than a right, even an obligation. The various explicit restrictions and penalties pertaining to the election of *parnasim* make proper sense only in the context of such a 'class' prerogative. The forbidden degrees of consanguinity gain poignancy in view of the relatively small class of

[80] GAA, PIG 21, pp. 396–9 (21 Tevet 5487/14 Jan. 1727).

[81] Don Manuel de Belmonte was treated exceptionally in other respects as well. He was the only man under 50 allowed to retain a most coveted seat in the Esnoga, between the large columns close to the *hekhal*: GAA, PIG 19, p. 829 (18 Adar 5440/18 Feb. 1680).

[82] The age requirements were formalized in the *reformação* of 1727 but had probably been implicit before: GAA, PIG 21, pp. 396–9 (21 Tevet 5487/14 Jan. 1727).

[83] GAA, PIG 21, pp. 394 (27 Shevat 5487/18 Feb. 1727), 399 (21 Tevet 5487/14 Jan. 1727).

[84] Theoretically 175 posts were available during this period; only 174 were filled as there were only five *parnasim* and one *gabai* in 5456. The *finta* figures were derived from the tables in GAA, PIG 19, pp. 779–83 (5438/1677/8); GAA, PIG 20, pp. 13–17 (5441/1680/1), 121–4 (5448/1687/8), 153–5 (5452/1691/2), and 185–7 (5455/1694/5).

Table 4.2. The composition of the Mahamad, 1675–1700

Finta	No. of fintados[a]	% fintados	No. of parnasim	Cumulative number of terms on Mahamad[b]	% total terms
≥100	14–24	3.2–5.9	25	74	42.5
50–99	26–55	6.4–12.4	26	53	30.5
30–49	48–68	11.7–14.7	19	40	23
<30	309–349	71.2–79.3	5	7	4

[a] The range gives the lowest and highest number of individuals in a particular *finta* category during the quarter-century under consideration.

[b] During this period a given *parnas* might serve several terms. This column lists the cumulative totals for each *finta* category.

largely intermarrying individuals who constituted prime Mahamad material. Indeed, seemingly minor changes in the rules of consanguinity highlight the increasing frequency of intermarriage as well as the caste-like contraction of the elite of Amsterdam's Portuguese Jewish community. In this respect the most significant alteration occurred in 1695, after the heyday of geographical and social mobility had passed. In that year it was decided that the forbidden degrees of relationship (*grados de parentesco*) should follow not only the lines of consanguinity but also those of affinity. At the same time it was resolved that *parnasim* of these forbidden *grados* should be allowed to succeed one another from one Mahamad to the next.[85] On the one hand, the ever-increasing intermingling of blood and marriage ties made a sham of the primary intentions of haskamah 2; on the other, the ever-decreasing number of candidates made it necessary to relax some of its secondary implications. Such was the paradoxical situation of an aristocratic governing body pretending to represent the community as a whole.

The obligatory nature of service on the Mahamad comes through most clearly in the penalties for refusal. Originally, refusal entailed a fine of 200 gulden, removal from candidacy for three years, and suspension of synagogue honours for a number of months or years. In 1656 the term of removal from candidacy was extended to six years; in 1699 it was again reduced to three; in 1722 it was abolished, if the person in question paid his fine.[86] This penalty, meanwhile, had been raised to 400 gulden in 1694 and was further increased to 600 gulden in 1744.[87] Obviously, removing persons from candidacy was a self-defeating measure and had to be abolished as refusals became more numerous. Fines were perhaps more effective, but appear to have been difficult to collect at times. In a curious

[85] GAA, PIG 20, p. 190 (7 Nisan 5455/23 Mar. 1695).

[86] GAA, PIG 19, p. 405 (19 Iyar 5416/3 May 1656); GAA, PIG 20, p. 276 (25 Heshvan 5460/ 10 Aug. 1700); p. 287 (7 Tishrei 5483/18 Sept. 1722).

[87] GAA, PIG 20, p. 181 (11 Elul 5454/1 Sept. 1694); GAA, PIG 22, p. 156 (12 Nisan 5504/25 Mar. 1744).

Table 4.3. *Yehidim* who refused to join the
Mahamad, 1639–1710

Year CE	Year AM	Name
1660/1	5421	Ishac Penso
1665/6	5426	Joseph d'Azevedo
1676/7	5437	Ishac de Meza
1681/2	5442	Jacob Pinedo
1688/9	5449	Moseh de Pinto
1691/2	5452	Abraham Lopes Berahel
1695/6	5456	Selomo Abarbanel Sousa
1698/9	5459	David Imanoel de Pinto
1699/1700	5460	Aron Alvares
		Selomo Curiel
1700/1	5461	Abraham Bueno Vivas
1703/4	5464	Abraham del Sotto
1706/7	5467	Ishac Curiel

incident in 1689 Abraham del Sotto paid the fine of 200 gulden owed by Moseh
de Pinto, who had flatly refused to serve, in order that de Pinto's refusal and non-
payment of the fine should not set 'a bad example'. Neither a relative nor, in all
likelihood, a friend, del Sotto probably sought to embarrass de Pinto.[88] Like debts,
monetary fines must have been a delicate issue among these merchants, potentially
involving questions of trust and honour. In general, of course, these fines were not
commensurate with the amount of force needed to persuade *yehidim* to accept their
appointment to the Mahamad: for 90 per cent of the Kahal Kados would not have
been able to afford the fine for declining an office which the same 90 per cent would
have regarded as the greatest honour. The level of the fine presupposed the socio-
economic status of the group from which the *parnasim* were drawn and was meaningful only in that context. The fact that the penalty was raised on several occasions
indicates the increasing reluctance of members of the Portuguese Jewish elite to
fulfil their obligation.

   During the final decade of the seventeenth century and the first decade of the
eighteenth, refusal to serve on the Mahamad assumed endemic proportions. Particularly numerous among those who refused were members of the most prominent
Portuguese Jewish families such as the de Pintos, the Curiels, and the del Sottos;
families which in previous years had furnished a very large number of *parnasim*.
Other prominent individuals such as Moseh Machado, Jacob Pereyra, and Imanoel
Levi Mendes had moved to The Hague and were thus never available for selection.

[88] GAA, PIG 20, p. 134 (8 Kislev 5450/20 Nov. 1689). Abraham del Sotto had recently been
readmitted as a *yahid* after he and several of his relatives had been excommunicated in the 1670s:
GAA, PIG 19, p. 839 (17 Sivan 5440/14 June 1680). In the next chapter we will have occasion to say
more on the excommunication of the del Sotto family.

Indeed, matters got so bad that in 1706 the Mahamad was forced to suspend the semi-annual election of three *parnasim*.[89] The office of *parnas* which had once been an aristocratic prerogative had become a burden, and the rewards of social status formerly attending supremacy within the Kahal Kados were sought—and found—elsewhere, within the larger confines of Dutch society, whether in Amsterdam or, especially, in The Hague and on quasi-aristocratic estates in the country.

Wealth may have been the most conspicuous determinant of 'worthiness' for the Mahamad, as suggested by Table 4.2; but it was by no means the only criterion on which status within the community was assessed. A cursory examination of the individuals who served as *parnas* or *gabai* reveals a far more variegated social reality than could be imagined on the basis of the *finta* figures alone. At the very top of the *finta* ladder it is impossible to separate wealth and status. Among the lower echelons, however, two other important features of status stand out to illumine significant dimensions of the social reality of Amsterdam's Portuguese Jewish community: lineage and occupation.

Among those who paid lower levels of *finta* are relatives of some at the top. Jeosua Abas was married to Ribca Curiel, a sister of Moseh Curiel alias Jeronimo Nunes da Costa. It was not simple affinity as such, however, which promoted Abas's rise to a level where he was eligible to become a *parnas* so much as the nature of that affinity. For the Curiel family was famous for marrying only with the Abas family. Six of Jacob Curiel's children married Abases.[90] Daniel Levi de Barrios speaks of 'the noble Sosas, the pure [*limpios*] Sarfatines, and the fortunate [*felizes*] Curiels who resemble those of the tribe of Manasseh in trying not to mix themselves by way of marriage except with those of their own stock' ('no procurando mezclarse en los Matrimonios sino con los de su estirpe').[91] The Abarbanel Sousa family was similarly partial to endogamous practices. And, though not among the wealthiest, several Abarbanel Sousas figured prominently among the members of the Mahamad. Endogamy rather than affinity appears to have been an important determinant of these families' worthiness to serve on the Mahamad.

Through endogamy, family clans seem primarily to have affected aristocratic airs. For narrow endogamy was indeed the common practice in Spain and Portugal, from the high aristocracy down to local elites.[92] Some families may have adopted endogamy to protect their New Christian identities, avoiding the risk of denunciation by keeping the inner family circle restricted. These endogamous practices

---

[89] GAA, PIG 20, p. 469 (29 Elul 5467/26 Sept. 1707).

[90] Jacob Curiel had a total of nine children. One son, Arão, died a bachelor. One daughter, Rachel, married Abraham Naar, of another family to which the Curiels were close. Gracia married Selomo Levi Ximenes. Sara, Moseh, Selomo, David, Ribca, and Abigail married, respectively, Ishac, Ribca, Sara, Lea, Jeosua, and Imanoel Abas. Members of the Abas alias Dias Jorge family, moreover, were elevated to the nobility by Emperor Mathias in 1614. See Révah, 'Pour l'histoire des "Nouveaux Chrétiens"', 304–5; Kellenbenz, *Sephardim*, 35, 489.

[91] De Barrios, *Triumpho del govierno popular*, 460.

[92] Bennassar, *The Spanish Character*, 182–91.

may have given such families a kind of unwritten distinction as to the deep roots of their Jewish origins. Some merchants may also have attempted to guard against dissipation of the family fortune by repeated intermarriage within the family.[93] The eligibility of the endogamous and less wealthy Curiels and Abarbanel Sousas for service on the Mahamad, however, must almost certainly be attributed to the aristocratic associations attending their marriage practices. The fact that their endogamy bore marks of both Iberian social and Jewish distinction may have given it the inflated importance such affectations otherwise lacked.

Endogamy was not the only means by which Portuguese Jews laid claim to a quasi-noble lineage. Two brothers of the Franco Mendes family, David and Mordehay, served a total of six terms on the Mahamad; yet their *finta* contributions never exceeded 40 gulden, while the sons and daughters of Abraham Franco Mendes had contracted marriages with partners from a wide variety of families. In this case, the nobility of the Franco Mendes lineage derived from its claim to descent from one of the thirty Jewish families whom Manoel of Portugal had allowed to settle in Oporto following the expulsion of the Jews from Spain in 1492.[94] (In a similar vein, the Abarbanel Sousas may have claimed descent from Don Isaac Abrabanel, one of the most prominent Jews of the expulsion period.) The Franco Mendes family, moreover, could boast to have been among the first Jewish settlers in Amsterdam and to have been prominent in communal affairs for several generations.[95]

In various forms, 'noble' lineage—with or without wealth—constituted an important source of social status. To us the quasi-noble claims of many Portuguese Jewish families may seem peculiar, even somewhat preposterous. Not only were they often based on the flimsiest of evidence, their intangibility and seeming lack of real consequence also contrast sharply with the mundane realities of mercantile and expatriate life. Yet the Portuguese Jewish passion for nobility was more than an atavistic survival of Iberian values and sensibilities. It should not be treated in isolation, but must await a fuller examination in a wider context.

Occupation, too, determined social status, both positively and negatively. For example, the brokers are conspicuous by their absence from the Mahamad, while the small group of physicians supplied quite a large number of *parnasim*; and yet the brokers constituted an important and fairly wealthy segment of the Portuguese Jewish community, whereas the physicians were economically of minor

[93] Smith, 'Mercantile Class', 137–55, also notes 'the construction of extended families' as a phenomenon mostly among the New Christians of Lisbon. He attributes it primarily to the inability of New Christians to marry into the nobility.

[94] De Barrios, *Triumpho del govierno popular*, 457.

[95] Belchior Mendes and his son, Francisco Mendes, are first encountered in notarial deeds during the very first years of the seventeenth century; NRPJA 81 (15 Feb. 1601), 107 (14 Feb. 1603), 109 (8 Mar. 1603). On 12 November 1623 the *imposta* board voted to have *escava* (requiem) said for Ishac Franco every Rescodes (Rosh Hodesh) and on Yom Kippur for his contribution to the purchase of the cemetery at Ouderkerk.

significance and financially relatively poor.[96] In economic and public life the sub-ordinates of the merchants, the brokers were assigned an inferior social position. The physicians, on the other hand, stood apart. Their relationship to the merchants was essentially non-economic and private. Untainted by economic involvement and in some sense a 'friend' of the family, the physician was found worthy of communal trust where other subordinates were not. Notwithstanding this acknowledgement of their status, however, physicians were not generally regarded as appropriate suitors for the daughters of the wealthy, nor did the sons of the wealthy choose a career in medicine.

CHARITY, WORSHIP, AND EDUCATION

Haskamah 1 leaves little doubt concerning the extent of the authority of the Mahamad. It is worth quoting in full:

The Mahamad will have authority and superiority over everything. No person may go against the resolutions taken and made public by the said Mahamad nor sign papers to oppose it. Those who do will be punished with *herem* [excommunication]. Therefore it is ruled that the Mahamad which serves every year has to be supreme in the governing of the Kahal and the *nação* and its dependencies. It can condemn disobedient persons to penalties it deems fit and make them ask forgiveness publicly from the *teva* [raised platform from which the Torah is read]. The Mahamad or whichever member of it is present in the synagogue (in case he finds it necessary to prevent the occurrence of discord) may also order (even under penalty of *herem*) any person or persons of this Kahal to leave the synagogue, to keep silent, or to calm down, or not to leave their house until ordered. Neither in these cases nor in others that may occur will a father take the side of his son, nor a son the side of his father, nor a relative that of a relative. Above all they will see to it that the order of the Mahamad be obeyed and executed, for thus it behoves the good government, peace, and tranquillity of this Kahal Kados. May God bless her.

Characteristically, this *haskamah* nowhere attempts to circumscribe precisely the spheres of authority within which the Mahamad ruled supreme. The actual dimensions of authority must be extracted from the regulations defining the specific rights and duties of the Mahamad. They may be subsumed under the broad and constantly shifting categories of charity, worship, education, and morality. Perhaps the weightiest duty of the Mahamad was the collection and administration of taxes to pay for the many services provided by the congregation. True to their mercantile background, the *parnasim* regulated the management of the various communal funds with meticulous detail. No Mahamad was allowed to

[96] Some of the most successful licensed brokers of the period paid *fintas* between 40 and 62 gulden: David de Abraham Cardoso 62 (in 5438/1677/8), David Hamis 62 (in 5438/1677/8), Abraham da Fonseca 50 (in 5452/1691/2), and Eliau Aboab 40 (in 5438/1677/8). In 5441 (1680/1) the physicians listed paid *fintas* between 3 and 24 gulden: Moseh Salom 24, Ishac Rocamora 17, Ishac Orobio de Castro and Selomoh Rocamora 12, Aron Bueno 10, David Sarfati 8, Daniel Semah Aboab 4, and Abraham Frois 3.

spend annually 'more than the revenue of the Kahal and the *imposta*' (cap. 38). At the end of each term, on Shabat Hagadol (the Sabbath preceding Passover), the *gabai* had to read, from the *teva*, a complete account of the financial management of the departing Mahamad (hask. 8). The revenue of Talmud Tora derived from obligatory taxes and voluntary contributions. The time and place for the collection of each were carefully prescribed.

The obligatory taxes, the *finta* and the *imposta*, constituted the mainstay of the Kahal's financial structure. The *finta* was assessed on the general wealth of each *yahid*, and the Mahamad had to update its *finta* assessments every two or three years (cap. 14). With regard to the *imposta*, the previous rules and regulations remained in effect (cap. 15 and hask. 48). A final tax was levied on the sale of kosher meat. The slaughter (*sehita*) and inspection (*bodeca*) of kosher meat was supervised by the Mahamad and the distribution of kosher meat restricted to 'the hall of the nation' (hask. 35).

The collection of voluntary contributions, elicited for special funds and on special occasions, was regulated equally punctiliously. The first was generally called a *nedava*, the second a *promessa*. *Nedavot* were collected for the Holy Land on Shabat Nahamu (the Sabbath following Tisha Be'av), for the *vestiaria* (for the clothing of poor students) on Hanukah, and for Bikur Holim (a charitable society for the care of the sick) and the *cautivos* (the ransom of captives) on Shabat Mikamokha (better known as Shabat Zakhor, the Sabbath before Purim) (hask. 13).[97] A general *nedava* for 'the poor of the *nação*', the so-called *nedava de selos peamim*, was collected before each of the three *Pascoas*, Pesah (Passover), Shavuot, and Sukkot (hask. 12). And finally, 'there will be a *nedava* whenever the Mahamad sees fit', in effect whenever there was an unforeseen shortage of funds or extraordinary expenditure (hask. 13). *Promessas* were not tied to any specific fund or time; the revenue went into the general charity chest, the *sedaca*, as did fines. *Promessas* were made by individual *yehidim* on the occasion of a personal celebration or of a religious honour (caps. 23, 28, and 29). On Purim, a special collection of *ma'ot purim* (Purim coins) was made to be distributed immediately among the poor (hask. 14). Moreover, three collection boxes were placed near the door of the synagogue: one for the *sedaca*, the second for the Holy Land, and the third for the *cautivos*; a fourth 'for the wax to be used on Yom Kippur' was added only on Rosh Hashanah (hask. 30). Finally, the Mahamad strictly prohibited a *yahid* from privately soliciting funds for another private individual.

These—plus testamentary bequests—were the sources of revenue for Talmud Tora. No extra-communal taxes were ever collected by the Mahamad. Amsterdam's Portuguese Jews paid municipal and state taxes as individuals, not collectively through the congregation. Almost the entire revenue collected by means of

---

[97] Shabat Zakhor is known among Portuguese Jews as Shabat Mikamokha, because the morning service is marked by the complete recitation of the *piyut Mi kamokha* of R. Yehudah Halevi: Dobrinsky, *Treasury*, 388.

the *finta*, *imposta*, *nedavot*, and *promessas* was spent within the community itself, excepting the funds for the Holy Land, for the redemption of captives, and for an occasional expenditure in favour of a foreign Jewish community struck by misfortune.

By and large, the collection of taxes does not appear to have given the Mahamad much trouble. In the years before the unification of the Kahal it had been necessary on several occasions to remind the *yehidim*, in fairly harsh terms, of their duty to pay the *imposta*.[98] As a general tax which concerned 'general' issues, it was not, perhaps, viewed with the same urgency as the *finta*, *nedavot*, and *promessas* that addressed more immediate, parochial concerns. After the unification, these periodic reminders were no longer required. *Finta* assessments, of course, had to be adjusted almost constantly, ostensibly at the request of the individuals involved. But the records reveal no opposition or any reluctance to pay the *finta* or the *imposta*, notwithstanding the fact that the highest *finta* assessments seem distinctly more formal than real. For, excepting the *finta* of 5438 (1677/8) when Ishac de Pinto was assessed at 386 gulden and his son David at 227 gulden, the maximum *finta* never exceeded 200 gulden at any point during the period from 1675 to 1700.[99] (The minimum was always 2 gulden.) As the wealthy merchants also paid substantially larger sums of *imposta*, the *parnasim* may have felt justified in setting the *finta* ceiling arbitrarily at 200 gulden. As it was, the top five of 409 *fintados* in 5452 (1691/2) paid more than 10 per cent of the total *finta* of 9,781 gulden.[100] Only with regard to the *imposta* on the buying and selling of shares in the two India companies did compliance fall short of regulations. As this trade had been uncommon at the time of the drafting of the original *imposta* statutes, it became subject to the tax only in 1641.[101] As trade became more common and the 1641 rate of *imposta* was found to be so high as to have occasioned evasion, the *parnasim* wisely decided in 1662 to lower the rates.[102] No individual was ever excommunicated for failure to pay communal taxes. Whether the *parnasim* were reluctant to broadcast such insubordination or whether compliance was indeed almost exemplary is hard to ascertain.

In respect of *nedavot* the Mahamad encountered a few minor 'inconveniences'. In particular it felt the need to prohibit, strenuously and repeatedly, the collection of alms on behalf of specific individuals (*pobres particulares*) during Purim.[103] It was also unhappy with *seluhim* (emissaries) arriving from the Holy Land to solicit

---

[98] Vlessing, 'New Light', 61. Her transcription of the relevant *haskamot* is faulty in places and her assertion that a list of taxpayers, identifying those who were in arrears, was posted in the synagogue is mistaken. It is nowhere mentioned in the sources.

[99] For the 5438 *finta*, see GAA, PIG 19, pp. 779–83.

[100] For the 5452 *finta*, see GAA, PIG 20, pp. 153–5.

[101] GAA, PIG 19, p. 103 (27 Elul 5401/2 Sept. 1641).

[102] Ibid., p. 507 (22 Elul 5422/6 Sept. 1662).

[103] Ibid., p. 61 (14 Adar 5400/8 Mar. 1640); GAA, PIG 20, pp. 200 (7 Adar II 5456/11 Mar. 1696), 539 (5471/1710/11).

funds in person.[104] Such spontaneous acts of charity particularized the problem of poverty to the detriment of the Mahamad's concern for 'the general poor' and undermined its authority. In matters of charity the Mahamad applied a strict and paternalistic conception of *bom governo* (good government).

The most severe and persistent difficulties arose in connection with the relatively minor tax on kosher meat. As an indirect tax, this levy provoked a certain measure of opposition, although it is difficult to pinpoint from which quarters. With the immigration of German and Polish Jews, it became possible to avoid this tax and purchase kosher meat elsewhere. Not surprisingly, the prohibition against buying meat from Tudescos or outside the *carniseria* (butchers' hall) of the *nação* was one of the most frequently reiterated *haskamot* of Talmud Tora.[105] On several occasions the Mahamad even found it necessary to add smoked meat and poultry to the list. The prohibition against poultry caused such a stir that it brought about, as we shall see in Chapter 5, the excommunication of Joseph Abarbanel Barboza. In prohibiting the purchase of kosher meat from German or Polish Jewish butchers, the Mahamad never explicitly referred to the tax issue as their motive. Instead they argued that such meat was *terephah e nevelah* (ritually unclean), a judgement which they expanded, on one occasion, by expressing doubts regarding the trustworthiness of Ashkenazi butchers.[106] It would seem that raising the matter of tax evasion was inappropriate inasmuch as those tempted to purchase meat from Ashkenazi butchers were motivated by poverty: kosher meat from these butchers was cheaper. Presenting a façade of religious propriety was more in line with the Mahamad's paternalism and rendered opposition to the prohibition a more acutely sensitive issue of authority.

The taxes collected were primarily used to pay for the Kahal's synagogue and its officers, its schools and teachers, and its multifarious charitable or social welfare expenditures. The lion's share, unquestionably, went for charity. Charity was also the communal concern over which the Mahamad retained for itself the tightest control. A myriad of associations provided a distinct number of general and specific services for the poor and the less fortunate. Some services the Mahamad itself controlled directly, others stood under their supervision, and a few others were independently organized. Several associations combined charitable with other activities. Funds were derived from the *finta* and *imposta*, from special annual *nedavot*, from membership fees, and from voluntary contributions.[107]

---

[104] GAA, PIG 19, p. 505 (19 Elul 5422/3 Sept. 1662).

[105] Ibid., pp. 15 (10 Sivan 5399/12 June 1639), 20 (21 Tamuz 5399/22 July 1639), 36 (13 Tevet 5400/8 Jan. 1640), 204 (27 Shevat 5406/12 Feb. 1646), 260 (3 Adar 5409/15 Feb. 1649), 375 (7 Tishrei 5415/18 Sept. 1655), 400 (8 Shevat 5416/12 Jan. 1656), 611 (5430/1669/70), 767 (20 Sivan 5437/20 June 1677), 770 (6 Elul 5437/3 Sept. 1677); GAA, PIG 20, pp. 101 (23 Heshvan 5447/10 Nov. 1687), 488 (5468/1707/8).

[106] GAA, PIG 19, pp. 15 (10 Sivan 5399/12 June 1639), 36 (13 Tevet 5400/8 Jan. 1640).

[107] Levie Bernfeld, '"Caridade escapa da morte"', gives very important data on testamentary 'legacies to the poor', not a few of which were administered by the Mahamad.

General poor relief was almost entirely in the hands of the Mahamad, who had at their disposal for this purpose a large charity fund known as the *sedaca*. Only one regulation specifies the general practice of poor relief. According to capitolo 32, persons benefiting from the *sedaca* had to be of good conduct and manners (*peçoas de boa vida e custumez*) and were chosen by lot. The same chapter decreed that no household could receive more than 2–6 gulden per month. Other regulations deal with specific categories of needy persons. Mourners received 4–6 gulden for the first meal (cap. 31). Criminals apprehended by the judicial authorities could not count on any support from the Kahal: 'Neither time nor money of the *nação* may be spent on such persons. Nor will the gentlemen of the Mahamad assist in their liberation, but will allow them to be punished by the court according to their offences, as an example for the others. Thus, the harmful is removed from among us and God's people may be free' (hask. 45).

Some aid was semi-permanent, for example in many cases of widowhood. The Mahamad also afforded temporary assistance. In addition to these monetary contributions, the Mahamad frequently provided rent subsidies and, in winter, peat for heating the apartments or rooms of the poor. The Mahamad also administered, through a special functionary nominated for that purpose, an *emprestimo* (pawn shop), where less fortunate members of the Kahal could borrow small sums of money. The services of this *emprestimo* were explicitly restricted to members of Talmud Tora, and no member was allowed to pawn articles belonging to a non-member.[108] Besides the Kahal's *emprestimo* there existed an independent association, Honen Dalim, founded in 1625, which also advanced loans at no interest against pawns.[109] The Bikur Holim association assumed as an ancillary responsibility the distribution of clothing among the poor of the *sedaca* during Hanukah, which falls on the eve of winter.[110]

To assist the sick among the poor beneficiaries of the *sedaca*, the Mahamad provided the services of a physician. Other details of sick care were primarily in the hands of the *parnasim* of Bikur Holim. This association, whose officials were nominated by the Mahamad in conjunction with the departing board, furnished medicine and nursing services as well as moral support in the form of periodic bedside visits. In fact, these visits, the traditional function of such associations in Jewish society, were not limited to the poor and explicitly included the rich as well.

Another group singled out for special assistance were the students of the communal religious school. In 1637 the *parnasim* noted with dismay that a number of promising students were forced to break off their studies in order to earn a living. It was accordingly decided to found a brotherhood (*irmandade*) which would provide

---

[108] GAA, PIG 19, p. 758 (22 Tevet 5437/27 Dec. 1676); Teensma, 'Fragmenten', 139. The Kahal's *emprestimo* appears to have fallen into disuse later in the century: GAA, PIG 20, pp. 157 (26 Shevat 5452/26 Jan. 1692), 340 (13 Kislev 5463/3 Dec. 1702).

[109] Pieterse, *Daniel Levi de Barrios*, 106.

[110] The *haskamot* of Bikur Holim may be found in GAA, PIG 19, pp. 102–4 (33 Omer 5399/22 May 1639), and Pieterse, *Daniel Levi de Barrios*, 175–8; see also pp. 95–7.

'scholarships' in the form of a monthly *haspakah* (provision). The capital of this *irmandade* consisted of membership fees and voluntary contributions, especially *promessas* made by men called to read from the Torah. Funds were distributed according to the abilities and diligence of the students.[111]

Orphans constituted a special category. Many probably received some aid from the *sedaca*. But private, independent associations assumed responsibilities otherwise provided by parents. Thus Dotar furnished dowries for orphaned girls, and Aby Yetomim gave orphaned boys an opportunity to learn a trade or pursue an education.[112] The latter sodality had come into being in 1648 in protest against the Mahamad's assumption of control over the burial society Gemilut Hasadim. The reasons for the split are not known. It remains curious that the two most prominent and best-organized benevolent societies independent of the Mahamad—and ostensibly deliberately so—concerned themselves with the care of orphans. The assertion of private initiative here may have been inspired by expectation of otherworldly rewards, traditionally—in Judaism but especially in Christianity—associated with this particular form of charity. Or it may have been motivated by a more mundane concern that an impartial, bureaucratic board of communal elders might not treat the issue as sensitively as private persons who had a personal stake in the future of these orphans.

As for Gemilut Hasadim, it provided for a proper burial of the poor and the appropriate assistance to the mourners.[113] The administrator of Gemilut Hasadim was appointed by the Mahamad. Of all the charitable associations of the Kahal, Gemilut Hasadim may well have been the least successful. In the 1660s it was necessary to remind members not to excuse themselves from fulfilling their obligation without sufficient cause and to raise the number of *ḥaverim* (members) from seventy-two to eighty-five so that men would be available to provide this important service.[114] This somewhat lacklustre support stands in contrast to the importance of the Hebra Kadisha in traditional Jewish communities. Either the distance to the cemetery at Ouderkerk discouraged enthusiasm or, more probably, the nature of Portuguese Jewish society favoured personal loyalties over abstract communal responsibilities, especially where no private interests were at stake.

Aside from these societies more or less specifically dedicated to charity, there existed several mutual aid associations. Like the larger societies Aby Yetomim and Gemilut Hasadim, such sodalities as Maskil Dal, Sahare Zedek, Keter Sem Tob, and Bahale Tesuba combined charitable work with periodic study sessions discussing religious topics.[115] Their life-span was generally short, their membership

[111] Paraira and da Silva Rosa, *Gedenkschrift*, 24–33; Pieterse, *Daniel Levi de Barrios*, 97–105.

[112] On Dotar, see sources quoted in n. 42. On Aby Yetomim, see Pieterse, *Daniel Levi de Barrios*, 117–19.

[113] The *haskamot* of Gemilut Hasadim may be found in GAA, PIG 19, p. 162 (1 Kislev 5404/ 12 Nov. 1643).

[114] Ibid., pp. 525 (21 Heshvan 5424/21 Nov. 1663), 583 (3 Tevet 5428/18 Dec. 1667).

[115] Pieterse, *Daniel Levi de Barrios*, 125–31.

limited, and their charity mostly restricted to fellow members. Probably because of the exclusive nature of these clubs and the concomitant diminution in community-wide charity, the Mahamad prohibited the proliferation of *hebrot e irmandades* in 1660 and again in 1684.[116]

The charitable concerns of the Mahamad also extended beyond the Kahal Kados de Talmud Tora to include German and Polish Jews in Amsterdam as well as Jewish communities and individuals abroad. Beginning around 1635, German and Polish Jewish immigration into Amsterdam expanded so rapidly that by the end of the century their number already exceeded that of the Portuguese Jews.[117] Refugees from the tumults of the Thirty Years War and, later, from the massacres of the Chmielnicki revolt and the Russo-Swedish war, many of these Ashkenazi Jews were extremely poor and appealed for help to Portuguese Jewish individuals and the *parnasim* of Talmud Tora. Door-to-door begging by these Ashkenazi poor, whether for money or for 'bread and butter', provoked severe reprimands from the Mahamad. In 1639, 1645, 1658, and 1664, the *parnasim* re-published their prohibi-tion against giving alms to Tudescos begging at the door.[118] In 1639 they gave as their reason the fear that such support would encourage large-scale immigration and result in ever-increasing burdens on the Kahal. As a matter of fact, 'many' who had been 'sent through' (*encaminhado*) by the Mahamad to Poland returned to Amsterdam by way of Prague and Frankfurt. In 1664 the *parnasim* warned against the dangers of contamination by the plague from *pobres polacos* (Polish). To assist the Tudescos in more appropriate ways, the Mahamad established in 1642 a special association, Abodat aHessed ('que quer dizer Menisterio ou Manifactura de Caridade': 'which means Service or Labour of Charity'), charged with the admin-istration of a workhouse, in which the poor could learn a trade and make a modest living.[119] Funds were collected through membership fees, voluntary contribu-tions, and a loan from the *sedaca* and were distributed according to merit. Abodat aHessed also provided orphans with a place to sleep, the sick with medicine, and the needy with clothes. In 1670 the workhouse was abolished, the association dis-mantled, except for a *tesoreiro* (treasurer), and the interest on its capital distributed among certain poor of the Kahal.[120] By this time the number of German and Polish Jews, including more affluent ones, was deemed to have grown sufficiently for them to be expected to take care of their own poor.

Finally, the Kahal Kados de Talmud Tora lent aid to communities and individ-uals abroad. It maintained a special fund for the ransoming of captives, adminis-

---

[116] GAA, PIG 19, p. 482 (4 Tevet 5421/6 Dec. 1660); PIG 20, p. 76 (2 Shevat 5444/18 Jan. 1684).

[117] In 1720 the number of German and Polish Jews in Amsterdam was estimated at 9,000: Bloom, *Economic Activities*, 210.

[118] GAA, PIG 19, pp. 20 (28 Tamuz 5399/30 July 1639), 195 (5405/1644/5), 430 (6 Iyar 5418/9 May 1658), 533 (5424/1663/4).

[119] The *haskamot* of Abodat aHessed may be found in GAA, PIG 19, pp. 109–12 (1 Adar 5402/1 Feb. 1642). See also Pieterse, *Daniel Levi de Barrios*, 132.

[120] GAA, PIG 19, p. 614 (7 Nisan 5430/28 Mar. 1670).

tered by a treasurer nominated by the Mahamad. This fund probably originated in petitions from the Portuguese Jews of Venice, in whose geographical orbit most cases of captivity occurred. By and large, ransom was paid only for Portuguese Jews, preferably for relatives of *yehidim* of Talmud Tora, but occasionally also for Iberian New Christians captured in the Mediterranean while on their way to joining a Jewish community, and exceptionally for other Jews.

The Kahal maintained a special fund for aid to Jewish communities and individuals in the Holy Land as well as administering contributions from the Portuguese Jewish community of Pernambuco (while it lasted) and that of Bayonne (beginning around 1673) and bequests by individuals to their *yeshivot*.[121] *Terra Santa* aid was given to the communities of Jerusalem, Hebron, Safed, and Tiberias.[122] The individuals assisted appear all to have been residents of Jerusalem and were, without exception, Portuguese and Spanish Jews. A fairly typical and detailed enumeration of contributions for 5421 (1660/1) lists 140 *patacas* for the general poor of Jerusalem, 130 *patacas* for Safed, 40 for Hebron, 25 for Tiberias, and 381 for individuals in Jerusalem, making a total of 716 *patacas*.[123] Among the 110 individuals whose names appear on the list we encounter twenty-two *hahamim*, four widows of *hahamim*, nine other relatives of *hahamim*, fourteen widows, three orphans, one *rubissa das mulheres* (teacher of women), one female slave, one blind woman, thirty other women, and twenty-five men. Beginning in 5433 (1672/3), the list of annual contributions includes 112 *patacas* for the *jesiba* of David Vaz and 100 for that of Moseh Franco Drago. Occasionally, special sums were designated for 'Robissim e livros em Syon' (teachers and books); once, a contribution was made to the 'K.K. dos Esquenazim'; and once to the 'K.K. de Tudescos' of Safed.[124]

The *parnasim* also extended, in response to special pleas, extraordinary aid to foreign Jewish communities who were being held hostage or had been hit by some singular disaster. In 1643 the Mahamad allocated aid to the Jews of Creps in Moravia (probably Krems in present-day Austria); in 1669, to those in Oran in North Africa; in 1677, to Polish Jews taken captive to Constantinople; in 1687, to the Jews of Buda; in 1689, to those of Belgrade; in 1690, to the *kehilot* of Prague; and, in 1699, to the Jews of Sarajevo in Bosnia.[125]

---

[121] Regarding contributions from Pernambuco, see GAA, PIG 19, p. 102 (5401/1640/1); from Bayonne, ibid., p. 659 (5433/1672/3).

[122] Tiberias disappears from the list after 1661 and reappears only in 1742: GAA, PIG 22, pp. 150–1 (11 Heshvan 5503/8 Nov. 1742). Economic deterioration and wars between local rulers had led to the abandonment of Tiberias by Jewish as well as other inhabitants. The town was resettled only in the late 1730s, and Jewish settlers returned to the holy site with the immigration of R. Hayim Abulafia of Smyrna and his large family entourage in 1740. See Barnai, 'Jewish Settlement', 143, 150–2.

[123] GAA, PIG 19, p. 496.

[124] 'K.K. dos Esquenazim', GAA, PIG 19, p. 228 (5407/1646/7); 'K.K. de Tudescos', ibid, p. 318 (10 Adar 5412/19 Feb. 1652).

[125] GAA, PIG 19, pp. 157 (24 Menahem 5403/9 Aug. 1643), 607 (7 Av 5429/4 Aug. 1669), 765 (3 Iyar 5437/5 May 1677); PIG 20, pp. 105 (5447/1686/7), 131 (9 Sivan 5449/28 May 1689), 140 (5450/1689/90), 270 (8 Tamuz 5459/5 July 1699).

The next area of major business and expenditure concerned the administration of communal worship. In this sphere the control of the Mahamad was virtually absolute. The *parnasim* managed the house of worship; hired, fired, and assigned tasks to the various religious officers; allotted seats in the synagogue; and decided what was and what was not appropriate behaviour within and around the synagogue. Every *yahid* had his assigned seat, every rite its set time, every custom its fixed procedure; assigned, set, and fixed by the *parnasim*.

In 1639, with the unification of the three congregations, Talmud Tora chose and enlarged the synagogue of the former congregation Bet Israel. The synagogue of Bet Jacob was sold to David del Sotto and that of Neve Salom to Mosse Moreno Monsanto.[126] In view of the much expanded immigration of the mid-century, it comes as no surprise that this synagogue was soon found to be too small. On Sunday, 16 November 1670, therefore, Haham Ishac Aboab, on behalf of a majority of *yehidim*, submitted the following petition to the Mahamad:

You [*parnasim*] are very well acquainted with the many vexations [*desgostos*] which the *yehidim* of our holy congregation suffer daily as a result of the tightness of seats. [This tightness is] the principal reason that we do not accomplish, with devotion, to commend ourselves to our Creator. This has moved us [*nosos coraçoins*] to request that You, with proper zeal, see fit to decide that an Esnoga be built sufficient to allow all unanimous to ask His Divine Majesty remission of our sins. [From His] mercy we hope for a good end to this good beginning. Submitting ourselves in everything to Your best judgement, we will obey Your resolutions wholly. May God dispose everything for the good. Amen.[127]

The Mahamad responded positively and began collecting funds for the new Esnoga immediately, on the following Sabbath, by means of special *nedavot*. As a result of the French invasion of 1672 and temporary shortages of funds, it took until 1675 for the magnificent structure to be completed. It proved sufficiently large for all the generations to come, and became a major attraction on the tourist route of many a foreign visitor as well as on the Sunday strolls of Amsterdam residents.[128] According to Abraham Idanha, the Kahal employed two *shamashim* (beadles), 'whose task it is to light the candelabras and perform other labours', and 'a Christian, a Hollander, whose task it is to sweep and keep the synagogue clean and, on Sabbath and holidays, to light and extinguish the candelabras, for Jews are not allowed to do this then'.[129]

The main religious functionaries of the Kahal were hired by the Mahamad. First among these was the *ḥazan* (cantor), who led the service; next were the *darshanim* (preachers), who were assigned specific Sabbaths on which they had to

---

[126] GAA, PIG 19, p. 8 (28 Veadar 5399/4 Apr. 1639).

[127] Ibid., p. 622 (3 Kislev 5431/16 Nov. 1670).

[128] A list of foreign visitors to the synagogues may be culled from Jacobsen Jensen, *Reizigers te Amsterdam*. On Amsterdam Sunday strollers, see GAA, PIG 19, p. 186 (16 Adar 5405/14 May 1645). For information on the building of the Esnoga, see de Castro, *Synagoge*.

[129] Teensma, 'Fragmenten', 133.

darsar (preach), as it was called in Amsterdam's Portuguese parlance; and finally, at least in 1639, the *haham* in charge of the *misvot* such as circumcisions, weddings, and funerals. The pronunciation of *derashot* (preachings) rotated on a prescribed basis. In 1639 the arrangement was that Haham Saul Levi Morteira preached on three consecutive Sabbaths or holidays and Haham Menasseh ben Israel on the fourth. Others who wished to *darsar* had to have permission from the Mahamad and had to inform the *haham* whose turn it was 'so as to release him of his duty' (cap. 19). The *derashot* to be delivered on Shabat Hagadol (before Passover), Shabat Shirah (when the Song of the Red Sea (Exod. 15) is read, after Tu Bishevat), Shavuot, Shabat Nahamu (after Tisha Be'av), Shabat Teshuvah (between Rosh Hashanah and Yom Kippur), the Sabbath of Hanukah, and Shabat Mikamokha (before Purim) had to be preached by the *haham* whose turn it was. In addition to their preaching duties, the *hahamim* served as instructors at the Kahal's religious school and as members of the Bet Din, the religious court. Even so their earnings were rather meagre and some were forced to seek additional sources of income: Menasseh ben Israel, for example, in printing, Saul Levi Morteira in money-changing.[130] Whatever prestige posterity may have accorded these *hahamim*, in the seventeenth century they were no more than inadequately re-munerated employees of the Mahamad and the Kahal. In Amsterdam a wealthy merchant would never have consented to his daughter's marriage with a *haham*.

In its regulation of synagogue worship, the first order of the Mahamad's business concerned the allotment of seats. Every *yahid* had a fixed seat in the Esnoga, but he did not own it; the seats were the Mahamad's to allot 'with as much equality as possible' and theirs to change 'as they see fit' (cap. 13). Women were not allotted seats: 'They will have to take a seat they find vacant whenever there is a service' (cap. 13). Foreigners and persons newly arrived also received assigned seats from the Mahamad who, if possible, took into consideration the requests of *yehidim* who wished such persons to be seated next to them (hask. 28). The *parnasim* and the *hahamim* each had their own bench on which they were seated in the order in which they served as president or in order of seniority (for example, in 1639 the order was: first Haham Saul Levi Morteira, then Haham David Pardo, then Haham Menasseh ben Israel, and finally Haham Ishac Aboab) (caps. 9 and 18). *Yehidim* could not protest against their assignment of a particular seat; if they did, they would not receive another seat assignment for five years. In 1680 Isaque Henriques Coutinho alias Sebastião Coutinho protested against his seat assignment and was suspended from 'congregating' with the Kahal. Coutinho appealed to the justices of Amsterdam with the argument that the Mahamad's decision prevented him from fulfilling his obligations as a Jew. On 9 May 1680 the justices ruled 'that as long as he wishes to be a Jew he will have to abide by the regulations of the

---

[130] Regarding Menasseh ben Israel's career as a printer, see Roth, *Life of Menasseh ben Israel*, 73–83; and esp. Fuks and Fuks-Mansfeld, *Hebrew Typography*, i. 99–135. For Saul Levi Morteira as a money-changer, see GAA, PIG 19, p. 191 (20 Iyar 5405/16 May 1645).

church'.[131] Two intractable problems associated with this question continued to upset the Mahamad's intentions of *bom governo* throughout the seventeenth and eighteenth centuries. First, it was extremely difficult to prevent *yehidim* from constantly changing seats—as witness the reiterated exhortations to remain in the places assigned.[132] Second, seats often remained vacant for uncertain lengths of time, owing to non-attendance, temporary absence from the city, or emigration. These empty seats were often in desirable sections of the Esnoga. The Mahamad was therefore forced to limit and then to change the limit of the time a seat could be allowed to remain vacant.[133]

The Mahamad clearly valued the attendance of women less than that of men. In winter, women were not allowed to stay in the Esnoga after dark. The opening hours of the gates to the women's galleries were carefully regulated and sometimes restricted. Mulatto or black women were not allowed to take a seat before the arrival of the 'white' women. Tudescas were not welcome. These regulations reveal the little consideration men gave women, especially in matters of religion.[134]

As noted above, capitolo 13 stipulated that the Mahamad would allot seats 'with as much equality as possible'. One list which seems to have been drafted at some time between 1675 and 1685 allows us to subject the Mahamad's sense of equality to close scrutiny.[135] The list is incomplete, mentioning a total of only 285 names, whereas the *fintas* of that period list more than 400 names. But of the 285 names listed 214 correspond to *finta* assessments, and for at least 50 per cent of the *yehidim* we can establish some correlation between social status and the seats occupied in the Esnoga.

Seats in the Esnoga were on parallel benches lined up longitudinally along the axis of the *hekhal* (ark) on one side, and the *teva* on the other.[136] They may be divided into three sections: seats in the 'ship' (central space) of the Esnoga, seats between the large columns supporting the roof of the Esnoga, and seats between the small columns supporting the women's galleries. Our correlations work out well only with regard to the benches between the two types of columns. Too much is unknown, uncertain, or unclear regarding arrangements in the ship to allow us to speak with any confidence. The *finta* averages for the different benches, beginning with the one closest to the *hekhal*, are as follows:

[131] GAA, PIG 19, p. 837 (13 Nisan 5440/12 Apr. 1680); PIG 20, p. 5 (9 May 1680).

[132] GAA, PIG 19, pp. 97 (17 Sivan 5401/26 May 1641), 315 (6 Tishrei 5412/21 Sept. 1651), 362 (25 Nisan 5414/12 Apr. 1654), 364 (4 Iyar 5414/21 Apr. 1654), 434 (5418/1657/8). All these warnings date from before the building of the Esnoga and may reflect the cramped conditions of the old synagogue rather than unruly behaviour.

[133] GAA, PIG 19, p. 187 (19 Adar 5405/17 Mar. 1645); PIG 20, p. 248 (2 Nisan 5458/14 Mar. 1698).

[134] GAA, PIG 19, pp. 62 (14 Adar 5400/8 Mar. 1640), 80 (5401/1640/1), 214 (15 Elul 5406/26 Aug. 1646), 375 (13 Tishrei 5415/24 Sept. 1654), 754 (4 Heshvan 5437/11 Oct. 1677).

[135] GAA, PIG 333: 'Livro de Repartissão dos Lugares da Esnoga', pp. 1–3 (a *repartissão* or distribution of seats preceding one from 5447/1686/7).

[136] A plan of the Esnoga may be found in Henriques de Castro, *Synagoge* (repr. Meijer), 37, or in Gans, *Memorboek*, 102, 104.

between the large columns: 86, 59, 56.6, 16.5 gulden;
behind the large columns: 14.8, 12.5, 7.4 gulden;
between the small columns: 73.2, 29.4, 25.7 gulden.[137]

According to an explicit regulation of the Mahamad, the seats between the large columns were reserved for men over 50 years of age and, later, when there were not enough men of advanced age to fill them, also for *parnasim* under 50.[138] It is clear from the figures listed above that age was not the only, and probably not even the prime, criterion. The most coveted seats—apparently, the ones closest to the *hekhal* and with a view of the *hekhal*—were assigned to the wealthiest members of the Kahal. This preferential treatment of the wealthy, of course, is hardly surprising. Why, then, did the *parnasim* find it necessary to stress 'equality' in the original definition of their task?

Following the assignment of seats, the Mahamad did its best to 'legislate' for as orderly and decorous a service as it deemed appropriate. These regulations are so numerous that no more than a few important or characteristic principles can be enumerated. The Mahamad 'set the hours for the beginning of prayer, in accordance with the seasons of the year' (hask. 6). It determined the election and order of those called up to read from the Torah, within the limits of traditional law, by the drawing of lots, 'so as to avoid confusion, [extra] work for the *parnas*, and scandal in the Kahal' (cap. 25). Withdrawal of one's name from the drawing box was a common punishment for the transgression of minor *haskamot*. The Mahamad also ruled against addressing men called up to read from the Torah—whether a local or foreign *haham* or other dignitary—by their titles, 'so as to avoid embarrassments' (hask. 21).

Only rarely do these particular *haskamot* appear to have been disobeyed. On the delicate subject of titles, the Mahamad twice asserted its authority to punish a recalcitrant *yahid*. In 1640, Haham Menasseh ben Israel was very briefly—for one day—excommunicated because he had loudly and publicly protested against the *gabai*'s refusal to address Jona Abarbanel, his brother-in-law, properly as 'senhor'.[139] In 1682 a dispute regarding the appropriate title of David de Mercado at his funeral resulted in the Mahamad fining Jacob Pereyra 120 gulden.[140] During the seventeenth century refusals to accept and fulfil the honours allotted appear to have been rare. On one such occasion and for reasons unknown, in 1699 Moseh Machado alias Antonio Alvares Machado, the famous army purveyor, refused the honour of Hatan Torah (the person concluding the year's reading of the Torah).[141] In 1706, however, the *parnasim* saw fit to remind *yehidim* of their duties and threatened a fine of 50 gulden for refusal to fulfil the honour of a Torah reading.[142]

---

[137] The *finta* figures are those for 5438 (1677/8): GAA, PIG 19, pp. 779–83.

[138] GAA, PIG 19, p. 829 (7 Adar 5440/7 Feb. 1680); PIG 20, p. 313 (24 Menahem 5461/18 Aug. 1701).   [139] GAA, PIG 19, p. 70 (16 Iyar 5400/8 May 1640).

[140] GAA, PIG 20, pp. 42–3 (6 Tamuz 5442/12 July 1682).

[141] Ibid., p. 274 (4 Tishrei 5460/27 Sept. 1699).   [142] Ibid., p. 426 (5466/1705/6).

Setting synagogue procedure was one thing; creating and maintaining an atmosphere appropriate to religious devotion was quite another. In the first place, it proved difficult, if not impossible, to curtail the movement of individuals during the service, within and outside the Esnoga. Judging by the Mahamad's exhortations, common infractions occurred when individuals stood up while the congregation was seated; when congregants engaged in conversation or left after the Sefer Torah had been raised, failing to listen to the recitation; when Dutch maids ventured among the male worshippers to bring children to their fathers; when *yehidim* got up to welcome a non-Jewish friend or acquaintance; and when *yehidim* and their families strolled around in the vicinity of the Esnoga during the service.[143] Two particular forms of conversation were singled out for specific reprimands. First, brokers were not allowed to talk business 'either before or after the prayers' (hask. 22). Later in the century the Mahamad prohibited business (especially stock) transactions also within the patio and immediate vicinity of the Esnoga.[144] It also strongly opposed any and all forms of altercation, whether publicly against the resolutions of the Mahamad or privately with another *yahid* or non-Jewish visitor.[145] Haskamah 19 further envisaged the possibility of physical conflicts and ruled that:

No person may raise his hand to strike his fellow in the synagogue, [in the schools, within the gate of the synagogue, or within a certain distance from the building of the synagogue]; nor may anyone come to these places carrying a sword, dagger, stick, or other offensive weapon, except a walking stick needed to lean on. In case some person or persons carry said weapons or raise their hand against their fellow in said places, we will have them placed in *herem* and separated from all our brothers, as soon as it happens. They will not be admitted to the synagogue, even though they do penance, without first being voted upon by the Gentlemen of the Mahamad and each paying 20 pounds gross to the *sedaca*.

In case someone of our [*nação*] has a quarrel with non-Jews and needs to carry some weapon for his defence, he will inform the Gentlemen of the Mahamad; and, if they find the reason justified, they will give permission to carry it for his defence.

It is also noted that the knife used by everyone is not included in this prohibition. One who draws his knife to do harm with it will incur the heaviest penalty of this *haskamah*. The *herem* will be lifted within the chamber of the Mahamad.

By and large, excepting an occasional fist-fight, physical violence was successfully kept out of the Esnoga. Elsewhere, of course, whether in the Jewish quarter or at the Exchange, impulsive, violent reactions were not uncommon. Lack of attention, disruptive movement, conversations, verbal arguments, and business discussions, on the other hand, would appear to have been fairly constant features of the Esnoga service of Amsterdam's Portuguese Jews.

[143] GAA, PIG 19, pp. 30 (7 Tishrei 5400/5 Oct. 1639), 76 (26 Elul 5400/13 Sept. 1640), 97 (17 Sivan 5401/26 May 1641), 196 (22 Elul 5405/13 Sept. 1645), 291 (26 Tamuz 5410/25 July 1650), 382 (5415/1654/5).

[144] Ibid., pp. 57 (15 Shevat 5400/8 Feb. 1640), 765 (1 Iyar 5437/3 May 1677); GAA, PIG 20, p. 336 (1 Heshvan 5463/23 Oct. 1702).

[145] Haskamot 1, 19, 20; GAA, PIG 19, p. 149 (17 Nisan 5403/6 Apr. 1643).

Eyewitness accounts by strangers unfamiliar with Jewish practices are, of course, not to be taken at face value. All too often we learn more from travelogues about the preconceptions of their authors than about the peoples they purport to be describing. Strikingly, for instance, none but the German travellers who visited seventeenth-century Amsterdam seems to have noticed that the Portuguese Jews employed Christian maids. In the same vein, the contrast between Jewish and Christian worship must have struck Protestants differently from Catholics. On the other hand, this very sensitivity to things unfamiliar may have prompted some travellers to describe experiences others left unmentioned. On the whole, facts noted by strangers can be useful whenever confirmed by other sources, as in the case of Christian maids and— it would seem from the above resolutions—of unruly behaviour in the Esnoga.

Among the many seventeenth-century travellers who visited the Esnoga or another Portuguese Jewish synagogue, the English were at once the most curious—and the most elaborate in their accounts—and the least negatively pre-disposed. The depiction they give of the service meshes with the impressions gained from the resolutions of the Mahamad. Philip Skippon, a military man who visited the old synagogue in 1663, describes what he saw as follows:

We went to their synagogue, a large place above stairs; the women are not seen in it, but have a gallery round the top with lattice windows; they wear no such stuff (like a *Scotch* plaid) as the men do over their faces, and hats which they never pull off in their synagogue. He that reads stands in a great desk, and makes a tone in his reading; the people also read either in the *Hebrew* or *Portuguese* bible in a singing tone; some men that were married the day before came to the reader, and spoke something to him which our interpreter said was what they gave to the poor, which he presently published: Their law, and some parts of the Old Testament were folded up in rolls, within an embroidered covering, the tops of the umbilicus or stick they roll'd them on, were cover'd with silver, and had silver bells hanging at them, the bridegrooms came from that end of the synagogue where they are lock'd up in presses, and brought them severally to the reader's seat, where they were untied, and all this while there was great singing among the people; then the reader or rabbi read somewhat, and the bridegrooms return'd to their places. Towards the latter end of their service, the reader and all the bridegrooms went round to shew themselves, with the Law, etc., untied in their hands, and the boys were very earnest to touch the covering with their hands and faces, and all this time the company made loud singings; when they came to the presses they put in the Law, etc. and then one said somewhat in a tone, and lock'd them up. The rabbi, while he was reading, had a little silver rod in his hand; at one time, for a good while, read at a table. This devotion was begun early in the morning, and lasted till noon; after dinner they began again. We observed some of the *Jews* to bow at times, (*quer.* whether at the name of *Jehovah?*) they seemed very careless, discoursing and laughing with strangers in the midst of the service; when they were dismissed, many of them went down singing till they came to the street. The minister or priest hath his seat under the reader.[146]

Will Brereton, a Member of Parliament who visited a synagogue on the Sabbath, 14 June 1634, noted laconically: 'Here in this congregation, no good

[146] Skippon, *Account of a Journey*, 405–6.

order, no great zeal and devotion here appearing; much time spent in singing and in talking.'[147] John Northleigh, a physician, visited the Esnoga around the turn of the century and left us this report:

Near Two thousand Souls I saw in their great Church, all habited in White Silk Hoods over their Shoulders, Men and Boys; whilst two of them, that look no more like Priests than any of the rest, read the Law at the lower end of the Church. At the Periods of which they would still make their great Alla or Allaluhah; but at other times be laughing, talking, and idly wandering, as if about prophane Affairs, though in a Presence so sacred.[148]

Besides offering descriptions of disorderly services, these travelogues create the distinct impression that Esnoga services were generally well attended. None of the records of the Mahamad makes any reference to the issue of attendance, either favourably or unfavourably. Only from the resolution exhorting *yehidim* not to take strolls in the vicinity of the Esnoga during prayers might we conclude that attendance was occasionally slackening off. On the whole, it is reasonable to conclude that attendance at the Esnoga constituted an elemental and regular feature of Portuguese Jewish religious practice.

As far as education was concerned, the Mahamad left the details of its administration to the *parnasim* of the Talmud Tora society; later, the management of the Ets Haim brotherhood, which provided financial assistance to students of Talmud Tora, was added to their duties. In 1639 the various classes or grades of Talmud Tora employed seven teachers: four whose only function was teaching (primarily in the lower grades), one whose primary job was as *ḥazan* of the Esnoga, and two *hahamim* who taught the upper grades and also preached in the Esnoga. The salaries of these teachers were paid from the *sedaca*, and their hiring was in the hands of the Mahamad. For the remainder of its costs the Talmud Tora relied on membership fees and voluntary contributions.

The Talmud Tora school confined itself to the religious education of boys. Regarding attendance—who attended, for how long, and how regularly?—we know virtually nothing. The organization of the curriculum is better known. The school seems to have been divided into six or seven grades (*escuelas*). In proper order, the students were taught the Hebrew alphabet and spelling; learned to read the Torah and the Prophets in Hebrew and to translate from Hebrew into Spanish; were introduced to the commentary of R. Solomon ben Isaac (Rashi); and finally, in the two highest grades, generally referred to as the *jesiba*, studied the Talmud and Jewish law.[149] This programme entailed a large commitment of time:

The time of study is the same for all the rabbis and the pupils. In the morning, when the clock strikes eight, all the teachers and pupils go to their respective classes, where they study until it strikes eleven, when they all leave. When the clock strikes two, they return as

[147] Brereton, *Travels*, 61.
[148] Northleigh, *Topographical Descriptions*, 60–1.
[149] De Barrios, *Triumpho del govierno popular*, 589–630; Pieterse, *Daniel Levi de Barrios*, 97–105.

above and study until it strikes five; or, in winter, until the time of service in the synagogue.[150]

The soundness of this curriculum and the positive results it bore made another Ashkenazi visitor, R. Shabbetai Sheftel Hurwitz, exclaim: 'I burst out in tears: why does this not also happen in our land? May this method of education spread across all Jewish communities!'[151]

In addition to the exemplary provisions it made for the religious school, the Mahamad also hired, in a less formal fashion, teachers to instruct the sons of the poor in the fundamentals of reading and writing, Portuguese, and arithmetic. Until 1652 there appears to have been only one such teacher; from 1652 until 1673, two; and after 1673, four. According to the contract drawn up in 1673 with David Senior Coronel, Daniel Lopes Arias, Selomoh Marcos, and Jacob de Caceres, they were to teach 'in the morning, from eleven until half past twelve; and in the afternoon, in summer, from five until half past six and, in winter, after the evening service'—that is, hours contiguous with those of the religious school. Students received this special education for three years.[152]

These institutions apart, education was a private matter, and occurred in three forms: private tutors for the sons—and daughters, it appears—of the more affluent; adult study groups; and individual study. Little is known about the tutors of the wealthy. We may assume that most of them were Portuguese Jews. Some children, it seems, must have received private instruction from Dutch tutors, evidenced by the fact that some Portuguese Jews acquired a distinctly different, Dutch (i.e. Gothic) style of handwriting.[153] Curiously, the daughter of the renowned physician Dr Ishac Orobio de Castro alias Baltasar de Orobio may have been one such child.[154]

Adult study groups were a favourite pastime with many Portuguese Jewish men. Where the inspiration for these loosely organized clubs, ornamentally referred to as *jesibot* or, in Spanish, as *academias*, came from is uncertain; many seem to have been based on ties of friendship.[155] Some of these clubs—the wealthier, presumably—hired a teacher. For instance, Tora Hor, of which the very wealthy Abraham Pereyra had been one of the founders, availed itself of the services of Haham Ishac Aboab. This *jesiba* met daily for half an hour 'to explicate the book of Rabenu Moseh' and on the Sabbath for an hour 'to answer questions arising from the *parashah* [Torah reading] of the week'.[156] Another *jesiba*, Keter Tora, founded by Haham Saul Levi Morteira under the auspices of the benefactor Ishac Penso, organized disputations on subjects of Jewish law. This particular club, comprising

[150] Shabbetai Bass, quoted in Gans, *Memorboek*, 107.   [151] Ibid.
[152] GAA, PIG 19, pp. 334 (11 Heshvan 5413/13 Oct. 1653), 681 (21 Menahem 5433/2 Sept. 1673).
[153] See Ch. 6 below, pp. 284–5.   [154] GAA, DTB 692, p. 35 (1 Mar. 1680).
[155] Large parts of de Barrios' *Triumpho del govierno popular* are dedicated to singing the praises of these *academias*.
[156] De Barrios, *Triumpho del govierno popular*, 357–92; Pieterse, *Daniel Levi de Barrios*, 109–11.

some of the most learned members of the Kahal, met daily for two hours.[157] These few aside, we have little more of the numerous *academias* of the seventeenth century than names, lists of members, and some curt (and often enigmatic) notes by the poet Daniel Levi de Barrios.

Information about individual private study has come down to us in the form of advice bequeathed by Ishack de Matatia Aboab, a jeweller, to his sons, in a so-called 'ethical will', dated 10 Sivan 5437 (10 June 1677). It is worth quoting an extensive fragment of this substantial document to highlight the utter seriousness with which Portuguese Jews pursued the objective of religious enlightenment.

My sons, if you wish to have the proper knowledge of the Law of the Lord and its precepts and wish to understand what its declarations and mysteries contain—which will gladden your soul and please the Lord, your God—assign fixed hours for the study of the Law. Read (or have read to you) with the proper concentration and inquisitiveness the books I will cite you in which you will find each time more pleasure. If your soul gladdens you with an understanding of what they contain and comprise, you will be simultaneously esteemed in the eyes of God and in those of the nations [*gentes*]. And you will not be as the base people of this century who live like brutes, without knowledge or understanding, who are satisfied with the surface of things and shun the secrets and mysteries enclosed in them. You will not reach this understanding without effort, or as the Sage says: 'if you seek it like silver and search for it as for hidden treasures, then you will understand the fear of the Lord' (Prov. 2: 4–5).

First, you should read, for four days a week, in the *Miqra gedolah*: the text in Hebrew and in the vernacular, with the commentary of Rashi, and other commentaries, beginning at the beginning until the end, even though it may take three or four years. The rest of the week you should read the *Shulḥan arukh* and, perhaps, from the *Levush*, until you have read all of it, which may take two or three years.

Having completed the reading of all these books with great concentration, you should read, for three days a week, Rabbenu Mosse [probably, Moses Maimonides' *Mishneh torah* rather than his *Moreh nevukhim*] from beginning to end, however long it may take; for two days a week, in *Minḥah belulah* [of Abraham Menahem Hacohen of Oporto], and other exegetes of the Law; and for the rest of the week, in some of the infinite number of books about our sages and morality which most attract you.

You should read all the *Mishnayot* with the best commentary.

Before all the festivals, you should always particularly read the *dinim* [laws] pertaining to them. Two weeks before Purim, you should read exegetical commentaries on the Megillah. A month before and during Pesah, you should read *Zevah pesah* on the Haggadah; and after Pesah, exegetical commentaries on the *Perakim* [*Pirke avot*] until Shavuot.

Never neglect to visit the *jesibot*.

Never neglect to listen to *derashot* [sermons].

From time to time, you should read for a few hours Spanish books of an entertaining nature and documents [histories?]. And especially, you should read at least each of the following twice: *Vision delectable* [of Alfonso de la Torre], *Nomologia* of Imanuel Aboab, *Carrascon* [of Fernando Texeda], *Las excelencias de los Hebreos* by [Isaac] Cardoso, *Lugares*

---

[157] De Barrios, *Triumpho del govierno popular*, 341–56; Pieterse, *Daniel Levi de Barrios*, 106–9.

comunes dichos y çentençias [?], *Princepe perfecto* [?], *Palafox* [Juan de Palafox y Mendoza's *Historia de la conquista de la China* or his *Historia real sagrada*?], *L° oliveyra de mão de todas çiençias* [?], *L° contos de mão* [?], *L°ˢ templo* [the various *Tratados* and *Retratos* of Jacob Jeuda Leon Templo?], *Conciliador* [of Menasseh ben Israel], *Almenara de la luz* [by Isaac Aboab, translated by Jacob Hages], *Obrigaçam dos coraçoens* [by Bahya ibn Paquda, translated by Semuel de Yshac Abas], *Cuzary* [by Yehudah Halevi, translated by Jacob Abendana], *Sefer hanhagot hayim* [*Libro intitulado regimiento de la vida* by Moses Almosnino], sermons of Jeosua da Silva [his *Discursos predycaveys*], questions and sermons of Abraham Cohen Pimentel [his *Questões e discursos academicos*, presented in Keter Tora], *Livro da providencia divina* of Isac Jesurun, *Imagem da vida christam* by f. Heitor Pinto.

And having occupied yourself with the above-mentioned books for seven or eight years, you should also read other books of our sages (of the infinite number that exist), as you may be inclined, according to your study ability. May the Lord, God, help you in everything so that you may always do His holy will.[158]

The ideal held up by Ishack Aboab may not have been reached by any lay members of the Kahal, but it gives us an idea of the framework within which the diligent Portuguese Jew pursued his religious education in seventeenth-century Amsterdam.

ORTHODOXY AND MORALITY

As with the *imposta* board, the Mahamad did not limit its jurisdiction to the obvious and central domains of charity, worship, and education. As best it could, it also sought to impose a certain level of public orthodoxy as well as of public and private morality.

The provision of kosher meat had been a central concern from the earliest days. It not only served as a convenient source of revenue but also provided the most distinctly Jewish necessity not available otherwise. Apart from the reiteration, mentioned above, of the prohibition on purchasing kosher meat from Tudescos, little needed to be said or discussed on this subject. The fact that *yehidim* obviously contravened the prohibition means that they did not accept the Mahamad's verdict that such meat was ritually unacceptable. In the context of orthodoxy, these actions must be ranked among the most visible signs of an ostensibly widespread observance of *kashrut* among the Portuguese Jews. Otherwise, information on this observance is virtually non-existent. The records of the Mahamad once speak of kosher meat to be exported to Brazil, possibly for the use of the travellers, possibly for consumption overseas;[159] and we possess one stray mention of a Jew who kept kosher under less than ideal circumstances. A Swedish traveller who visited Holland during the 1680s recounts how he and his travel companions ate at the home of a French language teacher at Leyden. Among the guests was a Jewish

---

[158] Aboab, 'Documentos para todo estado e ydade', fos. 6ᵛ–7ᵛ, Ets Haim-Montezinos Library, Amsterdam, MS 48 D 9. The bibliographical data in brackets may be found in Kayserling, *Biblioteca Española-Portugueza-Judaica*.   [159] GAA, PIG 19, p. 34 (9 Kislev 5400/5 Dec. 1639).

student 'who cooked and prepared his own food, in his room, for he would not tolerate the food and dishes handled by a Christian'.[160] Did other Portuguese Jewish guests, especially on more formal occasions, act similarly? Did Jeronimo Nunes da Costa and Manuel de Belmonte, agents of the kings of Portugal and Spain respectively, keep a strictly kosher diet during their frequent visits to The Hague, in days when there was not yet a Jewish community there? What did Abraham Cohen, a wealthy Portuguese Jewish friend of Johan Maurice, the former Dutch governor of Brazil, eat at the festive banquet organized by the directors of the West India Company in 1670?[161] We may be inclined to believe that on such occasions—which were not uncommon—these prominent Portuguese Jews did not insist on the strictest observance of *kashrut*, but we have no way of knowing. Even if they did not then keep kosher, in the overall scheme of the observance of *kashrut* these must be counted as minor incidents.

The Mahamad does not seem to have regulated the sale of wine. We do know of some Portuguese Jews importing kosher wine into Amsterdam. In 1706 Rachel Mendes Colaso of Peyrehorade produced eighty hogsheads of kosher wine for her sons, Abraham and Selomoh Lopes Colaso, in Amsterdam.[162] The wine imported by Selomo Belmonte in association with Arnout Sweers, however, was probably not kosher. The Belmonte & Sweers company employed a non-Jewish labourer, Jacob Schulperoort, who was charged with the casking of the wine, and according to Jewish law, Schulperoort's casking would have rendered the wine non-kosher.[163] Possibly the Belmonte & Sweers wine was not intended for Jewish consumption. At least one notarial deed reveals that Portuguese Jews were accustomed to frequenting Amsterdam's cafés and drinking what we must presume was non-kosher wine. In 1673, Daniel de Pas, Jesaia de Sousa, and Joseph Salvador had a glass of wine at the home of Françoys Gyssen.[164] Moreover, we must assume that the Portuguese Jewish men who visited the city's brothels also consumed non-kosher wine. On the whole, the dietary laws regarding kosher wine would appear to have been less strictly observed than those regarding kosher meat. Quite possibly wine was much less prominently—if at all—associated with Christian worship in the minds of the Portuguese Jews than it was in those of Ashkenazi Jews.

With regard to the observance of the Sabbath our sources are somewhat more explicit, not only because the Mahamad published regulations on the subject but also because mention of the Sabbath occurs in the notarial documents. Even though the Mahamad's resolutions ostensibly highlight failures to observe the Sabbath properly, the fact that only a few needed to be repeated would indicate

[160] Schoeps, *Philosemitismus im Barock*, 182.
[161] Abraham Cohen's attendance at the banquet is recorded in Hulshof (ed.), 'Duitsch econoom', 77. On Abraham Cohen, see Wiznitzer, *Jews in Colonial Brazil*, 171.
[162] Pieterse, 'Abraham Lopes Colaso', 1.
[163] GAA, NA 2205, p. 525 (4 Oct. 1658; A. Lock).
[164] GAA, NA 4077 (22 Nov. 1673; D. v. d. Groe).

that compliance was generally the rule. The *parnasim* forbade children to be drawn in little carts on the Sabbath, even by non-Jewish servants; reprimanded Jacob Jeuda Leon for showing his model of the Temple on the Sabbath; and admonished *yehidim* not to embark on a trip when it was certain they would not arrive at their destination before the Sabbath.[165] Before 1659, when the Amsterdam courts exempted Jews from appearing on Saturdays, the Mahamad twice reminded the Kahal to desist from such *audiencias*.[166] Less compliant was the response to the prohibition on visiting cafés and 'taking tea and chocolate' on the Sabbath.[167] The most frequent infractions of all occurred in connection with business transactions or labour performed by a third party on behalf of Portuguese Jews on the Sabbath.[168] Though contrary to Jewish law, these violations were not directly committed by Portuguese Jews themselves.

The notarial and other sources also reveal a widespread observance of the Sabbath. In 1662 Ishac Mocatta hired Coenraed Windus, master diamond polisher, to instruct his son, Aron, in the art of diamond cutting. The contract specifically states that Windus did not have to work on the Sabbath or on Jewish holidays.[169] In 1666 Moise Pereyra drew up a contract for his father's voyage to Frankfurt. Lambert Vogels, the coachmaster, was to deliver his passengers every Friday at two o'clock at an inn where they would eat and stay until Sunday morning.[170] On 30 August 1686 Ishac Enriques Faro alias Manuel de Toralto declared that he would like to draw up his last will and testament 'but that, as it was about six o'clock in the afternoon and the Sabbath would soon begin, he did not have time to compose nor to write his will'.[171] These examples could easily be multiplied: numerous others unanimously point to a strict observance of the Sabbath.

The nature of Sabbath observance is such that it is generally not mentioned unless it was being carried out. In order to discover whether the Sabbath was broken we must work in reverse: that is, we must establish the Saturdays of a given period and what Portuguese Jews did on these dates. An examination of this sort, for the years 1690 and 1691, yields some surprising results. Ester Salom, widow of Dr Moseh Rephael Salom (who was several times a *parnas* during his life), drew up her last will on Saturday, 3 November 1691; Florenza Dias de Pas hers on

[165] GAA, PIG 19, pp. 126 (44 Omer 5402/28 May 1642), 493 (13 Av 5412/17 Aug. 1652); PIG 20, p. 134 (5450/1689/90).

[166] GAA, PIG 19, pp. 388 (23 Iyar 5415/30 May 1655), 453 (9 Nisan 5419/2 Apr. 1659); Noordkerk, *Handvesten*, ii. 472–3.

[167] GAA, PIG 19, p. 172 (8 Sivan 5404/12 June 1644); PIG 20, p. 115 (28 Adar 5448/23 Sept. 1688).

[168] GAA, PIG 19, p. 388 (23 Iyar 5415/30 May 1655); PIG 20, pp. 93 (6 Av 5445/5 Sept. 1685), 189 (5455/1694/5).

[169] GAA, NA 2212A, p. 615 (28 Mar. 1662; A. Lock).

[170] GAA, NA 2220, p. 406 (4 Mar. 1666; A. Lock). Moise Pereyra was the son of the famous Abraham Pereyra. The voyage in question concerned Abraham Pereyra's pilgrimage to Venice, whence he was to join Shabbetai Zevi in Turkey or in the Holy Land.

[171] GAA, NA 3689, p. 9 (30 Aug. 1686; F. Tixerandet).

Saturday, 17 November 1691.[172] It is possible, of course, that these wills were actually drawn up and signed after sundown. With regard to marriage registrations there are no such doubts. In the years 1690–1, no fewer than six of forty-one Portuguese Jewish couples registered their intention to marry and signed the registration on a Saturday.[173] These figures may not appear very significant, but they do demonstrate that beyond the immediate purview of the Mahamad laxity in Sabbath observance was not uncommon.

The only other transgressions of Jewish law explicitly mentioned in the records of the Mahamad concern the beard. Twice, in 1657 and again in 1686, the Mahamad saw fit to reiterate the biblical injunction against shaving one's beard with a razor.[174] In 1676 *yehidim* were reminded not to trim their beards between Pesah and Shavuot.[175] The *parnasim* took the issue with somewhat surprising seriousness. They appear to have asked the *hahamim* to sermonize on the subject, refer to the practice of shaving as 'a grave sin', and threaten excommunication against anyone transgressing more than once. The Mahamad's sensitivity on this issue may have stemmed from their Iberian past, when assimilation in all matters pertaining to costume and toilette had been complete.

The final items of communal concern bore little or no relation to Jewish rituals. Some of the moral problems addressed by the *parnasim* were confined to the Kahal; others sprouted from relations between Jews and Christians. The major communal issues were gambling, and marital and sexual relations; the civic issues concerned business conduct and physical or spiritual frictions between Jews and Christians.

Gambling was too ingrained a vice for the Mahamad to be very effective in curbing it. Alongside provisions on the purchase of kosher meat and reiterated admonitions against lavish processions to honour a Hatan Torah or a Hatan Bereshit, gambling figures among the top three issues discussed by the Mahamad in the course of the seventeenth century. Gambling was also prominent among the Portuguese vices most obnoxious to contemporary Spaniards. In 1631 one David Darredes, pursued by gambling debts, illegitimate children, and suspicions of theft, fled the city before the authorities were able to apprehend him.[176] In 1656 Abraham Coronel Coutinho, 'a vagabond, whoremonger, gambler, and swindler', fled to Morocco to escape prosecution.[177] In 1654 an Italian Jew, Eleazar 'Schabielie', was banished from Amsterdam for the duration of two years, apparently because he had gambled with false dice.[178] There were within the Kahal other Portuguese Jews who capitalized on the prevalence of this passion. Abraham

[172] GAA, NA 4241 (3 and 17 Nov. 1691; D. v. d. Groe).
[173] GAA, DTB 696, p. 417–DTB 697, p. 237. These years were chosen because the registers quite accidentally listed the day of the week.
[174] GAA, PIG 19, p. 419 (9 Iyar 5417/22 Apr. 1657); PIG 20, p. 100 (19 Elul 5446/8 Sept. 1686).
[175] GAA, PIG 19, p. 750 (7 Elul 5436/16 Aug. 1676).
[176] GAA, NA 941, fos. 497–9 (23 Dec. 1631; D. Bredan).
[177] GAA, NA 2271, fo. 756 (30 Oct. 1656; A. Lock).
[178] GAA, ORA 310, fo. 12ᵛ (14 Mar. 1654).

Mendes Vasques and Semuel Pereira maintained gambling houses where school-boys and irresponsible fathers squandered their money.[179]

Haskamah 42 of 1639 only forbade 'playing' on fast days, 'for it is a grave sin against God and His Law'. From 1658 the Mahamad took notice of the large sums of money lost in gambling and prohibited 'all card and dice games with bets'. Subsequently the Mahamad was forced several times to reiterate the prohibition, occasionally adding new games to the list of proscribed pastimes, such as 'draybort' (possibly some form of roulette) in 1702.[180] More serious and potentially more damaging to the community as a whole were wagers (*apostas*) on public events. In 1664 the Mahamad warned of the 'bad name, hatred, and ill will [*roin nome, odio e malquerencia*]' that might be generated against the *nação* by wagers on the weekly death toll from the plague. Adding insult to injury, organizers of such wagers collected the relevant statistics at the city hall on the Sabbath. In 1673, in the days of the French invasion, Portuguese Jews accepted wagers on the lives of military leaders and government officials, on the sites and seizure of garrisons, on battles, and on ships surviving their voyages.[181] It is highly likely that the uncommonly stern censures of the *parnasim* did little to put a halt to these unsavoury practices but merely forced them underground.

Prostitution and the fathering of illegitimate offspring were among the commonest of social problems—so common, indeed, that the Mahamad took no notice of the related transgressions of the laws of the city and of propriety. The first, transgressions of the 1616 statute forbidding Jews from having 'any carnal conversation . . . with Christian women or maidens . . . even when such are of ill repute', were dealt with by the municipal authorities. The second resulted, more often than not, in out-of-court settlements between the Portuguese Jewish father and the Christian maid.[182] A typical incident of the first kind was registered as follows: 'Abraham Pessoa, of Amsterdam, 15 years of age, Jew, and David Henriques alias Francisco Lorenso, of Antwerp, 17 years of age, were both found in a whorehouse in the company of two Christian whores, all four in undershirt. According to the whores, Pessoa and Henriques had had carnal conversation with them.'[183] Both confessed. Pessoa was fined 150 gulden; Henriques—perhaps because he was from out of town—100 gulden. Regarding the second impropriety, the sources tell interesting tales of intimacy rarely recorded in Jewish history. In 1654 Antonio Lopes Suasso denied before the commissioner of small claims ('kleine zaken') that he was the father of the child of Margareta Meurs. Afterwards, in an inn, he agreed to pay Margareta Meurs 24 gulden for the costs of childbirth and to take the child

[179] GAA, NA 2218, p. 788 (20 Apr. 1665; A. Lock); NA 2268, fo. 16ᵛ (8 Jan. 1653; A. Lock). On similar gambling establishments in Antwerp, see Pohl, *Portugiesen in Antwerpen*, 104–5.

[180] GAA, PIG 19, pp. 443 (10 Heshvan 5419/6 Nov. 1658), 519 (8 Av 5423/11 Aug. 1663), 554 (26 Heshvan 5426/4 Nov. 1665); PIG 20, p. 319 (13 Adar 5462/13 Mar. 1702).

[181] GAA, PIG 19, pp. 537 (20 Menahem 5424/11 Aug. 1664), 678 (1 Tamuz 5433/15 June 1673). [182] See above, Ch. 1, n. 22. [183] GAA, ORA 323, fo. 223ᵛ (30 July 1677).

off her hands in Antwerp, where he would arrange for it to be brought up at his expense.[184] In 1673 Styntje Thomas of Ditmarsen allowed her son, fathered by Jacob Orobio, to be circumcised and wanted the child to be brought up by his father.[185] In 1674 Selomoh de la Faya agreed to pay 100 gulden in alimony and support of the child of Marritge Barents.[186] Only when young Portuguese Jews, at late hours of the night, bothered Christian women in the street did the *parnasim* issue a warning.[187] They drew a clear line between private and public improprieties—*desonestidades e desaforos*, immorality and effrontery, in the terminology of the resolution.

Improprieties in relations between Portuguese Jewish men and women were another matter. In these cases the Mahamad acted promptly and severely. In 1644 Abraham Mendes was excommunicated for bigamy; two years later, in 1646, Semuel Marques committed adultery with Sara Cardosa and received the same punishment. Jacob Moreno, his wife, and Daniel Castiel appear to have had a particularly improper relationship, for all three were excommunicated in 1654. A few years after this, in 1667, Jacob's son Abraham Moreno was relieved of his *herem* on condition that he did not visit the home of Clara Hamis.[188] In treating these cases with such severity the Mahamad was applying a social rather than a religious double standard. Relations with Christian women were relations between social unequals. Similar relations with Portuguese Jewish maids probably occurred, but these were not punished either. The behaviour of Abraham Mendes and others like him, however, set a bad example and threatened the social fabric of the community.

With the same kind of severity the Mahamad punished couples who married without parental permission as well as the witnesses who were present at the ceremony. The prohibition against such marriages had to be repeated often and may be presumed to have had only limited success.[189] The Mahamad took a dim view of this practice inasmuch as it threatened the structure of authority within the Kahal; a structure which was modelled in more ways than one on that of parental authority.

Resolutions dealing with business ethics and proprieties have been mentioned above and reference was made to illegal trade in banned currencies and the alleged improprieties of tobacco pedlars and stock trading on Sundays.[190] The 1642

[184] GAA, NA 2269, fo. 514 (31 July 1654; A. Lock).
[185] GAA, NA 4077 (6 Dec. 1673; D. v. d. Groe).
[186] GAA, NA 4078 (18 Apr. 1674; D. v. d. Groe).
[187] GAA, PIG 19, pp. 193 (22 Sivan 5405/16 June 1645), 199 (20 Tishrei 5406/10 Oct. 1645); PIG 20, p. 92 (23 Tamuz 5445/25 July 1685).
[188] GAA, PIG 19, pp. 170 (18 Nisan 5404/26 Apr. 1644), 204 (6 Sivan 5406/20 May 1646), 368 (27 Av 5414/10 Aug. 1654), 578 (23 Elul 5427/12 Sept. 1667).
[189] GAA, PIG 19, pp. 447 (16 Tevet 5419/11 Jan. 1659), 765 (27 Nisan 5437/29 Apr. 1677); PIG 20, pp. 34 (8 Nisan 5442/16 Apr. 1682), 146 (5451/1690/1), 511 (5470/1709/10).
[190] See above, pp. 21, 155, 158–9, 184.

admonition to abide by the state proclamations on currency transactions was signed by the entire membership of the Kahal—a measure otherwise reserved only for the *capitolos* and *haskamot* establishing Talmud Tora in 1639.[191] Compliance with state law in this instance was regarded as a *sine qua non* of the *nação*'s *conservação*. It went to the root of the trust-based toleration of Amsterdam's authorities. It is doubtful whether the Mahamad's precautions did much to alter the basic propensities of the Portuguese Jewish merchants, but there is little question that, whatever these merchants' business practices, they did not measurably affect relations with their fellow Amsterdammers.

The level of tension between Portuguese Jews and Dutch Christians appears to have been relatively low. It is worth investigating this issue in sufficient depth to reach a clear impression, as several scholars have attributed the intolerance of the *parnasim*—as, for example, in the case of Spinoza—to their fear of Christian repercussions. In so far as tensions did exist they fall into two distinct categories: social and religious. Little is recorded of Christian hostility towards Jews. Philip Skippon, the English traveller mentioned above, recorded how 'Jews oftentimes meet with affronts in the street.'[192] The observation probably contained little exaggeration. Specific information, however, is very hard to come by and when it does exist refers to particular incidents, such as the near riot against a Portuguese Jew accused of pederasty by an angry mob of neighbours.[193] In various weak endeavours to curb the occurrence of 'affronts' the Mahamad occasionally asked *yehidim* not to make themselves too conspicuous. The greatest difficulty lay in containing the enthusiasm of Portuguese Jews on occasions of great joy. Repeatedly the Mahamad asked that only the immediate family accompany brides and grooms from their homes to the Esnoga.[194] Large and unruly crowds drew the attention of Christian neighbours and passers-by who were unfamiliar with Portuguese Jewish mores and viewed such behaviour with suspicion or ridicule. Similar considerations moved the *parnasim* to prohibit public celebrations of Purim in which children were 'dressed up as sailors or in masks' ('em vestidos de marinheiros e mascaras').[195] In these *haskamot* the *parnasim* revealingly use the argument of *quietação* (tranquillity) rather than the more basic one of *conservação* (preservation).

Once, in a related context, the Mahamad did raise the spectre of endangered *conservação*. On 10 December 1646 they issued a set of twenty-two exhortations entreating *yehidim* and their wives and children not to depart from certain standards of moderation in clothing.[196] These sumptuary statutes were to counter a

[191] GAA, PIG 19, pp. 118–25 (27 Omer 5402/ 12 May 1642).

[192] Skippon, *Account of a Journey*, 405.

[193] GAA, ORA 315, fo. 113ᵛ (3 July 1663).

[194] GAA, PIG 19, pp. 56–7 (15 Shevat 5400/8 Feb. 1640), 156 (21 Menahem 5403/6 Aug. 1643), 201 (25 Kislev 5406/12 Dec. 1645), 276 (5410/1649/50).

[195] GAA, PIG 20, p. 200 (5456/1695/6).

[196] GAA, PIG 19, pp. 217–19 (2 Tevet 5407/ 10 Dec. 1646 and 5 Adar 5407/ 10 Feb. 1647).

probably recent trend towards ever more 'superfluous and excessive' articles and embellishments of attire. This ostentation, according to the *parnasim*, did 'much harm to [their/our] funds' and threatened 'the preservation of our *nação* . . . inasmuch as we would thereby be envied and disliked by the people in whose land we live'. The twenty-two paragraphs set limitations—meticulously specifying the article of clothing and the category of person to which the prohibitions applied— on precious stones, gold, and silver, certain types of cloth such as silk and *pano* (a woven fabric of wool, silk, cotton, and linen), embroideries and lace, as well as certain colours such as scarlet, crimson, yellow, or orange. Individuals transgress- ing this edict would be admonished by the Mahamad; if recalcitrant, their names would be withdrawn from the ballot box for *misvot*, nor would they be allowed to celebrate an *asurah* (a festival such as a circumcision or a wedding) or serve any office within the Kahal. These sumptuary laws caused such a stir that the *gabai* was forced to note, on 5 Adar 5407 (10 February 1647), 'that in view of the fact that many people do not observe them the Mahamad resolved, in order to avoid discord, not to enforce the penalties and to allow everyone to comply or not as they wished'.

Twice frictions seriously endangered the prized tranquillity. In 1640 the Mahamad learned of complaints in government circles regarding Portuguese Jews making 'scandalous' remarks about Christianity.[197] This criticism in turn had pro- voked certain preachers to raise the subject from the pulpit, some even to call for the expulsion of the Jews. In 1676, a Synod at Dort and the Academy of Leiden again discussed the same subject and called upon the political authorities to take appropriate measures.[198] In the concomitant *haskamot* prohibiting any and all forms of criticism, the *parnasim* were naturally led to warn of the dangers to the *nação's conservação*. Both expressions of alarm were induced by fairly concrete manifestations of the possibility of mounting anti-Jewish sentiment among the political leadership. On the whole, the *parnasim* were not easily provoked to over-react in matters external to the Jewish community. Just as the burgomasters confined their deliberations regarding the Jews to concrete issues of proven con- tention, so the Mahamad did not worry unduly about transgressions and frictions of little or no social or political consequence. In the cases cited above the *parnasim* issued their warnings after, not before, a negative reaction (primarily from church officials) had become apparent. I see no reason or evidence to impute to the Portuguese Jews or their leaders undue anxiety over the possibility of a Christian backlash. Of course, in internal matters the issues were far more complex, and emotions as well as reason sometimes got out of hand, as we shall see in the next chapter.

---

[197] GAA, PIG 19, p. 93 (20 Sivan 5400/ 10 June 1640).

[198] Ibid., p. 769 (1 Elul 5437/29 Aug. 1677). Of course, the prohibition on speaking against Christianity had been part of the municipal by-law of 1616 and had been incorporated as hask. 38 into the Kahal's foundation statutes. Parts of the demands of the Dort Synod of 1676 are published in Koenen, *Geschiedenis der Joden in Nederland*, 263, 450–4.

DIMENSIONS OF *CONSERVAÇÃO*

When not referring to the Portuguese Jewish collectivity as a *natie*, the Amsterdam authorities were wont to employ the designation *Jodenkerck* (Jews' church). In their minds the synagogue was basically no different from any of the other churches in the city. The Kahal Kados de Talmud Tora of Amsterdam was first and foremost a voluntary association. The government neither enforced membership, nor taxed the Kahal as a separate legal body, nor surrendered to the Mahamad or the *hahamim* the rights of law enforcement. When in 1670, in confirming the prohibition on the establishment of another Portuguese Jewish *minyan*, the burgomasters saw fit to grant the Kahal a monopoly on Portuguese Jewish worship, they did so for strictly practical reasons without any consideration of possible theoretical principles. Prior to 1639 they had never voiced any opposition to the proliferation of congregations. The structure of the association was in no way dictated by government or municipal statute.

In its own perceptions the Kahal was and became far more than a mere *kerck*. It remained a foreign colony dedicated to maintaining its right to live in Holland and also became a charitable society providing a variety of non-religious social services. Dutch law provided no guidelines for these added functions. The right to exist was no concern of the Dutch authorities, as long as the premisses of trust upon which it was based were not violated. It required no explicit charter and certainly no special institution. Charity was a wholly internal matter and, as far as Dutch law was concerned, an obligation the Portuguese Jews had taken upon themselves voluntarily. If these non-ecclesiastical realities could thus largely be ignored by the burgomasters and the States of Holland, they could not fail to impose upon the *nação* the need for something more than a board of elders supervising synagogal affairs.

The *imposta* board, in consultation with the three Mahamadot and later the single Mahamad of the unified community, therefore assumed responsibility for all synagogal, charitable, and civic matters concerning the *nação*. Tacit agreement among the members of the association established this structure—in imitation of contemporary examples—and continued to determine the range of concerns over which the *parnasim* held sway. In so far as the Mahamad required authority to implement its views on how these matters were to be dealt with, its power ultimately derived from the same source of tacit agreement. It was limited by the membership's desire to remain affiliated with the association.

The humdrum fates of Sebastião Coutinho and the sumptuary laws illustrate these basic principles better than the dramatic confrontations to be discussed in the next chapter. Coutinho's case shows that he was susceptible to the dictates of the *parnasim* only as long as he wished to continue to worship in the Esnoga. No one forced him to be a member of the Kahal. Had he chosen to sever his ties with the Kahal—and several *yehidim* did, as we shall see—the Mahamad would have lost any authority over him. Conversely, when the *parnasim* passed the sumptuary laws, they were forced to back down because of a singular and stubborn lack of compliance on the part of the membership. Upon the individual such as Coutinho the Mahamad was able to impose its will; upon the majority of *yehidim* it was not.

Many resolutions fell somewhere between these extremes. Sometimes, in hindsight, an issue proved less urgent than had been originally envisaged, or its pursuance more trouble than it was worth. At other times non-compliance was limited to marginal individuals deemed unworthy of the *parnasim*'s concern or unthreatening to the issue at stake; or infractions occurred beyond the purview of the Mahamad's supervision, in secret or outside the confines of the Jewish quarter. Here and there the *parnasim* applied a social double standard; elsewhere the individual avoided crossing the Mahamad's path. In neither case were the irregularities of particular significance except in so far as they may clarify the nature of the authority of the Mahamad and that of the members' affiliation.

The essentially voluntary nature of affiliation does not imply that membership was entirely optional. Obviously, it was first and foremost a consequence of birth, and as such entailed far more—or less—than the spontaneous and deliberate decision to join a certain religious community in worship. By birth one entered a micro-society, an intricate web of social, economic, cultural, and religious affiliations and cross-affiliations. It is impossible to extricate the religious commitment from this micro-social network. The vast majority of Portuguese Jews slipped into the association as naturally as they had been born and thought as little of separating themselves from it as they did of disowning their parents. The voluntariness of their membership was almost completely over-shadowed by the forces that pushed and pulled them to associate.

As a community of kin relations the authority of the Mahamad was naturally defined in analogy to parental authority. In this context the several, explicit assertions that the authority of the *parnasim* over-rides that of the parent are telling. The Kahal may have been created in liberal Holland and defined as a voluntary association, but the reality of membership by birth and all that entailed rendered the Mahamad's power authoritarian rather than liberal. In other words, this authoritarianism was a function not of communal autonomy but of the forces compelling *yehidim* to desire affiliation.

The analogy of parental authority may have made sense during the earliest phase of congregational proliferation when the religious assemblies and their Mahamadot were structured primarily along familial lines, and made its way into the definition of the unified Mahamad which inherited most of its predecessors' functions. With the establishment of the *imposta* board and its assumption of responsibility for poor relief a more explicit rationale was called for to justify the board's authority to impose onerous taxes. This rationale was expressed in terms of a concern for the *nação*'s preservation. The *imposta* board never spelled out in what manner it feared that the refusal to absorb some of the burden of poor relief might endanger the *nação*'s preservation. We would be jumping to conclusions prematurely if we simply assumed that this concern was directly linked to fears of jeopardizing the *nação*'s right to exist in Amsterdam. Perhaps the manner in which the *nação* came to accept this responsibility can provide some clues. It may also illuminate the associations with which the notion of *conservação* subsequently became invested.

The evolution of the Portuguese Jewish community can be charted as having gone through several distinct phases. The first, notwithstanding the obscurity surrounding it, was characterized by private and familial gatherings of an almost exclusively religious nature. During the second an awareness of the permanence of expatriation took hold, and controlled attempts were made, notably in the foundation of Dotar in 1616, to alleviate isolation and maintain non-economic, supra-personal—though as yet preferably familial—ties with other expatriate communities. Whether as the unanticipated result of the overtures made by Dotar or for political and economic reasons, the Amsterdam settlement soon became the major centre of attraction among refugees from the Iberian peninsula. At first, during the third phase, the *nação* sought, through the re-emigration policies of the *imposta* board, to divest itself of those immigrants without means of livelihood in order to keep the charity rolls within bounds. In the end, without ever entirely abandoning the policy of re-emigration, the *nação* assumed the burden of charity more positively and restructured its internal affairs accordingly. This last and all-important about-face was inspired, I would argue, by the Dutch conquest of north-eastern Brazil and the subsequent settlement of a very sizeable community of Portuguese Jews there. Dutch Brazil did far more than siphon off some of the extra population of the Amsterdam settlement; it also provided the Amsterdam *nação* with a new theatre of operations, independent of the existing diaspora. In some circles, as we saw and will have occasion to see again, it engendered a major shift in basic orientations. Beside the Iberocentric view which could not but see Amsterdam as a dead end of limited and shrinking opportunities, there emerged a perspective which saw Amsterdam as the centre of a circle of expanding horizons within which new opportunities were opening up. Those without means of livelihood who had formerly been a burden now became a potential asset with which to conquer new worlds.

The process through which the Amsterdam *nação* came to accept the burden of poor relief was not, in the first instance, negatively inspired by fears of tarnishing its image of profitability to the economic well-being of the city. It signalled a positive acceptance of the reality of expatriation and a new confidence that Amsterdam might yet create new opportunities particularly suited to Portuguese Jewish exploration. The outcome was a community which was greater than the sum total of its familial parts. In this new configuration the erstwhile negative connotations of 'preservation'—sparse opportunities owing to the limitations of expatriation— were infused with positive associations highlighting the gains of expatriation and the interdependence of the community. The subsequent emphasis placed upon Judaism and especially upon public orthopraxis was intended to reinforce the benefits which had accrued from the migration, as reflected in the ideal historical legends of the Amsterdam *nação*'s origins. On the other hand, the somewhat misplaced avowal of equality, for example in the allotment of Esnoga seats, betokens the added dimension of communal solidarity acquired with the assumption of charitable responsibilities.

This is not, of course, to suggest that the new abstract meanings given to *conservação* and the concomitant redefinition of the Kahal obliterated all traces and vestiges of the primordial forces that had once been the mainstay of communal affiliation. In the selection of *parnasim*, for instance, the old and the new co-existed peacefully side by side—the latter in the pious phraseology and meticulous rules circumscribing the qualifications, the former in the process of co-optation and the persons deemed to qualify. But in the central fields of charity and worship too, primordial alliances continued to assert themselves as a supplement (rather than as an alternative) to the cenralized, bureaucratic management of the Mahamad. On the one hand, *yehidim* continued to feel an irrepressible urge to assemble privately and intimately and, the prohibition against external *minyanim* notwithstanding, contrived to do so under the cloak of *academias*, *jesibot*, or *hebrot* to whose proliferation the Mahamad took repeated exception. In claiming a monopoly on charity the *parnasim* were somewhat more successful. In this area they asserted their authority with singular persistence and supervised charitable activities most personally. This intense personal preoccupation with charity on the part of the Mahamad served to reconfirm the parental connotations of its authority. Yet there was one area of charity the *yehidim* did manage to set aside for private initiative. Poignantly this concerned the care of orphans, fatherless children. It is as if they felt that these unfortunate individuals lacked the kind of primordial attachment which every *yahid* knew to be a prerequisite of membership in the *nação*. However parental the authority of the Mahamad may have attempted to be, it was so ultimately only by analogy, by extension. Orphans who lacked the most rudimentary experience of parental care, therefore, required private supervision rather than the more distant management of an annually changing Mahamad.

The fully fledged Kahal Kados de Talmud Tora of Amsterdam as it came into its own after 1639 must not be viewed two-dimensionally as wedged between a staunch, inflexible commitment to Judaism and an ever-conditional and precarious acceptance by society at large. Its internal dynamics were relatively free from external pressures. They were moved by two sets of tensions: between familial bonds and communal responsibility, and between expatriation and Judaism. Within the bounds set by these tensions the Kahal may still be defined as a voluntary association. On the whole, the tensions served to integrate the association to the point of obscuring the voluntary dimension from our view. The conflicts that befell the Amsterdam *nação* will reveal the stress points of these internal dynamics and the forces of potential disintegration born of these tensions.

FIVE

'DISSONANT WORDS', 'BAD OPINIONS', AND 'SCANDALS'

Varieties of Religious Discord and Social Conflict

I would like you [synagogue elders] to answer one question: if these groundless fears which you instil in the minds of men are contrived to restrain their natural inclination to evil and to keep them from going astray, did it never occur to you that you then likewise are men full of malice, unable to do what is good, ever prone to evil, injurious, without compassion or mercy? But I see every one of you filled with rage at so insolent a question and justifying his own conduct. 'What, are we not all pious and merciful and strict adherers to truth and justice?' Either what you boastingly say of yourselves is false or your accusation of all other men, whose natural propensity to evil you pretend to correct with your fictitious terrors, is unjust.

URIEL DA COSTA

FOR some individuals, certain requirements of membership of the Kahal Kados de Talmud Tora were too onerous to be passed over in silence. The Mahamad, for their part, regarded some infractions as just too serious to be overlooked. Conflicts ensued. The Mahamad applied the only powers it possessed: the right to deny someone all or some of the privileges of membership of the Kahal, and excommunication, which not only cancelled a person's membership but also removed him from any and all interaction with the *nação*. The *yehidim* responded by swallowing their pride and settling their differences, or by severing their ties with the Kahal. In the latter option Amsterdam's Portuguese Jews possessed a latitude rarely encountered in pre-modern Jewish communities. This relative freedom, in turn, imposed clear and immediate restraints upon the exercise of authority by the *parnasim*. Too incongruous or indiscriminate an application of force might alienate a *yahid* and result in his departure from the Kahal.

There existed little by way of an independent court to adjudicate in communal conflicts, whether between individuals or between *yehidim* and *parnasim*. The records do occasionally refer to a rabbinical court, but its mandate appears to have been limited to strictly religious matters. Capitolo 20 of the communal agreement has the following to say about the Bet Din, the rabbinical court:

All the *dinim* that will present themselves and that will have to be decided upon will be seen and examined by the salaried *hahamim*, according to a majority vote. In case there is a tied vote, the arguments will be heard by the Mahamad, before whom it will be decided. The Mahamad, gathering information as it sees fit, will side with those with whom it agrees. Thus the issue will be settled. If one of the *hahamim* asserts or writes anything against what was decided and two witnesses condemn him, he will lose his salary and will be removed from his post in the congregation and will never be admitted to that office again.

No records of the Bet Din have survived, so we will never know exactly what kinds of *dinim* it decided upon.[1] We have every reason to assume, however, that the term *dinim* restricted the Bet Din's jurisdiction—advice is probably a more appropriate term—to matters of purely religious law only. Whenever the resolutions of the Mahamad refer to consultations with the 'Senhores Hahamim' the issue always concerns an interpretation of a point of halakhah (Jewish law): as for example in clarifying the Jewishness of New Christians who died en route to Amsterdam or in specifying what kinds of activities were not allowed on the Sabbath.[2] Halakhah here must be understood in the strictest sense, for the issuance of bills of divorce, traditionally everywhere else but in Italy a rabbinical prerogative, was explicitly reserved for the Mahamad (hask. 47).[3]

Regarding non-religious matters the *imposta* board had drafted in 1632 a set of procedures for the intra-communal settlement of conflicts between *yehidim*.[4] 'In accordance with the custom of our city,' the board appointed itself the first and last arbiter of disputes among members of the *nação*. Twenty elaborate articles laid down the ground rules of this compulsory *judicatura* and threatened excommunication for non-compliance. This is the closest the community elders ever came to an autonomy similar to that upon which most other Jewish communities of Europe were based. The board's *termo* (resolution), however, would appear to have gone the same way as the sumptuary laws. Unlike other important *termos* of the *imposta* board, this resolution was never signed, neither by the members of the board nor by the council of fifteen elders of the three Mahamadot. More importantly, the *capitolos* and *haskamot* of 1639 are virtually silent on the subject. Capitolo 33 obliged any Jew with a financial claim against a fellow Jew to submit his case to voluntary arbitration by 'honourable judges' to be named by the parties involved, and to do everything possible to settle the claim. 'If the honourable judges cannot make them settle,' however, 'the parties remain free to procure and defend their justice wherever they want and see fit.' No specific punishment was threatened against those neglecting to make 'the prior effort'—an 'oversight' which, given the Mahamad's readiness to impose severe penalties, only confirms the relative insignificance of the issue. Not surprisingly, the procedures outlined in this *capitolo* conform to those already customary in mercantile circles in general. Obviously the

---

[1] The halakhic questions put to 'H. H. Ribi Ishack Aboab' in GAA, PIG 139, may contain the remnants of records related to the Bet Din.

[2] GAA, PIG 19, pp. 191 (4 Sivan 5405/29 May 1645), 388 (23 Iyar 5415/30 May 1655).

[3] Baron, *Jewish Community*, ii. 73–6.

[4] GAA, PIG 13, pp. 88–91 (15 Kislev 5393/28 Nov. 1632).

merchant *yehidim* had been unwilling to surrender their professional autonomy to comply with traditional Jewish practice.

If and when *yehidim* heeded the Mahamad's call for arbitration, they did so entirely voluntarily. To cite the single case of this sort registered in the Mahamad's *Manual*, in 1641, Abraham Israel Pereira Chuchou and Ishac Israel Pereira Chuchou, two brothers, appeared before the Mahamad and declared they would abide by the verdict of Daniel de Caceres and David Salom (neither a member of the Mahamad at the time).[5] For added 'assurance' the *parnasim* called in Haham Saul Levi Morteira and had the brothers swear an oath on the Holy Scripture. Another instance came to light accidentally. In 1671 Selomoh Levy Ximenes, acting on behalf of his son-in-law David de Ishac de Castro of Hamburg, and Abraham Abendana de Britto as the husband of Anna Ester de Castro were prompted, at the instigation of the Mahamad, to suspend their court case, apparently involving an inheritance dispute.[6] They were to try for six weeks to come to an agreement, and then, if no agreement had been reached, they would proceed to move their case in court. Cases like these undoubtedly occurred quite frequently. It must often have been a more convenient and less costly procedure than a court trial before unfamiliar justices. It remained, however, a voluntary avenue of adjudication, and no one, to the best of my knowledge, was ever excommunicated for failure to comply with the Mahamad's request for arbitration.

These examples—like most others potentially falling within the scope of this kind of arbitration—concerned merchants, in other words the social equals of the *parnasim*. With individuals socially or economically dependent upon the mercantile establishment, however, the dictates of the Mahamad were asserted with greater force and carried greater weight. Haskamah 34, for instance, stipulated that neither licensed nor unlicensed brokers were allowed to bring disputes regarding the collection of brokerage fees before a non-Jewish court, under penalty of 12 gulden to be paid into the *sedaca*. This stipulation, of course, served the self-interest of the merchant *parnasim* and was enforceable as the brokers were their clients. In some respects the issue of censorship, to be discussed later, resembles the operation of a statute rendered compelling by force of a patron–client relationship.

No mechanism existed to resolve conflicts between the Mahamad and individual *yehidim*. Haskamah 1 quite emphatically stated that 'the Mahamad will have authority and superiority over everything'. On occasion, however, as in the case of Sebastião Coutinho, members who felt themselves wronged by a verdict of the Mahamad appealed to the city courts. In these few instances, the court did not as a matter of course side with the *parnasim*, but tried as urgently as necessary to mediate and counsel moderation. Few *yehidim*, however, availed themselves of this option. More often than not, because of the essentially personal nature of the

---

[5] GAA, PIG 19, p. 101 (24 Av 5401 / 31 July 1641).
[6] GAA, NA 2235, p. 716 (31 Mar. 1671; A. Lock).

association, the advantages of membership were in themselves sufficiently attractive to induce *yehidim* to mend their ways. Only in a few, isolated circumstances was the price of membership too high or the issue too personally significant to allow a *yahid* to back down.

MATTERS OF CONTENTION

Of course, many dissatisfactions experienced by members of the *nação* had nothing to do with the manner in which the Mahamad defined and governed the Kahal. Some individuals simply and painfully encountered grave difficulties in gaining a livelihood. They were often left little choice but to try their luck elsewhere, abroad or within the non-Jewish community. The choice of either alternative frequently depended less on the degree of their commitment to Judaism than on the depth of their social and cultural roots within the *nação*. The poor and the unskilled had the least freedom of choice. Ethnic ties and linguistic and cultural affinities meant that they almost always stood a better chance of employment within the *nação* than anywhere else. In 1666 Abraham Hereira, a messenger boy, declared that 'he had been a Jew from his youth, had then become a Christian and was still a Christian in his heart, but pretended to be a Jew in order to be able to make a living among the Jews'.[7] Unskilled labourers like Hereira might attach themselves to a Portuguese Jewish merchant and travel abroad or accept the Mahamad's offer to pay for their emigration to Italy, Turkey, or the Caribbean. Mostly their economic woes forced them to remain obedient members of the Kahal, hope for an occasional hand-out, and make ends meet as best they could.

Occasionally matters got out of hand. Such appears to have been the case with Ishac da Costa alias Jacques Gedellian, nicknamed 'the devil of Vloyenburgh', and his associate, Antonio Sanches de Pas alias Semuel Aboab.[8] During the turbulent 1650s, these two made contact with the Spanish ambassador in The Hague and Spanish authorities abroad, in nearby Brabant. In exchange for a substantial reward, they offered to denounce the commercial practices of Portuguese Jewish merchants harmful to the interests of the Spanish Crown. Antonio Sanches de Pas, born in Jerusalem and 28 years of age at the time of his arrest in 1657, was unskilled and lived at the home of his uncle's widow, Rachel Salom, from whom he may occasionally have stolen small items. Asked why he had gone to The Hague and to Brabant, he answered: 'Because the Jews were giving him a very hard time here.' At Gedellian's instigation, Sanches had opened the mail of certain Portuguese Jewish merchants, and the two conspirators had drafted letters promising to divulge sensitive information ostensibly related to illegal transactions in the wool trade. Antonio Sanches was released on his own recognizance, 'promising not to harm the persons whom he had threatened'. Jacques Gedellian, who had already

---

[7] GAA, ORA 317, fos. 62, 64ᵛ (15, 22 July 1666).
[8] GAA, ORA 312, fos. 10ᵛ–13 (23 Oct. 1657).

once been arrested for whoremongering, was gaoled, notwithstanding efforts by the Spanish ambassador to claim him as his domestic.[9] The costs of his confinement were defrayed by the Kahal.

Spying and denunciations of this sort were not uncommon, and occasionally more substantial individuals engaged in such practices. In the course of the 1640s and 1650s Lopo Ramirez, formerly an active agent of the Portuguese rebels, defected to the Spaniards and eventually settled in Antwerp for some time.[10] In the late 1650s or early 1660s Andres de Belmonte (and, later, Manuel de Belmonte) became a spy for the Spanish government and reported on arms purchases made by the Portuguese Crown through Portuguese Jewish merchants.[11] Unlike the scheming of Gedellian and Sanches, the services of these successful merchants do not appear to have been motivated by resentment over their economic ill-fortune within the *nação*.

A more serious form of social and economic protest consisted in the public distribution of defamatory pamphlets, a form of voicing disagreement common throughout the seventeenth-century Republic. Such washing of one's dirty linen in public not only harmed the image of the Portuguese in the eyes of the local authorities, it also undermined the relative peace of the community and posed a real danger of igniting factional disputes—the micro-society's equivalent of civil war. Rarely does the documentation allow us to reconstruct the course of these events very clearly. The notations in the records of the Mahamad mention the nature of the defamation in general terms only, and occasionally the author of the pamphlet; rarely the two together.

In very strong words, hinting primarily at the internal dangers of the offence, haskamah 43 stated:

No person may venture to publish libels or defamatory pamphlets. Whoever commits such an outrage [*desaforo*] or has it committed by someone else will be placed in *herem* and separated from the *nação* with all the curses of our sacred Law, as befits him as a disturber [*perturbador*] of our *nação*, for he commits a crime both against the most sacred Law and against his fellow. Moreover, he will be punished rigorously at the discretion of the Gentlemen of the Mahamad.

Several times the *haskamah* was repeated without further details, though probably provoked by specific recurrences.[12] In the spring of 1666, while many members of the Kahal were in the throes of Sabbatean enthusiasm, sometimes violent altercations broke out between believers in the messiahship of Shabbetai Zevi and unbelievers. According to Jacob Sasportas, one unbeliever, Abraham de Souza, 'boldly risked his life [by appearing] before the people who detested him and his

---

[9] Swetschinski, 'Spanish Consul', 161.
[10] Swetschinski, 'Amsterdam Jewish Merchant-Diplomat', 13–14, and, more fully, Israel, 'Lopo Ramirez (David Curiel)'.
[11] I am planning to publish a more detailed account of Manuel de Belmonte's career shortly.
[12] GAA, PIG 19, p. 768 (21 Sivan 5437/21 June 1677); PIG 20, p. 141 (5451/1690/1).

family . . . He suffered indescribable abuse and harassment because of this, and but for the grace of God which protected him they would have killed him, for many a time they were lying in wait to get hold of him.'[13] Others vented their feelings in words. On 28 Nisan 5426 (3 May 1666) the *parnasim* issued a stern reprimand (with the obligatory threat of a *herem*) against 'the person or persons who composed or helped compose a certain *papel* which was printed and sold today at the Exchange; [a *papel*] concerning the unbelievers and, most scandalously, concerning the honour of the name of *el Dio Bendito* and the expectation of the coming of our Messiah' ('s[re] os incredulos, e com escandalo, s[re] a honra do nome del D. B[to] e a esperança da vinda de nosso Messiah').[14] A contemporary affidavit, dated 10 May 1666, speaks of *pasquillen* (lampoons) 'containing lists of the gentlemen unbelieving Jews, printed in Dutch and Spanish, one beneath the other'.[15] On the basis of this affidavit, I am inclined to believe that the Mahamad's warning was directed against over-zealous Sabbateans rather than against unbelievers. Whatever the case may have been, it was the publication of the material that probably most offended the Mahamad. In another instance equally involving honour, in 1709, the *parnasim* requested information about the author(s) of 'a certain *pasquim* or defamatory and scandalous libel, printed in Dutch, prejudicial and demeaning to the young women of Israel over whose honour we must truly watch'.[16] No denunciations were forthcoming. In both these cases the threats in themselves were probably sufficient to subdue emotions and put a stop to the 'outrage'.

In the case involving Daniel Rachão and Israel da Cunha we know their names but not the nature of the defamation. In 1640 both were excommunicated for having authored (Rachão) and distributed (da Cunha) 'certain *pasquins* or defamatory papers [affixed] to the gates of the synagogue, the bridge, the Exchange, and in other places'. Rachão's *herem* was revoked the following week; on da Cunha's we have no further information.[17] Two years later, Daniel Rachão was again found

[13] As cited and translated in Scholem, *Sabbatai Sevi*, 520. Scholem refers to Abraham de Souza as 'one of the wealthiest merchant princes of Amsterdam'. According to the *finta* of 5435 (1674/5) Abraham de Sosa was taxed at 17 gulden; in 5441 (1680/1) and 5448 (1687/8), at 8. The Abraham de Souza mentioned by Jacob Sasportas was almost certainly the book-keeper of 'the very wealthy merchant prince' Jacob de Pinto. De Pinto had very extensive commercial contacts in the eastern Mediterranean between Ancona and Smyrna. Much information regarding Shabbetai Zevi probably passed through his hands and was thus read by de Souza and passed on by the latter to Sasportas. GAA, NA 1522, p. 168 (12 Apr. 1673; J. V. Oli); see also *Gedrukte resolutiën . . . Holland*, 10 Dec. 1676, 17 Dec. 1676, 8 July 1677, in which Jacob de Pinto represents the community of Jewish merchants against the Dutch consul at Smyrna. The irrepressible temptation to label any and all Portuguese Jews—as in the case of Spinoza's father—'wealthy' illustrates richly how one-sidedly outsiders have viewed and continue to view the community.
[14] Kaplan, 'Attitude of the Leadership', 200–3
[15] GAA, NA 2221, p. 54 (10 May 1666; A. Lock). It has become a cliché to regard the leadership of the Amsterdam Kahal as wholly committed to the cause of Shabbetai Zevi. The case, it seems to me, deserves closer scrutiny and may ultimately prove to have been more complex than hitherto envisaged.
[16] GAA, PIG 20, p. 500 (5469/1708/9).
[17] GAA, PIG 19, pp. 55, 56 (17, 23 Shevat 5400/10, 16 Feb. 1640).

guilty and excommunicated for 'having written a defamatory letter abroad, full of falsehoods and lies, against honoured and distinguished members of our *nação*, both alive and dead'. Rachão confessed to having been motivated 'by hatred, deep resentment, and animosity' for these individuals and to having threatened to become a *malsin* (an informer 'of the most reprehensible sort').[18] This *herem*, too, was annulled a week later, after Rachão had expressed regrets and asked for forgiveness in the chamber of the Mahamad. All the incidents discussed so far apparently represented passing disturbances for the most part, involved people of dubious character, and were treated with relative mildness, in not pursuing the culprits too vigorously or in lifting the ban privately without requiring public penance.

Of a somewhat more serious nature was the conflict that resulted in the excommunication of the Haham Menasseh ben Israel. The basic facts are simple enough. On 16 Iyar 5400 (8 May 1640) Menasseh ben Israel was put in *herem* for one day. He had acted improperly in the synagogue in publicly and loudly having protested against the fact that his brother-in-law, Jona Abarbanel, had not been addressed as 'senhor'.[19] (On 8 Elul 5407/8 September 1647, the page registering his *herem* was glued over with a blank page 'out of proper respect'.) The names of Jona Abarbanel and Mosse Belmonte were being read from the *teva* as they had been found guilty of having published certain pamphlets 'on the subject of Brazil' ('sobre o sogeito do Brazil') in which they had named many names, some in veiled terms.[20] This would seem to be a fairly clear case of 'defamation' by Abarbanel and Belmonte and of impropriety and insubordination by Menasseh ben Israel. 'The subject of Brazil' was a vexing problem, however, that caused tensions again a few years later. In 1645

it came to the attention of the Gentlemen of the Mahamad that certain particulars regarding the affairs of Brazil, confused allegations against the ambassador of Portugal, have been spoken and have caused scandal and that others have been written with little consideration for what they say . . . Thus they order, under penalty of *beraha* [here another term for *herem*], that no one venture to speak or write similar things, for the harm such may elicit is great and prejudicial to the whole *nação*.[21]

At approximately the same time, Jeronimo Nunes da Costa, recently appointed an agent of Portugal, complained in a similar vein about the behaviour of his fellow members of the *nação*.

I will always show myself a good Portuguese and faithful servant of His Majesty [the king of Portugal]. I can be proud of this. And may all those who say the contrary be known as liars who want to gain a reputation by demeaning what others have accomplished. I speak of this

[18] GAA, PIG 19, pp. 131, 132 (28 Av 5402/26 Aug. 1642).

[19] GAA, PIG 19, p. 70 (16 Iyar 5400/8 May 1640); Roth, *Life of Menasseh ben Israel*, 51–7; and the documents published in Gebhardt, *Schriften des Uriel da Costa*, 212–22. Lewis Feuer, who first drew my attention to the possible significance of Menasseh ben Israel's excommunication, interprets the conflict in terms much too broad: *Spinoza*, 6, 11–13.

[20] GAA, PIG 19, p. 69 (16 Iyar 5400/8 May 1640).

[21] GAA, PIG 19, p. 196 (22 Elul 5405/13 Sept. 1645).

with great passion. It is good, therefore, that I do not know who says these things for he would not be secure enough to improve upon his performance.[22]

For reasons already discussed above, the Portuguese Jews of Amsterdam followed events in Brazil very closely. The documents referred to here reveal a deep rift within the *nação*. On the one hand there were those loyal to Spain, before 1640, and to Portugal thereafter; on the other, some identified themselves equally strongly with the Dutch West India Company.

There exists circumstantial evidence to show that Menasseh ben Israel was motivated by stronger emotions than a more or less laudable concern for his brother-in-law's honour. During the month of May 1640, the stock of the West India Company reached its highest level ever since the early days of exaggerated expectations in 1628–30.[23] This explosion of optimism regarding the company's future was the direct result of the defeat by a greatly outnumbered Dutch fleet of the Castilian–Portuguese armada off Itamaracá on 12 January 1640.[24] Spanish and Portuguese hopes of reconquering the Dutch-occupied part of Brazil around Pernambuco were dashed and unlikely to resurface in the foreseeable future. The *pasquins* authored by Jona Abarbanel, a licensed broker, and Mosse Belmonte 'on the subject of Brazil' almost certainly related to these recent events. And if Menasseh ben Israel's words and actions are to be taken at all seriously as more than expressions of hurt pride, it would appear that Abarbanel and Belmonte had voiced a pro-Dutch sentiment contrary to the pro-Iberian views of a powerful segment of the *nação*, if not of the Mahamad itself.

During late 1639 and early 1640 Menasseh ben Israel very seriously considered migrating to Dutch Brazil, where his brother had already established himself. The well-known exchange of letters between Hugo de Groot and Gerard Joannes Vossius on this matter speaks mostly of the lack of generosity shown by the *parnasim* in underpaying their *haham* and thereby forcing him into this drastic measure.[25] In the same context, Vossius' letter tellingly expresses suspicions regarding the international connections of the Amsterdam Portuguese and alludes to dangers which might 'arise here or in the Spanish lands' (possibly as a result of the Brazilian wars).[26] Apparently Menasseh ben Israel had conveyed to Vossius more than complaints about his low salary. Not yet having a vested economic interest as did most of his merchant employers, Menasseh ben Israel was free to espouse the Dutch cause and take the alternative of a move to Brazil seriously. In 1639 he dedicated the Latin translation of his *De termino vitae* to the Dutch West India Company. Even more defiantly, in 1641, shortly after his run-in with the *parnasim*, he also dedicated the second volume of his Spanish edition of the

---

[22] Swetschinski, 'Amsterdam Jewish Merchant-Diplomat', 15.
[23] Van Dillen, 'Effectenkoersen', 9–12.
[24] Boxer, *Dutch in Brazil*, 84–94.
[25] Roth, *Life of Menasseh ben Israel*, 59–60.
[26] Katchen, *Christian Hebraists*, 106–7.

Conciliador, intended primarily for Portuguese Jewish consumption, to 'the most noble, very wise, and illustrious Gentlemen of the Council of the West Indies'; the other three volumes, printed at different times, were dedicated to Portuguese Jewish dignitaries.[27] The accompanying dedicatory epistle briefly summarizes the successes of the West India Company, mainly against the Spanish 'tyrant'. Menasseh ben Israel humbly offers 'this fruit of [his] mind' amid the honours already bestowed by an amazed and admiring world. And then, in baroque sentences addressing himself indirectly to his Portuguese Jewish contemporaries, he makes the following confession:

particularly at the time that the Benign King, Don João IV, has returned to his native and hereditary Kingdom which another possessed, unjustly, until now, and when the old hatred [between the Republic and Portugal] ceases [a preliminary cease-fire treaty had been signed on 12 June 1641], the desired peace will follow, for which I—a Portuguese with a Batavian spirit [*animo*]—will be most grateful . . . And in the same manner in which until now, under the most extensive and never sufficiently lauded reign of the States General, we have been protected against the tyranny of Spain—for which benefice neither I nor those of my nation can give sufficient thanks—[in that manner] I trust to live [in Brazil?] under your protection, Gentlemen. May we take the occasion, with your benevolence, to thank you and show you the true nature of our spirit.

Clearly this introduction was written after the Portuguese rebellion of December 1640, when the subject of Brazil was no longer as clear-cut as it had been earlier that year. Menasseh ben Israel explicitly reveals the roots of his 'Batavian spirit' in expressing profound and sincere gratitude for the Republic's toleration of the Jews and exhorts his fellow Portuguese to do the same.

The interest, for us, in the conflict between the Mahamad and Menasseh ben Israel lies in its revelation not of conflicting economic interests—many such conflicts existed, though none produced much of a public flare-up—but of the radically different rationales that motivated Portuguese Jews. The *parnasim*, no doubt, were no less appreciative of Dutch toleration than Menasseh ben Israel; however, unlike their *haham*, they also possessed as merchants distinct and prior economic interests centred on the Iberian world. Fortunately for the *nação*, occasions when loyalty to Holland and commercial self-interest collided were few and far between. In fact, the otherwise virtually complete absence of truly divisive economic rivalries may be one of the most noteworthy aspects of the *nação*'s internal dynamics.

Among merchants, of course, competition was a way of life and legal proceedings a hazard of the trade. The merchant *yehidim* may well have rejected the Mahamad's attempt to impose a compulsory judicial panel specifically in order to keep the divisiveness of commercial competition and litigation out of the communal life of the *nação*. Merchants also possessed far greater freedom to manoeuvre themselves out of difficulties than did the less independent members of the community, whose

[27] Menasseh ben Israel, *Conciliador*, ii. 6.

social and economic fortunes were more directly tied to their place within the *nação*'s micro-society. Physicians and brokers in particular appear occasionally to have found the restrictions *nação* membership imposed upon them too stifling or not worth the price.

In Portugal and Spain physicians were frequently and conspicuously the most distrusted element of the New Christian population and consequently became a favourite target of inquisitorial prosecution.[28] (Quite possibly—and for reasons which would lead us too far from our subject if investigated here—medical schools were one of the major and most successful recruiting grounds of proselytizing Judaizers.[29]) It is not surprising, therefore, to find among the Portuguese refugees who settled in Amsterdam a disproportionate number of physicians. For linguistic and cultural reasons as well as implicit guild restrictions, the potential clientele of these physicians was almost wholly restricted to the *nação*. Consequently there were, more or less chronically, too many physicians for that relatively small number of potential patients; and this, in turn, created tensions and a search for other markets.

Dr Paulo de Lena had received his medical degree from the University of Coimbra. Shortly thereafter he had apparently been condemned by the Lisbon Inquisition and, upon his release, had fled to Hamburg and then to Amsterdam 'in order to reconvert to Judaism and enjoy the freedom Jews have there'. For a while he visited the synagogue regularly. Soon he began to complain 'that he had no means to stay in Amsterdam because here in Amsterdam there were other Portuguese physicians older than him, and he was, therefore, unable to earn his livelihood'. 'To his great regret' he was forced to leave Amsterdam and move to Rouen, 'where one did not enjoy the freedom to confess Judaism openly as in this city'. These pious confessions notwithstanding, once in Rouen Dr Paulo de Lena turned against his fellow Judaizing New Christians there and became one of the most hostile witnesses for the pro-Catholic prosecution during the 1633 Rouen conflict discussed above.[30]

An even more remarkable, if somewhat less dramatic, story has as its protagonist one of the semi-legendary figures of the Amsterdam *nação*. To begin with the version of the life of Vicente alias Ishac de Rocamora as it circulated among his contemporaries, we may turn to the account of Abraham Idanha, written only three years after de Rocamora's death and addressed to a friend in Spain:

By way of example let me adduce that many Spanish theologians who came here realized through their studies how much they had erred in their religion. They abandoned it and begged, with many tears, of the Jews to allow them to join them. They were circumcised and bathed in accordance with the precept of the Law of God. Although they arrive at this request voluntarily, it is granted to only a very few, for the Law of God does not force any-

[28] Caro Baroja, *Judíos en la España moderna*, ii. 175–204.
[29] Révah, 'Marranes portugais', 520.
[30] Vaz Dias, 'Blik in de Marranen-historie', *VA* 9: 108; Révah, 'Autobiographie', 62, 72, 80.

one to abandon the religion in which his parents brought him up unless he is of the People of Israel, for they are born with that obligation. Once a reverend Christian friar, a great theologian who had been the confessor of the Empress, came here and asked to be admitted to the congregation. Because he was a person of such importance, his request was granted. After having been circumcised and bathed he studied medicine and in a few years gained his medical degree. He married a Portuguese Jewish woman with whom he had children. During the thirty years of his life [here] he was a member of the congregation. He died three years ago. During his life he worked as a physician and, having had not a penny when he began, improved his station such that he left his children 50,000 gulden when he died. One of his sons has already obtained his medical degree and follows in his father's footsteps.[31]

According to other, more plausible traditions, Fray Vicente de Rocamora had been the confessor of the Infanta Maria.[32] Otherwise, the biographical outline reported by Abraham Idanha conforms accurately with what contemporary Portuguese Jews thought and knew of the man.

Dr Ishack de Rokamora (as he eventually took to signing his name) was born Vicente de Rocamora in Valencia around 1609 and became a Dominican priest and confessor at the royal court. For reasons unknown, Fray Vicente settled in Amsterdam in the early 1640s, converted to Judaism, and adopted the name of Ishack Ysrael Rokamora. In 1647 he married Abigail Toura and in 1665, after her death, contracted a second marriage to Sara Toura. He was never elected to the Mahamad nor ever appointed to any of the subaltern boards (possibly because, as Idanha seems to suggest, he was of Old Christian descent). But he was a member of the literary salon of Don Manuel de Belmonte, the famous Academia de los Sitibundos. His son Selomoh and his grandson Ishac both became physicians. Dr Ishak de Rocamora (as the inscription on his gravestone spells his name) died in 1684.[33]

When Vicente de Rocamora arrived in Amsterdam and converted to Judaism he was already fairly advanced in age and without a marketable skill. Having been an 'intellectual' all his life, he more or less naturally chose the only intellectual pursuit—outside of the rabbinate—open to Jews and registered to study medicine at the University of Leiden in 1645. After two years of study he completed his medical education but was unable to graduate for lack of funds. He turned for help to Menasseh ben Israel, who introduced him to his friend Gerard Joannes Vossius. On 29 March 1647 Vossius addressed the following letter to a friend:

Yesterday, Rabbi Menasseh ben Israel came to see me accompanied by Isaac Rocamora, a Portuguese Jew. The latter has been studying medicine for the last two years, and has made

---

[31] Teensma, 'Fragmenten', 135–6 (Dutch), 148–9 (Spanish).

[32] Brugmans and Frank (eds.), *Geschiedenis der Joden in Nederland*, 657–8.

[33] Kayserling, *Sephardim*, 291–2; Pieterse, *Daniel Levi de Barrios*, 82–3. The following archival sources provide additional information: GAA, PIG 19, p. 227 (8 Elul 5407/8 Sept. 1647) (*pessoas novamente fintadas*: persons newly added to the *finta* or whose *finta* was changed); GAA, DTB 679, p. 105 (10 July 1647), 686, p. 237 (23 May 1665); GAA, Weeskamer 32, fos. 42, 407 (16 July 1665; 30 Mar. 1677).

such progress that he is confident that his standard is such as to qualify him for the highest degree in the subject. Owing to his slender means, he prefers the Academy where the fees of graduation are the least. This Rocamora has been warmly recommended to me by your friend, Menasseh, who I know has no deficiency in your eyes excepting for his religion. I, for my part (and I would say this of few, not only of that sect, but of any other), consider him a man of true worth, albeit he lives in darkness. He has requested me to write you a letter informing you of his protégé's intention. Unless I am mistaken, religion is no impediment to the conferring of a degree: for, while you were still in your native city, this honour was bestowed by the University of Leyden upon David Haro. I remember, moreover, having heard from my old colleague Adolf van Voorst (God rest his soul!), in talking of this matter, that medical knowledge only comes into the question, and not religious belief; especially in these parts, where the Jews are licensed to practise the art.[34]

Ishack de Rokamora accordingly graduated from the Academy of Franeker, a minor university in the provinces where Jews hardly ever came. The medical degree, however, did not alleviate Ishack's financial difficulties. Neither did his marriage to the daughter of a respectable mercantile family from Rotterdam, apparently, bring him an adequate dowry. At this point Dr de Rokamora sought to resolve his financial predicament by courting the Christian community.

On 12 May 1650 the Reverend Wachtendorp reported to the Amsterdam Church Council

that he had again been approached by D. Vincentius de Roca Mora, Spaniard, who had lapsed into Judaism in this city and was married to a Jewish woman. [D. Vincentius de Roca Mora's] conscience was very troubled and vexed, and he showed himself inclined to desert Judaism and accept the Reformed religion. But [his conversion] appeared to be hampered because he did not know how he would make a living once the Jews had learned of his decision, for he and his children were supported by them.

The Church Council, however, was not ready to offer the doctor definite financial guarantees, and

thought fit not to decide on his acceptance so lightly, as we have so often been defrauded by such persons. He [de Rokamora] will be notified that, if he sincerely repents from his abominable apostasy, he will have to show so and desert Judaism publicly. And when it appears in every respect that his intentions are sincere, he may rest assured that God, the Lord, will not leave him unprovided for.

A week later Revd Wachtendorp reported back to the Church Council regarding his meeting with Dr de Rokamora, who appeared 'to have expected some assurance of support'. The council determined 'to wait for what he will intend to do in the future'. Dr Ishack Ysrael Rokamora never converted.[35] As is clear from Idanha's praises, his financial situation improved dramatically in later years, probably through an inheritance rather than purely as the result of hard work. A

---

[34] Vossius' letter is quoted in Roth, *Life of Menasseh ben Israel*, 121. De Rokamora's academic peregrinations may be followed in *Album Studiosorum Academiae Lugduno Bataviae*, 361; and *Album Studiosorum Academiae Franekerensis*, 137.   [35] Zwarts, 'Uriel da Costa tragedie'.

seventeenth-century physician could hardly be expected to have amassed such a fortune by dint of his medical practice alone. De Rokamora's decision not to convert ante-dated this welcome reversal of his misfortune. If in 1650 he remained a member of the *nação*, it was because as a Spanish physician he could count on some—however slight—financial support from the Kahal, whereas the Christian community had little to offer but uncertainties, in terms of either direct assistance or potential clients.

Guild restrictions limited Portuguese Jewish brokers to transactions involving one or more Portuguese Jewish merchants. In that market, although they probably never attained a monopoly, they were quite successful and assured of a more or less steady demand for their services. Conflicts between merchants and brokers, of course, were inevitable and perhaps even daily occurrences. By and large, though, the dependence of the brokers upon their patrons and the fierce competition among brokers were so great as to prevent any controversy from ever getting out of hand. As mentioned above, this dependence forced the brokers to swallow the humiliation of not being allowed to take their financial grievances to the city court. It had also allowed the *imposta* board and the Mahamad to dictate that no licensed broker should denounce an unlicensed interloper of the *nação*. On the other hand, because of their extensive dealings with non-Jewish merchants, brokers were among the few who could conceivably risk severing their ties with the *nação*.

I know of only one Portuguese Jewish broker who converted to Christianity. He was perhaps also the most substantial member of the community to do so during the seventeenth century. Jacob Netto had already been an interloper for many years when he became a licensed broker on 5 February 1670. Then suddenly, on 11 December 1674, he was taken off the roll of Jewish brokers because he 'had become a Christian'.[36] Most probably he remained a member of the guild. Otherwise we know only that in 1666 Jacob Netto was reprimanded by the Mahamad—and made to apologize publicly—for 'scandalous utterances' ('palabras escandalosas').[37] There is no immediately apparent connection between this reprimand and Netto's conversion eight years later. For the time being, if not for ever, the reasons for this conversion must remain in the dark.

Another broker, Jean Cardoso, married a non-Jewish wife, Janneke Dorrevelts, who, at the registration of their marriage in 1649, declared that she had converted to Judaism four years earlier.[38] Apparently the marriage caused some stir at the city hall, and in 1650 the *parnasim* refused the request of Elião Uziel alias Jean Cardoso to circumcise his son and bathe his daughter and prohibited his wife from coming to the synagogue.[39] It is uncertain whether Cardoso and the *parnasim* ever patched

---

[36] GAA, PA 366, no. 1190, p. 86 (11 Dec. 1674).
[37] Ets Haim-Montezinos Library, Amsterdam, MS 48 E 64, fo. 12ᵛ (Nisan 5426/1666). Since I last saw this manuscript it has been transferred to the PIG collection at GAA.
[38] GAA, DTB 680, p. 180 (17 Dec. 1649).
[39] GAA, PIG 19, p. 297 (8 Tishrei 5411/3 Oct. 1650).

up their differences. But it is clear that Cardoso remained a Jew and that several of his children later chose to convert to Christianity, some in the face of their father's protests, others after his death.[40] As we know nothing of the broker's motivations, it is impossible to say whether they were inspired by communal tensions or by personal predilection.

Aside from economic strains, the *nação* also suffered its share of familial conflicts. Some resulted from the misbehaviour of one of the partners; a more frequent cause was inheritance disputes. The ways in which these often bitter confrontations were resolved were as diverse as their causes. The vastness of this subject prevents us from discussing it in any detail; for present purposes it will suffice to consider some of the most immediate and apparent communal consequences of a few selected cases.

Not infrequently Portuguese Jews embroiled in serious domestic squabbles chose to emigrate rather than suffer the dishonour or humiliation of public disclosure. To cite a few examples, Ishac Ergas alias Sebastião da Cunha left for Venice 'because of the suit filed against him by his wife'; a suit inspired by the infidelities of her husband, who had acquired quite a reputation among prostitutes, who, for one reason or another, had nicknamed him 'the French Crown'.[41] Conversely, the infamous reputation of being a loose woman acquired by Rachel Nunes induced her husband to move to Livorno.[42] Not unlike the impending threat of bankruptcy or a negative sentence for a major offence, confrontations of this sort destroyed a person's status within the small community and left him or her little choice but to seek fortune or pleasure elsewhere. The Mahamad could do little to prevent these excesses and intervened, as we have seen, only when the individuals, as it were, flaunted their vice, and their adultery became a matter of public knowledge and affront.

Contrary to the cases of marital infidelity which drove partners apart, inheritance disputes tended to lock opponents into battles from which they could not easily extricate themselves. Many acrimonious fights, occasional physical violence, and lengthy and costly court proceedings ensued. Again the Mahamad was powerless to avert confrontations of this sort. They were a normal constituent of life, especially among the wealthy. Without a truly exhaustive and comparative investigation it is impossible to ascertain whether this seemingly excessive disputatiousness was more rampant in Holland as a result of some measure of social disintegration engendered by the expatriation than it had previously been in Portugal and Spain.[43]

The dispute between father and sons Pereyra over his wife's and their mother's

---

[40] On Cardoso and his descendants, see van Eeghen, 'Gereformeerde Kerkeraad', 172; GAA, DTB 685, p. 52 (29 Apr. 1661); DTB 497, p. 393 (12 Feb. 1672); GAA, NA 2166, pp. 65, 73, 76 (10–11 Apr. 1661; A. Lock); NA 2222, p. 60 (8 Sept. 1666; A. Lock).

[41] GAA, NA 2268, fo. 525ᵛ (27 Aug. 1653; A. Lock).

[42] GAA, NA 2272, fo. 11 (4 Jan. 1657; A. Lock).   [43] Kagan, *Lawsuits and Litigants*, 16–20.

inheritance has been mentioned above. The *parnasim*, we may recall, made no immediate effort to settle the dispute but merely attempted to clear the air of possible illegalities so that a fair settlement could be attained. A similar motivation prompted the Mahamad to interfere in an inheritance dispute unleashed by the death of Francisco Ramires Pina alias Ishac Naar in 1641. Here too it was the potential for serious communal repercussions created by certain unsavoury aspects of the affair that induced the *parnasim* to act.

Francisco Ramires Pina's first wife had died childless.[44] In accordance with the norm among contemporary Portuguese Jews there had been no community of property between him and his second wife, his niece Sara Naar. Thus, when Ramires Pina died, he left as his sole heir a 4-month-old daughter, Ribca. The Amsterdam Orphans' Chamber appointed Lopo Ramirez alias David Curiel and Manuel Dias Henriques alias Matatia Aboab, both married to sisters of the deceased, as Ribca's legal guardians and managers of her estate. In later years the estate was estimated to be worth at least 150,000 gulden, even after a substantial portion had been wasted under the management of Ribca's guardians. In 1649–50 Ramirez and Dias Henriques sought to disown their niece and claim the inheritance for Ramires Pina's sisters—and themselves. For reasons unknown, Francisco Ramires Pina and Sara Naar had not seen fit to ratify their marriage at the city hall and had contented themselves with the synagogal ceremony only. This negligence allowed Ramirez and Dias Henriques to declare Ribca an illegitimate child because, according to Dutch law, she had been born out of wedlock. At this point, Ribca's other relatives as well as the *parnasim* stepped in to prevent this blatant miscarriage of justice and flagrant breach of familial ranks. The case went through the city court and on appeal to the Court of The Hague, and attracted widespread attention among some of the highest authorities of the city and the state. A settlement was forced by Ribca's marriage, at age 15, to her cousin Jacob Abas of Hamburg. Though still a minor, Ribca was rendered by marriage legally of age and entitled to claim her inheritance. On 30 September 1656 the States of Holland retroactively declared all marriages previously solemnized according to Jewish law only, as well as the children therefrom, legal and legitimate and thereby settled the lawsuit in favour of Ribca de Pina.

On the communal front, the *parnasim* placed Ramirez and Dias Henriques under the 'small ban', denying them access to the synagogue. Ramirez and Dias Henriques protested against this exclusion to the burgomasters of Amsterdam, who accepted their plea and ordered the *parnasim* to allow the two to worship as usual. When Ramirez and Dias Henriques reappeared in the synagogue, however, they had to contend, as they left after the service, with verbal abuse—some young members shouted 'turncoats, turncoats' ('verklikkers, verklikkers')—and a brawl ensued in which Matatia Aboab became so angry as to draw his sabre. In order to

---

[44] The following account is based on Vaz Dias, 'Merkwaardige erfenisquaestie', and Fuks, 'Rechtstrijd'.

avoid further incidents of this sort, the Mahamad in 1658 and again in 1660 prohibited *yehidim* from submitting their cases to the Court of The Hague without
prior effort at arbitration by the Mahamad or the city court. The Hague Court,
it would seem, was less likely than the communal and municipal authorities to
adjudicate matters 'realistically' and probably tended to be stricter in its application of the letter of the law.

During 1651 the widowed Lopo Ramirez declared his intention to marry Rachel
Aboab, the daughter of his fellow guardian, Manuel Dias Henriques. Lopo's niece,
Sara Curiel, daughter of his sister Abigael Curiel, registered a protest against the
marriage with the *parnasim* and, eventually, the city court. Sara claimed that Lopo
had promised to marry her and had fathered her son Abraham. The *parnasim* took
Sara's part and refused to allow Lopo's and Rachel's marriage to be celebrated
in the Esnoga. In the end, Lopo married Rachel Aboab in 1651 and won the suit
instigated by Sara Curiel in the city court in 1653. But the matter did not rest there.
In 1679 Abraham Curiel asked, on the occasion of his wedding, for a requiem
prayer to be said in honour of his alleged father, David Curiel alias Lopo Ramirez.
Lopo's widow and children protested against the implicit claims made in that
action. Notwithstanding the sound advice of Amsterdam and Italian rabbis declaring Abraham's claims null and void, the *parnasim* again chose to side against
Lopo's immediate family. In the end, in 1682, after an appeal against the city
court's ruling by Sara and Abraham Curiel, the case was settled by the Court of
Holland, upon the advice of experts from the University of Leiden, which forbade
Abraham ever to assert his claim to being Lopo Ramirez' son in any form or
fashion.

Shortly after the first conflict Lopo Ramirez had left Amsterdam and had gone
to live in Antwerp, where he continued to live as a Jew. He returned to Amsterdam
in 1666 (possibly because of Sabbatean expectations) and was allowed to rejoin the
Kahal after paying a fine of 1,000 gulden.[45] Ramirez' emigration probably had little
to do with the insults he had suffered from the *parnasim* and fellow *yehidim*. In the
course of the 1640s he had increasingly become more sympathetic to the Spanish
cause and had begun to run into serious problems with the Portuguese ambassador, who had not a good word to spare for 'the rascal [*velhaco*]', as well as with his
own brother and nephew, Duarte and Jeronimo Nunes da Costa, who were the
major advocates and financiers of the Portuguese effort in northern Europe.[46]
Whether the various alienations—from his family, from his community, and from
his erstwhile loyalties—are somehow interrelated it is impossible to say. Lopo's is a
singular case, revealing first and foremost the complexity of the psyche of this
proud and wilful man—in many ways, a very good and characteristic Portuguese
Jew—and little of the inner social dynamics of his community.

[45] GAA, PIG 19, p. 562 (15 Sivan 5426/18 June 1666).
[46] On Nunes da Costa's diplomatic activities, see Swetschinski, 'Amsterdam Jewish Merchant-
Diplomat', and Israel, 'Diplomatic Career'.

Lopo Ramirez' migration to Antwerp points up another problem the Amsterdam *nação* faced, particularly during the second half of the century, as the Peace of Westphalia (1648) normalized relations between the Republic and Spain, and traffic between Amsterdam and Antwerp intensified. The conflicts discussed so far were generated by social and economic tensions within the community, intensified by the limited, village-like confines of the Kahal. Some members had been led to emigrate; others somehow survived the conflict and remained. With the reopening of relations with the Southern Netherlands, a third option arose by which *yehidim* could absent themselves from the Kahal without losing contact with the *nação*. This option no doubt entailed a slackening of Jewish observance and the danger of the temptation of entering, temporarily or not, into more or less intimate relations with Christians, ranging from a friendly visit to Sunday mass to intermarriage. These dangers were all the more real as many Portuguese Jews had only recently extricated themselves from a New Christian existence, with all its dubious and ambiguous compromises, and had been driven to settle in Amsterdam as much by inquisitorial pressure as by personal choice. Taking Jewish observances with less than complete seriousness and considering Christian practices to be no immediate threat to one's salvation came natural to ex-*conversos* and a certain degree of latitudinarianism was unavoidable, even in Amsterdam. But Antwerp harboured special dangers. It lacked an organized Jewish community—a fixed and stable centre of gravity—and was peopled with many Iberians—cultural compatriots, if not soulmates—who might tempt Portuguese Jews into reverting to their old ways.

In 1644 the Amsterdam Mahamad took action to discourage these and all flirtations with latitudinarianism.[47] In that year the *parnasim* considered 'the very grave sin [*o gravissimo pecado*] that idolatry is—for who commits it is as one who negates and transgresses the entire Law (and, therefore, is obligated to sacrifice his life rather than fall into [this sin]—[and the fact that] nonetheless there is no lack of people who, without taking the horridness of such a crime into consideration [*sen atentar hun tão orendo crime*], go to lands where they are "forced" to commit it'. They resolved that any Jew who had visited 'lands of idolatry' would not be readmitted to the Kahal without prior and public expression of deep regrets. The following penitential declaration, read in the Esnoga from the *teva*, became more or less standard

I mounted this *teva* at the order of the Gentlemen of the Mahamad in order to ask of the Lord of the World and His sacred Law forgiveness for the wrong that I have done in going to a land of idolatry. And of this entire congregation, people of God, I also beg forgiveness for the scandal that I have caused, for which I am very sorry, with all my heart. And I will fulfil the penance they will impose, obeying in everything and asking that God forgive us. May there be peace on Israel.[48]

[47] GAA, PIG 19, p. 172 (12 Sivan 5404/16 June 1644).
[48] Declaration read by Daniel de Barrios, GAA, PIG 19, p. 554 (9 Tishrei 5426/10 Oct. 1665); the text is published in Révah, 'Écrivains', p. lxxxii.

Between 1645 and 1725 eighty men (two twice) mounted the *teva* to make this declaration.[49] Only a very few of their declarations of penance (*palavras*) mention the land of idolatry in question. Abraham Israel Rodrigues, Daniel Thomas (both in 1645), and David Navarro (in 1647) had visited Spain; Abraham Zuzarte o mosso (in 1668) Portugal. Most of the other cases almost certainly involved the Southern (Spanish) Netherlands. For instance, Daniel de Barrios, who mounted the *teva* on 18 September 1665, had spent all or the greater part of that year in Brussels supervising the publication of his collection of poetry, *Flor de Apolo*, by the Brussels printer Balthasar Vivien.[50] The fact that Antwerp (and, very occasionally, Brussels) was the 'place of idolatry' frequented most often explains why 'this very grave sin' virtually disappears from the records after 1668, excepting a brief resurgence between 1695 and 1703. For in the course of the 1650s something like a semi-officially recognized Jewish community emerged in Antwerp, thereby no longer 'forcing' Portuguese Jews to commit idolatry.[51]

Even between 1645 and 1668, however, the Mahamad's treatment of the problem had been decidedly mild. The preamble to the 1644 resolution cited above might have prepared one for very severe punishments. The public expression of regrets was certainly no minor disgrace. It represented—perhaps intentionally—a very attenuated version of the infamous declarations demanded of penitents at *autos-da-fé*. If the act of asking forgiveness was no doubt humiliating to the individual involved, its purpose was more likely the intimidation of those who listened. The fact that many who were thus punished belonged to the lower strata of Portuguese Jewish society may indicate that the less affluent members of the *nação* were more inclined, often for reasons of economic necessity, to overstep the bounds of Jewish propriety. It is also possible that the Mahamad applied a double standard. Lopo Ramirez alias David Curiel, for instance, lived in Antwerp for almost a decade and was never made to make the declaration from the *teva*. Perhaps his 1,000 gulden fine bought him the dispensation. Whether because the individuals involved were often marginal members to begin with or for reasons of simple common sense, too heavy-handed a response from the Mahamad would certainly have been counter-productive. The most the *parnasim* could realistically hope for was to intimidate the *yehidim* sufficiently to make them think twice before committing this 'very grave sin' and 'horrid crime'.

The fear of latitudinarianism was not confined to actions only. There was a distinct tendency on the part of the Mahamad to keep anything smacking of Catholicism or reminiscent of New Christian inclinations to imitate Catholic ways out of the Kahal and the *nação*. In 1632 the *imposta* board forbade the staging of festival plays in the synagogues.[52] The reason given was that they were disruptive. More likely the board objected to the tendency to imitate, in however Jewish a

[49] Kaplan, 'Travels of Portuguese Jews'.
[50] Pieterse, 'Daniel Levi de Barrios', 19–20.   [51] Israel, 'Lopo Ramirez'.
[52] GAA, PIG 13, p. 86*b* (25 Tishrei 5393/10 Oct. 1632); published in Pieterse, *Daniel Levi de Barrios*, 155.

fashion, the Iberian *auto sacramental*. The Mahamad may have been successful in banning such blatantly Iberian imitations from the synagogue. The *nação*'s thirst for theatrical performances and frivolous poetic tournaments was satisfied elsewhere. Warehouses were rented to perform plays, and the forbidden *enigmas* (poetic variations on the theme of a riddle) found their illustrious home in the salons of Don Manuel de Belmonte.[53] Against the prominent Baron de Belmonte the Mahamad was powerless, and the theatrical performances were too few and far between to give much cause for alarm. Moreover and more importantly, these activities occurred in private and stirred up no scandal.

The printed word was a more serious matter. Published texts were there for everyone to see and might reflect negatively upon the *nação* as a whole. The right to censorship had first been claimed in 1632 by the *imposta* board in connection with the religious writings of Yosef Delmedigo. It was asserted most vigorously against several Portuguese Jewish poets writing secular poetry. The occasions reveal the measures of propriety applied by the *parnasim* to judge certain works unworthy of publication and show where the limits of latitudinarianism were drawn.

In 1656 the Mahamad prohibited the distribution and reading of Manuel de Pina's *Chanças del ingenio y dislates de la musa*, notwithstanding its dedication to Jeronimo Nunes da Costa, 'Cavallero hijodalgo de la caza de Su Magestad El Rey Don Juan IV de Portugal, y su agente en los Estados de Holanda'.[54] The *parnasim* had learned that the book 'had caused great scandal' and therefore prohibited (literally, excommunicated) it 'on account of the enormous *deshonistidadez* [probably, obscenities] contained in it'. In 1665, the first year during which Moseh Curiel alias Jeronimo Nunes da Costa served on the Mahamad, the ban on de Pina's *Chanças* was lifted. But in 1669 the original interdiction was again confirmed. Little else is known about the book, except that Manuel de Pina himself later personally denounced Daniel de Ribeira for possessing a copy.[55]

We are much better informed regarding the censorship to which the poetic creations of Miguel de Barrios alias Daniel Levi de Barrios were subjected. Hardly any work composed by de Barrios—the most prolific of all of Amsterdam's Portuguese Jewish writers—escaped the scrutiny of the *parnasim* and the *hahamim*. On several significant occasions these censors have left us their actual reports on the perceived demerits of de Barrios' work. These reports constitute the most explicit source revealing what imitation of Iberian models the guardians of the *nação*'s propriety found particularly objectionable.

Miguel de Barrios, a former captain in the Spanish army, arrived in Amsterdam at the end of 1662 or the beginning of 1663.[56] Shortly after his arrival de Barrios asked permission of the *parnasim* to have a collection of his poems, entitled *Flor de*

---

[53] See below, pp. 287, 300–1.
[54] GAA, PIG 19, p. 407 (25 Av 5416/15 Aug. 1656); Révah, 'Écrivains', pp. lxxiv–lxxvii.
[55] Révah, 'Aux origines de la rupture spinozienne', 407.
[56] For a biography of de Barrios, see Scholberg, *Poesia religiosa*, 3–42; Pieterse, *Daniel Levi de Barrios*, 15–30.

Apolo, printed in Amsterdam. The Mahamad submitted the text to the very pious Dr Ishac Naar for examination. The following was Dr Naar's report:

Magnificos Senhores. On your orders I examined a book, entitled *Flor de Apolo*, composed by Miguel de Barrios, in which—not to mention the fact that its overall theme concerns amorous and lascivious verses that any Jew would have little justification in publishing—I made the following observations: first, that he invokes Gentile deities and attributes divinity to them (albeit for poetic reasons). I am of the opinion that one should not tolerate to be said in jest things which, if said in truth, are so criminal. Furthermore, that in some places he exceeds all bounds of modesty and propriety [*honestidade*] and in others addresses particular and known persons. I think these need to be corrected. On examining his changes, one may grant him permission.

Following Dr Naar's report, the Mahamad heard de Barrios' response and referred the manuscript, 'corrected . . . in conformity with what he had been ordered', to Haham Ishac Aboab and Dr Ishac Naar. The examiners' unanimous opinion was that the book ought not to be allowed to be printed in Amsterdam; and so the Mahamad refused to give permission.[57] As a result of his difficulties with the Amsterdam censors, de Barrios settled in Brussels and had his *Flor de Apolo* printed there, in 1665, by Balthasar Vivien. During the same year, as we have seen, he returned to Amsterdam, where he was made to mount the *teva* and ask forgiveness for his having gone to 'a land of idolatry' and, presumably, having transgressed God's sacred Law.[58]

A few years later (the exact date is not known), de Barrios submitted another poetic manuscript, entitled *Coro de las musas*, for examination. The work was scrutinized by the religious leaders Ishac Aboab, Moseh Rephael de Aguilar, and Abraham Cohen Pimentel. The following was their very detailed report:

Report of the dissonant [*mal sonantes*] matters in the book *Coro de las musas* both contrary to the honour of our Jewish faith and lascivious:

Firstly, throughout the book there are three matters which, though not completely prohibited, are somewhat scandalous, to wit:

1. the naming of planets and other created things gods, in the manner of ancient paganism [*gentilidade antiga*];
2. the entitling of idolaters and foul [*imundos*] Christian saints;
3. the statement in various parts that the souls of deceased Christians and idolaters are in heaven partaking of the glory [*gozando de gloria*] . . .;

However, these three points could have been excused (assuming the book is printed), if there had not been other matters more scandalous, to wit:

1. the author states in praise of Charles V that he was a new Elijah when he was taken to heaven;

---

[57] The censorship of de Barrios' works is discussed—and the relevant documents are published—in Révah, 'Écrivains', pp. lxxvii–xc.

[58] GAA, PIG 19, p. 554 (9 Tishrei 5426/10 Oct 1665); published in Révah, 'Écrivains', p. lxxxiii.

2. he says in praise of Dona Maria of Portugal that she surpassed Rachel, Ruth, Hannah, and Dinah in perfection;

3. he says that Aguila (who represents Christianity) rose with the wings of faith to contemplate the heavenly things, but that the Turk considers the earthly things until he gathers them in the breath of his vanity [*no ar de sua vanidade*];

4. he says: 'he, zealous champion of the faith, founded the Holy Inquisition', and that because of it more than 800 thousand Hebrews were exiled;

5. he says: 'the damned idolater, Julian the Apostate, abandoned the Evangelical faith';

6. he says: '[the great Constantine] enlightened the celebrated Council which condemned the Arian heresy . . . to the coveted Cross he gave a serious cult';

7. he says: 'Illustrious pilgrims reached Rome, royal bird, faithful dove, great star'; he explains the epithet 'faithful dove' referring to its remaining close to its faith without allowing another, and what he calls an illustrious pilgrim and the epithet 'great star' [*gran luzero*] requires no explanation, for it refers to the Christian faith which he calls light [*luz*];

8. he calls the faith of the Christians 'Christian light', as above;

9. he says regarding an idolatrous king: 'the victory he achieved, trusting more in his faith than in his sword';

10. he says that King Ferdinand established the Holy Brotherhood;

11. he says that the good King supports the true religion; and says this regarding King Ferdinand, whom he calls 'a pillar of the Christian faith' . . .;

12. speaking of the King of England, he says: 'in persecution, in patience a Catholic David, a forewarned Job'; this is certainly unseemly, for today the name 'Catholic' is only given to a Christian;

13. he says: 'The Moon shines with the rays which it takes from the sun. The Ottoman represents it [taking the Moon as a device on its arms], pursuing in plunders the laurel that crowned the Romans in triumphs. But the time will come when this verse of David will be fulfilled: "In his days let the righteous flourish and abundance of peace, till the moon be no more" [Ps. 72: 7].' It seems from these words as if the punishment that the Turk is to receive is for the plunder which he unjustly inflicts upon the Romans and that these [the Romans] are the just who will flourish;

14. he calls Rome the Metropolis of the World and that at the present time when she no longer dominates the whole world; but he wants to say that she is the head and queen of the whole world spiritually;

15. speaking of Titus when he destroyed Jerusalem, he says: 'With strong squadrons he punished the crime of the rebels, with such virtue did he reign in their hearts.' Improper words for a Jew, calling his people rebels and the tyrant who destroyed us virtuous;

16. speaking in praise of Rome, he says: '[star] of wisdom, of valour, and of armed faith';

17. he invokes Jupiter and other deities. This is unseemly if only because he calls them gods, but it is very dissonant [*mal sonante*] to pray to them and invoke them.

Finally, the censors list the page references to a number of 'lascivious items which are not specified, for the sake of decency'.[59]

The page references which accompany this report are identical with the pagination of the version of *Coro de las musas* printed by Balthasar Vivien in Brussels in 1672. It would appear that the book had already been printed before it was examined by the Amsterdam rabbis. Probably the report drawn up by Ishac Aboab, Moseh Rephael de Aguilar, and Abraham Cohen Pimentel inspired the Mahamad's decision that 'the book *Coro de las musas* which he [Daniel Levi de Barrios] had printed in Brussels not be sold in Amsterdam and that the copies already distributed be returned'.[60]

This incident did not signify the end of de Barrios' clashes with Amsterdam's Portuguese Jewish censors. In 1679 de Barrios observed: 'None of the works which I have published was censored as thoroughly as that one [*Coro de las musas*] and that which I am publishing now, entitled *Harmonia del mundo*.'[61] Another testimony regarding the censoring of *Harmonia del mundo* comes from R. Jacob Sasportas. Notwithstanding de Barrios' Sabbatean sympathies, R. Jacob maintained very cordial relations with the poet and seems to have been among the few who were more favourably disposed towards his work. In the *Sefer tsitsat novel tsevi* Jacob Sasportas furnishes the following account of de Barrios' *Harmonia del mundo*:

> One of them [i.e. of the Sabbatean believers] was a man by the name of Daniel Levi de Barrios who wrote poetry in the vernacular and who was called a *poeta*. He composed many works of poetry, including a Pentateuch in verse, entitled 'Melody of the World' [*Niggun Olam*], *Harmonia del mundo*, which he had divided into 12 parts each of which he dedicated to a duke, such as the Duke of Leghorn, and to the princes of Holland, Portugal, Spain, and England. All of these promised to reward him and sent him their picture, their banner, their coat of arms, and the glory [*tiferet*] of their forebears to be printed and sent him money for the publication of the book . . . And, because he consulted with me regarding all his affairs and the matter of his books and because I was among those who supported him [in his bid] to get permission to have the book published, while part of the Mahamad and most of the rabbis opposed it saying that the book contained phrases which were not in accordance with our Torah and, also, that he transformed our Torah into gentile, secular literature by copying it in verse form, therefore [because of Sasporta's favourable disposition], he revealed to me all his affairs and all his dreams and vanities.[62]

According to the records of the Kahal, the Hahamim Ishac Aboab, Benjamin Musaphia, and Josiau Pardo had been entrusted with the examination of *Harmonia del mundo*. On 23 April 1673, responding to a request from de Barrios, the *parnasim* decided that 'the part or parts of the manuscript seen by the *hahamim* can be printed once they have been initialled and that the author would be obliged to give the first printed pages which come off the press to the said Gentlemen in order that

[59] Révah, 'Écrivains', pp. lxxxv–lxxxvi; documents in GAA, PIG 66A.
[60] Ets Haim-Montezinos Library, Amsterdam, MS 48 E 64, fo. 27ᵛ (MS transferred to GAA, PIG).
[61] Révah, 'Écrivains', p. lxxxvii.   [62] Sasportas, *Sefer tsitsat novel tsevi*, 363–4.

they may be examined to see if they agree with the originals initialled by the *hahamim*.[63] Two editions of *Harmonia del mundo* (or, as it was called by its full title, *Imperio de Dios en la harmonia del mundo*) appeared, but unfortunately the title pages indicate neither where nor when. Possibly de Barrios had not accepted the compromise put forward by the *parnasim*, for on 28 June 1677 'Danyel de Bayros digo Levy de Bayros' received 25 gulden from the *sedaca* 'on account of a book that he wrote and that the Gentlemen did not want to approve'.[64] This sum looks like a consolation for the Mahamad's refusal to allow de Barrios' version of *Harmonia del mundo* to be printed. From about that period onwards, Daniel Levi de Barrios received financial aid from the *sedaca* more or less regularly.

Even these financial arrangements did not end de Barrios' censorship problems. Even as his poetry adopted a more religious tone and concentrated on more 'orthodox' material, the *parnasim* found occasion to examine and confiscate his *Desembozos de la verdad contra las máscaras del mundo*, in 1675.[65] In 1690 the Mahamad prohibited the possession, sale, presentation, or shipping abroad of 'the conclusions' of a book entitled *Arbol de vidas*.[66] Finally, in 1691, the Mahamad reprimanded de Barrios for having printed, without their permission, a *daras* (exposition) dedicated to the *Yesiba de Neve Sedeck*.[67] No further details are available regarding the precise nature of the material that elicited the Mahamad's negative responses.

Besides providing us with an entire catalogue of Portuguese Jewish sensibilities, the various clashes between the *parnasim* and rabbis on the one side and Daniel Levi de Barrios on the other also serve to show how one important Portuguese Jewish writer reacted to censorship and how the *parnasim* responded to his evasions. Almost all of de Barrios' early (pre-1680) works were published in the Spanish Netherlands, either by Balthasar Vivien in Brussels or by Jerome & Jean-Baptiste Verdussen or Jacob van Velsen in Antwerp. They were published under the name of Don Miguel de Barrios and, as the various reports indicate, appealed to a large extent to a non-denominational audience. After 1680, more or less coincidentally with the period during which de Barrios received financial aid from the *sedaca*, all of his works were published in Amsterdam by David de Castro Tartas or by Jacob de Cordova. These works were generally of more strictly Jewish content and were dedicated, by and large, to the grandees of Amsterdam's Portuguese Jewish community.[68] In 1678 de Barrios declared in a letter to the Mahamad of the Kahal Kados de Talmud Tora of Amsterdam that he had suffered financially from the prohibitions levelled against his works. 'The fear of God', he writes, 'keeps me

[63] Ets Haim-Montezinos Library, Amsterdam, MS 48 E 64, fo. 30 (MS transferred to GAA, PIG).
[64] Pieterse, *Daniel Levi de Barrios*, 22, 144–5.
[65] Ets Haim-Montezinos Library, Amsterdam, MS 48 E 64, fo. 33ᵛ (MS transferred to GAA, PIG).
[66] GAA, PIG 20, p. 173 (5453/1692/3); Révah, 'Écrivains', p. lxxxviii.
[67] Ibid., p. lxxxix.
[68] Scholberg, *Poesia religiosa*, 56–80; Pieterse, *Daniel Levi de Barrios*, passim.

within Judaism and makes me not heed the vanities of the world that applauds my writings.'[69] For the Amsterdam prohibitions on *Flor de Apolo* and *Coro de las musas* deprived him of an important market and a potential source of patronage. During the 1670s de Barrios gambled on the generosity of the Spanish noblemen in Brussels; a gamble he lost, it seems. Towards the end of the 1670s, more than ten years after he first joined the Kahal, he decided to change tack and seek the support and patronage of Amsterdam's Portuguese Jews, whose aristocratic tastes were becoming more and more pronounced. De Barrios' choice of the place and the content of his publications was governed by financial considerations. The Mahamad's decisions hurt him financially, but they did not ruin him (or, at first, did not threaten to ruin him), for the very simple reason that as an ex-*converso* de Barrios was not wholly dependent upon the Jewish community for economic security. His subsequent dependence is underscored by the aid he received from the *sedaca*. The case of de Barrios demonstrates that censorship existed only in so far and for so long as the author was willing or forced to submit himself to it. During the 1670s de Barrios was neither willing nor forced to do so, and—surprisingly, yet typically—the Mahamad accepted without further action what might otherwise have seemed a serious degree of insubordination.

Not only did the Mahamad desist from taking any action against Daniel Levi de Barrios, it went out of its way to support him financially. In the light of the facility with which the Mahamad wielded the weapon of excommunication, this restraint and generosity must strike one as somewhat unexpected. To some extent, the influence of de Barrios' wealthy patrons may account for the circumspection with which his 'disloyalties' were handled. For even during the 1670s de Barrios seems to have been in touch with such highly esteemed Portuguese Jews as Manuel de Belmonte, Jeronimo Nunes da Costa, and Dr Ishac Orobio de Castro, with whom he frequented the Academia de los Sitibundos, a literary salon founded in 1676.[70] A more important reason for the *parnasim*'s calmness resides, it seems to me, in the nature of the material censored. For none of the many objections raised in the reports relates in any direct manner to Judaism itself. The *hahamim* found de Barrios' use of Christian metaphors 'dissonant', 'inappropriate', and 'improper': they never faulted him for any mishandling of Jewish concepts, only on his overly positive estimation of Christianity and Christians. De Barrios' cast of mind, the *parnasim* realized, was not sceptical but naïvely latitudinarian. They grasped the opportunity to bind him more closely to the Jewish community when the very proud poet was forced to solicit their assistance. Only once, in 1697, did the *parnasim* raise their voice against Daniel Levi de Barrios, threatening him with excommunication when they learned that he had written a letter to the magistrate of Hamburg 'containing [I quote the Mahamad's summary; the letter itself has not

[69] Da Silva Rosa, 'Eigenhandige brief', 106–11, repr. in Scholberg, *Poesia religiosa*, 27; Révah, 'Écrivains', p. lxxxvii; Pieterse, *Daniel Levi de Barrios*, 143–4.

[70] Scholberg, 'Miguel de Barrios', 141–50.

been preserved] matters that could cause scandal and prejudice the peace and preservation of our nation residing in that city'.[71] Clearly, de Barrios had gone beyond latitudinarianism and had actually endangered, at least potentially, the status of the sister Portuguese Jewish community of Hamburg.

Atypical as the case of Miguel alias Daniel Levi de Barrios may have been in its details, it none the less highlights certain basic dynamics of the communal life of the Amsterdam *nação*. It demonstrates the danger presented by the availability of Antwerp as an alternative market and a centre of cultural attraction. It re-emphasizes the importance of economic interdependence as a primary constituent in the life of the *nação*. As in the reactions to 'idolatrous transgressions' abroad, it reveals the tolerance of the Mahamad for a certain degree of latitudinarianism as long as the latter remained basically unassociated with the Kahal. And finally, it discloses how rapidly so pagan an imagination as de Barrios' could be refurbished to think in fairly orthodox Jewish terms. Like many others of its kind, that conversion owed much not only, negatively, to the exigencies of survival but also, positively, to the strong and distinct social and religious principles upon which the Amsterdam *nação* was founded.

CHALLENGING AUTHORITY

Up to this point none of the conflicts discussed questioned the authority of the Mahamad directly, nor did any revolve around one or another of the elemental principles of community membership. The discord was disturbing, but the *parnasim* succeeded in preventing it from dividing the *nação* and endangering its *quietação* or, even, *conservação*. Some other disturbances touched the more basic principles of the Kahal and created accordingly a great deal of acrimony.

A very small number of excommunications concerned offences of unknown quantity. Juda Cohen Berberisco came under pressure to leave the city for reasons unknown.[72] Moseh Hamis Dorta had committed 'a grave offence' in Hamburg for which he had been excommunicated there; he fled to Amsterdam where he was excommunicated again.[73] Johanan de Leão's 'enormous vices' were so great that the *parnasim* did not bother or were reluctant to list them.[74] A few other cases of this sort could be cited.[75] About most other conflicts we have data allowing us to classify the offence and speculate about the Mahamad's motivation for its response.

It is somewhat difficult to gauge exactly what was at stake on the several occasions on which the *parnasim* stated some form of 'insubordination' as the

[71] Révah, 'Écrivains', p. lxxxix.

[72] GAA, PIG 13, pp. 102, 118, 129 (11 Av 5393/18 July 1633; 18 Elul 5395/1 Sept. 1635; 12 Sivan 5396/15 June 1636).   [73] GAA, PIG 19, pp. 32–3 (5400/1639/40).

[74] Ibid. 209, 212 (20 Sivan 5406/3 June 1646; 7 Elul 5406/18 Aug. 1646).

[75] For a fuller discussion of the *herem*, a complete list of persons *enheremadas* before 1683, and details about some specific cases, see Kaplan, 'Social Functions of the *Herem*'.

reason behind their punitive action. Undoubtedly in some cases it was as much the inspiration behind the refusal to obey or the content of the altercation as the act itself which upset the *parnasim*. 'Insubordination' was the Mahamad's last resort in imposing its will upon recalcitrant *yehidim*. Ishac Peralta, Abraham de Jacob Levi, Moseh Jesurun d'Oliveira, and Joseph Mendes da Silva were variously punished for having had words with, 'having insulted', one or more of the *parnasim*, within or outside the synagogue.[76] David Nassy was excommunicated for having 'abused' the Haham Ishac Aboab.[77] On one occasion where the sources are more explicit than usual, Ishac Mendes da Silva insulted the president and vice-president of the Mahamad as they came to fetch him at his home to accompany him as Hatan Bereshit to the Esnoga. Apparently Mendes da Silva became upset and felt demeaned by the fact that the *parnasim* appeared at his door not with Ishac Mendes Penha, who was to be part of the same honorary procession as Hatan Torah, but with Mendes Penha's son because the father had fallen ill.[78] Undoubtedly the *parnasim* deeply resented such public displays of disrespect for their authority. These innocent incidents may also serve as reminders of how fragile the authority of the Mahamad could be.

This authority was based upon a gentlemen's agreement, on ill-defined implicit assumptions. Yet it was invested with burdensome civic responsibilities, particularly those of charity and the concomitant imposition of taxes. Among the most basic assumptions underlying the Mahamad's position was the implied analogy between parental and communal authority. Just as the burgomasters of Amsterdam and other towns were known as the city fathers, so the *parnasim* viewed themselves as the parents of a large, extended family—an analogy underscored many times over by the reality of a widely intermarried *nação*. In April 1636 the justices of Amsterdam called in the elders of the *nação*, protested against the disorderly behaviour of certain Portuguese Jewish youths, and asked the Mahamadot to inform their congregants of measures the city was planning to take to prevent these excesses. The elders successfully requested the justices to give them an opportunity, in this instance, to deal internally with the unruly and recalcitrant youths. In their proposal, the *parnasim* speak of these young men who deserve to be punished severely 'for their unwillingness to accept the restraint of their elders', and in parentheses, revealingly, 'parents and relatives; [an unwillingness] from which easily other greater vices could come'.[79] In later years, implicitly applying the same analogy, the Mahamad took a very dim view of the wilful erosion of parental authority. In 1659 the *parnasim* adopted a stern resolution prohibiting marriages without parental consent or, where neither parents, nor grandparents, nor

---

[76] On Peralta, see GAA, PIG 19, p. 16 (1 Tamuz 5399/3 July 1639); on Levi, see PIG 20, p. 28 (18 Tishrei 5442/30 Sept. 1682); on Jesurun, see ibid. 298 (12 Heshvan 5461/25 Oct. 1701); on Mendes, see ibid. 403 (5465/1704/5).   [77] GAA, PIG 19, p. 765 (3 Iyar 5437/5 May 1677).

[78] GAA, PIG 20, p. 151 (28 Tishrei 5452/21 Oct. 1691).

[79] GAA, PIG 13, pp. 123–6 (5396/1635/6).

brothers, nor uncles were alive or available, that of the *haham*. This *haskamah* was provoked by the actions of Jacob Semah Cortisos, who surreptitiously married the daughter of 'Madama' Tavares—behaviour all the more dishonourable as he and the Tavares family belonged to the upper echelons of the *nação*. In subsequent years this prohibition had to be repeated periodically and more *yehidim* were excommunicated or otherwise punished for transgressing it than for any other single *haskamah*.[80]

The weakness of parental and communal authority represented by these cases constituted a fairly abstract, indirect problem and the problems it posed remained within bounds. A far greater threat to communal authority and unity was posed by the rebellion of higher-status *yehidim* against the Mahamad's monopoly on the sale of kosher meat and poultry. The increasing numbers of German and Polish Jews had organized their own community and built their own substantial synagogue. The existence of this community offered rebellious Portuguese Jews the possibility of severing their ties with the Kahal without leaving the city and without having to forsake Jewish worship. The Ashkenazi community's butchers, moreover, supplied an alternative and cheaper source of kosher meat. In the 1670s Portuguese Jews availed themselves of both these options. On 30 June 1670 Abraham de Ishac Bueno, a wealthy jeweller, informed the *parnasim* that he no longer wished to be counted a member of the *nação* and was joining the German Jewish community. Whether or not he carried his threat through is uncertain, but in 1680 he was still or again at odds with the Mahamad.[81] In 1677 Joseph Abarbanel Barboza had publicly and loudly denounced the Mahamad's declaration that poultry sold by Ashkenazi butchers was unfit for Portuguese Jewish consumption. Abarbanel Barboza contested the halakhic justification of the prohibition and was duly excommunicated for 'insubordination'. Abarbanel Barboza, however, took his case to court and refused to do the required penance. He was soon joined in his rebellion by others who formally, through a notary, informed the Mahamad that they were cancelling their membership in the Kahal.[82] Although Abraham Bueno's name is not mentioned in this context, his second clash with the *parnasim*, in 1680, may have been part of the same or a parallel rebellion. For Abraham Bueno, too, was joined by friends and relatives in leaving the Portuguese Jewish community.[83] However, as all their various names recur in the *finta* list of 5444 (1683/4), we must assume that eventually all returned to the Kahal.

In view of the low esteem generally accorded by the Portuguese Jews to the German Jews, these implied or executed threats to join the latter's community

[80] GAA, PIG 19, pp. 445, 447 (5419/1658/9).

[81] Ets Haim-Montezinos Library, Amsterdam, MS 48 E 64, fo. 23 (26 Av 5430/12 Aug. 1670) (MS transferred to GAA, PIG); GAA, NA 3586, p. 970 (30 June 1670; J. Snel).

[82] Kaplan, 'Social Functions of the *Herem*', 147–50; GAA, PIG 19, p. 810 (8 Shevat 5439/21 Jan. 1679).

[83] GAA, NA 4094 (24 Apr. 1680; D. v. d. Groe); 4097 (23 Jan., 22 Feb. 1681; D. v. d. Groe).

must not be taken lightly. It is curious, too, that the *yehidim* implicated in this rebellion were almost all well-regarded members of the Kahal; several had even been members of the Mahamad. The issue at stake was obviously not a purely religious one. In threatening to defect to the German Jewish community Abraham Bueno, Joseph Abarbanel Barboza, and their friends gave voice to their dissatisfaction with the Kahal, not to a preference for the religious or dietary views of the German Jews. Their mutiny was the protest of a rival faction against the leadership claims of even wealthier, and often more recent, immigrants. Discontent may have been aggravated by the recent building of the magnificent Esnoga, which had placed great financial burdens upon the Kahal as a whole. The distribution of that burden may have fostered discontent particularly among individuals who expected to bask in the glory of that Esnoga but were unlikely to do so.

Bueno, Abarbanel Barboza, and their friends were eventually forced to swallow their pride. Their number was too small or lacked sufficient solidarity and the *nação*, even under the leadership of another coterie, simply much more attractive, socially and economically, than the Ashkenazi community. They had nevertheless gained a small, but not insignificant, victory in having been able to force the Mahamad to lighten its heavy hand and restrict the impulsive use of the *herem*. For in 1683 the burgomasters of Amsterdam, 'without wishing to interfere in the internal affairs of the congregation', expressed the expectation that henceforth the punishment of *herem* be applied 'with moderation'.[84]

Only once during the seventeenth century did a relatively small group of *yehidim* successfully challenge the authority of the Mahamad. (The failed mutinies discussed in the previous paragraphs may very well have been inspired by the climate created by this challenge, which preceded them chronologically.) On the surface no more than another factional squabble, this particular contest of wills throws into sharp relief some of the most basic facts and dynamics of seventeenth-century Portuguese Jewish life. The 'del Sotto affair' constitutes, as it were, a micro-history of the Amsterdam *nação*.

Jacob Delmonte alias Jacob del Sotto alias Cornelis Cox Dircksz. died in Amsterdam on 29 March 1670. Jacob Delmonte (as he is most commonly referred to in the documents) was one of the patriarchs of a very numerous and extremely wealthy family, the great majority of whose members lived in Amsterdam at the time of his death. The del Sotto family originated from Portugal—from Bragança, it appears. After leaving Portugal the family had settled in France, in Bordeaux and in Rouen. In Bordeaux, as yet still known as Mendes or Mendes Sotto, the family aligned itself with that of Dr Francisco Lopes, professor in the faculty of medicine at Bordeaux. The wife of Dr Francisco Lopes was a Mendes Sotto and two of their daughters and one of their sons married two brothers and one sister of Jacob Delmonte. Antonio Lopes Suasso, another son of Dr Francisco Lopes and Isabel Mendes, hispanicized Sotto to read Suasso. In Rouen the del Sotto family

---

[84] GAA, PIG 20, p. 67 (21 Jan. 1683; 14 May 1683).

aligned itself with the Rodrigueses. Subsequent generations of the Rodrigues family assumed different family names depending on the name of the patriarch. Thus the children of Salvador Rodrigues alias Josua Jesurun Rodrigues adopted the family name Salvador; the children of Martin Rodrigues alias Joseph de los Rios, Salvador Rodrigues' brother, the family name de los Rios. The Jesurun and Alvares families were also intermarried with the del Sottos. In Rouen various members of the del Sotto family had been embroiled, as Judaizing New Christians, in the 1633 upheaval discussed earlier. Quite possibly these Lopes, Rodrigues, and Mendes families had already been interrelated before they left Portugal.[85]

Jacob Delmonte (b. 1612, Rouen) was the son of Francisco and Francisca Mendes Sotto alias Abraham and Sara del Sotto. In 1638 in Amsterdam he married Isabel Mendes (b. 1612, Bayonne), the widow of Bartolomeo Rodrigues. Isabel Mendes was the daughter of Bartolomeo's sister, Francisca Mendes alias Ester Jesurun Rodrigues, who was married to Dr Antonio Luis Alvares. Another daughter of Francisca Mendes, Gracia Nunes (b. 1615, Rouen), married (in 1637 in Amsterdam) Jacob Delmonte's brother, David alias Salvador del Sotto (b. 1613, Rouen). Jacob Delmonte's sister, Leonora Mendes alias Lea del Sotto, was married (in 1628 in Rouen) to Martin Rodrigues, brother of Bartolomeo Rodrigues and Francisca Mendes. Jacob Delmonte's wife, Isabel Mendes alias Ribca del Sotto, died in 1665; and Jacob Delmonte remarried (in 1666 in Amsterdam) his niece Mariana, daughter of his brother, David del Sotto, and Lucretia, daughter of Manuel Martinez Dormido. Neither Isabel Mendes nor Mariana del Sotto bore Jacob Delmonte any children.[86]

Shortly before his death Jacob Delmonte had been negotiating with the *parnasim* of the Kahal regarding a loan for the construction of the new Esnoga. Already heavily burdened with an extensive *sedaca* roll and having very little liquid capital at its disposal for such a large undertaking, the Mahamad had decided to appeal to private *yehidim*. Thus began the negotiations with the very wealthy and childless Jacob Delmonte. Delmonte was willing to furnish about 100,000–150,000 gulden for the building of the synagogue on condition that the *parnasim* would pay him and, after his death, his heirs interest at a modest rate. So far the condition was quite acceptable to the *parnasim*. But Jacob Delmonte insisted on the further stipulation that every year the new *parnasim* would be obliged to renew the obligation personally so that Jacob Delmonte and his heirs would know precisely from whom to collect the annual interest. This stipulation the *parnasim* could not

---

[85] For the alias of Jacob Delmonte, see GAA, NA 3586, p. 566 (3 June 1670; J. Snel). For the family background, see Malvezin, *Histoire des Juifs à Bordeaux*, 137 n. 1; Roth, 'Marranes à Rouen', 120, 126; Révah, 'Autobiographie', 73, 79; and esp. 'Genealogia do velho M. Lopes', an eighteenth-century manuscript presently in private hands.

[86] On the various family relations mentioned in this paragraph, see GAA, DTB 674, p. 286 (20 Nov. 1637); DTB 675, p. 37 (1 July 1638); DTB 687, p. 19 (30 Oct. 1666); GAA, NA 2165, p. 224 (4 June 1660; A. Lock); NA 2177, p. 78 (7 May 1672; A. Lock); NA 2218A, p. 173 (17 Jan. 1665; A. Lock); NA 2222, p. 56 (8 Sept. 1666; A. Lock); NA 3587, p. 797 (30 Mar. 1670; J. Snel).

accept. They did not want to bind themselves personally to repay either the capital or the interest, but were willing only to offer the goods of the synagogue as collateral. This did not satisfy Jacob Delmonte, and the negotiations ended.[87] Shortly thereafter Jacob Delmonte fell ill and died. The funds for the construction of the new synagogue were ultimately collected in a special *nedava* by a surtax on the *finta*; the lion's share was borrowed from Ishac de Pinto.[88]

Upon the death of Jacob Delmonte the *parnasim* had expected to be nominated, in his last will and testament, executors of a substantial bequest on behalf of the Kahal's poor. Requesting to see the will of Jacob Delmonte, the *parnasim* were told that there was none. According to the testimonies of David de Aguilar, the deceased's bookkeeper, Mariana del Sotto, his widow, and Abraham Jesurun, the husband of one of his nieces, Jacob Delmonte had decided to change his will as early as the turn of the year; but because of the death of a child of Abraham de los Rios, the husband of another of his nieces, and his own subsequent illness, he had not had a chance to draw up a new will 'in favour of his common heirs and friends [i.e. relatives]'. And so, according to the testimony of Abraham Jesurun,

on Tuesday night at about 11 or 12 o'clock, before the Saturday on which Delmonte died, Mariana del Sotto was in the room with him, the witness, when Delmonte asked her to give him his will, which she did. Delmonte then said that he had always thought that he would recuperate from this present illness in order to change his will and that this will was weighing heavily on his mind. Thereupon he told Mariana to throw the will in the fire, which she did, whereupon Delmonte said: 'Keep it secret.'

Otherwise confirming the testimony of Abraham Jesurun, that of Mariana del Sotto adds that, though the will had originally been sealed, Jacob Delmonte had later (two weeks after the onset of his illness) endorsed the will, 'at the persuasion of his physician Isaack Orobio', with a signed note saying that the will was not closed. For obvious reasons, the *parnasim* were not satisfied with the version of the story given by Jacob Delmonte's heirs and threatened them with excommunication 'if they refused to declare what the *parnasim* wanted to hear', as one partial witness put it. According to the *parnasim*, someone among Delmonte's heirs had intentionally burned or embezzled the will in order to prevent the large bequest from being made.[89]

To make matters even more complicated, the del Sottos appear to have felt that the *parnasim*'s disbelief or subsequent intransigence had been inspired in part by the vindictiveness of the Salvador family. The Salvadors were not among Jacob

[87] GAA, NA 2233, p. 48 (7 May 1670; A. Lock); NA 3586, p. 673 (9 May 1670; J. Snel).

[88] De Castro, *Synagoge* (1950 edn.), 30–3.

[89] GAA, NA 3586, p. 510 (14 Apr. 1670; J. Snel); NA 3586, p. 504 (13 Apr. 1670; J. Snel); NA 3586, p. 506 (13 Apr. 1670; J. Snel); NA 3586, p. 676 (9 May 1670; J. Snel). A great many documents relating to the 'del Sotto affair' are assembled in GAA, PIG 520A, pp. 68–324: 'Papeis do pleito & ajusto com os herdeiros de Jacob Delmonte alias Del Sotto'. A typescript chronology and index of these documents was prepared by Mr Silvio van Rooy (dated 9 May 1973) and is available at the Amsterdam city archives.

Delmonte's heirs, but were very intimately related to the de los Rios family, which did stand to gain from the disappearance of Jacob Delmonte's will. Whatever the precise involvement of the Salvadors in the proceedings against the del Sottos, the heirs of Jacob Delmonte found it necessary to register testimony regarding the persistent animosity between Jacob Delmonte and the Salvadors. From this testimony we learn that Ishac and Abraham Salvador had accused Jacob Delmonte of being 'a knave and thief'; that Abraham Salvador had drawn his dagger in a vain attempt to wound Jacob Delmonte and Ishac de los Rios; and that Jacob Delmonte had referred to Salvador Rodrigues as 'the man I hate more than anyone else in the world'.[90] The events preceding the actual 'del Sotto affair' furnished all the ingredients for a highly emotional and bitter conflict.

Excommunication of the heirs of Jacob Delmonte ultimately ensued, but not before they had formally transgressed the most hallowed statute of the Kahal Kados. At first the *parnasim* obtained a court order placing the entire estate of Jacob Delmonte in receivership. They were also able to persuade the bailiff of Amsterdam to share their suspicions of the heirs of Jacob Delmonte. These actions provoked a lengthy and complicated legal battle before the city court of Amsterdam, the Court of Holland, and the High Court. Aside from the purely legal actions, both sides employed subterfuges in the attempt to force a decision or some satisfaction in its favour. The del Sottos insisted that the court appoint Christians as administrative supervisors over their management of Jacob Delmonte's estate. When the court had the estate temporarily sealed, the del Sottos did not hesitate to break the seals. But the *parnasim* possessed heavier guns. They threatened with excommunication anybody who refused to come forth with any information that he possessed regarding Jacob Delmonte's will. Next they threatened with excommunication anybody who came to the aid of the del Sottos. They forbade Jacob Marques, a solicitor, to give counsel to the heirs. They even went so far as to solicit the aid of the German and Polish Jewish communities and asked their *parnasim* to threaten their members with excommunication likewise. (The German and Polish *parnasim* refused to get involved.) The *parnasim*'s ally, the bailiff, was more successful and obtained a court order permitting him to see all affidavits notarized on behalf of Jacob Delmonte's heirs. Individual Portuguese Jews, acting upon personal initiative, were able to intercept letters addressed to the heirs of Jacob Delmonte.[91]

[90] On the vindictiveness of the Salvadors, see GAA, NA 3586, pp. 672, 677 (9 May 1670; J. Snel). On the del Sotto–de los Rios connection, see GAA, DTB 686, p. 42 (8 Feb. 1664); DTB 687, p. 99 (19 Aug. 1667); GAA, NA 643, p. 21 (7 May 1631; S. Cornelisz); NA 2178, p. 45 (14 Mar. 1673; A. Lock); NA 2234, p. 854 (9 Dec. 1670; A. Lock).

[91] In order of the facts' appearance in this paragraph, see GAA, NA 3586, p. 618 (30 Apr. 1670; J. Snel); NA 3586, p. 877 (7 June 1670; J. Snel); NA 2233, p. 146 (19 May 1670; A. Lock); NA 2233, p. 1018 (27 Aug. 1670; A. Lock); GAA, PIG 520A, p. 202 (29 Apr. 1670); GAA, NA 3586, p. 884 (7 June 1670; J. Snel); Ets Haim-Montezinos Library, Amsterdam, MS 48 E 64, fo. 22ᵛ (11 Nisan 5430/1 Apr. 1670), fo. 23 (14 Nisan 5430/4 Apr. 1670) (MS transferred to GAA, PIG); GAA, NA 3586, p. 938 (22 June 1670; J. Snel); NA 3586, p. 447 (3 Apr. 1670; J. Snel); NA 3586, p. 945 (24 June 1670; J Snel); NA 2233, p. 44 (7 May 1670; A. Lock); NA 3587, p. 84 (11 July 1670; J. Snel).

The general climate of harassment created by the *parnasim* and the bailiff and aggravated by the actions of individual *yehidim* completely alienated the del Sottos from the synagogue. On Friday, 22 August 1670, therefore, the heirs of Jacob Delmonte decided to organize their own *minyan* (prayer meeting of at least ten adult males). Ishac del Sotto the Elder served as its *parnas* and Abraham del Sotto as the cantor. The creation of this *minyan* was a direct provocation of the *parnasim* of the Kahal and furnished them with the legal argument they had lacked so far to justify excommunicating the heirs of Jacob Delmonte. For, in organizing the private *minyan*, the heirs had contravened capitolo 2 of the merger agreement of 1639 forbidding the establishment of any congregation outside the unified Kahal Kados de Talmud Tora. On the following 27 August, Ishac Levy Ximenes, *gabai*, publicly revealed, from the *teva*, the names of the ten men who had participated in this private *minyan* and who were thereby excommunicated. They were:

Ishac del Sotto, brother of Jacob Delmonte;
David del Sotto, brother of Jacob Delmonte;
Abraham del Sotto, son of Ishac del Sotto;
Ishac de David del Sotto, son of David del Sotto;
Ishac de los Rios, son of Martin Rodrigues and Leonora Mendes, sister of Jacob Delmonte;
Jacob de los Rios, another son of Martin Rodrigues, and husband of Sara del Sotto, daughter of David del Sotto;
Abraham de los Rios, another son of Martin Rodrigues, and husband of Sara del Sotto, daughter of Joseph del Sotto, deceased brother of Jacob Delmonte;
Josuah de los Rios, another son of Martin Rodrigues;
Abraham Jesurun, husband of Ester del Sotto, daughter of David del Sotto;
Aron Dormido, brother of Lucretia, second wife of David del Sotto, and husband of Reyna del Sotto, daughter of David and Lucretia del Sotto.

Now formally cut off from the Kahal and its services, on 30 August 1670 the heirs of Jacob Delmonte purchased their own private cemetery immediately adjacent to the Bet aHaim of the Kahal.[92]

However successfully the proud heirs of Jacob Delmonte managed their separation from the Kahal, excommunication entailed certain consequences they had not bargained for. According to traditional Jewish law, the *herem* cuts the excommunicated off from all forms of communication with the members of the religious community other than his most immediate relatives. Contact with the excommunicated results in the excommunication of the transgressor. And in the 'del Sotto affair' the *parnasim* made absolutely certain that every *yahid* clearly understood the meaning of excommunication. The *parnasim* forbade Simon de Pool, a German

    [92] GAA, PIG 520A, p. 75 (7 Sept. 1670); Ets Haim-Montezinos Library, Amsterdam, MS 48 E 64, fo. 23ᵛ (7 Elul 5430/23 Aug. 1670), 23ᵛ (11 Elul 5430/27 Aug. 1670) (MS transferred to GAA, PIG); GAA, PIG 520A, p. 222 (30 Aug. 1670).

Jew, to serve his del Sotto masters. Dr Reynoso, a physician, and Ishac Baruh, a barber, refused to visit the son of David del Sotto and the widow of Jacob Delmonte 'for fear of also being excommunicated'. Ishac Baruh later received permission from the Mahamad, but was expressly forbidden to speak with his client. Much worse was the refusal of Portuguese Jewish merchants to speak with any del Sotto about business matters. Addressed by a del Sotto, Portuguese Jewish merchants turned their backs without uttering a word. On 4 September 1670 this refusal to communicate actually led to a physical clash between certain heirs and some Portuguese Jewish merchants.

Abraham del Sotto, Abraham Jesurun, and Ishac de David del Sotto accompanied by a court clerk had appeared at the Exchange to discuss certain matters pertaining to the estate of Jacob Delmonte, and received the usual silent treatment. The clerk thereupon subpoenaed the Portuguese Jewish merchants to appear before the Court of Holland. Pandemonium broke out among the Portuguese nation. They yelled 'matta matta esta canalja dos Sottos' which translated means 'kill, kill that del Sotto riff-raff'. Those of the Portuguese Jewish nation then violently attacked [the del Sottos] who were at the Exchange. Henrico Mendes Silva hit Abraham del Sotto, and the eldest son of Jacob Bueno de Mesquita Abraham d'Aron Jesurun. The Jewish nation attacked them with such force and violence that [the del Sottos] became apprehensive and feared for their lives. Greater harm would certainly have come their way if [the del Sottos] had not been assisted by various Dutch merchants who had joined [in the dispute]. The Exchange officer, too, defended them with his stick as much as he could. The first to call 'matta matta' were Jacob Pereira, Samuel Pereira, and Mordochay Senior.

A few days later Abraham Coronel testified that certain Portuguese Jews had said that they would persecute the del Sottos until they surrendered to the *parnasim* and that they would not rest before one of the del Sottos was dead.[93]

Obviously suffering greatly from the ban, the ten excommunicated men decided to contest the legality of capitolo 2 of the merger agreement before the burgomasters of Amsterdam. On 17 November 1670 the burgomasters decreed that capitolo 2 of the merger agreement was valid and legal, but that it could not be applied against the heirs of Jacob Delmonte. The excommunication of the del Sottos was immediately annulled.[94]

At the instigation of the High Court and with the mediatory assistance of Rephael de Arredondo, husband of Sara de los Rios, daughter of Martin Rodrigues, the heirs of Jacob Delmonte and the *parnasim* finally settled their dispute on 2 October 1671. According to this agreement the heirs of Jacob Delmonte would bequeath to the Kahal 40,000 gulden, the interest on which was to be used for general poor relief. The agreement stipulated that the 40,000 gulden had to be

---

[93] GAA, NA 3586, p. 907 (15 June 1670; J. Snel); NA 2233, p. 1008 (27 Aug. 1670; A. Lock); NA 2233, p. 1034 (29 Aug. 1670; A. Lock); NA 2233, p. 1024 (28 Aug. 1670; A. Lock); NA 2234, p. 26 (4 Sept. 1670; A. Lock); NA 3587, p. 358 (6 Sept. 1670; J. Snel); NA 2234, p. 67 (9 Sept. 1670; A. Lock).

[94] Noordkerk, *Handvesten*, ii. 473; Ets Haim-Montezinos Library, Amsterdam, MS 48 E 64, fo. 24 (27 Elul 5430/ 12 Sept. 1670) (MS transferred to GAA, PIG).

invested in East India Company shares and was never to be converted into other stock. In a separate agreement, David del Sotto committed himself to paying 6,000 gulden in cash to the Kahal. The heirs also agreed to transfer three-quarters of the cemetery they had purchased to the *parnasim*; one-quarter would remain in the possession of Leonora Mendes and Abraham de los Rios to serve as a private cemetery for their descendants. This part of the Portuguese Jewish Bet aHaim is still known today as the 'Bet aHaim dos Sottos'.[95]

The little private cemetery later caused another conflict between the heirs of David del Sotto and the *parnasim*, who were apparently unhappy with the del Sotto cemetery and attempted to have it transferred and incorporated into the rest of the cemetery. The del Sottos resisted. The *parnasim* then tried to make it difficult for them to reach their own cemetery, whose only approach was across the Bet aHaim. In 1679 the Mahamad temporarily denied several del Sotto women entrance to the synagogue. But all harassment was to no avail. In the end the del Sottos were able to retain possession of their own private cemetery.[96]

One final aspect of the affair needs to be noted to round off the account. 'The heirs of Jacob Delmonte' were not simply Jacob Delmonte's intestate heirs. On 30 March 1670, the day after Jacob Delmonte's death, eight individuals agreed to divide his estate into eight equal parts, regardless of the degree of relationship of the individual heirs. Five were indeed intestate heirs: Ishac del Sotto, a brother; Leonora Mendes, a sister; David del Sotto, a brother; Abraham de los Rios, husband of Sara del Sotto, only daughter of Joseph del Sotto, a brother; and Francisco de Liz, husband of Francisca Mendes Sotto, a sister. The three others—Jacob de los Rios, Abraham Jesurun, and Ishac de David del Sotto—were children or married to children of David and his first wife, Gratia del Sotto. Gratia del Sotto was a sister of Isabel Mendes, first wife of Jacob Delmonte. Since, as the agreement states, the estates of Jacob Delmonte and Isabel Mendes had been irretrievably mixed up, the respective heirs had decided upon this simple division into eight equal shares. In another agreement, made two weeks later, the heirs of Jacob Delmonte committed themselves to an elaborate set of provisions of marital gifts for several friends and relatives of the deceased. These less immediate relatives, who had undoubtedly been named in Jacob Delmonte's will, stood to lose most from the disappearance of his will and had to be provided for.[97]

[95] Pieterse, *Daniel Levi de Barrios*, 86; GAA, DTB 685, p. 147 (10 Mar. 1662); GAA, NA 2234, p. 854 (9 Dec. 1670; A. Lock); GAA, PIG 19, pp. 649–51 (17 Veadar 5432/16 Mar. 1672); PIG 520A, pp. 121 (7 Oct. 1672), 156 (letter dated 1 Oct. 1672); GAA, NA 2237, p. 1118 (24 Dec. 1671; A. Lock); GAA, PIG 520A, p. 151 (30 Dec. 1671).

[96] GAA, NA 2252, p. 322 (1 June 1677; A. Lock); NA 2254, p. 59 (24 Jan. 1678; A. Lock); NA 2256, p. 243 (5 Apr. 1679; A. Lock); Ets Haim-Montezinos Library, Amsterdam, MS 48 E 64, fo. 48 (20 Nisan 5439/2 Apr. 1679), fo. 49ᵛ (16 Tamuz 5439/26 June 1679) (MS transferred to GAA, PIG); GAA, NA 2256, p. 247 (5 Apr. 1679; A. Lock).

[97] GAA, NA 3587, p. 797 (30 Mar. 1670; J. Snel); NA 3586, p. 413 (30 Mar. 1670; J. Snel); NA 3586, p. 499 (13 Apr. 1670; J. Snel); NA 3587, p. 527 (8 Oct. 1670; J. Snel).

The 'del Sotto affair' as described above reveals all the workings of a clan. The endogamous marriages of several generations of del Sottos had created an elaborate network of extremely tight relationships with its centre in Amsterdam and branches in France, Spain, and England. The clan also showed typical signs of social strain, especially with members who had married exogamously such as Salvador Rodrigues. The Nunes da Costa family experienced similar conflicts in its relations with Lopo Ramirez. The del Sotto clan was perhaps the most extensive of all the wealthy Portuguese Jewish families in Amsterdam. Possibly the unpleasant events of 1633 in Rouen had driven more members of the clan to Amsterdam than had been intended. Generally the affairs of such a clan produced little conflict with the outside world, for theirs was a self-contained unit having every interest in co-operating with those in its immediate social surroundings.

Jacob Delmonte's childless death disturbed the normal workings of the clan. As he had no natural heirs, his fortune would not necessarily remain within the clan group. Moreover, shortly before his death Delmonte had actually been thinking of bequeathing a substantial part of his fortune to the community. We have no way of knowing whether he ever really changed his mind once death appeared imminent. It is by no means implausible. Whatever the case may have been, his sudden death left the clan very few options to rectify the damage done—damage mostly in the form of (possibly false) expectations on the part of the *parnasim*. In opposing the Mahamad the clan acted as an admirably tight and loyal unit. It stuck to its guns in the face of substantial hardships. It was sufficiently extensive and numerous—perhaps the only clan of its kind in Amsterdam—to be able to survive even the harsh pronouncement of excommunications. The heirs of Jacob Delmonte needed neither to emigrate nor to join the German Jewish community, although Ishac del Sotto the Elder seems to have done the latter briefly. They were able to oppose the authority of the *parnasim* on terms chosen by the heirs themselves. The only other case of such successful opposition involved the lone figure of Spinoza.

QUESTIONING TRADITION

The final class of conflicts to be discussed concerns the religious question or, more precisely, the manner in which the *parnasim* and certain individuals disagreed about the definition of the Jewish content of the association. Here is not the place to enter into the protracted debates of religious history. The question whether or not Uriel da Costa or Spinoza is to be seen as a deist or forerunner of deism lies outside the scope of this social history. Here we can seek only to elucidate the social dimensions of these religious conflicts and to offer an assessment to complement the deliberations of the historians of ideas.

To a certain extent these religious disputes have suffered from over-exposure. They are, of course, a natural target of scholarly scrutiny. By virtue of their intellectual content they are in some deceptive ways the easiest to reconstruct. However, in the total scheme of conflicts that riddled the *nação* they were few in number and caused only brief and minor disruption. Measured by the usual standards of frequency, level of disturbance, and numbers of people involved, religious controversies do not rank high on the list of communal stress points. If the unnatural, ambiguous, twisted history of the Iberian New Christians must be invoked in this context at all—to account, for instance, for whatever measure of heterodoxy did crop up—the very high level of orthodoxy ought to occasion far more surprise than the few incidents of religious deviance.[98]

Some divergence of religious opinions was accepted. The very lively controversy concerning 'the eternality of punishment', for instance, appears not to have provoked any public disturbance.[99] And even though the debate involved only the *hahamim*, the issue as to whether past sins could be redeemed was undoubtedly of great existential import. For as ex-Marranos all the Portuguese Jews, without exception, had lived lives of sin; and whether they had done so under compulsion or not was to them far less immediately important than whether or not the consequences were irreparable. On another occasion, in 1653, the Mahamad reprimanded Saul Levi Morteira and Menasseh ben Israel for having made their disagreement public and temporarily suspended them, without pay, from their duties.[100] The records do not say what their clash was about. Even the explosion of Sabbatean enthusiasm in 1666 caused no major communal disruption. Subsequently, it is true, the *parnasim* guarded against any resurgence of Sabbatean sympathies. In late 1666, presumably shortly after Shabbetai Zevi's apostasy became known in Amsterdam, they censured the dissemination of a printed collection of Sabbatean sermons, *Fin de los dias*, by Moseh de Gideon Abudiente of Hamburg, on the grounds that their subject matter was 'contrary to the truth of our sacred Law'.[101] In 1667 the *parnasim* enlisted the support of the Amsterdam burgomasters to expel one Sabbatay Raphael, 'a Jew, 24 years of age, of Sicilian parents, born in Jerusalem, claiming to be a prophet with supra-human knowledge and the ability to make himself invisible, who threatens to cause a great deal of disunity within the community'. Under questioning Raphael denied that he had made these claims, but insisted that a 'three-eyed' prophet Elijah had appeared and spoken to him in a cloud in a 'church' (no doubt a synagogue is meant) in Jerusalem.[102] In 1671 the *parnasim* forced the Haham Ishac Aboab, once a staunch Sabbatean himself, to denounce and prohibit, from the *teva*, 'a letter written by Dr Abraham Cardoso of Tripoli . . . concerning essential issues of our sacred Law',

[98] The point is made forcefully in Yerushalmi, *Re-education of the Marranos*.

[99] On this theological dispute, see Altmann, 'Eternality of Punishment'.

[100] GAA, PIG 19, pp. 344, 356, 358 (Heshvan 5414/1653).

[101] Ets Haim-Montezinos Library, Amsterdam, MS 48 E 64, fo. 26 (MS transferred to GAA, PIG); Kaplan, 'Attitude of the Leadership', 204–7; Scholem, *Sabbatai Sevi*, 440, 548–88.

[102] A copy of the expulsion order may be found in GAA, PIG 119.

because it contained 'dissonant' [*mal soante*] and scandalous doctrines'.[103] After the conversion of Shabbetai Zevi, the heresy of continued Sabbatean speculations was fairly cut and dried and could be disposed of briskly and unopposed. The cases we are about to discuss, then, must have had quite far-reaching implications to have elicited such strongly negative responses.

Only the religious views and opinions expressed by Yosef Delmedigo, Uriel da Costa, and Daniel alias Juan de Prado and his cohorts, Daniel de Ribeira and Bento de Spinoza, provoked truly severe communal strictures. Arriving at a precise judgement as to what attracted such censure is, however, far from straightforward. The condemnations formulated by the *parnasim* are singularly vague and insufficiently explicit to enable us to home in on the views being castigated; several of these individuals thus attacked, by contrast, have left us a veritable treasury of writings outlining their views in great detail. Between the reticence of the Mahamad and the prolific outpourings of the condemned lies a vast gap allowing for much speculation about which particular issue, idea, or statement may have most offended the communal leadership. Here we will focus on what appears a more or less recurrent theme variously expressed by all five individuals concerned.

To enter this maze of speculations we may take our cue from the observations made by Dr Ishac Orobio de Castro following the excommunications of Daniel de Prado and Bento de Spinoza. Orobio de Castro had known de Prado in Spain at the University of Alcalá and wrote his former acquaintance an open letter in which he observed:

Those who withdraw from Idolatry to the [United] Provinces where liberty is granted to Judaism are of two kinds:

Some who, upon reaching the desired haven and receiving the seal [of circumcision], direct all their will to love the Divine Law and try to learn, within the grasp of their understanding, that which is necessary in order to scrupulously observe the sacred precepts, laws, and ceremonies, which they and their forebears had forgotten in Captivity. They humbly listen to those who, raised in Judaism and having learned the Law, are able to explain it. As soon as they can, they make themselves proficient—each one according to his state and capability—in the laudable modes, traditions, and customs, which Israel observes throughout the world, so as to order their lives in the service of God and avoid the errors which were formerly committed by ignorance. They come ill with ignorance, but, since they are not accompanied by the horrible sickness of pride, they recuperate easily, tasting the holy and healing medicine which the compassion of their brothers offers to them. For, when they arrive, all of the latter, from the greatest rabbi to the most minor layman, try to teach them so that they shall not err in the observance of the Divine Law.

Others come to Judaism who, while in Idolatry, had studied various profane sciences such as logic, physics, metaphysics, and medicine. These arrive no less ignorant of the Law of God than the first, but they are full of vanity, pride, and haughtiness, convinced that they are learned in all matters, and that they know everything; and even though they are ignorant

---

[103] Ets Haim-Montezinos Library, Amsterdam, MS 48 E 64, fo. 26 (MS transferred to GAA, PIG); Kaplan, 'Attitude of the Leadership', 207–11.

of that which is most essential, they believe they know it all. They enter under the felicitous yoke of Judaism and begin to listen to those who know that of which they are ignorant, [but] their vanity and pride do not permit them to receive instruction so that they may emerge from their ignorance. It seems to them that their reputation as learned men will diminish if they allow themselves to be taught by those who are truly learned in the Holy Law. They make a show of great science in order to contradict what they do not understand, even though it be all true, all holy, all divine. It seems to them that, by making sophistic arguments without foundation, they are reputing themselves to be ingenious and wise. And the worst of it is that they also spread this opinion among some who, because of either their youth or bad nature, presume themselves clever, and who, even though they don't understand a thing of that which the foolish philosopher says against the Law of God, act nonetheless as if they understood him, in order not to admit that they do not understand him, and thus still to be regarded as understanding. These succeed in making such a philosopher even more prideful. His pride grows, so does his impiety, so that without much effort the ignorant philosopher, as well as those who hold him in affection, falls into the abyss of apostasy and heresy.[104]

Much may be said about this curious passage. As an explanation of the source of heterodox tendencies it will not do. Ishac Orobio de Castro was himself one 'who, while in Idolatry, had studied various profane sciences' and one who by his own logic ought to have inclined towards heresy.[105] What the passage loses in explanatory force, however, it gains in descriptive value. For in trying so hard to proffer an explanation Orobio de Castro reveals the essence of the conflict. Before any discussion of specific arguments and counter-arguments we are here reminded that there were some who accepted tradition and others who did not. (Orobio de Castro's negative references to pride, incidentally, only expose his basic conservatism more starkly.[106]) Orobio de Castro's inadvertent characterization of this most elementary dichotomy may go some way towards explaining the negative response of the *parnasim*. For the individuals characterized as having been unwilling to accept tradition did not merely question this or that particular tradition but attacked the very principles of traditionalism; and it is this wholesale attack upon tradition that makes these individuals stand out in the history of Jewish heretics.

Yosef Shlomoh Delmedigo was born on Crete in 1591, studied at the University of Padua, and then embarked on a life of wanderings through Egypt, Turkey, Lithuania, and Hamburg which landed him for a time in Amsterdam in 1626. From 1626 until 1629 he served as the *haham* of the congregation Bet Israel. In 1629 his unorthodox views met with such strong opposition from the *imposta* board and the other *hahamim* that he left for Frankfurt. He died in Prague in 1655.[107]

---

[104] Révah, *Spinoza et le Dr Juan de Prado*, 89–90; trans. in Yerushalmi, *From Spanish Court*, 45–6.

[105] For the biography of Ishac Orobio de Castro, see Kaplan, *From Christianity to Judaism*.

[106] On 'pride' and 'self-esteem' as used in the seventeenth century, see Lovejoy, *Reflections on Human Nature*.

[107] See *Encyclopedia Judaica*, v. 1478–81; and, more fully, Barzilay, *Yoseph Shlomoh Delmedigo*.

In 1629 the *imposta* board decided to scrutinize the publication of Delmedigo's *Sefer elim* and *Ma'ayan ganim* by Menasseh ben Israel's recently established printing press. On 13 May it asked Menasseh ben Israel to appear before its assembly. Following the discussion, it was decided that Ruby Joseph Salom, the cantor of Bet Jacob, would translate Delmedigo's work verbatim in the presence of Menasseh ben Israel ('to facilitate translation of doubtful passages'), Haham Abraham Cohen Herrera, and one member of each of the three Mahamadot. Cohen Herrera and the three *parnasim* would then submit their opinion to the board. Menasseh ben Israel, meanwhile, obtained approbations from the Venetian rabbis: Leone Modena, Simhah Luzzatto (both dated 10 Menahem 5389/30 July 1629), Nehemiah Saraval (dated the week of 18–25 August), and Jacob Lebet Halevi (undated). The Venetian rabbis saw only the first part of Delmedigo's work entitled *Sefer elim*. The objectionable material, it appears, formed part of *Ma'ayan ganim*. On 27 August 1629 Menasseh ben Israel completed the printing of *Sefer elim*. On 2 September he was again called before the *imposta* board, which decided to have the printed as well as the yet unprinted parts of the book examined once more. Were the examiners to find anything 'contrary to the honour of God and His sacred Law and to good manners' they were to report this in writing, whereupon Menasseh ben Israel was to respond 'whether he agreed or give reasons why such statements were not prohibited'. The board would then make its ultimate decision. The sources fail to yield any more data, but judging from the lack of a complete printing of *Ma'ayan ganim* and Delmedigo's departure the decision was negative.[108]

Ma'ayan ganim was intended as a response to various questions raised by Zerah bar Nathan of Troki, a Karaite whose acquaintance Delmedigo made in Lithuania—questions which formed the main body of the text of *Sefer elim*. *Ma'ayan ganim* contains answers to only three of the twelve questions. Most conspicuous by their absence are two particular chapters which were to deal respectively with the occult sciences and the kabbalah, and with a number of major theological issues.

Yosef Delmedigo's attitude towards the kabbalah confused many of his readers. Even modern scholars cannot agree on whether he condemned all or only the practical kabbalah. Delmedigo contradicts himself repeatedly on the issue. For instance, the manuscript version of the introduction of *Ma'ayan ganim*, the so-called '*Ahuz* letter, condemns the kabbalah outright, but the printed edition labels the theoretical kabbalah 'the wisdom of the Divine'. The changes in the '*Ahuz* letter were probably due to the presence in Amsterdam and on the review board of Abraham Cohen Herrera, one of the seventeenth century's most important adepts of the theoretical kabbalah, or to the moderating influence of Menasseh

---

[108] This and the following account is based on d'Ancona, 'Delmedigo', where all the relevant documentary evidence has been published. Surprisingly, Barzilay's recent biography makes no mention of the censorship of *Ma'ayan ganim* or of d'Ancona's article. The relevant archival sources are GAA, PIG 13, pp. 50, 53.

ben Israel.[109] If Delmedigo thus shows himself ready to qualify his criticism of the kabbalah under pressure from the Amsterdam examiners, we must incline towards the inference that the other missing chapter, on major theological issues, contained the insurmountable stumbling-block.

According to the question raised by Zerah bar Nathan, this chapter was to discuss matters of no less import than the existence of God, his unity, his providence, *creatio ex nihilo*, the angels and the *sefirot*, paradise and hell, and the problem of faith and reason. The mere raising of these questions may have alarmed the *imposta* board, as well as, perhaps, the implied criticism by the Karaite of certain talmudic traditions regarding these issues. On the other hand, we have every reason to suspect that Delmedigo's answers were highly unorthodox, for his general frame of mind did not augur well for a staunch, unequivocal defence of traditional Judaism.

Barzilay's characterization of Yosef Delmedigo as 'a *maskil* before the age of the Haskalah' may be misleading, but there can be no doubt that Delmedigo represents seventeenth-century rationalism at its most confused. Delmedigo's plea for freedom of conscience defines him well:

These bad, foolish people should have realized that the will cannot dominate the forces of the soul like a master over his slaves, but only as a king over his subjects: for although they listen to the will of man, they have the freedom to resist it, as Aristotle writes in the *Ethics*. Sometimes there may exist conceptions in the soul so strong that the will is unable to dispel them. Political philosophers determined that there is nothing which one desires that has not first been thought through, for reason rules over the will and inspires the will. How, then, is it possible that one would want that which he does not understand or that which is contrary to what he understands? The will is not what one pretends to say, but what one wills in his heart. How can we disapprove of someone who does not want to believe that which is contrary to what he imagines in his mind or something the impossibility of which reason has demonstrated? This is a grave illness; the Supreme Being will not punish him for it, for injustice is far from Him. The civil laws, too, bear only on those who make their opinions known to the masses and cause the public to err, but not on what one thinks.[110]

How far a cry is Delmedigo's sympathetic understanding of the 'illness' of a conscience that cannot believe other than what its reason tells it from Orobio de Castro's harsh indictment of the 'illness' of pride! In his quest for 'truth', Yosef Delmedigo devoted most of his energies to exposing the errors of tradition and to shaking the confidence of his contemporaries in received truths, among which the fairy-tales of the practical kabbalah were a favourite target. To mention a few pertinent issues: he recommends the study of Latin, for most of Hebrew literature is but a faint reflection of the scientific riches to be found in the original sources. He depreciates the miracle stories of the rabbis: 'Has anything of this sort been heard

[109] On Abraham Cohen Herrera, see Scholem's introduction to *Das Buch Shaar ha-Shamayim*, trans. Hänssermann; Krabbenhoft, 'Structure and Meaning'; Altmann, 'Lurianic Kabbala'.

[110] Quoted in d'Ancona, 'Delmedigo', 122.

with regard to Aristotle or Avicenna, Ibn Rushd or Alexander, Themistius and Johanan the Grammarian, in the course of their metaphysical speculations? The sages of other nations deal all day long with such matters, and yet not a wing moves.'[111] He equates the Mosaic Law with the legal propositions of Solon, Socrates, Plato, and Aristotle, in their common aim towards 'the welfare of man and society, and the enhancement of peace and prosperity'. He claims that Jewish leaders have mystified the Law so as to secure greater obedience. And, to cite one final and crucial example, he dismisses the particularistic doctrine which limited the immortality of the soul to Jews who keep the commandments as too parochial, and, at times, expresses rational doubt regarding even the very immortality of the soul.[112]

Each and every one of the issues raised by Yosef Delmedigo could have elicited a negative response from the *imposta* board. His all-inclusively critical stance undermined tradition in general and the kabbalah in particular; it reduced the stature of the Torah; and it questioned the uniqueness of Israel. Delmedigo clashed at virtually every turn and twist of his restless soul with the intellectual premises upon which the majority of Amsterdam's Portuguese Jews based their religious and communal existence. Menasseh ben Israel may have found Delmedigo's rationalism challenging, the *yehidim* of Bet Israel may have been attracted to his extensive Jewish learning at a time when such knowledge was in short supply; but in the end his blend of commitment to Judaism with universalist aspirations collided head-on with the Portuguese Jews' recent recovery from unforced assimilation and their treasured discovery of Jewish uniqueness.

Yosef Delmedigo, of course, had never been a New Christian or Marrano, and much of the conflict between him and the *imposta* board may be explained by their widely differing histories, though Delmedigo's ideas would have encountered severe resistance in almost every Jewish community of that era. Uriel da Costa, Daniel de Prado, and Daniel de Ribeira had all grown up on the Iberian peninsula and yet raised some of the very same issues. Obviously the critique and defence of traditionalism transcended biographical differences reducible either to more or less education in the secular sciences or to the presence or absence of a New Christian background.

The only Amsterdam *herem* registered against Uriel da Costa speaks of 'many erroneous, false, and heretical opinions contrary to our most sacred Law' and notes how the *hahamim* had failed in their attempts to bring da Costa back to the 'truth'. 'Because of his sheer obstinacy [*pertinacia*; the term reeks of inquisitorial jargon] and arrogance', his earlier excommunication, dating from 1618 in Hamburg, was confirmed.[113] Daniel de Prado was condemned twice in fairly rapid succession. The first ban records the words of penance he spoke from the *teva* on the orders of

---

[111] Quoted in Barzilay, *Yoseph Shlomoh Delmedigo*, 258. [112] Ibid. 317.
[113] GAA, PIG 13, pp. 25–6 (30 Omer 5383/ 15 May 1623); Gebhardt, *Schriften des Uriel da Costa*, 181–3.

the *parnasim* and lists 'bad opinions [*mas opinions*] and having shown little zeal in the service of God and His sacred Law': 'I have sinned and committed crimes, both in words and in deeds, against *El Dio Bendito* and His sacred Law and, thereby, scandalized this Kahal Kados.' The second recounts unsuccessful attempts by the *parnasim* to make de Prado agree to emigrate, with the financial aid of the Mahamad, and registers his excommunication 'for having relapsed, with considerable scandal, into seeking "to seduce" various persons with his very bad opinions [*pesimas opinioims*] contrary to our sacred Law'.[114] Spinoza, who was excommunicated shortly after de Prado's first condemnation, was charged with 'bad opinions and deeds' and with having continued, after reprimand, 'to practise and teach his abominable heresies and to commit "enormous" deeds'. The registration of Spinoza's *herem* contains a horrific formula of curses absent from the others:

With the judgement of the Angels and with that of the Sages, we excommunicate, cut off, curse, and anathematize Baruch de Espinoza, with the consent of *El Dio Bendito* and that of this entire Kahal Kados, before these sacred Sefarim [Scrolls of the Torah], with the six hundred and thirteen precepts written therein, with the *herem* inveighed by Jehosuah against Yeriho, with the curse Elisah laid upon the children, and with all the curses written in the Law. Cursed be he by day and cursed be he by night; cursed be he in sleeping and cursed be he in waking; cursed be he in leaving and cursed be he in entering. May Adonai not pardon him; may the wrath and zeal of Adonai be aroused against this man; may all the curses written in the book of the Law fall upon him; may Adonai blot out his name from under the skies; and may Adonai cut him off from all the tribes of Israel with all the curses of the heavens written in the book of the Law. And you who are attached to Adonai, your God, you are all alive today.[115]

There is very little in the dry recordings of these excommunications to go by. Only concerning Daniel de Prado and Daniel de Ribeira do we actually possess a dossier compiled by the prosecution—primarily Haham Saul Levi Morteira—containing testimonies by seemingly trustworthy witnesses regarding the views and teachings of these two 'heretics'.

His own personal circumstances apart, the background of Uriel da Costa's family was quite typical of the first generation of Portuguese New Christian settlers in Amsterdam. Gabriel, as Uriel was baptized in 1583–4, and his brothers and sister were born in Oporto, to parents who hailed from nearby Braga. The father was a merchant and sometime tax farmer who spent a brief time in Brazil in the 1570s and acquired a minor noble title in the first decade of the seventeenth century. On and off, between 1600 and 1608, Gabriel studied canon law at the University of Coimbra and served as a clerk at the archbishopric. Returning to Oporto after his father's death in 1608, he became the treasurer of the collegiate church of San Martinho de Cedofeita, took minor orders, and received the

---

[114] GAA, PIG 19, pp. 407, 427–8; Révah, *Spinoza et le Dr Juan de Prado*, 57–60.
[115] GAA, PIG 19, p. 408; Révah, *Spinoza et le Dr Juan de Prado*, 57–8; Salomon, 'La Vraie Excommunication'.

tonsure. In 1611 he briefly went to Lisbon to settle with his father's major creditor. He returned with a settlement and a fiancée, Francisca de Crasto, whom he married on 5 March 1612. It would appear that, in so far as a conversion to crypto-Judaism occurred, Gabriel's happened in Lisbon. In 1614 the family suddenly packed its bags and took a boat to Amsterdam. As New Christian emigration was severely restricted at the time, their departure was brought to the attention of the officials; the consequent investigations concluded that the motive had been strictly economic and no further action was taken against Gabriel's sister and her husband who had stayed behind. In his autobiography Uriel da Costa emphasizes his wish to return to Judaism as the motive for his departure and mentions how he had, reluctantly, informed his relatives of that desire, nowhere hinting that his mother and brothers were of like mind. On the contrary, his remarks on the subject incline one rather to think that they were not. He also never speaks of any proselytizing, however mild, he may have engaged in on behalf of Judaism prior to his departure. Yet a number of more distant relatives who were imprisoned by the Inquisition after 1618 denounced Gabriel da Costa as the one who had led them to Judaism.[116] Pointing the finger at relatives who had fled the country and were beyond the grasp of the Inquisition was a favourite tactic by which accused men and women were able to satisfy the inquisitors' hunger for denunciations without endangering the lives of anyone living within their jurisdiction. Uriel da Costa's silence on this point and his subsequent falling out with members of his family lead one to believe that the self-consciousness of his return to Judaism was part of a personal quest. Once in northern Europe the two oldest da Costa brothers, Jacome alias Abraham and Gabriel alias Uriel, settled with their mother in Hamburg; two younger brothers, Miguel alias Mordecai and João alias Joseph, remained in Amsterdam—a common arrangement in those days. Barely a year after his arrival in Hamburg, Uriel da Costa made a brief and rather slapdash list, known as *Propostas contra a tradição*, of legal and ritual practices he considered at odds with biblical dictates, and forwarded his findings to the Ponentine Jewish community of Venice, then still considered the intellectual centre of the Portuguese Jewish diaspora.[117] The leaders of that community passed them on in turn to Leone Modena, rabbi of Venice's Ashkenazi community. On the advice of the Venetian rabbis, the Hamburg community excommunicated Uriel da Costa in 1618. In 1623 Uriel and

[116] Révah, 'La Religion d'Uriel da Costa', 54–5.

[117] *Propostas contra a tradição* is the name Carl Gebhardt gave to the text; see *Schriften des Uriel da Costa*, 1–32. Gebhardt thought that a text of that name by Moseh Rephael de Aguilar was a transcription of Uriel da Costa's work. As a matter of fact, de Aguilar's text is a translation of Leone Modena's quotations from Uriel da Costa followed by de Aguilar's counter-arguments (see Salomon's introduction to da Costa, *Examination*, 11). Uriel's text may very well not have had a title at all; it was not meant to be published. *Propostas* remains convenient and is here used for that reason. The word 'Ponentine' was invented to distinguish these Portuguese and Spanish Sephardim from the Levantine Sephardim of Greece and Turkey. 'Ponentine' refers to the west, where the sun 'sets', in contradistinction to 'Levantine', meaning east, where the sun 'rises'.

his mother returned to Amsterdam, ostensibly to prepare the edition of his book *Exame das tradições phariseas*, in which he elaborated on the discrepancies he had earlier sent to Venice, adding a new and much larger section arguing against a biblical foundation for the doctrine of the immortality of the soul. As noted above, the Hamburg *herem* had already been applied in Amsterdam too, from 15 March 1623. After the book appeared in print Uriel was briefly imprisoned, for, as he says, 'the elders and officials of the Jews [*Senatores & Magistratus Judaicus*] agreed to make a complaint against me before the public magistrate, asserting that I had published a book to disprove the immortality of the soul in order to subvert not only the Jewish, but also the Christian religion'. His treatise was condemned to public burning, and Uriel left, with his mother, to live in Utrecht. After her death in 1628 he returned to Amsterdam, effected some reconciliation with the *parnasim*, and seems to have resumed a life in commerce. Then, over ten years later, a crisis of some kind came to a head. Uriel transferred ownership of all his belongings to his maid and common-law wife, and committed suicide in April 1640. Philip van Limborch, the editor of Uriel's autobiography, reports the following unsubstantiated sequence of events:

[Uriel da Costa] seems to have finished [*Exame das tradições phariseas*] a few days before his death and after he had determined to put an end to his life. For burning with a desire of being revenged on his brother (others say his cousin) by whom he thought himself injured, he came to a resolution to shoot him and then himself. Accordingly, as his relative was going by his house one day, he levelled a pistol at him, but missing fire and feeling himself discovered, he immediately clapt too [shut] the door and, taking up another pistol which lay ready for that purpose, he shot himself and died in a terrible manner. In the house of the deceased this manuscript [*Exemplar humanae vitae*] was found.[118]

Until the late 1980s it was believed that the communal leaders had been successful in their effort to obliterate any and all traces of Uriel da Costa's writings. Recently, however, a copy of the printed edition of the *Exame* has been found and republished, enabling us to be much less speculative than scholars have hitherto been in sketching Uriel da Costa's intellectual odyssey, if such a term may be applied to his outbursts. There are clearly two distinct stages: first, a core of observations presented in the *Propostas*, reiterated, rearranged, and elaborated in the *Exame*; and second, a major attack on the doctrine of the immortality of the soul plus a set of counter-arguments, together constituting the greater part of the *Exame*, against Leone Modena and Dr Semuel da Silva. Leone Modena had, in a Hebrew manuscript entitled *Magen vetsinah* (*Shield and Buckler*), responded to Uriel's *Propostas*. Da Silva had somehow gained access to Uriel's draft of the *Exame* and published his refutation of Uriel's arguments against the immortality of the soul in his *Tratado da imortalidade da alma* (Van Ravesteyn, 1623), before Uriel had had a chance to bring out his *Exame*. An offhand remark of Leone Modena's—'Where [in the Torah] do we find clearly set out the survival of the

---

[118]   Quoted in Salomon's introduction to da Costa, *Examination*, 23.

soul?'—apparently inspired the ruminations on the immortality of the soul on which past historians of Uriel's offensiveness had focused most of their attention. It is the part of the *Exame* that gave rise to his brief imprisonment, but it cannot have inspired his excommunications. True, in the *Exemplar humanae vitae*, Uriel speaks of a lifelong preoccupation with the fear of damnation, going back to his childhood. But this is probably better read as a description of his state of anguish on the eve of his suicide. And after the publication of the *Exame* the doctrine of the immortality of the soul found frequent defenders among other learned members of the Amsterdam community. Besides Dr da Silva, Menasseh ben Israel published his *De la resurreccion de los muertos*, Saul Levi Morteira and Moseh Rephael de Aguilar wrote manuscript refutations, and others digressed on the issue in other contexts.[119] But we need not therefore jump to the conclusion that those were indeed the opinions of Uriel's most objectionable to contemporary *parnasim*. Altogether, the *parnasim*'s ready denunciation of Uriel da Costa to the Amsterdam authorities must banish, once and for all, the thought that their actions, against this or any other heretic, were motivated by a fear that the discovery of such critical notions would offend Dutch Christians. Denying the immortality of the soul was a serious matter, and the response of the *parnasim* was appropriately measured.

'A tradição, que se chama lei de boca, não he verdadeira tradição, nem teve principio com a lei': thus, with this most pugnacious sentence, Uriel da Costa opens his *Exame*. 'The tradition called the Oral Torah is not a truthful tradition, nor did it originate with the Torah.' The *Propostas* had treated this subject as a conclusion to a number of discrepancies between traditional practices and interpretations and their biblical origins; in the later work these follow in a different order, da Costa having reversed the sequence following criticism from Leone Modena that he proceeded in the *Propostas* from the particular to the general. In the *Propostas* he treats six contradictions, in the *Exame* twelve, of which six deal with ritual matters and six with punishments for criminal acts. There seems to be little system or reason behind da Costa's choice of discrepancies to highlight: the use of *tefillin*, the cut of circumcision, the *lulav*, meat which may be eaten, the prohibition on eating meat with milk, the calculation of the months and festivals. They are all fairly elementary ritual provisions, but others might have been selected. Da Costa's strictures seek to establish the falsity of those who currently set the rules. All of those rules pertaining to criminal acts—an eye for an eye, intentional homicide, the culpability of the owner of an ox which gored a man, the punishment for a man who sleeps with a woman and her mother, the redemption of sold property, the stealing of an ox—evince a staunch and harsh fundamentalism in obdurate opposition to those authorities who sought to soften the extremism of biblical legislation. If in ritual matters rabbinic tradition has added constraints, in matters criminal it has

[119] Saperstein, 'Saul Levi Morteira's Treatise'; de Jong, ' "Tratado da immortalidade" '; Martins, 'Inédito Judaico-Português'. Spinoza addresses the issue in the *Tractatus theologico-politicus*, and Orobio de Castro in his *Amica collatio* with Philip van Limborch.

mellowed the biblical dictates. Uriel da Costa likes neither trend. He is opposed to any and all tampering with the divine word.

Not surprisingly, Uriel da Costa's *Exame* has the flavour of counter-reformatory Catholicism, the ideology in which he had been brought up. At the same time, all of his writings are permeated with a personal problematic that is nowhere fully explicated, not even in his autobiographical *Exemplar humanae vitae*. A psychologically knowledgeable historian or, better yet, a historically inclined psychiatrist would probably have a field day with the *Exemplar*, as the record of a wounded narcissist. But there is not much of social significance that can be made of these observations. The ideology of counter-reformatory Catholicism and narcissism undoubtedly infiltrated other precincts of Portuguese Jewish life in seventeenth-century Amsterdam. Neither would have been particularly offensive to the *parnasim*. None of the particular discrepancies publicized by da Costa would have elicited strong censure. They are of the sort that might have been discussed in any of the *jesibot*. It was the conclusion he drew that was so particularly offensive. Propounding the worthlessness of rabbinic tradition and the falsehood of its guardians is what got Uriel da Costa into trouble. Which of the two assertions weighed more heavily with the *parnasim* we cannot say. The two tend to go hand in hand.

Dr Semuel da Silva's point-by-point refutation of da Costa's views regarding the soul confirms this interpretation. In the opening dedication he sketches the following development:

> Out of respect for the honourable family to which this man belongs I am not revealing his name, although he is not deserving of such consideration. I watched and registered the course of his life; his insolent and haughty manner of speaking, his hypocrisy and deceitfulness during the time he haunted our places of worship—pretending to champion their holy rules and regulations—and the subterfuges which were the first samples of the poison he was distilling. The final proof of his attitude came when he did not hesitate to draw up and distribute a declaration in which he denied tradition and the Oral Torah given by God to Moses on Mount Sinai—the true explanations of the Written Torah—saying that they are deceptions and frauds and that the Torah has no need of such explanations and that he and others like him can give better ones.

At the very end of the *Tratado da imortalidade da alma* the author steps back a little from the particulars of their controversy and makes this general observation: 'All that men know and can know [is arrived at] by one of three roads: by authority, by reason, by experience.' And he concludes the *Tratado* by arguing for the superiority of experience ('using our physical senses' and merely 'confronted by anomalies') over reason ('analysing, distinguishing, and examining', but truly 'beset by a thousand shoals') and, more extensively, for that of authority, in other words tradition, over experience.[120] Uriel da Costa wedded his quest to reason—da Silva's lowest

---

[120] Semuel da Silva, *Tratado da imortalidade da alma*, 147–54.

order of knowledge—and, whether he did so to bolster his opposition or whether his commitment to rationalism ineluctably led to the confrontation with the *parnasim*, it is impossible to know.

Of the careers of Daniel de Prado, Daniel de Ribeira, and Baruh de Spinoza, it is unquestionably Spinoza's that elicits the greatest curiosity. But his early life as a Portuguese Jew, before his excommunication in 1656, contains little of interest for a social history of the community. Nothing in it explains the course his creativity was to take later. Even his altercation with the *parnasim* remains largely obscure. We have the unusual text of his *herem*, his association with the much older Daniel de Prado, and the *Tractatus theologico-politicus*, but little other evidence to satisfy our curiosity. To distil from the *Tractatus* an embryonic philosophy that clashed with that of the *parnasim* appears a far more roundabout and intellectually shakier procedure than to identify the young Spinoza with the 'doctrines' propounded by de Prado, about which we have more or less reliable documentation. There is no way around the irony that in this history of Amsterdam's Portuguese Jewish community its most famous son must largely remain unnamed.

Daniel de Prado was born around 1614, apparently in Andalusia. He studied at the University of Alcalá and obtained his medical degree at that of Toulouse in 1638. In 1654 he briefly lived in Hamburg before coming to Amsterdam in 1655. Of Daniel de Ribeira's life we know virtually nothing. He appears to have settled in Amsterdam at approximately the same time as de Prado. De Prado clearly had difficulty establishing himself as a physician, for he received financial assistance from the *sedaca* on several occasions during 1656–7. De Ribeira was hired to give basic education to poor children and received a small salary. De Prado was first excommunicated in July 1656 but then made the penance mentioned above and was re-admitted, thereafter even being supported financially. The Mahamad, at the instigation of Haham Saul Levi Morteira, then began to doubt the sincerity of his repentance and started to collect evidence from students who were in contact with him and de Ribeira. The evidence assembled gave rise to de Prado's second excommunication and his subsequent departure from Amsterdam for Antwerp. Daniel de Ribeira left before the *parnasim* had a chance to formalize the charges against him, and nothing more is heard of him. The evidence against Daniel de Prado and Daniel de Ribeira has survived among the archives of the Kahal and constitutes our most reliable source regarding the heterodox beliefs for which they—and probably also their student Baruh de Spinoza—were censured.[121]

The evidence reports the denunciations made by various students against either Daniel de Prado or Daniel de Ribeira. Among the acts denounced were specific transgressions of Jewish law. Both had ignored the Sabbath laws by smoking, carrying money, and lighting a fire on the Sabbath. De Ribeira also ate non-kosher

---

[121] On Daniel de Prado and Daniel de Ribeira, see Révah, *Spinoza et le Dr Juan de Prado*; id., 'Spinoza et les hérétiques'; id., 'Aux origines de la rupture spinozienne'. These articles published the evidence assembled against de Prado and de Ribeira.

food. During Hanukah de Ribeira pronounced not the proper benediction but instead either 'oculis, coculis, calavernis' or 'al anismi' and then 'calavernis, cogues'. He went so far as to say that had he arrived on Hanukah or Pesah he would not have become a Jew, for it was all a fable. Daniel de Ribeira also 'never prayed, never put on *tefillin*, never went to the synagogue', except on Mondays and Thursdays. Daniel de Prado derided the Hebrew language 'for there was neither rhyme nor reason to anything written in it'.

Both Daniel de Prado and Daniel de Ribeira held a cynical and deprecatory view of the Law of Moses. They questioned its adherents, its teachers, and its author. Asked once to join his friends in building a *sukkah* (tabernacle) 'for it is meritorious', Daniel de Ribeira responded that 'he did not want to deserve merit for that', and when his friends insisted, saying that it was a duty and everyone did it, he retorted that 'therefore he would do it, not for the merit, but because everyone did it'. Jews, Daniel de Prado used to say, went to the synagogue three times a day 'thinking thereby, and by seeing the Law raised, to be saved immediately'. Both men derided the fact that you were allowed to handle a needle without a point on the Sabbath but not one with a point. The rabbis, moreover, did not explain why you could not light a fire on the Sabbath; instead they lectured about the age of Rachel or Jacob. Scripture may state: 'You shall do what they command you,' which is said to refer to our sages, but it could also be understood to refer to the sages of the Karaites; the text makes no distinction.

From these haphazard critiques of the Jews and their rabbis, Daniel de Prado and Daniel de Ribeira moved to a nearly complete indictment of the Law of Moses. Before the revelation of the Law people such as Cain knew by natural reason that it was a sin to copulate with one's mother and to kill; Moses merely added the sacrifices. The sacred Law was a law for children because of the ceremonies it contained. Moses was a sorcerer who 'made such precepts as he made for his own profit and that of his brother such as the tithes, evaluations of persons promised to God, redemptions and primacy, priesthood, and the best and most profitable offices of the nation'. The sacred Law was a falsehood and should not be given more credence than those of Muhammad or Jesus. In order to prove that the Law was given by God, the *haham* said that it was the same as our belief that there was a duke of Alva: because the history books said so. Daniel de Prado replied that that was no proof, for there was also a Peter who said that God had talked to him, but that was not true.

Daniel de Prado and Daniel de Ribeira went beyond their expressions of doubt regarding the value and divine inspiration of the Law to a critique of the biblical representation of God itself. They denied God's particular and general providence. The Jews, Daniel de Ribeira said, are not God's children. God is without power, 'for had He been powerful He would have saved His people from the Inquisition'. God has not created the world; 'the world was always as it is now and will always be'. The Chinese erect a column every year and count more than 10,000 years from the creation of the world. Why are there then only 5,000 and so many years according to the count of Moses?

Finally, in a more philosophical vein, Daniel de Prado and Daniel de Ribeira argued against the immortality of the soul and for the autonomy of human reason. 'The soul dies with the body.' The *hahamim* may say that the dead move under the earth; according to our understanding that is impossible. Rhetorically, no doubt, Daniel de Prado used to ask 'whether a person should be led in what touched his conscience by what others told him or by what his understanding dictated; and having to follow one's understanding, why should a man do what others said and not what his understanding said?' The *hahamim* say that simply by being a philosopher a man is immediately bad. But, says Daniel de Prado, 'as soon as one says "yes is yes, for no is no," he already speaks philosophically'.

Daniel de Prado and Daniel de Ribeira were clearly upset by the investigations initiated against them. They often spoke of an inquisition established by the Portuguese Jews of Amsterdam. On several occasions they 'threatened' to emigrate either to Antwerp or even to Portugal. They bore a particularly severe grudge against Haham Saul Levi Morteira. David de Prado, a son of Daniel de Prado, informed the *parnasim* of 'the hatred with which H[aham] Morteira treats him [Daniel de Prado], offending, mistreating, and destroying him not with demonstrations of [wanting to] correct and amend him, but by acting as he has done with others, of which we have sufficient knowledge. For, as h[aham], he should have taught him if he needed it and not say to him that he shouldn't argue with him.'[122] On one occasion Daniel de Prado even contemplated a large-scale rebellion in the synagogue against the *hahamim*, whom, he joked, it was just to kill. The Mahamad, too, was criticized by Daniel de Ribeira. Responding to Jacob de Pina's charge that he was not allowed to possess a copy of de Pina's 'excommunicated' book, de Ribeira replied: 'The Mahamad could not have excommunicated it, for, according to philosophy, two preconditions must be met to make it valid: first, a justification of the charge, and, second, the competence of those who excommunicate. Neither was met in this case.'

The specific views and deeds of de Prado and de Ribeira denounced by their students and peers have all the spontaneity and fragmentariness of colloquial speech and everyday behaviour. Notwithstanding their lack of coherence, it is not difficult to recognize a fairly consistent pattern of criticism. And since the publication of this evidence, there can no longer be any doubt that some of the basic elements of Spinoza's highly sophisticated critique of tradition, as formulated in the *Tractatus theologico-politicus*, were first acquired in the company of Daniel de Prado. The mixture of social resentment and intellectual self-assertion sounding through de Prado's and de Ribeira's phrases may reveal more of what the Mahamad responded to so negatively than the highly polished, emotionally controlled sentences of Spinoza. On the one hand, there is the ridicule of the religious

<hr>

[122] Révah, 'Aux origines de la rupture spinozienne', 397.

sentiments of fellow *yehidim*, the animosity towards the *hahamim*, and the invalidation of the Mahamad's authority; on the other, an indictment of traditional Jewish law and even of the truthfulness of the Bible, as well as an avowal of the superiority of philosophy, making it clear that these 'heretics' were not quibbling over this or that interpretation, but were indeed espousing a radical independence from tradition.

The social resentment voiced by Daniel de Prado and Daniel de Ribeira leaves us with an interesting question. For there are some striking social similarities between the individuals excommunicated on the basis of their critique of tradition. Each and every one of these so-called heretics was somehow unsatisfactorily integrated, socially and economically, into the *nação*. Yosef Delmedigo was a 'foreigner' who arrived and left alone and who never gained more than a meagre salary as a *haham*. Although Uriel da Costa had some relatives and his family was fairly highly regarded, he seems also to have been at odds with close relatives and somewhat of a social outsider even before his clashes with the *parnasim*. Daniel de Prado came and left with a small family and, like Paulo de Lena before him, failed to make a living as a physician. Daniel de Ribeira was a poor teacher of poor students. Spinoza may appear at first sight to be an exception, often accorded a fairly elevated status in the community. Yet, although a merchant and one-time *parnas*, Spinoza's father certainly did not belong to the upper echelons of Portuguese Jewish society. Besides, by the 1650s Spinoza's parents had died, and the family's commercial enterprises had come to a halt. All these individuals, moreover, were trained intellectuals; in that respect Orobio de Castro's observation is correct. The combination of relative social isolation, economic failure, and intellectual self-esteem (with its more appropriately modern connotations than 'pride') certainly accounts much better for the alienation of these men from tradition than their ubiquitously cited Marrano background. If and when such individuals as, apparently, Uriel da Costa and Daniel de Prado brought their critique with them from the Iberian peninsula, it may have been because similar dynamics were at work there.[123] In the end only Spinoza, who had been born in Amsterdam and who had, perhaps, in some sense imbibed the positive values of Portuguese Jewish life in seventeenth-century Amsterdam, was able to transcend the stage of criticism and produce a philosophical *œuvre* of lasting importance.

INTERNAL TENSIONS AND COMMUNAL IDENTITY

On 22 July 1665 the Mahamad passed an appealingly revealing *reformação* in which it was decided to annul the penalty of *herem* previously imposed in fourteen

---

[123] From the evidence published by I. S. Révah, in his *Spinoza et le Dr Juan de Prado* and 'La Religion d'Uriel da Costa', portraits emerge of two militant proselytizers for Judaism prior to their departure from the Iberian peninsula. It would perhaps be worth pursuing the similarities rather than the differences between the Iberian and the Amsterdam situations.

haskamot.[124] The *haskamot* in question covered a great span of sins or errors, ranging from the prohibition on writing public pamphlets against the ambassador of Portugal to others threatening excommunication against persons failing to testify to a transgression such as the use of a razor to shave one's beard. None governed any particularly important issues. The significance of the *reformação* lies in signalling a change of attitude on the part of the Mahamad, in its expression of the realization that in the recent past the threat of the *herem* had been used unnecessarily frequently. In subsequent years the threat was used ever more sparingly.

In the *reformação*, the decade of 1654–64—from which eleven of the revised *haskamot* dated—stands out as a particularly contentious or heavy-handed period. These were the years, too, of the political skirmishings of Lopo Ramirez and Andres de Belmonte, of Menasseh ben Israel's overtures to Cromwell, of the beginnings of the censorship of the secular literary creations of Manuel de Pina and Miguel de Barrios, and, of course, of the excommunications of Daniel de Prado and Baruh de Spinoza. At the beginning of the decade the *parnasim* had settled a disruptive disagreement between the two temperamentally as well as intellectually very different *hahamim*, Saul Levi Morteira and Menasseh ben Israel—generally in favour of the former.[125] The efforts to curtail travel to 'lands of idolatry', we may recall, throve from 1644 to 1668. Socially, too, the two decades from the mid-1640s to the mid-1660s were the tensest of the entire seventeenth century. They witnessed the large-scale immigration of Portuguese New Christians from Spain whose great wealth and cosmopolitan culture would give the Amsterdam community its celebrated distinction. The 1650s also saw the return of more than a thousand Portuguese Jewish colonists from Dutch Brazil. At no other point in the history of the Portuguese Jews of seventeenth- or eighteenth-century Europe did so many from such socially and culturally varied backgrounds simultaneously seek to make their home in one religious community. It is certainly not too far-fetched to suspect some relation between the intellectual ferment and these social changes within the community itself—especially as there exists absolutely no indication anywhere that either the recent, large-scale immigration of German and Polish Jews or unrecorded and subtle tensions in Jewish–Christian relations exerted even the mildest pressure on the leaders of the Portuguese Jewish community.

The censorious words and punitive actions of the Mahamad represent, of course, in the first place a concerted effort to protect a community that threatened to be torn in all directions by the most recent political and demographic changes, a

---

[124] GAA, PIG 19, p. 551 (10 Menahem 5425/22 July 1665; 25 Menahem 5425/6 Aug. 1665). The Mahamad convened, as it did on other weighty occasions, in conjunction with the *haham* and the six *adjuntos*, i.e. former *parnasim*.

[125] GAA, PIG 19, pp. 341 (19 Adar 5413/16 Feb. 1653), 344 (13 Veadar 5413/12 Mar. 1653), 346 (6 Nisan 5413/3 Apr. 1653), 356 (19 Heshvan 5414/9 Nov. 1653), 358 (3 Nisan 5414/21 Mar. 1654), 363 (25 Nisan 5414/12 Apr. 1654). Unfortunately the resolutions of the Mahamad give us no inkling as to the nature of the disagreement.

distinct struggle to circumscribe the 'boundaries' of Portuguese Jewishness. The growing heterogeneity of the community forced the *parnasim* to explicate themselves much more than had ever been necessary before. But there is more hidden behind the veil of religious orthodoxy. For what gave the new formulations a possibly questionable aura was that they were now heavily influenced by a wholly new class of *parnasim*. Although we will never know the precise nature of the insults the children, relatives, and friends of Abraham Franco Mendes and Abraham Israel Pereyra hurled at each other in 1654, it is irresistibly tempting to see in the altercation between the old and relatively modest family of Franco Mendes, which had established itself in Amsterdam from the earliest days of the seventeenth century, and the newly arrived, immensely wealthy Pereyras a revealing sign of the times.[126] As these wealthier immigrants acquired their positions in the Mahamad, the tone of resolutions gained an unmistakably authoritarian edge from which the *parnasim* in 1665 sought to distance themselves once the changing of the guard had become a *fait accompli*. Furthermore, what may have made the authority of the Mahamad during this period particularly irksome was the scant religious 'legitimacy' of the new *parnasim*. For, notwithstanding the ultra-pious assertions of such as Abraham Pereyra in his famous moral treatises, contemporaries knew all too well how flimsy the attachment of these grandees to Judaism had been in many cases and how tainted with hypocrisy, by implication, their impositions of orthodoxy. An educated Spanish New Christian like Daniel de Prado, who discovered his studies to yield so dismally little by way of livelihood or social status and who may even have been a fairly active Judaizer in his student days at Alcalá de Henares, showed himself singularly incapable of humbly accepting, as Orobio de Castro insinuated, his fate.

The critique of tradition voiced by da Costa, de Prado, de Ribeira, and Spinoza went beyond undermining the bases upon which the *parnasim* established their authority, although it clearly meant to do that as well. On another social front, it questioned the foundation of contemporary Jewish identity. For without a legitimate tradition collective identity becomes a hollow construct. Most emphatically in their rejection of the election of Israel, but also in other caustic asides—as in the denigration of Abraham and the disdain for the Sabbath regulations—we can see a striving to break with traditional particularism and an inclination, perhaps, towards cosmopolitanism. As, on the one hand, the *parnasim* are engaged in defining their fragile identity to fend off a disintegration threatened by unsettling social and cultural shifts, so are these 'heretics', on the other, belabouring, as it were, the precariousness of that same identity. Both are addressing the same problem from different points of view. In the end, the fact that these two opposing views were harboured within the same community tells us more about what truly preoccupied the Portuguese Jew of seventeenth-century Amsterdam during those crucial mid-

---

[126] GAA, PIG 19, p. 365 (29 Iyar 5414/16 May 1654).

century years than any number of monotonously pious ordinances. And the fact that a few highly educated individuals, economically as well as socially peripheral to the community, preferred a more cosmopolitan version of Portuguese Jewishness over the staunchly particularist definition of the successful merchants says more about their society than any number of other differences between the antagonists that modern scholars may choose to highlight.

It is wrong to portray the Portuguese Jews, as Yovel does, as having been almost continuously struggling to define their collective identity throughout the seventeenth century.[127] The question did not arise out of the necessity to provide the refugees from the Iberian inquisitions, the ex-Marranos, with a clearly orthodox, unambiguously Jewish ideal to which to conform—one, allegedly, so sorely needed as to disallow any and all questioning of the traditions upon which the Kahal founded itself. By and large, as Orobio de Castro had already noted, the reintegration of former New Christians into a Jewish community proceeded rather smoothly. (And the fact that modern scholars have trouble accepting that verity says more about our generation than that of Spinoza.) The matter of collective identity became a burning issue, tellingly, only in Amsterdam and only during the brief period from the early 1640s until the mid-1660s, solely because only then and there did several so diverse groups of New Christians come together to form a single social, cultural, and religious entity.

[127] Yovel, *Spinoza and Other Heretics*, i. 12–13.

SIX

A PATCHWORK CULTURE

Iberian, Jewish, and Dutch Elements in Peaceable Coexistence

> *Merchant*: Mercurius, the god of merchants, is rightly portrayed with wings on head and feet. For, although some merchants have neither head nor feet, most seem to have wings on their feet witnessing the speed with which they move about and wings on their head considering the flight of their thoughts . . .
>
> I have to admit that I thought myself in the Tower of Babel hearing the mixture and confusion of languages you [the stockdealer] created: *optio* in Latin, *bichile* in Dutch, *surplus* in French . . .
>
> Athenaeus says that those who talk a lot suffer from the disease of logodiarrhea . . . I would call your ailment fluxorrhea or nilorrhea for you seem to be making more noise than the flood and to be having more mouths than the Nile . . .
>
> *Stockdealer*: As to the mixture of languages, it is not my fault. Necessity brought these idioms into being, use spread them and appropriateness gave them authority. I am giving them to you for what they cost me, with no profit other than the trouble to present them and the hard work to explain them.
>
> JOSEPH PENSO DE LA VEGA

IN studying Amsterdam's Portuguese Jews we tend to become overwhelmed by the many and profound changes the émigrés must have experienced. They moved from one country and climate to another, 'converted' from one religion to another. They had to cope with greatly different economic realities. They found themselves suddenly estranged from society at large, and engaged in the establishment of a novel association. Amid the hustle and bustle of these changes certain basic continuities tend to be lost. Some of these continuities pertained to the economic endeavours of the Portuguese Jews; others, no less significant, touched their cultural life.

LANGUAGES AND NAMES

Amsterdam's Portuguese Jews spoke primarily Portuguese. All the records of the Kahal Kados were kept in Portuguese; most notarial documents, too, were drafted in Portuguese. Only a few Portuguese Jews seem to have preferred Spanish. For

An earlier version of this chapter, entitled 'The Portuguese Jews of Seventeenth-Century Amsterdam: Cultural Continuity and Adaptation', was published in F. Malino and P. Cohen Albert (eds.), *Essays in Modern Jewish History: A Tribute to Ben Halpern* (Rutherford, NJ: Associated University Presses, 1982).

instance, Abraham Pereyra, formerly a long-time resident of Madrid and author of two moral treatises in Spanish, was addressed in Spanish by a notary.[1] His sons, however, Jacob Pereyra and Moise Pereyra, both of whom were born in Madrid, wrote to the Mahamad in Portuguese.[2] Daniel Levi de Barrios, a native of Spain and a former captain in the Spanish army, was the only Portuguese Jew to read his declaration of penance for having visited 'a land of idolatry' in Spanish.[3] Abraham Gomez Silveyra, a native of Madrid, wrote private letters and public sermons in Spanish.[4] The use of Spanish, therefore, was not an affectation. It can be documented only for a distinct and small number of Portuguese Jews who were natives or long-term residents of Spain. Ladino, the Spanish Jewish dialect, was not spoken in Amsterdam.

The knowledge of Hebrew among Amsterdam's Portuguese Jews is difficult to gauge. Its use was restricted to the synagogue, where not all the *yehidim* were equally adept in the reading of Hebrew. Some needed the guidance of the *hazan* to participate in the prayers. In particular, recently arrived immigrants must have lacked the necessary proficiency. Presumably all Amsterdam-born Portuguese Jews eventually received a Hebrew education sufficient to enable them to participate in Jewish worship, but the knowledge of Hebrew acquired by adult immigrants after settlement in Amsterdam cannot be estimated. The Hebrew phrases quoted in the poetry of Daniel Levi de Barrios could easily have been transcribed from the works of Menasseh ben Israel.[5] On the other hand, in an unpublished poem de Barrios fancifully equates *España* with *Pania* and *Panim* (Hebrew for 'face') to read *España* into the second verse of the first chapter of Genesis: 'And the spirit of God hovered over the face of the waters.'[6] This and other similarly ludicrous plays on words may bear witness to a more personal competence in Hebrew, unless they were picked up in discussions at any one of the *jesibot*. Some knowledge of Hebrew was undoubtedly acquired by adult immigrants, but it is doubtful whether many of them ever attained much more than prayer-book proficiency. After twenty years of residence in Amsterdam, Ishac Orobio de Castro, the noted apologist of Judaism and a most eager student of the rabbis,

---

[1] GAA, NA 2268, fo. 545 (8 Sept. 1653; A. Lock); the choice of Spanish may have been the notary's, of course. On Abraham Pereyra in general, see Kayserling, *Biblioteca Española-Portugueza-Judaica*, 87; Scholem, *Sabbatai Sevi*, 529–30; van Praag, *Gespleten zielen*; Méchoulan, 'Abraham Pereyra, juge'; id., 'La Pensée d'Abraham Pereyra'; id., *Hispanidad y judaísmo*.

[2] Autograph letters of Moise Pereyra and Jacob Pereyra may be found in GAA, PIG 780, 'Papers of the Estate of Abraham and Sara Pereira'.

[3] GAA, PIG 19, p. 554 (9 Tishrei 5426/18 Sept. 1665).

[4] The letters of Abraham Gomez Silveyra may be found in GAA, PIG 66A. On his writings, see n. 86 below.

[5] I have no real evidence to substantiate the possibility that Daniel Levi de Barrios actually borrowed these phrases from the writings of Menasseh ben Israel; this is merely a plausible suggestion. De Barrios' quotations may have come from any of a host of compilations. For a similar problem in tracing the Jewish sources of Isaac Cardoso, see Yerushalmi, *From Spanish Court*, 362–4.

[6] Unpublished poem dedicated to the Conde de Oropesa among the dispatches of Manuel de Belmonte; BN Madrid, MS 9403, no. 30 (dated Amsterdam, 4 July 1689).

appears to have acquired familiarity with the Hebrew script but to have been unable to read the Hebrew sources in the original.[7]

Although Amsterdam was in the seventeenth century one of the most cosmopolitan cities in Europe, Portuguese Jews of various occupations could not—nor wished to, probably—avoid the use of Dutch. Portuguese Jewish brokers in particular must have been able to conduct business in Dutch. It is difficult to measure exactly how widespread the knowledge of Dutch was. For instance, Jeronimo Nunes da Costa, who had been fairly young when his parents settled in northern Europe, knew Dutch; Abraham Pereyra and Abraham Jesurun did not.[8] Even the learned Haham Saul Levi Morteira was not completely at home in Dutch after some forty years of residence in Amsterdam.[9] The many Portuguese Jews who were unfamiliar with Dutch could, at a pinch, rely on more or less professional translators. A significant element of the service rendered by such Portuguese Jewish solicitors as David Torres, Jacob Marques, and Ishac Abeniacar consisted in helping Portuguese Jews overcome the language barrier.[10] Knowledge of Dutch, though unquestionably not a rarity, was certainly not ubiquitous.

There are other, more interesting—and more positively demonstrable—signs of Dutch 'cultural' inroads into Portuguese Jewish life. The echoes may be faint, but the spelling, naming, and writing customs adopted by Amsterdam's Portuguese Jews point unmistakably in the direction of their cultural adaptation of certain Dutch manners.

In the seventeenth century spelling had not yet been standardized, either in Portugal and Spain or in Holland. None the less, certain types of spelling can easily be distinguished as commonly Iberian or as commonly Dutch. And the spelling of Portuguese Jewish names—forenames as well as surnames—can definitely be shown to have been influenced by Dutch spelling. (To the best of my knowledge, no Portuguese Jew in the seventeenth century adopted a Dutch name as his non-Jewish forename, except as part of an alias.) The favourite forenames of Amsterdam's Portuguese Jews were those of the patriarchs: Abraham, Isaac, and Jacob. Each of these could be and was spelled in any number of ways: for instance, Abraham as Abraham, Abraam, Abram, or Abraõ and Jacob as Jacob, Jaacob, Jahacob or Yahacob, Yaacob, or Yacob.[11] None of these spellings betrays any

[7] Yerushalmi arrived at the same conclusion with regard to Isaac Cardoso; see *From Spanish Court*, 365.

[8] On Jeronimo Nunes da Costa, see GAA, NA 2226, p. 268 (31 Jan. 1668; A. Lock). On Abraham Jesurun, see GAA, NA 2234, p. 26 (4 Sept. 1670; A. Lock).

[9] GAA, NA 2271, fo. 205 (30 Mar. 1656; A. Lock). Saul Levi Morteira settled in Amsterdam in 1616. See Pieterse, *Daniel Levi de Barrios*, 61–2.

[10] For examples, see GAA, NA 2209, p. 303 (16 Sept. 1660; A. Lock); NA 2228, p. 1023 (12 Dec. 1668; A. Lock); NA 2234, p. 26 (4 Sept. 1670; A. Lock); NA 2237, p. 456 (27 Oct. 1671; A. Lock); NA 2271, fo. 73 (10 Feb. 1656; A. Lock); NA 2271, fo. 246ᵛ (19 Apr. 1656; A. Lock).

[11] These spellings have been taken from the signatures appended to the marriage registrations and from the *finta* lists. The latter, of course, tend to show consistent spellings within individual lists drawn up by the same current *gabai*, but various *gabayim* spelled the names differently.

distinct linguistic characteristics. Only for the name Isaac can we, perhaps, determine some faint Dutch influences. Of the 444 men registered on the Jewish
community's tax list of 5435 (1674/5)—to take the random year of the opening of
the new Esnoga—seventy-one were called Isaac or 'so-and-so, son of Isaac'; 188
Portuguese Jewish bridegrooms between 1598 and 1699 were similarly named.
The signatures appended to the marriage registrations yield a total of twenty-seven
different spellings. The two basic forms were Ishac, with the 'h' in the middle as a
reference to the original Hebrew spelling of Yitshak, and Isaque, the standard form
in Romance languages. The most common variants substituted 'c', 'que', 'cq', or
'q' at the end of the name, of either Ishac or Isaque, or applied a 'z' instead of an 's'
in Isaque and a 'Y' instead of 'I' at the beginning of either Ishac or Isaque, con-
forming to a common practice in Romance languages at the time, when these letter
pairs were often used interchangeably.[12] These modulations represent standard
Romance language principles and account for only eleven of the spellings. The
replacement of the final 'c' or 'que' by 'k' or 'ck' and the duplication of the 'a', in
conjunction with the standard variations, added another sixteen spellings. Both
the 'k' and the 'aa' are used very uncommonly in Portuguese or Spanish. They are,
of course, very commonly used in Dutch. And the occurrence of these elements in
the spelling habits of Amsterdam's Portuguese Jews may perhaps serve as a first
modest sign of acculturation. No fewer than sixty-seven of the 188 Isaacs (35.6 per
cent) had adopted a 'k'.[13] A surprising twenty-nine (15.4 per cent) preferred the
'aa'.[14] It may seem to lead too far to suggest, on the basis of the mere occurrence of
a 'k' or 'aa' in only one of at least a dozen common forenames, that about one-sixth
to one-third of the Portuguese Jewish population had become acculturated. On the
other hand, the fact that several Ishacks also adopted 'Dutchisms' in their
surnames, in their handwriting style, or in other small ways raises the incidence
above the level of a more or less curious accident. Isaack Baruh Roos, for example,
changed Rosa to Roos; Ishack de Rokamora applied the 'k' also in his surname. In
the case of de Rokamora we may have little doubt that he made his steps to acculturation at the universities of Leiden and Franeker; for most others in our sample
we can only guess where they acquired their 'Dutchisms': at the Exchange, in some
workshop, in a tavern?[15]

Other Portuguese Jews similarly altered the vocal or consonantal spelling of
their surname. For instance, Sousa became Suza or Susa; de Pina, de Pinna; de

---

[12] In order of decreasing frequency: Ishac (29), Isaque (27), Izaque (17), Ysaque (8), Ishaq (4),
Yzaque (4), Yshac (3), Isaq (2), Isac (2), Ishaque (1), Isacq (1).

[13] Isack (18), Ishack (16), Ishak (10), Isaack (6), Izack (3), Isaak (3), Izak (2), Isak (2), Ysack (2), and
Yshak, Ysak, Ysaack, Ysaak, Ysake (once each).

[14] Isaac (16), Isaack (6), Isaak (3), and Ysaack, Ysaak, Isaaq, Isaacq (once each).

[15] GAA, DTB 687, p. 307 (8 Feb. 1669), marriage of Isaack Baruh Roos; DTB 686, p. 237 (23 May
1665), marriage of Ishack de Rokamora; *Album Studiosorum Academiae Lugduno Bataviae*, 361; *Album
Studiosorum Academiae Franekerensis*, 137.

Lima, de Limma; Toura, Torra; Cardoso, Cardose or Cardosse.[16] More distinctly
Dutch are the consonant changes in Mocadt (instead of Mocata or Mocatta),
Delmondt (Delmonte), de la Penja (de la Penha), and Rodriges or Roderyges
(Rodrigues).[17] The spellings Rodriges and especially Roderyges even suggest
changes in pronunciation.[18] Unmistakably Dutch are Sinjoor for Senior and
Dewart for Duarte.[19] At most these spelling changes reveal sensitivity to the sound
of the Dutch language without ever truly disguising the Iberian character of the
surname. Some names, however, were changed so radically as to lose virtually
every echo of their Portuguese or Spanish source. Members of the de Caceres family appear to have 'Dutchified' their name to Keizer ('emperor').[20] Some Zuzartes
adopted Swaert or Swart ('sword' or 'black').[21] Rachel Kasteel ('castle') may have
been either Castiel or Castello.[22] Schaep ('sheep') appears to have been Escapa.[23]
In all these cases acoustic similarity suggested the particular Dutch name chosen.
The reasons for these radical name changes are indeterminable. There is nothing

[16]   For Suza or Susa, see GAA, DTB 686, pp. 30 (11 Jan. 1664), 363 (10 July 1666); DTB 694, p. 37
(10 Feb. 1684). For de Pinna, see GAA, DTB 690, p. 275 (26 Mar. 1677); DTB 691, p. 60 (17 Sept.
1677); DTB 693, p. 454 (28 Oct. 1683). For de Limma, see GAA, DTB 695, p. 223 (9 Aug. 1686). For
Torra, see GAA, DTB 686, p. 237 (23 May 1665). For Cardose or Cardosse, see GAA, DTB 695,
p. 291 (21 Nov. 1686); DTB 696, p. 69 (27 Feb. 1688).

[17]   For Mocadt, see GAA, DTB 688, p. 284 (6 Nov. 1671). For Delmondt, see GAA, DTB 691,
p. 80 (19 Nov. 1677). For de la Penja, see GAA, DTB 693, p. 42 (24 Dec. 1681); DTB 696, pp. 62
(13 Feb. 1688), 74 (12 Mar. 1688). For Rodriges, see GAA, DTB 693, p. 265 (11 Dec. 1682); DTB 695,
pp. 174 (26 Apr. 1686), 287 (15 Nov. 1686), 341 (14 Mar. 1687). For Roderyges, see GAA, DTB 690,
p. 137 (29 Nov. 1675).

[18]   The disappearance of the 'u' would indicate a change in the pronunciation of the 'g'. The 'gu'
does not exist in Dutch. 'Rodrigues', therefore, may in Dutch have been pronounced as 'Rodriges',
with 'kh' for 'gu'. After the change in pronunciation the change in orthography follows. The spelling
'Roderyges' reflects a further accommodation to Dutch pronunciation.

[19]   For Sinjoor, see GAA, DTB 691, p. 117 (22 Apr. 1678). For Dewart, see GAA, DTB 681,
pp. 125 (7 Sept. 1651), 274 (31 Jan. 1653).

[20]   GAA, DTB 688, p. 361 (13 May 1672), marriage of David Keizer and Ester Dias. On the suggested connection between Keizer and de Caceres, see GAA, PIG 700, 'Papers of the Estate of Abigail
Dias da Fonseca alias Beatris de Caceres'. According to these papers, a host of descendants of Abigail
Dias da Fonseca were called Keizer. I have nowhere found explicit evidence of the equation Keizer =
de Caceres.

[21]   GAA, DTB 692, p. 27 (9 Feb. 1680), marriage of David Swaert and Sara Gaon; DTB 693, p. 302
(12 Feb. 1683), marriage of Salomon van Abraham Swart and Judith Barzilay. Both David Swaert and
Salomon Swart were accompanied by their mother, Refika Swart. On 14 August 1648, Abraham
Zuzarte and Refika Zuzarte registered their marriage: GAA, DTB 680, p. 20. Moreover, the *fintas* of
5441 (1680/1) and 5448 (1687/8) list a David de Abraham Zuzarte and a Selomoh de Abraham
Zuzarte. These facts leave no doubt that the names Swaert and Swart are indeed bastardizations of
Zuzarte.

[22]   GAA, DTB 693, p. 353 (7 May 1683), marriage of Daniel Peres and Rachel Kasteel.

[23]   GAA, DTB 692, p. 96 (5 July 1680), marriage of Ymanuel Torres and Ester Schaep; Ester,
unfortunately, does not sign her name. Also GAA, DTB 694, p. 133 (23 June 1684), marriage of
Abraham Schaep and Simha Belmonte. Both Ester and Abraham Schaep were accompanied by their
father Salomon Schaep. On 30 July 1652 one Salamão Escapa registered his marriage with Rachel
Macabea: GAA, DTB 681, p. 231.

in the records to suggest that these Portuguese Jews had converted or were about to convert. If anything, it seems more plausible to assume that these were poorer Portuguese Jews about to be swallowed up in the increasingly more important German Jewish community.[24] To my knowledge, the only Portuguese Jewish family with a non-acoustic, truly translated Dutch equivalent of its surname that was not an alias were the wealthy Belmontes, also known as Schonenberg.[25]

Apart from spelling changes and the adoption of Dutch-sounding surnames, Portuguese Jews also modified the 'son of' designation attached to their first names. The first names given to Portuguese Jewish children followed rather strict rules. The first son received the name of his paternal grandfather, the second that of his maternal grandfather; third and following sons were similarly named either after great-uncles or after great-grandfathers. For instance, Abraham Israel Suasso alias Francisco Lopes Suasso (d. 1710), son of Ishac Israel Suasso alias Antonio Lopes Suasso (d. 1685), married Rachel da Costa (d. 1749), daughter of Jacob alias Alvaro da Costa. Their seven sons were named Ishac (1695–1775), Jacob (d. 1751), Manuel (d. 1773), Moseh (1700–41), Aron (d. 1740), David (d. 1705), and Abraham (1710–70).[26] Except for David, who died an infant, and Abraham, who had no sons, all remaining five sons named their first-born sons Abraham, after the children's paternal grandfather. The second son of Moseh was named Joseph after Joseph de Lima, father of Rachel, Moseh's wife; the second son of Aron, Jacob after Jacob de Pinto, father of Eliseba, Aron's wife. Both third sons of Moseh and Aron were called Ishac, presumably after Ishac Israel Suasso, the children's great-grandfather, for their grandfather, Abraham, had had no brothers. As a result of these naming practices, Portuguese Jews came to use a relatively small number of names—around a dozen—over and over again. The *finta* list of 5463 (1702/3) establishes the following frequencies: Abraham—79, Ishac—69, Jacob—61, David—50, Moseh—44, Joseph—32, Semuel—21, Aron—19, Binjamin and Selomoh—16 each, Daniel—13, and Imanuel—10; these total 91 per cent of the community. In order to distinguish the various Abrahams, Ishacs, and Jacobs with the same surname, therefore, Portuguese Jews added their father's first name to their own with the Spanish or Portuguese preposition 'de'. Thus the five Abraham Israel Suassos were known as Abraham de Ishac, Abraham de Jacob, etc. During the last quarter of the seventeenth century, however, Portuguese Jews began to substitute the Dutch preposition 'van' for the Spanish 'de'. Thus we find such signatures as David van Mardohay Pintto, Jacob van Abraham Nunes Henriques,

[24] The persons under discussion may all be found on the *finta* lists of the Kahal. The same *fintas*, however, also show them to have been among the poorer members of the Kahal. Abraham Zuzarte, father of David Swaert and Salomon Swart, was a tobacco dealer; Daniel Peres, husband of Rachel Kasteel, a teacher.

[25] GAA, PIG 641, 'Papers of the Estate of Rachel Belmonte alias Schonenberg'. The Christian branch of the family also used the name Schonenberg; see Gottheil, *The Belmont–Belmonte Family*.

[26] 'Genealogia do velho M. Lopes que foy o mais antigo assendente conhecido da familia dos s^res Suasso vindo de Espanha e cazada com N. Mendes Sotto e deixou 5 filhos e 5 filhas [a genealogy in private hands]'.

and Moses van Isaack Senior Coronel.[27] In the eighteenth century, it appears, this 'Dutchism' gained even wider currency, without ever completely supplanting the Iberian form.

Finally, the two most significant adaptations to Dutch culture that can be positively identified concern the addition to the surname of the Dutch 'de Jonghe' instead of 'junior' or 'o moço' and the adoption of Dutch handwriting. The appellation 'junior' is rare in any form. The Dutch form 'de Jonge' or 'de Jonghe' occurs four times: in Thomas Fernandes de Jonghe (as early as 1623), Jeosuah Abaz de Jonge, Ishak Navarro de Jonghe, and Isaak de Jonge.[28] Isaac de Jonge appears as the Dutchified name of Isaaq van Benjamin Jesurun.

The adoption of Dutch handwriting may reveal much more than the acquisition of Dutch spelling and speaking manners. In the seventeenth century Dutch handwriting may be quite easily distinguished from that common in Spain and Portugal. Virtually all Portuguese Jews, male and female, used the Roman script. In sheer numerical terms, the twenty-eight men and women who signed their names in Gothic script may seem insignificant. But the Gothic handwriting must have been acquired through a Dutch education, and thus the few examples immediately gain in significance. They indicate that certain Portuguese Jews, in addition to the physicians who studied at Dutch universities, stepped outside their community for an education; in other words, that some sought acculturation more actively than the above examples of more or less passive adaptation. Spinoza's study at the Dutch (Latin) school of Francis van den Enden is generally regarded as a meaningful sign of his estrangement from the Portuguese Jewish community.[29] Spinoza (who used Roman script) appears not to have been alone. Ironically, perhaps, the daughter of the physician Ishac Orobio de Castro, the one and only contemporary Portuguese Jew to have proffered a philosophical critique of Spinozan ideas, was among those who had learned the Gothic script.[30] Unfortunately, neither the conditions nor the motivations of these apparently Dutch-educated men and women can be distilled from the records.

Two general observations must nevertheless be made, for this is after all a significant issue. First, it is surprising that twelve of the twenty-eight Gothic-script writers were women. Female literacy was always substantially lower than that of males; and, as the signatures to the marriage registrations reveal, female illiteracy was higher among Amsterdam-born brides than among any of those born abroad, excepting the women immigrants from Italy. The decline in female literacy may have been caused by the social uprooting that attended the migration, by the

[27] GAA, DTB 690, p. 141 (13 Dec. 1675); DTB 694, p. 159 (10 Aug. 1684); DTB 696, p. 307 (30 Apr. 1689).

[28] GAA, DTB 669, p. 141 (14 Jan. 1623); DTB 683, pp. 22 (4 May 1656), 83 (20 Oct. 1656); DTB 696, p. 151 (26 June 1688).

[29] Francès, *Spinoza dans les pays néerlandais*, 243–5.

[30] Polak, 'De betekenis der Joden voor de wijsbegeerte'; Kaplan, *From Christianity to Judaism*, 263–70.

Kahal's undervaluation of female education, by a shortage of competent instructors, or by any combination of these factors. Whatever the case may have been, it seems plausible to relate the increase in female illiteracy to the evidence of a Dutch education enjoyed by several Portuguese Jewish daughters. Dutch instructors may have filled the gap between the high educational standards imported from the home country and the lack of communal (Jewish) facilities and private (Iberian) options in Amsterdam. The second observation concerns the coincidence of various 'Dutchisms' within one person or within one family. Several of the men and women who used Gothic script had also accepted some of the Dutch adaptations to their names: for instance, Samuel de Soesa, Leonora Dewart, Sara Torra, Ysaack Hoeb, David Swaert, Salomon van Abraham Swart, and Rachel Kasteel.[31] 'Dutchisms' also appear to have run in families such as the de Rocamoras, the de Sousas, the Seniors, and the Touros; the de Rocamora and Touro families, moreover, were interrelated.[32] These facts suggest, on the one hand, that the various 'Dutchisms' sketched above—however faint their echoes—must be taken as serious indications of acculturation, and on the other, that this acculturation transcended personal idiosyncrasy and constituted a somewhat diffused social phenomenon whose precise social location cannot, unfortunately, be pinpointed more accurately.

Having weighted our analysis in favour of acculturation by stressing Dutch cultural inroads, we must redress the balance and reconsider the overall cultural picture. Thus the dominant and persistent Portuguese tone appears as the most striking feature of Amsterdam's Portuguese Jewish culture. In almost every form of expression the Portuguese Jews remained consciously and distinctly Iberian. The first conspicuous change came in their adoption of Hebrew (that is, biblical) forenames. At first mainly the Jewish equivalent of more commonly used Iberian names, the Hebrew names eventually replaced their Christian counterparts completely. Only in the second instance, that is to say, after Judaization of the

[31] GAA, DTB 680, p. 203 (25 Feb. 1650): Samuel de Soesa; DTB 681, pp. 125 (7 Sept. 1651), 274 (31 Jan. 1653): Leonora Dewart; DTB 686, p. 237 (23 May 1665): Sara Torra; DTB 685, p. 195 (30 June 1662): Ysaack Hoeb; DTB 692, p. 27 (9 Feb. 1680): David Swaert; DTB 693, p. 302 (12 Feb. 1683): Salomon van Abraham Swart; DTB 693, p. 353 (7 May 1683): Rachel Kasteel.

[32] Samuel de Soesa signed in Gothic, and Ribca Susa, Ester de Suza, and Samuel de Suza changed the spelling of their names: see GAA, DTB 680, p. 203 (25 Feb. 1650); DTB 686, p. 363 (10 July 1666); DTB 694, p. 37 (10 Feb. 1684); DTB 686, p. 30 (11 Jan. 1664). Salomon Rocamora signed in Gothic, and Ishack de Rokamora adopted a spelling with 'k': GAA, DTB 688, p. 150 (31 Oct. 1670); DTB 686, p. 237 (23 May 1665). Sara Torra signed in Gothic and changed the spelling; Moses van Samuel Touro replaced 'de' with 'van': GAA, DTB 686, p. 237 (23 May 1665); DTB 693, p. 376 (4 June 1683). Joseph Sinjoor changed the spelling, and Jeuda van Mardohay Senior replaced 'de' with 'van': GAA, DTB 691, p. 117 (22 Apr. 1678); DTB 693, p. 465 (20 Nov. 1683).

Regarding the relationships between the Touro and the de Rocamora families: Ishack de Rokamora was first married to Abigel Tora (GAA, DTB 679, p. 105 (10 July 1647)); after Abigel's death, he married Sara Torra (GAA, DTB 686, p. 237 (23 May 1665)); and finally, Salomon Rocamora, son of Ishack de Rokamora, married Abigail Toura (GAA, DTB 687, p. 361 (28 June 1669)).

Portuguese immigrants had run its course, did Dutch culture make headway; and never, it seems, was acculturation intended to mask the individual's Jewish identity.

WRITING, READING, PERFORMING, AND THE ARTS

The pursuit of pleasure and entertainment played a great part in Portuguese Jewish life, both private and public—a mark of their relative wealth, of their sense of comfort in the city, of their temperament. Their frequenting of coffee-houses, brothels, and gambling establishments is not unexpected and well documented. Very little more needs to be said about these diversions here. Suffice it to say that some coffee- and gambling-houses existed within the Portuguese Jewish community itself, as establishments run by and for Portuguese Jews.[33] There do not appear to have been any Portuguese Jewish brothels or prostitutes, though the sources do mention an occasional German Jewish prostitute.[34]

As characteristically Portuguese, allegedly, as the penchant for womanizing and gambling was the Portuguese Jews' attraction to the theatre. We need only recall the hundreds of *comedias* and *autos sacramentales* of Lope de Vega, Tirso de Molina, and Calderón to remind ourselves of the pre-eminence of drama in Iberian cultural and religious life. The Iberian émigrés retained this appetite and satisfied it whenever and wherever the opportunity presented itself. The earliest dramatic performances by and for Portuguese Jews were staged in the synagogue. We know of the *Dialogo dos montes* by Rehuel Jesurun, performed in the synagogue of Beth Jacob on Shavuot of 1624.[35] In this play, a kind of *auto mosaico* (that is, a Jewish version of the Iberian *auto sacramental*), seven Portuguese Jewish amateur actors represented seven biblical mountains singing the praises of God, the Law of Moses, and Israel. But on 10 October 1632 the *imposta* board forbade the celebration of such feasts in the synagogue.[36] Subsequently, the board's resolution was adopted as haskamah 16 of Talmud Tora: 'There will be neither feasts nor *enigmas* [poetic variations on the theme of a riddle] in the synagogue, neither on Simhat Torah nor at any other time.'[37] The city authorities of Amsterdam also placed severe obstacles in the way of Portuguese Jewish theatrical performances, for the city council had given a virtual theatrical monopoly to the 'Dutch Academy', whose box-office receipts accrued to the city's orphanage and old men's home.[38] Other troupes were allowed to perform only during the weeks of the annual

---

[33] One mentioned was run by Abraham Mendes Vasques (GAA, NA 2268, fo. 16ᵛ (8 Jan. 1653; A. Lock)) and another by Semuel Pereira (NA 2218B, p. 788 (20 Apr. 1665; A. Lock)). Jacques Richard in his correspondence refers to the 'chocolaterie' of one Pacheco; AGR, Brussels, microfilm 725, no. 351 (in letters dated 5, 22 Feb., 19 Dec. 1657).

[34] GAA, NA 2268, fo. 525ᵛ (27 Aug. 1653; A. Lock); NA 2220, p. 353 (23 Feb. 1666; A. Lock).

[35] Pieterse, *Daniel Levi de Barrios*, 68–9; van Praag ' "Dialogo dos montes" '.

[36] GAA, PIG 13, p. 86 (25 Tishrei 5393/9 Oct. 1632); Pieterse, *Daniel Levi de Barrios*, 155.

[37] GAA, PIG 19, p. 107.   [38] Zumthor, *Daily Life in Rembrandt's Holland*, 205–7.

Kermis (fair or carnival). Notwithstanding these community and city restrictions, Amsterdam's Portuguese Jews somehow found ways to satisfy their hunger for *comedias* and *enigmas*. In 1667 Aron de la Faya, Benjamin Henriques, Jacob Navarro, Abraham Israel, Daniel Levi de Barrios, and Semuel Rosa performed a play before an audience of more than thirty persons in a warehouse rented from Semuel Pereira.[39] Among the spectators were the children of the then burgomaster Gillis Valckenier. During the 1670s and 1680s various Portuguese Jewish intellectuals and merchants founded a private literary salon that appears to have specialized in the 'staging' of *enigmas*. In 1696 Francisco Rodrigues Henriques rented a warehouse for theatrical performances. In 1708 'devotees of Spanish comedies' requested the magistrature to allow them to continue the performances they had been giving every Wednesday during the last nine years. At about the same time Amsterdam's German Jews received permission to stage their comedy— apparently a *purimshpiel*—again.[40]

Unfortunately, we have no information regarding the plays that were performed in these Portuguese Jewish 'theatres'. They may have been the hits of the Iberian stage or the generally more mediocre creations of an illustrious Marrano playwright such as Antonio Enriquez Gomez, written prior to his settlement in Amsterdam.[41] We simply do not know. We do not even know whether the plays composed locally by Amsterdam's Portuguese Jewish poets were ever staged. Moseh Zacuto's *Yesod olam* and Joseph Penso's *Asirei hatikvah* were both written in Hebrew and may have been intended primarily as intellectual exercises.[42] With regard to the anonymous Spanish *purimshpiel Comedia famosa de Aman y Mordochay* we may assume a greater likelihood of actual stage production.[43] Perhaps the mention of Daniel Levi de Barrios among the Portuguese Jewish actors of 1667 points to an actual performance of a play by this local Portuguese Jewish playwright, though it is no guarantee that they actually performed one of his own plays.

De Barrios' plays fall into two categories. There are first the cloak-and-dagger comedies (*comedias de capa y espada*), probably written prior to his permanent settlement in Amsterdam: *Pedir favor al contrario*, *El canto junto el encanto*, and *El español de Oran*, all published in his *Flor de Apolo* (Brussels, 1665).[44] We do not know whether these were ever performed in Amsterdam or elsewhere. Otherwise,

---

[39] GAA, NA 3580, pp. 100, 131 (1, 8 Feb. 1667; J. Snel).   [40] Kossmann, *Nieuwe bijdragen*, 136–8.

[41] On Antonio Enriquez Gomez, see Kayserling, *Biblioteca Española-Portugueza-Judaica*, 49–51; Besso, *Dramatic Literature of the Sephardic Jews of Amsterdam*, 58–68; Rubio, 'Antonio Enríquez Gómez'; Révah, 'Un pamphlet'.

[42] On Moseh Zacuto, see Besso, *Dramatic Literature of the Sephardic Jews of Amsterdam*, 41–4; Melkman, 'Het eerste drama in de Joodse literatuur'; id., 'Moses Zacuto en zijn familie'. On Joseph Penso de la Vega, see nn. 75 and 82 below.

[43] Besso, *Dramatic Literature of the Sephardic Jews of Amsterdam*, 69–72.

[44] On Miguel de Barrios' *comedias*, see ibid. 73–84; Scholberg, *La poesia religiosa de Miguel de Barrios*, 48–9.

de Barrios composed several *comedietas* (short, one-act plays) for certain more or less solemn occasions. From de Barrios' pre-Amsterdam days date a theatrical *panegírico* for Charles II and Catherine of England and an *epitalamio* presented on the occasion of the marriage of the Emperor Leopold and the Infanta Margarita.[45] The latter had been commissioned by the Marquesa de Caracena, wife of the former governor-general of the Spanish Netherlands, and actually appears to have been performed in the palace at Brussels. In Amsterdam, de Barrios composed *comedietas*—variously termed *auto sacro, diálogo harmonico, auto mosayco, academia sacra*, or simply *diálogo*—for a number of charitable and educational associations within the Amsterdam Kahal—Honen Dalim, Maskil Dal, Tora Hor, Me'irat Henaim, and Ets Haim.[46] These are very brief allegorical dramas praising the goal and members of the association in question. For instance, in the *auto mosayco* 'Tora Hor', Learning (*la Ciencia*), Study (*el Estudio*), Prophecy (*el Vaticinio*), Charity (*la Caridad*), and Israel persuade Wealth (*la Riqueza*) to follow the Law (*la Ley*), and Music informs him that the Law is in 'Tora Hor'. The various allegorical 'characters' also use this opportunity to praise the administrators and members of the association by name. Thus, if these *autos* were performed, they can only have been staged during the year's term of any particular administration, unless we assume the unlikely possibility that de Barrios re-wrote his rhymes with every change of the board.

De Barrios' *comedietas* do not provide much of a clue to the plays performed on Amsterdam's Portuguese Jewish stage. Only one of his extant works–a three-act allegorical *comedia* entitled *Contra la verdad no hay fuerza* ('No Force is a Match for the Truth') can be considered a fully fledged, non-occasional dramatic creation composed specifically and exclusively for a Portuguese Jewish audience.[47] The play celebrates the martyrdom of Abraham Atias, Yahacob Rodriquez (Caseres), and Rahel Nunez Fernandez, who were burned at the stake in Córdoba on 29 June 1665, and is dedicated to Ishac Penso, a wealthy merchant in Amsterdam and a native of Espejo in the province of Córdoba.[48] Here the place occupied in Christian *autos sacramentales* by the apotheosis of the eucharist is taken by the glorification of *kidush hashem* (the sanctification of the Name [of God]), that is, martyrdom.[49] Daniel Levi de Barrios gave a distinctly Iberian and typically Catholic form an unmistakably Jewish content. To us, the clash between Jewish ideas and Catholic modes of expression may seem so striking that we might be led to impute to de Barrios a conscious polemical intention; but when we consider his work as a whole, *Contra la verdad no hay fuerza* appears as just one more example of the Portuguese Jewish predilection for Iberian cultural modes.

[45] Besso, *Dramatic Literature of the Sephardic Jews of Amsterdam*, 83–4 (with source references).

[46] *Triumpho del govierno popular*, 217–40, 277–312, 369–92, 412–36, 594–630.

[47] The text of *Contra la verdad no hay fuerza* has been reprinted in Scholberg, *La poesia religiosa de Miguel de Barrios*, 249–341; Eng. trans., entitled 'Truth Triumphs in the End', in Lazar (ed.), *The Sephardic Tradition*, 153–218.   [48] Roth, 'Abraham Nuñez Bernal', 40–1.

[49] Scholberg, *La poesia religiosa de Miguel de Barrios*, 119.

As with the other plays mentioned above, we have no way of knowing whether *Contra la verdad no hay fuerza* was ever actually performed. It has been inferred from the fact that only three incomplete copies of the *comedia* have come down to us that the play was probably censored;[50] but none of the censorship records of de Barrios' works refers to this work, nor does anything in the play appear sufficiently objectionable to warrant censorship. As it stands, *Contra la verdad no hay fuerza* remains the sole example of a *comedia* composed in Amsterdam that was most probably also performed on the local stage.

Very occasionally we are afforded a glimpse into the homes of Portuguese Jews through the inventories of the estates of deceased men and women. Some of these allow us to establish what kinds of religious and art objects were more or less usually encountered in Portuguese Jewish homes. Common objects such as kiddush cups, menorot, or even two separate sets of dishes are presumably subsumed under 'household effects'. By and large, only objects of value—in the present context, books and paintings—are specified in some detail. As for books, those in Hebrew were more often than not simply treated together as so many 'Hebrew books', because of the notaries' inability to read Hebrew or the heirs' lack of interest. For instance, the inventory of the estate of Joseph de los Rios lists 'about sixty printed Hebrew books, both large and small and in good as well as in bad condition—55 guilders'.[51] Paintings were mostly listed by title or description rather than by painter.

Certain wealthy Jews possessed private Sifrei Torah (Torah scrolls). It is difficult to ascertain how widespread the custom was. Jean Cardoso, the inventory of whose estate lists 'five books of Moses called Sefer Torah with the appertaining ornaments', maintained a private synagogue at his country home in Soest.[52] The heirs of Jacob Delmonte, in whose house visitors reported seeing 'a flower-patterned mantle, embroidered with gold and silver, for the books of Moses', had established their private *minyan* in the wake of a dispute with the *parnasim*, discussed in Chapter 5 above.[53] These Sifrei Torah were used for specific, identifiable purposes. 'A book of Moses with all its appurtenances' and 'two ivory arms for use with a book of Moses', listed in the inventory of Abraham da Fonseca's estate, cannot be connected with any known extra-synagogal activity. From nineteenth-century sources we learn that private Torah mantles and ornaments were loaned to the Esnoga for use on special occasions.[54] These were kept at home when not used, because of their great value, because the Esnoga lacked the proper storage facilities, or because their owners simply wished to keep them in their personal vicinity.

Bibles and prayer-books were, of course, much more widespread and often lavishly ornamented: 'a prayer-book bound in green shagreen with golden locks';

---

[50] Ibid. 110. [51] GAA, NA 2261B, p. 1120 (2 Mar. 1665; A. Lock).
[52] GAA, NA 2261B, pp. 952–1007 (9 May 1661; A. Lock).
[53] GAA, NA 2254, p. 372 (29 Apr. 1678; A. Lock).
[54] GAA, NA 4256 (24 Jan. 1712; D. v. d. Groe); Swetschinski, *Orphan Objects*, 123–5.

'a Jewish prayer-book with ribbon, gilt-edged'; 'two Hebrew *kerckboeckjens* [literally church books] with silver-plated clasps and locks'. Some inventories specify that the bibles had been printed by Athias. Spanish translations of the Bible are also mentioned, both in the Athias edition and in the large Ferrara one.[55]

Books, in particular, promise a more direct and richer insight into the heart of Portuguese Jewish culture. We can know what the local printers published, what some people had in their personal libraries, and which authors were cited—and read, presumably—by the local literati.[56] There are, of course, hazards associated with each of these sources. Whether a given book printed in Amsterdam or in someone's library or cited in a footnote somewhere was actually read remains an elusive question; and what impact it made lies beyond any but the deepest analyses.

Without figures to indicate the size of a given edition or the number of copies sold, a mere listing of published titles would give a distorted impression of Amsterdam's Portuguese Jewish culture—all the more so as so much of what came off the presses of the local printing establishments was intended for the German and Polish Jewish markets. Unless the text is in Spanish or Portuguese, or refers specifically in some way to the rites or customs of the Portuguese Jewish community, or was written by a Portuguese Jew or Jewess, it is difficult to decide whether to include it in our summary or not. A part of Imanoel Benveniste's edition of the Babylonian Talmud was financed by Gerrit Verduyn (a Christian), another by David del Sotto.[57] No conclusion as to the intended market can be drawn from that information. On the other hand, titles financed by Ashkenazi merchants from abroad can generally be assumed not to have been aimed at local Portuguese Jewish clients, though they may, of course, still have been read by them. Approbations were very frequently issued by Portuguese Jewish rabbis for works unquestionably and primarily aimed at an Ashkenazi readership, especially where the printer was a Portuguese Jew, as the approbation frequently also conferred an exclusive licence for a given period of time. Only with regard to a few rare dedications may we perhaps be a little more inclined to believe that they also indicate the intended audience. As we do not know with any degree of accuracy how widespread the knowledge of Hebrew was among the Portuguese Jews, it would be a mistake to exclude most Hebrew publications from our summary. We might hesitate here and

[55] GAA, NA 2261B, pp. 952–1007 (9 May 1661; A. Lock); NA 4242 (28 Oct. 1692; D. v. d. Groe); NA 4249, p. 925 (20 Nov. 1703; D. v. d. Groe); NA 4256 (24 Jan. 1712; D. v. d. Groe).

[56] I have found the following inventories of personal libraries: of Abraham da Fonseca, GAA, NA 4256 (24 Jan. 1712; D. v. d. Groe); of Joseph Jenes, GAA, NA 4249, p. 925 (20 Nov. 1703; D. v. d. Groe); of Jean Cardoso, GAA, NA 2261B, pp. 952–1007 (9 May 1661; A. Lock); of Spinoza, Servaas van Rooyen (ed.), *Inventaire des livres formant la bibliothèque de Bénédict Spinoza*, and, more recently and more conveniently, Aler (ed.), *Catalogus van de bibliotheek der vereniging Het Spinozahuis*, 19–32; of Ishac Aboab da Fonseca, *Catalogus variorum . . . librorum* (David de Castro Tartas, 1693), of which the library of the Jewish Theological Seminary in New York has a copy. Da Fonseca's library contained some 256 titles. Abraham da Fonseca, himself a broker and jeweller, appears to have inherited this library from his grandfather of the same name, the former *haham* of Hamburg.

[57] Fuks and Fuks-Mansfeld, *Hebrew Typography*, i. 161.

there, and think a given title too esoteric ever to have had much appeal for Portuguese Jewish readers; but it would defeat the purpose of this summary if we excluded on principle all data that do not conform to some more or less well-founded preconceptions.

Bibles were printed—and no doubt read—locally in Hebrew as well as in Spanish. Printed bibles contained either all the books of the Torah, Prophets, and Hagiographa, with or without the Targum Onkelos—very occasionally, also with the Targum Jonathan and in one case with the three Targumim together (Menasseh ben Israel, 1638–40)—and with or without the commentary of Rashi; or the Torah only with the Megillot and Haftarot, in the editions by Uri Phoebus Halevi of 1674, 1679–80, and 1680, according to both the Portuguese Jewish and Ashkenazi *minhagim*. Two other biblical books were singled out, because of their ritual uses, for separate publication: Psalms—once with an accompanying Spanish translation (1670–1)—and the Song of Songs, preferably with the Targum and the *Pirkei avot* and once with a Ladino translation of the Song and a Spanish translation of the Targum (David de Castro Tartas, 1664). The Targum of the Song of Songs was also published on its own by David de Castro Tartas, in 1663 and 1683. In accordance with Amsterdam Portuguese Jewish custom, it is read during Sabbath services between Pesah and Shavuot. The inventory of the estate of Ester Abendana, widow of Joseph Jenes, lists 'a Bible of the Old and New Testament in Dutch, a book of Ruby Franco' (possibly Joseph Franco Serrano's *Los cinco libros de la Sacra Ley*, Amsterdam, 1695).[58] A New Testament in Dutch was also found among the books of Spinoza, and Haham Ishac Aboab possessed a copy of the 'Evangelium' in four languages, Hebrew among them. Spinoza's reading of the New Testament comes as no surprise; Aboab owned quite a number of Christian publications in Spanish and Portuguese, as we will see, and his copy of the New Testament may have been part of that general interest or a curiosum—it is hard to say. The copy in the home of Joseph Jenes similarly may represent a more or less common phenomenon or have been a fluke; there is no way of knowing as yet. All in all, there are no surprises here, excepting, perhaps, the ready availability of translations. Prayer-books, whether for daily or festival use, also came as often as not with an accompanying Spanish translation. For most of the seventeenth century, it would appear, the knowledge of Hebrew in a substantial segment of the population was sufficiently wanting to justify such relatively expensive editions.

Amsterdam's Portuguese Jews did not evince a great and profound interest in the halakhah. The libraries of Ishac Aboab and Abraham da Fonseca, the grandson of the Hamburg *haham*, contained all the requisite codes, compendia, responsa, and other halakhic literature. But these were the working libraries of men who sat on the Bet Din, the communal court of religious law. Joseph Jenes's library contained only 'a *dinim* of Isaac Athias' and 'two books of *dinim de mantimiento del alma*'; Spinoza's, *Ḥidushei harav rabeinu nisim* (Riva di Trento, 1558), Joseph Ibn

---

58 GAA, NA 4249, p. 925 (20 Nov. 1703; D. v. d. Groe).

Verga's *Sefer she'erit yosef*, on the methodology of the Talmud, Joshua Levita's *Halikhot olam sive Clavis talmudica* with a translation by Constantin l'Empereur (Leiden, 1634), and Nathan ben Yehiel's *Sefer musaf he'arukh* (Benveniste, 1655). Nathan's introductory manual may have been the text used to teach students of the Talmud Tora school. Jean Cardoso possessed no halakhic works at all. Compendia similar to that of Hamburg's Yshac Athias (*Tesoro de preseptos*, Venice, 1627, or Amsterdam, 1649) were also compiled and published, in Amsterdam, by Abraham Farar (*Declaração das seiscentas e treze encommendanças da nossa Santa Ley*, Amsterdam, 1627), Menasseh ben Israel (*Thesouro dos dinim*, 1645), and David Pardo— born in Amsterdam, but a *haham* in London (*Compendio de dinim*, Amsterdam, 1689). David Pardo also edited a Hebrew anthology of *Shulḥan arukh* texts, entitled *Shulḥan tahor* (Uri Phoebus Halevi, 1686), dedicated to the *parnasim* of the London congregation Sha'ar Hashamayim.[59] The Amsterdam *haham* of the later seventeenth century Selomoh de Oliveyra drafted—for purposes of teaching, it would seem—an alphabetical list of talmudic expressions and a brief summary of the thirteen principles expounded by Maimonides in his *Sefer hamitsvot* (*Darkhei no'am*, David de Castro Tartas, 1688) as well as an alphabetical list of the 613 *mitsvot* (*Darkhei hashem*, Uri Phoebus Halevi, 1688).[60] The other book of *dinim* referred to in the Joseph Jenes inventory may have been Moseh Altaras' *Libro de mantenimiento de la alma* (Venice, 1609), a manual similar to the ones published in Amsterdam. In a more general, theoretical vein, David Cohen de Lara made a Spanish translation of Maimonides' *Yesodei hatorah* (*Tratado de los articulos de la Ley Divina*, Amsterdam, 1652). These relatively superficial and mostly utilitarian manuals were apparently quite popular. They were needed, of course, to help new returnees to Judaism establish a modicum of halakhically correct behaviour.

Amsterdam's Jewish printers also issued several editions of the Mishnah, Benveniste one of *Hilkhot rav alfasi* (1643) and a monumental one of the Babylonian Talmud (1644–7), and Athias one of Maimonides' *Sefer hamitsvot* (1660) and two of the *Shulḥan arukh* (1661–4 and 1697–8). In 1661–4 Athias printed, on orders from David de Mercado, the *Shulḥan arukh* in an edition of 3,000 copies—clearly too many if he was aiming solely at the Portuguese Jewish communities of northern Europe and the Caribbean. Students in the highest classes of the Talmud Tora school did, as we have seen, study the Talmud, and Ishack de Matatia Aboab recommended that his sons read the *Shulḥan arukh* and the *Mishneh torah* as well as the Mishnah; he does not mention the Talmud. But whether any Portuguese Jews other than the rabbis, teachers, and students were drawn to study these halakhic works cannot be established. Our inventories are simply too few and show no hint of a pattern.

With regard to other works from the Jewish past, Portuguese Jewish tastes tended to run towards the moralistic and the polemical. Joseph Jenes's library lists

---

[59] Fuks and Fuks-Mansfeld, *Hebrew Typography*, ii. 281–2.
[60] Amzalak, 'Selomoh de Oliveyra', 110.

'a book of Cuzari . . . a book of the Obligation de los corasones'.[61] Jean Cardoso
owned three highly unusual volumes: 'a printed book of Philo Judaeus, first
volume, in French; a same of the second volume; a printed book of Flavius
Josephus, in French, in folio'.[62] Even Spinoza's library contained no more than a
few idiosyncratic texts: Maimonides' *Moreh nevukhim*, Meir Ibn Aldabi's *Sefer
shevilei emunah* (Daniel de Fonseca, 1627), Menahem Recanati's *Perush al hatorah*,
and Leone Ebreo's *Los dialogos de amor*. Haham Aboab, of course, possessed the
whole spectrum of traditional Jewish literature among the more than 400 Hebrew
titles in his library. He also owned, in the vernacular, copies of a Spanish translation of Josephus' *Contra Apion* and of the indispensable *Dialogos de amor*.
(Surprisingly, perhaps, the translations produced locally of Jewish sources from
the past did not find their way into the *haham*'s library.) Bahya Ibn Paquda's *Hovot
halevavot* seems to have been particularly popular and appeared in two editions.
The first, in a Spanish translation written with Hebrew characters, *Libro intitulado
obligacion de los coraçones* (1610), was ascribed to 'el grande rabbenu Moseh de
Aegipto' and translated or rather copied by David Pardo from a Constantinople
translation;[63] the second, *Obrigaçam dos coraçoens* (David de Castro Tartas, 1670),
is one of the few works translated (by Semuel Abas) into Portuguese rather than
Spanish, which must certainly be counted a mark of the moral treatise's popular
appeal. No Hebrew edition was printed in Amsterdam. Two separate translations
of Maimonides on penitence—a favourite theme among Amsterdam's Portuguese
Jews even before the advent of Shabbetai Zevi—were issued in Spanish translations: *Livro intitulado Thesuba que he contrition* (1613), by Semuel da Silva, and
Tratado de penitencia (Leiden, Johan Zacharias Baron, 1660), by David Cohen de
Lara. Cohen de Lara also published in Leiden a Hebrew riddle by Abraham Ibn
Ezra with notes and a Latin translation, *Sefer divrei david* (Johan Zacharias Baron,
1658); a parallel edition without the Latin translation is dedicated, in Spanish, to
Jacob de Pinto.[64] One Hebrew edition of Jonah Gerondi's *Sefer hayirah* was
printed by Menasseh ben Israel in 1627, and a Spanish translation of parts of his
Sha'arei teshuvah, entitled *Sendroe de vidas*, by Benveniste in 1638. The kabbalist
Eijah de Vidas was printed twice: first in a Spanish translation, by David Cohen de
Lara, of the first chapter of his *Reshit hokhmah*, *Tratado del temor divino* (Menasseh
ben Israel, 1633), and then in a Hebrew abridgement of that work entitled *Totsa'ot
hayim* (Benveniste, 1650). Yehudah Halevi's famous philosophical apology,
Hakuzari or 'the book of argument and proof in defence of a despised religion',
appeared in a translation by Jacob Abendana, under the title *Cuzary libro de grande*

[61] GAA, NA 4249, p. 925 (20 Nov. 1703; D. v. d. Groe).
[62] Philo of Alexandria, *Les Œuvres de Philon Juif . . . contenant l'exposition Literale & Morale des
livres sacrez de Moyse & des autres Prophetes, & plusieurs divers mysteres, pour l'instruction d'un chacun en
la pieté & aux bônes mœurs*, ed. Federic Morel (Paris: Bessin, 1619); Josephus Flavius, *De l'antiquité
judaique*, trans. Guillaume Michel (Paris: Cousteau, 1534).
[63] Offenberg, 'Exame das tradições', 57–8.
[64] Fuks and Fuks-Mansfeld, *Hebrew Typography*, i. 49–50.

sciencia y mucha doctrina (1663). Again no Hebrew edition was printed. 'Captain' Joseph Semah Arias translated Josephus' *Contra Apion* into Spanish (David de Castro Tartas, 1687). In Hebrew, and therefore perhaps not primarily for Portuguese Jewish consumption, Menasseh ben Israel printed Sa'adiah Gaon's *Sefer ha'emunot* (1647), and several other printers issued editions of Rashi's *Perush* (commentary on the Bible). There remains only the publication, in Hebrew, of several treatises by Isaac Abarbanel dealing with the messianic question and more or less directly countering Christian arguments about the messiahship of Jesus: *Perush al nevi'im aharonim* (Benveniste, 1641–2), *Sefer mashmia yeshuah* (Benveniste, 1644), and *Ma'ayanei hayeshuah* (Menasseh ben Israel, 1647). In view of the persistent anti-Christian polemic for which Amsterdam's Portuguese Jews are justly famous, it would appear that these publications were, in the first place, meant for them. Their anti-Christian implications may have inspired the cautious publication in Hebrew rather than any gentile language. The predominant publication of traditional Jewish literature in translation may have been dictated by the need for such literature especially on the part of men and women recently re-converted to Judaism. It may simply not have made economic sense to re-issue the same works in a second Hebrew edition for those who had mastered that language. Or it may just be that the majority of Portuguese Jews never got beyond the rudimentary level of prayer-book Hebrew—an interpretation perhaps favoured by the fact that they created so very little literature of their own in Hebrew.

As to more or less contemporary religious literature bought and published, so far as we can tell most was created locally and only a few salient items were imported from elsewhere. Haham Aboab, who again owned the greatest collection of both local and foreign such literature, was entirely atypical of his congregation in this regard. To begin with the latter, Joseph Jenes's inventory mentions 'two books of Manuel Aboab'; Spinoza's and Cardoso's none at all. Imanuel Aboab's famous *Nomologia*, first published in an Amsterdam edition in 1629, was much revered among Portuguese New Christians returning to Judaism. The printers published only two short works of the other contemporary luminary, Judah di Modena, both in Hebrew: *Sod yesharim* (Menasseh ben Israel, 1649) and *Sur mera* (Leiden, 1656), as well as Isaiah Hurwitz's *Shenei luhot haberit*, in Hebrew (Benveniste, 1648–9) and in a partial Spanish translation (*Libro yntitulado Enseña a pecadores*, David de Castro Tartas, 1666). Local authors published religious works in Hebrew, Spanish, and Portuguese. Of those in Hebrew only the two treatises by Yosef Delmedigo, *Sefer elim* (Menasseh ben Israel, 1629) and *Ma'ayan ganim* (Menasseh ben Israel, 1629), and Menasseh ben Israel's *Nishmat hayim* (Menasseh ben Israel, 1651)—and, possibly, Moseh de Mercado's *Perush 'al sefer kohelet utehilim* (Benveniste, 1653)—were actually written in Hebrew. The philosophico-kabbalistic ruminations of Abraham Cohen Herrera, *Sha'ar hashamayim* (Benveniste, 1655) and *Beit elohim* (Benveniste, 1655), had been translated, from Spanish, by Haham Ishac Aboab da Fonseca while in Brazil. And Saul Levi Morteira's collected fifty sermons, *Givat sha'ul* (Benveniste, 1645), were in all likelihood originally delivered in Portuguese. Portuguese was not a language used very often in any but the most popular or colloquial publications. Sermons were perhaps the only class of religious literature where it recurs, as most of them had been delivered in Portuguese to begin with. There are Portuguese sermons by most of the local *hahamim*—Saul Levi Morteira, Jacob Sasportas, Ishac Aboab da Fonseca, Selomoh de Oliveyra, Selomoh Jeuda Leon, Daniel Belilhos, and David Nunes Torres of The Hague— including a collection of the sermons delivered on the occasion of the opening of the Esnoga in 1675 as well as others by Semuel Jahia of Hamburg and Jeosua da Silva of London.[65] On a few special occasions, individuals who were not professional preachers also published sermons: Ishac and Selomoh Lousado's father had his sons' bar mitzvah 'sermons' printed as *Sermoens pregados na celebre Esnoga de Amsterdam* (Dias, 1691), one in Dutch, the other in Portuguese; and Abraham Gomez Silveyra, who had literary pretensions, published his *Sermones* (1677) at his own expense—the only ones to appear in Spanish, but then Gomez Silveyra was actually a native of Spain, who had undoubtedly delivered his sermons before the Yesibà Jeneral de los Huerfanos (the orphans' society) and at funerals in Spanish.[66]

The fact that both Semuel da Silva's *Tratado da imortalidade da alma* (Van Ravesteyn, 1623) and Uriel da Costa's *Exame das tradições phariseas* (Van Ravesteyn, 1624) came out in Portuguese may indicate no more than the polemic impulsivity with which they were published. In Spanish, Menasseh ben Israel published his own writings: *Conciliador* (1632–51), *De la resurreccion de los muertos* (1636), *De la fragilidad humana* (1642), *Esperança de Israel* (1650), and *Piedra gloriosa o de la estatua de Nebuchadnesar* (1655). The very wealthy merchant Abraham Pereyra, of course, had no trouble seeing his personal religious ruminations into print as *La certeza del camino* (David de Castro Tartas, 1666) and *Espejo de la vanidad del mundo* (Amsterdam: Alexander Jansen, 1671). Like Menasseh ben Israel, Moseh Dias was a printer, most of whose output seems to have consisted of occasional sermons, and who had no problem publishing his own *Meditaciones sobre la historia sagrada del Genesis* (1698 and, in a second augmented edition, 1705). Which leaves us, beside Yosef Delmedigo's treatises and the sermons of

[65] Saul Levi Morteira, *Sermão funeral* [Moseh de Mercado] (Benveniste, 1652); Jacob Sasportas, *Eleh divrei* [the only funeral sermon in Hebrew, Moseh de Mercado] (Benveniste, 1652); Ishac Aboab da Fonseca, *Exortação* (David de Castro Tartas, 1680); Selomoh de Oliveyra, *Sermam funeral* [Ishac Aboab da Fonseca] (Dias, 1710); Daniel Belilhos, *Sermoens* (Dias, 1693); Selomoh Jeuda Leon, *Serman moral* (Dias, 1694); also *Sermam funeral* [Selomoh de Oliveyra] (Dias, 1694); David Nunes Torres, *Sermam funeral* [Sara de Pinto] (Dias, 1686); also *Sermam funeral* [Mordechai Franco Mendes] (Dias, 1690), *Sermão apologetico* (Dias, 1690), and *Sermões* (Dias, 1690); Semuel Jahia, *Trinta discursos* (n.p., 1629); Jeosua da Silva, *Discursos predicaveys* (Jacob de Cordova, 1688).

[66] Kayserling, *Biblioteca Española-Portugueza-Judaica*, also lists a (Spanish?) *Sermon moral del fundamento de nuestra ley* (Amsterdam, 1691) by Hisquiau da Silva, an itinerant *haham* who solicited funds for the Holy Land, and a *Sermão no dia de Pascoa* (1690) by one Semuel da Silva de Miranda.

Saul Levi Morteira, with only the latter's colleague Ishac Aboab da Fonseca's *Paraphrasis comentado sobre el Pentateucho* (Jacob de Cordova, 1681) as examples of publications not financed by the author himself. Of these publications, the libraries of Cardoso possessed none; that of Joseph Jenes only 'a book of Haham Isaack Aboab' (i.e. the *Paraphrasis*); and that of Spinoza only Yosef Delmedigo, but in an undated Basle edition of the *Collectanea decerpta*, and Menasseh ben Israel's *Esperança de Ysrael*. Surprisingly, Aboab appears not to have possessed a copy of his own *Paraphrasis*.

As most of these local publications were financed by the authors themselves, it is difficult to use them as a gauge of anything other than the urgency of their authors' particular religious preoccupations. A penchant for reading ascetic writings was apparent also in the Portuguese Jews' preferences among traditional literature; yet, except for Abraham Pereyra, none of the other writers exhibited much of a similar predilection. Menasseh ben Israel at times appears like an author in search of an audience. On various occasions he addresses a general, interested Christian audience, humanist scholars, millenarians, or his fellow Portuguese Jews. It would be risky to draw any conclusions about the religious interests of the Portuguese Jews from his publications. Abraham Cohen Herrera's Neoplatonic interpretations of the kabbalah may or may not have been shared by Ishac Aboab—Menasseh ben Israel also veers in that direction—but it does not follow that they found a widespread following. When all is said and done, the sources reveal an incontrovertible bias in favour of succinct summaries of the nature of Judaism, ascetic and penitential contemplations, and a more or less constant effort, personally and often, to pursue a Jewish interpretation of the Bible.

Works of biblical or linguistic scholarship and Ibero-Jewish history constitute the final class of Jewish literature that held a particular attraction for Portuguese Jews. Spinoza owned copies of Moses Qimhi's *Sefer dikduk* and Joseph Jenes 'one [book] called *Excelencia de los Hebreos*', and Haham Aboab, for obvious reasons, a great number of the publications listed below. Isaac Uziel, Moseh Rephael de Aguilar, and Selomoh de Oliveyra published Hebrew grammars; Menasseh ben Israel, Benjamin Musaphia, David Cohen de Lara, Jacob Sasportas, and Selomoh de Oliveyra published various linguistic studies and vocabularies or compiled indexes; and Jacob Jeuda Leon 'Templo' wrote a number of studies on the 'architecture' of the Tabernacle, the Temple, the Ark of the Covenant, and the Cherubim in the Holy of Holies.[67] Their own personal Spanish and Portuguese

---

[67] Isaac Uziel, *Ma'aneh lashon* (Menasseh ben Israel, 1627); Moseh Rephael de Aguilar, *Epitome da grammatica Hebrayca* (Leiden: Johan Zacharias Baron, 1660; Athias, 1661); Selomoh de Oliveyra, *Livro da grammatica Hebrayca & Chaldaica* (David de Castro Tartas, 1688); Menasseh ben Israel, *Sefer penei rabah* (Menasseh ben Israel, 1628); Benjamin Musaphia, *Zekher rav* (Menasseh ben Israel, 1635), a poetic version of the story of creation using every possible Hebrew root and, also, lexicographical addenda to Nathan ben Yehiel's *Musaf he'arukh* (Benveniste, 1655); David Cohen de Lara, *Ir david* (Van Ravesteyn, 1638); Jacob Jeuda Leon Templo, *Retrato del templo de Selomo* (Middelburg, 1642), *Tavnit heikhal* (Amsterdam, 1650), *Retrato de la arca del testamento* (Van Ravesteyn, 1653),

Jewish history received attention, too, principally in three editions of Selomoh Ibn Verga's *Shevet yehudah*: two in Hebrew (Menasseh ben Israel, 1638; Benveniste, 1655) and one in Spanish, *La Vara de Iuda* (Benveniste, 1640). By contrast, Samuel Usque's *Consolaçam as tribulações de Ysrael*, which addresses the period of the expulsion and the establishment of the Inquisition more extensively, was printed only once in 1611. Isaac Cardoso's *Las excelencias de los Hebreos* (David de Castro Tartas, 1679) was published in Amsterdam, while the author was still alive and living at Verona in Italy. The work was dedicated to Jacob de Pinto of Amsterdam, who had extensive business dealings with Italy and probably paid for the printing. The publication of *Las excelencias* in Amsterdam—and in Amsterdam alone—stands not only as a mark of the city's toleration (the book is a classic of Jewish apologetics) but also of the presence of a system for sponsoring such publications and of a readership, including merchants like Joseph Jenes, that Jacob de Pinto must have had in mind when he opened his wallet. Contemporary history was treated by Daniel Levi de Barrios, as we will have occasion to see shortly, in Moseh Pereyra de Paiva's rather brief *Notisias dos Judeus de Cochin* (Uri Phoebus Halevi, 1687), and in a collection of poems with the self-explanatory title *Elogios que zelosos dedicaron a la felice memorià de Abraham Nunez Bernal que fue quemado vivo santificando el Nombre de su Criador en Cordova a 3 de Mayo 5415* (Elegies dedicated by pious men to the happy memory of Abraham Nuñez Bernal, who was burned alive [a martyr], sanctifying the name of his creator, in Cordova on 3 May 5415[/1655]) (Amsterdam, no date). These few works, we do well to remember, are dwarfed in number by comparison with the general history devoured by Amsterdam's Portuguese Jews. It certainly comes as some surprise that, in contrast with other major persecutions in Jewish history, Amsterdam's Portuguese Jews addressed their own immediate past far less than their biblical ancestry. As I have argued elsewhere, the memories of that immediate past were too individualistic, too heterogeneous, to be very easily communicable and certainly to be distilled into a collectively acceptable form.[68]

Over and above the religious literature received from traditional and contemporary sources, Amsterdam's Jewish printers also published a host of secular writings by local authors. The total volume of such publications may even have equalled that of the religious publications. The existence and bulk of this literature must certainly be considered one of the distinguishing features of Amsterdam's Portuguese Jewish community. No other Portuguese Jewish settlement ever harboured as many belletrists as Amsterdam did during the second half of the

Retrato del tabernaculo de Moseh (Amsterdam, 1654), *Tratado de los cherubim* (Van Ravesteyn, 1654); Jacob Sasportas, *Toledot ya'acov* (Menasseh ben Israel, 1652); Selomoh de Oliveyra, *Igeret . . . lehavin mashal umelitsah* (David de Castro Tartas, 1665), *Shareshet gavelut* (Tartas, 1665), *Mikra'ei kodesh* (Uri Phoebus Halevi, 1670), an introduction on cantillation to editions of Psalms (Tartas, 1670; Halevi, 1689), *Sefer or tov* (Tartas, 1675), and *Sefer ets ḥayim* (Tartas, 1682–3).

[68] Swetschinski, 'Un refus de mémoire'.

seventeenth century. Here we must restrict ourselves to an examination of the types of literature most popular among these writers and, perhaps, in greatest demand among Amsterdam's Portuguese Jewish readership.

An astonishingly large part of the Portuguese Jewish literature written in Amsterdam is of a purely occasional character. The superabundance of this kind of poetry among the works of Daniel Levi de Barrios has earned him the title of poet laureate of Amsterdam's Portuguese Jewish community. Occasional poetry then occupied the place that special occasion photography occupies today, with weddings and deaths most frequently thus commemorated. Communal organizations, their administrators, and their members were also immortalized in this fashion. Some less common occasions, too, invited lyrical attention: for instance, Don Rephael de Arredondo's mediation in the del Sotto dispute and the temporary absence of Moseh Nunes Marchena's bride-to-be.[69] Not all of this poetry celebrated wealthy Portuguese Jewish merchants; de Barrios also poetically adorned a few non-Jewish weddings.[70] Finally, a great many poems by Miguel de Barrios, Jose de la Vega, and Duarte Lopes Rosa (alias Moseh Rosa) sang the praises of contemporary heads of state such as John III Sobieski of Poland (on the occasion of his defeat of the Ottomans at Vienna in 1683), Charles II of Spain, Peter II of Portugal, Louis XIV of France, William Henry Prince of Orange, the Emperor Leopold, William III of England, and Cosimo III, grand duke of Tuscany—not to mention the host of officials from the Spanish Netherlands and various Spanish and Portuguese embassies; hence the use of their Christian names.[71] All this occasional poetry was exclusively for commercial purposes—not necessarily because there existed a large readership for such publications, but because they were tailored for a wealthy sponsor. This was the means by which a poet such as de Barrios provided for his family. Most such verse was written as automatically as Parisian street artists draw portraits.

But Amsterdam's Portuguese Jewish writers also produced more serious literature. Second only to the volume of occasional poetry was their output of religious

[69] De Barrios' opuscula are not always bound together in the same fashion and also appear as parts of several 'collected editions'. It is therefore necessary, when citing a particular text, to specify the copy in which it was found. The examples cited here may be found, respectively, in *Triumpho del govierno popular*, 571, and *Estrella de Jacob sobre flores de lis*, no pagination (copy in BN Madrid, Raros 5214).

[70] The non-Jewish weddings celebrated are those of Lorenso Besels and Clara Reyniers, Adam de Besels and Sara van Ray, and Gilberto and Jacob de Flines and Catalina and Isabel de Gelder. The poems may be found in *Estrella de Jacob* and *Luna opulenta de Holanda* (copy in BN Madrid, Raros 12313).

[71] To mention one example: *Sol de la vida* (copy in BN Madrid, Raros 5837) contains poems dedicated to Don Phelipe de Sasportas y Moscoso, Don Manuel de Lyra, Don Bernardo de Salinas, Don Fernando de Mascareñas, Don Sancho Manuel, Conde de Villaflor, Conde de la Torre, Mariscal de Turena, Duarte Ribero de Macedo, Don Henrique de Tabares y Sousa, Don Bernardino Sarmiento y Soto Mayor, Don Francisco de Mora y Corte Real, D. Sebastian Enriques de Castro, Don Juan Luis de la Ceda, and Don Francisco de Silva.

poetry. The overwhelming majority of these poems deal with the Law—a favourite Portuguese New Christian/Jewish shorthand for Judaism.[72] De Barrios, Penso de la Vega, and, in his prosaic way, Ishac Orobio de Castro all created their variations on the theme of the Law's perfection, eternity, and superiority. De Barrios focused in particular on 'the permanence and superiority of Judaism, the durability of Israel in the face of all efforts to destroy her, and the special protection extended by God to the Hebrew'.[73] He also composed some additional religious poetry, possibly reflecting more personal preoccupations: a lengthy poem on free will, a collection of ten poems entitled *Dias penitenciales* (the ten days between Rosh Hashanah and Yom Kippur), vernacular *seliḥot* or 'acts of contrition' (as de Barrios subtitled the poems), a sort of poetic version of the Torah entitled *Imperio de Dios en la harmonia del mundo*, and the *comedia* discussed above, *Contra la verdad no hay fuerza*.[74]

If de Barrios' most personal creations focused on religious themes, Joseph Penso de la Vega (who was not a neophyte) concentrated on lighter genres. His *Rumbos peligrosos* (Jacob de Cordova, 1683) contains three novellas and his *Ideas posibles* (David de Castro Tartas, 1692) twelve, five of which are (rather free) translations of Italian originals. His most famous work, *Confusion de confusiones* (David de Castro Tartas, 1688), remains the most erudite seventeenth-century description of the mechanics of the stock market, of which de la Vega had the best firsthand knowledge.[75] Isabella Correa also translated an Italian original into Spanish: Guarini's *Pastor Fido* (Amsterdam, van Ravesteyn, 1694).[76] On the whole, truly recreational literature was not the forte of Amsterdam's Portuguese Jews; outside Iberian sources probably kept up a steady supply.

The literary output summarized above is impressive enough. But, when all is said and done, the authors who created it were only a meagre handful. If Amsterdam none the less deserves the epithet of poetic capital of the Portuguese Jewish diaspora, it is because of the two literary academies organized by Don Manuel de Belmonte: the first, in 1676, called Academia de los Sitibundos (Academy of the

---

[72] Yerushalmi, *From Spanish Court*, 400–2.

[73] Scholberg, *La poesia religiosa de Miguel de Barrios*, 83–4.

[74] De Barrios' religious poetry has been analysed and collected in Scholberg, *La poesia religiosa de Miguel de Barrios*. For bibliographical references to works of de Barrios, see Roest, 'De opuscula van Daniel Levi (Miguel) de Barrios'; Kayserling, *Biblioteca Española-Portugueza-Judaica*, 16–26; Peeters-Fontainas, *Bibliographie des impressions espagnoles des Pays-Bas méridionaux*, i. 52–7, ii. 717–22; den Boer, 'Spanish and Portuguese Editions', *SR* 23 (1989), 45–64. For studies of de Barrios' life and works, see Zwarts, 'De Joodsche dichter-troubadour'; Gates, 'Three Gongoristic Poets'; Rubio, 'Notas sobre la vida y obras del capitán Miguel de Barrios'; Wilson, 'Miguel de Barrios and Spanish Religious Poetry'; Glaser, 'Two Notes on the Hispano-Jewish Poet Don Miguel de Barrios'; Pieterse, *Daniel Levi de Barrios*.

[75] Kayserling, *Bibliotheca Española-Portugueza-Judaica*, 85–7; Peeters-Fontainas, *Bibliographie des impressions espagnoles des Pays-Bas*, 108–9; den Boer, 'Spanish and Portuguese Editions', 152–4; the editions of *Confusion de confusiones*: Spanish original with Dutch trans.: de la Vega, *Confusion de confusiones*, intr. Smith, trans. Geers; German trans. Pringsheim, *Die Verwirrung der Verwirrungen: Vier Dialoge über die Börse in Amsterdam*; partial Eng. trans. Kellenbenz, '*Confusion de confusiones*' by Joseph de la Vega, 1688.   [76] Cabezas Alguacil, 'Doña Isabel de Correa'.

Thirsty), the second, in 1685, Academia de los Floridos (Academy of the Flowery/ Select).[77] Daniel Levi de Barrios gives us the following unusually terse description of the first *academia*:

In the year 1676 Ishac Nunez alias Don Manuel de Belmonte, Count Palatine and resident of the king of Spain in the Netherlands, organized a poetic academy of which he was a judge with two renowned individuals: Doctor Ishac de Rocamora alias Fray Vicente de Rocamora—Dominican, a native of Valencia, and preacher to the Empress Dona Maria of Austria—and Ishac Gomez de Sosa—famous Latin poet and nephew of Doctor Samuel Serra who imitated Virgil in Latin poetry. I was the *mantenedor de la justa poetica* [overseer of poetic contest]. And the *aventureros* [contestants] were Abraham Henriques, Mosseh Rosa, Mosseh Dias, and Abraham Gomez Silveyra. Jacob Castelo, expert in the liberal arts, inspired her [the Academy] with his odd *enigmas* [riddles] and Abraham Gomez Arauxo and other noble minds [did the same] with their explications.[78]

These academies were clearly modelled on the Spanish *tertulias literarias*, examples of which abounded in almost every major city of the peninsula.[79] They also have something of our contemporary debating clubs about them, though the academies' style was more typically literary and their discussion often totally frivolous. The academies held regular meetings where the *aventureros* would read their poetry (and, occasionally, prose) on a topic assigned at the previous meeting. Frequently the poetry readings were in the form of a real contest (*justa poetica* or *certamen*) in which the victor won a prize. The customary rules and regulations of the Amsterdam academies have not been preserved. We do not know whether the Portuguese Jewish academicians adopted fictitious names, as was the practice in Spain; whether women were allowed to participate in the academies; how often meetings were scheduled; or why the academies appear to have had such a short life-span.

We do, however, know a great many of the topics 'discussed' and have a fairly extensive membership list of the Academia de los Floridos. The topics constitute a mixed bag. Some were simply and characteristically light-hearted, others more serious and even religious. Among the frivolous topics were: Does love outweigh vengeance? Which is the noblest of the senses? Which is worse, a spendthrift or a miser? Which is preferable, poverty with children or riches without them? During the absence of Moseh Nunes Marchena's bride-to-be, the academy discussed whether 'the lover suffers more from not possessing the woman he sees or from not seeing the woman he loves while awaiting her to be his wife'. Arguing the case of the lover who suffered from not seeing his bride-to-be, de Barrios composed a short dialogue between Cupid, Hymen (the god of marriage), and Music.[80] Among the more serious discussions the academy addressed itself to the question: 'If man

[77] Scholberg, 'Miguel de Barrios and the Amsterdam Sephardic Community', 141–4; Kaplan, *From Christianity to Judaism*, 286–302.

[78] *Triumpho del govierno popular*, p. 458 of copy 9 E 43 in the Ets Haim-Montezinos Library.

[79] King, 'The Academies and Seventeenth-century Spanish Literature'; Sánchez, *Académias literárias*.   [80] *Estrella de Jacob* (copy in BN Madrid, Raros 5214).

is born of woman, why did God create man first?' In 1684, on the election of David Bueno de Mesquita as Hatan Bereshit, de Barrios composed an *Enigma del principio* in the form of a 'hieroglyph' depicting 'a rose in the mouth of a Hebrew and the head of the giant Goliath in the hand of David'. The rose (Spanish *rosa*)—through a play on the Hebrew word *roshah*, 'its beginning', in Daniel 7: 1—symbolizes the beginning of prophecy, and the head of Goliath—man is a microcosm and, therefore, the macrocosm is a giant—the beginning of the world. The enigma, a suitable 'hieroglyph' for the honoured Hatan Bereshit, was best explained by Joseph Penso, who won a beaver hat as a prize.[81] Some of the academic exercises of Daniel Levi de Barrios and Joseph Penso de la Vega appeared in print; those of Moseh Rosa are listed by Kayserling as having existed in manuscript.[82] The overwhelming majority of academic literature was never published and was probably never intended to be.

The academies brought together three fairly distinct groups within Amsterdam's Portuguese Jewish community: the intellectuals, the 'new' merchants, and the aristocrats. Similar groupings also characterized the Iberian academies. In Amsterdam the intellectuals were represented by the writers and the physicians; the merchants by jewellers, speculators, and army purveyors, in other words, that group of 'entrepreneurs' whose rise characterized the 'new' Portuguese Jewish economy of the late seventeenth century; and the aristocrats by the two most successful diplomats, Manuel de Belmonte and Jeronimo Nunes da Costa.[83] The

---

[81] Ibid.

[82] The extant academic writings of Daniel Levi de Barrios specifically identified as such include: 'Si pesa mas el amor que la fuerça del agravio', in his *Bellomonte de Helicona* (copy in BN Madrid, Raros 10386); 'Enigma del principio', 'Ansias de Epytalamio', and 'Enigma', in his *Estrella de Jacob* (copy in BN Madrid, Raros 5214); 'soneto peregrino' and 'Triumpho del color celeste', in his *Libre alvedrio y harmonia del cuerpo* (copy in BN Madrid, Raros 12815). Joseph de la Vega's academic works are collected in his *Discurso academico, moral y sagrado* (Amsterdam, 1683); *Discurso academico* (Amsterdam, 1683); and *Discursos academicos, morales, retoricos, y sagrados* (Antwerp [= Amsterdam], 1685). Regarding Moseh Rosa's *Luzes de la idea y academicos discursos*, see Kayserling, *Bibliotheca Española-Portugueza-Judaica*, 95.

[83] The following persons are mentioned by Daniel Levi de Barrios in 'Relacion de los poetas y escritores españoles de la nacion judayca amstelodama', in his *Triumpho del govierno popular* (copy in Ets Haim-Montezinos Library, Amsterdam, 9 E 43), 451–8; and published in Kayserling, 'Une histoire de la littérature juive de Daniel Lévi de Barrios' (I have used here the Hispanic spellings provided by de Barrios): Don Manuel de Belmonte, Geronimo Nunez (da Costa) ('aristocrats'); Ishac Gomez de Sosa, Mosseh Dias, Joseph Nunez Marchena, Francisco de Lis, Manuel Levi (Valle), Joseph Atias, Abraham Penso, Ishac Pesoa, Moseh Machado, David Franco Mendez, Moseh Pereyra, Joseph Israel Alvarez, Raphael del Castillo, Moseh Nunez Marchena, Antonio Gabriel, Jacob de Chaves ('merchants'); Ishac de Rocamora, Daniel Levi de Barrios, Mosseh Rosa, Abraham Gutierrez, Joseph Penso Vega, Mosseh Orobio de Castro, Balthasar Orobio, Abraham Froys ('intellectuals'); Abraham Henriques, Abraham Gomez Silveyra, Jacob Castelo, Abraham Gomez Arauxo, Simon Levi de Barrios, Manuel de Lara, David Xamiz Vaz, Abraham Lumbrosso, Semuel Semah, Gabriel Moreno, Joseph Jesurum Lobo, Ishac Villegas, Aaron de Medina, Ishac Carillo, David Ximenez; Jacob de Avilar Cardoso, Jacob de Gama, Aron Henriquez, Jacob Gabay Isidro, Duarte Blandon de Silva (category uncertain).

academies themselves, of course, owed their formation to the emergence of
Manuel de Belmonte as Amsterdam's most prominent Portuguese Jewish
aristocrat in the wake of the Hispano-Dutch alliance of the 1670s. It provided the
bachelor Don Manuel with an entourage—a court and, perhaps, a 'family'. For
Manuel de Belmonte was particularly keen on flaunting his aristocratic pretensions. In 1673 he had been nominated a count palatine by the German Emperor
Leopold II in recognition of his efforts on behalf of the defence of the Spanish
Netherlands, but when de Belmonte's Jewishness was brought to the emperor's
attention the issuance of the diploma was cancelled. Don Manuel de Belmonte
none the less steadfastly continued to refer to himself, for the rest of his life, as a
'Conde Palatino'.

The academies represent more than an exercise in aristocratic imitation.
Perusing the list of some forty-seven individuals reported to have been members,
we are struck by the predominance of Spanish-born Jews, a predominance rendered even more marked if we add to the number actually born in Spain those born
in the Spanish Netherlands or in France with immediate family ties to Spain. If the
academies symbolize the 'aristocratization' of Amsterdam's Portuguese Jewish
community, their membership reveals this feature to have been of distinctly
Spanish inspiration. Furthermore, as secular equivalents of the *jesibot*, they constituted the only truly extra-synagogal associations established by Portuguese Jews in
Amsterdam. This extra-synagogal activity does not represent a diminution of
Jewish loyalties. None of the academicians ever voiced any criticism of Judaism.
On the contrary, Ishac Orobio de Castro and Abraham Gomez Silveyra displayed
their Jewish allegiance very proudly in their apologetic writings. The topics given
poetic treatment at academic meetings resemble the 'dissonant' ideas for which the
works of Manuel de Pina and Daniel Levi de Barrios were censored. As de Barrios
was forced to publish his *Flor de Apolo* and *Coro de las musas* in Antwerp, so the
academicians had to establish private associations outside the framework of the
synagogue to engage in levity and frivolity. The negative attitude of the Kahal
towards secular Spanish poetry accounts, on the one hand, for the establishment of
private salons to celebrate an inherited Spanish tradition and, on the other, for the
relative scarcity of academic publications. The academies rescued for Amsterdam's Portuguese Jewish cultural life the Spanish flavour of the expatriates' past
that might otherwise have been lost in the Mahamad's partriarchal sense of propriety.

Judging from the sources quoted in the published writings of Portuguese Jews,
they were most avid readers of classical and contemporary literature. The inventories confirm the phenomenon to have been quite widespread. That of the library
of Abraham da Fonseca lists no vernacular literature at all. Joseph Jenes possessed
'a history of Palafox' (Juan de Palafox y Mendoza's *Historia de la conquista de la
China por el Tartaro* or his *Historia real sagrada*), 'a history book of Emanuel
van Meteren' (*Commentarien ofte memorien van den Nederlandtschen staet, handel,*

oorlogh ende geschiedenissen van onsen tijden), 'a history of Prince Frederick Henry', 'a Spanish–Dutch dictionary', and 'a few other booklets of little value'. Even if in its superabundance of Jewish and Hebrew titles Haham Aboab's library was generally atypical, with regard to his secular taste the published auction catalogue shows him to have been similarly inclined towards some classical standards and, especially, towards historical narratives. In these areas it lists:

Alma & Aphorismos de C. T. [*Alma o Aphorismos de Cornelio Tacito* (Antwerp, 1651)]
Eneydas de Virgilio
La Vlisea de Homero
Obras de Cayo Velello Patreculo
Estephanus, Pinedo [Stephanus of Byzantium, *Stephanus De Urbibus; quem primus Thomas de Pinedo Lusitanus Latii jure donabat* (Amsterdam, 1678)]
Os cinco livros de Coronica de Aragão [Jerónimo Zurita, *Los cinco libros postreros de la primera parte de los Anales de la Corona de Aragon* (Zaragoza, 1610) or *Los cinco libros postreros de la segunda parte de los Anales de la Corona de Aragon* (Zaragoza, 1610)]
Historia de Carlos V. 2 voll. [Prudencio de Sandoval, *Historia de la vida y hechos del Emperador Carlos V*, 2 vols. (Pamplona, 1614; and many other places and dates)]
Caracteres antigos de España
Direytos del Rey D. Pedro de Portugal
Marco Paulo, letra Gotica [*Marco Paulo. Ho livro de Nycolao veneto* (Lisbon, 1502)]
Panegirico del Rey D. Pedro de Portugal
Decadas de Alexandro Farnese, Principe de Parma, 3 Tom. Fig. [Famiano Strada, *Primera decada de las Guerras de Flandes* (Cologne, 1681); id., *Segunda decada de las Guerras de Flandes* (Cologne, 1681); Guglielmo Dondini, *Tercera decada de lo que hiço en Francia Alexandro Farnese* (Cologne, 1681)]
Monarchia Eclesiastica, 4 Tom. [Juan de Pineda, *Monarchia eclesiastica o historia universal del mundo* (Barcelona, 1606–20)]
Coronica del Rey Dom Joaõ de Portugal
Historia general del Perù [Garcilaso de la Vega, *Historia general del Peru* (1609)]
Panegirico del Rey Guillelmo.

The library of Jean Cardoso, in his working life a broker, reveals a similar cosmopolitan orientation. The inventory of his estate lists the following titles:

Jorge de Montemayor, *Diana*
Francesco Guicciardini, *Histoire des guerres d'Italie*
Famianus Strada, *Histoire de la guerre de Flandre*
De l'estat et succes des affaires de France
Résolutions politiques et maximes d'estat
The Memoirs of Queen Margaret (in French)
Tacitus (in French)

L'Incertitude vainte et abus des sciences
Histoire de France of Henry IV
Appian Alexandrin, [*Des Guerres des Romains*]
Philippe de Comines, *Mémoires*
Les Œuvres de C. Saluste
The Commentaries of Julius Caesar (in French)
A small book of Hugo de Groot (in French)
Conincklijck Memoriael of Carolus Stuart (in Dutch)
A history of the decadence of the empire of the Greeks and the rise of the Turk
Seneca (in French)
The history of the Romans (in French)
A history of Emanuel de Metere (in French)
Theodore Agrippa d'Aubigné, *L'Histoire universelle*
A history of England (in French)
Livy (in French)
The History of Thucydides Athenian (in French)
Tractatus de hispaniorum nobilitate (in Latin)
P. C. Hooft, *Cronijck van Hendrick den Grooten* (in Dutch)
Les Vies des hommes illustres (in French)
L'Enéide of Virgil (in French)
Petrarcha (in Spanish)
The Voyage of King Charles II through Holland (in French).

As noted above, Jean Cardoso's marriage to a Dutchwoman who converted to Judaism renders his library—especially in its paucity of volumes of Jewish interest and, possibly, the very presence of some in Dutch—atypical of the Jewish community; and the superabundance of French volumes makes his collection unrepresentative of the largely Spanish-reading community. Yet, as far as his 'taste' in literature is concerned, he must most certainly be counted a member of the Amsterdam Portuguese Jewish community. For Joseph Jenes, Jean Cardoso, and Haham Aboab shared an interest in history, the history not merely of their immediate surroundings but of western Europe in general, and, mostly, contemporary history. Contemporary political treatises figure in the libraries of Jean Cardoso and Spinoza; Cardoso's contained French political maxims, Spinoza's the Dutch discourses of the brothers de la Court. Spinoza's library also contained the more theoretical works of Niccolò Machiavelli, Thomas More, and Diego da Saavedra Fajardo. Contemporary political thought appears a more or less general Portuguese Jewish interest whose depth and focus varied according to the individual's educational background. Spinoza's theoretical interests were more particularly his own. The libraries of Jean Cardoso and Spinoza also contained a great many of the works of classical antiquity.[84] Both possessed copies of Livy and Virgil—of whom

---

[84] On Aboab, see Berger, 'Codices Gentium'.

Haham Aboab also owned a translation—as well as works of Julius Caesar, Sallust, Tacitus, Seneca, and Josephus; Cardoso also the history of Appian, copies of Thucydides and, surprisingly, Philo; Haham Aboab what seems like a translation of the historian Velleius Paterculus. Spinoza, on the other hand, preferred philosophy, science, and, perhaps unexpectedly, poetry: Aristotle, Cicero, Diophantus, Epictetus, Euclid, Hippocrates, Lucan, Martial, Homer, Ovid, Petronius, Plautus, and Pliny the Younger. Aboab liked poetry, history, and geography: Homer, Velleius Paterculus, Herodotus, Polybius, Diodorus Siculus, Dionysius of Halicarnassus, Plutarch, Strabo, Pausanias, Arrianus, and Dio Cassius. The same extensive classical erudition may be gleaned from the publications of Amsterdam's Portuguese Jews. Astonishingly, none of the inventories mentions the name of Plato, who was seen by Menasseh ben Israel as closest in spirit to the Jewish tradition, especially that of the kabbalah.

With regard to the Spanish and Portuguese literature read by Portuguese Jews, Spinoza proves a more reliable guide than Cardoso. Only one Spanish belletristic work is listed in the inventory of the latter's library: the pastoral novel *Diana* by Jorge de Montemayor (d. 1561), a Portuguese who wrote in Spanish. Haham Aboab also did not incline towards the *belles-lettres*. His library contained only a copy of Lope de Vega's 'Jerusalem Conquistada' (Madrid, 1609) and the famous playwright's *Cantos* (possibly his *Rimas* (Lisbon, 1605), *Rimas humanas y divinas* (Madrid, 1634), or *Rimas sacras* (Madrid, 1614)). Spinoza owned many of the classics of Spanish Golden Age literature: Luis de Góngora's *Obra* (two copies), Baltasar Gracián's *El criticón*, Alvaro Pérez's *Obras y relaciones*, a *comedia famosa* of Juan Pérez de Montalván, Francisco de Quevedo's *Obras*, *Poesias*, and *La Cuna*, and João Pinto Delgado's *Poema de la Reyna Ester*.

The above assessment of the reading preferences of Amsterdam's Portuguese Jews leaves a great deal to be desired. For one thing, it lacks measurable dimensions. But it is not totally devoid of significance, for its findings coincide in part with the data to be drawn from the citations found in contemporary Portuguese Jewish literature. All the classical authors and Spanish belletrists found in the libraries of Cardoso and Spinoza are cited recurrently in the works of Daniel Levi de Barrios, Joseph Penso de la Vega, and Ishac Orobio de Castro. Contemporary historical and political literature is cited too. But, in contrast to the French and Dutch preferences of Cardoso and Spinoza, our Portuguese Jewish authors seem to have limited their reading almost exclusively to such Spanish works as, to name a few:

José de Acosta, *Historia natural y moral de las Indias*
Bernardo José Aldrete, *Varias antiguedades de España, Africa y otras provincias*
Juan Calvete de Estrella, *El felicissimo viaje del . . . Principe Don Phelippe*
Luis de Camões, *Os Lusíadas*
Manuel de Faria y Souza, *Comentarios a la Lusiada de Luis de Camões*

Sebastian Manrique, *Itinerario de las missiones que hizo . . . en varias missiones del India Oriental*

Pedro Medina, *Libro de grandezas y cosas memorables de España*

Pedro Mexia, *Historia imperial y cesarea*

Juan de Pineda, *Monarquia eclesiástica, o historia universal del mundo*

Juan de la Puente, *De la conveniencia de las dos monarquias Católicas*

Jerónimo de Quintana, *A la muy antigua, noble y coronada villa de Madrid*

Bernardino de Rebolledo, *Selva militar y politica*

Diego de Saavedra Fajardo, *Corona gothica, castellana y austriaca*

Pedro Teixeira, *Relaciones . . . de los reyes de Persia.*

As suggested above, an interest in historical and political literature appears to have been widespread among Portuguese Jews. The particular literature chosen naturally varied according to the reader's biographical and educational background.

One final class of literature frequently cited in Portuguese Jewish literature is conspicuously almost completely absent from the library inventories: the literature of the Church. Perhaps no single author is cited in Portuguese Jewish literature so frequently and ubiquitously as Augustine, but only Spinoza's library lists a copy of his *Opera omnia* (Augsburg, 1537). (Spinoza also owned a Spanish translation of Calvin's *Institutio.*) Other Church Fathers such as Jerome, Ambrose, and Tertullian are mentioned more sporadically. Of the medieval doctors of the Church, Thomas Aquinas' name recurs most often, but Albertus Magnus, Duns Scotus, and Nicholas of Lyre are also cited. Surprisingly, perhaps, Haham Aboab's library is the only inventory to record a substantial number of more or less modern Christian works. In addition to the collections of sermons by 'Padre Galvão', 'Padre Peres', 'P. Andrade', 'Samora', 'Feo', and 'Fonseca', which I have as yet been unable to identify with any degree of certainty, the catalogue lists:

Introduccion del simbolo de la Fé [Luis de Granada, *Introduccion del simbolo de la fe* (Salamanca, 1583)]

Declaracion de los 7 Psalmos Penitenciales [Pedro de Vega, *Declaracion de los siete psalmos penitenciales* (Madrid, 1602)]

A vida de Francisco Xavier [João de Lucena, *Historia de vida do padre Francisco de Xavier* (Lisbon, 1600)]

Flos Santorum, segunda parte [Alonso de Villegas, *Flos sanctorum, segunda parte y historia general en que se escrive la vida de la Virgen* (Toledo, 1582)]

Philosophia Moral de Principes [Juan de Torres, *Philosophia moral de principes* (Lisbon, 1602)]

Amor de Ds. Fonseca 2 voll. [Christóbal de Fonseca, *Tratado del amor de Dios* (Salamanca, 1592)].

Christóbal de Fonseca's *Tratado del amor de Dios* and Luis de Granada's *Introduccion del simbolo de la fe* are also cited by Portuguese Jewish authors, in addition to such luminaries as Juan Eusebio Nieremberg and Antonio Vieira. Very little of this literature is cited specifically for polemical purposes. Only in the apologetic writings of Ishac Orobio de Castro is Christian literature refuted with any consistency. But even so resolute an anti-Christian polemicist as Orobio de Castro quotes Augustine—and Augustine only—in support of his doctrine of free will.[85] Presumably, Amsterdam's Portuguese Jews had read and studied most of this Christian literature prior to their settlement in Amsterdam, while still New Christians in Spain or Portugal. The Christian works in Aboab's library—at least, the ones that can be identified—date from before his settlement in Amsterdam. Even so, the fact that he or his parents decided to bring them along to Amsterdam—if that is indeed how he acquired them—hints at more than a purely rudimentary interest. Whether or not the chapter-and-verse citations found in de Barrios' and Orobio de Castro's works indicate that they actually had this literature at hand in their libraries we cannot say. It seems quite possible. In any case, the absence of such literature from the libraries of Joseph Jenes, Jean Cardoso, and Spinoza can easily be explained by their never having been in Spain or Portugal. There are certain indications that some works can only have been read in Amsterdam, that is, by former New Christians after settlement in Amsterdam or by Portuguese Jews who had never been educated in Spain or Portugal. For instance, Antonio Vieira is mentioned by Daniel Levi de Barrios, Joseph Penso de la Vega, and Abraham Gomez Silveyra. Most of Vieira's works were published after de Barrios came to Amsterdam. Moreover, Joseph Penso de la Vega and Abraham Gomez Silveyra both grew up in Amsterdam, and so their familiarity with the works of Vieira can only have been gained there.[86] Then again, Vieira may have been an exceptional case. He had personally been in direct communication with Amsterdam's Portuguese Jews and was a known defender of Portugal's New Christians.[87] Abraham Gomez Silveyra's manuscript, however, also reveals him to have been more or less familiar with Thomas Aquinas, Fray Juan Marquez (*El gobernador christiano*), Jerome (commentary on the Bible), and Cyprian (*De unitate*

---

[85] Van Limborch, *De veritate religionis*, 82–6.

[86] On Abraham Gomez Silveyra, see Kayserling, *Bibliotheca Española-Portugueza-Judaica*, 102–3. Only two of Gomez Silveyra's works appeared in print: *Sermones* (Amsterdam, 5437/1676/7); and *Bejamen que dio Don Diego Gomez Silveyra* (Antwerp?, 1682?). A great many manuscripts attributed (some disputably) to Abraham Gomez Silveyra have also survived, among them *Entretenimientos gustozos o dialogos burlescos: entre un Judio, Turco, Reformado, y Catolico* (Jewish Theological Seminary, no. 2527); *Preliminarias que deven anteceder a todo genero de controversias en materia de religion* (Ets Haim-Montezinos Library, MS 48 A 18); *Disertaciones sobre el Mesias, donde se prueva a los Cristianos que J. D. no es el Mesias* (Ets Haim-Montezinos Library, MS 48 B 15); *Libro quinto o quinta Piedra del Zurron de David* (Ets Haim-Montezinos Library, MS 48 A 22); *Silveyrados: dialogos theologicos en versos poco-series* (Ets Haim-Montezinos Library, MS 48 B 14); *Libro mudo, donde se alegan muchas authoridades divinas y humanas para todas las controversias en materia de religion* (Ets Haim-Montezinos Library, MS 48 B 18); and *Libro quarto: El juez de las controversias, donde se manifiesta el juez de la verdad y se halla la sentencia verdadera* (Ets Haim-Montezinos Library, MS 48 B 17).

[87] Révah, 'Les Jésuites portugais contre l'Inquisition'.

ecclesiae). At present we cannot determine whether this familiarity was more than superficial, and, if so, whether it extended beyond such philosophically inclined individuals as Abraham Gomez Silveyra.[88]

With regard to paintings, there appears to have existed a greater disparity in tastes. There is no indication that Portuguese Jews as a group preferred paintings of distinctly Jewish or even biblical themes. In 1693 two Portuguese Jews bought a number of paintings in Antwerp from the estate of Diego Duarte.[89] Carlos Delmonte acquired two portraits by Rubens: one of 'the Infanta, the mother of the present Emperor', the other of Louis XIII of France. Jacques Vaz Faro, a former *parnas* of the Kahal, bought nine paintings: two portraits by Anthony van Dyck of two English noblewomen, a landscape with Pan and Syrinx by Paul Bril, a portrait of a praying man by Jan Mabuse, a feast of the gods by Georg Pencz, a 'last judgement' by 'Jacques de Backer' (Jacob Adriaensz. Backer?), a peasants' fair by David Teniers, and two paintings by Sebastian Vrancx. Nothing in the records tells us whether the paintings were purchased for personal use or to be traded. We may be inclined to assume the latter, but there is nothing in the subjects of the paintings as such that would strongly point in that direction. Otherwise our information about paintings owned by Portuguese Jews comes from estate inventories, which tell us more about the precise location of a painting's 'use' than they do about the painters. Here we encounter, interspersed among studies of secular subjects, paintings with biblical motifs such as King Ahasuerus, the children of Israel (mentioned twice), the Temple of Solomon, the prophet Elijah (twice), Tobias (twice), Noah's Ark, and the death of Rachel.[90] Jean Cardoso clearly preferred secular paintings and Aron Querido biblical ones. In the cursory notation typical of inventories, Cardoso's paintings are listed as: kitchen, ships, *straatsvaarder* (a ship used in Mediterranean traffic) attacking Turkish galleys, battle or raid of soldiers, Noah's Ark, pagan sacrifice (by Van Campen), Bacchus, old man and woman with glasses, *zeetge* [seascape] *van Percellus*, horseman (by Jan Baptist Weenix), fruit, landscape with woman and horse, horseman shot from his horse, lute-player, battle, Rachel dying, night, portrait of the deceased, rooster, sea with ship, landscape, man pushing, *vrouwtroonje* [woman's face], battle, (portrait) girl, girl, (portrait) woman, homestead of the deceased, fire, *zeetge van Percellus*, farmer drying tobacco, pub (by Brouwer), siege of Naerden, castle, farmyard, . . . a large painting of Tobias, and a painting over the mantelpiece of the prophet Elijah. Querido, on the other hand, possessed 'a painting of the Red Sea; of Abraham and Hagar; of Moses; another of Abraham and Hagar; of Abraham and Lot; of Abraham and the

---

[88] There are some indications that Amsterdam's Portuguese Jews continued to keep abreast of intellectual developments in the Iberian peninsula. Thus we find among the books in the library of Aron Colaso senior, in 1783, many of the works of Fray Benito Jerónimo Feijóo; see Pieterse, 'Abraham Lopes Colaso', 56.

[89] E. Samuel, 'Disposal of Diego Duarte's Stock of Paintings'.

[90] GAA, NA 2261A, p. 505 (26 Mar. 1654; A. Lock); NA 2261B, p. 844 (11 July 1661; A. Lock); NA 2261B, pp. 952–1007 (9 May 1661; A. Lock).

angels; of Solomon's judgement; of King Balthasar; of the meeting of Jacob
and Esau; of Absalom; of Abigail; of Abraham's sacrifice; of Rebecca; of the Ten
Commandments; of Queen Esther; another of Queen Esther; a portrait of a
woman'.[91] Either, of course, may have been inspired by contemporary examples—
Cardoso by secular Dutchmen, Querido by more devout ones. For want of more
inventories it is not clear in which collection the majority of Portuguese Jews
would have felt better at home.

As we have learned from other sources, confirmed by various inventories,
Amsterdam's Portuguese Jews had no objection to having their portraits painted.
We even possess portraits of the Hahamim Menasseh ben Israel, Ishac Aboab, and
Jacob Sasportas.[92] That of Menasseh ben Israel was drawn by a Portuguese Jewish
painter, Salom Italia (notwithstanding his name, originally from Castelo Branco in
Portugal), who lived in Amsterdam during the 1640s. Another Portuguese Jew,
Moseh Belmonte, drew an amateurish portrait of his mother.[93] Amsterdam's
Portuguese Jews clearly adhered to the 'liberal' interpretation of the second com-
mandment that linked the prohibition against representational art directly and
solely to idolatry.

They displayed the same liberality when it came to ornamenting their gravestones. Quite a few of the marble stones at the Bet aHaim of Ouderkerk are embel-
lished with bas- or haut-reliefs, mostly of biblical scenes appropriate to the name of
the deceased. For instance, the gravestone of Ribca (d. 1694), wife of Semuel Levy
Ximenes, depicts Rebecca coming to the well to draw water for herself and her
camels. The gravestone of Samuel Senior Teixeira (d. 1717) portrays Samuel's
vision in the Temple, including a depiction of God—the only such depiction in all
of Jewish art! That of his wife, Rachel Teixeira de Mattos (d. 1716), shows Rachel
dying at the time of Benjamin's birth. The sumptuous gravestone of Mosseh de
Mordecay Senior (d. 1730) represents no fewer than eleven scenes, among which
are Moses with the two stone tablets and Mordechay on horseback.[94] Unlike the
painted portraits, the sculpted gravestones represent only a passing vogue, from
the very end of the seventeenth century through the first three or four decades of
the eighteenth. Only relatively few of the wealthiest Portuguese Jews indulged in
these extravagant burial monuments. The portraits were a European phenomenon
and were generally painted by Dutch artists; the gravestones resemble those from
southern Europe and were probably imported from Italy. The gravestones with
their biblical representations are, perhaps, laden with more possible meanings than
most other contemporary cultural expressions of Amsterdam's Portuguese Jews.
They reveal wealth and conspicuous consumption, and coincide with the aristoc-

---

[91] GAA, NA 2261B, pp. 952–1007 (9 May 1661; A. Lock).

[92] Reproductions of these portraits may be found in Gans, *Memorboek*, 40, 73, 99, 100. On Salom
Italia, see da Silva Rosa, 'Salom Italia'.   [93] Gans, *Memorboek*, 31.

[94] Examples of these gravestones are reproduced in Gans, *Memorboek*, 124–5, 127; and (with much
clearer photographs) Alvares Vega, *Beth Haim*, esp. 37, 40–1, 45, 48, 50, 54.

ratization of the community. They are associated with the Iberian past and may reflect a third-generation nostalgia for the land of origin. Their biblical figures may be read as Jewish variants of the Christian patron saint and reveal a predilection for private familial devotions. The biblical themes recall the biblical dimensions of the *nação* and are in their religious unorthodoxy emblems of Jewish ethnic awareness. No single one of these meanings truly recommends itself more strongly than another. Together they symbolize the multifarious facets of Portuguese Jewish history.

CULTURAL CONSERVATISMS, EXORCISMS, AND FLIRTATIONS

Two different aspects of Portuguese Jewish culture stand out and yet need to be underscored. First, there is the widespread and wholesale retention of Iberian culture; second, the simultaneous flirtations, often in one and the same person, with 'rationalism' and 'mysticism'.

If a culture is to survive on foreign soil, it needs a community that has attained a certain critical mass, that is more or less isolated from the rest of society by one barrier or another, and that is relatively self-sufficient socially and economically. In the early modern period migrations of sizeable numbers of people who continued to function in 'exile' as a more or less cohesive unit, though cut off in unnatural ways from their roots, were relatively rare. Apart from the much smaller and far more utilitarian and temporary settlements of foreign merchants, who were moreover in constant touch with their home country and frequently travelled back and forth, only the Huguenots and the Jews—Portuguese, German, and Polish—fit the bill. In the modern era migrations have become far more commonplace. At the same time, what were once more or less natural forces of acculturation turned into politically and socially charged pressures, from both within and without, to assimilate. We have as a result become simultaneously much more familiar with and less understanding of the cultural dynamics of earlier migrations. Hence the great surprise, until the most recent past, of many Jewish historians at the retention of so much Iberian culture by these Portuguese and Spanish New Christian/Jewish refugees.

As marvel gave way to observation, the first order of business was to inventorize, dispassionately, the various manifestations of Iberian culture retained by the first and later generations of Portuguese Jews. 'A treasure-house of values and concepts' or 'cultural baggage' are now the far more positive descriptions of the cultural conservatism exhibited in the continued use of Iberian ideas and modes of expression after settlement in Amsterdam. Yet 'treasure-house' and 'baggage'— and even 'conservatism'—may still mislead, perhaps, in suggesting too passive an attitude on the part of the Portuguese Jews. For, approaching the matter more analytically, the first thing one notices is that not all retentions are of one and the same sort.

Some of it no doubt was passive. But even among the purely passive retentions there are distinctly different forms. Where no conflict existed between inherited Iberian culture and Jewish modes of thought, perception, or action, continued use of the Iberian form posed no problem and depended basically on personal predilections, as in the adoption of a Spanish or Portuguese or Hebrew or Dutch name, and social appropriateness. On occasion the religious leaders defined appropriateness differently from the congregation, as when they forbade theatrical performances in the Esnoga, took umbrage at the shaving practices of the *yehidim*, or tried to restrain the exuberance of public celebrations. Clearly, where a particular Iberian model served a familial function, *yehidim* were slow to yield to the strictures of their communal leadership. The importance of the public processions accompanying the Hatan Torah or Hatan Bereshit was so great that no number of warnings succeeded in curbing the practice. In the end, whether such practices made sense within a Dutch context probably influenced their survival rate more than the raising of rabbinic eyebrows.

Patterns of thought are sometimes relatively easy to eradicate, at other times more difficult. Philosophical doctrines once learned at a Catholic university are not easily translated into Jewish terms, even if their basic positions are quite similar or even identical. Ideas cannot simply be abstracted from their previous context. They are often part of the ideational infrastructure of consciousness. Additionally and more importantly, the vast majority of Portuguese Jews did not in the least feel that their return to Judaism called for a radical overhaul of consciousness. Whether crypto-Judaism is a myth or a reality, most Portuguese Jews viewed themselves as, in some form or other, continuing a Jewish tradition. Paradoxically, perhaps, the stress on this Jewish continuity laid the groundwork for the Iberian cultural conservatism that seemed at first glance so contradictory. Ishac Orobio de Castro's turning to Augustine to defend his belief in the freedom of the will, for example, triggered no alarms, because, in his own mind, his Augustianism and his Judaism had always existed side by side before his return to Judaism. On the other hand, as Abraham Pereyra plagiarized Christian authors he cautiously purged the texts he 'borrowed' of their specifically Christian content.[95] Apparently he believed that the moral teachings he sought to recommend to his Jewish audience transcended religious differences. His use of Iberian models betrays, at best, a blindness to the real differences between the ethics of two similar, but different religious traditions, at worst, a laziness or haste perhaps induced by the Sabbatean expectations Pereyra so heartily embraced. As we might say today, Abraham Pereyra got away with it because of the pervasively permissive atmosphere created by the widespread retention of Iberian social models and the belief in the continuity from crypto-Judaism to Judaism that also characterized Orobio's Christian usages.

---

[95] Van Praag, *Gespleten zielen*; Kaplan, *From Christianity to Judaism*, 323.

Many of these purely passive retentions disappeared quite naturally. Christian authors ceased to be part of the educational diet. And with them, for better or worse, we might add parenthetically, Portuguese Jewish forays into philosophy died. For, however widely praised the school system of the Kahal may have been, it was never intended to go beyond the equivalent of high school, so that future generations of Portuguese Jews rarely proceeded beyond that initial level in their introduction to philosophy. And although Dutch universities were open to Jewish enrolment, Portuguese Jews availed themselves of that educational opportunity only to pursue a medical career, now defined more narrowly than in the scholastic-ally inspired curricula of Iberian universities.

Amsterdam's Portuguese Jews clearly went beyond the various passive forms of Iberian cultural retention. Their dogged linguistic conservatism, in particular, required substantial effort to maintain. At a minimum, it forced every member of the community to become bilingual. The German and Polish Jewish communities continued throughout the eighteenth century to grow, and large segments of their populations who never ventured outside the Jewish quarter could get by with one language only. The Portuguese Jewish community never had that luxury. Its num-bers were never large enough to allow them to isolate themselves from the rest of society and, if anything, declined in the course of the next century. But Portuguese (or some hybridized form of Spanish–Portuguese) played such a vital role in shoring up familial and religious attachments—and the boundaries between these two spheres were kept so intentionally vague that the two reinforced one another—that the 'hardship' of bilingualism appeared but a small price to pay. Ironically, there exists an unmistakable parallel between this continued use of Portuguese in the diaspora and the erstwhile, imagined or real, preservation of Jewish customs in Portugal and Spain. If in the past the stigma of New Christianhood had come to define their uniqueness, the only way to preserve the sense of that uniqueness now was through the continued use of Portuguese as the language of intra-familial and intra-communal communication, through acts and decisions of active con-servatism.

There exists yet another class of Iberian cultural retentions. The theatrical creations represented by the *Dialogo dos montes* and *Contra la verdad no hay fuerza*, the literary academies organized by the Baron de Belmonte, and the richly ornate gravestones of the very wealthy represent, it seems to me, something more than an indulgence of an unquenchable Iberian taste. To view the academies and the gravestones as manifestations that slipped past rabbinic censorship because of the great wealth and power of those who indulged in their sponsorship misses, per-haps, an important insight. Are we simply and repeatedly drawn to contemplate these examples because they are so rare in Jewish history, because they are so strikingly at odds with Jewish sensibilities as defined by central and eastern European traditions, or because they exude a real originality, a palpable vitality that less creative emulations of Iberian models lack? *Poser la question* . . . Each of these cultural expressions lies on the sensitive fault-line between the personal and the social, where private Iberian desires ran into communal Jewish censure. The resultant creations are more than a surrender to Iberian urges; they are truly creative resolutions. As many writers are wont to say, the ultimate wellspring of creativity resides in the desire or need to rid oneself of inner demons or to repair a personal hurt. The gravestones, plays, and academic exercises have all the hall-marks of such exorcism. If they all bear unmistakably and quintessentially Iberian imprints, the gravestones and plays none the less succeed in expressing vital aspects of Judaism as experienced by Amsterdam's Portuguese Jews: the biblical past and Jewish hopes in the face of martyrdom. The first redeems the relative absence of a Jewish past, the second the loss of a homeland which most Portuguese New Christians would rather not have quit.[96]

The Sabbatean enthusiasm that swept the community off its feet in 1666–7 arguably represents another such creative, exorcising moment in the history of Amsterdam's Portuguese Jews. All too often the susceptibility of Amsterdam's level-headed, rationalistic Jews to the pretensions of a false messiah is interpreted in purely Jewish instead of Iberian terms. Shabbetai Zevi offered, so it is argued, two important ointments for the wounded spirits of erstwhile New Christians: a confirmation that their rejection of the messiahship of Jesus had been correct and a chance to redeem the sins of their past through penitential prayer and fasts.[97] But penitential fasts were a very Iberian Catholic phenomenon, that had already been favoured by New Christians with Jewish loyalties. Fasting means rejection: for a Catholic, a renunciation of the lures of worldly existence, for a Judaizing New Christian, a renunciation of Catholicism. The fasting of Judaizers had the added advantage that it was often undetectable. Whether or not Judaizers were aware of the ironic beauty of their act remains doubtful. But when Shabbetai Zevi called again for fasting as a means to redemption it touched a responsive Iberian chord that had found scant acknowledgement and few outlets since the re-conversion to

[96] On the relative absence of a Jewish past, see Swetschinski, 'Un refus de mémoire'.

[97] Scholem, *Sabbatai Sevi*, 464–7, lists five factors: (1) that the messianic call came from the Holy Land; (2) that the messianic manifestation was accompanied by a renewal of prophecy; (3) that the message combined traditional apocalyptic elements as well as their kabbalistic reinterpretation; (4) that the prophet called for repentance; and (5) that the messianic tide engulfed the whole people, without differentiation. Elsewhere (pp. 485–6) Scholem remarks: 'Yet the fact remains that in the great centers of former marranos (Salonika, Leghorn, Amsterdam, Hamburg, to name only the most important), the Sabbatian gospel was eagerly received; it evidently struck a chord in the hearts of those who had themselves, or whose parents had, been through the misery of a life of forced hypocrisy and dissimulation in Spain and Portugal. There was not a little of the desire to atone for their Christian past in the messianic enthusiasm of the marranos, for although their conscious attitude was anti-Christian, the Sabbatian awakening provided them with a Jewish and hence "legitimate" equivalent of the devout messianic fervor which they had known in their Spanish youth.' If I understand the convoluted syntax of the last sentence correctly, Scholem recognizes an Iberian dimension in the displacement of devout messianic fervour from Jesus to Shabbetai Zevi. I do not recognize, in any of the sources with which I am familiar, echoes—conscious or otherwise—of devout Christian messianic fervour, but I do find many traces of a preoccupation with asceticism, even before the advent of Shabbetai Zevi.

Judaism, other than in the reading of the ascetic writings of Bahya ibn Paquda and the penitential treatise of Maimonides.

Of course, precisely because something appears so irrational it becomes inaccessible to rational control. But there would seem to be something more behind the surrender to Sabbateanism by such enthusiasts as the practical merchant Abraham Pereyra and the scientifically inclined Haham Selomoh de Oliveyra—to name but two famous examples. Abraham Pereyra could not have become as wealthy as he did without a large dose of practical common sense, and Haham Selomoh de Oliveyra is best known for a number of publications of biblical scholarship on such non-religious topics as rhyme and metre and the like. Two very different examples may be cited to confirm the same mentality. Earlier in the century, Abraham Cohen Herrera had written two treatises outlining the principles of Lurianic kabbalah in Neoplatonic terms. It was an attempt to demonstrate the congruence of the Jewish mystical tradition with an important European philosophical, 'rational' tradition. The Cambridge Neoplatonists similarly saw in the Jewish mystical tradition a means to bridge the gap between faith and reason. In the writings of Ishac Orobio de Castro, one encounters elements of both scholasticism and fideistic scepticism.[98] The simultaneous flirtation with rationalism and mysticism appears to be a widespread characteristic of Portuguese Jewish culture. It, too, was to some degree an Iberian transplant—or, more plausibly yet, another Iberian Christian propensity which, like the example of fasting, served the New Christians especially well in their efforts to contemplate two religious traditions simultaneously and forge the necessary modicum of peaceful co-existence between them. Transplanted to Amsterdam, it continued to give rise to various ruminations on the subject of Jewish–Christian reconciliation, whether in the form of mutual respect or a common messianic future, or, as in Spinoza, an *amor dei intellectualis* that transcends any and all religious differences. The faith in such a possibility carried Amsterdam's Portuguese Jews further towards a cosmopolitan ideal than either their Iberian classmates or their Jewish co-religionists of the time were able, willing, or daring enough to project.

[98] Kaplan, *From Christianity to Judaism*, 313–22.

CONCLUSION

RELUCTANT COSMOPOLITANS
Jewish Ethnicity in statu renascendi

> Tradition is not something a man can learn; not a thread he can pick up when he feels like it; any more than a man can choose his own ancestors. Someone lacking a tradition who would like to have one is like a man unhappily in love.
>
> LUDWIG WITTGENSTEIN

> It is the natural condition of exile, putting down roots in memory.
>
> SALMAN RUSHDIE

> Arriving at each new city, the traveller finds again a past of his that he did not know he had: the foreignness of what you no longer are or no longer possess lies in wait for you in foreign, unpossessed places.
>
> ITALO CALVINO

To everyone but themselves, it would seem, the Portuguese Jews of seventeenth-century Amsterdam were living a contradiction—or alternatively, representing trends of which they were naturally unaware, and which they might not have favoured. These two perspectives, no doubt, underlie the 'strangeness' experienced by historians of an earlier generation in approaching the Portuguese Jews of the early modern era.

The most blatant contradiction—reiterated more frequently than any other—was summarized most famously in Gebhardt's pithy phrase: 'The Marrano is a Catholic without faith and a Jew without knowledge, but a Jew by will.'[1] Some took the view that the loss of Catholic faith served to undermine subsequently any and all forms of faith, including the one to which the Marranos aspired, and that the lack of Jewish knowledge may conveniently hold the key to all manner of erratic or curious behaviour. And yet actual evidence for the difficulties Amsterdam's Portuguese Jews—or even the previous generation of Marranos—felt in living with a so-called split conscience is difficult to come by. Either they were unaware that a particular opinion on any issue was more attuned to Catholic traditions than Jewish ones, or they thought the splitting of opinions into separate traditions unnatural or meaningless. Even in the criticism of Daniel Levi de Barrios' latitudinarianism the emphasis was entirely on flagrant misappropriations of Catholic

---

[1] Gebhardt, *Schriften des Uriel da Costa*, p. xix.

imagery or attributions. The critics were more concerned about public impropriety than about any alleged exhibition of 'false consciousness'. The divided
national loyalties of the Portuguese Jews are another 'hidden yet apparent' contradiction occasionally brought into play to illuminate actions that seem foreign to our
modern view. But the distinction made by the Portuguese Jews between a hatred
of the Inquisition and all it stood for and a general appreciation for the secular
authorities and Iberian culture in general was not a mask covering an irresolvable
deeper tension. Seventeenth-century merchants did not generally think in terms
so nationalistic as to exercise an overriding influence on individual commercial
decisions. Whether or not a given action profited one government or another was
usually a secondary consideration at a time when the role of national governments
in local and international economies had barely begun to make itself felt. The
notion that as new immigrants the Portuguese Jews were held or held themselves
to a higher standard of national loyalty than applied to native Dutchmen would not
have occurred to a seventeenth-century merchant or official. Even the earl of
Shrewsbury spoke in 1690 of the 'advantage' the London Jews might expect from
making 'suitable returns of affection and gratitude for the kindness they have
received', when pressing them to lend more money to a Portuguese Jewish army
purveyor enlisted in the English campaigns in Ireland.[2] He viewed the possibility
as a concrete *quid pro quo*, not in the abstract terms of modern nationalism. Nor is
there any evidence that the Portuguese Jews sensed any conflict between their non-
religious Iberian culture and that of Holland. They happily retained much of the
first and borrowed from the latter as they saw fit, without misgivings about its
appropriateness. No doubt, Amsterdam's Portuguese Jews, as well as others of the
early modern era, often experienced within one life-span two distinct and in some
respects antagonistic religious traditions, lived under the authority of two or more
often hostile governments, and had been forced to make themselves at home as
best they could in a variety of cultures. Yet, more often than not, the tensions
engendered by these changes were resolved quite smoothly and gave rise to no
apparent psychological trauma nor to repressed undercurrents of social pathology.

As mentioned in the Introduction, the effort to identify the Portuguese Jews of
seventeenth-century Amsterdam as the first modern Jews has a venerable pedi-
gree; and it has been lent particular force through having initially been made by the
other 'first modern Jews' themselves—Moses Mendelssohn and his contemporaries. Yet the unambiguous and unapologetic openness to secular culture and
political assertiveness that these German Jews praised and sought to emulate can
only be seen as a natural and unavoidable outgrowth of their previous lives as
Marranos. If, therefore, one wishes to retain the view of the Portuguese Jews as
the first modern Jews, one must acknowledge the unexemplary nature of what was,
in the first instance, a historical fluke and, as such, both inimitable and of very limited analytical value. Jitzhak Baer saw in Amsterdam's Portuguese Jews the first

---

[2] As cited in Ch. 3 above, pp. 139–40.

sign of a break with traditional Jewish historical consciousness. At the very end of the seventeenth century Moses Hagiz, a *shaliaḥ* (envoy) from Palestine, reported that many of Holland's Portuguese Jews were quite comfortable living in the *golah* (exile, that is, the historical reality), no longer regarded *galut* (exile, the metahistorical principle) as divine punishment, and interpreted the messianic call for the return of the Jews to the Holy Land as intended for the poor alone.[3] In a similar vein Jacques Bernard, the editor of the *Nouvelles de la République des Lettres*, mentioned in 1707 in passing how a very wealthy Jew, in a conversation about the Messiah and the return of his nation to the land of Canaan, had responded 'that, as far as he was concerned, he would not be so foolish [*assez fou*] as to leave Holland where he lived very well [*il se trouvoit fort bien*] in order to go to Judea where he would certainly not be as comfortable [*si à son aise*]'.[4] Baer saw these radical changes as essentially a product of the new rationalism ingested in liberal Holland and England and explicitly steered clear of drawing a parallel with the scepticisms of Uriel da Costa and Spinoza which had their roots in native Marrano traditions or experiences. In failing to recognize the change in historical consciousness as the outcome of an internal dynamic, Baer repeated a common mistake of his generation and missed an opportunity to reveal a truly distinctive feature of Portuguese Jewish history.

Paradoxically, the contradictions that were there have been ignored, and the first hints of a peculiarly Jewish modernity overlooked: the first because they belonged to a sphere somewhere between concrete everyday historical reality and modern metahistorical abstractions, the latter because it flew in the face of the aspirations of most modern Jews. The advantages that any kind of 'split soul'— Gebhardt used the term *Bewußtsein*—may have brought are almost totally ignored. On the most mundane level, an ability to present oneself in any number of guises created opportunities in smuggling in an era in which embargoes and monopolies were common occurrences, especially in the Iberian world. Both in trade between Holland and the Iberian peninsula and in the interloping trade in Spanish and Portuguese America, the Portuguese Jews enjoyed an inestimable advantage that propelled them into a prominence far beyond their numbers. Similarly, the diplomatic successes of Don Manuel de Belmonte, Jeronimo Nunes da Costa, and, especially, Antonio Lopes Suasso, Baron d'Avernas-le-Gras, owed almost everything to their ability to function in very different, often hostile cultural environments. The example of Antonio and Francisco Lopes Suasso, moreover, illustrates the even greater heights that could be attained when former enemies decide to act in concert. The benefits of biculturalism were obviously not restricted to situations of antagonism. Another creative application of cultural traits acquired in one life and deployed in another may even have contributed to the prominence of the Portuguese Jews in stock trading. For even if Joseph Penso de la Vega had not relished the comparison between stock trading and gambling as

---

[3] Baer, *Galut* (Eng. edn.), 112–14.   [4] *Nouvelles*, juillet–décembre 1707, 274.

much as he did, we would have understood—albeit not without some discomfort—the link between a newly developing Dutch innovation and what was an often-remarked cultural Portuguese trait. And, in the final analysis, the wealth and status generated by 'illegal' trading practices, participation in international political negotiations, and an advanced understanding of the dynamics of the Amsterdam stock exchange did much to call forth the special attention lavished on the Kahal Kados de Talmud Tora of seventeenth-century Amsterdam. It is ironic that, at least in my analysis, the conflicts to explain which the notion of a split soul was most often invoked were themselves more probably a by-product of the social tensions resulting from the great disparity of wealth that came to characterize the Amsterdam community more strongly than any other. Even de Barrios' latitudinarianism would have remained without expression but for the relative abundance of patrons. To reiterate: it makes no sense to posit all manner of split souls/ identities/personalities or 'psychocultural' problems when the historical persons in question themselves give so little direct or even indirect evidence of having suffered from their alleged 'splitness'—unless every conflict be judged *ipso facto* a sign of the presence of at least one troubled soul.[5] Especially not if such an analysis stands in the way of acknowledging the trauma, if it may be so called temporarily for the sake of this argument, that actually did occur.

RELIVING MEMORIES

> . . . one memory
> Certainly hides another, that being what memory is all about,
> The eternal reverse succession of contemplated entities.
>
> KENNETH KOCH

Somewhere in the welter of surprises elicited by Amsterdam's Portuguese Jews, one of the more obvious ones remains unstated, as far as I know. How is it that the descendants of New Christians—who had immersed themselves almost totally in non-Jewish culture and society, who had at best but a very rudimentary knowledge and understanding of Judaism—came to act so much like Jews; so naturally, indeed, that to Moses Mendelssohn and his generation and many thereafter they could even be considered in some sense exemplary? It is a tricky, even awkward question, and one to which I have no ready answer. If it were not already too fashionable, I might have preferred to view the Portuguese Jews as a group *sui*

---

[5] In the first volume of *Spinoza and Other Heretics* Yovel details, all too eloquently, the psychocultural dimensions of the Marrano soul/mind, all on the basis, essentially, of his exposition of one single play by an author of uncertain Marrano loyalties. Poetry undoubtedly has a place in history. The flights of Yovel's poetic fancy, however, do nothing but manipulate the very real physical and psychological pain as well as the excitement of creative subterfuges experienced, in innumerable varieties of intensity and self-consciousness, by the Marranos. Yovel's psychocultural findings are, in some sense, reminiscent of the very recent 'discoveries' of multiple incidences of child abuse by so-called experts. The well-trained eye must always guard against seeing too much.

generis—one to whom the problematics of Jewish history do not apply and in whom we do not need to seek the roots of patterns that will characterize their historically very different brethren elsewhere in subsequent stages of their development. Yet I can divest myself no more than any other Jewish historian of the very real sense that the Portuguese Jews lived the constraints and possibilities of Jewish history as richly as any other Jews and that the creative solutions they forged are, therefore, as valid *exempla iudeae vitae* as any. Hence I cannot resist emphasizing one particular element in their spiritual evolution whose significance, if my interpretation is correct, transcends the *sui generis* confines of New Christian and Portuguese Jewish history.

Of all the possible ruptures or contradictions to be selected, one stands out as having been passed over hitherto in almost complete silence. For notwithstanding all the talk of the loss or renewal of the ancestral Jewish traditions, no one speaks of what the migration from the Iberian peninsula to Holland and the conversion from Roman Catholicism to Judaism, not to mention a host of other more personal traumas, did to the memory of these Portuguese Jews. Just as positivistically as Gebhardt was able to define his actors in terms of faith, will, and knowledge, so certain are we, despite our general state of confusion, that memory plays a crucial role in human life—both individual and social—and particularly in the formation of that sense of identity that is so glibly posited as having been the most existentially urgent and socially significant issue in Portuguese Jewish history and at the crux of many a contentious matter. All too often memory means little more than the reservoir of accumulated traces or imprints of past events: entirely passive, devoid of a dynamic of its own. Yet it is in grasping the peculiarity of Portuguese Jewish memory that we will begin fully to sense—almost concretely, as we will see—the contours of their quest for identity. Surprisingly, we may discover this memory to be a close cousin of Gebhardt's will; for there exists, in some respect, such a profound link between hope and memory that neither should be studied independently of the other. And in the end, out of the seemingly unusual course of Portuguese Jewish memory, we can—'by a double process of repetition', to quote Sir Lewis Namier's epigraph to the Introduction—rescue the possibility of an insight into their modernity.

Paradoxically, it was much less the loss of the memory of Jewish traditions than the rejection of the memory of their Marrano past that helped define the Portuguese Jews of seventeenth-century Amsterdam.[6] For it must strike one as a little odd—or counter-intuitive, in the current phrase—that so few Portuguese Jews made any personal references to their Marrano past; and odder yet (and confirming the pattern) that one of the two autobiographical manuscripts that we have comes from an Old Christian who converted to Judaism in Amsterdam in the wake of several geographical and spiritual peregrinations.[7] The other memoir we owe to

---

[6] The following re-works in the main the ideas formulated in Swetschinski, 'Refus de mémoire'.

[7] Teensma, 'Levensgeschiedenis van Abraham Perengrino'.

the very wealthy Ishac de Pinto, who set down family traditions and personal recollections, mostly extolling the social and economic successes of his ancestors, in 1671 (or shortly thereafter) for internal consumption within his 'clan'.[8] Otherwise we are left with stray references in the occasional poetry of Daniel Levi de Barrios and the oft-cited, pious generalizations of Abraham Pereyra in his ethical treatises that do more to obscure than to reveal the ambiguities of the (and his) Marrano past—and, I suspect, were in some sense intended to do so.[9] All in all, it is a surprisingly meagre harvest for a group of people who had undergone such a tumultuous past. I see the paucity of autobiographical revelations as a sign, perhaps, of repression of past nightmarish traumas—or, more likely, of an inability to forge out of the great diversity of very personal memories a collective memory. The manner in which any given individual or family had made his or her or its religious accommodations while still under the authority of the Church was so particular, so personal, as to preclude any sharing beyond the closest of relatives or friends. And memories that cannot be shared tend to fade or recede into the background.[10] Additionally, the Portuguese Jews remained loyal to their Iberian culture to a surprisingly large extent and for a surprisingly long time.[11] The refusal of the Marrano past was clearly not simply part and parcel of a larger process of cutting any and all ties with the past. The spiritual transformation entailed not only a jettisoning of certain parts of the past and a retention of others, it also involved the adoption of new elements. For, in the absence of a collective religious past, the Portuguese Jews resorted to a 'renaissance' of their biblical heritage, as it were. They identified themselves far more directly and far more concretely with their biblical ancestors than is common in Jewish communities already accustomed to accord to the Bible and its heroes a place of special honour.

Amsterdam's Portuguese Jews saw their return to Judaism not simply as a

[8] Salomon, ' "De Pinto" Manuscript'. It seems to me that Ishac may have been motivated to write down these recollections at a time when he had risen to a very prominent position within the Kahal Kados as chairman of the committee in charge of the financing of the new Esnoga—a prominence he greatly relished, judging by the list of honorary posts in the community with which he ends the manuscript. Perhaps typically, he makes no great show of the de Pinto family's Jewish loyalties through several generations; but he does firmly establish his descent from one Rodrigo Alvares Pinto—'This gentleman was a native of Spain,' states the opening sentence—who himself or through his father, we learn later, 'was converted in adulthood to Christianity, but there is no information about anything of this sort'. Antiquity and nobility rank higher than religious matters.

[9] See Pereyra's *La certeza del camino* (Amsterdam, 1666) and *Espejo de la vanidad del mundo* (Amsterdam, 1672). These works have been the subject of several studies by Henry Méchoulan: 'Abraham Pereyra, juge des marranes'; 'La Pensée d'Abraham Pereyra'; and *Hispanidad y judaísmo*, which is also an annotated edition of *La certeza del camino*. Unfortunately the many questions regarding the gap between the Pereyra of these writings and the Pereyra known from other sources remain unanswered. They must none the less make one pause before taking the sincerity of the writings at face value.

[10] The entire thrust of Maurice Halbwachs's two books on the subject of collective memory is to stress the primary importance of sharing in memory altogether, not merely in collective memory.

[11] For details see Kaplan, 'On the Relation of Spinoza's Contemporaries', and Ch. 6 above.

continuation of a tie temporarily interrupted, but clearly as a new beginning. They adopted the names of the patriarchs to underscore their sense of opening a new chapter. The oldest male or the first one in the family to convert to Judaism adopted the name of Abraham, and so on down the line. Even in the imaginary dialogues describing the process of religious conversion, not only did they prefer to invoke the biblical example of Abraham, but also they did not hide the rupture with the past this action represented.[12] Nowhere, perhaps, is this sense of a new beginning thrown into sharper relief than in the story of the refugees blown off course and forced to land in Emden. For in that story, by the simple application of a biblical frame, the author compared the settlement of the New Christians in Amsterdam to the exodus from Egypt. We may recall how, after the refugees made contact with Moses Uri Halevi, it was his son Aron who spoke with them and not Moses himself, because Moses (so the author alleges) did not know any Spanish. This parallels strikingly the biblical story where Moses at first refuses to tell the people that God has appeared to him, saying: 'I have never been a man of ready speech . . . I am slow and hesitant of speech' (Exod. 4: 10), whereupon God responds: 'Have you not a brother, Aaron the Levite? . . . He will do all the speaking to the people for you, he will be the mouthpiece' (4: 14, 16); and where, finally, after Aaron has told the people everything: 'They heard that the Lord had shown his concern for the Israelites and seen their misery' (4: 31). The adoption of a biblical frame not only demonstrates how naturally the identification with the biblical past was made; it is here employed directly to transform an otherwise mundane memory into the story of the birth of a new people.

In other instances the Portuguese Jews of Amsterdam made their identification with the biblical past even more concrete. In the building of the new Esnoga, completed in 1675, the communal elders allowed their design to be inspired by the miniature model of the Jerusalem Temple that one of the teachers of the Kahal, Jacob Jeuda Leon 'Templo', had built and about which he had published a pamphlet.[13] Biblical motifs are certainly not new in synagogue architecture.[14] In other cases, though, the association is more or less intentionally kept at the symbolic level, whereas in the Amsterdam Esnoga the Portuguese Jews created a truly biblical locus, a place that literally embodied their identification with the Hebrew Bible. Elsewhere, in the cemetery, certain very wealthy Portuguese Jews at the end of the seventeenth century allowed themselves to be carried away by their enthusiasm and covered their grave sites with elaborate stones on which were carved, in bas-relief, depictions of biblical scenes often associated with the biblical namesake of the person buried there.[15] Thus they gave another expression to their

[12] Wilke, 'Conversion ou retour?'
[13] Rosenau, 'Jacob Judah Leon Templo's Contribution'; Offenberg, 'Jacob Jehuda Leon'.
[14] Krinsky, *Synagogues of Europe*, 7–9.
[15] Photographs of these and other gravestones may be found in Henriques de Castro, *Keur van grafstenen*, and Alvares Vega, *Beth Haim*.

pride in being the descendants of biblical heroes. Here again it is misleading to view these sculptured stones, as Yovel does, as another manifestation of the split soul.[16] On the contrary, they exhibit, it seems to me, a rather strong and healthy urge to overcome spiritual wounds. It is in the very concreteness of these manifestations of biblical identification, as well as their appearance at strategic points—concerning the 'face' they put on to the world—both public and private that we must recognize the true significance of these actions, which are too readily dismissed as of little more than folkloric interest. Halbwachs has shown how memory attaches itself to place more readily than to time.[17] The Esnoga as well as the gravestones must be considered 'place' aids or empirical spaces for memories to dwell in, so to speak, as the Portuguese Jews used the common heritage of the biblical past—with which, of course, they had no spatial associations—to replace a Marrano past they could not share.

The Portuguese Jews of seventeenth-century Amsterdam concentrated their intellectual creativity principally in two distinct areas: in the refutation of Christianity and in the elucidation of the Bible—areas in which they chose to define their identity as no longer being Christians and as descended from the deceptively familiar, yet entirely foreign, personages of the Bible. Such was the depth of their identity crisis. In many of these biblical explorations, moreover, we may recognize the striking theme of a desire for a world of greater religious harmony. Uriel da Costa expressed his wish for a simpler, a more direct road to salvation. Menasseh ben Israel entertained the hope of resolving contradictions and putting an end to religious disputes, between individuals as between religions. Spinoza explored the possibilities of a more truly ethical existence, inspired by a religion freed of its temporal powers. And Daniel Levi de Barrios straightforwardly entitled his poetic rendition of the Bible *Harmonia del mundo*. The hopes of religious harmony echoed in their writings most certainly did not arise from the conflicts these authors experienced within the Portuguese Jewish community. These hopes are too universal, almost too ecumenical, for that. More likely they ante-dated the conversion to Judaism or the conflict with the community's leaders, and reflect visions of the future as entertained by New Christians, for whom nothing was more odious than the intolerance of a religion unwaveringly and oppressively convinced of its own truth. Memories of the Marrano past thus come through in these optimistic aspirations towards a harmonious future more clearly than in the pious generalizations of Abraham Pereyra—only to confirm Sir Lewis Namier's dictum about an imagined past and a remembered future.

There is, in the final analysis, something unexpectedly Jewish and modern in these two simultaneous endeavours: the universalist, 'cosmopolitan' striving towards religious or ethical harmony and the more particularistic, 'reluctant' definition of a Portuguese Jewish identity. The latter especially, it seems to me,

[16] Yovel, 'Marranisme et dissidence', 78.
[17] Halbwachs, *The Collective Memory*, ch. 4, 'Space and the Collective Memory'.

deserves to be stressed as the hallmark of Portuguese Jewish modernity. For in mobilizing the biblical past to support a contemporary social identity, the Portuguese Jews, in essence, created anew an ethnic identity neither Iberian nor Jewish; a hybrid identity in which the fusion of disparate religious and cultural elements occurred after the original union was given up as too ambivalent to be shared and as offering, moreover, no simple continuity, religious or other, from past to present. In other circumstances we can easily imagine the creation of an ethnic identity occurring for different reasons, although perhaps always in some sense because of important memories that cannot be shared. Ethnicity, if the Portuguese Jews are to serve as our example, most certainly—as every essay on the subject will underscore—involves shared memories; but these are invented memories, not actual ones, for the latter cannot be shared. And this ethnicity, based on the invention of shared memories, makes the social bond at once closer, in actually requiring the participants to contribute to its maintenance, and looser, in not offering the safeguards of primordiality beyond the immediate family to which one belongs. This is not the place to ask whether all ethnicities are of this configuration or whether the Portuguese Jewish version is only one type among several. Regardless of the answer to that question, it is clear that not all ethnic Jews must be seen as retaining inert elements from the past, simply because it is in the nature of inert elements to be retained or for any other psychological or social reason. What is ethnic about the Portuguese Jews is not their retention of a great deal of Iberian culture, but their coupling of that culture with a Judaism that was no part of it, the generic ancestral Judaism of the Bible. Their ethnicity is a new, modern concoction, for which there existed no antecedents in Jewish history.

Appendix
Details of Freight Contracts

The following tables give details of contracts entered into in Amsterdam by Portuguese Jews. Numbers given are for contracts relating to each town, city, or country listed in each year. If a contract lists several towns, each is included; consequently, the total of contracts is not the same as the total of places listed.

Table A.1. Ports mentioned in freight contracts, 1596–1621 (listed alphabetically by country or region)

	1596	1597	1598	1599	1600	1601	1602	1603	1604	1605	1606	1607	1608	1609	1610	1611	1612	1613	1614	1615	1616	1617	1618	1619	1620	1621	Total
Barbary Coast[a]	1	—	—	—	—	—	—	—	—	—	—	—	—	—	—	—	—	—	—	—	—	—	—	—	—	—	1
France[b]	—	—	—	1	—	—	—	—	—	—	—	—	—	—	—	—	—	—	—	—	—	1	—	—	—	—	2
Italy																											
Livorno[c]	1	—	—	—	—	—	—	—	—	—	3	5	—	—	—	—	1	—	—	—	1	2	1	3	—	—	17
Palermo	—	—	—	—	—	—	—	—	—	—	—	—	—	—	—	—	—	—	—	—	—	—	—	1	—	—	1
Venice[d]	—	—	—	—	—	—	—	—	—	—	—	3	2	—	—	—	—	—	—	2	1	1	—	1	—	—	10
North Africa[e]	—	—	—	—	—	—	—	—	—	—	—	—	—	—	—	—	—	—	—	—	2	1	—	—	1	—	4
Portugal																											
Algarve[f]	—	1	2	1	—	—	—	2	3	—	2	—	2	5	5	1	2	2	2	—	5	5	2	6	1	—	49
Aveiro[g]	—	—	3	1	—	—	—	1	—	1	—	—	1	2	3	—	—	2	2	1	4	7	1	3	4	1	36
Lisbon[h]	—	—	10	—	—	—	—	1	—	—	—	1	3	1	—	—	—	—	—	—	1	6	3	5	5	1	32
Oporto[h]	—	—	9	—	2	—	—	—	—	1	—	—	2	3	4	2	3	2	—	—	2	5	1	13	1	—	52
Setúbal	—	—	—	—	2	4	—	—	1	—	—	—	2	2	2	—	1	—	1	6	38	53	19	3	2	—	132
Portug. colonies																											
Azores	—	—	—	—	—	—	—	—	—	—	—	—	—	—	—	1	—	—	—	—	—	—	—	—	—	—	1
Brazil	—	—	—	—	—	—	—	—	—	—	—	—	—	—	—	—	—	—	—	—	1	—	—	—	—	—	1
Guinea (W. Africa)	—	—	—	—	—	—	—	—	—	—	—	—	—	1	—	1	1	—	—	—	—	—	—	—	—	—	3
Madeira	—	—	2	—	—	—	—	—	—	—	—	—	—	—	1	—	—	—	—	—	—	—	—	—	—	1	4
Portuguese N. Africa[i]	—	—	—	—	—	—	—	—	—	—	—	—	—	—	—	—	—	—	—	1	2	6	5	5	1	—	20
Spain																											
Alicante	—	—	—	—	—	—	—	—	—	—	—	—	—	—	1	—	—	—	—	1	1	—	1	—	—	—	3
Canary Isles[j]	—	—	—	—	—	—	—	—	—	—	—	—	—	1	1	1	—	—	—	—	—	1	—	3	1	—	9
Galicia[k]	—	—	—	—	—	—	—	—	—	—	—	—	—	1	2	—	—	4	—	—	—	—	1	6	1	—	15
Málaga[l]	—	—	—	—	—	—	—	—	—	—	—	—	—	—	—	—	—	—	—	3	1	3	2	4	6	1	20
Seville[m]	—	—	—	—	—	—	—	—	—	—	—	—	—	—	—	—	—	—	—	—	1	1	1	1	—	—	4
Other																											
Alexandria, Egypt	—	—	—	—	—	—	—	—	—	—	—	—	—	—	—	—	—	—	—	—	—	1	—	—	—	—	1
Constantinople, Turkey	—	—	—	—	—	—	—	—	—	—	—	—	—	—	—	—	—	—	—	—	—	—	—	—	1	—	1
TOTAL NO. OF FREIGHT CONTRACTS	1	—	21	2	3	5	—	3	5	2	3	9	9	14	16	6	7	7	5	13	51	76	30	26	42	7	

[a] Including Capo Ghir and Safi [b] Including La Rochelle and Saint-Jean-de-Luz [c] Including Civitavecchia, Genoa, La Spezia, and Viareggio [d] Including Gar and Malamocco [e] Including La Goulette, Sousa, and Tunis [f] Including Albufeira, Ayamonte, Castro Marim, Faro, Lagos, Portimão, and Tavira [g] Including Buarcos [h] Including Caminha, Viana do Castelo, and Vila do Conde [i] Including Ceuta, Mazagan, and Tangier [j] Including Garachico, Gomera, La Orotava, and Santa Cruz (de Tenerife or de la Palma) [k] Including Bayona, Betanzos, La Coruña, Muros, Padrón, Pontevedra, and Vigo [l] Including Adra, Almuñécar, Estepona, Motril, Salobreña, Torrox, and Vélez Málaga [m] Including Cádiz and San Lúcar

Table A.2. Ports mentioned in freight contracts prepared by notary J. V. Oli, 1638–1676 (listed alphabetically by country or region)

	1638	1639	1640	1641	1642	1643	1644	1645	1646	1647	1648	1649	1650	1651	1652	1653	1654	1655	1656
Barbary Coast[a]	—	1	1	1	3	4	3	2	7	6	5	1	1	1	—	—	—	3	3
Brazil (Dutch)[b]	—	—	—	—	—	—	—	—	—	—	2	—	—	1	3	—	—	—	
France (south-west)[c]	—	1	1	—	—	—	—	—	3	1	2	—	2	1	—	—	—	—	1
Italy																			
Livorno[d]	1	1	1	3	4	3	3	4	2	1	2	—	1	—	—	—	—	—	—
Venice[e]	—	3	2	1	—	1	—	—	—	—	—	—	—	—	—	—	—	—	—
North Africa[f]	—	—	—	—	—	—	—	—	—	—	—	—	—	—	—	—	—	—	—
Portugal																			
Algarve[g]	—	—	—	2	1	3	2	4	5	5	3	6	12	10	4	3	6	5	3
Aveiro	—	—	—	—	—	—	—	—	—	—	—	—	1	—	1	2	3	3	—
Lisbon	—	—	1	1	1	5	5	6	17	5	1	—	7	16	7	6	8	7	5
Oporto[h]	—	1	—	—	—	—	4	—	—	2	2	2	3	11	3	2	2	1	5
Setúbal[i]	—	3	3	4	3	3	4	2	4	1	—	—	2	1	4	—	4	7	4
Portug. colonies																			
Azores[j]	—	—	—	—	3	4	2	5	3	3	2	1	4	3	2	—	1	2	1
Brazil (Portuguese)[k]	—	—	—	—	—	—	—	—	—	—	—	—	—	1	—	—	—	—	—
Madeira	—	—	—	—	—	—	1	2	4	1	1	—	1	—	2	—	1	1	—
Portuguese N. Africa[l]	1	3	2	4	3	3	3	2	—	—	2	—	—	—	—	1	—	—	—
São Tomé	—	—	—	—	—	—	—	—	—	—	—	—	—	—	—	—	—	—	—
Spain																			
Alicante[m]	—	—	—	—	—	—	—	—	—	—	—	—	—	—	—	—	—	1	—
Barcelona	—	—	—	—	—	—	—	—	—	—	—	—	—	—	—	—	—	—	—
Canary Isles[n]	—	—	—	—	—	2	—	—	—	—	1	4	1	2	2	—	2	—	—
Málaga[o]	—	—	—	1	—	1	1	1	2	2	—	2	2	2	—	—	—	—	3
Santander[p]	1	1	2	—	—	—	—	1	—	—	9	4	4	6	—	1	3	2	2
Seville[q]	—	—	—	—	1	—	—	—	—	—	1	8	—	3	1	—	2	3	1
TOTAL NO. OF FREIGHT CONTRACTS	2	7	6	9	12	21	23	21	36	22	36	20	40	47	23	15	26	26	26

[a] Including Agadir, Mogador, Oualidia, Safi, and Salé   [b] Including Pernambuco   [c] Including Bayonne, Bordeaux, and Saint-Jean-de-Luz   [d] Including Genoa   [e] Including Ancona and Gar   [f] Including Algiers   [g] Including Albufeira, Faro, Lagos, (Vilanova de) Portimão, and Tavira   [h] Including Viana do Castelo   [i] Including Almada   [j] Including Faial, São Miguel, and Terceira   [k] Including Bahia, Cabo de Santo Agostinho, and Tamandaré   [l] Including Tangier and Tétuan   [m] Including Valencia   [n] Including Garachico, La Orotava, Las Palmas de Gran Canaria, Rambles, and Santa Cruz de Tenerife   [o] Including Almuñécar, Estepona, Motril, Salobreña, Torrox, and Vélez Málaga   [p] Including Bilbao and San Sebastian   [q] Including Cádiz, El Puerto de Santa Maria, Huelva, and Sanlúcar de Barrameda

1657	1658	1659	1660	1661	1662	1663	1664	1665	1666	1667	1668	1669	1670	1671	1672	1673	1674	1675	1676	Total
1	—	1	2	1	5	1	2	—	—	—	2	—	1	4	—	1	1	—	1	65
—	—	—	—	—	—	—	—	—	—	—	—	—	—	—	—	—	—	—	—	6
2	—	—	—	—	1	1	—	1	—	—	—	—	—	—	—	—	—	—	—	17
—	—	—	—	—	—	—	—	—	—	—	—	—	—	—	—	—	—	—	—	26
—	—	—	—	—	—	—	—	—	—	3	—	—	1	—	—	—	—	—	—	11
—	—	—	—	—	—	—	1	—	—	—	—	—	—	—	—	—	—	—	—	1
3	4	5	10	4	5	4	2	3	1	4	2	1	1	1	—	—	—	2	2	128
—	—	—	—	—	—	—	—	—	—	—	—	—	—	—	—	—	—	—	—	10
1	—	1	1	1	2	—	1	3	—	—	2	1	2	—	2	—	—	—	—	115
1	3	1	—	—	1	7	3	1	—	3	2	—	1	—	—	—	1	—	—	62
2	—	6	8	6	2	2	1	—	—	—	—	1	—	3	4	—	—	—	—	84
2	—	2	—	4	—	2	—	—	1	3	1	—	1	1	—	—	—	—	—	53
—	—	—	—	1	—	—	—	—	—	—	—	—	—	—	—	—	—	—	—	2
—	2	—	—	8	2	2	—	—	—	2	—	—	1	—	—	—	—	—	2	33
—	—	—	—	—	—	—	—	—	—	—	—	—	—	—	—	—	—	—	—	24
—	—	—	—	—	—	—	1	—	—	—	—	—	—	—	—	—	—	—	—	1
—	—	—	1	—	—	—	1	—	—	—	—	—	—	—	—	—	—	—	—	3
—	—	—	1	—	—	—	—	—	—	—	—	—	—	—	—	—	—	—	—	1
—	—	—	2	1	—	—	—	—	—	1	—	—	—	—	—	—	—	—	—	18
—	2	4	2	2	2	3	1	—	1	—	—	—	—	—	—	—	—	—	—	34
—	1	1	1	—	—	1	1	—	—	—	—	—	—	—	—	—	—	—	—	41
—	—	1	—	—	—	1	—	—	—	—	—	—	—	—	—	—	—	—	—	22
11	11	20	27	28	20	23	13	8	3	15	10	3	8	9	6	1	2	2	5	652

Bibliography

ABBOU, ISAAC D., *Musulmans andalous et judéo-espagnols* (Casablanca, 1953).

ABOAB, ISHACK DE MATATIA, 'Documentos para todo estado e ydade', MS 48 D 9, Ets Haim-Montezinos Library, Amsterdam.

ADLER, CYRUS, 'A Contemporary Memorial Relating to Damages to Spanish Interests in America Done by Jews of Holland 1634', *PAJHS* 17 (1909), 45–51; repr. in M. A. Cohen (ed.), *The Jewish Experience in America* (Waltham, Mass., and New York, 1971), ii. 178–84.

ADLER, E. N., 'The Jews of Amsterdam in 1655', *TJHSE* 4 (1903), 224–9.

ALBO, JOSEPH, *Sefer ha'ikarim*, ed. and trans. I. Husik (Philadelphia, 1946).

Album Studiosorum Academiae Franekerensis (1585–1811, 1816–1844) (Franeker, n.d.).

Album Studiosorum Academiae Lugduno Bataviae MDLXXV–MDCCCLXXV (The Hague, 1875).

ALER, J. M. M., *Catalogus van de bibliotheek der vereniging Het Spinozahuis te Rijnsburg* (Leiden, 1965).

ALTMANN, ALEXANDER, 'Eternality of Punishment: A Theological Controversy within the Amsterdam Rabbinate in the Thirties of the Seventeenth Century', *PAAJR* 40 (1972), 1–88.

—— *Moses Mendelssohn: A Biographical Study* (University, Ala., 1973).

—— 'Gewissensfreiheit und Toleranz: Eine begriffsgeschichtliche Untersuchung', *Mendelssohn Studien*, 4 (1979), 9–46.

—— 'Moses Mendelssohn on Excommunication: The Ecclesiastical Law Background', in id., *Essays in Jewish Intellectual History* (Hanover, NH, and London, 1981), 170–89.

—— 'Lurianic Kabbala in a Platonic Key: Abraham Cohen Herrera's "Puerta del Cielo" ', *HUCA* 53 (1982), 317–55.

ALVARES VEGA, L., *Het Beth Haim van Ouderkerk: Beelden van een Portugees-Joodse begraafplaats* (Assen, 1975).

ALVES, FRANCISCO MANUEL, *Os judeus no distrito de Bragança*, Memórias Arqueológico-Históricas do Distrito de Bragança 5 (Bragança, 1981; repr. Bragança, 1985).

AMZALAK, M. B., 'Selomoh de Oliveyra: Noticia biobibliográfica', *Revista de Estudos Hebraicos*, 1 (Lisbon, 1928), 96–118. Also pub. separately, Lisbon, 1928.

D'ANCONA, J., 'Delmedigo, Menasseh ben Israel en Spinoza', *BMGJWN* 6 (1940), 105–52.

—— 'Komst der Marranen in Noord-Nederland. De Portugese gemeenten te Amsterdam tot de vereniging (1639)', in H. Brugmans and A. Frank (eds.), *Geschiedenis der Joden in Nederland* (Amsterdam, 1940), 201–69.

—— 'De Portugese gemeente "Talmoed Tora" te Amsterdam tot 1795', in H. Brugmans and A. Frank (eds.), *Geschiedenis der Joden in Nederland* (Amsterdam, 1940), 270–305.

VAN APELDOORN, L. J., *Geschiedenis van het Nederlandsche huwelijksrecht voor de invoering van de Fransche wetgeving* (Amsterdam, 1925).

APPLEBY, JOYCE OLDHAM, *Economic Thought and Ideology in Seventeenth-Century England* (Princeton, 1978).

ARIÈS, PHILIPPE, *Centuries of Childhood: A Social History of Family Life*, trans. R. Baldick (London, 1962).

BAER, JIZCHAK (YITZHAK) FRITZ, *Galut* (Berlin, 1936); Eng. trans. *Galut* (New York, 1947).

BAIÃO, ANTONIO, *Episódios dramáticos da Inquisição portuguesa*, 3 vols. (Oporto, Rio de Janeiro, and Lisbon, 1919–38).

——*A Inquisição de Goa*, 2 vols. (Coimbra and Lisbon, 1930–45).

BAILYN, BERNARD, *The New England Merchants in the Seventeenth Century* (Cambridge, Mass., 1955).

BAINTON, ROLAND H., *et al.*, *Castellioniana: Quatre études sur Sébastien Castellion et l'idée de la tolérance* (Leiden, 1951).

BALBIAN VERSTER, J. F. L., 'Waar was het hof van Baron de Belmonte?', *Jaarboek Amstelodamum*, 25 (1928), 177–90.

BARBOUR, VIOLET, *Capitalism in Amsterdam in the Seventeenth Century* (Baltimore, 1950).

BARNAI, JACOB, 'The Jewish Settlement in Palestine in the 17th and 18th Centuries', in *The Jewish Settlement in Palestine 634–1881*, ed. A. Carmel, P. Schäfer, and Y. Ben-Artzi (Wiesbaden, 1990), 142–64.

BARNOUW, P. J., *Philippus van Limborch* (The Hague, 1963).

BARON, SALO W., *The Jewish Community: Its History and Structure to the American Revolution*, 3 vols. (Philadelphia, 1942).

——*A Social and Religious History of the Jews*, 1st edn., 3 vols (New York, 1937); 2nd rev. edn., 18 vols. to date (New York, London, and Philadelphia, 1952–).

——'Medieval Heritage and Modern Realities in Protestant–Jewish Relations', *Diogenes*, 61 (1968), 32–51.

——KAHAN, ARCADIUS, *et al.*, *Economic History of the Jews*, ed. N. Gross (New York, 1975).

DE BARRIOS, DANIEL LEVI, *Triumpho del govierno popular y de la antiguedad holandesa* (Amsterdam, 1683–4), copy of the Rosenthalia Library, Amsterdam, Ros. 19G12.

BARTAL, I., and KAPLAN, Y., 'Emigration of Indigent Jews from Amsterdam to Erets Yisrael (Palestine) at the Beginning of the Seventeenth Century' (Heb.), *Shalem*, 6 (Jerusalem, 1992), 177–93.

BARZILAY, ISAAC, *Yoseph Shlomoh Delmedigo (Yashar of Candia): His Life, Works and Times* (Leiden, 1974).

BAUER, HELGA, 'Die Predigt als Spiegel politischer und sozialer Ereignisse: Zur "Judenfrage" im Jahre 1630 in Portugal', *Aufsätze zur portugiesischen Kulturgeschichte, Portugiesische Forschungen der Görresgesellschaft*, 1st ser., 11 (1971), 26–67.

BEINART, HAIM, 'The *Converso* Community in 16th and 17th Century Spain', in R. D. Barnett (ed.), *The Sephardi Heritage: Essays on the History and Cultural Contribution of the Jews of Spain and Portugal* (London, 1971), 457–78.

—— 'The Exodus of Conversos from the Iberian Peninsula in the Fifteenth to Seventeenth Centuries' (Heb.), in R. Bonfil (ed.), *Scritti in memoria di Umberto Nahon* (Jerusalem, 1978), 63–106.

BENNASSAR, BARTOLOMÉ, *Valladolid au siècle d'or: Une ville de Castille et sa campagne au XVIᵉ siècle* (Paris and The Hague, 1967).

—— *The Spanish Character: Attitudes and Mentalities from the Sixteenth to the Nineteenth Century* (Berkeley, 1979).

—— (ed.), *L'Inquisition espagnole XVᵉ–XIXᵉ siècle* (Paris, 1979).

VAN DEN BERG, J., *Joden en christenen in Nederland gedurende de zeventiende eeuw* (Kampen, 1969).

—— 'Eschatological Expectations Concerning the Conversion of the Jews in the Netherlands during the Seventeenth Century', in Peter Toon (ed.), *Puritans, the Millennium and the Future of Israel: Puritan Eschatology 1600 to 1660* (Cambridge and London, 1970), 137–53.

—— 'Church and State Relations in the Netherlands', in J. A. Hebly (ed.), *Lowland Highlights: Church and Oecumene in the Netherlands* (Kampen, 1972), 32–9.

—— and VAN DER WALL, ERNESTINE G. E., *Jewish–Christian Relations in the Seventeenth Century: Studies and Documents* (Dordrecht, 1988).

BERGER, SHLOMO, 'Codices Gentium: Rabbi Isaac Aboab's Collection of Classical Literature', *SR* 29 (1995), 5–13.

BESSO, HENRY V., *Dramatic Literature of the Sephardic Jews of Amsterdam in the XVIIth and XVIIIth Centuries* (New York, 1947).

BLOK, F. F., 'Quelques humanistes de la Jérusalem de l'Occident', in *Humanists and Humanism in Amsterdam: Catalogue of an Exhibition in the Trippenhuis, Amsterdam, 20–25 August 1973* (Amsterdam, 1973), 9–32.

—— 'Caspar Barlaeus en de Joden: De geschiedenis van een epigram', *Nederlands Archief voor Kerkgeschiedenis*, 57 (1977), 179–209; 58 (1978), 85–108.

BLOK, P. J., *Michiel Adriaanszoon de Ruyter*, 3rd edn. (The Hague, 1947).

BLOM, J. C. H., FUKS-MANSFELD, R. G., and SCHÖFFER, I. (eds.), *Geschiedenis van de Joden in Nederland* (Amsterdam, 1995).

BLOOM, HERBERT I., 'A Study of Brazilian Jewish History, 1623–1654, Based Chiefly upon the Findings of the Late Samuel Oppenheim', *PAJHS* 33 (1934), 43–125.

—— *The Economic Activities of the Jews of Amsterdam in the Seventeenth and Eighteenth Centuries* (Williamsport, Pa., 1937).

BLUMENKRANZ, BERNHARD, 'Augustin et les juifs, Augustin et le judaïsme', *Recherches Augustiniennes*, 1 (1958), 225–41.

—— (ed.), *Histoire des Juifs en France* (Toulouse, 1972).

BODIAN, MIRIAM, 'The "Portuguese" Dowry Societies in Venice and Amsterdam: A Case Study in Communal Differentiation within the Marrano Diaspora', *Italia*, 6 (Jerusalem, 1987), 30–61.

—— 'Amsterdam, Venice, and the Marrano Diaspora in the Seventeenth Century', *Dutch Jewish History*, 2 (Jerusalem, 1989), 47–65.

BODIAN, MIRIAM, ' "Men of the Nation": The Shaping of *Converso* Identity in Early Modern Europe', *Past & Present*, 143 (1994), 48–76.

——*Hebrews of the Portuguese Nation: Conversos and Community in Early Modern Amsterdam* (Bloomington, Ind., 1997).

DEN BOER, HARM, 'Spanish and Portuguese Editions from the Northern Netherlands in Madrid and Lisbon Public Collections', *SR* 22 (1988), 97–143; 23 (1989), 38–77, 138–77.

BOGUCKA, MARIA, 'Amsterdam and the Baltic in the First Half of the Seventeenth Century', *Economic History Review*, 2nd ser., 26 (1973), 433–7.

BONGER, H., *De motivering van de godsdienstvrijheid bij Dirck Volckertszoon Coornhert* (Arnhem, 1954).

BONTEMANTEL, HANS, *De regeeringe van Amsterdam soo in 't civiel als crimineel en militaire (1653–1672)*, ed. G. W. Kernkamp, 2 vols. (The Hague, 1897).

BOONACKER, V. F. J., 'Iets uit de handelingen der classis van Rhenen en Wijk in de jaren 1670–1673: Deels betreffende maatregelen tot bekeering van joden en heidenen . . .', *Nieuw Archief voor Kerkelijke Geschiedenis*, 2 (Leiden, 1854), 281–94.

BORGES COELHO, ANTÓNIO, *Inquisição de Evora*, 2 vols. (Lisbon, 1987).

BOVENKERK, FRANK, 'Shylock of Horatio Alger: Beschouwingen over de theorie der handelsminderheden', in L. Dasberg and J. N. Cohen (eds.), *Neveh Ya'akov: Jubilee Volume Presented to Dr Jaap Meijer* (Assen, 1982), 148–64.

BOVENKERK, H., 'De Joden gezien door middeleeuwse en zestiende-eeuwse schrijvers', in H. Brugmans and A. Frank (eds.), *Geschiedenis der Joden in Nederland* (Amsterdam, 1940), 105–56.

——'Nederlandsche schrijvers tijdens de Republiek over de Joden', in H. Brugmans and A. Frank (eds.), *Geschiedenis der Joden in Nederland* (Amsterdam, 1940), 714–71.

BOXER, C. R., 'Padre António Vieira, SJ and the Institution of the Brazil Company in 1649', *Hispanic American Historical Review*, 29 (1949), 474–94.

——*The Dutch in Brazil 1624–1654* (Oxford, 1957).

——*The Dutch Seaborne Empire 1600–1800* (London, 1965).

——*The Portuguese Seaborne Empire 1415–1825* (London, 1969).

BOYAJIAN, JAMES C., *Portuguese Bankers at the Court of Spain 1626–1650* (New Brunswick, NJ, 1983).

BRANDT, GERARD, *The History of the Reformation and other Ecclesiastical Transactions in and about the Low-Countries*, 4 vols., trans. J. Chamberlayne (London, 1720–23); repr. with intr. by J. W. Smit (New York, 1979).

BRANTS, V., 'Une page de sémitisme diplomatique et commercial: Incidents de la vie d'Amsterdam au XVIIᵉ siècle', *Académie Royale de Belgique: Bulletin de la Classe des Lettres et des Sciences Morales et Politiques et de la Classe des Beaux Arts*, 7 (1905), 575–96.

BRAUDEL, FERNAND, *The Mediterranean and the Mediterranean World in the Age of Philip II*, trans. S. Reynolds, 2 vols. (New York, 1972–3).

——*The Wheels of Commerce: Civilization and Capitalism 15th–18th Century*, vol. ii, trans. S. Reynolds (New York, 1982).

——and ROMANO, R., *Navires et marchandises à l'entrée du port de Livourne (1547–1611)* (Paris, 1951).

BRERETON, WILL, *Travels in Holland, the United Provinces, England, Scotland and Ireland, MDCXXXIV–MDCXXXV*, ed. E. Hawkins (n.p., 1844).

BRUGMANS, H., *Opkomst en bloei van Amsterdam* (Amsterdam, 1944).

——*Geschiedenis van Amsterdam*, 7 vols. (1930–3; repr. Utrecht and Antwerp, 1972).

——and FRANK, A. (eds.), *Geschiedenis der Joden in Nederland* (Amsterdam, 1940).

BUISSON, FERDINAND, *Sébastien Castellion: Sa vie et son œuvre (1515–1563)*. *Étude sur les origines du protestantisme libéral français*, 2 vols. (Paris, 1892; repr. Nieuwkoop, 1964).

CABEZAS ALGUACIL, C., 'Doña Isabel de Correa, traductora y poetisa sefardí', *Miscelánea de Estudos Arabes y Hebraicos*, 10 (1961), 111–29.

Calendar of State Papers, Domestic Series, of the Reign of William and Mary, ed. W. J. Hardy, 5 vols. (London, 1895–1906) [i. 13 Feb. 1689–April 1690; ii. May 1690–Oct. 1691; iii. 1 Nov.–end of 1692; iv. 1693; v. 1694–1702].

Calendar of Treasury Books, vols. ix–xxiv, ed. W. A. Shaw (London, 1931–52).

CARO BAROJA, JULIO, *Los Judíos en la España moderna y contemporánea*, 3 vols. (Madrid, 1962).

——*La sociedad criptojudía en la corte de Felipe IV* (Madrid, 1963); repr. in id., *Inquisición, brujería y criptojudaísmo* (Barcelona, 1970).

CASTILLO, ALVARO, 'Dans la monarchie espagnole du XVIIᵉ siècle: Les Banquiers portugais et le circuit d'Amsterdam', *Annales*, 19 (1964), 311–16.

DE CASTRO. *See* HENRIQUES DE CASTRO MZ., D.

Catalogus variorum atque in insignium in quavis facultate & lingua, librorum, praecipus theologicorum & miscellaneorum, hebraica, graeca, latina, & hispanica, clarissimi doctissimique viri D. Isaaci Abuab, rabini primarii, sanctae theologiae, inter Judaeos professoris (Amsterdam, 1693).

CHOURAQI, ANDRÉ, *Histoire des Juifs en Afrique du Nord* (Paris, 1985).

CHRISTENSEN, AKSEL E., *Dutch Trade to the Baltic about 1600: Studies in the Sound Toll Register and Dutch Shipping Sources* (Copenhagen and The Hague, 1941).

COHEN, ROBERT, 'Jewish Demography in the Eighteenth Century: A Study of London, the West Indies, and Early America', Ph.D. thesis (Brandeis University, 1976).

——'Passage to a New World: The Sephardi Poor of Eighteenth-century Amsterdam', in L. Dasberg and J. N. Cohen (eds.), *Neveh Ya'akov: Jubilee Volume Presented to Dr Jaap Meijer* (Assen, 1982), 31–42.

——(ed.), *The Jewish Nation in Surinam: Historical Essays* (Amsterdam, 1982).

——' "Memoria para os siglos futuros": Myth and Memory on the Beginnings of the Amsterdam Sephardi Community', *Jewish History*, 2 (1987), 67–72.

COHEN HERRERA, ABRAHAM, *Das Buch Shaar ha-Shamayim oder Pforte des Himmels*, intr. G. Scholem, trans. F. Hänssermann (Frankfurt, 1974).

CONTRERAS, JAIME, *El Santo Oficio de la Inquisicion de Galicia: Poder, sociedad y cultura* (Madrid, 1982).

COORNHERT, DIRK VOLCKERTSZ., *Weet en rust: Proza van Coornhert*, ed. H. Bonger and A.-J. Gelderblom (Amsterdam, 1985).

COPPENHAGEN, J. H., *Menasseh Ben Israel—Manuel Dias Soeiro (1604–1657): A Bibliography* (Jerusalem, 1990).

DA COSTA, ISAAC, BREWSTER, BERTRAM, and ROTH, CECIL, *Noble Families among the Sephardic Jews* (London, 1936).

DA COSTA, URIEL, *Examination of Pharisaic Traditions—Exame das tradições phariseas: Facsimile of the Unique Copy in the Royal Library of Copenhagen*, intr. and trans. H. P. Salomon and I. S. D. Sassoon (Leiden, 1993).

DE COSTER [COSTERUS], ABRAHAM, *Historie der Joden die tzedert der verstooringhe Jerusalems in alle Landen verstroyt zijn* (Rotterdam, 1608; repr. Amsterdam, 1658).

DE LA COURT, PIETER, *The True Interest and Political Maxims of the Republic of Holland and West-Friesland* (London, 1746).

CROSS, HARRY E., 'Commerce and Orthodoxy: A Spanish Response to Portuguese Commercial Penetration in the Viceroyalty of Peru, 1580–1640', *The Americas*, 35 (1978/9), 151–67.

CUNO, FR. W., *Franciscus Junius der Aeltere, Professor der Theologie und Pastor (1545–1602): Sein Leben und Wirken, seine Schriften und Briefe* (Amsterdam, 1891).

CUVELIER, JOSEPH, and LEFÈVRE, JOSEPH, *Correspondance de la Cour d'Espagne sur les affaires des Pays-Bas*, 6 vols. (Brussels, 1923–37).

DAVID-PEYRE, YVONNE, *Le Personnage du médecin et la relation médecin–malade dans la littérature ibérique, XVIe et XVIIe siècle* (Lille, 1971).

DEDIEU, JEAN-PIERRE, 'Les Causes de foi de l'Inquisition de Tolède (1483–1820): Essai statistique', *Mélanges de la Casa de Velázquez*, 14 (1978), 143–71.

—— ' "Christianisation" en Nouvelle Castille: Catéchisme, communion, messe et confirmation dans l'archevêché de Tolède', *Mélanges de la Casa de Velázquez*, 15 (1979), 261–94.

—— *L'Administration de la foi: L'Inquisition de Tolède (XVIe–XVIIIe siècle)*, Bibliothèque de la Casa de Velázquez 7 (Madrid, 1989).

DENUCÉ, J., 'Een geheime synagoge te Antwerpen in de XVI^{de} eeuw', *Antwerpsch Archievenblad*, 3rd ser., 4 (1929), 151–4.

VAN DEURSEN, A. TH., *Het kopergeld van de Gouden Eeuw*, 4 vols. (Assen, 1978–81); Eng. trans. *Plain Lives in a Golden Age: Popular Culture, Religion and Society in Seventeenth-century Holland*, trans. M. Ultee (Cambridge, 1991).

DIAMOND, A. S., 'Problems of the London Sephardi Community, 1720–1733', *TJHSE* 21 (1968), 39–63.

—— 'The Community of the Resettlement, 1656–1684: A Social Survey', *TJHSE* 24 (1975), 134–50.

VAN DILLEN, JOHAN G., 'Effectenkoersen aan de Amsterdamsche beurs 1723–1794', *Economisch-Historisch Jaarboek*, 17 (1931), 1–46.

—— 'Vreemdelingen te Amsterdam in de eerste helft der zeventiende eeuw: I. De Portugeesche Joden', *Tijdschrift voor Geschiedenis*, 50 (1935), 4–35.

——'De economische positie en betekenis der Joden in de Republiek en in de Neder-landsche koloniale wereld', in H. Brugmans and A. Frank (eds.), *Geschiedenis der Joden in Nederland* (Amsterdam, 1940), 561–616.

——'Omvang en samenstelling van de bevolking van Amsterdam in de 17ᵉ en 18ᵉ eeuw', in id., *Mensen en achtergronden* (Groningen, 1964), 484–97.

—— *Van rijkdom en regenten: Handboek tot de economische en sociale geschiedenis van Nederland tijdens de Republiek* (The Hague, 1970).

——(ed.), *Bronnen tot de geschiedenis van het bedrijfsleven en het gildewezen van Amsterdam*, 3 vols. (The Hague, 1929–74).

DOBRINSKY, HERBERT C., *A Treasury of Sephardic Laws and Customs*, rev. edn. (Hoboken, NJ, and New York, 1988).

DOMÍNGUEZ ORTIZ, ANTÓNIO, 'El proceso inquisitorial de Juan Nuñez Saravia, banquero de Felipe IV', *Hispania*, 61 (1955), 559–81.

—— *Política y hacienda de Felipe IV* (Madrid, 1960).

——'Los extranjeros en la vida española durante el siglo XVII', *Estudios de Historia Social de España*, 4/2 (1960), 291–426.

—— *Los Judeoconversos en España y América* (Madrid, 1971).

DUBNOV, SIMON M., *History of the Jews in Russia and Poland from the Earliest Times until the Present*, trans. I. Friedlaender, 3 vols. (Philadelphia, 1916–20).

VAN EEGHEN, I. H., *Inventarissen der archieven van de gilden en van het Brouwerscollege* (Amsterdam, 1951).

——'De Gereformeerde Kerkeraad en de Joden te Amsterdam', *Maandblad Amstelodamum*, 47 (1960), 169–74.

——'De kinderen van Hansken Hangebroek', *SR* 11 (1977), 33–9.

——'Mr. Daniel Mostart en de "Huwelijkse Zaken" ', *SR* 17 (1983), 15–21.

ELKAN, ALBERT, 'Über die Entstehung des niederländischen Religionsfrieden von 1578 und Mornays Wirksamkeit in den Niederlanden', *Mitteilungen des Instituts für österreichische Geschichtsforschung*, 27 (1906), 460–80.

EMMANUEL, ISAAC S., *Histoire des Israélites de Salonique* (Paris, 1936).

——and EMMANUEL, SUZANNE A., *History of the Jews of the Netherlands Antilles*, 2 vols. (Cincinnatti, 1970).

Encyclopedia Judaica, 15 vols. (Jerusalem, 1971).

ENDELMAN, TODD M., *The Jews of Georgian England 1714–1830: Tradition and Change in a Liberal Society* (Philadelphia, 1979).

ETTINGER, S., 'The Beginnings of the Change in the Attitude of European Society towards the Jews', *Scripta Hierosolymitana*, 7 (1961), 193–219.

VAN EYSINGA, W. J. M., 'De Groots Jodenreglement', *Mededeelingen der Koninklijke Akademie van Wetenschappen, Afd. Letterkunde*, NS 13/1 (Amsterdam, 1950), 1–8.

FABIÃO, LUIS CRESPO, 'O caso de David Curiel com o alemão (Curioso manuscrito inédito seiscentista, da autoria dum Judeu português d'Amsterdão)', *Biblos*, 38 (1965), 1–53.

FERGUSON, WALLACE K., 'The Attitude of Erasmus toward Toleration', in id., *Renaissance Studies* (London, Ont., 1963), 75–81.

FERRO TAVARES, MARIA JOSÉ PIMENTA, *Os Judeus em Portugal no século XV* (Lisbon, 1982).

FEUER, LEWIS, *Spinoza and the Rise of Liberalism* (Boston, 1958).

FITA, FIDEL, 'El judío errante de Illescas (1484–1514)', *BRAH* 6 (1885), 130–40.

FORTUNE, STEPHEN A., *Merchants and Jews: The Struggle for British West Indian Commerce, 1650–1750* (Gainesville, Fla., 1984).

FRANCÈS, MADELEINE, *Spinoza dans les pays néerlandais de la séconde moitié du XVII siècle* (Paris, 1937).

FRANCISQUE-MICHEL, ROLAND, *Les Portugais en France, les Français en Portugal* (Paris, 1882).

DE FREITAS, GUSTAVO, *A Companhia Geral do Comércio do Brasil, 1649–1720* (São Paulo, 1951); 'separata' from *Revista de Historia*, 2 (São Paulo, 1951), 307–28; 3 (1951), 85–110, 313–44.

FUKS, L., 'Een rechtstrijd onder Amsterdamse Sefardim', in ' '*T Exempel dwinght'*: *Opstellen aangeboden aan I. Kisch ter gelegenheid van zijn zeventigste verjaardag* (Zwolle, 1975), 175–89.

——'The Inauguration of the Portuguese Synagogue of Amsterdam, Netherlands, in 1675', *Arquivos do Centro Cultural Portugues*, 14 (Paris, 1979), 489–507.

——'Jewish Libraries in Amsterdam in 1640', in *Aspects of Jewish Life in the Netherlands: A Selection from the Writings of Leo Fuks*, ed. R. G. Fuks-Mansfeld (Assen, 1995), 38–57.

——and FUKS-MANSFELD, R. G., *Hebrew and Judaic Manuscripts in Amsterdam Public Collections*, 2 vols. (Leiden, 1973).

—— ——*Hebrew Typography in the Northern Netherlands, 1585–1815: Historical Evaluation and Descriptive Bibliography*, 2 vols. (Leiden, 1984–7).

FUKS-MANSFELD, R. G. 'Bevolkingsproblematiek in joods Amsterdam in de zeventiende eeuw', *SR* 18 (1984), 134–42.

——*De Sefardim in Amsterdam tot 1795: Aspecten van een joodse minderheid in een Hollandse stad* (Hilversum, 1989).

GACHARD, M., *La Bibliothèque nationale à Paris: Notices et extraits des manuscrits qui concernent l'histoire de Belgique*, 2 vols. (Brussels, 1875).

GALANTE, ABRAHAM, *Histoire des Juifs d'Istanbul*, 2 vols. (Istanbul, 1941–2).

GANS, MOZES H., 'Don Samuel Palache als Morè en zeerover, grondlegger onzer gemeenschap', in *Opstellen, opperrabbijn L. Vorst aangeboden ter gelegenheid van zijn installatie* (Rotterdam, 1959), 15–23; Heb. trans. *Studies on the History of Dutch Jewry*, 1 (Jerusalem, 1975), 33–9.

——*Memorboek: Platenatlas van het leven der joden in Nederland van de middeleeuwen tot 1940* (Baarn, 1971); Eng. trans. *Memorbook: A History of Dutch Jewry from the Renaissance to 1940* (Baarn, 1977).

GARCÍA CÁRCEL, RICARDO, *Herejía y sociedad en el siglo XVI: La inquisición en Valencia 1530–1609* (Barcelona, 1980).

GATES, EUNICE JOINER, 'Three Gongoristic Poets: Anastasio Pantaleón de Ribera, Juan de Tamayo Salazar, and Miguel de Barrios', in *Estudios dedicados a Menedez Pidal*, 7 vols. (Madrid, 1950–62), ii. 383–5.

GEBHARDT, CARL (ed.), *Die Schriften des Uriel da Costa* (Amsterdam, Heidelberg, and London, 1922).

GEBHARDT, J. F., 'Het "aansprekers-oproer" van 1696', *Amsterdamsch Jaarboekje* (1899), 100–57.

VAN GELDER, H. A. ENNO, *De levensbeschouwing van Cornelis Pietersz. Hooft* (Amsterdam, 1918).

——*Getemperde vrijheid* (Groningen, 1972).

GEYL, PIETER, *The Netherlands in the Seventeenth Century*, 2 vols. (London and New York, 1961).

——*The Revolt of the Netherlands, 1555–1609* (London, 1962).

GLASER, EDWARD, 'Two Notes on the Hispano-Jewish Poet Don Miguel de Barrios', *REJ* 124 (1965), 201–11.

GOITEIN, S. D., *A Mediterranean Society: The Jewish Communities of the Arab World as Portrayed in the Documents of the Cairo Geniza*, 3 vols. (Berkeley and London, 1967–78).

GONSALVES DE MELLO, JOSE ANTONIO, NETO, *Tempo dos Flamengos: Influencia da ocupação holandesa na vida e na cultura do Norte do Brasil* (Rio de Janeiro and São Paulo, 1947).

GORIS, J. A., *Étude sur les colonies marchandes méridionales (Portugais, Espagnols, Italiens) à Anvers de 1488 à 1567: Contribution à l'histoire des débuts du capitalisme moderne* (Louvain, 1925).

GOTTHEIL, RICHARD J. H., *The Belmont–Belmonte Family: A Record of Four Hundred years* (New York, 1917).

GRAETZ, HEINRICH, *Geschichte der Juden von den ältesten Zeiten bis auf die Gegenwart*, vol. x: *Von der dauernden Ansiedlung der Marranen in Holland bis zum Beginne der Mendelssohnschen Zeit (1750)*, 3rd edn. (Leipzig, n.d.).

——*The Structure of Jewish History and Other Essays*, trans., ed., and intr. I. Schorsch (New York, 1975).

GRAMULLA, GERTRUD SUSANNA, *Handelsbeziehungen Kölner Kaufleute zwischen 1500 und 1650* (Cologne, 1972).

DE GROOT, HUGO, *Inleidinge tot de Hollandsche rechts-geleerdheid*, ed., S. J. Fockema Andreae and L. J. van Apeldoorn, 2 vols. (Arnhem, 1926).

——*Remonstrantie nopende de ordre dije in de landen van Hollandt ende Westvrieslandt dijent gestelt op de Joden*, ed. J. Meijer (Amsterdam, 1949).

GUGGISBERG, HANS R., 'Veranderingen in de argumenten voor religieuze tolerantie en godsdienstvrijheid in de zestiende en zeventiende eeuw', *Bijdragen en Mededelingen betreffende de Geschiedenis der Nederlanden*, 91 (1976), 177–95.

HAAG, E. and E., *La France protestante ou vies des Protestants français*, 10 vols. (1846–59; repr. Geneva, 1966).

VAN DER HAAR, C., *De diplomatieke betrekkingen tussen de Republiek en Portugal 1640–1661* (Groningen, 1961).

HALBWACHS, MAURICE, *La Topographie légendaire des Évangiles en Terre Sainte* (Paris, 1941).

HALBWACHS, MAURICE, *La Mémoire collective*, ed. Jeanne Alexandre, *née* Halbwachs (Paris, 1950); Eng. trans. *The Collective Memory*, intr. Mary Douglas (New York, 1980).

HALEVI, URI BEN ARON, *Narração da vinda dos Judeos espanhões a Amsterdam, 1711*, ed. J. S. da Silva Rosa (Amsterdam, 1933).

HALPERN, BEN, 'Modern Jews and their History', *Commentary*, 56 (Aug. 1973), 72–4.

HAMPSHIRE, STUART, *Spinoza* (New York and Baltimore, 1952).

HART, SIMON, 'Enige statistische gegevens inzake analfabetisme te Amsterdam in de 17ᵉ en 18ᵉ eeuw', *Maandblad Amstelodamum*, 55 (1968), 3–6.

——'Historisch-demografische notities betreffende de huwelijken en migratie te Amsterdam in de 17ᵉ en 18ᵉ eeuw', *Maandblad Amstelodamum*, 55 (1968), 63–9.

—— *Geschrift en getal* (Dordrecht, 1976).

HASSINGER, ERICH, 'Wirtschaftliche Motive und Argumente für religiöse Duldsamkeit im 16. und 17. Jahrhundert', *Archiv für Reformationsgeschichte*, 49 (1958), 226–45.

HEERES, J. E. (ed.), 'Jörg Franz Müller's reisindrukken', *De Navorscher*, 52 (1902), 187–205, 343–59.

HEIBER, HELMUT, *Walter Frank und sein Reichsinstitut für Geschichte des neuen Deutschlands* (Stuttgart, 1966).

HENNINGSEN, GUSTAV, 'El "Banco de datos" del Santo Oficio: Las relaciones de causas de la Inquisición española (1550–1700)', *BRAH* 174 (1977), 547–70.

HENRIQUES, H. S. Q., *The Jews and the English Law* (London, 1908; repr. Clifton, NJ, 1974).

HENRIQUES DE CASTRO MZ., D., *De synagoge der Portugeesch-Israelietische Gemeente te Amsterdam: Een gedenkschrift ter gelegenheid van haar tweede eeuwfeest* (The Hague, 1875); repr., ed. J. Meijer (Amsterdam, 1950).

—— *Keur van grafstenen op de Nederl.-Portug. Israel. begraafplaats te Ouderkerk aan de Amstel* (Leiden, 1883).

HENRIQUEZ PIMENTEL, M., *Geschiedkundige aanteekeningen betreffende de Portugeesche Israelieten in Den Haag en hunne synagogen aldaar* (The Hague, 1876).

HENRY, LOUIS, *Techniques d'analyse en démographie historique* (Paris, 1980).

HERCULANO, ALEXANDRE, *History of the Origin and Establishment of the Inquisition in Portugal*, trans. J. C. Banner (Stanford, Calif., 1926); repr., intr. Y. H. Yerushalmi (New York, 1972).

HERKS, J. J., *De geschiedenis van de Amersfoortse tabak* (Amsterdam, 1967).

HERRERO GARCIA, MIGUEL, *Ideas de los españoles del siglo XVII* (Madrid, 1966).

HERRERO MARTÍNEZ DE AZCOITIA, GUILLERMO, 'La población palentina en los siglos XVI y XVII', *Publicaciones de la Institución 'Tello Téllez de Meneses'*, 15 (1956), 7–30.

HERSHKOWITZ, LEO, 'Some Aspects of the New York Jewish Merchant and Community, 1654–1820', *AJHQ* 66 (1976/7), 10–34.

HERTZBERG, ARTHUR, *The French Enlightenment and the Jews: The Origins of Modern Anti-semitism* (New York, London, and Philadelphia, 1969).

HES, HINDLE S., *Jewish Physicians in the Netherlands 1600–1940* (Assen, 1980).

HEYD, URIEL, 'The Jewish Communities of Istanbul in the Seventeenth Century', *Oriens*, 6 (1953), 299–314.

HIRSCHBERG, H. J., *A History of the Jews in North Africa* (Heb.), 2 vols. (Jerusalem, 1965; rev. Eng. trans. Leiden, 1974–81).

HIRSCHEL, L., 'Een godsdienstdispuut te Amsterdam in het begin der 17ᵉ eeuw', *VA* 6 (1929/30), 178–80, 197–200.

OP 'T HOF, W. J., *De visie op de joden in de Nadere Reformatie tijdens het eerste kwart van de zeventiende eeuw* (Amsterdam, 1984).

——'Een pamflet uit 1623 betreffende de bekering der joden', *Nederlands Archief voor Kerkgeschiedenis*, 65 (1985), 35–45.

HOLLINGSWORTH, T. H., *Historical Demography* (Ithaca, NY, 1969).

HOOFT, CORNELIS PIETERSZ., *Memoriën en adviezen*, 2 vols. [vol. 2 ed. H. A. Enno van Gelder] (Utrecht, 1871–1925).

HORDES, STANLEY M., 'The Inquisition as Economic and Political Agent: The Campaign of the Mexican Holy Office against the Crypto-Jews in the Mid-Seventeenth Century', *The Americas*, 39 (1982), 23–38.

HUBERT, E., *De Charles-Quint à Joseph II: Étude sur la condition des protestans en Belgique* (Brussels, 1882).

HUIZINGA, JOHAN, 'Hugo de Groot en zijn eeuw', in id., *Verzamelde werken* (Haarlem, 1948), ii. 389–403.

HULSHOF, A. (ed.), 'Een Duitsch econoom in en over ons land omstreeks 1670', *Onze Eeuw*, 10 (1910), 65–96.

HUUSSEN, AREND H., JUN., 'The Legal Position of Sephardi Jews in Holland, circa 1600', *Dutch Jewish History*, 3 (1993), 19–41.

HYAMSON, ALBERT M., *The Sephardim of England: A History of the Spanish and Portuguese Jewish Community 1492–1951* (London, 1951).

IJZERMAN, J. W. (ed.), *Journael van de reis naar Zuid-Amerika (1598–1610) door Hendrik Ottsen* (The Hague, 1918).

ISRAEL, JONATHAN I., 'The Portuguese in Seventeenth-Century Mexico', *Jahrbuch für Geschichte von Staat, Wirtschaft und Gesellschaft Lateinamerikas*, 11 (1974), 12–32; repr. in id., *Empires and Entrepots: The Dutch, the Spanish Monarchy and the Jews, 1585–1713* (London, 1990), 311–32.

——'Spain and the Dutch Sephardim, 1609–60', *SR* 12 (1978), 1–61; repr. in id., *Empires and Entrepots: The Dutch, the Spanish Monarchy and the Jews, 1585–1713* (London, 1990), 355–415.

——'The Jews of Spanish North Africa, 1600–1669', *TJHSE* 26 (1979), 71–86.

——'Some Further Data on the Amsterdam Sephardim and their Trade with Spain during the 1650s', *SR* 14 (1980), 7–19.

——'Spanish Wool Exports and the European Economy, 1610–40', *Economic History Review*, 2nd ser., 33 (1980), 193–211.

——*The Dutch Republic and the Hispanic World 1606–1661* (Oxford, 1982).

ISRAEL, JONATHAN I., 'The Diplomatic Career of Jeronimo Nunes da Costa: An Episode in Dutch–Portuguese Relations of the Seventeenth Century', *Bijdragen en Mededelingen betreffende de Geschiedenis der Nederlanden,* 98 (1983), 167–90.

——'The Economic Contribution of Dutch Sephardi Jewry to Holland's Golden Age, 1595–1713', *Tijdschrift voor Geschiedenis,* 96 (1983), 505–35; repr. in id., *Empires and Entrepots: The Dutch, the Spanish Monarchy and the Jews, 1585–1713* (London, 1990), 417–47.

——'An Amsterdam Jewish Merchant of the Golden Age: Jeronimo Nunes da Costa (1620–1697), Agent of Portugal in the Dutch Republic', *SR* 18 (1984), 21–40.

——'The Changing Role of the Dutch Sephardim in International Trade, 1595–1715', in J. Michman and T. Levie (eds.), *Dutch Jewish History* (Jerusalem, 1984), 31–51.

——*European Jewry in the Age of Mercantilism 1550–1750* (Oxford, 1985).

——'Manuel López Pereira of Amsterdam, Antwerp and Madrid: Jew, New Christian, and Adviser to the Conde-Duque de Olivares', *SR* 19 (1985), 109–26; repr. in id., *Empires and Entrepots: The Dutch, the Spanish Monarchy and the Jews, 1585–1713* (London, 1990), 247–64.

——'Gregorio Leti (1631–1701) and the Dutch Sephardi Elite at the Close of the Seventeenth Century', in A. Rapoport-Albert and Steven J. Zipperstein (eds.), *Jewish History: Essays in Honour of Chimen Abramsky* (London, 1988), 267–84.

——'Sephardic Immigration into the Dutch Republic, 1595–1672', *SR* 23 (1989), 45–53.

——'The Dutch Republic and its Jews during the Conflict over the Spanish Succession', *Dutch Jewish History,* 2 (Jerusalem, 1989), 117–36.

——'Dutch Sephardi Jewry, Millenarian Politics and the Struggle for Brazil (1640–1654)', in J. I. Israel and D. S. Katz (eds.), *Sceptics, Millenarians and Jews* (Leiden, 1990), 76–97.

——'Een merkwaardig literair werk en de Amsterdamse effectenmarkt in 1688: Joseph Penso de la Vegas "Confusion de Confusiones" ', *De zeventiende eeuw,* 6 (1990), 159–65.

——*Empires and Entrepots: The Dutch, the Spanish Monarchy and the Jews, 1585–1713* (London, 1990).

——'Spain, the Spanish Embargoes, and the Struggle for the Mastery of World Trade, 1585–1660', in id., *Empires and Entrepots: The Dutch, the Spanish Monarchy and the Jews, 1585–1713* (London, 1990), 189–212.

——'The Amsterdam Stock Exchange and the English Revolution of 1688', *Tijdschrift voor Geschiedenis,* 103 (1990), 412–40.

——'Dutch Sephardi Jewry and the Rivalry of the European States 1640–1713', in A. Haim (ed.), *Society and Community: Proceedings of the Second International Congress for Research into the Sephardi and Oriental Heritage 1984* (Jerusalem, 1991), 173–95.

——'The Sephardi Contribution to Economic Life and Colonization in Europe and the New World (16th–18th Centuries)', in H. Beinart (ed.), *The Sephardi Legacy,* 2 vols. (Jerusalem, 1992), ii. 365–98.

——'The Sephardim in the Netherlands', in E. Kedourie (ed.), *Spain and the Jews: The Sephardi Experience 1492 and After* (London, 1992), 189–212.

—— 'Lopo Ramirez (David Curiel) and the Attempt to Establish a Sephardi Community in Antwerp in 1653–1654', *SR* 28 (1994), 99–119.

JACOBSEN JENSEN, J. N., *Reizigers te Amsterdam: Beschrijvende lijst van reizen in Nederland door vreemdelingen voor 1850* (Amsterdam, 1919; suppl., Amsterdam, 1936).

JANSEN, CLIFFORD, 'Some Sociological Aspects of Migration', in J. A. Jackson (ed.), *Migration* (Cambridge, 1969), 60–73.

JASPERS, G. J., 'Schets van Abraham Costerus' leven en werken', *Nederlands Archief voor Kerkgeschiedenis*, 57 (1976/7), 31–61.

DE JONG, M., 'O "Tratado da immortalidade da alma" de Moses Rephael de Aguilar', *Biblos*, 10 (1934), 488–99.

JORDAN, W. K., *The Development of Religious Toleration in England*, 4 vols. (Cambridge, Mass., 1932–40).

JUSTER, JEAN, *Les Juifs dans l'empire romain: Leur condition juridique, économique et sociale*, 2 vols. (Paris, 1914).

KAGAN, RICHARD L., *Lawsuits and Litigants in Castile, 1500–1700* (Chapel Hill, NC, 1981).

KAMEN, HENRY, *The Rise of Toleration* (New York and Toronto, 1967).

—— *Spain in the Later Seventeeth Century 1665–1700* (London and New York, 1980).

—— 'The Mediterranean and the Expulsion of Spanish Jews in 1492', *Past & Present*, 119 (1988), 30–55.

—— 'The Expulsion: Purpose and Consequence', in E. Kedourie (ed.), *Spain and the Jews: The Sephardi Experience 1492 and After* (London, 1992), 74–91.

—— *The Spanish Inquisition* (New York, 1966); rev. edn., *Inquisition and Society in Spain in the Sixteenth and Seventeenth Centuries* (Bloomington, Ind., 1985); rev. edn., *The Spanish Inquisition: An Historical Revision* (London, 1997).

KAPLAN, YOSEF, 'The Attitude of the Leadership of the Portuguese Community in Amsterdam to the Sabbatean Movement, 1665–1671' (Heb.), *Tsiyon*, 39 (1974), 198–216.

—— 'Nueva información sobre la estancia de Juan de Prado en Amberes', *Sefarad*, 35 (1975), 159–63.

—— 'Rabbi Saul Levi Morteira's Treatise "Arguments against the Christian Religion" ' (Heb.), *Studies on the History of Dutch Jewry*, vol. i (Jerusalem, 1975), 9–31.

—— 'Jewish Students at Leiden University in the Seventeenth Century' (Heb.), in *Studies on the History of Dutch Jewry*, vol. ii (Jerusalem, 1979), 65–75.

—— 'Jewish Proselytes from Portugal in Seventeenth-Century Amsterdam: The Case of Lorenzo Escudero' (Heb.), in *Proceedings of the Seventh World Congress of Jewish Studies* (Jerusalem, 1981), 87–101.

—— 'The Portuguese Jews of Amsterdam: From Forced Conversion to a Return to Judaism', *SR* 15 (1981), 37–51.

—— *From Christianity to Judaism: The Life and Work of Isaac Orobio de Castro* (Heb.) (Jerusalem, 1982); Eng. trans. *From Christianity to Judaism: The Story of Isaac Orobio de Castro*, trans. R. Loewe (Oxford, 1989).

—— 'The Social Functions of the *Herem* in the Portuguese Jewish Community of Amsterdam in the Seventeenth Century', in J. Michman and T. Levie (eds.), *Dutch Jewish History* (Jerusalem, 1984), 111–55.

KAPLAN, YOSEF, 'On the Relation of Spinoza's Contemporaries in the Portuguese Jewish Community of Amsterdam to Spanish Culture and the Marrano Experience', in C. de Deugd (ed.), *Spinoza's Political and Theological Thought* (Amsterdam, 1984), 82–94.

——'The Portuguese Community of Amsterdam in the Seventeenth Century: Between Tradition and Change' (Heb.), *Proceedings of the Israel Academy of Sciences and Humanities*, 7/6 (Jerusalem, 1985); rev. Eng. trans. 'The Portuguese Community of Amsterdam in the Seventeenth Century: Tradition and Change', in A. Haim (ed.), *Society and Community: Proceedings of the Second International Congress for Research into the Sephardi and Oriental Heritage 1984* (Jerusalem, 1991), 141–71; Spanish trans. in id., *Judíos nuevos en Amsterdam: Estudio sobre la historia social e intelectual del judaísmo sefardí en el siglo XVII* (Barcelona, 1996), 23–55.

——'The Travels of Portuguese Jews from Amsterdam to the "Lands of Idolatry" ', in id. (ed.), *Jews and Conversos: Studies in Society and the Inquisition* (*Proceedings of the Eighth World Congress of Jewish Studies*) (Jerusalem, 1985), 197–224.

——'Relations between the Portuguese and Ashkenazi Jews of Amsterdam in the Seventeenth Century' (Heb.), *Proceedings of the Ninth World Congress of Jewish Studies*, division B, vol. i: *The History of the Jewish People (from the Second Temple Period until the Middle Ages)* (Jerusalem, 1986), 159–64.

——'Amsterdam and the Ashkenazic Migration in the Seventeenth Century', *SR* 23 (1989), 22–44.

——'The Portuguese Community in 17th-Century Amsterdam and the Ashkenazi World', *Dutch Jewish History*, 2 (Jerusalem, 1989), 23–45; Spanish trans. in id., *Judíos nuevos en Amsterdam: Estudio sobre la historia social e intelectual del judaísmo sefardí en el siglo XVII* (Barcelona, 1996), 78–106.

——'Political Concepts in the World of the Portuguese Jews of Amsterdam during the Seventeenth Century: The Problem of Exclusion and the Boundaries of Self-identity', in id. *et al.* (eds.), *Menasseh ben Israel and his World* (Leiden, 1989), 45–62; Spanish trans. in id., *Judíos nuevos en Amsterdam: Estudio sobre la historia social e intelectual del judaísmo sefardí en el siglo XVII* (Barcelona, 1996), 56–77.

——'The Intellectual Ferment in the Spanish-Portuguese Community of Seventeenth-century Amsterdam', in H. Beinart (ed.), *The Sephardi Legacy*, 2 vols. (Jerusalem, 1992), ii. 284–314.

——'Deviance and Excommunication in the Portuguese Community of Eighteenth-century Amsterdam', *Dutch Jewish History*, 3 (Jerusalem, 1993), 103–15.

——'Familia, matrimonio y sociedad: Los casamientos clandestinos en la diáspora sefardí occidental', *Espacio, Tiempo y Forma*, 4th ser., 6 (1993), 129–54; repr. in id., *Judíos neuvos en Amsterdam: Estudio sobre la historia social e intelectual del judaísmo sefardí en el siglo XVII* (Barcelona, 1996), 107–38; Fr. trans. in *XVIIIe siècle*, 183 (1994), 255–78.

——*Judíos nuevos en Amsterdam: Estudio sobre la historia social e intelectual del judaísmo sefardí en el siglo XVII* (Barcelona, 1996).

——Méchoulan, Henry, and Popkin, Richard (eds.), *Menasseh ben Israel and his World* (Leiden, 1989).

Karner, Frances, *The Sephardics of Curaçao: A Study of Socio-Cultural Patterns in Flux* (Assen, 1969).

Kasher, Asa, and Biderman, Shlomo, 'Why was Baruch de Spinoza Excommunicated?', in J. I. Israel and D. S. Katz (eds.), *Sceptics, Millenarians and Jews* (Leiden, 1989), 98–141.

Katchen, Aaron L., *Christian Hebraists and Dutch Rabbis: Seventeenth Century Apologetics and the Study of Maimonides' 'Mishneh Torah'* (Cambridge, Mass., 1984).

Katz, D. S., *Philo-Semitism and the Readmission of the Jews in England 1603–1655* (Oxford, 1982).

——*The Jews in the History of England 1485–1850* (Oxford, 1994).

Katz, Jacob, *Die Entstehung der Judenassimilation in Deutschland und deren Ideologie* (Frankfurt, 1935); repr. in id., *Emancipation and Assimilation: Studies in Modern Jewish History* (Westmead, 1972), 195–276.

——*Exclusiveness and Tolerance: Jewish–Gentile Relations in Medieval and Modern Times* (London, 1961).

——*Tradition and Crisis: Jewish Society at the End of the Middle Ages* (Glencoe, Ill., 1961).

——*Out of the Ghetto: The Social Background of Jewish Emancipation* (Cambridge, Mass., 1973).

Katz, Solomon, *The Jews in the Visigothic and Frankish Kingdoms of Spain and Gaul* (Cambridge, Mass., 1937).

Kayserling, Meyer, *Sephardim: Romanische Poesien der Juden in Spanien. Ein Beitrag zur Literatur und Geschichte der spanisch-portugiesischen Juden* (Leipzig, 1859).

——'Une histoire de la littérature juive de Daniel Lévi de Barrios', *REJ* 18 (1889), 276–89; 32 (1896), 88–101.

——*Biblioteca Española-Portugueza-Judaica* (Strasbourg, 1890; repr. Nieuwkoop, 1961; repr., intr. Y. H. Yerushalmi, New York, 1971).

Kedourie, Elie (ed.), *Spain and the Jews: The Sephardi Experience 1492 and After* (London, 1992).

Kellenbenz, Hermann, *Unternehmerkräfte im Hamburger Portugal- und Spanienhandel 1590–1625* (Hamburg, 1954).

——'Spanien, die nördlichen Niederlanden und der skandinavisch-baltische Raum in der Weltwirtschaft und Politik um 1600', *Vierteljahrschrift für Sozial- und Wirtschaftsgeschichte*, 41 (1954), 289–332.

——*Sephardim an der unteren Elbe* (Wiesbaden, 1958).

——*A participação da Companhia de Judeus na conquista holandesa de Pernambuco* (Paraíba, 1964).

——'Tradiciones nobilarias de los grupos sefardíes', in I. M. Hassán (ed.), *Actas del Primer Simposio de Estudios Sefardíes* (Madrid, 1970), 49–54.

King, Willard F., 'The Academies and Seventeenth-century Spanish Literature', *Publications of the Modern Language Association*, 75 (1960), 367–76.

KISCH, GUIDO, *The Jews in Medieval Germany: A Study of their Legal and Social Status* (Chicago, 1949).

—— *Zasius und Reuchlin: Eine rechtsgeschichtlich-vergleichende Studie zum Toleranzproblem im 16. Jahrhundert* (Constance, 1961).

—— *Erasmus' Stellung zu Juden und Judentum* (Tübingen, 1969).

KISTEMAKER, RENÉE, and LEVIE, TIRTSAH (eds.), *Exodo: Portugezen in Amsterdam 1600–1680* (Amsterdam, 1987).

KLEEREKOPER, M. M., and VAN STOCKUM, W. P., *De boekhandel te Amsterdam voornamelijk in de 17ᵉ eeuw: Biografische en geschiedkundige aanteekeningen*, 2 vols. (The Hague, 1914–16).

KNUTTEL, W. P. C., *Acta der particuliere synoden van Zuid-Holland*, Rijksgeschiedkundige Publicatiën, Kleine Serie, vols. iii, v, viii, xi, xv, xvi (The Hague, 1908–16).

KOEN, E. M., 'Duarte Fernandes, koopman van de Portugese natie te Amsterdam', *SR* 2 (1968), 178–92.

—— 'The Earliest Sources Relating to the Portuguese Jews in the Municipal Archives of Amsterdam up to 1620', *SR* 4 (1970), 25–42.

—— 'Waar en voor wie werd de synagoge van 1612 gebouwd?', *Maandblad Amstelodamum*, 57 (1970), 209–12.

—— 'Nicolaes van Campen als huiseigenaar van de Portugees-Israelietische synagoge', *Maandblad Amstelodamum*, 58 (1971), 117.

KOENEN, H. J., *Geschiedenis der Joden in Nederland* (Utrecht, 1843).

KOSSMANN, E. F., *Nieuwe bijdragen tot de geschiedenis van het Nederlandsche toneel in de 17ᵉ en 18ᵉ eeuw* (The Hague, 1915).

KOSSMANN, E. H., *Politieke theorie in het zeventiende-eeuwse Nederland*, Verhandelingen der Koninklijke Akademie van Wetenschappen, Afd. Letterkunde, NS 67/2 (Amsterdam, 1960).

—— and MELLINK, A. F. (eds.), *Texts Concerning the Revolt of the Netherlands* (London, 1974).

KRABBENHOFT, KENNETH, 'Structure and Meaning of Herrera's "Puerta del Cielo" ', *SR* 16 (1982), 1–20.

KRIEGER, LEONARD, 'Authority', in Philip P. Weiner (ed.), *Dictionary of the History of Ideas*, 5 vols. (New York, 1973), i. 141–62.

—— 'The Idea of Authority in the West', *American Historical Review*, 82 (1977), 249–70.

KRINSKY, CAROL H., *Synagogues of Europe: Architecture, History, Meaning* (Cambridge, Mass., 1985).

KUHN, ARTHUR K., 'Hugo Grotius and the Emancipation of the Jews in Holland', *PAJHS* 31 (1928), 173–80.

LAPEYRE, HENRI, *Une famille de marchands: Les Ruiz* (Paris, 1955).

—— *Géographie de l'Espagne morisque* (Paris, 1959).

LAZAR, MOSHE (ed.), *The Sephardic Tradition: Ladino and Spanish Jewish Literature*, trans. D. Herman (New York, 1972).

LEA, HENRY CHARLES, *A History of the Inquisition of Spain*, 4 vols. (New York, 1906–7).

LECLER, JOSEPH, *Toleration and the Reformation*, trans. T. L. Westow, 2 vols. (London, 1960).

—— and VALKHOFF, MARIUS-FRANÇOIS (eds.), *A l'aurore des libertés modernes: 'Synode sur la liberté de conscience', 1582 par Thierry Coornhert* (Paris, 1979).

LEFÈVRE, JOSEPH, *La Secrétairerie d'État et de Guerre sous le régime espagnol (1594–1711)*, Académie Royale de Belgique, Classe des Lettres etc., Mémoire, coll. in octavo, 36/1 (Brussels, 1934).

LEON, ABRAM, *The Jewish Question: A Marxist Interpretation*, trans. E. Germain, 2nd edn. (New York, 1970).

LÉON, HENRY, *Histoire des Juifs de Bayonne* (Paris, 1893).

LEVIE BERNFELD, TIRTSAH, ' "Caridade escapa da morte": Legacies to the Poor in Sephardi Wills from Seventeenth Century Amsterdam', *Dutch Jewish History*, 3 (Jerusalem, 1993), 179–204.

LIEBMAN, SEYMOUR B., 'The Great Conspiracy in Peru', *The Americas*, 28 (1971/2), 176–90.

—— 'The Great Conspiracy in New Spain', *The Americas*, 30 (1973/4), 18–31.

VAN LIER, R. A. J., 'The Jewish Community in Surinam: A Historical Survey', in R. Cohen (ed.), *The Jewish Nation in Surinam: Historical Essays* (Amsterdam, 1982), 19–27.

VAN LIMBORCH, PHILIPPUS, *De veritate religionis amica collatio cum erudito Judaeo* (Gouda, 1687); Dutch trans. *Vriendelijke onderhandeling met een geleerden Jood* (Amsterdam, 1723).

LINDEBOOM, J., 'Erasmus' Bedeutung für die Entwicklung des geistigen Lebens in den Niederlanden', *Archiv für Reformationsgeschichte*, 43 (1952), 1–12.

LOCKE, JOHN, *The Correspondence of John Locke*, ed. E. S. de Beer (Oxford, 1976–89).

LOCKHART, JAMES, and SCHWARTZ, STUART B., *Early Latin America: A History of Colonial Spanish America and Brazil* (Cambridge, 1983).

LOEB, ISIDORE, 'Notes sur l'histoire des Juifs en Espagne', *REJ* 22 (1891), 104–11.

LOKER, ZVI, 'Jewish Presence, Enterprise and Migration Trends in the Caribbean', in S. J. K. Wilkerson (ed.), *Cultural Traditions and Caribbean Identity: The Question of Patrimony* (Gainesville, Fla., 1980), 177–204.

—— 'Juan de Yllan, Merchant Adventurer and Colonial Promoter: New Evidence', *SR* 17 (1983), 22–6.

LOVEJOY, ARTHUR O., *Reflections on Human Nature* (Baltimore, 1961).

LUCIO D'AZEVEDO, J., *História de António Vieira*, 2 vols. (Lisbon, 1918–20).

—— *História dos Cristãos Novos portugueses* (Lisbon, 1921).

MAARSEN, I., 'De responsa als bron voor de geschiedenis der Joden in Nederland', *BMGJWN* 5 (1933), 118–46.

MACPHERSON, C. B., *The Political Theory of Possessive Individualism: Hobbes to Locke* (London, Oxford, and New York, 1962).

MAGALHAES-GODINHO, VICTORINO, 'L'Émigration portugaise du XVᵉ siècle à nos jours', in *Conjoncture économique, structures sociales: Hommage à Ernest Labrousse* (Paris and The Hague, 1974), 253–68.

MAHLER, EDUARD, *Handbuch der jüdischen Chronologie* (Leipzig, 1916).

MAHLER, RAPHAEL, *A History of Modern Jewry, 1780–1815* (London and New York, 1971).

MALINO, FRANCES, *The Sephardic Jews of Bordeaux: Assimilation and Emancipation in Revolutionary and Napoleonic France* (University, Ala., 1978).

MALKIEL, DAVID, *A Separate Republic: The Mechanics and Dynamics of Venetian Jewish Self-Government, 1607–1624* (Jerusalem, 1991).

MALVEZIN, THÉOPHILE, *Histoire des Juifs à Bordeaux* (Bordeaux, 1875).

MANSFIELD, BRUCE, *Phoenix of his Age: Interpretations of Erasmus c.1550–1750* (Toronto, Buffalo, and London, 1979).

MANUEL, FRANK E., *The Broken Staff: Judaism through Christian Eyes* (Cambridge, Mass., 1992).

MARCUS, JACOB R., *The Colonial American Jew 1492–1776*, 3 vols. (Detroit, 1970).

MÁRQUEZ VILLANUEVA, FRANCISCO, 'El problema de los conversos: Cuatro puntos cardinales', *Hispania Judaica*, 1 (Barcelona, 1980), 51–75.

MARTINS, A., 'Um inédito Judaico-Português de Amsterdam: "Tratado da imortalidade da alma" ', *Revista Portuguesa de Filosofia*, 5 (1950), 201–20.

MATHOREZ, J., 'Notes sur les Espagnols en France depuis le XVIe siècle jusqu'au règne de Louis XIII', *Bulletin Hispanique*, 16 (1914), 337–71.

MATTINGLY, GARRET, *Renaissance Diplomacy* (Boston, 1955).

MAURO, FRÉDÉRIC, *Le Portugal et l'Atlantique au XVIIe siècle, 1570 1670: Étude économique* (Paris, 1960).

MÉCHOULAN, HENRY, 'Morteira et Spinoza au carrefour du socinianisme', *REJ* 135 (1976), 51–65.

—— 'Abraham Pereyra, juge des marranes et censeur de ses coreligionnaires à Amsterdam au temps de Spinoza', *REJ* 138 (1979), 391–400.

—— '*Le herem* à Amsterdam et "l'excommunication" de Spinoza', *Cahiers Spinoza*, 3 (1979/80), 117–34.

—— 'Diego de Estella, une source espagnole de l'œuvre d'Abraham Pereyra', *SR* 15 (1981), 178–87.

—— 'La Pensée d'Abraham Pereyra dans "La Certeza del Camino" ', in J. Michman and T. Levie (eds.), *Dutch Jewish History* (Jerusalem, 1984), 69–85.

—— *Hispanidad y judaísmo en tiempos de Espinoza: Estudio y edición anotada de 'La certeza del camino de Abraham Pereyra'*, *Amsterdam 1666*, Acta Salmanticensia, Filosofía y letras 175 (Salamanca, 1987).

—— *Être juif à Amsterdam au temps de Spinoza* (Paris, 1991).

MEIJER, JAAP, 'Provéditeur Pereira', *Maandblad voor de Geschiedenis der Joden in Nederland*, 1 (1947/8), 151.

—— *Encyclopaedia Sefardica Neerlandica* (Amsterdam, 1949).

—— 'Hugo Grotius' "Remonstrantie" ', *JSS* 17 (1955), 91–104.

—— *Zij lieten hun sporen achter: Joodse bijdragen tot de Nederlandsche beschaving* (Utrecht, 1964).

—— 'Barlaeus overgewaardeerd: Joodse bijdrage tot de 350ste verjaardag van onze universiteit' (Heemstede, 1982).

MELKMAN, J., *David Franco Mendes: A Hebrew Poet* (Amsterdam, 1951).

—— 'Het eerste drama in de Joodse literatuur', *BMGJWN* 8 (1960), 54–5.

—— 'Moses Zacuto en zijn familie', *SR* 3 (1969), 145–55.

—— 'Between Sephardim and Ashkenazim in Amsterdam', in I. Ben-Ami (ed.), *The Sephardi and Oriental Jewish Heritage* (Heb.) (Jerusalem, 1982), 135–49.

MENASSEH BEN ISRAEL, *Conciliador o de la conveniencia de los lugares de la S. Escriptura que repugnantes entre si parecen*, 4 vols. (Amsterdam, 1632, 1641, 1650, 1651).

—— *Thesouro dos dinim, que o povo de Israel he obrigado saber e observar*, 2 vols. (Amsterdam, 1645–7).

—— *Espérance d'Israel*, intr. and trans. H. Méchoulan and G. Nahon (Paris, 1979); Eng. trans. by Moses Wall, *The Hope of Israel*, intr. trans. Richenda George (Oxford, 1987).

MENDES DOS REMEDIOS, JOAQUIM, *Os Judeus em Portugal*, 2 vols. (Coimbra, 1895–1928).

—— *Os Judeus portugueses em Amsterdam* (Coimbra, 1911).

MENKMAN, W. R., 'Slavenhandel en rechtsbedeling op Curaçao op het einde der 17e eeuw', *West-Indische Gids* [XVII^de Jaargang (1935/6)], 18 (1936), 11–26.

VAN METEREN, EMANUEL, *Historie van de oorlogen en geschiedenissen der Nederlanderen, en derzelver naburen, van 1315 tot 1611* (Gorinchem, 1748–63).

MICHMAN, J., *see* MELKMAN, J.

MILANO, ATTILIO, *Storia degli Ebrei in Italia* (Turin, 1963).

MOTLEY, JOHN L., *The Rise of the Dutch Republic*, 4 vols. in 2 (Philadelphia, 1898).

NAHON, GÉRARD, 'Inscriptions funéraires hébraïques et juives à Bidache, Labastide-Clairence (Basses-Pyrénées) et Peyrehorade (Landes): Rapport de mission', *REJ* 127 (1968), 223–52, 347–65; 128 (1969), 349–75; 130 (1971), 195–230.

—— 'Les Rapports des communautés judéo-portugaises de France avec celle d'Amsterdam au XVIIᵉ et au XVIIIᵉ siècles', *SR* 10 (1976), 37–78, 151–88.

—— 'Recherches sur les relations intercommunautaires: Amsterdam et la diaspora séfarade au XVIIᵉ siècle', *Annuaire de l'École Pratique des Hautes Études, Vᵉ section. Sciences religieuses*, 85 (1977/8), 235–45; 87 (1978/9), 241–53.

—— 'Une source pour l'histoire de la diaspora séfarade au XVIIIᵉ siècle: Le "Copiador de Cartas" de la communauté portugaise d'Amsterdam', in *The Sephardi and Oriental Jewish Heritage: The First International Congress on Sephardic and Oriental Jewry* (Jerusalem, 1981), 109–22.

—— *Les 'Nations' juives portugaises du sud-ouest de la France (1684–1791): Documents* (Paris, 1981).

NANNINGA UITTERDIJK, J., *Een Kamper handelshuis te Lissabon 1572–1594: Handelscorrespondentie, rekeningen en bescheiden* (Zwolle, 1904).

NETANYAHU, BENZION, *Don Isaac Abravanel: Statesman and Philosopher* (Philadelphia, 1968).

—— *The Origins of the Inquisition in Fifteenth Century Spain* (New York, 1995).

NOORDKERK, HERMANUS, *Handvesten ofte privilegien . . . der stad Amstelredam*, 2 vols. (Amsterdam, 1748).

NORTHLEIGH, JOHN, *Topographical Descriptions: with Historico-political, and Medico-physical Observations: Made in Two Several Voyages through Most Parts of Europe* (London, 1702).

Nouvelles de la République des Lettres, 40 vols. (Amsterdam, 1684–1718).

NOVINSKY, ANITA, 'A Historical Bias: The New Christian Collaboration with the Dutch Invaders of 17th Century Brazil', in *Proceedings of the Fifth World Congress of Jewish Studies*, 5 vols. (Jerusalem, 1972), ii. 141–54.

—— and PAULO, AMILCAR, 'The Last Marranos', *Commentary*, 43 (May 1967), 76–81.

OBERMAN, HEIKO A., *Wurzeln des Antisemitismus: Christenangst und Judenplage im Zeitalter von Humanismus und Reformation* (Berlin, 1981); Eng. trans. *The Roots of Anti-Semitism in the Age of Renaissance and Reformation* (Philadelphia, 1984).

OELMAN, TIMOTHY (trans. and ed.), *Marrano Poets of the Seventeenth Century: An Anthology* (Oxford, 1982).

OFFENBERG, ADRI K., 'Exame das tradições: Een bibliografisch onderzoek naar de publikaties der eerste Sefardim in de Noordelijke Nederlanden, met name in Amsterdam (1584–1627)', in R. Kistemaker and T. Levie (eds.), *Exodo: Portugezen in Amsterdam 1600–1680* (Amsterdam, 1987), 56–63.

——' Jacob Jehuda Leon (1602–1675) and his Model of the Temple', in J. van den Berg and E. G. E. van der Wall (eds.), *Jewish–Christian Relations in the Seventeenth Century: Studies and Documents* (Dordrecht, 1988), 95–115.

DE OLIVEIRA, ANTÓNIO, *A vida económica e social de Coimbra de 1537 a 1640*, 2 vols. (Coimbra, 1971–2).

——'O motim dos estudantes de Coimbra contra os cristãos-novos em 1630', *Biblos*, 57 (1981), 597–627.

D'OLIVEIRA FRANÇA, EDUARDO, 'Um problema: A traição dos cristãos-novos em 1624', *Revista de Historia*, 41/83 (1970), 21–71.

DE OLIVEIRA MARQUES, A. H., *History of Portugal*, 2 vols. (New York and London, 1972).

OPPENHEIM, SAMUEL, 'The Early History of the Jews in New York, 1654–64', *PAJHS* 18 (1909), 1–92.

OROBIO DE CASTRO, ISAAC (BALTASAR), *Certamen philosophicum propugnata veritatis divina ac naturalis adversus Joh. Bredenburg principia in fine annexa* (Amsterdam, 1684); repr. in *Réfutation des erreurs de Bénoit de Spinosa, par Fénélon, le père Lami, bénédictin, et par le Comte de Boulainvilliers*, ed. Lenglet-Dufresnoy (Brussels, 1731); Spanish trans., ed. Joaquim de Carvalho, *Memorias da Academia das Ciencias de Lisboa, Clase de Lettras*, 2 (1937), 253–300.

—— *La observancia de la divina ley de Moseh*, ed. M. B. Amzalak (Coimbra, 1925).

—— *La observancia de la divina ley de Mosseh*, ed. J. I. Garzón (Barcelona, 1991).

PARAIRA, M. C., and DA SILVA ROSA, J. S., *Gedenkschrift uitgegeven ter gelegenheid van het 300-jarig bestaan der onderwijsinrichtingen Talmud Torah en Ets Haïm bij de Port. Israël. Gemeente te Amsterdam* (Amsterdam, 1916).

PARKES, JAMES, *The Conflict of the Church and the Synagogue: A Study in the Origin of Anti-semitism* (London, 1934).

PAULO, AMILCAR, *Os criptojudeus* (Oporto, n.d.).

PEETERS-FONTAINAS, JEAN, *Bibliographie des impressions espagnoles des Pays-Bas* (Louvain and Antwerp, 1933).

—— *Bibliographie des impressions espagnoles des Pays-Bas méridionaux*, 2 vols. (Nieuwkoop, 1965).

PENELLA, JUAN, 'Le Transfert des Moriscos espagnols en Afrique du Nord', in M. de Epalza and R. Petit (eds.), *Recueil d'études sur les Moriscos andalous en Tunisie* (Madrid and Tunis, 1973), 77–88.

PERES, DAMIÃO, 'O Conselho da Fazenda e as alterações monetárias do reinado de D. João IV', *Anais* (da Acad. Port. da Historia), 14 (1954), 1–294.

PIETERSE, WILHELMINA CHR., *Inventaris van de archieven der Portugees-Israëlietische gemeente te Amsterdam 1614–1870* (Amsterdam, 1964).

—— *350 jaar Dotar* (Amsterdam, 1965).

—— *Daniel Levi de Barrios als geschiedschrijver van de Portugees-Israëlietische gemeente te Amsterdam in zijn 'Triumpho del govierno popular'* (Amsterdam, 1968).

—— (ed.), *Livro de Bet Haim do Kahal Kados de Bet Yahacob* (Assen, 1970).

—— 'Abraham Lopes Colaso en zijn zoon Aron, kooplieden te Amsterdam en Bayonne van ca. 1700 tot 1774', *SR* 7 (1973), 1–7.

—— and KOEN, E. M. (eds.), 'Amsterdam Notarial Deeds Pertaining to the Portuguese Jews up to 1639', after *SR* 3/2 (1969) entitled 'Notarial Records Relating to the Portuguese Jews in Amsterdam up to 1639', *SR* 1/1 (1967), 111–15 [nos. 1–6]; 1/2 (1967), 110–22 [nos. 7–36]; 2 (1968), 111–26 [nos. 37–85], 257–72 [nos. 86–119]; 3 (1969), 113–25 [nos. 120–55], 234–54 [nos. 156–223]; 4 (1970), 115–26 [nos. 224–68], 243–61 [nos. 269–345]; 5 (1971), 106–24 [nos. 346–422], 219–45 [nos. 423–536]; 6 (1972), 107–23 [nos. 537–600], 229–45 [nos. 601–71]; 7 (1973), 116–27 [nos. 672–730], 266–79 [nos. 731–97]; 8 (1974), 138–45 [nos. 798–839], 300–7 [nos. 840–71]; 10 (1976), 95–104 [nos. 872–931], 212–31 [nos. 932–1081]; 11 (1977), 81–96 [nos. 1082–1190], 216–27 [nos. 1191–1259]; 12 (1978), 158–79 [nos. 1260–1383]; 13 (1979), 101–14 [nos. 1384–1473], 220–40 [nos. 1474–1607]; 14 (1980), 79–102 [nos. 1608–1753]; 15 (1981), 143–54 [nos. 1754–1821], 245–55 [nos. 1822–81]; 16 (1982), 61–84 [nos. 1882–2013], 196–218 [nos. 2014–2125]; 17 (1983), 66–79 [nos. 2126–2200], 210–17 [nos. 2201–43]; 18 (1984), 61–73 [nos. 2244–2312], 159–76 [nos. 2313–93]; 19 (1985), 79–90 [nos. 2394–2448], 174–84 [nos. 2449–99]; 20 (1986), 109–30 [nos. 2500–2600]; 21 (1987), 105–15 [nos. 2601–57], 198–203 [nos. 2658–88]; 22 (1988), 58–67 [nos. 2689–2739], 189–96 [nos. 2740–75]; 23 (1989), 110–17 [nos. 2776–2815], 203–9 [nos. 2816–50]; 24 (1990), 68–77 [nos. 2851–2900], 216–25 [nos. 2901–50]; 25 (1991), 107–18 [nos. 2951–3000], 176–89 [nos. 3001–52]; 27 (1993), 171–81 [nos. 3053–99]; 28 (1994), 204–15 [nos. 3100–49]; 29 (1995), 100–12 [nos. 3150–99], 214–30 [nos. 3200–70]; 30 (1996), 304–18 [nos. 3271–3326]; 31 (1997), 139–51 [nos. 3327–84].

POHL, HANS, 'Die Zuckereinfuhr nach Antwerpen durch portugiesische Kaufleute während des 80jährigen Krieges', *Jahrbuch für Geschichte von Staat, Wirtschaft und Gesellschaft Lateinamerikas*, 4 (1967), 348–73.

——*Die Portugiesen in Antwerpen (1567–1648): Zur Geschichte einer Minderheit* (Wiesbaden, 1977).

POLAK, LEO, 'De betekenis der Joden voor de wijsbegeerte', in H. Brugmans and A. Frank (eds.), *Geschiedenis der Joden in Nederland* (Amsterdam, 1940), 680–713.

POPKIN, RICHARD H., 'The Historical Significance of Sephardic Judaism in 17th-Century Amsterdam', *The American Sephardi*, 5 (1971), 18–27.

——'Menasseh ben Israel and Isaac La Peyrère', *SR* 8 (1974), 59–63; 18 (1984), 12–20.

POSTHUMUS, N. W., *Nederlandsche prijsgeschiedenis*, vol. i: *Goederenprijzen op de beurs van Amsterdam 1585–1914; Wisselkoersen te Amsterdam 1609–1914* (Leiden, 1943).

VAN PRAAG, J. A., 'El "Dialogo dos montes" de Rehuel Jessurun', in *Mélanges de philologie offerts à Jean-Jacques Salverda de Grava* (Groningen, 1933), 242–55.

——*Gespleten zielen* (Groningen, 1948); Spanish trans. 'Almas en litigio', *Clavileño*, 1 (1950), 14–26.

——'Los Protocolos de los sabios de Sion y la Isla de los Monopantos de Quevedo', *Bulletin Hispanique*, 51 (1949), 169–73.

PRESTAGE, EDGAR, DE AZEVEDO, PEDRO, and LARANJO COELHO, P. M. (eds.), *Correspondencia diplomática de Francisco de Sousa Coutinho durante a sua embaixada em Holanda*, 3 vols. (Coimbra, 1920–6; Lisbon, 1955).

PRICE, J. L., *Culture and Society in the Dutch Republic During the 17th Century* (New York, 1974).

PRIEBATSCH, FELIX, 'Die Judenpolitik des fürstlichen Absolutismus im 17. und 18. Jahrhundert', in *Forschungen und Versuche zur Geschichte des Mittelalters und der Neuzeit (für Dietrich Schäfer)* (Jena, 1915), 564–651.

PRINS, IZAK, *De vestiging der Marranen in Noord-Nederland in de zestiende eeuw* (Amsterdam, 1927).

——'Prince William of Orange and the Jews' (Heb.), *Tsiyon*, 15 (1950), 93–105.

PULLAN, BRIAN S., *Rich and Poor in Renaissance Venice: The Social Institutions of a Catholic State, to 1620* (Oxford and Cambridge, Mass., 1971).

——'"A Ship with Two Rudders": "Righetto Marrano" and the Inquisition in Venice', *Historical Journal*, 20 (1977), 25–58.

——'The Inquisition and the Jews of Venice: The Case of Gaspar Ribeiro, 1580–1581', *Bulletin of the John Rylands University Library*, 62 (1979/80), 207–31.

——*The Jews of Europe and the Inquisition of Venice, 1550–1670* (Oxford, 1983).

TEN RAA, F. J. G., and DE BAS, F., *Het staatsche leger, 1568–1795*, 8 vols. (The Hague, 1911–64).

RABINOWITZ, L., *The Herem Hayyishub: A Contribution to the Medieval Economic History of the Jews* (London, 1945).

RADEMAKER, C. S. M., *Life and Work of Gerardus Joannes Vossius (1577–1649)* (Assen, 1981).

RAMOS-COELHO, JOSÉ, *Historia do Infante D. Duarte, irmão de El-Rei D. João IV*, 2 vols. (Lisbon, 1889–90).

RAU, VIRGÍNIA, *A exploração e o comércio do sal de Setúbal: Estudo de historia económica* (Lisbon, 1951).

——'Subsidios para o estudo do movimento dos portos de Faro e Lisboa durante o século XVII', *Anais* (da Acad. Port. da Historia), 2nd ser., 5 (1954), 199–277.

——'O Pe António Vieira e a fragata "Fortuna" ', *Studia*, 2 (1958), 91–102.

——'A embaixada de Tristão de Mendonça Furtado e os arquivos notariais holandeses', *Anais* (da Acad. Port. da Historia), 2nd ser., 8 (1958), 95–151.

——'Feitores e feitorias: "Instrumentos" do comércio internacional português no século XVI', *Brotéria*, 81 (1965), 458–78.

—— and GOMES DA SILVA, MARIA FERNANDA (eds.), *Os manuscritos da Casa de Cadaval respeitantes ao Brasil* (Coimbra, 1955).

VAN RAVESTEYN, W., jun., *Onderzoekingen over de economische en sociale ontwikkeling van Amsterdam gedurende de 16de en het eerste kwart der 17de eeuw* (Amsterdam, 1906).

RAVID, BENJAMIN C., 'The First Charter of the Jewish Merchants of Venice, 1589', *AJS Review*, 1 (1976), 187–222.

——*Economics and Toleration in Seventeenth Century Venice: The Background and Context of the 'Discorso' of Simone Luzzatto* (Jerusalem, 1978).

REESSE, J. J., *De suikerhandel van Amsterdam van het begin der 17de eeuw tot 1813: Een bijdrage tot de handelsgeschiedenis des vaderlands* (Haarlem, 1908).

REIJNDERS, CAROLUS, *Van 'Joodsche natiën' tot joodse Nederlanders: Een onderzoek naar getto- en assimilatieverschijnselen tussen 1600 en 1942* (Amsterdam, n.d.).

RÉVAH, ISRAEL S., 'Le Premier Établissement des Marranes portugais à Rouen (1603–1607)', *Annuaire de l'Institut de Philologie et d'Histoire Orientales et Slaves*, Université Libre de Bruxelles, 13 (1955; Mélanges Isidore Lévy), 539–52.

——'Les Jésuites portugais contre l'Inquisition: La Campagne pour la fondation de la Compagnie Générale du Commerce du Brésil (1649)', *Revista do Livro*, 34 (1956), 29–53.

——'Spinoza et les hérétiques de la communauté judéo-portugaise d'Amsterdam', *RHR* 154 (1958), 173–218.

——*Spinoza et le Dr Juan de Prado* (Paris and The Hague, 1959).

——'Les Marranes', *REJ* 118 (1959/60), 30–77.

——'Pour l'histoire des "Nouveaux Chrétiens" portugais: La Relation généalogique d'I. de M. Aboab', *Boletim internacional de bibliografia luso-brasileira*, 2 (1961), 276–310.

——'Autobiographie d'un Marrane: Édition partielle d'un manuscrit de João (Moseh) Pinto Delgado', *REJ* 119 (1961), 41–130.

——'La Religion d'Uriel da Costa, Marrane de Porto, d'après des documents inédits', *RHR* 161 (1962), 45–76.

——'Un pamphlet contre l'Inquisition d'Antonio Enríquez Gómez: La Seconde Partie de la *Politica Angelica* (Rouen, 1647)', *REJ* 121 (1962), 81–168.

RÉVAH, ISRAEL S., 'Le Premier Règlement imprimé de la "Santa companhia de dotar orfans e donzelas pobres" (Amsterdam, 1615–1616)', *Boletim internacional de bibliografia luso-brasileira*, 4 (1963), 650–91.

——'Pour l'histoire des Marranes à Anvers: Recensements de la "Nation Portugaise" de 1571 à 1666', *REJ* 122 (1963), 123–47.

——'Aux origines de la rupture spinozienne: Nouveaux documents sur l'incroyance dans la communauté judéo-portugaise d'Amsterdam à l'époque de l'excommunication de Spinoza', *REJ* 123 (1964), 359–431.

——'Les Écrivains Manuel de Pina et Miguel de Barrios et la censure de la communauté judéo-portugaise d'Amsterdam', *Otsar yehudei sefarad / Tesoro de los Judíos Sefardies*, 8 (1965), pp. lxxiv–xci.

——'Les Marranes portugais et l'Inquisition au XVIᵉ siècle', in R. D. Barnett (ed.), *The Sephardi Heritage* (London, 1971), 479–526.

RIBEIRO SANCHES, A. N., *Christãos Novos e Christãos Velhos em Portugal*, ed. R. Rêgo (Lisbon, 1956).

RODRIGUEZ, MARIE-CHRISTINE, and BENNASSAR, BARTOLOMÉ, 'Signatures et niveau culturel des témoins et accusés dans les procès d'inquisition du ressort du Tribunal de Tolède (1525–1817) et du ressort du Tribunal de Cordoue (1595–1632)', *Cahiers du monde hispanique et luso-brésilien*, 31 (1978), 17–46.

ROEST, M., 'De opuscula van Daniel Levi (Miguel) de Barrios', *De Navorscher*, NS 11 (1861), 301–6.

DE ROEVER, N., *Uit onze oude Amstelstad: Schetsen en tafereelen* (Amsterdam, 1889).

ROMEIN, JAN and ANNIE, *De Lage Landen bij de zee: Geïllustreerde geschiedenis van het Nederlandsche volk*, 4 vols. (Zeist, 1961).

VAN ROODEN, P. T., and WESSELIUS, J. W., 'The Early Enlightenment and Judaism: The "Civil Dispute" between Philippus van Limborch and Isaac Orobio de Castro (1687)', *SR* 21 (1987), 140–53.

—— ——'Two Early Cases of Publication by Subscription in Holland and Germany: Jacob Abendana's "Mikhlal Yofi" (1661) and David Cohen de Lara's "Keter Kehunna" (1668)', *Quaerendo*, 16 (1986), 110–30.

ROORDA, D. J., 'De joodse entourage van de Koning-Stadhouder', in id., *Rond Prins en patriciaat* (Weesp, 1984), 143–55.

ROOSEN, WILLIAM JAMES, *The Age of Louis XIV: The Rise of Modern Diplomacy* (Cambridge, Mass., 1976).

ROSENAU, HELEN, 'Jacob Judah Leon Templo's Contribution to Architectural Imagery', *Journal of Jewish Studies*, 23 (1972), 72–81.

ROSENBERG, A. W., 'Hugo Grotius as Hebraist', *SR* 12 (1978), 62–90.

ROSENBLOOM, JOSEPH R., 'Notes on the Jews' Tribute in Jamaica', *TJHSE* 20 (1964), 247–54.

ROTH, CECIL, 'Quatre lettres d'Élie de Montalte', *REJ* 87 (1929), 137–65.

——'Les Marranes à Rouen: Un chapître ignoré de l'histoire des Juifs de France', *REJ* 88 (1929), 113–55.

——— *Venice* (Philadelphia, 1930).

——— 'The Religion of the Marranos', *JQR* 22 (1931/2), 1–33.

——— *A History of the Marranos* (Philadelphia, 1932).

——— 'Immanuel Aboab's Proselytization of the Marranos', *JQR* 23 (1932), 121–62.

——— *A Life of Menasseh ben Israel: Rabbi, Printer, and Diplomat* (Philadelphia, 1934).

——— 'Abraham Nuñez Bernal et autres martyrs contemporains de l'Inquisition', *REJ* 100bis (1936), 38–52.

——— 'The Strange Case of Hector Mendes Bravo', *HUCA* 18 (1944), 221–45.

——— *The History of the Jews of Italy* (Philadelphia, 1946).

——— 'The Role of Spanish in the Marrano Diaspora', in F. Pierce (ed.), *Hispanic Studies in Honour of I. González Llubera* (Oxford, 1959), 299–308.

——— 'The Resettlement of the Jews in England in 1656', in V. D. Lipman (ed.), *Three Centuries of Anglo-Jewish History* (Cambridge, 1961), 1–25.

——— 'An Elegy of João Pinto Delgado on Isaac de Castro Tartas', *REJ* 121 (1962), 355–66.

RUBIO, JERÓNIMO, 'Antonio Enríquez Gómez, el poeta judaizante', *Miscelánea de Estudios Arabes y Hebraicos*, 4 (1955), 187–217.

——— 'Notas sobre la vida y obras del capitán Miguel de Barrios', *Miscelánea de Estudios Arabes y Hebraicos*, 5 (1956), 199–224.

RÜRUP, REINHARD, 'Jewish Emancipation and Bourgeois Society', *Leo Baeck Institute Year Book*, 14 (1969), 67–91.

RUSSELL-WOOD, A. J., *Fidalgos and Philanthropists: The Santa Casa da Misericordia of Bahia, 1550–1715* (Berkeley and Los Angeles, 1968).

SALOMON, HERMAN, P. (ed. and intr.), 'The "De Pinto" Manuscript: A 17th Century Marrano Family History', *SR* 9 (1975), 1–62.

——— 'Haham Saul Levi Morteira en de Portugese Nieuw Christenen', *SR* 10 (1976), 127–41.

——— 'Baruch Spinoza, Ishac Orobio de Castro and Haham Mosseh Rephael d'Aguilar on the Noachites: A Chapter in the History of Thought', *Arquivos do Centro Cultural Portugues*, 14 (Paris, 1979), 253–86.

——— *Portrait of a New Christian: Fernão Alvarez Melo (1569–1632)* (Paris, 1982).

——— 'The Portuguese Background of Menasseh ben Israel's Parents as Revealed through the Inquisitorial Archives at Lisbon', *SR* 17 (1983), 105–46.

——— *Os primeiros portugueses de Amesterdão: Documentos do Arquivo Nacional da Torre do Tombo 1595–1606* (Braga, 1983).

——— 'La Vraie Excommunication de Spinoza', in H. Bots and M. Kerkhof (eds.), *Forum Litterarum: Miscellânea de estudos literários, linguísticos e históricos oferecida a J. J. van den Besselaar* (Amsterdam, 1984), 181–99.

——— *Saul Levi Morteira en zijn 'Traktaat betreffende de waarheid van de Wet van Mozes'* (Braga, 1988).

——— 'Myth or Anti-myth? The Oldest Account Concerning the Origin of Portuguese Judaism at Amsterdam', *Lias*, 16 (1989), 275–316.

SAMUEL, EDGAR R., 'Portuguese Jews in Jacobean London', *TJHSE* 18 (1958), 171–230.

—— 'The First Fifty Years', in V. S. Lipman (ed.), *Three Centuries of Anglo-Jewish History* (Cambridge, 1961), 27–44.

—— 'New Light on the Selection of Jewish Children's Names', *TJHSE* 23 (1971), 64–86; 24 (1975), 171–2.

—— 'The Disposal of Diego Duarte's Stock of Paintings 1692–1697', *Jaarboek 1976 Koninklijk Museum voor Schone Kunsten-Antwerpen*, 305–24.

—— 'Manuel Levy Duarte (1631–1714): An Amsterdam Merchant Jeweller and his Trade with London', *TJHSE* 27 (1982), 11–31.

—— 'The Curiel Family in 16th-Century Portugal', *TJHSE* 31 (1990), 111–36.

—— 'The Readmission of the Jews to England in 1656, in the Context of English Economic Policy', *TJHSE* 31 (1990), 153–69.

SAMUEL, WILFRED S., 'A Review of the Jewish Colonists in Barbados in the Year 1680', *TJHSE* 13 (1936), 1–111.

SÁNCHEZ, JOSÉ, *Académias literárias del Siglo de Oro español* (Madrid, 1961).

DE SANTA CRUZ, ALFONSO, *Cronica de los Reyes Catolicos*, ed. J. de Mata Carriazo (Seville, 1951).

SAPERSTEIN, MARC, 'Saul Levi Morteira's Treatise on the Immortality of the Soul', *SR* 25 (1991), 131–48.

SARAIVA, ANTONIO JOSÉ, *A politica de discriminação social e a represão da heterodoxia*, 3 vols. (Lisbon, 1950–62); 'separata' of his *Historia da Cultura em Portugal* (Lisbon, 1950), i. 9–189.

—— *Inquisição e Cristãos-Novos* (Porto, 1969).

SASPORTAS, JACOB, *Sefer tsitsat novel tsevi* (Heb.), ed. Y. Tishby (Jerusalem, 1954).

SCHAMA, SIMON, *The Embarrassment of Riches: An Interpretation of Dutch Culture in the Golden Age* (Berkeley, 1988).

SCHOCHET, GORDON J. (ed.), *Life, Liberty, and Property: Essays on Locke's Political Ideas* (Belmont, Calif., 1971).

SCHOEPS, HANS-JOACHIM, *Philosemitismus im Barock: Religions- und geistesgeschichtliche Untersuchungen* (Tübingen, 1952).

—— 'Isaak Orobio de Castros Religionsdisput mit Philipp van Limborch', *Judaica*, 2 (1946/7), 89–105.

—— *The Jewish–Christian Argument: A History of Theologies in Conflict*, trans. D. E. Green (New York, 1963).

SCHOLBERG, KENNETH R., 'Miguel de Barrios and the Amsterdam Sephardic Community', *JQR* 53 (1962), 120–59.

—— *La poesia religiosa de Miguel de Barrios* (Madrid, n.d.).

SCHOLEM, GERSHOM, *Sabbatai Sevi: The Mystical Messiah 1626–1676* (Princeton, 1973).

SCHOUTEN, H. J., 'Het geslacht Belmonte', *Maandblad De Nederlandsche Leeuw*, 10 (1892), 41–5.

SCHRAA, P., 'Onderzoekingen naar de bevolkingsomvang van Amsterdam tussen 1550 en 1650', *Jaarboek Amstelodamum*, 46 (1954), 1–33.

SEELIGMANN, SIGMUND, 'Het Marranen-probleem uit oekonomisch oogpunt', *BMGJWN* 3 (1925; Feestbundel L. Wagenaar), 101–36.

—— *Bibliographie en historie: Bijdrage tot de geschiedenis der eerste Sephardim in Amsterdam* (Amsterdam, 1927).

—— 'De gilden en de Joden', *VA* 5 (1928), 135–7.

Sermões que pregarão os doctos ingenios do K. K. de Talmud Torah desta cidade de Amsterdam no alegre estreamento publica celebridade da fabrica que se consegrou a Deos para caza de oração cuja entrada se festejam em Sabath Nahamú anno 5435 (Amsterdam, 1675).

SERRÃO, JOAQUIM V., *Les Portugais à l'Université de Toulouse (XIII–XVII siècles)* (Paris, 1970).

SERVAAS VAN ROOYEN, A. J., *Inventaire des livres formant la bibliothèque de Bénédict Spinoza* (The Hague, 1888).

SHILLINGTON, V. M., and WALLIS CHAPMAN, A. B., *The Commercial Relations of England and Portugal* (London and New York, 1907).

SICROFF, ALBERT A., *Les Controverses des statuts de 'pureté de sang' en Espagne du XVe au XVIIe siècle* (Paris, 1960).

DA SILVA, SEMUEL, *Tratado da imortalidade da alma*, ed. P. Gomes (Lisbon, n.d.), Eng. trans. in Uriel da Costa, *Examination of Pharisaic Traditions—Exame das tradições phariseas: Facsimile of the Unique Copy in the Royal Library of Copenhagen*, intr. and trans. H. P. Salomon and I. S. D. Sassoon (Leiden, 1993), 427–551.

DA SILVA CARVALHO, AUGUSTO, 'Um agente de Portugal em França: Francisco Mendes Gois', *Anais* (da Acad. Port. da Historia), 2nd ser., 2 (1949), 213–40.

DA SILVA ROSA, JAKOB DE SAMUEL, 'Een eigenhandige brief van Daniel Levi de Barrios: Bijdrage tot eene biographie van dezen dichter-geschiedschrijver', in *Festskrift i anledning af profesor David Simonsens 70-aarige fødselsdag* (Copenhagen, 1923), 106–11.

—— *Geschiedenis der Portugeesche Joden te Amsterdam 1593–1925* (Amsterdam, 1925).

—— 'Van Marrano tot Joodsch apologeet, Dr. Isaac (Balthazar) Orobio de Castro', *VA* 3 (1926), 6–9, 21–3.

—— 'Van Marranen tot Portugeesche Joden te Amsterdam: Een economisch of religieus motief', *Maandblad Amstelodamum*, 20 (1933), 30–2.

—— 'Joseph Athias (1635–1700): Ein berühmter jüdischer Drucker', *Soncino-Blätter*, 3 (1930; Festschrift Heinrich Brody), 107–12.

—— 'Salom Italia', *Maandblad voor Geschiedenis der Joden in Nederland*, 1 (1947/8), 214–22.

SIQUEIRA, SONIA A., *A Inquisição Portuguesa e a sociedade colonial* (São Paulo, 1978).

SKIPPON, PHILIP, *An Account of a Journey Made thro' Parts of the Low Countries, Germany, Italy, and France*, in A. Churchill (ed.), *A Collection of Voyages and Travels*, vol. vi (London, 1732).

SMITH, DAVID GRANT, 'Old Christian Merchants and the Foundation of the Brazil Company', *Hispanic American Historical Review*, 54 (1974), 233–59.

SMITH, DAVID GRANT, 'The Mercantile Class of Portugal and Brazil in the Seventeenth Century: A Socioeconomic Study of the Merchants of Lisbon and Bahia', Ph.D. thesis (University of Texas at Austin, 1975).

SNAPPER, F., *Oorlogsinvloeden op de overzeese handel van Holland* (Amsterdam, 1959).

SOMBART, WERNER, *Die Juden und das Wirtschaftsleben* (Leipzig, 1911).

SONNE, ISAIAH, 'Da Costa Studies', *JQR* 22 (1932), 247–93.

——'Leon Modena and the Da Costa Circle in Amsterdam', *HUCA* 21 (1948), 1–28.

SPEET, B. M. J., 'De middeleeuwen', in Blom *et al.* (eds.), *Geschiedenis van de Joden in Nederland* (Amsterdam, 1995), 19–49.

SPINOZA, BENEDICT (BARUH), *The Chief Works*, trans. R. H. M. Elwes, 2 vols. (London, 1883–4).

——*Opera*, ed. C. Gebhardt, 4 vols. (Heidelberg, 1925).

——*The Political Works*, ed. and trans. A. G. Wernham (Oxford, 1958).

STERN-TAEUBLER, SELMA, 'Die Vorstellung vom Juden und vom Judentum in der Ideologie der Reformationszeit', in *Essays Presented to Leo Baeck on the Occasion of his Eightieth Birthday* (New York, 1954), 194–211.

——*The Court Jew: A Contribution to the Period of Absolutism in Central Europe* (Philadelphia, 1950; repr. New Brunswick, NJ, 1985).

SUÁREZ FERNÁNDEZ, LUIS (ed.), *Documentos acerca de la expulsión de los judíos* (Valladolid, 1964).

——*Judíos españoles en la Edad Media* (Madrid, 1980).

SWETSCHINSKI, DANIEL M., 'The Spanish Consul and the Jews of Amsterdam', in M. A. Fishbane and P. R. Flohr (eds.), *Texts and Responses: Studies Presented to Nahum N. Glatzer on the Occasion of his Seventieth Birthday by his Students* (Leiden, 1975), 158–72.

——'Conflict and Opportunity in "Europe's Other Sea": The Adventure of Caribbean Jewish Settlement', *American Jewish History*, 72 (1982), 212–40.

——'An Amsterdam Jewish Merchant-Diplomat: Jeronimo Nunes da Costa alias Moseh Curiel (1620–1697), Agent of Portugal', in L. Dasberg and J. N. Cohen (eds.), *Neveh Ya'akov: Jubilee Volume Presented to Dr. Jaap Meijer on the Occasion of his Seventieth Birthday* (Assen, 1982), 3–30.

——'Marranos', in Mircea Eliade (ed.), *The Encyclopedia of Religion*, 16 vols. (New York and London, 1987), ix. 210–18.

——'Wetenschap en vooroordelen', *Ter Herkenning*, 16/2 (1988), 90–100.

——'Worthy Merchants, Keen Bankers, Loyal Courtiers: The Suassos and the House of Orange', in id. (with Loekie Schönduve), *De familie Lopes Suasso, financiers van Willem III / The Lopes Suasso Family, Bankers to William III* (Zwolle, 1988), 9–64.

——'Tussen middeleeuwen en Gouden Eeuw, 1516–1621', in Blom *et al.* (eds.), *Geschiedenis van de Joden in Nederland* (Amsterdam, 1995), 53–94.

——'Un refus de mémoire: Les Juifs portugais d'Amsterdam et leur passé marrane', in E. Benbassa (ed.), *Mémoires juives d'Espagne et du Portugal* (Paris, 1996), 69–77.

——*Orphan Objects: Facets of the Textiles Collection of the Joods Historisch Museum, Amsterdam* (Amsterdam and Zwolle, 1997).

SZAJKOWSKI, ZOSA, 'Trade Relations of Marranos in France with the Iberian Peninsula in the Sixteenth and Seventeenth Centuries', *JQR* 50 (1959/60), 69–78.

TAYLOR, R. C., 'Migration and Motivation: A Study of Determinants and Types', in J. A. Jackson (ed.), *Migration* (Cambridge, 1969), 99–133.

TEENSMA, BENJAMIN N., 'De levensgeschiedenis van Abraham Perengrino, alias Manuel Cardoso de Macedo', *SR* 10 (1976), 1–36.

——'Fragmenten uit het Amsterdamse convoluut van Abraham Idaña, alias Gaspar Méndez del Arroyo (1623–1690)', *SR* 11 (1977), 127–55.

——'Sefardim en Portugese taalkunde in Nederland', *SR* 19 (1985), 39–78.

——'De taal der Amsterdamse Sefardim in de 17e en 18e eeuw', in R. Kistemaker and T. Levie (eds.), *Exodo: Portugezen in Amsterdam 1600–1680* (Amsterdam, 1987), 70–2.

——'Van Marraan tot Jood: 17e en 18e-eeuwse Amsterdamse Sephardim en hun Iberische achtergrond', *Jaarboek Amstelodamum*, 80 (1988), 105–25.

——'Resentment in Recife: Jews and Public Opinion in 17th-Century Brazil', in J. Lechner (ed.), *Essays on Cultural Identity in Colonial Latin America: Problems and Repercussions* (Leiden, 1988), 63–78.

——'The Suffocation of Spanish and Portuguese among the Amsterdam Sephardi Jews', *Dutch Jewish History*, 3 (Jerusalem, 1993), 137–77.

TEICHER, JACOB, 'Why was Spinoza Banned?', *Menorah Journal*, 45 (1957), 41–60.

TEMPLE, SIR WILLIAM, *Works*, 4 vols. (London, 1814; repr. New York, 1968).

TERRASSE, HENRI, *Histoire du Maroc des origines à l'établissement du Protectorat français*, 2 vols. (Casablanca, 1949–50).

VAN TIJN, TH., 'Pieter de la Court: Zijn leven en zijn economische denkbeelden', *Tijdschrift voor Geschiedenis*, 69 (1956), 304–70.

TODOROV, NIKOLAI, *The Balkan City, 1400–1900* (Seattle and London, 1983).

TREVELYAN, MARY CAROLINE, *William the Third and the Defense of Holland 1672–74* (London, New York, and Toronto, 1930).

USQUE, SAMUEL, *Consolation for the Tribulations of Israel*, trans. M. A. Cohen (Philadelphia, 1965).

VASCO RODRIGUES, ADRIANO, 'Judeus portuenses no desenvolvimento económico dos portos atlânticos, na época moderna', *Revista de Historia*, 2 (Porto, 1979), 19–26.

VAZ DIAS, A. M., 'Joden in den Amsterdamschen diamanthandel in het begin der 18e eeuw: Eenige nieuwe gegevens', *VA* 6 (1929/30), 280–3.

——'Een blik in de Marranen-historie: Gegevens uit het notarieel archief van Amsterdam (IIe reeks)', *VA* 7 (1930/1), 154–6; 9 (1932/3), 77–80, 108–10, 121–3.

——'De scheiding in de oudste Amsterdamsche Portugeesche gemeente Beth Jaacob (1618)', *VA* 7 (1930/1), 386–8, 402–4; 8 (1931/2), 7–9, 22–3.

——'Het approviandeeren der legers van den Stadhouder, Prins Willem III', *VA* 7 (1930/1), 413–15.

——'De stichters van Beth Jaacob: De eerste Joodsche Gemeente in Amsterdam', *VA* 8 (1931/2), 195–7, 222–4, 238–40, 247–9.

VAZ DIAS, A. M., 'Een merkwaardige erfenisquaestie: Episode uit het bloeitijdperk der Amsterdamsche Port. Joodse Gemeente', *Ha-Ischa*, 8 (1936), 196–8.

——'Over den vermogenstoestand der Amsterdamsche Joden in de 17e en de 18e eeuw', *Tijdschrift voor Geschiedenis*, 51 (1936), 165–76.

——'Het Amsterdamsche Jodenkwartier', in *Gedenkschrift der Stichting 'Bouwfonds Handwerkers Vriendenkring'* (Amsterdam, 1937), 17–40.

——'Een verzoek om de Joden te Amsterdam een bepaalde woonplaats aan te wijzen', *Jaarboek Amstelodamum*, 35 (1938), 180–202.

——and VAN DER TAK, W. G., *Spinoza mercator & autodidactus: Oorkonden en andere authentieke documenten betreffende des wijsgeers jeugd en diens betrekkingen* (The Hague, 1932).

VAZQUEZ DE PRADA, V., *Lettres marchandes d'Anvers*, 4 vols. (Paris, n.d.).

DE LA VEGA, JOSEPH (PENSO), *Confusion de Confusiones*, intr. M. F. J. Smith, trans. G. J. Geers (The Hague, 1939).

——*Confusion de Confusiones*, ed. and trans. Hermann Kellenbenz (Boston, 1959).

——*Die Verwirrung der Verwirrungen: Vier Dialoge über die Börse in Amsterdam*, trans. Otto Pringsheim (Breslau, 1919).

VEIGA TORRES, JOSÉ, 'Uma longa guerra social: Os ritmos da repressão inquisitorial em Portugal', *Revista de História Económica e Social*, 1 (1978), 55–68.

VERDOONER, DAVE, and SNEL, HARMEN, *Trouwen in Mokum/Jewish Marriage in Amsterdam 1598–1811* (The Hague, 1991).

VIGNOLS, L., 'Le Commerce hollandais et les congrégations juives à la fin du XVIIᵉ siècle', *Revue Historique*, 44 (1890), 329–39.

VLESSING, ODETTE, 'New Light on the Earliest History of the Amsterdam Portuguese Jews', *Dutch Jewish History*, 3 (Jerusalem, 1993), 43–75.

——'The Portuguese-Jewish Merchant Community in Seventeenth-century Amsterdam', in C. Lesger and L. Noordegraaf (eds.), *Entrepreneurs and Entrepreneurship in Early Modern Times: Merchants and Industrialists within the Orbit of the Dutch Staple Market* (The Hague, 1995), 223–43.

VOGELSTEIN, HERMANN, *Rome*, trans. M. Hadas (Philadelphia, 1941).

WÄTJEN, HERMANN, *Das Judentum und die Anfänge der modernen Kolonisation: Kritische Bemerkungen zu Werner Sombarts 'Die Juden und das Wirtschaftsleben'* (Berlin, 1914).

——*Das holländische Kolonialreich in Brasilien: Ein Kapitel aus der Kolonialgeschichte des 17. Jahrhunderts* (The Hague and Gotha, 1921).

WEBER, MAX, *Gesammelte Aufsätze zur Religions-Soziologie*, vol. ii, 2nd edn. (Tübingen, 1923).

WERNHAM, A. G. *See* SPINOZA

WESSELIUS, J. W., 'Herman P. Salomon on Saul Levi Mortera', *SR* 23 (1989), 93–8.

WIJBRANDS, A. W., 'Overgang tot het Jodendom', *Studiën en bijdragen op 't gebied der historische theologie*, 3 (1876), 455–75.

WILKE, CARSTEN LORENZ, 'Conversion ou retour? La Métamorphose du nouveau chrétien en Juif portugais dans l'imaginaire sépharade du XVIIᵉ siècle', in E. Benbassa (ed.) *Mémoires juives d'Espagne et du Portugal* (Paris, 1996), 53–67.

WILSON, EDWARD, M., 'Miguel de Barrios and Spanish Religious Poetry', *Bulletin of Hispanic Studies*, 40 (1963), 176–80.

WIZNITZER, ARNOLD, 'The Number of Jews in Dutch Brazil, 1630', *JSS* 16 (1954), 107–14.

——'The Merger Agreement and Regulations of Congregation Talmud Torah of Amsterdam (1638–1639)', *Historia Iudaica*, 20 (1958), 109–32.

——*Jews in Colonial Brazil* (Morningside Heights, NY, 1960).

WOLF, LUCIEN, 'Status of the Jews in England after the Resettlement', *TJHSE* 4 (1901), 177–93.

——'Jews in Elizabethan England', *TJHSE* 11 (1928), 1–91.

WOOLF, MAURICE, 'Foreign Trade of London Jews in the Seventeenth Century', *TJHSE* 24 (1975), 38–58.

WRIGHT, IRENE A., 'The Coymans Asiento (1685–1689)', *Bijdragen voor Vaderlandsche Geschiedenis en Oudheidkunde*, 6th ser., 1 (1924), 23–62.

YERUSHALMI, YOSEF HAYIM, *From Spanish Court to Italian Ghetto: Isaac Cardoso. A Study in Seventeenth-Century Marranism and Jewish Apologetics* (New York and London, 1971).

——'Conversos Returning to Judaism in the Seventeenth Century: Their Jewish Knowledge and Psychological Readiness' (Heb.), *Proceedings of the Fifth World Congress of Jewish Studies*, 5 vols. (Jerusalem, 1972), ii. 201–9.

——'Jews in Post-expulsion Spain and Portugal', in *Salo Wittmayer Baron Jubilee Volume*, 3 vols. (Jerusalem, 1974), ii. 1023–58.

——*The Lisbon Massacre of 1506 and the Royal Image in the 'Shebet Yehudah'*, HUCA supplement no. 1 (Cincinnati, 1976).

——*The Re-education of the Marranos in the Seventeenth Century*, Rabbi Louis Feinberg Memorial Lecture no. 3 (Cincinnati, 1980).

——*Assimilation and Racial Anti-Semitism: The Iberian and the German Models*, Leo Baeck Memorial Lecture no. 26 (New York, 1982).

——*Zakhor: Jewish History and Jewish Memory* (Seattle and London, 1982).

——'Spinoza's Remarks on the Existence of the Jewish People' (Heb.), *Proceedings of the Israel Academy of Sciences and Humanities*, 6/10 (Jerusalem, 1984).

YINGER, J. MILTON, *Ethnicity: Source of Strength? Source of Conflict?* (Albany, NY, 1994).

YOGEV, GEDALIA, *Diamonds and Coral: Anglo-Dutch Jews and Eighteenth-Century Trade* (n.p., 1978).

YOVEL, YIRMIAHU, 'Why Spinoza was Excommunicated', *Commentary*, 64 (Nov. 1977), 46–52.

——'Marranisme et dissidence: Spinoza et quelques prédécesseurs', *Cahiers Spinoza*, 3 (1979/80), 67–99.

——*Spinoza and Other Heretics*, vol. i: *The Marrano of Reason* (Princeton, 1989).

ZERNATTO, GUIDO, 'Nation: The History of a Word', *Review of Politics*, 6 (1944), 352–5.

ZIMMELS, H. J., *Die Marranen in der rabbinischen Literatur: Forschungen und Quellen zur Geschichte und Kulturgeschichte der Anusim* (Berlin, 1932).

ZIMMELS, H. J., *Ashkenazim and Sephardim: Their Relations, Differences, and Problems as Reflected in the Rabbinical Responsa* (London, 1958).

ZUMTHOR, PAUL, *Daily Life in Rembrandt's Holland* (New York, 1963).

ZWARTS, JACQUES, 'De eerste rabbijnen en synagogen van Amsterdam naar archivalische bronnen', *BMGJWN* 4 (1928), 145–271.

—— *Hoofdstukken uit de geschiedenis der Joden in Nederland* (Zutphen, 1929).

—— 'De Uriel da Costa tragedie van een monnik-biechtvader te Amsterdam (1650)', *Centraal Blad voor Israëlieten in Nederland*, 50/13 (24 May 1934).

—— 'De Joodsche dichter-troubadour De Barrios op Rembrandt's Het Joodse Bruidje', *Gedenkboek 5695–1935, Centraal Blad voor Israëlieten in Nederland* (Amsterdam, 1935), 60–72.

Index of Persons

A

Abarbanel, Jona 207, 231–2
Abarbanel Barboza, Joseph 199, 251–2
Abarbanel Sousa family 194–5
Abarbanel Sousa, Selomo 193
Abas (alias Dias Jorge) family 194
Abas, Imanoel 194 n.
Abas, Ishac 194 n.
Abas, Jacob 239
Abas, Jeosua 194
Abas, Lea 194 n.
Abas, Ribca 194 n.
Abas, Sara 194 n.
Abas, Semuel de Yshac 213, 293
Abaz, Jeosuah, de Jonge 284
Abendana, Ester 291
Abendana, Jacob 213, 293
Abendana de Britto, Abraham 227
Abeniacar, Ishac 280
Aboab, Eliau 196 n.
Aboab, Imanuel 212, 294
Aboab, Isaac 213
Aboab, Ishack de Matatia 212–13, 292
Aboab, Matatia, see Dias Henriques, Manuel
Aboab, Rachel 240
Aboab, Semuel, see Sanches de Pas, Antonio
Aboab da Fonseca, Ishac (Haham) 169, 204, 211, 250, 260
  as censor 244, 246
  initiatives on behalf of new Esnoga 1, 204
  library of 291, 293–6, 303–7
  migrates to Brazil 115
  portrait painted 309
Abrabanel, Isaac 56, 195, 294
Abrabanel, Judah, see Leone Ebreo

Abraham Menahem Hacohen 212
Abudiente, Moseh de Gideon 260
Abulafia, Hayim 203 n.
Acosta, José de 305
Aguilar, David de 154, 254
Aguilar, Moseh Rephael de 115, 244, 267 n., 269, 296
Albertus Magnus 306
Aldrete, Bernardo José 305
Alewijn, Abraham 117 n.
Almosnino, Moses 213
Altaras, Moseh 292
Alvares, Antonio Luis (Dr) 253
Alvares, Aron 193
Alvares Machado, Antonio (alias Moseh Machado) 138–40, 193, 207
Alvares Pinto, Rodrigo 320 n.
Ambrose 306
Anckerman, Hendrick 155 n.
Appianus 304–5
Aquinas (Thomas) 306–7
Ares da Fonseca, Estevan de 114
Aristotle 264, 305
Arredondo, Rephael de 129, 257, 298
Arrianus 305
Athias, Immanuel 154
Athias, Isaac 291–2
Athias, Joseph 149–50, 152–4, 290
Atias, Abraham 288
Aubigné, Theodore Agrippa d' 304
Augustine 9, 306–7
Azevedo, André de, & Pas, João de 109, 123
Azevedo, Joseph d' 193

B

Backer, Jacob Adriaensz. 308
Barents, Marritge 218

Barlaeus, Caspar 29–32
Baron, Johan Zacharias 293
Barrios, Daniel (Levi) de (alias Miguel de Barrios) 152, 241 n., 307, 318, 322
  censored 242–9, 275
  communal historian 169–70, 177, 194
  member of literary academies 212, 300–2
  plays by 287–8
  poetry by 279, 297–9
Barrios, Miguel de, see Barrios, Daniel (Levi) de
Baruh, Ishac 257
Baruh, Izaque 155 n.
Baruh Roos, Isaack 281
Barzilay, Judith 282 n.
Bassan, Abraham 188 n.
Bassan, Ishac 188 n.
Bassan, Jacob 188 n.
Bassan, Moseh 188 n.
Bastaer, Annetien 85 n.
Belilhos, Daniel 295
Belmonte, Andres de 133–4, 229, 275
Belmonte, Manuel de (alias Ishac Nunes Belmonte) 191
  diplomatic career 133–7, 229, 317
  patron of literary academies 243, 248, 299–302
Belmonte, Mosseh 231–2, 309
Belmonte, Selomo 214
Belmonte, Simha 282 n.
Benveniste, Imanoel 151, 290, 292–4, 297–8
Bodin, Jean 39
Brandon, Ishac 104
Brereton, Will 90, 209
Bril, Paul 308
Brouwer, Adriaen 308
Bruyning, Jan 153
Bueno, Abraham de Ishac 251–2

Index of Subjects

Inquisition, Spanish 56, 114
  pursuing Portuguese New Christians in
    Spain 62–4, 72, 75, 77, 120, 122
  spying on New Christians in France 79, 81
Inquisition, Spanish American 62–4
insurance underwriting 142, 147–8
Ireland 138–9
Italian Jews 188–9
Italy 183, 186
  Iberian Jewish settlements in 55–6, 59–61,
    66, 77, 93, 100
  immigration from 68–9, 82–3, 86, 88
  trade relations with 107–8, 110–12, 114, 129
  see also individual towns

J

Jamaica 83, 95, 126–8
Jerusalem (Palestine) 85, 184, 203
jesiba (pl. *jesibot*) 203, 210–12
jewellers 136, 143–4, 212, 301
  see also trade: in jewels
Jewish historiography 297
Jewish law 19, 212, 226
  see also Bet Din
judiciary, communal, *see* autonomy; Bet Din
Justinian code 36

K

kabbalah 173, 263–4, 293–4, 296, 305, 314
kashrut, see orthodoxy
Keter Sem Tob (association) 201
Keter Tora (*jesiba*) 211, 213
kin relations, *see* family
Königsberg (East Prussia) 109
kosher meat 172–3, 177, 183, 213, 251
  tax on 197, 199
Krems (Moravia) 203

L

La Rochelle (France) 78
Labastide–Clairence (France) 65, 79, 94, 98
Ladino (language) 279
Lagos (Portugal) 73, 109
Lamego (Portugal) 72
languages, use of, *see* Dutch; Hebrew; Ladino;
  Portuguese; Spanish
latitudinarianism 241–6, 248–9
lawyers, *see* solicitors
legends 100–1, 168–71
lineage, *see* nobility
Lisbon (Portugal) 141

immigration from 73–4
New Christians in 57–8, 63, 72, 114
trade relations with 106, 108–10, 117, 119,
  123, 125
literacy 88–9, 284
literature 290–9, 302–8
  Christian 306–8
  classical 302–5
  contemporary Iberian 302, 305
  contemporary Jewish 294–6
  historiographical 302–6
  political 304–6
  secular 297–306
  traditional Jewish 292–4
  in translation 291–4, 297
  see also bible(s): 'scholarship'; Jewish
    historiography; kabbalah; poetry
Livorno (Italy) 66, 82, 93, 107–8, 130
Llerena (Spain) 77
London (England) 98, 136, 139–40, 143, 292
  emigration to 92
  'immigration' from 67, 69, 85, 88–9
  Jewish settlement in 51, 65, 94–5, 126–7,
    158, 174–5
  trade relations with 105–6, 120, 123, 130

M

Madeira 60, 73, 97, 106, 123
Madrid (Spain) 108, 133
  immigration from 75
  New Christians in 60, 63, 72–3, 77, 80
  trade with 118, 120–2
Mahamad 190–1, 196
Málaga (Malaga) 60, 75, 111
Mantua (Italy) 184
marriage 66, 87–8, 141, 178, 240
  intermarriage with Ashkenazim 188–9
  regulated by Dutch law 18–19, 36, 239
  under supervision of Mahamad 218,
    250–1
  see also divorce; endogamy; family; sexual
    relations
Martinique 83
Masa (Barbary coast) 85
Maskil Dal (association) 201, 288
Me'irat Henaim (association) 288
Mennonites 33
Mexico 61–2, 83, 112
Middelburg (Zeeland) 64–5, 94, 96
modernity 2–3, 6–7, 316–19
Mogadouro (Portugal) 72
Moncorvo (Portugal) 72